Lecture Notes in Computer Science 9733

Commenced Publication in 1973
Founding and Former Series Editors:
Gerhard Goos, Juris Hartmanis, and Jan van Leeuwen

More information about this series at http://www.springer.com/series/7409

Masaaki Kurosu (Ed.)

Human-Computer Interaction

Novel User Experiences

18th International Conference, HCI International 2016
Toronto, ON, Canada, July 17–22, 2016
Proceedings, Part III

 Springer

Editor
Masaaki Kurosu
The Open University of Japan
Chiba-shi, Chiba
Japan

ISSN 0302-9743   ISSN 1611-3349 (electronic)
Lecture Notes in Computer Science
ISBN 978-3-319-39512-8   ISBN 978-3-319-39513-5 (eBook)
DOI 10.1007/978-3-319-39513-5

Library of Congress Control Number: 2016939993

LNCS Sublibrary: SL3 – Information Systems and Applications, incl. Internet/Web, and HCI

Printed on acid-free paper

This Springer imprint is published by Springer Nature
The registered company is Springer International Publishing AG Switzerland

Foreword

The 18th International Conference on Human-Computer Interaction, HCI International 2016, was held in Toronto, Canada, during July 17–22, 2016. The event incorporated the 15 conferences/thematic areas listed on the following page.

A total of 4,354 individuals from academia, research institutes, industry, and governmental agencies from 74 countries submitted contributions, and 1,287 papers and 186 posters have been included in the proceedings. These papers address the latest research and development efforts and highlight the human aspects of the design and use of computing systems. The papers thoroughly cover the entire field of human-computer interaction, addressing major advances in knowledge and effective use of computers in a variety of application areas. The volumes constituting the full 27-volume set of the conference proceedings are listed on pages IX and X.

I would like to thank the program board chairs and the members of the program boards of all thematic areas and affiliated conferences for their contribution to the highest scientific quality and the overall success of the HCI International 2016 conference.

This conference would not have been possible without the continuous and unwavering support and advice of the founder, Conference General Chair Emeritus and Conference Scientific Advisor Prof. Gavriel Salvendy. For his outstanding efforts, I would like to express my appreciation to the communications chair and editor of *HCI International News*, Dr. Abbas Moallem.

April 2016   Constantine Stephanidis

HCI International 2016 Thematic Areas
and Affiliated Conferences

Thematic areas:

- Human-Computer Interaction (HCI 2016)
- Human Interface and the Management of Information (HIMI 2016)

Affiliated conferences:

- 13th International Conference on Engineering Psychology and Cognitive Ergonomics (EPCE 2016)
- 10th International Conference on Universal Access in Human-Computer Interaction (UAHCI 2016)
- 8th International Conference on Virtual, Augmented and Mixed Reality (VAMR 2016)
- 8th International Conference on Cross-Cultural Design (CCD 2016)
- 8th International Conference on Social Computing and Social Media (SCSM 2016)
- 10th International Conference on Augmented Cognition (AC 2016)
- 7th International Conference on Digital Human Modeling and Applications in Health, Safety, Ergonomics and Risk Management (DHM 2016)
- 5th International Conference on Design, User Experience and Usability (DUXU 2016)
- 4th International Conference on Distributed, Ambient and Pervasive Interactions (DAPI 2016)
- 4th International Conference on Human Aspects of Information Security, Privacy and Trust (HAS 2016)
- Third International Conference on HCI in Business, Government, and Organizations (HCIBGO 2016)
- Third International Conference on Learning and Collaboration Technologies (LCT 2016)
- Second International Conference on Human Aspects of IT for the Aged Population (ITAP 2016)

Conference Proceedings Volumes Full List

Human-Computer Interaction

Program Board Chair: **Masaaki Kurosu, Japan**

- Jose Abdelnour-Nocera, UK
- Sebastiano Bagnara, Italy
- Simone Barbosa, Brazil
- Kaveh Bazargan, Iran
- Adriana Betiol, Brazil
- Simone Borsci, UK
- Michael Craven, UK
- Henry Duh, Australia
- Achim Ebert, Germany
- Xiaowen Fang, USA
- Stefano Federici, Italy
- Ayako Hashizume, Japan
- Wonil Hwang, Korea
- Yong Gu Ji, Japan
- Mitsuhiko Karashima, Japan
- Heidi Krömker, Germany
- Glyn Lawson, UK
- Tao Ma, USA
- Cristiano Maciel, Brazil
- Naoko Okuizumi, Japan
- Philippe Palanque, France
- Alberto Raposo, Brazil
- Eunice Sari, Indonesia
- Dominique Scapin, France
- Milene Selbach Silveira, Brazil
- Guangfeng Song, USA
- Hiroshi Ujita, Japan
- Fan Zhao, USA

The full list with the program board chairs and the members of the program boards of all thematic areas and affiliated conferences is available online at:

http://www.hci.international/2016/

HCI International 2017

The 19th International Conference on Human-Computer Interaction, HCI International 2017, will be held jointly with the affiliated conferences in Vancouver, Canada, at the Vancouver Convention Centre, July 9–14, 2017. It will cover a broad spectrum of themes related to human-computer interaction, including theoretical issues, methods, tools, processes, and case studies in HCI design, as well as novel interaction techniques, interfaces, and applications. The proceedings will be published by Springer. More information will be available on the conference website: http://2017.hci.international/.

General Chair
Prof. Constantine Stephanidis
University of Crete and ICS-FORTH
Heraklion, Crete, Greece
E-mail: general_chair@hcii2017.org

http://2017.hci.international/

Contents – Part III

Narratives and Visualization

Wayfinding, Mobility, and Transport

Media, Entertainment, Games, and Gamification

User Studies

Emotions in HCI

Warmth and Affection: Exploring Thermal Sensation in the Design of Parent-Child Distant Interaction

Sunmin Lee[✉] and Thecla Schiphorst

School of Interactive Arts and Technology, Simon Fraser University,
Suite 250-13450 102 Ave., Surrey, British Columbia V3T 0A3, Canada
{sla38,thecla}@sfu.ca

Abstract. Within HCI there is a history of investigating how wearable technologies provide the promise of creating intimate experiences in distant interactions. Through an iterative design process, we developed a wearable prototype for parent-child remote communication that explored warmth as a metaphor for affection. In our field study, we discovered that children interpreted thermal messages in several ways, constructing their own meanings of messages which support thoughtful interaction with design artifacts. Our findings suggest multiple uses of thermal interaction can arise by engaging the parents in reconsidering the roles of meaning-making in their everyday environment. We discuss how these findings exemplify an emerging design space akin to *non-finito products* underlying user values and creativity. Furthermore, our findings show how parents and children in different families practicing with the same prototype co-created a set of distinct and unique meaning based on their own creative application of their values surrounding warmth and affection.

Keywords: Somaesthetics · Parent-child distant communication · Thermal sensation · Affection · Ambiguity · Non-finito products

1 Introduction

Current video chat systems such as Skype or Apple's FaceTime afford high quality of auditory and visual cues by allowing users to communicate with others anytime and anywhere. However, it is still a challenge for parents and their young children to maintain and develop an intimate relationship as physical intimacy that plays a vital role in social-emotional development for the children is filtered out of the process in the video conversation. Considerable research studies [4, 6, 7, 19] on infant development have revealed that a lack of touch from caregivers causes emotional, behavioral and social problems for children.

To address this problem, we consider an alternate way to provide interpersonal touch in remote communication between parents and their children. We developed a wearable system to augment physical intimacy for parent-child remote communication. Concerning the issues carried by the absence of physical contact in remote communication, we focused on one-way form of communication, from a parent to a child, to understand the child experiences and perspectives of warm messages. Through several

© Springer International Publishing Switzerland 2016
M. Kurosu (Ed.): HCI 2016, Part III, LNCS 9733, pp. 3–14, 2016.
DOI: 10.1007/978-3-319-39513-5_1

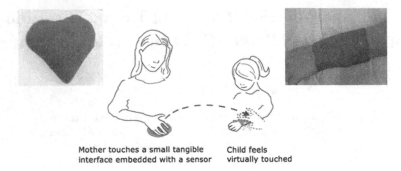

Mother touches a small tangible
interface embedded with a sensor

Child feels
virtually touched

Fig. 1. The overview of final prototype system that generates thermal sensation as a metaphor for physical intimacy

design iterations with various tactile feedback, we investigated thermal sensation in the design of parent-child distant interaction. Based on a somaesthetic design framework underlining the aesthetics of somatic experience, our design prototype allows parents to send children heat messages as a poetic metaphor for interpersonal touch (see Fig. 1). Through a qualitatively focused methodological approach, we conducted a field study of working families in which parents in the work-force spent time away from their children. Our findings reveal each user group in the field study developed different strategies of using the same device with their own meanings and contexts of interaction.

In this paper, we discuss the process of designing our design prototype, *TouchMe*, and present the methodology used to understand its emerging usages and interpretations in user personal experiences. We then show our findings and how these findings reveal an emerging design space, *non-finito products*, which highlights user values and creativity in the practical cases of deploying the system as a resources for design [12].

2   Related Work

Several HCI researchers [1, 3] attempt to support physical interaction for remote communication by exploring wearable technologies. Lee and Lim fabricated a heat application as a pair of wearable devices to enhance social connectedness in remote communication [9]. They recruited two groups of participants who are in intimate relationships and asked them to report the situation and purpose of using the prototype within the context of everyday routines for a day. The findings from their study suggested that heat expression has its own unique attributes such as abstract degrees of thermal perception, positive preconceptions on warmth and unobtrusiveness in sending and receiving the thermo-messages. Similarly, YourGlove, HotHands and HotMits designed by Gooch and Watts [5] involve a wearable technology that simulates tangible presence such as a physical representation of hand-holding, interaction. Gooch and Watts conducted a semi-structured interview to understand the qualities of individual design factors on the systems. Most participants found that all three prototypes assisted them to share a connection with their partners, evoking personal memories. Nonetheless, the participants stated that the representation of hand-holding with thermal cues was more compelling.

Although the researchers suggested wearable technology could illustrate physical metaphors of interpersonal touch using thermal sensation in order to reinforce affective communication and contribute to sustain close social relationship, they heavily focused on long distance romantic relationships instead of parents and their children. Few researchers including Teh et al. [15] sought for a more effective method to foster physical interaction in interpersonal communication between parents and child. However, most of their prototypes were not evaluated to get insight into the users' expectations and experiences.

3   System Design

In a research through design process, we iterated our design with two artifacts. Addressing the issues carried by the absence of physical contact from a caregiver in remote interaction, we designed a wearable and tangible system that supports one-way form of communication, from a parent to a child.

3.1   First Prototype with Various Tactile Feedback

To illustrate physical intimacy, we first explored three types of tangible information; vibrotactile cues, thermal feedback, and combination of both vibrotactile and thermal feedback. The system was designed to simulate tactile sensation in particularly the forearm which is sensitive to light touch [16].

We designed a wearable technology that can evoke the sensation of subtle movements next to our skin [11, 15, 18]. The system comprises a pair of devices; one (tangible input device) is for a parent to send tactile information to a child, and the other (wearable output device) is for the child to receive the messages (see Fig. 2).

When a parent touches the tangible interface worn on his or her arm, it detects the tactile movement and transfers the data wirelessly to the child for up to 10 km. The child then receives the information from the wearable system. Both input and output feedbacks are accompanied by light cues to indicate the real-time state of sending or receiving intimate information at a glance. The prototype was built with soft circuits using conductive thread and small mobile programmable computers (see Fig. 3).

Fig. 2.   The initial prototype comprises a tangible input device (left) and a wearable output device (right).

Fig. 3. The system is composed of soft circuits (left) with LilyPad Arduino (right)

Therefore, target users for the wearable communication system are (1) either a full or part time working parent who tends to spend less time with his or her child, and (2) a child in the age group of 7 to 11 years. The system was geared specifically towards school-aged children experiencing rapid progress in all areas of development and skills [2]. She claimed that in this stage, the child begins to have activities outside the family and explore independence, yet they still need "warm, supportive, and engaged parents" to develop "secure emotional attachments, healthy peer relationships, high self esteem, and a strong sense of morality."

In order to understand which form of tactile information is more emotive and convincing on users, we pursued a preliminary pilot user study with eight participants having various careers such as a housewife and an electrical engineer. In the study, we simply asked the participants to interact with both input and output devices and report their experiences including feelings on three different tactile feedbacks. Interestingly, all participants responded that they only felt vibrotactile cue when it was given with heat feedback. On the other hand, when either vibrotactile or heat reaction was separately occurred, every participant could identify the information. Although vibrotactile cue illustrated in our prototype was more prevailing in stimulating the users' sensory experiences compared with heat feedbacks, the participants perceived it as an alarming or notifying message instead of physical intimacy. Suhonen et al. confirmed this result by arguing that thermal signal may be more suitable in the contexts of communicating emotional information such as interpersonal touch [14]. Therefore, our new prototype focused on only thermal sensation.

3.2 Final Prototype

Focusing on thermal sensation, we modified the wearable communication system framed within the context of somaesthetics for more expressive tactile interaction in remote communication between parent and child. By adopting a somaesthetic design framework of tactile interaction proposed by Schiphorst et al. [10], the wearable communication device explores four underlying themes; *experience, poetics of interaction, materiality and semantics.*

It focuses on *somatic sensory experience* of the wearer to evoke positive interpersonal reactions for remote communication between parents and child. The tangible feedback exhibited by the Peltier thermoelectric heat pump in the system not only induces thermal sensibility but also brings physical comfort, which is essential to the formation of social bonds as well as psychological development of the child [Harlow]. The *poetic concepts* of embodied communication form the foundation of designing fundamental features and functionality of wearable systems. The output device conveys thermal feedbacks as a metaphor of interpersonal warmth accompanied by skin-to-skin interaction. The system expresses two interaction modes with symbolic displays of visual aesthetics. A pulsating LED light pattern in a non-interaction mode symbolizes the pulse of other wearer to signify his or her physical presence at a distance. In interaction mode when the wearer interacts with the interface, LED emits the brightest sparks which visualizes the meaning of lighting up social relationship. The device emphasizes its *physical material properties* including textile, shape and color that engrosses emotive experience of interaction between the wearer and the system. The heart shape (see Fig. 1) underlines a metaphorical sense as the center of a child's emotions and affection towards the child, offering more meaningful interaction. It formulates *semantics* of thermal sensory qualities in interpersonal touch, exploring the meaning of heat feedbacks in remote communication. Thermal sensation simulated by the system highlights connotative values derived from our social experience. The patterns of thermal information bring up new interpretations of remote interaction and reflect the values of physical presence in intimate relationship.

4   Methodology

4.1   Participants

Through snowball sampling, we recruited seven families with young children responded to participate in the study. Table 1 provides an overview of the participant demographics including employment status, working/school hours, and the amount of time they spend interacting with children using communication devices per day. Adult participants were 1 male and 6 female parents between the ages of 32 and 41, whereas child participants were 4 male and 3 female elementary students.

4.2   Methods

Our research involves an exploratory approach where researchers observe how people use and adopt a new technology to gain an in-depth understanding of its use patterns and key problems [8]. Consequently, qualitative research methodology was applied in a user study to understand how parents and child utilize the thermal wearable application to share a feeling of connection. The evaluation methods were composed of semi-structured interviews, field trial, diary study, and survey. The two-week field trial study was designed with diary studies to collect empirical data in a natural setting. The survey study was planned with paper-based questionnaires to measure a participant's general experiences in using the prototype. All methods took place at participants' houses or any other locations convenient to the participants.

Table 1. Overview of participant demographics

User group	Participants	gender	age	Employment status	Working/ school schedule	Average time spent on remote communication
Family 1	Parent 1	Female	41	Full time	10 a.m. ~ 7 p.m.	15 min
	Child 1	Male	9	Student	8 a.m. ~ 3 p.m.	
Family 2	Parent 2	Female	33	Full time	9 a.m.~ 5 p.m.	Less than 15 min
	Child 2	Female	8	Student	8 a.m. ~ 2 p.m.	
Family 3	Parent 3	Female	34	Full time	12 p.m.~ 8 p.m.	50 min
	Child 3	Female	9	Student	8 a.m. ~ 3 p.m.	
Family 4	Parent 4	Female	40	Part time	4 p.m.~ 8 p.m.	40 min
	Child 4	Male	7	Student	8 a.m. ~ 1:45 p.m.	
Family 5	Parent 5	Male	35	Full time	9 a.m.~ 5 p.m.	10 ~ 15 min
	Child 5	Female	8	Student	8 a.m. ~ 2 p.m.	
Family 6	Parent 6	Female	32	Full time	10 a.m. ~ 7 p.m.	15 ~ 20 min
	Child 6	Male	8	Student	8 a.m. ~ 2 p.m.	
Family 7	Parent 7	Female	36	Full time	4 p.m.~ 12 p.m.	30 min
	Child 7	Male	9	Student	8 a.m. ~ 2 p.m.	

4.3 Procedure

The study began with semi-structured interviews asking current experiences in communication devices and general concept of thermal sensation. We then conducted a short prototype trial session where both parent and child were asked to experience thermal messages on their forearm and describe the first impression of thermal information. Additionally, the adult participants were requested to thermally interact with children using the prototype for 30 min (see Fig. 4). After the trial session, they were given a series of questionnaires with two open-ended questions to understand their overall experience in the first prototype use.

Due to the limited range of wireless communication in the prototype, we considered the distances between the participants' houses and work/school and their daily activity routine. With that in mind we carefully designated four families (Family 1, 2, 6 and 7) from the user groups to pursue a field trial and diary studies. A prototype was provided to each selected user group and they were asked to use it as an interpersonal

Fig. 4. A short prototype trial session

communication device in their daily lives for two weeks. The participants were also inquired to report their experiences or context of prototype usage including intention, duration, feeling or reaction in a diary format. For the reporting method, they wrote a diary on a study web page (called Online Diary). The parents were requested to record the children's experiences of thermal messages by asking them if they encounter any challenges to access or achieve the tasks. After the field trial periods, we revisited the participants and conducted a debriefing interview to gain additional information about use experiences and values that we were not able to extract from the diary study.

5   Results

5.1   Usage Patterns of Thermal Wearable System

During a two-week period of the field trial, four parents in the user groups reported that they sent a total of 151 thermal messages to their children; this indicated on average, 2.69 thermal messages were conveyed to children by an individual parent each day. Each user group showed different patterns on the daily usage of prototype. However, most parents sent fewer thermal messages during the weekend. They sent the thermal information at diverse locations such as home, a coffee shop and grocery store as there was no limitation on the time and manner of use.

The thermal messages were delivered for a variety of purposes. Each parent in the user groups showed her own distinct patterns of using the prototype. Parent 1 sent the thermal information at a specified time including lunchtime as a greeting message. Another participant, Parent 2, used it to encourage her child for special occasions such as when he took an exam. The participants, Parent 6 and Child 6, predefined system use cases so the parent used it accordingly. On the other hand, Parent 7 sent the messages with physical affectionate expressions to her child.

Based on the above usage patterns, our analysis revealed that users accessed the thermal wearable system as a method to (1) express affection towards their children and (2) notify the children.

As a way to convey affection
The results of diary study showed parents in the field study groups predominantly used the thermal wearable system in order to express affection which refers to a feeling of loving and caring for children. During the debriefing interview, Parent 1 mentioned that thermal message is another "loving expression" that she was able to share with her child. She explained warmth that the messages contained reminded her child a feeling of love. The parent and child in Family 6 came up with their own values of thermal messages. For instance, they defined two short signals of thermal information as "I am so proud of you" and one long signal as "I love you." When the child was at school and slept over at his friend's house, these interpersonal expressions were delivered to him through the thermal wearable system. She stated that the way of sending thermal messages was much more comfortable for her to communicate how much she loves and cares about him than verbally saying the phrases.

As a way to notify children

The quality of current message in the system merely involves thermal display and light indication which amplifies the feature of heat cue. In addition, there is no difference in the degree of temperature. However, the participants in the field trial group reported that they utilized the system to deliver distinct information in different contexts. Parent 2 presented their ideas on particular topics within specific time frames. For example, Parent 2 sent the messages to her child playing with friends in the playground at dinner time in order to let him know "it is time for dinner." Parent 6 gave a disciplinary notice to her child to limit his certain actions by sending the thermal messages. Though she shares a physical space with her child, she sent the thermal messages to her child to distract or redirect his attention by restricting his behaviors.

Children's perceptions and experiences of thermal messages

Each group of parents and children provided different responses when they were verbally given a term "warmth" in the first semi-structured interview. Most children came up with objects or materials that contain or convey physical sensation of being warm; for example, they answered, "heater", "jacket", "sun", "fire" and "mom and baby." Nonetheless, a majority of child participants positively assessed thermal feedbacks generated in the wearable device (see Fig. 5), and recalled feelings of interpersonal warmth.

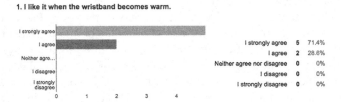

1. I like it when the wristband becomes warm.

I strongly agree	5	71.4%
I agree	2	28.6%
Neither agree nor disagree	0	0%
I disagree	0	0%
I strongly disagree	0	0%

Fig. 5. The results of survey questionnaire in the first semi-structured interview indicate most of child participants positively reacted to thermal cues in the system.

As a loving attention

In particular, children perceived the quality of heat messages with its metaphorical meanings involving parents' presence and attention. For instance, Child 1 and Child 6 experienced the physical presence of mother at a distance with thermal messages. In the beginning of field study, Child 1 considered the message notified him that his mother was physically close to him when he received it. On the other hand, Child 6 explained the first impression of warmth in the system reminded him "mom's cuddles." He said warm temperature of message suggested him a feeling of comfort which he experienced in cuddling with his mom, even though the warmth was simulated on his wrist. In addition, Child 2 referred to the thermal messages as physical protection from her mother. She expressed that when she was anxious about her test or scared of thunderstorm, she felt more secure and confident after getting the messages from her parent. Child 7 elicited the parent's loving attention from the thermal information. He believed the fact of getting a heat message indicated his mother attempted to physically interact with him regardless of the fact that she was located at a different place.

Playfulness

The results of the field study presented that the prototype also encouraged children to have playful and explorative experiences. The system embraced some degree of inherent playfulness not only for adults who interact with the prototype, but also for children who experience the feedback. The feature of playful interaction was characterized by unique tangible values of thermal information. By way of illustration, Child 1 said, "It's not like a text message I can read, so I have to guess what she is trying to say (through the heat)." Child 6 experienced thermal interaction in a playful and affectionate manner. Unlike Child 1 speculating the connotations of message, Child 6 designated its values as affectionate verbal expressions with his parent, by employing the relative length of thermal signals. He described the thermal messages sent by his parent was unique information which can be only decrypted by him.

As a disciplinary note

The thermal wearable system fostered intimate atmosphere in parent-child communication, but it also allowed children to have unfriendly experiences. On the whole, child user groups reported they perceived thermal messages as moderate and sympathetic sensory information. However, the perceived quality of thermal stimulus was interpreted in a negative way according to the context of situation in which the child received the message. The children tended to feel that the tone of thermal interaction was fierce and intense when they confronted unsupportive communication climates. For instance, as Parent 6 gave the disciplinary notification to her child in order to limit the time he spent playing video games, he discerned her furious feelings through the message. He mentioned in the interview, "She didn't tell me stop playing game, but I could feel she was pretty angry at me (through the message)." He also added that the intensity of thermal expression was higher at that moment.

6   Discussion

The results from the study revealed fundamental values of thermal messages and system usages by highlighting two underlying themes; 1) Unobtrusive way to express a feeling of affection towards a child and 2) Thermal message as action trigger. We also discovered unexpected system usage patterns of parents and children's multiple interpretations on thermal information.

According to Sengers and Gaver [13], "People appropriate and reinterpret systems to produce their own uses and meanings, and these are frequently incompatible with design expectations and inconsistent within and across groups." Complexity in advancing technologies has shifted a fundamental practice of designing interaction in a more meaningful and interpretable way [17]. Seok et al. suggested an emerging design space, *non-finito products*, by highlighting user's own values and creativity in the practical cases of using the system as interaction design resources [12]. They argued that purposefully incomplete design artifacts stimulate users to complete the interaction based on their own contexts and choices.

From the findings, we found that our prototype, *TouchMe* manifestly encompasses the properties of *non-finito products* by allowing the parents and children to manipulate thermal interaction and interpret the metaphorical meanings of thermal expression in their own manner. *TouchMe* is designed to support parents and children to share a feeling of connectedness using thermal sensation as a metaphor for physical intimacy. Nevertheless, the system let the users build their own usages to achieve the specific goals. A majority of the parent participants used the system to express affectionate feelings towards their children by recalling their experiences and the children's reactions in the first field trial.

Furthermore, the thermal wearable communication system was used to convey non-emotional information to children. For instance, some parents sent thermal messages non-verbally to persuade the children into performing certain actions such as stop playing video games and return home for dinner. Thermal sensation triggers the children's creativity and imagination to create their own meaning of messages, and it simultaneously provokes their intuitions to understand the intentions of thermal interaction. The thermal message was occasionally perceived as multiple degrees of temperature based on the situational contexts in which the child experienced the message.

TouchMe was not intended to foster a *non-finito product*. However, with the ambiguous quality of sensory information, *TouchMe* evolving through several processes of a user study and somaesthetic design framework may spontaneously fit into the new design space that provokes user's creativity and values in the actual contexts of deploying the systems.

As pointed out by Seok et al., the old paradigm of designing finished and closed systems based on designer's single interpretation hardly satisfies user's individual needs. Consequently, researchers should consider to develop the systems to be more open, interpretable and customizable through multiple design processes by focusing on users' somatic experiences, like *TouchMe*.

7 Conclusion

Our prototype, *TouchMe* opens a space for interpretation and functionality in metaphors of warmth and affection through thermal communication between parents and children. The ambiguous information of thermal sensation provides a creative space that initiates the children's imagination enabling them to construct their own meaning for the messages. Thoughtfully designed artifacts suggests multiple uses by engaging the parents in reconsidering the roles of system in their daily environment.

Thermal feedback in distance interaction system was employed in an unobtrusive way to express affection towards a parent's child. It was also used as an action trigger in certain contexts. For instance, in one case the thermal feedback non-verbally persuaded the children to stop playing video games and returned home to have dinner. While the physical sensation of warmth in the messages supported the children's feeling of emotional warmth, the act of sending the messages to the children and expecting them to experience not only the sensation of warmth but also the feeling of warmth allowed parents to maintain connection in simple yet 'anytime' moments while in the workplace. Lastly, despite the stability of the thermal temperature, a child's emotional response was affected by their perceived interpretation of the meaning of the thermal sensation.

This explores the proposition of Seok et al. [12] which focuses on a user's value-creating approach in the design process. The dynamic feedbacks of *TouchMe* discloses users' needs and values in thermal communication and allows them to have continuous experiences within their everyday contexts. Our research affords insight for a more effective and flexible design in thermal interfaces to provoke user's values and creativity.

References

1. Adcock, M., Boch, M., Harden, V., Harry, D., Poblano, R.V.: Tug n' talk: a belt buckle for tangible tugging communication. In: CHI 2007. San Jose, USA (2007)
2. Bennett, T.: Dr. Bennett's Developmental Psychology Crash Course (Ages 7–11 Years) (2014). http://getkidsinternetsafe.com/blog/crash-course-for-7-to-11/
3. Choi, Y., Tewell, J., Morisawa, Y., Pradana, G., Cheok, A.: Ring*U: a wearable system for intimate communication using tactile lighting expressions. In: ACE 2014 Proceedings of the 11th Conference on Advances in Computer Entertainment Technology, Article No. 63 (2014)
4. Field, T.: Infants' need for touch. Hum. Dev. **45**, 100–103 (2002)
5. Gooch, D., Watts, L.: YourGloves, HotHands and HotMits: devices to hold hands at a distance. In: Proceedings of UIST 2012, pp. 157–166. ACM Press (2012)
6. Grunwald, M.: Human Haptic Perception. Basics and Applications. Birkhäuser, Berlin (2008)
7. Harlow, H.F., Harlow, M.K., Hansen, E.W.: The maternal affectional system of Rhesus monkeys. In: Rhinegold, H.L. (ed.) Maternal Behaviors in Mammals, pp. 254–281. Wiley, New York (1963)
8. Hesse-Biber, N.S., Leavy, P.: The Practice of Qualitative Research, 2nd edn. Sage Publications Inc., Thousand Oaks (2011)
9. Lee, W. Lim, Y.: Thermo-message: exploring the potential of heat as a modality of peripheral expression. In: CHI EA 2010, pp. 4231–4236. ACM (2010)
10. Schiphorst, T., Seo, J., Jaffe, N.: Exploring touch and breath in networked wearable installation design. In: MM2010 Proceedings of the International Conference on Multimedia, Extended Abstracts on Human Factors in Computing Systems, pp. 1399–1400. ACM Press, Firenze, Italy, 25–29 October 2010
11. Schiphorst, T.: Tendrils: exploring the poetics of collective touch in wearable art. In: Proceedings of TEI 2011, pp. 397–398. ACM Press (2011)
12. Seok, J., Woo, J., Lim, Y.: Non-finito products: a new design space of user creativity for personal user experience. In: Proceedings of the SIGCHI Conference on Human Factors in Computing Systems, Toronto, Ontario, Canada, 26 April–01 May 2014
13. Sengers, P., Gaver, B.: Staying open to interpretation: engaging multiple meanings in design and evaluation. In: Proceedings of the DIS 2006. ACM Press (2006)
14. Suhonen, K., Väänänen-Vainio-Mattila, K., Mäkelä, K.: User experiences and expectations of vibrotactile, thermal and squeeze feedback in interpersonal communication. In: Proceedings of the BCS-HCI 2012, British Computer Society, pp. 205–214 (2012)
15. Teh, J.K.S., Cheok, A.D., Peiris, R.L., Choi, Y., Thuong, V., Lai, S.: Huggy pajama: a mobile parent and child hugging communication system. In: International Conference on Interaction Design and Children, pp. 250–257. ACM Press, New York (2008)
16. Vrontou, S., Wong, A.M., Rau, K.K., Koerber, H.R., Anderson, D.J.: Genetic identification of C fibers that detect massage-like stroking of hairy skin in vivo. Nature **493**, 669–673 (2013)

17. Wakkary, R., Desjardins, A., Hauser, S.: Unselfconscious interaction in the home: a construct. Interacting with Computers (2015, Submitted for publication)
18. Wang, R., Quek, F.: Touch and Talk: contextualizing remote touch for affective interaction. In: Proceedings of TEI 2010, pp. 13–20. ACM Press (2010)
19. Weiss, W.J., Wilson, P.W., Morrison, D.: Maternal tactile stimulation and the neuro development of low birth weight infants. Infancy 5, 85–107 (2004)

From Internet Memes to Emoticon Engineering: Insights from the Baozou Comic Phenomenon in China

Xiaojuan Ma[✉]

The Hong Kong University of Science and Technology, Kowloon, Hong Kong
mxj@cse.ust.hk

Abstract. Baozou comic, a.k.a. rage comic internationally, has been widely used as a form of visual communication of emotions in social media, advertisement, entertainment, and many other domains in China. In particular, Chinese netizens have converted this type of Internet memes into emoticons and use them extensively in Instant Messaging applications. This paper discusses the potential socio-economic context of the Baozou comic phenomenon in China. Baozou comic is a unique combination of cuteness and parody, and can serve as a vehicle to convey out-of-control, subtle, complicated, or hidden emotions. Its ugly aesthetics reflects the self-perception of a new generation of Chinese Internet users. The grassroots emoticon engineering process, including easy production, replication, and customization, also contributes to the growing popularity of Baozou comic in China. Analysis on miscommunication over Baozou emoticons reveal some related issues such as the need to balance ambiguity and emotional depth in expressions.

Keywords: Internet memes · Baozou comic · Rage comic · Emoticon · Stickers

1 Introduction

On October 1, 2015, the city police of Nanjing, China published a set of anti-fraud booklets in a Baozou comic (i.e., rage comic in China)[1] style on its Weibo[2] and WeChat[3] account (Fig. 1 Left). Just in one day, the booklets received over 200,000 clicks online. Many news media, including the CCTV (China Central Television) news website, reported the success of this campaign [4]. In the same month, the Weibo account of the official Taobao Store of the Forbidden City Museum[4] posted an article titled "Enough, Leave me Alone" (Fig. 1, right). The article told the story of the last emperor of the Ming Dynasty with Baozou comics [7]. The purpose was to advertise for the museum's lucky souvenirs. Over 1.27 million people have read the post and many left a like.

---

[1] Chinese website of Baozou comic: http://baozoumanhua.com.
[2] Chinese Microblogging platform: http://www.weibo.com/.
[3] A online social networking tool by Tencent: http://www.wechat.com/.
[4] Forbidden City's official Taobao store: https://gugong1925.world.taobao.com/.

© Springer International Publishing Switzerland 2016
M. Kurosu (Ed.): HCI 2016, Part III, LNCS 9733, pp. 15–27, 2016.
DOI: 10.1007/978-3-319-39513-5_2

Fig. 1. Left: screenshot from the anti-fraud booklet (Copyright ©weibo.com/njga); right: screenshot of the microblogging article by Forbidden City's official Taobao store (Copyright ©weibo.com/gugongtaobao).

These events have demonstrated the well-recognized ability of Baozou comic to evoke public attention in China, regardless of the heated debates on the appropriateness of using this new style of visual communication in scenarios that are often considered to be formal or serious. Compared to stylish graphics carefully crafted by designers, Baozou comics are unpolished, rough, ugly (in the conventional sense) sketches or images made usually by amateurs exploiting materials available over the Internet (see examples of comparison in Fig. 1 right). However, despite its "minimal effort" aesthetic [6] and potential legal issues [17] as a type of Internet memes, Baozou comic has swept all kinds of online communications, from instant messaging (IM) such as WeChat (Fig. 2) and QQ[5], micro blogs, e-bulletin boards, to forums.

The popularity of Baozou comic is a reflection of an emerging fad of emoticon (particularly digital stickers in IM) engineering [25] in China. More and more Chinese Internet users are involved in the creation and dissemination of static images as well as animated GIFs of facial expressions, many of which are in the style of Baozou comics. There has been some research on the spread of Internet memes globally [2, 18]. However, not much work has looked into (1) why are Chinese people who have the tradition of making and keeping "face" (miànzǐ 面子 in Chinese) [10] willing to depict themselves in ugly drawings? (2) What kinds of emotions do Chinese people intend to express through these comics, given that their culture is rich in affects [26] but encourages emotion restraint [1]? And (3) why and how can the emoticon engineering practices be widely adopted?

QQ is another instant messaging tool of Tencent: http://im.qq.com/.

Fig. 2. Left: WeChat Cute Pets stickers in conventional Internet meme style; right: WeChat Bubbly Chatter stickers in Baozou style. (Copyright © Tencent).

This paper aims to address these questions. I use the Baozou comic phenomenon in China as a lens to explore the potential socio-economic factors behind the indulgence in emotion expression in the form of a parody. I investigate the different types of emotions commonly depicted in Baozou comics, and tactics to craft such illustrations. In the end, I discuss some insights into emoticon engineering and its social implications in the situated cultural context.

2 Background

This section reviews the history of Baozou comic from its root Internet meme and more specifically rage comic, the use of emoticons, kaomoji, and emoji in online communication, and the fad of sticker in Asia.

2.1 Internet Meme, Rage Comic, and Baozou Comic

An Internet meme is "a form of visual entertainment" [2], which gains "influence through online transmission" [5] and gets "replicated via evolution, adaptation or transformation of the original meme vehicle" [12]. More specifically, an Internet meme can be a static image, an animated GIF, a video clip, or a remix of different modalities reproduced or repackaged by anyone out of any existing materials available online [2, 18]. Therefore, Internet memes are usually lightweight with low visual quality, which to a certain extent makes them easier to access, replicate, adapt, and spread across the Internet. The memes tend to be simple in style, directing readers to emphasize on the embedded message rather than the aesthetic value of the graphics [2]. Note that the message expressed in a meme often deviates from the intent of the original source. It can be explicitly presented as additional text or implicitly conveyed through the graphical content, sometimes with special effects as visual cues. A commonly seen example of Internet memes is lolcats, i.e., humorous photos of cat(s) with superimposed text, from the Caturday tradition of 4Chan[6]. More examples can be found on the website Know Your Meme (knowyour-meme.com).

Rage comic is a special genre of Internet memes, originating from an amateur-made four-panel web comic strip about an angry experience published on 4Chan in 2008. It mainly consists of a stick figure-style character with a crudely drawn face (a.k.a. rage face) to "show universal emotions" – not restricted to anger or rage – "of varying degrees under a wide variety of circumstances" [15]. A rage face can be a freehand sketch or copy-pasted from some other sources such as photo, video, cartoon and Japanese manga [6]. Some of the most popular rage faces include Forever Alone, Trollface, and Rageguy[7]. Creators can compose elaborate comic strips using rage face(s) to depict some personal story with a humorous punch line.

Rage comic was first introduced to China as bàozǒu mànhuà (or Baozou comic 暴走漫画) in 2008[8], and has become increasingly popular among Chinese Internet users since then. The term bàozǒu means out of control, which implies the simple and crude style of the visuals on one hand and its use as a venting channel on the other hand. Initially, Baozou comics were mostly amateur comic strips submitted to the baozou-manhua.com website, telling stress-buster jokes or real-life stories that everyone can somehow resonate with [3]. In recent years, another form of Baozou comic has emerged and gained popularity even outside the baozoumanhua.com community.

As part of the fad of sticker in Chinese social media [25], still or animated Baozou figures are used as emoticons in electronic and web messages (Fig. 2 right). Besides the classic rage faces, Baozou comic creators have added to the collection some new facial expressions extracted from online photos and videos of (Internet) celebrities, such as the famous Yao Ming face. By changing text descriptions and/or varying the background, the same face can express different affects. For example, a friend living in

---

[6] An image-based bulletin board: http://www.4chan.org.
[7] See http://knowyourmeme.com/memes/rage-comics for more examples.
[8] The copyright of rage comics in China is owned by Xi'an MOMO IT Ltd., the owner of the website baozoumanhua.com.

Beijing sent me a Baozou style WeChat sticker[9] on the coldest day this winter to tease the north-south divide of central heating in China. The top character in Northern China is showing off while the bottom one in Southern China is pretending to be strong, but they actually share the same face. I call this process emoticon engineering, since users mainly customize existing Baozou faces to indicate their feelings.

2.2   Emoticon, Kaomoji, Emoji, and Sticker

In the narrowest sense, "emoticon" refers to typographic smileys[10]. Kaomoji[11] are Japanese-style emoticons that make full use of the Japanese character set in addition to the common symbols. In many occasions, the definition of emoticon is extended to include other versions of smileys such as drawings and pictographs. In the scope of this paper, I use "emoticon" as a general term, i.e., a visual representation of a facial expression, especially as a kind of grassroots creation.

In contrast, emoji are stylish graphics originally developed by the Japanese communication company NTT DoCoMo for online communication. The contents of emoji range from living being and everyday objects to signs and symbols, no longer limited to facial expressions. Although the vocabularies are more or less the same, companies tend to have their own design of the graphics. For example, iOS emoji have a different look from those on an Android phone.

Another related concept is sticker – illustrations or animations of characters sometimes attached with witty words and phrases that can be sent in instant messaging (IM) applications to express emotions. In other words, stickers are emoticon designed for IM services. The depiction of facial and bodily expressions in stickers is more elaborate, expressive, and comprehensive than the traditional typographic symbols.

A picture is worth a thousand words. Users find digital stickers beneficial especially in East Asian cultures, because sending a sticker is less cumbersome than typing out the entire message in a logographic script like Chinese [8, 21, 22]. Furthermore, it can increase the sense of intimacy [24, 25], and convey feelings that may be awkward to say in words [21]. Therefore, the fad of sticker quickly spreads across Japanese, Korean, and Chinese users of Asia-based IM services such as Line [21] and WeChat [25], and extends to other platforms such as Facebook Messenger [8].

Most of stickers feature a cute style [8, 21]. However, under the influence of Baozou comic, stickers in China have established a special type of "cuteness" that is very different from the Hello Kitty Japanese kawaii style, i.e., vulgar, wacky appearance with anarchic wit to achieve a parody effect [13, 25]. Take WeChat as an example. Not only do many third-party sticker packs ready for download have some Baozou flavor, but it is also common that users convert Baozou-style images and GIF animations from the web into stickers or simply make their own. One can find the use of Baozou emoticons in other online media as well, ranging from forum and blog posts (Fig. 1 right) to Internet

---

[9] See http://ww1.sinaimg.cn/bmiddle/6807d621gw1f0dxsyyh9sj20bc0m8ta5.jpg for the image.
[10] See this article for details: http://www.theguardian.com/technology/2015/feb/06/difference-between-emoji-and-emoticons-explained.
[11] See http://kaomoji.ru/en/ for examples.

novels. Exploring the socio-economic context of contemporary China can provide some insights into the popularity of Baozou emoticons.

3   Socio-Economic Factors of the Rise of Baozou Emoticons

Baozou comic was first adopted by young Chinese netizens to vent about amusing or frustrating experiences. Later, it was accepted by a more general population as emoticons. The ugly aesthetics of Baozou comic reflects the self-perception of ordinary Chinese Internet users and meets their need for expression in a face-keeping culture.

3.1   Subculture of Diǎosī

A nation-wide survey by Sohu showed that 64, 81 and 70 percent of respondents in their 20 s, 30 s and 40 s, respectively, considered themselves as a diǎosī (屌丝) – a nobody [11]. Diǎosī is an epithet that was originally an insult but has now evolved to be a universal self-ascribe identity, meaning someone born in an ordinary family, with a mediocre look, and having a humble job [20]. Although often used comically as the polar opposite of the upper-class gāofùshuài (高富帅, literally means a "tall, rich, and handsome" male) and báifùměi (白富美, a "fair-skinned, wealthy, and beautiful" female) [11, 20], diǎosī actually denotes an average person. According to the 2013 survey, 76 % of the respondents from Shanghai, China took on the diǎosī label [11], many of whom had college education and a middle-class income.

In other words, a diǎosī is not a loser in the traditional sense. Rather, it is a self-perception that one's socio-economic status is far from perfect in "a pretty person's world" (看脸的世界) where "only the rich can live a willful life" (有钱才能任性). On one hand, diǎosī usually admit such imperfection through self-belittlement such as ǎicuǒqióng (矮矬穷, i.e., short, ugly, and poor) or humorous satire such as "look at how I look rather than my look" (主要看气质, Fig. 3 right) [20]. On the other hand, they share the disillusionment of low socio-economic mobility through ègǎo (恶搞, i.e., parody, see Fig. 1 right for an example) [20]. For example, the diǎosī character portrayed in popular Chinese web series such as "Unexpectedness (万万没想到)" is usually a guy with no background, no money, and no future in reality, but always keeps the daydream of moving up the socio-economic ladder. As one of the famous lines from Unexpectedness says, "[I] believe that very soon I will get a promotion and raise, be appointed as the manager, become the CEO, marry a báifùměi, and reach the peak in life. [I] get a bit excited just thinking about it."

Baozou comic as a unique combination of cuteness and parody [25] fits the multifacet image of diǎosī. First, it is vivid but not very offensive to depict the self-mockingly vulgar appearance and life of diǎosī using crude, cheap-looking Baozou-style characters (Fig. 3 left). Sometimes the visuals come with captions in both Chinese and Chinglish ("give you some color to see see" in Fig. 2 left) as a self-belittler. Second, Baozou comic has a sense of humor in its gene, and thus can be leveraged to convey the playful nature of diǎosī especially in the form of ègǎo (Fig. 3 right).

Fig. 3. Left: WeChat Horse and Frog stickers that illustrate a diǎosī's self-perception; right: examples of ègǎo using Hey Good Thinking stickers. (Copyright © Tencent).

3.2 Subculture of Tǔcáo

Diǎosī often like to tease themselves or assorted phenomena in daily life. The use of mockery is called tǔcáo (吐槽 in Chinese and tsukkomi in Japanese). This term comes from Manzai, a type of team comedy in Japan in which the tsukkomi player points out and corrects the errors and misunderstandings of the boke player in a direct, sharp manner [19]. These days, tsukkomi has become a common archetype in Japanese light novels and modern anime. Through these channels, Chinese netizens got introduced to the act of tǔcáo and have adopted it in everyday scenarios.

However, tǔcáo is a challenge to traditional face-keeping culture in China. Self-teasing in public may impair one's own image, while mocking others may be considered as offensive and consequently cause aversion reaction. Using Baozou comic for tǔcáo can be an effective risk mitigation strategy. For one thing, Baozou faces are universal. People are less likely to associate the characters with a specific person. For another, the exaggerated facial expressions in Baozou comic are a well-known device to achieve a comedic effect. As a result, people often view Baozou-style tǔcáo as a mockery of some common experiences or phenomena rather than a targeted insult. For example, there are two stickers from the same WeChat sticker pack specially made to welcome the year of 2016. One is an ordinary New Year wish, "A whole new year, a whole new me." The other is a tǔcáo that can be sent when someone posts that wish, which says "In a few days, someone would post self-deception messages such as 'A whole new year, a whole new me' again."

4 Emotions Expressed in Baozou Emoticons

Chinese Internet users, especially those identifying themselves as diǎosī, often use Baozou emoticons in parody (ègǎo) and mockery (tǔcáo) of different emotions. This section discusses the underlying rationales, based on 400 Baozou faces retrieved from baozoumanhua.com and over 300 Baozou stickers collected from WeChat messages.

4.1 "Out of Control" Emotions

Chinese people have the tradition of educating children the culturally appropriate way to display and react to emotions [23]. On one hand, Chinese people value the negative emotions such as surprise, angry, and dissatisfaction that they perceive as signals of violation of social norm or unfulfillment of social obligations [26]. On the other hand, they are encouraged to regulate the expression of such emotions in terms of duration, intensity, and frequency, so as not to disrupt interpersonal relationship and social harmony [1]. Contemporary Chinese are less reluctant to speak out especially online. But still many people feel that venting through emoticons is more socially acceptable in many occasions than directly saying things in words. It is because emoticons were initially invented to differentiate jokes from serious content online, meaning that the expressions should not be taken very seriously [16].

Before the introduction of Baozou emoticons, kaomoji was a popular means (and still is in many places) to communicate feelings in forums, games, chat rooms, etc. It employs a bigger character set than the single-byte typographic emoticons, and can convey richer affects with faces, actions, objects, and special effects (Fig. 4 bottom). However, kaomoji are considered as kawaii icons and thus favored far more by females [9]. In comparison, Baozou emoticons are relatively gender-neutral. They can apply similar visual cues to kaomoji and use exaggeration more extensively as a rhetorical device (Fig. 4 bottom).

Surprise "lightning strike"   Embarrassment "hang oneself"   Anger "throwing table"

Σ(ﾟ 口 ﾟ)   (o-_-o)   (ﾉ ﾟ 益 ﾟ)ﾉ 彡 ┻━┻

Fig. 4. Top: Curly Pete sticker (Copyright © Tencent); bottom: corresponding kaomoji.

Besides showing facial expressions as ordinary emoticons do, Baozou emoticons can indicate a strong surge of emotion by comically visualizing the intended feeling getting out of control, such as lightning strike (rúléihōngdǐng 如雷轰顶) for surprise and throwing table (xiānzhuō 掀桌) for anger. Although 14 of the 19 emotion categories in baozoumanhua.com are negative, the same technique can be used to signify positive affect. For example, Fig. 5 (top) shows various "thank you, boss" stickers that I collected from WeChat messages when participating in digital red packet activities during the Lunar New Year[12]. Characters in the stickers bow, kneel, or kowtow to the sender of the red packet – the boss – for even just a few cents, which hilariously demonstrates appreciation under the diǎosī mentality. Such behaviors, however, would be perceived as a severe loss of face in real life.

Fig. 5. Top row: various professional red packet-related stickers with the message "Thank you, boss"; bottom row: various user-made stickers related to red pocket (from screenshots of WeChat messages, Copyright © Tencent).

4.2 Subtle or Complicated Emotions

Although the Chinese language has already had a rich vocabulary of emotional terms [26], netizens keep inventing new idiom-like Internet slangs to express more subtle or complicated emotions, such as rénjiānbùchāi (人艰不拆, "Some lies are better not exposed, as life is already so hard")[13]. While existing textual emoticons and emoji aim to show common feelings, Baozou characters tend to have more emotional depth. Many Baozou faces consist of salient features from different basic emotions [14], e.g., the Curly Pete guy in Fig. 6 (left). Some even deliberately introduce ambiguities. For instance, it is hard to tell if the character is smiling or crying with one hand over the face if the tears are not drawn (Fig. 6 right). Since such designs can lead to different interpretations of the encoded emotion, it leaves room for users to customize the message by attaching different witty phrases and/or adding visual cues (Fig. 6 right).

Fig. 6. Left: the Curly Pete face consists of salient facial features of three basic emotions; right: an examples of one sticker with different messages (Copyright © Tencent).

4.3 Internal "Overlapping Sound"

Sometimes people do not mean what they say. Chinese Internet users have been using a technique called "overlapping sound (OS)" to illustrate tǔcáo as an internal mental

---

[13] NYTimes article: http://sinosphere.blogs.nytimes.com/2013/10/27/better-than-a-tweet-using-four-characters-young-chinese-create-internet-idioms-with-a-new-world-of-meaning/?_r=0.

activity. OS appears in text such as posts, Internet novels, and news, with the words to be said written in Chinese and the real message written in Pinyin. In the example of 心(è)疼(gǎo) in Fig. 7, the article says that people "feel sorry for (心疼)" Leonardo Dicaprio but it actually means "making fun of (ègǎo)" him. Ambiguous facial expressions in Baozou emoticon can serve as good indicators of OS.

Fig. 7. An example of textual "overlapping sound (OS)" (screenshot of a NetEase news article. Copyright © NetEase).

5   DIY Emoticon Engineering

In addition to being expressive and evoking, the ability to turn users from pure consumers to producers is another reason why Baozou emoticons can quickly gain wide adoption. Depicting facial expressions is usually the most critical and the most difficult part of emoticon design. Baozou emoticons make it easier by allowing amateurs to exploit pre-made faces of biǎoqíngdì (表情帝, an individual with rich expressions) from online comics, photos, and videos. Some of the popular examples include the well-known Yao Ming Face and Jackie Chan's Duang[14]. Some celebrities even published their own Baozou-style sticker pack (Fig. 8 left).

Fig. 8. Left: a professional sticker of idol Luhan; middle: example of simple customization of Bubble Pup stickers to fit the Lunar New Year theme; right: examples of how adding simple graphical elements can help disambiguate the emotion, while combining multiple elements can express complicated feelings. (Copyright © Tencent).

---

[14] BBC article about "Duang": http://www.bbc.com/news/blogs-trending-31689148.

To make a Baozou emoticon, creators can simply crop out the character from a web image or a screenshot, turn a photo into a line drawing, or convert a selected video segment to an animated GIF. Alternatively, they can copy and paste the face onto different cartoon figures, and add other graphical elements such as sweat, flush, shadow, symbols, motion lines props, and text to further customize the emoticon (Fig. 8 middle and right). This emoticon engineering process can be carried out with ordinary image editing tools such as Microsoft Paint and Photoshop, or a dedicated Baozou comic generator (a.k.a. ragemaker).

6 Discussion

Baozou comic strips encourage readers to put themselves in the character's shoes and reflect upon their own experiences. Baozou emoticons instead allow both senders and receivers to separate their image in real life from the representations. For example, in the fourth sticker from the left in the bottom row of Fig. 5, the sender drew an arrow with a "that's me" remark towards the panda that is kowtowing at the fastest pace. The receiver recognizes and accepts the sticker as an expression of appreciation, but will not expect the sender to perform the illustrated action in reality. Such mutual understanding gives Baozou sticker users more freedom of choice. My senior male colleagues actually sent Baozou sticker of cute girls and babies (Fig. 5 bottom right).

The fad of stickers has penetrated different age groups. In a Taiwanese talk show called University (大学生了没), the college students shared stories of their parents who are in their 50 s and 60 s flooding the IM services with stickers. There are similar blog posts on Chinese social media. While the parents seem to master the motivational poster-type of stickers pretty well, Chinese young netizens have discovered a new type of generation gap called "your mom don't understand your Baozou sticker."

There are several reasons for this, which also reveals potential issues in emoticon engineering. First, older Internet users are not very familiar with the newly invented Internet slangs, and thus they often intuitively take the witty phrases accompanying the emoticons in their literal meaning. For example, a common caption for the "hand-over-face" emoticon (Fig. 6 right) is wǒyěshìzuìle (我也是醉了, I am drunk). It actually means a person is speechless or knocked out by something shocking, and can be mistaken as a complaint of overdrinking. Misunderstanding frequently occurs when a sticker receiver does not realize that the message uses metaphor or hyperbole. Second, the emphasis of a Baozou emoticon is the face, but people may get distracted by other things in the scene. For example, a mother replied "Don't smoke" to the sad Baozou sticker (a crying man taking a cigarette) sent by her son. Third, as mentioned earlier, many Baozou expressions are subtle and complicated. Without sufficient visual cues and/or knowledge about the original source of the face, readers may find the emotion difficult to interpret. Fourth, readers may not notice that the emoticon is showing an affect that is different from what is being said; that is, the visual is serving as the overlapping sound of the words. In the end, the usual response of the younger generation to such miscommunication is, "Never mind. It is just an emotional expression."

7 Conclusion and Future Work

In summary, the Baozou emoticon phenomenon in China exemplifies an ongoing grassroots creation movement. Its emergence satisfies the need of expression of a new generation of Chinese Internet users. Its ugly aesthetics reflects the self-perception of the users, and is a unique component of the trend of cuteness in many East Asia countries. Easy production, replication, and customization further boost the popularity of Baozou emoticons. In the future, I plan to conduct more systematic studies on the creation and use of emoticons and related gender, cultural, and socio-economic issues.

References

1. Bond, M.H.: Emotions and their expression in Chinese culture. J. Nonverbal Behav. **17**(4), 245–262 (1993)
2. Börzsei, L.K.: Makes a meme instead: a concise history of internet memes. New Media Stud. Mag. **7**, 152–189 (2013)
3. Chen, S.W.: Baozou manhua (rage comics), Internet humour and everyday life. Continuum **28**(5), 690–708 (2014)
4. China Central Television News (CCTV): Nanjing Police Teach Anti-Fraud Methods using "Ye Liangchen Baozou Comics" (in Chinese) (2015). http://news.cntv.cn/2015/10/02/ARTI1443771338069299.shtml
5. Davison, P.: The language of internet memes. In: The social media reader, pp. 120–134 (2012)
6. Douglas, N.: It's supposed to look like shit: the internet ugly aesthetic. J. Vis. Cult. **13**(3), 314–339 (2014)
7. Forbidden City's Taobao Store: Enough, Leave me Alone (in Chinese). http://www.weibo.com/p/1001593903583732031574?from=page_100606_profile&wvr=6&mod=wenzhangmod
8. Guilford, G.: This company is betting millions that you'll use cartoon bears instead of English, Quartz. http://qz.com/156030/line-is-betting-millions-that-virtual-bears-and-bunnies-will-sweep-the-west/
9. Hjorth, L.: Mobile Media in the Asia-Pacific: Gender and the Art of Being Mobile. Routledge, New York (2008)
10. Hu, H.C.: The Chinese concepts of "face". Am. Anthropol. **46**(1), 45–64 (1944)
11. Kan, K., Tiscione, J.: 'Diaosi': Understanding China's Generation X. That's Beijing. (2013). http://online.thatsmags.com/post/diaosi-understanding-chinas-generation-x
12. Knobel, M., Lankshear, C.: Memes and affinities: Cultural replication and literacy education. In: Annual Meeting of the National Reading Conference, vol. 30 (2005)
13. Li, J.: The Sticker Wars: WeChat's creatives go up against Line. http://www.88-bar.com/2014/02/the-sticker-wars-wechats-creatives-go-up-against-line/
14. Ma, X., Forlizzi, J., Dow, S.: Guidelines for depicting emotions in storyboard scenarios. In: 8th International Design and Emotion Conference (2012)
15. Morris, K.: Making rage comics? Just fine with this English teacher. The Daily Dot (2011). http://www.dailydot.com/culture/rage-comics-teach-english/
16. Randall, N.: Lingo online: A report on the language of the keyboard generation. MSN Canada (2002). http://www.arts.uwaterloo.ca/~nrandall/LingoOnline-finalreport.pdf
17. Schiphorst, R.F.: The Author and The Digital Craftsman (2013)

18. Shifman, L.: Memes in a digital world: Reconciling with a conceptual troublemaker. J. Comput. Mediated Commun. **18**(3), 362–377 (2013)
19. Stacker, J.F.: Manzai: Team Comedy in Japan's Entertainment Industry. In: Understanding Humor in Japan, p. 51 (2006)
20. Szablewicz, M.: The 'losers' of China's Internet: Memes as 'structures of feeling' for disillusioned young netizens. China Inf. **28**(2), 259–275 (2014)
21. Tabuchi, H.: No Time to Text? Say It With Stickers. New York Times. http://www.nytimes.com/2014/05/26/technology/no-time-to-text-apps-turn-to-stickers.html
22. Walther, J.B., D'Addario, K.P.: The impacts of emoticons on message interpretation in computer-mediated communication. Soc. Sci. Comput. Rev. **19**(3), 324–347 (2001)
23. Wang, Q.: "Did you have fun?": American and Chinese mother–child conversations about shared emotional experiences. Cogn. Dev. **16**(2), 693–715 (2001)
24. Wang, S.S.: More than words? The effect of line character sticker use on intimacy in the mobile communication environment. Soc. Sci. Comput. Rev. (2015)
25. Xinhua News: Face-loving Chinese Find New Facial Expression Fad. http://news.xinhuanet.com/english/2016-01/28/c_135054074.htm
26. Yik, M.: How unique is Chinese emotion. In: The Oxford Handbook of Chinese Psychology, pp. 205–220 (2010)

Designing Responsive Interactive Applications by Emotion-Tracking and Pattern-Based Dynamic User Interface Adaptation

Christian Märtin[✉], Sanim Rashid, and Christian Herdin

Faculty of Computer Science, Augsburg University of Applied Sciences, An der Hochschule 1, 86161 Augsburg, Germany
{Christian.Maertin,Sanim.Rashid,Christian.Herdin}@hs-augsburg.de

Abstract. Model-based user interface development environments (MB-UIDEs) can be enhanced by pattern-based frameworks to allow for richer design capabilities and more flexible responsive behavior during the runtime of the implemented target application. In this paper an experimental system prototype for integrating facial analysis and eye-tracking into a pattern-based dynamic user interface adaptation process is discussed. The resulting system evaluates the emotional state of the system users to trigger the HCI-pattern-based adaptation of the user interface. By monitoring the emotional states of the users over longer time periods, while the system changes its behavior and its appearance, conclusions about the perceived quality dimensions of the interactive application can be drawn.

Keywords: Model-based development · MB-UIDE · Pattern-based development · HCI-patterns · Responsive design · Eye tracking · Facial analysis · Emotion tracking · Adaptive user interface

1 Introduction and Related Work

Model-based approaches have a rich history in HCI and can be fruitfully applied for building media-rich and flexible interactive systems [12]. In addition to classic model-based and model-driven approaches, in recent years the descriptive characteristics and powers of HCI patterns [11, 14], pattern languages [4, 9], and generic software pattern-based approaches, [10], were increasingly exploited for modeling structure, behavior, and presentational aspects of interactive systems.

The PaMGIS framework [5, 7] combines the model-based user interface development paradigm with a pattern-based modeling and design approach conforming to the CAMELEON reference model [2]. In PaMGIS the modeling and semi-automated construction of interactive applications is centered around a pattern repository that allows storage of and access to domain-independent and domain-dependent HCI pattern languages that are specified in the PPSL pattern specification language [6]. These patterns can be exploited for advanced user interface modeling and design purposes together with various other model types and modeling artifacts, e.g. task models [13], user models, context models, and environment models. So far, applications for various

© Springer International Publishing Switzerland 2016
M. Kurosu (Ed.): HCI 2016, Part III, LNCS 9733, pp. 28–36, 2016.
DOI: 10.1007/978-3-319-39513-5_3

application areas, e.g. web-shops, knowledge sharing systems and travel information systems have been constructed using the PaMGIS approach and tool environment. For these areas not only usable and functional application prototypes could be developed, but also the mapping of the same abstract and semi-abstract models to different target platforms and target devices was demonstrated.

In this paper we aim to go a step further in our view of the usefulness of the pattern-based modeling approach for interactive system design. In order to arrive at true context-aware software services, new software engineering approaches are required that couple standard or agile requirements engineering techniques with methods that monitor the users' behavior, emotions, and possibly their changing mental states at runtime in order to decipher their intentions during their interaction with software services in a sequence of situations starting with the desire to reach a certain goal and finishing with the goal-satisfying situation. For studying the requirements engineering process and the software engineering life-cycle for situation-aware software, the Situ framework was constructed [3]. Studies with the Situ framework involve the monitoring of humans-in-the-loop and could produce so called Situ_patterns and building blocks for runtime adaptation of the observed software services. The information gathered could later be used for situation-responsive design without the direct monitoring of a user's mental states.

In the more elementary approach, presented in this paper, we aim at demonstrating that a pattern-based approach generally is apt for arriving at adaptive interactive applications with highly responsive design and runtime-reconfiguration capabilities. For this purpose we use abstract and semi-abstract HCI-patterns from our repository as models and templates for runtime-adaptive user interfaces. Our experimental system controls the choice of layout and presentation characteristics by evaluating user behavior and user emotions during runtime. The feasibility of this new approach is demonstrated for a prototypical interactive application, where the PaMGIS pattern repository is coupled with highly interactive system components for behavior and emotion evaluation based on face reading and eye-tracking technology.

2   Application Prototype

The aim of this project was to develop a prototype which is able to adapt a web page dynamically in order to control the user experience, so that the interests and satisfaction of the user persist as long as possible. The adaptation should happen on the basis of facial analysis and the gaze motion. For changing the appearance of the user interface the PaMGIS pattern repository can be accessed dynamically. To gain deep insights into consumer behavior, eye tracking was used as a sensor technology. For the facial analysis the FaceReader 6.1, developed by Noldus, was used. The resulting software system can be seen as a test bed for studying user emotions and mental states of users during inter-action with web applications. It can also be used for evaluating the impact of runtime-adaptable user interfaces on the mood and mental states of users.

2.1 Technologies and Tools

As one of our goals was the rapid development of the target system with state-of-the art software technologies, the following tools and systems were used for the implementation of the prototype. The ASP.NET MVC web application framework, developed by Microsoft, implements the Model-View-Controller (MVC) pattern. The open-source Java-Script Framework AngularJS was used for running the resulting single page application. AngularJS basically does not implement the MVC in the traditional sense, but rather close to the MVVM (Model-view-view-model) pattern. With AngularJS, HTML DOM can be extended with additional attributes, to be more responsive to user actions. Furthermore it allows rapid prototyping by supporting data binding and dependency injection. All the relevant application parts are implemented within the browser. Therefore a complete client-side solution is created that is ideally fit for coupling it to any server technology [1] and eases all aspects of implementing user privacy. The Cascading Style Sheets (CSS) describe the design of the elements from the HTML page. The elements are derived from HCI patterns. They represent the platform-dependent final user interface and can be retrieved from the pattern repository at runtime.

The facial expression analysis software FaceReader 6.1 was employed for analyzing users' emotions. The software tracks six different basic facial expressions (happy, sad, surprised, disgusted, angry and scared) [8]. The gaze directions, head orientation and person characteristics (gender and age) can also be logged automatically [8]. An Application Programming Interface is also included in the FaceReader 6.1 software. The language binding assembly for the .NET Framework is the FaceReaderAPI.dll. This API serves as an interface between the different software programs and eases integration. The framework allows other software components to respond instantly to the emotional state of the participant. The API includes real-time export of detailed state log data, which enables the facial analysis, tagging and inference of cognitive affective mental states from facial video [8].

For the eye-tracking the Tobii eye-tracker X-2-60 was used. For the development of eye-tracking applications Tobii provides the Tobii Analytics SDK. This SDK includes an application programming interface, which is implemented as a core library, "tetio", and a set of language bindings which are built on top of the core. The language binding assembly for the .NET Framework is the Tobii.EyeTracking.IO.dll [17]. The Tobii eye-tracker presents itself on the LAN by using a technology called "zero configuration networking" (zeroconf). It automatically creates a usable computer network based on the Internet Protocols Suite (TCP/IP) when computers or network peripherals are interconnected [16]. No manual operator intervention or special configuration servers are required. An instance of the EyeTrackerBrowser class is created and started to consider the connected eye tracker in the network.

2.2 Software Architecture

The UXDataControlForm in Fig. 1 illustrates the Windows Form application, which has access to the data of the eye tracker and FaceReader in real-time due to the APIs [15]. When the application is connected to the FaceReader, it is possible to control the Face

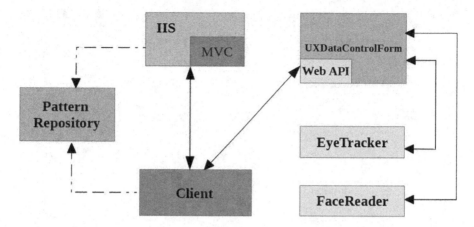

Fig. 1. Software architecture of the prototype. The dashed lines indicate that information in the pattern repository is interpreted to access the needed concrete implementation of patterns that may reside in the client or the server.

Reader software and its actions like start and stop of a facial analysis, enable detailed log and state log. The detailed log contains all the classifications enabled in the logging settings [8]. The state log shows the dominant expressions of the participant. If the eye tracker is connected to the local area network, the application automatically detects the tracker and a connection can be established. The application allows the user to start/stop tracking and run the eye-tracker calibration. Figure 2 shows a snapshot of the UXDataControlForm [15]. The Windows Form Application is not really the main part of the project. It only offers the possibility to access the hardware and to retrieve user experience data (emotion, gaze points).

The central part of our prototype architecture is the Client, the browser that accesses the real-time data. To enable data access, the browser needs a connection to the UXDataControlForm. For this purpose there were no separate Internet Information Services (IIS) required. The connection was implemented using a self-host Web API inside the Windows Form application.

The application listens to the http://localhost:8080/ address. The Web API Controller "UXDataController", which is defined in the application, uses the GET action and returns the FaceReader and Eye Tracker data via an interface.

The prototype of the web application, which handles the user experience state, is basically implemented as a client-side application in AngularJS. AngularJS allows dynamic changes in the page without having to load the whole page again. Via the API Angular requests the data and evaluates it in the directive. A directive is essentially a function that executes, when the Angular compiler finds it in the DOM (Document Object Model) [1].

The structure of the web application is kept simple. The web application implements a railway link map system where railway link maps according to the user´s desired destination are shown. Figure 3 shows a snapshot of the web application, where a timetable information has to be entered in order to get a link map. The link map data are

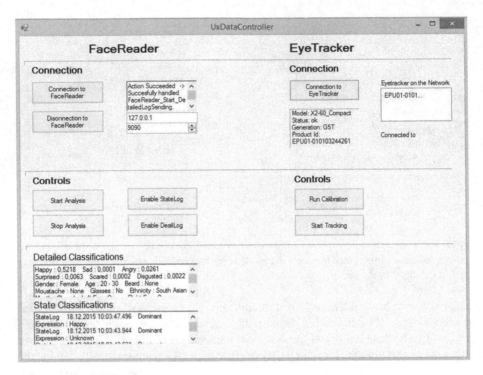

Fig. 2. WinForms Application as a Web API host application

requested and retrieved from a database. Every web page of the application has a controller and a directive in AngularJS. Main functions are defined in services that are accessed in directives. The service, e.g., fetches the eye-tracker and Face Reader data.

Every single page is segmented in panels (Fig. 3) and has a specifically defined directive, which is given to each panel. For each panel there is a defined update-method in the directive.

With the help of the eye tracker, which is adjusted to the screen size, the eye motion positions of the user can be easily retrieved. To get the most exact positions, a calibration procedure can be executed by the user in the UXDataController (see Fig. 2).

If the user looks at a specific panel (in Fig. 3), the directive automatically calls the appropriate update-method of the panel. In the update-method the current emotion state of the user is retrieved from the Face Reader and analyzed. The analysis algorithm examines, how often the user has looked at a given panel and stores the result in an array together with the inherent emotion state at that time. The algorithm can be extended at any time for more sophisticated evaluations. The final dominant expression (over a specific time period), which is figured out by a statistical calculation, can be assigned to the panel. Once the dominant expression is assigned to a panel, the system designer can decide what the update-method should do. Dependent on the dominant expression and the situation (click behavior of the user) the page can change its color dynamically or some extra features can be added to give the user a better user experience. In addition

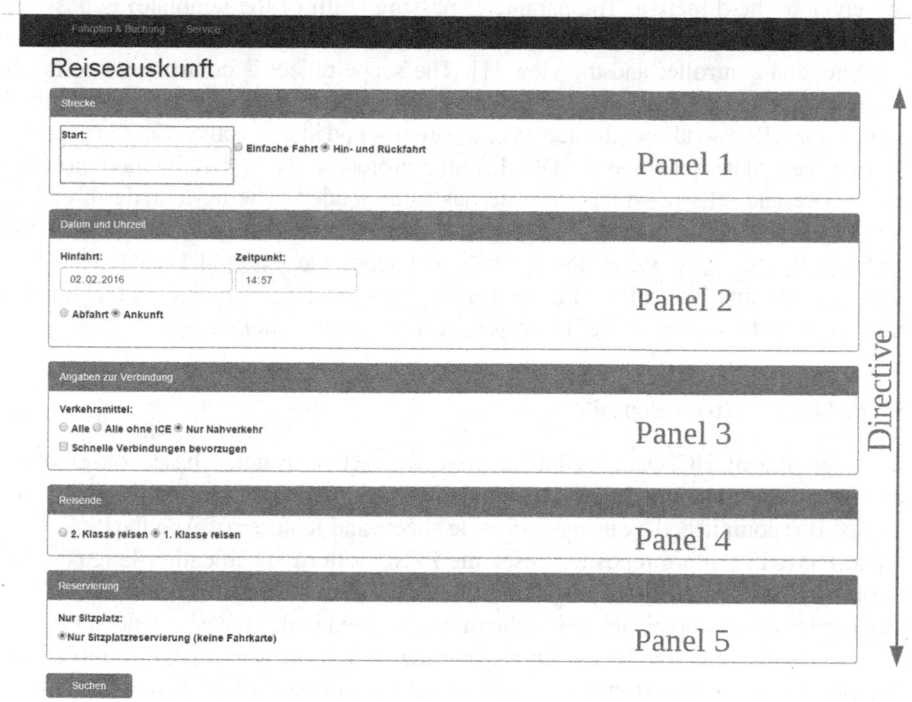

Fig. 3. Screenshot of the web application [15]

the user characteristics are exploited and the page can be adjusted even more precisely. For example the font size can be increased, if the user is aged [15].

To demonstrate the importance of an optimized user experience in the experimental setting some errors were installed into the web application. In Fig. 3, for example, there is no destination field, so it is not possible to enter data. This is an attempt to upset the user and change his or her emotional state to "angry". If the emotional state is "angry", the background color will be changed to an enjoyable color and the layout will be adjusted by the CSS-based UI implementation of a user experience pattern to mollify the user and manipulate his mind and mood. The prototype also includes several external HTML pages, modeled after HCI-patterns that can offer help services, if needed. They are dynamically placed on the site, to help the user in a specific situation. In this web application example the destination field is required, to reach the intended goal. The display of an external HTML template is realized by using features of AngularJS directives. Directives are very powerful concepts in Angular. HTML itself does not support embedding HTML pages within HTML pages. To achieve this functionality, the directives in AngularJS can be exploited. The directives allows to load dynamic templates into the web page [1]. In this example an external HTML page, which contains the option to select a destination is added.

The display of the external HTML page is also done in the current directive and update-method of the panel. Here the system designer has to decide, which template has to be given to the directive. The parameter passing (path of the template) is possible with scope. Scope is an object that refers to the application model. It is a link between the application controller and the view [1]. The scope object is controller-specific. If some model data in the view are changed, the controller automatically gets the modified value. AngularJS also allows the access of a parent scope in a directive. So it is possible to render the updated value to the DOM. In the prototype the update-method calls the parent scope and tells it, which template has to be loaded. The ng-include directive, which is defined in the main HTML page, contains the scope object (the path of the template). By getting a value, the ng-include fetches the external HTML resource, compiles it and finally includes it in the HTML page. The ng-include directive creates a new scope, but it can also refer to the parent scope with $parent.scope.

2.3 PaMGIS Pattern Repository

The integration of HCI-patterns for adaptive interactive systems based on emotion tracking and the mentioned technologies and their implementation for the final user interface is accomplished by using CSS style sheets and features of AngularJS.

The PaMGIS pattern repository uses the PPSL pattern specification language for describing HCI patterns on all abstraction levels [7]. The CSS style sheets and HTML pages used in the prototypical Web application presented in this paper are modeled after structural and presentation HCI patterns. In order to link the actual pattern implementation code to the patterns from which they are derived, the specification language offers the *Deployment* element. This specification element contains powerful specification attributes to describe the more implementation-related aspects like concrete code and model fragments which can also be used for automated user interface generation. In the context of the discussed prototype they also contain the links to the runtime environment that interprets the CSS stylesheet or HTML code for each pattern accessed by the update methods of the applications.

The prototypical application in Fig. 3 implements user interface adaptation by constructing the displayed HTML page from two interpreted patterns. The first pattern is responsible for the structure of the first panel of the input form. The second is responsible for the color experience of the entire form.

Figure 3 shows the initial page setup. For each panel a pattern is available in the repository. For the pattern *Panel1* the initial pattern implementation is *Panel1:Travel-Start*. For the pattern *TimeTableInformationColor*, the initial setup uses its implementation *TimeTableInformationColor:Neutral*. If the mood of the user changes to "angry", the structure will be adapted by executing the HTML code of the pattern implementation *Panel1:TravelStartDestination* and changing the color of the complete page by accessing the pattern implementation *TimeTableInformationColor:Mollifying*. For each pattern a PPSL specification is available in the repository. The PPSL top level element <*Deployment*> [7] contains a list of all implementations of a given pattern. The update method accesses the selected implementation by entering an identifier. As a result, a link to the relevant HTML code is returned. An alternative would be the direct storage of the implementation code fragment within the repository, which is also supported by PPSL.

In order to allow for the most flexible architectures for all types of resulting interactive applications, the PaMGIS pattern repository can be accessed either by the client side or the server side.

3   Conclusion

In this paper an architecture for building adaptive interactive systems by introducing emotion tracking, flexible client technologies for dynamic and responsive application design and integrating a pattern-repository into the design environment was demonstrated. This architecture will serve as an experimental platform for testing the PaMGIS framework as a basis for modeling and constructing a wide spectrum of domain-dependent and independent adaptive applications for various target platforms, contexts, and devices.

In the prototype a relatively simple railway timetable information system was implemented as an exemplary interactive application. In the future any type of web-based application, e.g. web shops, games, apps for personal communication, etc., can serve as a target for pattern-based dynamic adaptation triggered by the monitoring of user emotions. The monitoring interface is also open for additional sensor-based gathering of emotional and mental states of the user. Wearable devices could provide bio-signals in addition to the already integrated facial analysis and eye-movement data.

In addition, experiments with more intelligent algorithms for drawing conclusions about the hidden mental states from the observed emotional, eye movement and biological data will be carried out.

One of the next steps towards a reliable system will be a thorough measurement and usability-lab-based evaluation of the mood-changing effects of emotion-state-triggered dynamically adapted user interfaces on diverse users and over longer time periods, when interacting with an extended version of the prototypical railway timetable application. Measurements of this kind will allow both, a reliable identification of diverse quality characteristics of the application in use, and, at the same time open the way to find out more about the hidden mental states of the users in different situations and contexts of use.

References

1. AngularJS Documentation. https://docs.angularjs.org. Accessed 21 Dec 2015
2. Calvary, G., Coutaz, J., Bouillon, L. et al.: The CAMELEON Reference Framework (2002). http://giove.isti.cnr.it/projects/cameleon/pdf/CAMELEON%20D1.1RefFramework.pdf. Accessed 15 April 2015
3. Chang, C.K.: Situation analytics: a foundation for a new software engineering paradigm. Computer **49**, 24–33 (2016)
4. Deng, J., Kemp, E., Todd, E.G.: Managing UI pattern collections. In: Proceedings of the 6th ACM SIGCHI New Zealand Chapter's International Conference on Computer-Human Interaction: Making CHI Natural, pp. 31–38. ACM (2005)
5. Engel, J., Märtin, C.: PaMGIS: Framework for pattern-based modeling and generation of interactive systems. In: Proceedings of HCI International 2009, San Diego, U.S.A., pp. 826–835 (2009)

6. Engel, J., Herdin, C., Märtin, C.: Exploiting HCI pattern collections for user interface generation. In: Proceedings of PATTERNS 2012, pp. 36–44 (2012)
7. Engel, J., Märtin, C., Forbrig, P.: A concerted model-driven and pattern-based framework for developing user interfaces of interactive ubiquitous applications. In: Proceedings of First International Workshop on Large-scale and Model-Based Interactive Systems, Duisburg, pp. 35–41 (2015)
8. FaceReader 6 Application Programming Interface. Technical Note
9. Fincher, S., Finlay, J.: Perspectives on HCI patterns: concepts and tools (introducing PLML). Interfaces **56**, 26–28 (2003)
10. Gamma, E., et al.: Design Patterns Elements of Reusable Object-Oriented Software. Addison-Wesley, Reading (1995)
11. Kruschitz, C., Hitz, M.: Human-computer interaction design patterns: structure, methods, and tools. Int. J. Adv. Softw. **3**(1 & 2) (2010)
12. Meixner, G., Calvary, G., Coutaz, J.: Introduction to model-based user interfaces. W3C Working Group Note 07 January 2014. http://www.w3.org/TR/mbui-intero/. Accessed 27 May 2015
13. Paternò, F.: The ConcurTaskTrees notation. In: Model-Based Design and Evaluation of Interactive Applications, pp. 39–66. Applied Computing. Springer, Berlin (2000)
14. Seffah, A.: The evolution of design patterns in HCI: from pattern langauges to pattern-oriented design. In: Proceedings of the 1st Interational Workshop on Pattern-Driven Engineering of Interactive Computing Systems (PEICS 2010), pp. 4–9 (2010)
15. Rashid S.: Entwicklung eines Prototypen zur User Experience Optimierung auf der Basis von Emotions- und Blickanalyse im Bereich E-Commerce. M.Sc. Thesis, Augsburg University of Applied Sciences (2016)
16. Zero Configuration Networking (ZeroConf). http://www.zeroconf.org/. Accessed 18 Dec 2015
17. Tobii Studio SDK. Developer Guide, 8 May 2013

fNIRS as a Method to Capture the Emotional User Experience: A Feasibility Study

Kathrin Pollmann[1,2(✉)], Mathias Vukelić[1,2], Niels Birbaumer[3,4], Matthias Peissner[2], Wilhelm Bauer[2], and Sunjung Kim[3]

[1] Institute of Human Factors and Technology Management IAT, University of Stuttgart, Stuttgart, Germany
{kathrin.pollmann,mathias.vukelic}@iat.uni-stuttgart.de
[2] Fraunhofer Institute for Industrial Engineering IAO, Stuttgart, Germany
[3] Institute of Medical Psychology and Behavioral Neurobiology, University of Tübingen, Tübingen, Germany
[4] Istituto di Ricovero e Cura a Carattere Scientifico, Ospedale San Camillo, Venice, Italy

Abstract. User experience (UX) has become a key factor in interface design. Still, so far, no satisfying solution exists for measuring the emotional user experience (UX) during human-technology interaction (HTI) and linking them to design elements of the interface. Non-invasive brain imaging techniques are promising tools to assess the underlying causes and generation of emotional experiences in the brain. Against this background, especially functional near-infrared spectroscopy (fNIRS), a rather new and portable method, appears to have strong potential for measuring UX in real-world HTI settings. However, so far fNIRS has scarcely been used in emotion research. The present research evaluates the feasibility of using fNIRS to detect emotional user responses during HTI by comparing it to the well-established method of fMRI which, due to its set-up, is difficult to use in HTI context. Our feasibility study shows that fNIRS can detect brain activity patterns which are similar to those obtained using fMRI and can be used to distinguished positive and negative emotional reaction in an HTI context and displays brain activities which cannot be examined when fMRI is used. Future research should investigate whether similar results can be found when fNIRS is used in less controlled and more realistic HTI scenarios.

Keywords: User experience · Emotion research · Non-invasive brain-imaging · fNIRS · Human-technology interaction

1 Introduction

1.1 Measuring User Experience

In the past years human-technology interaction (HTI) research has started to direct more attention towards emotional and affective user reactions. Nowadays, usability is no longer the only important factor for successful interface design. There is an increased interest in designing products which do not only support the users in efficiently reaching their goals, but also maximize their positive experience during the

© Springer International Publishing Switzerland 2016
M. Kurosu (Ed.): HCI 2016, Part III, LNCS 9733, pp. 37–47, 2016.
DOI: 10.1007/978-3-319-39513-5_4

interaction. Recent studies in the field of HTI showed that users are more inclined to use or buy a technical product that induces a positive user experience (UX) compared to those products that do not [1, 2]. Still, until now, no satisfying solution has been proposed for identifying moments of positive and negative emotional experience during human-technology interaction (HTI). It is hence difficult to determine whether a technical product really has the intended emotional effect on its users and causes a positive UX. Furthermore, it is hard to find reliable solutions for linking the emotional state of the user to design elements of the interface.

Taking into account the distinct subjective nature of emotions, HTI mainly makes use of subjective methods like surveys, questionnaires or self-reports to assess UX. However, the value of these methods for measuring UX during HTI is limited: Subjective methods can either be employed in retrospective after the interaction or require the interruption of the interaction process. Both approaches are prone to attribution errors and cognitive biases and thus likely to yield a distorted image of the real UX [3]. Subjective measures also fail to identify emotional changes occurring over time [4]. Moreover, given that humans show limited abilities for introspection, subjective reports do not yield information about those emotional reactions that are rather implicit results from unconscious cognitive processing [5].

Subjective data can be complemented by results from behavioral methods such as observing the user or their task performance, which can be employed to continuously monitor the user's emotional reactions during HTI. In addition, video-based face recognition tools can be used to deduce the user's emotional state from their mimics [6]. However, like subjective measures, behavioral methods might fail to detect implicit emotional reactions which are most likely too subtle to be reflected in human behavior or mimics [5].

In addition, psychophysiological measures such as electrocardiography (ECG), electromyography (EMG) electrooculography (EOG) or electrodermal activity (EDA) are emerging as quantitative metrics to identify cognitive and emotional state changes underlying UX [7]. Psychophysiological methods detect electrical activity in the peripheral nervous system right after the user experiences an emotional event. Based on the measured activity the emotional reaction can be characterized on different dimensions such as its valence and the level of arousal, and based on the revealed patterns the emotional state can be inferred. However, psychophysiological methods are currently the least feasible approach for UX measurements as they require the attachment of sensors to the user's body, which restricts their comfort and wellbeing, and might ultimately alter the experience. Although psychophysiological methods are more suitable than subjective or behavioral methods to assess implicit emotional user reactions, activity measured from the peripheral nervous system only yields indirect information about the UX, as the main processing of the emotional event and generation of an emotional state takes place in the brain.

Thus, the more promising approach for measuring UX appears to be to focus on the immediate source of the user's emotional reaction by investigating neural activity in the brain rather than in the peripheral nervous system.

1.2   fNIRS: A New Tool for Emotion Research

Non-invasive brain imaging techniques, primarily developed for clinical settings, are powerful tools for assessing the source of mental and emotional states. Being able to detect and visualize changes in neuronal activity during task performance, brain imaging is becoming a realistic tool for HTI research. The most common method to gain deeper insights into emotional processing is functional Magnetic Resonance Imaging (fMRI) [8]. fMRI measurements provide three-dimensional functional images of the brain showing hemodynamic changes in blood volume and oxygenation, the so called blood oxygen level-dependent (BOLD) hemodynamic response, which occurs in relation to a stimulus. Using strictly controlled experimental set-ups fMRI studies were able to show that different emotional states can be distinguished from each other [9, 10]. However, having been designed for clinical or strictly controlled set-ups, fMRI has limitations regarding the applicability to real-world interaction scenarios and external validity and is hence less suitable to be used in an HTI context. The stationarity, set-up and functionality of fMRI scanners require participants to lie down in unnatural positions restricting their movements and the extent to which the interaction can be performed, thus distorting the UX.

Against this background, functional near-infrared spectroscopy (fNIRS), a rather new and portable method, appears to have strong potential for measuring UX in real-world HTI settings. Unlike other imaging techniques fNIRS does not require a strictly controlled environment and does not have as many restrictions such as stationarity, long set-up time or intolerance to movement.

Similarly to fMRI, fNIRS is a non-invasive, optical brain imaging technique that detects hemodynamic responses based on blood oxygen changes in the brain. To do so, it employs near-infrared light (wavelengths usually in the range from 760 nm to 850 nm) to measure concentration changes of oxygenated-hemoglobin (oxy-Hb) and deoxygenated-hemoglobin (deoxy-Hb) after local neuronal activations. Being based on similar physiological mechanism as fMRI, fNIRS can be regarded as a reliable and valid measurement for detecting activations in cortical regions [11]. fNIRS has successfully been used to asses various mental states during HTI [12] and recent studies show that fNIRS can be employed to detect emotional brain responses [11, 13]. Still, these studies were performed with receptive stimuli and did not involve any interaction of the participant. It is hence still unclear whether fNIRS is a suitable method to detect emotional responses during HTI and link them to the user's experience throughout the interaction process.

1.3   Research Question

The current study was carried out as part of a larger research initiative investigating the neuronal underpinnings of emotional user reactions during realistic HTI environments. It is aimed at investigating the feasibility of using fNIRS as a UX measurement tool by comparing its performance to the results of an fMRI-study which was conducted by Kim and colleagues within the same research project [14]. Using fMRI, we found different cortical activation patterns and hemispheric differences for events that were positively and negatively rated by participants within an HTI context. In our fNIRS-study we expect to find concentration changes in oxygenated- and deoxygenated-hemoglobin that reflect similar brain activity as detected in the fMRI-study.

2   Methods and Materials

2.1   Subjects

Ten participants from the fMRI-study [14] were re-invited to take part in the present study (mean age: 24.90 ± 2.18 years, 4 females). All participants were right-handed. Participants gave their written informed consent before participation and received monetary compensation. The study protocol was approved by the local ethics committee of the Medical Faculty of the University of Tübingen.

2.2   Stimulus Material

Just like in the fMRI-study, participants were put into an HTI-scenario by confronting them with an interactive ideation tool, which was especially developed in a dedicated study [15].

There are two variations of the ideation tool (in the following referred to as "emotional 1" and "emotional 2") of which each contains certain graphical design elements that have shown to evoke different emotional states in the user and should ultimately cause a positive UX. The third variation of the tool contains none of these elements, thus causing an emotionally neutral UX (see Fig. 1).

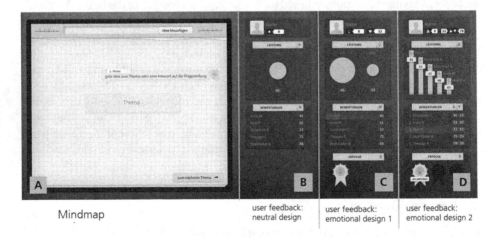

Fig. 1.   Screenshot of the ideation tool: **1A.** Exemplary shows the part of the screen designed for ideation in the form of a mind map which is placed next to an area that gives user feedback about their ideas. **1B, C and D.** show three different design variations of the user feedback area: the "neutral" version und two "emotional version" (from left to right).

As the physical set-up of the fMRI makes it difficult to realize a scenario were participants can interact with a technical system, in the fMRI-study for each of the three versions of the ideation tool five screenshots of the most prominent design elements were used as stimuli (15 screenshots in total). To guaranty the comparability of the fMRI and fNIRS results, the present study makes use of the exact same stimulus material and follows the same experimental procedure.

2.3 Experimental Procedure

In each session, participants were confronted with screenshots from all three versions of the ideation tool. To put these screenshots in the context of the whole tool, participants got an introduction to the tool and its functionalities at the beginning of each experimental session. Each session comprised two measurement blocks consisting of 15 trials each. Figure 2 shows the overview of the time course of one trial. Every trial consisted of a cued task design with different task epochs. The experiment procedure started with the presentation of the word "attention". This screen was only shown once to indicate the beginning of the experiment and direct the participant's attention to the screen. Each trial was initiated by a preparatory fixation phase followed by a short description of the area of the screen that the screenshot was taken from (e.g. user feedback category: performance). After another fixation phase, a screenshot of the ideation tool was visually presented. Each trial was completed by a rating period during which participants had to rate their emotional experience on a 10-point scale ranging from extremely negative (1–2: "I dislike it") to extremely positive (9–10: "I like it"). The selected screenshots were randomly sorted and each screenshot was presented twice to the participant.

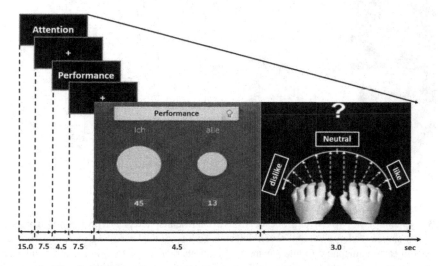

Fig. 2. Experimental paradigm showing the time course of each trial

2.4 Experimental Set-up

Participants were comfortably seated in a chair in front of a computer screen. Instead of a keyboard participants had a self-designed rating device, developed by the Institute of Medical Psychology and Behavioral Neurobiology and the MEG center, at the University of Tübingen, with ten keys lying on the table in front of them to perform the ratings for the different screen shots.

The changes of cerebral blood volume (CBV) in different brain regions during the interaction with the ideation tool were measured in the form of concentration changes of oxygenated- (oxy-Hb) and deoxygenated-hemoglobin (deoxy-Hb) by using a 30-optode fNIRS-system (ETG-400, Hitachi Medical Corporation, Japan). Two probe sets with 5*3 are used as a measurement mode, and the center position between them corresponds to Cz based on the international 10–20 system for electroencephalographic (EEG) electrode placement (Fig. 3). Each probe was composed of eight light sources and seven detectors, whereby a fixed distance of 30 mm between a source and a detector was ensured. Two wavelengths (695 and 830 nm) were used for measurement of the concentration of oxy-Hb and deoxy-Hb with a sampling period 0.1 s. The fNIRS system ETG-400 from Hitachi applies already the modified Beer-Lambert law [16] during data acquisition to obtain concentration changes of oxy- and deoxy-Hb.

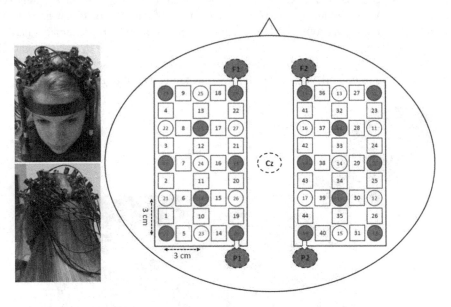

Fig. 3. Schema of the two fNIRS probe locations in each hemisphere: Each probe system included eight light source (red circles) and seven detectors (white circles) resulting in 22 measurement channels in each hemisphere (white squares). The number 27 (red circle) in the left hemisphere and the number 17 (red circle) in the right hemisphere are located so that the center between the both responds to Cz in the international 10–20 system for EEG electrode placement. Optode positions responding to the location of electrodes in the international 10–20 system are presented as red circles with dotted line (for example, the position of the number 28 in the left hemisphere responds to F1) (Color figure online).

2.5 Data Analysis

Subjective and Behavioral Data. First, we examined whether the emotional design of two versions of the ideation tool had an effect on participants' ratings. A repeated measures ANOVA with pairwise comparisons including emotionality of design as a with-in subject factor was used to compare participants' ratings for the screenshots of the three different version of the ideation tool.

In order to explore differences in participants' ratings and the response times between different emotional conditions, the screenshots with ratings 1 and 2 were categorized as dislike (D), the screenshots with ratings 3–8 as neutral (N) and the screenshots with ratings 9 and 10 as like (L). To examine differences between these three categories we performed a Kruskal-Wallis Test, as the data was not normally distributed. The response time was calculated by the time difference between the presentation of the rating task and participants' ratings. A participant's rating is considered correct, if the rating was performed within 3.0 s after the onset of the task. Otherwise, the rating was considered as missed and excluded from the analysis.

fNIRS Data. Offline fNIRS analysis was performed to examine the differences of activation levels (oxy-Hb and deoxy-Hb) between the different emotional graphical design elements of each trial and each channel. We focused one temporal window for the analysis of concentrations changes of oxy-Hb and deoxy-Hb: epoch of the visually presented screenshot of the ideation tool (3 s). Epochs in which the rating was missed have been excluded from further analysis. The epochs were pre-processed by high-pass filtering the raw data with a cut-off frequency of 0.02 Hz to eliminate baseline drifts and pulsation artifacts caused by heartbeat activity [17]. Next, the epochs were ordered according to the participants' rating belonging to each emotional category (D, L and N). Furthermore, we averaged the oxy- and deoxy-Hb changes across epochs on an individual basis for each emotional category. Finally, possible spatial differences of concentration changes during the respective time window were explored by analyzing statistical difference among the emotional categories (D > N, L > N, D > L) with the Mann-Whitney-U-Test, since data did not obey Gaussian distribution.

3 Results

3.1 Subjective and Behavioral Data

The statistical analysis showed an effect of emotionality of design on subjective ratings ($F(2, 1.82) = 24,06$, $p < .001$). Post-hoc pairwise comparisons revealed significant differences in participants' ratings between the "neutral" prototype ($M = 3.96$, $SD = 2.09$) and the "emotional 1" prototype ($M = 5.80$, $SD = 2.22$; $p < .001$) as well as between the "neutral" version and the "emotional 2" prototype ($M = 6.23$, $SD = 2.75$; $p < .001$). However, we did not observe any difference in evaluation rating between the two emotional versions of the ideation tool ($p = .675$).

Regarding intensity of the ratings, a Man-Whitney-U-Test revealed no significant difference between L ($Mdn = 2.0$) and D ratings ($Mdn = 2.0$; $U = 918.5$, $p = .065$).

The analysis of the response times indicated a tendency of participants to respond faster to L stimuli (Mdn = 0.78) than to N stimuli (*Mdn* = 1.03 and D stimuli (*Mdn* = 0.95), but no significant difference was found.

3.2 fMRI Results

The findings from the fMRI-study conducted by Kim et al. [14] indicate that the screen-shots taken from the three versions of the ideation tool activated a distributed network of interacting cortical and subcortical brain regions which are known to be involved during emotional processing.

We found a strong left-hemispheric activation of the parietal cortex, i.e. the supra-marginal gyrus for positively rated design elements, while negatively rated design elements mainly activated right-hemispheric midline (i.e. cingulum) and bi-hemispheric parietal cortical regions (i.e. supramarginal gyrus). Moreover, for negatively rated design elements the activated cortical brain regions showed a stronger involvement with subcortical brain regions (a network of putamen, thalamus and insula) than for positively rated design elements.

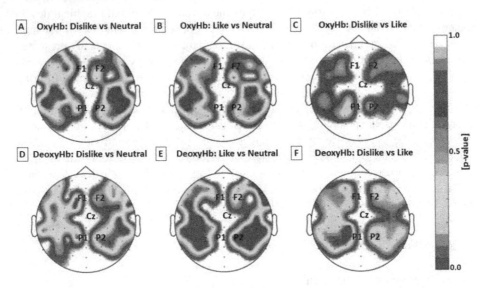

Fig. 4. Differences of the oxy- (**A-C**) and deoxy-Hb (**D-F**) concentration changes between the different emotional categories. **A:** Differences between Dislike (D) versus Neutral (N) showing higher concentration changes for D as compared to N. **B:** Differences between Like (L) versus Neutral (N) showing higher concentration changes for L as compared to N. **C:** Differences between Dislike (D) versus Like (L) showing no significant differences among these two categories. **D:** Differences between Dislike (D) versus Neutral (N) showing higher concentration changes for D as compared to N. **E:** Differences between Like (L) versus Neutral (N) showing higher concentration changes for L as compared to N. **F:** Differences between Dislike (D) versus Like (L) showing higher concentration changes for D as compared to L. Channels, showing significant differences in the Mann-Whitney-U-Test test, are indicated by colors (orange to red). Colors indicate different p-values (uncorrected) taken from the statistical test (Color figure online).

3.3   fNIRS Results

We observed significant changes of oxy-Hb for the emotionally loaded screenshots (dislike and like) as compared to the neutral one (Fig. 4A, B). Here, positively rated screenshots activated to a stronger degree left-hemispheric frontal, central and parietal regions and to some extend right-hemispheric central and parietal regions. On the other side, negatively rated screenshots activated bi-hemispheric central and parietal regions and to a minor extend left-hemispheric frontal regions. Furthermore, we found significant changes of deoxy-Hb for the emotionally loaded screenshots (dislike and like) as compared to the neutral one (Fig. 4D, E). Here, negatively rated screenshots activated bi-hemispheric central and parietal regions. For positively rated screenshots stronger activity was observed in bi-hemispheric central and parietal regions. Moreover, we observed significant changes of deoxy-Hb for the negatively loaded screenshots in comparison to the positively loaded ones (Fig. 4F). Here, the negative rated ones activated more left-hemispheric parietal regions.

4   Discussion

Participants' ratings reflected that the emotionally-loaded design elements induced positive and negative emotional states, while the neutral design elements did not. These findings are in line with the study by Sonnleitner and colleagues [15] who obtained similar results when initially evaluating the UX caused by the different versions of the ideation tool. From the fNIRS measurements we were able to distinguish on the cortical level positively rated design elements from negatively rated ones by comparing changes in oxy-Hb in frontal, central and parietal regions to neutrally rated ones. Here, similar to the results during the fMRI measurements positive design elements resulted in a stronger left-hemispheric activation, while negative design elements resulted in a bi-hemispheric activation pattern. Interestingly, the data revealed a strong involvement of deoxy-Hb concentration changes for the emotionally-loaded design elements i.e. a bi-hemispheric increase of central and parietal regions for positive rated design elements and right-hemispheric increase of central and parietal regions for negative rated design elements – a pattern that cannot be observed via fMRI measurements. The different activation patterns of oxy-Hb and deoxy-Hb in fronto-central and parietal regions between the two hemispheres show that fNIRS can be used to reliably differentiate between positive and negative emotional user reactions. Our results show that fNIRS is a potential, non-invasive and portable alternative method to fMRI measurements for sensing emotional states in realistic HTI settings. As mentioned in the introduction, the main benefit of fNIRS compared to fMRI is its portability, easy and fast set-up and low sensitivity to movement artefacts. However, in the present research these advantages of fNIRS only played a minor role. To assure comparability of the results between the fMRI and fNIRS measurements, our feasibility study was conducted as an exact replication of the fMRI-study, and thus only screenshots were used as stimulus material. These screenshots are merely snapshots from the actual interaction process and therefore have limited ecological validity.

To further evaluate the suitability of fNIRS as a tool for measuring UX, future studies will have to consider its use during ongoing interactions with a technical product, e.g. the ideation tool, rather than merely looking at receptive materials before drawing definite conclusions.

In addition, it would be interesting to compare the performance of fNIRS to other non-invasive brain imaging techniques, e.g. Electroencephalography (EEG) which is another portable and more popular neuroscientific method. To advance the approach of using non-invasive brain imaging techniques for UX measurement, it should be determined which portable method yields the best results and whether the informative value of the desired mental and emotional states could be enhanced by combining EEG and fNIRS.

Ultimately, the goal should be to develop a solution that is able to reliably detect and classify emotional user experience in real-time, thus providing the means to monitor the user throughout the whole interaction process. This would provide a suitable method to disclose moments of positive UX and to link them directly to the design elements of the technical system.

Acknowledgements. This research was supported by a grant from the Ministry of Science, Research and Arts of Baden-Wuerttemberg, Germany (Az: 32-729.63-0/5-14)

References

1. Kahneman, D.: Objective happiness. In: Kahneman, D., Diener, E., Schwarz, N. (eds.) Well-being. The Foundations of Hedonic Psychology, pp. 3–25. Russell Sage Foundation Press, New York (1999)
2. Spath, D., Peissner, M., Sproll, S.: Methods from neuroscience for measuring user experience in work environments. In: Proceedings of the International Conference on Applied Human Factors and Ergonomics (AHFE 2010) (2010)
3. Amelang, M., Schmidt-Atzert, L.: Psychologische Diagnostik und Intervention. Springer Medizin, Heidelberg (2006)
4. Hirshfield, L.M., Solovey, E.T., Girouard, A., Kebinger, J., Jacob, R.J.K., Sassaroli, A., Fantini, S.: Brain measurement for usability testing and adaptive interfaces: an example of uncovering syntactic workload with functional near infrared spectroscopy. In: Proceedings of the 27th International Conference on Human factors in Computing Systems, pp. 2185–2194. ACM, Boston, MA, USA (2009)
5. Minnery, B.S., Fine, M.S.: Neuroscience and the future of human-computer interaction. Interactions 16(2), 70–75 (2009)
6. Gerhäuser, H., Elst, G.: Detection of Faces and Facial Expressions Used in Market Research–ShoreTM. Fraunhofer Institute for Integrated Circuits IIS, Erlangen (2011)
7. Fairclough, S.H.: Fundamentals of physiological computing. Interact. Comput. 21(1), 133–145 (2009)
8. Braeutigam, S.: Neural systems supporting and affecting economically relevant behavior. Neurosci. Neuroecon. 1, 11–23 (2012)
9. Phan, K.L., Wager, T., Taylor, S.F., Liberzon, I.: Functional neuroanatomy of emotion: a meta-analysis of emotion activation studies in PET and fMRI. Neuroimage 16(2), 331–348 (2002). doi:10.1006/nimg.2002.1087

10. Sitaram, R., Lee, S., Ruiz, S., Rana, M., Veit, R., Birbaumer, N.: Real-time support vector classification and feedback of multiple emotional brain states. Neuroimage **56**(2), 753–765 (2011). doi:10.1016/j.neuroimage.2010.08.007

11. Ernst, L.H., Plichta, M.M., Lutz, E., Zesewitz, A.K., Tupak, S.V., Dresler, T., Ehlis, A.-C., Fallgatter, A.J.: Prefrontal activation patterns of automatic and regulated approach–avoidance reactions–a functional near-infrared spectroscopy (fNIRS) study. Cortex **49**(1), 131–142 (2013)

12. Girouard, A., Solovey, E.T., Hirshfield, L.M., Peck, E.M., Chauncey, K., Sassaroli, A., Fantini, S., Jacob, R.J.K.: From brain signals to adaptive interfaces: using fNIRS in HCI. In: Tan, D.S., Nijholt, A. (eds.) Brain-Computer Interfaces, Human-Computer Interaction Series, pp. 221–237. Springer, Heidelberg (2010)

13. Plichta, M.M., Gerdes, A.B.M., Alpers, G.W., Harnisch, W., Brill, S., Wieser, M.J., Fallgatter, A.J.: Auditory cortex activation is modulated by emotion: a functional near-infrared spectroscopy (fNIRS) study. Neuroimage **55**(3), 1200–1207 (2011)

14. Kim, S., Peissner, M., Bauer, W., Scheffler, K., Birbaumer, N.: Neural correlates of emotional preference in work environment. Front. Behav. Neurosci. (under review)

15. Sonnleitner, A., Pawlowski, M., Kässer, T., Peissner, M.: Experimentally manipulating positive user experience based on the fulfilment of user needs. In: Kotzé, P., Marsden, G., Lindgaard, G., Wesson, J., Winckler, M. (eds.) INTERACT 2013, Part IV. LNCS, vol. 8120, pp. 555–562. Springer, Heidelberg (2013)

16. Cope, M., Delpy, D.T.: System for long-term measurement of cerebral blood and tissue oxygenation on newborn infants by near infra-red transillumination. Med. Biol. Eng. Comput. **26**(3), 289–294 (1988)

17. Plichta, M.M., Herrmann, M.J., Baehne, C.G., Ehlis, A.-C., Richter, M.M., Pauli, P., Fallgatter, A.J.: Event-related functional near-infrared spectroscopy (fNIRS): are the measurements reliable? Neuroimage **31**(1), 116–124 (2006)

CAS(ME)²: A Database of Spontaneous Macro-expressions and Micro-expressions

Fangbing Qu[1,2], Su-Jing Wang[3], Wen-Jing Yan[4], and Xiaolan Fu[1(✉)]

[1] State Key Laboratory of Brain and Cognitive Science, Institute of Psychology,
Chinese Academy of Sciences, Beijing, China
{qufb, fuxl}@psych.ac.cn
[2] University of Chinese Academy of Sciences, Beijing, China
[3] Key Laboratory of Behavior Sciences, Institute of Psychology,
Chinese Academy of Sciences, Beijing, China
wangsujing@psych.ac.cn
[4] Institute of Psychology and Behavioral Sciences,
Wenzhou University, Wenzhou, China
yanwj@wzu.edu.cn

Abstract. Micro-expressions are facial expressions that are characterized by short durations, involuntary generation and low intensity, and they are regarded as unique cues revealing one's hidden emotions. Although methods for the recognition of general facial expressions have been intensively investigated, little progress has been made in the automatic recognition of micro-expressions. To further facilitate development in this field, we present a new facial expression database, CAS(ME)², which includes 250 spontaneous macro-expression samples and 53 micro-expression samples. The CAS(ME)² database offers both macro-expression and micro-expression samples collected from the same participants. The emotion labels in the current database are based on a combination of Action Units (AUs), self-reports of every facial movement and the emotion types of the emotion-evoking videos to improve the validity of the labeling. Baseline evaluation was also provided. This database may provide more valid and ecological expression samples for the development of automatic facial recognition systems.

Keywords: Mirco-expression recognition · Macro-expression recognition · Facial action coding system · Emotion labeling

1 Introduction

Facial expressions convey much information regarding individuals' affective states, statuses, attitudes, and their cooperative and competitive natures in social interactions [1–5]. Human facial expression recognition has been a widely studied topic in computer vision since the concept of affective computing was first proposed by Picard [6]. Numerous methods and algorithms for automatically recognizing emotions from human faces have been developed [7]. However, previous research has focused primarily on general facial expressions, usually called macro-expressions, which typically last for more than 1/2 of a second, up to 4 s [8] (although some researchers treat the

© Springer International Publishing Switzerland 2016
M. Kurosu (Ed.): HCI 2016, Part III, LNCS 9733, pp. 48–59, 2016.
DOI: 10.1007/978-3-319-39513-5_5

duration of macro-expressions as between 1/2 s and 2 s [9]). Recently, another type of facial expression, namely, micro-expressions, which are characterized by their involuntary occurrence, short duration and typically low intensity, has drawn the attention of affective computing researchers and psychologists. Micro-expressions are rapid and brief expressions that appear when individuals attempt to conceal their genuine emotions, especially in high-stakes situations [10, 11]. A micro-expression is characterized by its duration and spatial locality [12, 13]. Ekman has even claimed that micro-expressions may be the most promising cues for lie detection [11]. The potential applications in clinical diagnosis, national security and interviewing that derive from the possibility that micro-expressions may reveal genuine feelings and aid in the detection of lies have encouraged researchers from various fields to enter this area. However, little work on micro-expressions has yet been performed in the field of computer vision.

As mentioned above, much work has been conducted regarding the automatic recognition of macro-expressions. This progress would not have been possible without the construction of well-established facial expression databases, which have greatly facilitated the development of facial expression recognition (FER) systems. To date, numerous facial expression databases have been developed, such as the Japanese Female Facial Expression Database (JAFFE) [14]; the CMU Pose, Illumination and Expression (PIE) database [15] and its successor, the Multi-PIE database [16]; and the Genki-4 K database [17]. However, all of the databases mentioned above contain only still facial expression images that represent different emotional states.

It is clear that still facial expressions contain less information than do dynamic facial expression sequences. Therefore, researchers have shifted their attention to dynamic factors and have developed several databases that contain dynamic facial expressions, such as the RU-FACS database [18], the MMI facial expression database [19], and the Cohn-Kanade database (CK) [20]. These databases all contain facial expression image sequences, which are more efficient for training and testing than still images. However, all of the facial expression databases mentioned above collect only posed expressions (i.e., the participants were asked to present certain facial expressions, such as happy expressions, sad expressions and so on) rather than naturally expressed or spontaneous facial expressions. Previous literature reports have stated that posed expressions may differ in appearance and timing from spontaneously occurring expressions [21]. Therefore, a database containing spontaneous facial expressions would have more ecological validity.

To address the issue of facial expression spontaneity, Lucey et al. [22] developed the Extended Cohn-Kanade Dataset (CK +) by collecting a number of spontaneous facial expressions; however, this dataset included only happy expressions that spontaneously occurred between the participants' facial expression posing tasks (84 participants smiled at the experimenter one or more times between tasks, not in response to a task request). Recently, Mcduff et al. [23] presented the Affectiva-MIT Facial Expression Dataset (AM-FED), which contains naturalistic and spontaneous facial expressions collected online from volunteers recruited on the internet who agreed to be videotaped while watching amusing Super Bowl commercials. This database achieved further improved validity through the collection of spontaneous expression samples recorded in natural settings. However, only facial expressions that were understood to be related to a single emotional state (amusement) were recorded, and no self-reports on the facial movements were collected to exclude any unemotional movements that may contaminate the database, such as blowing of the nose, swallowing of saliva or rolling of the eyes. Zhang et al. [24] recently published a new facial expression database of 3D spontaneous elicited facial expressions, coded according to the Facial Action Coding System (FACS).

Compared with research on macro-expression recognition, however, studies related to micro-expression recognition are rare. Polikovsky et al. [25] used a 3D-gradient descriptor for micro-expression recognition. Wang et al. [26] treated a gray-scale micro-expression video clip as a 3rd-order tensor and applied Discriminant Tensor Subspace Analysis (DTSA) and Extreme Learning Machine (ELM) approaches to recognize micro-expressions. However, the subtle movements involved in micro-expressions may be lost in the process of DTSA. Pfister et al. [27] used a temporal interpolation model (TIM) and LBP-TOP [28] to extract the dynamic textures of micro-expressions. Wang et al. [29] used an independent color space to improve upon this work, and they also used Robust PCA [30] to extract subtle motion information regarding micro-expressions. These algorithms require micro-expression data for model training. To our knowledge, only six micro-expression datasets exist, each with different advantages and disadvantages (see Table 1): USF-HD [9]; Polikovsky's database [25]; SMIC [27] and its successor, an extended version of SMIC [31]; and CASME [32] and its successor, CASME II [33]. The quality of these databases can be assessed based on two major factors.

These micro-databases have greatly facilitated the development of automatic micro-expression recognition. However, all these databases only include cropped micro-expression samples, which was not very suitable for automatic micro-expression spotting. Besides, the methods used for emotion labeling was not consistent, which usually labeled the emotion according to FACS or the emotion type of elicitation materials or both. These methods left the possibility that may include some meaningless

Table 1. Previous micro-expression databases

Database		Number	Estimated emotions	Elicitation	Tagging
USD-HD		100	6 (basic emotions)	Posed	Micro/non-micro
Polikovsky's database		42	6 (basic emotions)	Posed	FACS
SMIC		77	3 (positive/negative/surprise)	Spontaneous	Emotion category
SMIC extension*	HS	164	3 (positive/negative/surprise)	Spontaneous	Emotion category
	VIS	71			
	NIR	71			
CASME		195	7 (basic emotions)	Spontaneous	Emotion/FACS
CASME II		247	5 (basic emotions)	Spontaneous	Emotion/FACS

* The SMIC extension database includes three subsets containing expressions recorded using different cameras: HS represents expression samples recorded using a high-speed camera at 100 fps, VIS corresponds to a normal visible-light camera, and NIR corresponds to a near-infrared camera. The latter two cameras were both operated at 25 fps.

facial movements into the database (such as the blowing of the nose, swallowing of saliva or rolling of the eyes). In this database, together with the FACS and emotion type of elicitation material, we collected participants' self-reports on each of their facial movements, which to the best extent guaranteed the purity of the database.

Considering the issues mentioned above, we developed a new database, CAS (ME)^2, for automatic micro-expression recognition training and evaluation. The main contributions of this database can be summarized as follows:

- This database is the first to contain both macro-expressions and micro-expressions collected from the same participants and under the same experimental conditions. This will allow researchers to develop more efficient algorithms to extract features that are better able to discriminate between macro-expressions and micro-expressions and to compare the differences in feature vectors between them.
- This database will allow the development of algorithms for detecting micro-expressions from video streams.
- The difference in AUs between macro-expressions and micro-expressions will also be able to be acquired through algorithms tested on this database.
- The method used to elicit both macro-expressions and micro-expressions for inclusion in this database has proven to be valid in previous work [33]. The participants were asked to neutralize their facial expressions while watching emotion-evoking videos. All expression samples are dynamic and ecologically valid.
- The database provides the AUs for each sample. In addition, after the expression-inducing phase, the participants were asked to watch the videos of their recorded facial expressions and provide a self-report on each expression. This procedure allowed us to exclude almost all emotion-irrelevant facial movements, resulting in relatively pure expression samples. The main emotions associated with the emotion-evoking videos were also considered in the emotion labeling process.

2 The CAS(ME)^2 Database Profile

The CAS(ME)^2 database contains 303 expressions — 250 macro-expressions and 53 micro-expressions — filmed at a camera frame rate of 30 fps. The expression samples were selected from more than 600 elicited facial movements and were coded with the onset, apex, and offset frames[1], with AUs marked and emotions labeled [35]. Moreover, to enhance the reliability of the emotion labeling, we obtained an additional emotion label by asking the participants to review their facial movements and report the emotion associated with each.

Macro-expressions with durations of more than 500 ms and less than 4 s were selected for inclusion in this database [8]. Micro-expressions with durations of no more than 500 ms were also selected.

---

[1] The onset frame is the first to change from the baseline (usually a neutral facial expression). The apex frame is the first to reach the highest observed intensity of the facial expression, and the offset frame is the first to reach the baseline.

The expression samples were recorded using a Logitech Pro C920 camera at 30 fps, and the resolution was set to 640×480 pixels. The participants were recorded in a room with two LED lights to maintain a fixed level of illumination. The steps of the data acquisition and coding processes are presented in following sections. Table 2 presents the descriptive statistics for the expression samples of different durations, which include 250 macro-expressions and 53 micro-expressions, defined in terms of total duration. Figure 1 shows examples of a micro-expression (a) and a macro-expression (b).

Table 2. Descriptive statistics for macro-expressions and micro-expressions

Expression type	N	Total duration	
		Mean (ms)	Standard deviation
Macro-expression	250	1305.87	657.6
Micro-expression	53	418.82	65.87

2.1 Participants and Elicitation Materials

Twenty-two participants (16 females), with a mean age of 22.59 years (standard deviation = 2.2), were recruited. All provided informed consent to the use of their video images for scientific research.

Seventeen video episodes used in previous studies [36] and 3 new video episodes downloaded from the internet were rated with regard to their ability to elicit facial expressions. Twenty participants rated the main emotions associated with these video clips and assigned them arousal intensity scores from 1 to 9 (1 represents the weakest intensity, and 9 represents the strongest intensity). Based on the ability to elicit micro-expressions observed in previous studies, only three types of emotion-evoking videos (those evoking disgust, anger, happiness) were used in this study, and they ranged in length from 1 min to approximately 2 and a half minutes. Five happiness-evoking video clips were chosen for their relatively low ability to elicit micro-expressions (see Table 3). Each episode predominantly elicited one type of emotion.

Table 3. Participant's ratings of the 9 video clips

Clip no.	Duration	Main emotion(s)	Rate of selection	Mean score
1	1'07"	Disgust	0.86	4.14
2	1'35"	Disgust	0.92	4.33
3	1'57"	Anger	0.75	4.5
4	2'24"	Anger	0.77	3.92
5	1'18"	Happiness	0.92	4
6	1'32"	Happiness	0.86	3.07
7	1'16"	Happiness	0.86	3.28
8	1'48"	Happiness	0.73	3.64
9	1'09"	Happiness	0.71	3.17

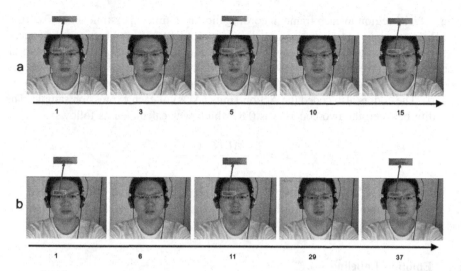

Fig. 1. Examples of a micro-expression (a) and a macro-expression (b). The apex frame occurs at approximately frame 5 for the micro-expression and frame 11 for the macro-expression, both of which represent the negative emotion anger. The AU related to these two expressions are all AU4 (inner brow).

2.2 Elicitation Procedure

Because the elicitation of micro-expressions requires rather strong motivation to conceal truly experienced emotions, motivation manipulation protocols were needed. Following a procedure used in previous studies [32], the participants were first instructed that the purpose of the experiment was to test their ability to control their emotions, which was stated to be strongly related to their social success. The participants were also told that their payment would be directly related to their performance. To better exclude noise arising from head movements, the participants were asked not to turn their eyes or heads away from the screen.

While watching the videos, the participants were asked to suppress their expressions to the best of their ability. They were informed that their monetary rewards would be reduced if they produced any noticeable expression. After watching all nine emotion-eliciting videos, the participants were asked to review the recorded videos of their faces and the originally presented videos to identify any facial movements and report the inner feelings that they had been experiencing when the expressions occurred. These self-reports of the inner feelings associated with each expression were collected and used as a separate tagging system, as described in the following section.

2.3 Coding Process

Two well-trained FACS coders coded each frame (duration = 1/30th of a second) of the videotaped clips for the presence and duration of emotional expressions in the upper and lower facial regions. This coding required classifying the emotion exhibited in each facial region in each frame; recording the onset time, apex time and offset time of each expression; and arbitrating any disagreement that occurred between the coders. When the coders could not agree on the exact frame of the onset, apex or offset of an expression, the average of the values specified by both coders was used. The two coders achieved a coding reliability (frame agreement) of 0.82 (from the initial frame to the end). The coders also coded the Action Units (AUs) of each expression sample. The reliability between the two coders was 0.8, which was calculated as follows:

$$R = \frac{2 \times AU(C_1 C_2)}{AA}$$

where AU(C1C2) is the number of AUs on which Coder 1 and Coder 2 agreed and AA is the total number of AUs in the facial expressions scored by the two coders. The coders discussed and arbitrated any disagreements [33].

2.4 Emotion Labeling

Previous studies of micro-expressions have typically employed two types of expression tagging criteria, i.e., the emotion types associated with the emotion-evoking videos and the FACS. In databases with tagging based on the emotion types associated with the emotion-evoking videos, facial expression samples are typically tagged with the emotions happiness, sadness, surprise, disgust and anger [32] or with more general terms such as positive, negative and surprise [31]. The FACS is also used to tag expression databases. The FACS encodes facial expressions based on a combination of 38 elementary components, known as 32 AUs and 6 action descriptors (ADs) [34]. Different combinations of AUs describe different facial expressions: for example, AU6 + AU12 describes an expression of happiness. Micro-expressions are special combinations of AUs with specific local facial movements indicated by each AU. In the $CAS(ME)^2$ database, in addition to using the FACS and the emotion types associated with the emotion-evoking videos as tagging criteria, we also employed the self-reported emotions collected from the participants.

When labeling the emotions associated with facial expressions, previous researchers have usually used the emotion types associated with the corresponding emotion-evoking videos as the ground truth [31]. However, an emotion-evoking video may consist of multiple emotion-evoking events. Therefore, the emotion types estimated according to the FACS and the emotion types of the evoking videos are not fully representative, and many facial movements such as blowing of the nose, eye blinks, and swallowing of saliva may also be included among the expression samples. In addition, micro-expressions differ from macro-expressions in that they may occur involuntarily, partially and in short durations; thus, the emotional labeling of micro-expressions based only on the FACS AUs and the emotion types of the evoking videos is incomplete. We must also consider the inner feelings that are reflected in the self-reported emotions of the participants when labeling micro-expressions. In this database, a combination of AUs, video-associated emotion types and self-reports was considered to enhance the validity of the emotion labels. Four emotion categories are used in this database: positive, negative, surprise and other (see Table 4).

Table 4. Criteria for labeling each type of emotion and their frequencies in the database

Emotion category	Criteria	Number	Macro-expressions	Micro-expressions
Positive	AUs needed for Happiness, at least AU6 or AU12	93	87	6
Negative	AUs needed for Anger (AU4 + AU5), Disgust (AU9, AU10 or AU4 + AU7), Sadness (AU1), or Fear (AU1 + AU2 + AU4 or AU20)	114	95	19
Surprise	AUs needed for Surprise (AU1 + AU2, AU25, or AU2)	22	13	9
Other	Other facial movements*	74	55	19

*The 'other' category includes facial expressions that cannot be classified as related to basic emotions, such as those associated with tension and control, hurt, sympathy, confusion and helplessness. Consistent with previous studies, the emotion labeling in this database is partially based on the AUs because micro-expressions are typically partial and of low intensity. In addition, the participants' self-reports and the contents of the video episodes were also considered.

Table 4 predominantly presents the emotion labeling criteria based on the FACS coding results; however, the self-reported emotions and the emotion types associated with the emotion-evoking videos were also considered during the emotion labeling process and are included in the CAS(ME)^2 database.

3 Dataset Evaluation

To evaluate the database, we used Local Binary Pattern histograms from Three Orthogonal Planes (LBP-TOP) [28] to extract dynamic textures and used a Support Vector Machine (SVM) approach to classify these dynamic textures.

Among the 303 samples, the number of frames included in the shortest sample is 4, and the longest sample contains 118 frames. The frame numbers of all samples were normalized to 120 via linear interpolation. For the first frame of each clip, 68 feature landmarks were marked using the Discriminative Response Map Fitting (DRMF) method [37]. Based on these 68 feature landmarks, 36 Regions of Interest (ROIs) were drawn, as shown in Fig. 2. Here, we used Leave-One-Video-Out (LOVO) cross-validation, i.e., in each fold, one video clip was used as the test set and the others were used as the training set. After the analysis of 302 folds, each sample had been used as the test set once, and the final recognition accuracy was calculated based on all results.

We extracted LBP-TOP histograms to represent the dynamic texture features for each ROI. Then, these histograms were concatenated into a vector to serve as an input to the classifier. An SVM classifier was selected. For the SVM algorithm, we used LIBSVM with a polynomial kernel, $\mathcal{K}(x_i, x_j) = (\gamma x_i^T x_j + coef)^{degree}$ $\gamma = 0.1$, with

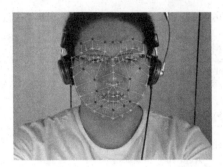

Fig. 2. Thirty-six Regions of Interest (ROIs).

degree = 4 and *coef* = 1. For the LBP-TOP analysis, the radii along the X and Y axes (denoted by R_x and R_y) were set to 1, and the radii along the T axis (denoted by R_t) were assigned various values from 2 to 4. The numbers of neighboring points (denoted by P) in the XY, XT and YT planes were all set to 4 or 8. The uniform pattern and the basic LBP were used in LBP coding. The results are listed in Table 5. As shown in the table, the best performance of 75.66 % was achieved using $R_x = 1$, $R_y = 1$, $R_t = 3$, p = 4, and the uniform pattern.

Table 5. Performance in the recognition of micro-expressions with LBP-TOP feature extraction

		Basic LBP		Uniform pattern	
		P = 4	P = 8	P = 4	P = 8
Rx = 1, Ry = 1	Rt = 2	71.05	65.79	71.05	65.13
	Rt = 3	75.00	65.46	75.66	65.13
	Rt = 4	74.67	67.76	74.01	66.45
Rx = 2, Ry = 2	Rt = 2	71.38	68.75	71.38	68.09
	Rt = 3	72.37	67.43	72.37	67.76
	Rt = 4	72.37	68.42	72.37	69.74
Rx = 3, Ry = 3	Rt = 2	70.72	69.41	70.72	69.41
	Rt = 3	72.04	69.74	72.04	70.39
	Rt = 4	74.01	69.41	73.68	71.71
Rx = 4, Ry = 4	Rt = 2	71.05	70.72	71.05	70.39
	Rt = 3	73.03	70.39	73.03	71.71
	Rt = 4	73.36	69.74	73.36	73.36

4   Discussion and Conclusion

In this paper, we describe a new facial expression database that includes macro-expression and micro-expression samples collected from the same individuals under the same experimental conditions. This database contains 303 expression samples, comprising 250 macro-expression samples and 53 micro-expression samples. This database may allow researchers to develop more efficient algorithms to extract features that are better able to discriminate between macro-expressions and micro-expressions.

Considering the unique features of micro-expressions, which typically occur involuntarily, rapidly, partially (on either the upper face or the lower face) and with low intensity, the emotional labeling of such facial expressions based only on the corresponding AUs and the emotion types associated with the videos that evoked them may not be sufficiently precise. To construct the presented database, we also collected self-reports of the subjects' emotions for each expression sample and performed the emotion labeling of each sample based on a combination of the AUs, the emotion type associated with the emotion-evoking video and the self-reported emotion. This labeling method should considerably enhance the precision of the emotion category assignment. In addition, all three labels are independent of one another and will be accessible when the database is published in the future, to allow researchers to access specific expressions in the database.

In the current version of the database, because of the difficulties encountered in micro-expression elicitation and the extremely time-consuming nature of manual coding, the size of the micro-expression sample pool may not be fully sufficient. We plan to enrich the sample pool by eliciting more micro-expression samples to provide researchers with sufficient testing and training data.

Acknowledgments. This project was partially supported by the National Natural Science Foundation of China (61375009, 61379095) and the Beijing Natural Science Foundation (4152055). We appreciate Yu-Hsin Chen's suggestions in language.

References

1. DePaulo, B.M.: Nonverbal behavior and self-presentation. Psychol. Bull. **111**(2), 203 (1992)
2. Ekman, P., Friesen, W.V.: Constants across cultures in the face and emotion. J. Pers. Soc. Psychol. **17**(2), 124 (1971)
3. Friedman, H.S., Miller-Herringer, T.: Nonverbal display of emotion in public and in private: Self-monitoring, personality, and expressive cues. J. Pers. Soc. Psychol. **61**(5), 766 (1991)
4. North, M.S., Todorov, A., Osherson, D.N.: Inferring the preferences of others from spontaneous, low-emotional facial expressions. J. Exp. Soc. Psychol. **46**(6), 1109–1113 (2010)
5. North, M.S., Todorov, A., Osherson, D.N.: Accuracy of inferring self-and other-preferences from spontaneous facial expressions. J. Nonverbal Behav. **36**(4), 227–233 (2012)
6. Picard, R.W.: A. Computing, and M. Editura. MIT Press, Cambridge, MA (1997)
7. Tong, Y., Chen, J., Ji, Q.: A unified probabilistic framework for spontaneous facial action modeling and understanding. Pattern Anal. Mach. Intell. **32**(2), 258–273 (2010)
8. Ekman, P.: Emotions Revealed: Recognizing Faces and Feelings to Improve Communication and Emotional Life. Macmillan, New York (2007)
9. Shreve, M., et al.: Macro-and micro-expression spotting in long videos using spatio-temporal strain. In: 2011 IEEE International Conference on Automatic Face and Gesture Recognition and Workshops (FG 2011). IEEE (2011)

10. Ekman, P., Friesen, W.V.: Nonverbal leakage and clues to deception. Psychiatry **32**(1), 88–106 (1969)
11. Ekman, P.: Telling Lies: Clues to Deceit in the Marketplace, Politics, and Marriage. WW Norton & Company, New York (2009). (Revised Edition)
12. Porter, S., Ten Brinke, L.: Reading between the lies identifying concealed and falsified emotions in universal facial expressions. Psychol. Sci. **19**(5), 508–514 (2008)
13. Rothwell, J., et al.: Silent talker: a new computer-based system for the analysis of facial cues to deception. Appl. Cogn. Psychol. **20**(6), 757–777 (2006)
14. Lyons, M., et al.: Coding facial expressions with Gabor wavelets. In: 1998 Proceedings of Third IEEE International Conference on Automatic Face and Gesture Recognition. IEEE (1998)
15. Sim, T., Baker, S., Bsat, M.: The CMU pose, illumination, and expression (PIE) database. In: 2002 Proceedings of Fifth IEEE International Conference on Automatic Face and Gesture Recognition. IEEE (2002)
16. Gross, R., et al.: Multi-pie. Image Vis. Comput. **28**(5), 807–813 (2010)
17. Whitehill, J., et al.: Toward practical smile detection. IEEE Trans. Pattern Anal. Mach. Intell. **31**(11), 2106–2111 (2009)
18. Bartlett, M.S., et al.: Automatic recognition of facial actions in spontaneous expressions. J. Multimedia **1**(6), 22–35 (2006)
19. Pantic, M., et al.: Web-based database for facial expression analysis. In: 2005 IEEE International Conference on Multimedia and Expo ICME 2005. IEEE (2005)
20. Kanade, T., Cohn, J.F., Tian, Y.: Comprehensive database for facial expression analysis. In: Proceedings of Fourth IEEE International Conference on Automatic Face and Gesture Recognition. IEEE (2000)
21. Schmidt, K.L., Cohn, J.F.: Human facial expressions as adaptations: evolutionary questions in facial expression research. Am. J. Phys. Anthropol. **116**(S33), 3–24 (2001)
22. Lucey, P., et al.: The extended cohn-kanade dataset (CK +): a complete dataset for action unit and emotion-specified expression. In: 2010 IEEE Computer Society Conference on Computer Vision and Pattern Recognition Workshops (CVPRW). IEEE (2010)
23. McDuff, D., et al.: Affectiva-MIT facial expression dataset (AM-FED): naturalistic and spontaneous facial expressions collected "In-the-Wild". In: 2013 IEEE Conference on Computer Vision and Pattern Recognition Workshops (CVPRW). IEEE (2013)
24. Zhang, X., et al.: BP4D-Spontaneous: a high-resolution spontaneous 3D dynamic facial expression database. Image Vis. Comput. **32**(10), 692–706 (2014)
25. Polikovsky, S., Kameda, Y., Ohta, Y.: Facial micro-expressions recognition using high speed camera and 3D-gradient descriptor (2009)
26. Wang, S.-J., et al.: Face recognition and micro-expression recognition based on discriminant tensor subspace analysis plus extreme learning machine. Neural Process. Lett. **39**(1), 25–43 (2014)
27. Pfister, T., et al.: Recognising spontaneous facial micro-expressions. In: 2011 IEEE International Conference on Computer Vision (ICCV). IEEE (2011)
28. Zhao, G., Pietikainen, M.: Dynamic texture recognition using local binary patterns with an application to facial expressions. IEEE Trans. Pattern Anal. Mach. Intell. **29**(6), 915–928 (2007)
29. Wang, S.-J., et al.: Micro-expression recognition using dynamic textures on tensor independent color space. In: Pattern Recognition (ICPR). IEEE (2014)
30. Wang, S.-J., Yan, W.-J., Zhao, G., Fu, X., Zhou, C.-G.: Micro-expression recognition using robust principal component analysis and local spatiotemporal directional features. In: Agapito, L., Bronstein, M.M., Rother, C. (eds.) ECCV 2014 Workshops. LNCS, vol. 8925, pp. 325–338. Springer, Heidelberg (2015)

31. Li, X., et al.: A spontaneous micro-expression database: Inducement, collection and baseline. In: 2013 10th IEEE International Conference and Workshops on Automatic Face and Gesture Recognition (FG). IEEE (2013)
32. Yan, W.-J., et al. CASME database: a dataset of spontaneous micro-expressions collected from neutralized faces. In: 2013 10th IEEE International Conference and Workshops on Automatic Face and Gesture Recognition (FG). IEEE (2013)
33. Yan, W.-J., et al.: CASME II: an improved spontaneous micro-expression database and the baseline evaluation. PLoS ONE 9(1), e86041 (2014)
34. Ekman, P., Friesen, W., Hager, J.: Facial Action Coding System: The Manual on CD-ROM Instructor's Guide. Network Information Research Co, Salt Lake City (2002)
35. Yan, W.-J., et al.: For micro-expression recognition: database and suggestions. Neuro-computing 136, 82–87 (2014)
36. Yan, W.-J., et al.: How fast are the leaked facial expressions: the duration of micro-expressions. J. Nonverbal Behav. 37(4), 217–230 (2013)
37. Asthana, A., et al.: Robust discriminative response map fitting with constrained local models. In: 2013 IEEE Conference on Computer Vision and Pattern Recognition (CVPR). IEEE (2013)

Micro-Expression Recognition for Detecting Human Emotional Changes

Kazuhiko Sumi$^{(\boxtimes)}$ and Tomomi Ueda

Aoyama Gakuin University, Sagamihara, Kanagawa 252-5258, Japan
sumi@it.aoyama.ac.jp

Abstract. We propose a method estimating human emotional state in communication from four micro-expressions; mouth motion, head pose, eye sight direction, and blinking interval. Those micro-expressions are picked up by a questionnaire survey of human observers watching on video recorded human conversation. Then we implemented a recognition system for those micro-expressions. We detect facial parts from a RGB-Depth camera, measure those four expressions. Then we apply decision-tree style classifier to detect some emotional state and state changes. In our experiment, we gathered 30 videos of human communicating with his/her friend. Then we trained and validated our algorithm with two-fold cross-validation. We compared the classifier output with human examiners' observation and confirmed over 70 % precision.

1 Background and Objectives

In recent years, face recognition application to communications media and human interface, as well as research for human face recognition has been active in computer science. Studies of facial expression recognition by computer system, especially technique for still face image expression recognition, have been popular in these 15 years. More recently, studies have proceeded toward video face images.

Quantitative description of facial expression was first studied by Ekman [1]. He developed face behavioral description method, which is referred to as Facial Action Coding System (FACS). In FACS, the face area is divided into three areas; top: around eyebrow, central: around eye, bottom: around mouth. In those three areas, he defined standard unit movement of facial parts, in other word the movement of the muscles of the face, which is referred to as Action Unit (AU). AUs were classified into 44 types. Human six major facial expression, "happiness", "fear", "dislike", " surprise", "sadness", and "anger" are described by the combination of several AUs.

However, the above-mentioned six major expressions are somewhat very distinctive, intentionally posed expression. In our daily communication, natural facial expression is more subtle and delicate. It is so called micro-expression. Micro-expression, also explained by Ekman, is the rapid change of facial expression and appears only in a short-period. However, detailed description of micro-expression

© Springer International Publishing Switzerland 2016
M. Kurosu (Ed.): HCI 2016, Part III, LNCS 9733, pp. 60–70, 2016.
DOI: 10.1007/978-3-319-39513-5_6

or relationship between emotion and micro-expression is not yet established. Current studies are focusing on searching clue for estimation of emotional state, not limited to the face, speech and body motion, and voice.

In this study, we look for facial motion and head motion that becomes a clue for emotion estimation appeared in human-to-human conversation and communication. We described the useful micro-expression and relationship between emotion and micro-expression from the analysis of questionnaire survey of observers watching on human conversation videos. We implemented the observer's analysis into computer and compared its estimation with human observer's one. Although, it is a subjective judgment and there is no evidence that the analysis is exact to the mental state of test subjects, there is correlation between human observer's estimation and computer outputs. We expect this system can be applied to machine-to-human communication that have the power of empathy and warm atmosphere.

2   Related Work

Most of the existing studies on human emotion recognition are based on automatic facial expression recognition. Ekman and Friesen developed the Facial Action Coding System (FACS)[1]. 44 facial action units (AU) are defined to describe facial expression. Basic emotions, i.e., happiness, surprise, anger, sadness, fear, and disgust are corresponding to prototypic facial expressions.

Based on this idea, many studies of automatic recognition of prototypic facial expressions were carried out. For example, Black [3] detected prototypic expressions by combination of facial parts motion and deformation. Facial parts are detected by facial part image templates. Mase [2] detected prototypic expressions from optical flow on the face image. Essa [4] detected facial control points and detected AUs from the motion of control points. Donato compared the performance of several features and classification approach i.e., optical flow, PCA, LFA, FLD, ICA, and their local patch versions. They also compared automatic method with human estimation. He concluded that ICA and Gabor Jets based approach are the best performance. However, images are frontal face image, cropped, normalized, and marked manually. Those studies were principle but cannot be applied to real applications. Tian et.al., developed multi-state feature-based AU recognition [6]. Their method could recognize non-frontal faces if all the AU muscles were seen. However, there is a manual facial feature point refinement process and it is not fully automatic.

So far, face analysis methods are classified into three types according to the facial features. First is geometric feature (shape of facial parts) approach. For example, Chang et.al., used 58 facial landmarks [8]. Second is facial feature point based approach. For example, Pantic et.al., used facial characteristic points around facial parts [9]. Third is facial texture features approach. For example Bartlett et al., uses Gabor wavelets to describe facial shape changes [7]. More recently, those features are integrated and the precision of recognition is improved [13,14].

There are few approaches that integrate information from facial expressions and head motion. Body motion, such as head pose or hand gesture is more visible rather than a small change of facial expression, and appears to be corresponding to a certain emotional state. For cxample, Asteriadis et.al, integrated eye gaze state and head pose to describe e-learners' behavior [10]. Gunes combined facial expressions and body motion to estimate human affect recognition [12].

In these 5 years, human-to-machine interface, usage of RGB-Depth (RGBD) camera has become popular. Compared with standard RGB camera, advantages of RGBD camera for face recognition is robustness and performance [15]. However, most of the studies remain in basic study, and emotion recognition in a natural conversation environment is still a big challenge. In this study, we aim at finding useful emotion categories and corresponding facial/body expressions appearing in hume-to-human communication in real world situation.

3   Proposed Method

In the conventional technique, facial expressions that have been recognized are obvious expressions, while a human in daily life read more delicate emotions. To realize such delicate emotion recognition, we utilize not only obvious facial expression but also micro-expressions and other body motion. Micro-expression is that of the moment appear relatively natural facial expressions and facial behavior in expression. Detecting micro-expression is considered to be important information on changes in the human delicate emotions. Therefore, rather than the change of motion in three areas used in the conventional AU technique (eyebrows, eyes, and mouth), we look for new micro-expression AUs for micro-expressions.

To simplify the problem, we focus on estimating emotion during communication or conversation, and try to find several emotion classes that can be stably observed by both human and computer.

To find such emotion class, we conducted a preliminary experiment with 10 test human observers. First, we recoded video of a person in communication and showed it to 10 observers. Each observer was asked to describe what kind of emotions he/she estimated about the person in the video. By analyzing all the observers' description and fining common descriptions, we come to a conclusion that the following five emotions are appearing in conversations; "friendly[1]", "boring", "a little depression", "shocked", and "a little surprised".

Then we looked for corresponding micro expression to those five emotions. We showed the video to the observers again and asked to describe which of the five emotions he/she discovered and the clue why he/she discovered the emotion. By analyzing all the observers' description again, we correlated the following micro-expression to the five emotions; mouth motion, face direction, eye sight direction, and blinking interval. Details are described in Sect. 3.1.

---

[1] We define friendly is a mental attitude attracted by the partner's talk or the partner him/herself.

We implemented face parts recognition and above emotion estimation with RGBD camera images. Figure 3 shows the schematic diagram of our proposed method. (Figs. 1, 2, 4, 5, 6, 7, 8, 9 and 10)

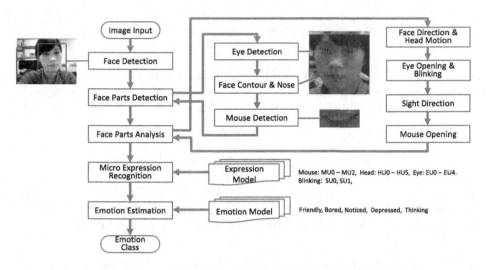

Fig. 1. Schematic Diagram of Emotional Estimation

The input is a pair of a 3D range and a RGB texture image of a human, taken by RGBD camera. First, the face region is detected by a combination of depth peak and facial pattern. In the figure, red rectangle in the left picture denotes the detected face region. Then eye and face contour are detected using the face texture model and the depth edge. In the figure, green dots on the right picture denote eye contours and red dots denote face contour and other facial parts contour. Once, facial parts and their locations are detected, we perform measurement of facial components; head direction, eye opening and blinking, line of sight direction, and mouth opening. Those measurements are matched with micro-expression model, which is built from the observers questionnaires. Finally, we estimate emotions and their changes from the emotion model.

Mouth Motion. According to emotional condition, mouth open width and stretched length are changing variously. For example, laughing is a obvious action. Laugh opens the mouth widely and the teeth are disclosed. On the other hand, smile, which is more delicate expression than laugh, raises the corner of the mouth just a little. In conversation, the mouth is changing its shape variously to speak. Thus it is not perfect estimating emotions only from mouth motion. Never the less mouth motion is very important information for estimating delicate emotions.

We focus on mouth open width, which is the distance between lower edge of the upper lip and upper edge of the lower lip m_y, and mouth stretch length, which

Fig. 2. Detecting mouth motion; opening width and stretching length

is the distance between the left and the right corner of the mouth m_x. If m_x, m_y exceeds a pre-determined threshold, we detect the following three motions; smiling (MU0), mouth slightly opening (MU1), and mouth closing (MU2) as in Eq. 1.

$$\text{MU} = \begin{cases} 0 \text{ (smile)} & \text{if } m_x \geq T_{MUx1} \text{ and } m_y \leq T_{MUy1} \\ 1 \text{ (slightly open)} & \text{if } m_x \geq T_{MUx2} \text{ and } m_y \geq T_{MUy2} \\ 2 \text{ (close)} & \text{if } m_x \geq T_{MUx3} \text{ and } m_y \leq T_{MUy3} \end{cases} \qquad (1)$$

where $T_{MUx1} = 0.22$, $T_{MUy1} = 0.00$, $T_{MUx2} = 0.19$, $T_{MUy2} = 0.05$, $T_{MUx3} = 0.17$, and $T_{MUy3} = 0.01$ of horizontal face size in our implementation.

Head Pose. Psychologists pointed out that lowers his head when sad and body tremble when he is scary. Empirically, we know the strong evidence that emotion affects head post. For example, head rotates naturally its direction toward an interested object or person. Head pose go up when feeling contemptuous of a person. Head pose go down when feeling shame, sadness, embarrassment, and bored. This is a non-verbal communication of "attitude", when we are in conversation.

We compute an average facial surface normal from a range image of the face region of the subject. Then compute three face directional angles; roll θ_x (rotation around X axis), pitch θ_y (rotation around Y axis), and yow θ_z (rotation around Z axis) respectively. Figure 3 shows the axis of the head. If those angle exceeds a pre-determined thresholds, we detect 6 face directional motion; directing front (HU0), directing left (HU1), directing right (HU2), directing up (HU3), directing down (HU4) and nodding (HU5) as in Eq. 2.

$$\text{HU} = \begin{cases} 0 \text{ (front)} & \text{if } \theta_x \leq T_{HUx1} \text{ and } \theta_y \leq T_{HUy1} \text{ and } \theta_z \leq T_{HUz1} \\ 1 \text{ (left)} & \text{if } \theta_y \geq T_{HUy2} \\ 2 \text{ (right)} & \text{if } \theta_y \leq -T_{HUy2} \\ 3 \text{ (up)} & \text{if } \theta_x \geq T_{HUx2} \\ 4 \text{ (down)} & \text{if } \theta_x \leq T_{HUx3} \\ 5 \text{ (nodding)} & \text{if } T_{HUx4} \leq \theta_x \leq T_{HUx5} \end{cases} \qquad (2)$$

where $T_{HUx1} = 9$, $T_{HUy1} = 8$, $T_{HUz1} = -3$, $T_{HUy2} = 24$, $T_{HUx2} = 15.6$, $T_{HUx3} = -8$, $T_{HUx4} = -7$, and $T_{HUx5} = -3$ degree in our implementation.

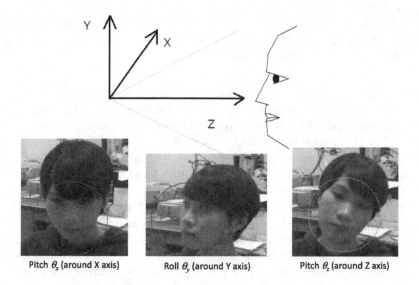

Pitch θ_x (around X axis)   Roll θ_y (around Y axis)   Pitch θ_z (around Z axis)

Fig. 3. Recognition of face/head pose (Color figure online)

Direction of Line of Sight. Among the expression, in particular eye produces significant and direct impression. We naturally feel that information from thoughtful eyes and their motion is equivalent to spoken words. Sometimes we are able to distinguish posed smile from a laughing face. This is because we are reading the movement of eyes. For example, if the line of sight is looking up, it implies remembering with the past experience or the landscape as seen previously. If eyes and facing up is moving left and right restlessly, it implies upset feelings. So, eye movements often represent the feelings unconsciously.

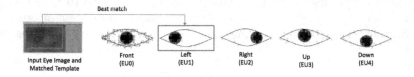

Fig. 4. Recognition of line of sight direction.

To detect line of sight or eye direction, we first detect each eye region (left and right). Then for each eye, we compare the region with 5 typical pre-determined template images expressing looking front (EU0), looking left (EU1), looking right (EU2), looking up (EU3) and looking down (EU4) as in Fig. 3 and Eq. 3. In Fig. 3, the left image is the detected eye region, red rectangle denotes highest match among 5 templates. In this case, template EU1 is the best match.

$$EU = \arg \max_{0 \leq k \leq 4} \max\{q(I(x,y), G(k))\} \tag{3}$$

where, k is the template number $(0 \leq k \leq 4)$, $G(k)$ is the k-th template image (size $w \times h$), $(I(x,y)$ is a $(w \times h)$ sub-region of each eye region starting from upper left corner at (x, y), and $q(I, G)$ is a correlation function. Our implementation uses normalized cross-correlation function as q.

Blinking. Blinks, usually 25 to 35 times per minutes, become more than 35 times, when an impact is applied to the eye or sudden emotional influence, such as upset and surprises. Blinking or frequency has a good correlation with mental state whether the person is nervous or relaxed.

To measure eye opening and blinking, we use skin color based approach. We compute the ratio of dark color (iris and pupil region) pixels and skin color pixels of the eye region of the test subject, then estimate eye opening and closing comparing with a pre-determined threshold. Figure 3 shows the scheme. In the figure, left upper image is the detected eye region, left middle and left bottom images are eye opened and closed image respectively. White pixel denotes that color is similar to skin. If the number of skin color pixels exceeds the threshold, we count one eye closing (pointed by red arrows in the figure). Then we count the number of eye closing in a few seconds and compute blinks per minutes n_b. If n_b is less than a threshold, we consider it is stable (SU0), if it is larger we consider it is nervous (SU1) as in Eq. 4.

$$SU = \begin{cases} 0 \text{ (stable)} & \text{if } T_{SU1} \leq n_b \leq T_{SU2} \\ 1 \text{ (nervous)} & \text{if } n_b > T_{SU2} \end{cases} \tag{4}$$

where, threshold $T_{SU1} = 25$ and $T_{SU2} = 35$ in our implementation.

3.1   Emotion Estimation

To build a mental state corpus, we recorded 30 cut of video of the test subject conversations with his/her friend. Then we showed the video to the evaluator subjects, and asked why they felt the five emotions. From their answers, we could find corresponding micro-expressions related with the five emotions as in Table 1.

Table 1. Correspondence between micro-expressions and emotions

	Eye-sight	Blinking	Face direction	Mouth motion
Feeling familiar	EU0	SU0	HU5	MU0
Bored	EU1 ∨ EU2	SU1	HU1 ∨ HU2	MU2
Noticing	EU0	SU1	HU3	MU1
Depressed	EU4	SU0	HU4	MU2
Thinking	EU3	SU0	HU3	MU2

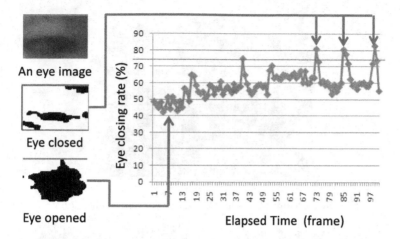

Fig. 5. Recognition of eye opening and blinking

According to the co-occurrence of the micro-expressions for each emotions in Table 1, we can build a decision tree, in which each node of the tree corresponds to a row of Table 1. If there is a match of AUs combination at a node, corresponding emotion is detected. (Tables 2 and 3)

Table 2. Emotional Transition and Corresponding Facial Action Units

emotion	Combination of Micro-expression	
Feeling Familiar	EU0 ∧ HU5 ∧ MU2	
Boredom	EU1 ∧ HU1	EU2 ∧ HU2
Noticed	EU0 ∧ HU5 ∧ MU1	SU1 ∧ MU1
Depressed	EU3 ∧ HU4	
Thinking	EU0 ∧ HU3	

4   Experiments

Using 30 video cuts generated from our video corpus, we performed two-fold cross-validation. We trained our system with half of the corpus. Then we examined the rest of the corpus for evaluation. We asked 10 experimenters, different persons from observers in the preliminary experiment in Sect. 3, to check a conversation video, in which each of scene cuts contains a single emotional expression. Then we evaluated computer's output with the human experimenters' results. The results are shown in Table 4.

As the second experiment, we aimed to detect multiple emotional expressions. In this case, experimenter (same as previous experiment) are asked to

Fig. 6. An example scene for single emotion evaluation

Fig. 7. Examples of friendly emotion estimation. Successfully estimated (left) and failure (right)

Fig. 8. Examples of bored emotion estimation. Successfully estimated (left) and failure (right)

Fig. 9. Examples of thinking estimation. Successfully estimated (left) and failure (right)

Fig. 10. Examples of noticed emotion estimation. Successfully estimated (left) and failure (right)

Table 3. Single emotion in a cut

Single Emotion	Recall Rate	Precision
Single Emotion	83 %	80 %

check if there is a transition of emotion. This means that in the first half of the video contains emotion A, while the second half of the video contains another emotion B. Of course it is more difficult task, because the algorithm as well as the experimenter have to estimate two emotion correctly. The results are shown in Table 4.

Table 4. Multiple emotions in a cut

Emotional Change	Recall Rate	Precision
Emotion A to B	74 %	70 %

Table 4 shows that a single emotion can be estimated more the 80 % from our method. This means that the facial parts recognition and micro-expression recognition proposed in Sect. 3.1 is working well and corresponding emotional state estimation is working too. However, Table 4 shows emotional changes is about 10 % less accurate than single emotion. This implies that our method is somewhat different from human estimation. We found that human evaluators have a tendency to feel continuous even after the first emotional cue distinguished. We should develop some hysteresis function in the future.

5   Conclusion

We proposed a method to micro-expression recognition for detection of human emotional changes. We focused mouth motion, face direction, eye-sight direction, and blinking as micro-expressions. Our experiments showed a good corresponding between our method and human evaluators. However, our method has some difference when human shows multiple emotions or changes their emotions.

References

1. Ekman, P., Friesen, M.V.: The Facial Action Coding System: A Technique for The Measurement of Facial Movement. Consulting Psychologist, Palo Alto (1978)
2. Mase, K.: Recognition of facial expression from optical flow. IEICE Trans. **E74**(10), 3474–3483 (1991)
3. Black, M., J., Yacoob, Y.: Tracking and recognizing rigid and non-rigid facial motions using local parametric models of image motion. In: International Conference on Computer Vision, pp. 374–381 (1995)
4. Essa, I., Pentland, A.: Coding, analysis, interpretation and recognition of facial expressions. IEEE Trans. PAMI **19**(7), 757–763 (1997)
5. Donato, G., Bartlett, M.S., Hager, J.C., Ekman, P., Sejnowski, T.J.: Classifying facial actions. IEEE Trans. PAMI **21**(10), 974–989 (1999)
6. Tian, Y., Kanade, T., Cohn, J.F.: Recognizing action units for facial expression analysis. IEEE Trans. PAMI **23**(2), 1–19 (2001)
7. Bartlett, M.S., Littlewort, G., Frank, M.G., Lainscsek, C., Fasel, I., Movellan, J.: Recognizing facial expression: machine learning and application to spontaneous behavior. In: IEEE Conference on CVPR, pp. 568–573 (2005)
8. Chang, Y., Hu, C., Feris, R., Turk, M.: Manifold based analysis of facial expression. J. Image Vis. Comput. **24**(6), 605–614 (2006)
9. Pantic, M., Patras, I.: Dynamics of facial expression: recognition of facial action-snand their temporal segments from face profile image sequence. IEEE Trans. SMCB **36**(2), 433–449 (2006)
10. Asteriadis, S., Tzouveli, P., Karpouzis, K., Kollias, S.: Estimation of behavioral user state based on eye gaze and head pose – application in an e-learning environment. Multimedia Tools Appl. **41**(3), 469–493 (2008)
11. Gunes, H., Piccardi, M.: Automatic temporal segment detection and affect recognition from face and body display. IEEE Trans. SMC. Part B, Cybern. **39**(1), 64–84 (2009)
12. Gunes, H., Pantic, M.: Dimensional emotion prediction from spontaneous head gestures for interaction with sensitive artificial listeners. In: Safonova, A. (ed.) IVA 2010. LNCS, vol. 6356, pp. 371–377. Springer, Heidelberg (2010)
13. Bartlett, M.S., Whitehill, J.: Automated facial expression measurement: recent applications to basic research in human behavior, learning, and education. In: Calder, A., et al. (eds.) Handbook of Face Perception. Oxford University Press, New York (2010)
14. Tian, Y., Kanade, T., Cohn, J.F.: Facial expression recognition. In: Li, S.Z., Jain, A.K. (eds.) Handbook of Face Recognition, pp. 487–520. Springer-Verlag, Berlin (2011). Chap. 11
15. Lemaire, P., Ardabilian, M., Chen, L., Daoudi, M.: Fully automatic 3D facial expression recognition using differential mean curvature maps and histograms of oriented gradients. In: International Conference on Automatic Face and Gesture Recognition, pp. 1–7 (2013)

Users' Sense-Making of an Affective Intervention in Human-Computer Interaction

Mathias Wahl[(✉)], Julia Krüger, and Jörg Frommer

Department of Psychosomatic Medicine and Psychotherapy, Medical Faculty,
Otto von Guericke University Magdeburg, Magdeburg, Germany
{mathias.wahl,julia.krueger,joerg.frommer}@med.ovgu.de

Abstract. This qualitative interview study builds on an empirical experiment in which an affective intervention was given to users in a critical dialog situation of human-computer interaction (HCI). The applied intervention addressed users on a personal level by asking for their thoughts and feelings. Since this is still an unusual behavior for a technical system, the aim of the present study was to investigate how users reason about this. Three different kinds of individual sense-making processes regarding the intervention were worked out. These clarify that a personal level of interaction between system and user is only appropriate for some users, whereas it also can have adverse effects on others. By explicating users' experiences and conceptions, this study contributes to research on affective interventions in HCI that in the past was mainly focused on measurements of effectiveness rather than on understanding users'inner processes regarding such interventions.

Keywords: Intervention · User experience · Qualitative research · Interviews · Affective computing · Human-Computer interaction

1 Introduction

The ability of technical systems' to recognize, respond to and even influence affective states of users is of growing importance for the human-computer interaction (HCI). Especially regarding interactions with personalized assistive technology that individually adapts its functionality to its users, like for instance in the case of Companion-systems [1, 2], the consideration of users' affect is crucial. When assisting a user in his or her everyday life, the complexity of tasks is very high and thus the risk to encounter critical dialog situations inducing negative emotions increases. In such cases, system's adequate reaction to users' needs is beneficial for comforting users, for keeping the interaction going and for improving users' attitude towards the system.

Affective interfaces that provide emotional support by applying affective interventions have been shown to be capable of relieving emotional states like stress [3] or frustration [4], enhancing the problem solving capabilities [5] and improving the willingness to further participate in a given task [6]. Although these studies demonstrate that synthetic emotions expressed by technical systems can help frustrated users, it is still poorly understood why this is the case [7]. In these studies, interventions' effectiveness

© Springer International Publishing Switzerland 2016
M. Kurosu (Ed.): HCI 2016, Part III, LNCS 9733, pp. 71–79, 2016.
DOI: 10.1007/978-3-319-39513-5_7

was measured by applying questionnaires (ratings of frustration, valence and arousal and ratings of the interaction in general on predefined scales), observing user behavior or analyzing user performance data. Besides these ratings that provide quantitative measurements of users' states or users' evaluation of the system, the question of what was going on in users' minds during the interaction and the intervention remained unanswered.

The aim of the present study is to help filling this research gap by exploring how users individually experienced an affective intervention, which was given to them in reaction to a critical dialog situation of HCI and hence to better understand what makes such an approach valuable. It is not the intention to either evaluate the applied system, or to test the effectiveness of the applied intervention. Instead, in an account of basic research, it is the aim to understand subjective sense-making processes regarding the affective intervention.

In order to design affective interventions in a way that supports each individual user, it is important to understand how users experience these and what they wish for regarding their design. In previous studies, we were able to demonstrate that users experience interactions with technical systems highly individual and that their experience was influenced by individual sense-making processes, which helped users to understand nature and behavior of their counterpart and thus to gain safety in the interaction [8–10]. Because individual sense-making processes are mostly represented on an implicit (i.e., barely consciously reflected) level of awareness, an adequate methodology is needed for their assessment. For this purpose, established methods of user research, which mostly rely on structured questionnaires or interviews with pre-formulated items, are suitable to only a limited extent. Instead, by using open question formats, narrations can be evoked in users, which in turn make it possible to access the initially hidden sense-making processes. The content of such processes is crucial for the acceptance of technical systems and especially for affective interventions. Thus, in this study, the sense-making processes underlying users' experiences of an intervention will be investigated. For this purpose, a qualitative research methodology that allows to consider users' individuality and the implicitness of their sense-making will be applied.

2   Empirical Investigations

The present study builds on a widely standardized empirical experiment in which a critical dialog situation of HCI was established. In reaction to this critical situation, an affective intervention was given to the participants. Subsequent to taking part in the experiment, participants were interviewed.

2.1   Wizard of Oz Experiment

In order to simulate a computer system capable of speech and individualized reactions, the empirical experiment was designed as a Wizard of Oz study [11]. The system was represented solely by a computer screen with a graphical user interface (without any interface agent) and a male machine-like sounding computer voice. The only possible way for the participants to interact with the system was via speech. In cooperation with the system, participants had to pack a suitcase for a holiday trip by selecting items from a catalogue depicted on a screen in front of them. At a certain point during the packing procedure, participants were informed about the actual weather conditions at the destination of their trip ('weather barrier'), which were contrary to what was suggested in the beginning. Therefore, participants were required to repack their suitcase under increasing time constraints, what was intended to cause feelings of stress and frustration. In reaction to this critical situation, an affective intervention was given to the participants (for a detailed description of the whole experimental design see [12, 13]).

2.2 Affective Intervention

The affective intervention was given to the participants right after the weather barrier. It consisted of three consecutive components (cf. Table 1), which basically refer to the common factors of psychotherapy (activation of positive resources, actualization of what is to be changed, active help for coping with the problem, motivational clarification), which were formulated by Grawe [14]. The intervention was realized as a solely text-based speech output and differed from the rest of the experiment in that the system firstly referred to itself as 'I' and secondly directly asked for participants' feelings. This was meant to change the level of interaction (from a primary factual to a more personal level) and to help participants in reflecting on their critical situation as well as to offer support for recovery.

Table 1. Intervention components and corresponding speech outputs

Intervention component	Speech output
1. Empathic understanding	"Because of an interruption in the data line the information about your destination could not be obtained earlier. Thus, your situation surprisingly changed. The items you chose suggest you had expected different weather conditions. If you had known the actual weather conditions of your destination, would you have chosen different items? I'm interested in your opinion"
2. Clarification of affect	"Did this situation also trigger any negative feelings? If so, can you describe them?"
3. Encouragement	"I hope your motivation to further contribute to this task was not affected by this too much"

2.3 User Interviews and Sample

The interviews aimed at investigating how participants experienced the interaction with the system and how they were affected by the intervention. For conducting the interviews, a semi-structured interview guide, including open narration generating questions, was used [15].

In total, there were 35 participants (17 female) who took part in the empirical experiment, received the affective intervention and were interviewed subsequently. They were between 18 and 75 years old (two age groups: 18-28 and 60 +) and had different educational backgrounds. By investigating such a heterogeneous sample, a wide range of experiences should be grasped. This corresponds to the rationale of qualitative research, which can be seen in the maximization of variance and in the generation of hypotheses rather than in testing those.

2.4 Analysis Procedure

Initially, the audio records of the interview sequences dealing with the experiences of the intervention of all 35 participants considered for this study were transcribed (which resulted in 232 transcript pages) and the transcripts were imported into the analysis software 'MaxQDA' [16]. Following the procedures of 'summarizing qualitative content analysis' [17], at first the text was broken down into 'meaning units' (MUs), which are segments of text that contain one main idea and are understandable by themselves [18]. Next, these MUs were assigned to the most suitable of five predefined categories (so-called 'first level categories': *experience of the context, experience of the system, experience of the relation to the system, experience of the intervention* and *self-related experience*). The assigned MUs were then compared to each other and grouped according to similarities. These groups constituted a set of subcategories ('third level categories'), which in turn could be arranged into main categories representing a higher abstraction level ('second level categories').

As a result of this procedure, a category system with 5 first level, 13 second level and 58 third level categories was worked out. With the help of this category system, users' subjective experiences were structured and patterns of individual sense-making processes regarding the affective intervention could be identified. Next, these patterns will be described in more detail.

3   Results

The analysis revealed a variety of subjective sense-making processes. Especially, the shift from a factual to a personal level of interaction was experienced with a lot of astonishment by the users. At first, the intervention was experienced as *"surprising"* (07-AJ)[1], *"unusual"* (28-CM) and *"strange"* (29-SG) and in a sense *"it fell out of the context"* (14-RT). For some users aim and purpose of the intervention were not clear, which led to some uncertainty. Being addressed on a personal level prompted users to question if this is even possible. For some users it was clear that a computer system is based on facts (*"for me computer programs are facts and no statements of feelings"*, 01-VL), that it functions according to its programming and that it is not capable of comprehending feelings (*"when a computer asks me if I am disappointed, sad or funny, it can maybe classify the words into categories, but nevertheless it cannot comprehend them"*, 05-KK). Others instead were convinced that the system can individually process information and react adequately (*"you always think that a computer is a predefined program,*

---

[1] User's initials are used in order to ensure anonymity. All quotes were translated from German into English.

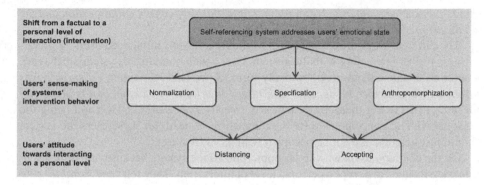

Fig. 1. Users' sense-making of the intervention and the resulting attitude towards interacting on a personal level.

but when it answers that individually, it is odd [...] it is admirable or strange that a computer can respond as we do", 08-BP).

After this initial astonishment and ambiguity concerning system and intervention, users tried to make sense of system's intervention behavior (cf. Fig. 1).

The sense making regarding the intervention differed significantly between the users, but in abstracting the individual experiences, three main tendencies could be identified.

Some users **normalized** system's behavior, which means that they considered system's self-referencing and addressing of users' emotions as an ordinary part of the interaction, which was not different from the rest. For these users it was simply a *"program point"* (17-VK) and a *"task"* (27-CD) that had to be worked off. They found nothing special about being asked after their feelings by a computer program (*"I just answered and that's it"*, 24-BS). By normalizing system's behavior, these users in a way negated system's interest in their emotional state (*"no matter what I say [...] the computer is not interested"*, 05-KK). This way they ruled out the possibility of interacting with the system on a personal level.

Other users **specified** system's behavior by clearly identifying it as, for instance, a *"documentation of feelings"* (03-MR), a *"critical evaluation"* (18-JK), a *"review of the actual situation"* (13-CK) or a *"confirmation of changed requirements"* (14-RT). For these users, the initial uncertainty regarding the intervention vanished as soon as they had figured out its aim and purpose. In a sort of routine they recognized the intervention as something they know from prior experience, for example as a situation in which they have been tested or asked for their opinion.

A third group of users **anthropomorphized** the system because of the behavior it displayed. For these users the system revealed *"human traits"* (09-EG), which resulted in not recognizing it as a machine any more (*"it is a computer, I didn't associate that, I felt that it was a person sitting there and asking me"*, 30-KM). In the case of anthropomorphization, the users regarded the intervention as a confirmation for system's personhood. This interpretation helped users to regain safety in the interaction, because interactions with human-beings are familiar and thus predictable. Moreover, anthropomorphizing the system enhanced the collaboration with it (*"it understood me, it noticed* *that I had problems and asked after these, I think this deepens the collaboration and the relationship with the program, too*", 26-SS).

The different ways of making sense of the intervention influenced users' attitudes towards further interacting with the system. Users, who normalized system's behavior, wanted to **distance** themselves from any form of personal interaction ("*I know it was programmed to be nice to me, but I don't need that from a machine, that is not useful for me*", 11-HG). For them the system is a "*service provider*" (11-HG) and being too personal with it is unconducive for the interaction. Instead, for these users the system should just function and not be occupied with users' feelings.

On the contrary, users who anthropomorphized the system because of the intervention were inclined to **accept** a personal level of interaction. They felt "*comfortable*" (06-UK) with the system and "*chitchatted*" (09-EG) with it. For them, a personal level of interaction with the system improves the interaction experience and helps to cope with negative emotional states.

Users, who specified system's behavior, either tended to distance themselves or to take part in a personal interaction. For these users, the functionality on a factual level is most important, but they also value a more intimate level of interaction ("*when it's going well on a factual level, then the emotional side is safe for me, too*", 25-SP). But still there a concerns like participant YD puts it: "*it is strange to tell an unemotional machine how I feel, because it can probably not emphasize with my situation*" (19-YD). Thus, these users remain somewhat undecided with regard to their preferred level of interaction with the system.

4   Discussion

In an account of basic research, the aim of the present study was to understand how users conceptualized and experienced an affective intervention, which was given to them by a system. Above relating to ratings on predefined categories or measurements of effectiveness, different ways of how users made sense of the intervention have been worked out. These indicate that a personal level of interaction, in which users' emotional state is addressed, is not advantageous for all kinds of users and that it can also have negative effects on users' willingness to further participate in the given task.

With the intervention, there was a shift from a task related factual level of interaction to a more reflective personal level. In different studies, Reeves, Nass and Moon [19, 20] were able to show that people readily engage in communicative behavior as they know it from human-human interaction, as soon as a computer gives basic social cues (like speech-based communication). With regard to the affective intervention, the research presented here confirms this tendency of users. However, the sense-making processes that have been worked out indicate that users reacted in individually different ways to the offer of a personal communication. While some users anthropomorphized the system ('anthropomorphization'), others did not react to the social behaviors of the system ('normalization') or identified it as something detached from the system ('specification'). Moreover, the data revealed that some users (those who normalized or specified system's behavior) denied any form of personal interaction with a technical system.

Especially for the further development of assistive technology, which aims at reacting adequately to needs and states of its users (like in the case of Companion-systems that are meant to provide an emotional dimension of the interaction in addition to a task-oriented formal one [1, 2]), this is an important fact that needs to be considered. Only if such systems are able to react to users' needs and actual emotions on an *appropriate interactional level*, systems will be perceived as individualized assistants and partners and thus will be able to support users in processing their affect and in reaching their goals.

The affective intervention applied in this research was intentionally kept relatively short and was given to the participants regardless of their current emotional state. This way it was possible to gather a differentiated view on experiences, since participants were not tempted to interpret the intervention in a certain way and moreover, the sense-making processes of all kinds of participants were included in the analysis. To validate the results, further research is needed. It will be interesting to find out, how users' sense-making processes change depending on (a) the critical situation they are in (e.g., stress, frustration, cognitive overload or boredom), (b) the time frame of the interaction with the system (single vs. multiple interactions) or (c) the representation of the system (e.g., anthropomorphic vs. artificial system voice; interface agent vs. no agent). Also different kinds of interventions (e.g., personal vs. factual) should be tested against each other to further investigate to which extent an intervention influences the experience of a system as a whole.

The implications of the present study can primarily be seen in generating an under-standing for the importance of individual sense-making processes in HCI. Already a relatively simple intervention was able to evoke a broad range of interpretations and moreover clarified that a 'one type fits all' solution is not inevitably appropriate for all kinds of users, because users draw on their own sense-making processes to arrive at reasonable explanations. These sometimes may seem pretty far-fetched from reality, but they enable users to participate in an efficient interaction with the system and thus to achieve their goals. Regardless of the best intentions of designers, in the end the user will decide about acceptance or denial of an intervention or even a system as a whole. This decision is based on individual experiences and attitudes, which are only to some extent consciously reflected. In HCI contexts, investigating such implicit ways of experience is only in its beginnings. Here, the user is mostly viewed as a computable variable, whose ways of experiences can be best described in quantified categories. The present study wants to contribute to a modified view on the user and his or her individual sense-making processes. In the future, more research based on an interpretative qualitative methodology will be needed to investigate user experience in HCI and thus to gain a differentiated view of users' interpretations regarding the system and its behavior. With regard to affective interventions, the sense making processes that have been worked out in this study can serve as a starting point for future research.

Acknowledgments. The present study is performed in the framework of the Transregional Collaborative Research Centre SFB/TRR 62 "A Companion-Technology for Cognitive Technical Systems" funded by the German Research Foundation (DFG). The responsibility for the content of this paper lies with the authors.

References

1. Wilks, Y.: Artificial companions. Interdiscipl. Sci. Rev. **30**(2), 145–152 (2005)
2. Wendemuth, A., Biundo, S.: A companion technology for cognitive technical systems. In: Esposito, A., Esposito, A.M., Vinciarelli, A., Hoffmann, R., Müller, V.C. (eds.) COST 2102. LNCS, vol. 7403, pp. 89–103. Springer, Heidelberg (2012)
3. Prendinger, H., Mayer, S., Mori, J., Ishizuka, M.: Persona effect revisited. In: Rist, T., Aylett, R.S., Ballin, D., Rickel, J. (eds.) IVA 2003. LNCS (LNAI), vol. 2792, pp. 283–291. Springer, Heidelberg (2003)
4. Hone, K.: Empathic agents to reduce user frustration: the effects of varying agent characteristics. Interact. Comput. **18**, 227–245 (2006)
5. Partala, T., Surakka, V.: The effects of affective interventions in human–computer interaction. Interact. Comput. **16**, 295–309 (2004)
6. Klein, J., Moon, Y., Picard, R.W.: This computer responds to user frustration: theory, design and results. Interact. Comput. **14**, 119–140 (2002)
7. Beale, R., Creed, C.: Affective interaction: how emotional agents affect users. Int. J. Hum.-Comput. St. **67**, 755–776 (2009)
8. Frommer, J., Rösner, D., Lange, J., Haase, M.: Giving computers personality? Personality in computers is in the eye of the user. In: Rojc, M., Campbell, N. (eds.) Coverbal Synchrony in Human-Machine Interaction, pp. 41–71. CRC Press, Boca Raton (2013)
9. Krüger, J., Wahl, M., Frommer, J.: Making the system a relational partner: users' ascriptions in individualization-focused interactions with companion-systems. In: Berntzen, L., Böhm, S. (eds.) CENTRIC 2015, The Eighth International Conference on Advances in Human-oriented and Personalized Mechanisms, Technologies, and Services, pp. 48–54. IARIA XPS Press/s.l (2015)
10. Wahl, M., Krüger, J., Frommer, J.: From anger to relief: five ideal types of users experiencing an affective intervention in HCI. In: Berntzen, L., Böhm, S. (eds.) CENTRIC 2015, The Eighth International Conference on Advances in Human-Oriented and Personalized Mechanisms, Technologies, and Services, pp. 55–61. IARIA XPS Press/s.l (2015)
11. Dahlbäck, N., Jönsson, A., Ahrenberg, L.: Wizard of Oz studies—why and how. Knowl.-Based Syst. **6**, 258–266 (1993)
12. Rösner, D., Frommer, J., Friesen R., Haase, M., Lange, J., Otto, M.: LAST MINUTE: a multimodal corpus of speech-based user-companion interactions. In: LREC Conference Abstracts, pp. 96–104. LREC, Istanbul (2012)
13. Frommer, J., Rösner, D., Haase, M., Lange, J., Friesen, R., Otto, M.: Project A3 prevention of Negative courses of dialogues: wizard of Oz experiment operator's manual. In: Working Paper of the Collaborative Research Project/Transregio 62 "A Companion Technology for Cognitive Technical Systems". Pabst Science Publication, Lengerich (2012)
14. Grawe, K.: Outline of a general psychotherapy. Psychotherapeut **40**, 130–145 (1995)
15. Lange, J., Frommer, J.: Subjektives Erleben und intentionale Einstellung in Interviews zur Nutzer-Companion-Interaktion [Subjective experience and intentional stance in interveiws regarding user-companion interaction (in German)]. In: Heiß, H.-U., Pepper, P., Schlinghoff, H., Schneider, J. (eds.) Informatik 2011. LNI, vol. 192, p. 240. Köllen, Bonn (2011)
16. Kuckartz, U.: MAXQDA: qualitative data analysis. VERBI Softw., Berlin (2007)
17. Mayring, P.: Qualitative content analysis: theoretical foundation, basic procedures and software solution, p. 143 (2014). http://nbn-resolving.de/urn:nbn:de:0168-ssoar-395173

18. Tesch, R.: Qualitative research analysis types and software tools. Palmer Press, New York (1990)
19. Reeves, B., Nass, C.: The Media Equation. How People Treat Computers, Television, and New Media Like Real People and Places. Cambridge University Press, Cambridge (1996)
20. Nass, C., Moon, Y.: Machines and mindlessness: social responses to computers. J. Soc. Issues **56**(1), 81–103 (2000)

Communication and Companionship

Impression Evaluation for Active Behavior of Robot in Human Robot Interaction

Okada Akiho and Midori Sugaya[(✉)]

Shibaura Institute of Technology, Computer Science and Engineering, Tokyo, Japan
{okada,doly}@shibara-it.ac.jp

Abstract. Behavioral design of robot is one of the concerns in the human-robot interaction [1, 2]. About the design of human-robot communicative interaction, there are lots of approaches have been presented for finding the preferable behaviors that are accepted by the people. In these studies, the users impressions of robots during interactions with them have been focused on the initiatives of the users, with users evaluating the response of the robot. Conversely, there have less studies on the evaluations on human impressions when a robot takes the initiative and performs active behavior towards a human. While creating events in which a robot explicitly performed active behavior, we reviewed human-robot interactions and presented our behavioral designs. Based on that, we implemented greeting functions for the robot. The objective of this study is to investigate the users' impressions on the robot especially with the activeness of the robot. We examined the differences in their impressions depending on with or without of active behavior of robot. The results show significant differences in activity, affinity, and intentionality.

Keywords: Human robot interaction · Active behavior of robot · Robot · Behavioral design of robot · Robot communication

1 Introduction

In recent years, robots that can communicate with people while interacting with them have become more common. There has been a call for increased development of robot technology, including things such as functional application in new areas, humanoid platforms and humanoid robots for entertainment. Prior to this study, studies of human-robot interactions suggested that we still need a large amount of study on evaluating the impressions that a robot leaves on people. Nakata et al. conducted an experiment on interpersonal valence based on the impressions people had after seeing the reaction a robot made after those touched the robot with their hands. The results revealed that when the robot interacted with those people in a way that showed a kind of emotional attachment to them, users had a positive impression of the robot [1]. Kakio et al. investigated the differences in user impressions depending on the reaction of a robot when they pushed the robot, which showed that they had different impressions depending on the robot's reactions [2]. Many of these studies on user impressions have been conducted as follows: users took the initiative and did something, and a robot reacted to that. In a

© Springer International Publishing Switzerland 2016
M. Kurosu (Ed.): HCI 2016, Part III, LNCS 9733, pp. 83–95, 2016.
DOI: 10.1007/978-3-319-39513-5_8

way, most of the studies focused on the passive behavior of the robots. When two people are communicating, two positions are assumed; one side is acting (the party which is currently active, as in speaking) and the other side is reacting to that (the party which is currently passive, as in listening). In previous studies, the robot side, which was the passive side, was not sufficiently studied. Thus, we defined behavior in which a robot takes the initiative and does something towards a human user as "active behavior", and studied the changes in the users' impressions depending on the presence or absence of that active behavior. In addition, the behavioral design model of our robot that performed active behavior was shown as an action state transition. There have been many studies on human-robot interactions [1–3, 8, 9]. However, there were not enough studies in which the behavior of a robot was determined to be "passive" or "active", and then their basic behavior was demonstrated, as an action guideline, in the form of a status model. That's what we attempted to do.

In this study, in accordance with our status model on active behavior, we conducted an experiment on greetings. We thought that with greetings, the intention of the robot would be easily understood, even if we included a variety of active behaviors. The reason is as follows: in a previous study, we investigated the movements of a robot that looked in the direction of a person, with settings for the robot's looking direction control [3]. However, in the evaluation items, "activity", "affinity" and "pleasantness" depending on the presence or absence of the looking direction control, statistically significant differences in impressions were not noticed.

The results didn't reveal that active behavior had an effect. Certain behavior levels are required if it can be recognized as active behavior. Thus, we focused on "greetings" as active behavior, which might lead to improvements in evaluations on impression, and we mounted this on a robot. To perform this greeting behavior, we mounted two optical sensors on RAPIRO [4] to create contact interaction between a user and the robot, which would react when touched by a user. To allow for interaction prior to the greeting action, we implemented a looking direction control action and a greeting action, in which the robot raised and lowered its arms. In the experiment, we carried out a questionnaire survey on the impressions that users had on the robot's behavior when it performed active behavior and when it didn't. The results showed that there were significant differences in "affinity", "activity" and "intent". The result shows that in human-robot interactions, the active behavior of robot will obtain the better impression when we design and implement the expected action.

This paper is organized as follows. Section 2 shows a point of debate from our previous study. Section 3 shows the design and proposal of active behavior in humanoid robots. Section 4 shows the implementation, experiment and discussion. Section 5 shows the summary and discusses future challenges.

It should be noted that in this paper, the terms "interaction", "contact interaction" and "communication" are used when we investigate the impressions that people have on robot actions or reactions, namely interaction and for correspondence and understanding, namely communication between robots and humans. In this study, greeting behavior was the main interaction; thus, we called interactions containing contact in the experiment "contact interactions" to reduce ambiguity in the paper.

2 Related Work

2.1 Hypothesis on Active Behavior

As the numbers of humanoid robots, including the ASIMO [5], Pepper [6], and Palro [7] models have become more and more common, a variety of study on human-robot interactions has been also conducted. Nakai et al. assumed that stuffed animals that have more realistic features might help to reduce boredom in interactions with users, and they studied the realism of stuffed animals that had fluctuation of the lights in their eyes [8]. In addition, Nakata et al. created a robot that showed receptive behavior (the ability to nod), repulsive behavior (dispelling behavior) and reactionless behavior with contact with a human hand, and investigated the affinity caused by interpersonal valence.

These prior studies have been conducted assuming an animal robot, and applications to a humanoid robot have not been fully considered. There is also some study on humanoid robots. Kakio et al. investigated the impression that users had on a robot's reactions when they pushed the robot, with the aim that whether the robot could naturally express its situation through the reactive action to the users push [2]. Yano et al. investigated the differences in impressions that users felt depending on the speed that a robot raised its arms up and down [9]. Both pieces of study required the preceding active behavior of the user towards a robot; then the users evaluated the robot's reaction to their actions. In a word, most of the previous studies are based on impressions in which the robots were reacting to users passively.

We attempted to explicitly understand the relationship between human-robot interactions using conventional studies determined to be "passive" or "active", and we aimed to conduct evaluations on user impressions of the robot's active behaviors. Eventually, based on these results, we aim to construct an interaction model that can be used with designing robot behavior.

2.2 Expectations with Active Robot

There is study in which users' opinions, regarding what kind of situations they feel affinity or pleasantness toward a robot in, were organized using the KJ method [10]. This study organized the following opinions into five stages: "What kind of behavior do humans expect from a robot when they see it for the first time?" and "What kind of robot actions do humans think are interesting or pleasant?" (Table 1).

Table 1. Actions that humans expect from a robot/sorted into groups using the KJ method

Stage	Expected actions	Concrete examples
1	Greetings	Bowing or a handshake
2	Entertainment	Dancing and acrobats
3	Human-like behavior	Smooth movements
4	Assisting daily life tasks	Ability to clean rooms and have a conversation with the user
5	Desire	Having common hobbies and showing signs of affection

Actions 1 to 5 show that people have a variety of expectations when it comes to robot behaviors, with a relatively passive attitude. Especially in 4 and 5, they expect a robot to support their daily life and become their partners. Thus, we thought that when a robot can actively carry out the actions shown in the examples, there will be improvements to the items in our evaluation on impressions, including in "trust" and "affinity". According to our definition, the active behavior of a robot means that it takes the initiative and does something for a user without prior commands or instructions from a user. This proactive action is similar to the spontaneous behavior in people. Since robots don't naturally have spontaneity, in order to realize this kind of spontaneous behavior, some procedures were necessary. Here, observation of the state of a person, performed by transmission of information from a sensor, and an action based on that observation, are defined as "active behavior", and we discuss this.

2.3 Effects of Active Behavior

Kanda et al. demonstrated examples of evaluations on impressions by using proactive actions such as a robot that has a looking direction function control action [3]. Kanda et al., investigated autonomous behavior in robots based on information from sensors without direct intervention from a user, so that the robot could leave an impression of intelligence on people that interacted with it. Their study is within the definition of active behavior shown in this present study. In the Kanda et al study, they set up a robot with a looking direction function control action and let the robot move freely back and forth in a hallway. They used the looking direction function control to have the robot look in the direction of students when it passed them. Then, the differences in the impressions left on the students were evaluated depending on the presence or absence of the looking direction function control. The results showed that there were no statistically significant differences in "activity", "affinity" and "pleasantness" in the active behavior with the action of looking a direction of a user.

Considering the results, a robot's "active behavior" does not necessarily lead to an improvement in one's impression. We focused on the part that concluded [there were no statistically significant differences in "activity", "affinity" and "pleasantness"] as a debatable point, and set up objectives and study tasks as written in the next chapter.

3   Design and Implementation

3.1 Issues and Objectives

We considered the reasons why there were no statistically significant differences in "activity", "affinity" and "pleasantness", and then we thought that the main reasons were as follows:

- The looking direction control action did not satisfy a level of action that users expect from a robot, based on the KJ method results.
- The intention of the robot's actions was not clear to the users, so the users did not find any meaning in that action itself.

In this study, we assumed the behaviors that users expect on a robot based on results using the KJ method as the robot's active behavior, as indicated in Sect. 2.2. We thought that improvements in impressions could be obtained when a robot actively carries out actions that users would expect. Thus, in this study, we decided to conduct evaluations on impressions of the active behaviors that people expect from robots in human-robot interactions.

3.2 Active Robot Behavioral Design

We defined those expected actions as the robot's active behavior, which were sorted into groups based on the previous study indicated in Sect. 2.2. The numbers indicate the level of each active behavior. This time we set the action of greeting in the first stage as level 1 and carried out our behavioral designs. We defined the robot's actions using the following three statuses: waiting for human actions (observation of human non-contact action), active behavior, and waiting for contact (observation of human contact action) (see Fig. 1).

Figure 1 (1)–(6) indicates the following:

(1) Detection of human behavior in a non-contact state (2) Detection of an action, and then activating the setting for active behavior. (3) Detection of an action, without activating active behavior. (4) Status changes from active behavior to waiting for contact. (5) Detection of human contact and the status of that contact, and reaction behavior for that contact (6) End of human contact and withdrawal.

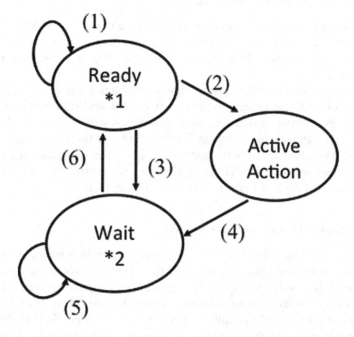

Fig. 1. An overall view of the design of the robot's active behavior, (*1 Observation of human non-contact action, *2 Observation of human contact action).

As mentioned in Sect. 2.2, active behavior in a robot means that the robot takes action against a user proactively. However, robots do not have spontaneity, so in order to simulate it, we set a state of waiting behavior where the robot observes user's actions while in a non-contact state. The transition to the next state happens as follows: the robot detects human action while in the non-contact state (1), that action triggers the robot's active behavior (2), and if active behavior has been confirmed, the robot will move on to the next step of active behavior. If active behavior has not been confirmed (3), the robot will move on to a step of mutual contact behavior. After finishing its active behavior, it will move on to a state of waiting for contact (4), where it will wait for contact again, and when a user provides contact action, it will react again (5). If the contact from a user seems to be over (there is no reaction for a certain period of time), the robot will determine contact to be over and will withdraw and move from (5) to (6). We define this as a behavioral model in which active behavior is added to a robot that is performing normal operations. Next, we implemented concrete actions using this model.

3.3   Procedure of Greeting Action

In this study, we try to implement an active behavior greeting action, the type of action that we thought users would expect. Generally, the process of greetings between people unfolds as follows:

1. One person notices the other person.
2. He waves his hand or says something.

To give someone a greeting, the robot has to initiate the action. In order to do that, it has to observe the subject in a non-contact state, and next, some active behavior that corresponds to the observation is necessary. This is consistent with the behavior model shown in Sect. 3.2.

In this study, in order to imitate natural human communication, we included looking direction control actions and greetings as our active behaviors. More specifically, when the robot notices a person by detecting their approach, it will act accordingly (turning towards the person and making a looking direction control action), and after that, it will wave its hand. This allows the robot to demonstrate active behavior more explicitly. The details of the greeting action, in accordance with the state transition model in Fig. 1, the robot is assumed to take action according to the above model.

3.4   The Design of Distance in Greeting Actions

This time, greeting action was used as a step prior to human-robot interactions. We assumed that people would like to have interaction with the robot, so the robot should approach them; thus, we implemented looking direction control actions and greeting actions. It was necessary to determine the distance between them. We defined this distance in accordance with the definition of personal space. According to Edward Hall, personal space is classified into four zones, each further divided into a close phase and a far phase [11].

Based on that, we chose the close phase in what is defined as socially active distance (120–200 cm) as the zone for the robot when it detects the approach of a person. We chose the far phase in personal distance (75–120 cm) as the zone for the robot when it starts to turn towards a person while performing its looking direction control action. We chose the close phase in personal distance (45–75 cm) as the zone for the robot when performing the greeting and interacting face to face. According to Nishida [12], people normally have daily conversations in these interpersonal distances, from 50 cm to 150 cm. Thus, we determined that our settings were appropriate.

3.5 Implementation

In this section, we describe the implementation of robot that achieves the active behavior about the hardware and software.

Robot: We used RAPIRO for the robot implementation, which is a humanoid robot kit [4]. Total dimensions $250 \times 200 \times 155$ (millimeters). 13 motors were mounted on its head, neck, shoulders, elbows, palms, waist, feet, and ankles. A dedicated arduino mounted in the RAPIRO operated these motors, which enabled it to act. In addition, LEDs were installed in its body, with colors that were adjustable by changing RGB values. Due to light emitting from its eyes, these color changes can be seen from outside the robot. In this experiment, we did not use the LEDs, because we thought that the color might affect the experiment results on greeting actions due to personal preferences for colors.

Sensors: For sensing the approach of a subject, two ultrasonic distance sensor modules (3 cm–4 m) were used. CDS cells (5 mm type) were used as optical sensors and attached to the RAPIRO body.

Operation settings: The following actions were set on the RAPIRO: (Fig. 2).

To return to the waiting state, the robot slightly spread both arms and both hands. It then repeated the cycle. In the looking direction control action, RAPIRO rotates its head 50 degrees to the direction where a subject is approaching, either left or right, and returns its head to the front direction after two seconds. In the greeting action when a subject stands in front of RAPIRO, it raises its right arm and waves its arm from left to right for two seconds, and then returns to the waiting state. The following are the three types of actions in the contact state:

– It moves its left and right hands up and down alternatively.
– It shakes its hands and feet.
– It raises its arms and continues to move its arms from right to left.

These contact interactions were repeated for all subjects in the same manner, without adding randomness. This experiment aimed to compare user impressions with and without greeting actions. So, we decided that there should be no differences in the contact interactions.

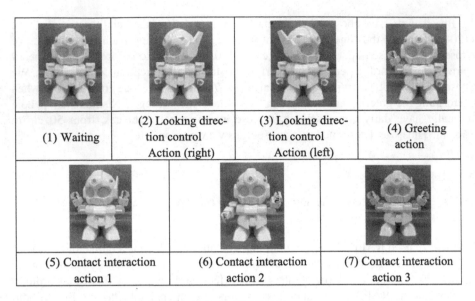

(1) Waiting	(2) Looking direction control Action (right)	(3) Looking direction control Action (left)	(4) Greeting action
(5) Contact interaction action 1		(6) Contact interaction action 2	(7) Contact interaction action 3

Fig. 2. Setting of RAPIRO's actions

4 Experimental Evaluation

We attempted to investigate whether or not there were improvements in user impressions in the situation where a robot takes the initiative and gives a greeting, prior to any interaction between the robot and the user. The detail of the experiment is as follows.

4.1 Experiment

The numbers of subjects were 10 students in our university: six of them were male and four of them were female. In this experiment, we divided the subjects into two groups of 5 people. The subjects on each team experienced both situations, meaning one situation where the robot performed greeting actions and one without them. Doing this let us examine the differences in impressions depending on the order of robot actions in the experiment.

– Team A: With greetings → Without greetings
– Team B: Without greetings → With greetings

The evaluation method is as follows. Each subject experienced both situations, with and without greetings, and answered a questionnaire immediately afterwards. They could select one of the following four levels for each question: I really thought so: 3; I kind of thought so: 2; I didn't really think so: 1; I didn't think so at all: 0. Questions 1 to 5 investigated "activeness", "pleasantness", "affinity", "intentionality", and "continuity" respectively.

Q1. Did you think the robot was active? (Activeness)
Q2. Did you think that the robot tried to entertain you? (Pleasantness)

Q3. Did you feel pleasant with the robot? (Affinity)

Q4. Did you feel that the robot had some sort of intention? (Intentionality)

Q5. Did you think that you would want to continue to play with the robot? (Continuity)

Q6. What do you think the robot's action of waving its arms at you when you were approaching it meant?

Q7. Additional comments

This time we told the subjects that the robot would "initiate active behavior", not specifically mentioning anything about "greeting actions". So question number 6 was to gauge how well the subjects understood the intent of the robot's active behavior.

The location was in a corridor with a 2 m width in front of our laboratory. The head motor on RAPIRO could not be moved up and down, so we put it on a table and adjusted its height so that its looking direction met the subject's looking direction. The ultrasonic sensors detected the approach and departure of the subjects. We placed RAPIRO against the wall, and installed ultrasonic sensors around 160 cm to the right side and left side of RAPIRO respectively. The initial position of each subject was outside of the ultrasonic sensors on both sides, about 2.5 m from the robot. The starting position of the subject could have been either on the left side or the right side.

The initial state of the robot was set to observation of a person in a non-contact state. When it detected the approach of a subject, it started performing active behavior if the setting for active behavior was initialized; else it changed modes and started detecting contact if active behavior was not initialized. When it detected a subject leaving on the opposite side of the ultrasonic sensor, it changed modes to not detecting contact mode. It returned to its original state of observing people in a non-contact state. The optical sensor was incapable of reacting even if something touched it, so the only way to set the sensor off was if a subject approached the robot a certain way.

We told the subjects to walk at a certain speed, and stop one time in front of RAPIRO. We had the subjects practice that. This was achieved by applying a delay() to the series of actions with RAPIRO's looking direction control to greet subjects face-to-face in the program. This time, we didn't include a program in which RAPIRO would judge if a subject was standing in front of it. So if the subject walked at a certain speed, we thought we could adjust the timing from its looking direction control action to its greeting. The flow of the experiment is shown in Fig. 3.

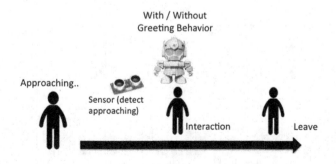

Fig. 3. The experiment flow

Firstly, the subject stood outside of the ultrasonic sensors (either to the left or right), and started walking straight toward RAPIRO (1). Then, the ultrasonic sensors reacted, and RAPIRO started a looking direction control action (2). When the subject stopped in front of RAPIRO, it started its greeting action (3). When the subject touched RAPIRO's optical sensor, it started contact interactions (4). The subject leaves RAPIRO (5). At that time, we instructed the subject to pass by the ultrasonic sensor on the opposite side. If there was no active behavior to be performed, RAPIRO skipped from (2) to (3).

Each subject performed this entire process (going and coming) 3 times for us. We programmed RAPIRO to ignore information from the ultrasonic sensor when a subject turned around, and also not to perform a looking direction control action at this time. We haven't determined the time period of the contact interactions.

4.2 Result

Figure 4 summarizes the results of the evaluations on impressions with and without active behavior from Q1 to Q5 that shown in the previous section, in the graph. Statistically significant differences are respectively shown in the each question. Figure 5 shows the results of the questionnaire that each subject answered. Subjects from *No. 1* to *No. 5* belonged to team A, subjects from *No. 6* to *No. 10* belonged to team B.

Result1: Statistically significant differences were observed in the following fields: "activeness", "pleasantness", "affinity", "intentionality" and "continuity", all of which were used in the preliminary experiment (**<0.01).

Result2: Where experimental procedures were different, we noticed there were some differences in the evaluations of the subjects between the presence of active behavior and the absence of it from both teams.

Result3: "Intentionality" changed in accordance with the presence or absence of active behavior in the answers of 70 % of the 10 subjects in the experiment.

Result4: Among all the subjects, there were some subjects who had exactly the same impressions regardless of the presence or absence of active behavior.

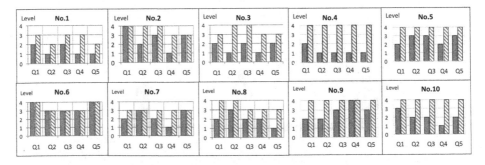

Fig. 4. Evaluations on impressions depending on with (left) or without (right) of active behavior

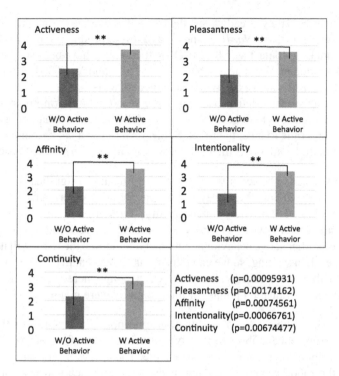

Fig. 5. Average score of impression difference with or without active behavior of robot

We investigated whether or not there are differences in the evaluations depending on the order of their experiences, and with or without active behavior. We performed a dual variance analysis on the average evaluation scores of each indicator from each team. The results showed that there were no interaction effects in all of the indicators.

4.3   Discussion

This section shows the summary of our discussions. Discussions 1-4 correspond to results 1-4 as described in previous section.

Discussion 1: In the evaluations on impressions depending on the presence or absence of the robot's active behavior, statistically significant differences were observed in all the following fields: "activeness", "pleasantness", "affinity", "intentionality" and "continuity". Therefore, implementing active behavior in a robot could be a factor that brings good results with impressions.

Discussion 2: We focused on the differences in the evaluations of each subject on the team. For subjects *No. 3* and *No. 4* from team A and subject *No. 10* from team B, the differences in their evaluations were greater than other subjects on their team depending on the presence or absence of active behavior. The reason might be as follows: subjects *No. 1, No. 2, No. 6, No. 7, No. 8* and *No. 9* understood how RAPIRO works and functions in this experiment, and they already knew the method and range of operation. However, for subjects *No. 3, No. 5*, and *No. 10,* at the time of this experiment it was only their first or second time making contact with RAPIRO. So there might have been some differences in their prior knowledge. We believed that subjects *No. 3* and *No. 4* had stronger impressions toward RAPIRO's active behavior than other subjects, so the differences between the presence or absence of active behavior were greater. Furthermore, subject *No. 5* provided high evaluations both in cases with and without active behavior, even though it was also his first time to meet the robot. Subject *No. 5* has a background in which he loves robot animation and robots themselves, which might have affected his evaluation.

Discussion 3: The active behavior we designed this time had a significant impact on the intentionality on the robot. We believed that the robot's performance of that active behavior itself helped it to have intentionality. Furthermore, even without active behavior, its intentionality was not zero, due to the robot's reaction in contact interactions. If there is neither active behavior nor contact interaction, the robot will not perform any action other than waiting, so we can expect that intentionality will be almost zero. However, since there was a reaction to contact, even though there was no active behavior it seemed that some evaluation points for intentionality were given.

Discussion 4: All of subject *No. 6*'s evaluations on impressions were exactly the same regardless of the presence or absence of active behavior. Some of subject *No. 7*'s answers to questions on their impressions were also same. Their answers for question 6 "what do you think the robot's action of waving its arms at you when you were approaching it meant?" were as follows: "a robot was facing me and making some kind of sign" (*No. 6*), and no answer (*No. 7*). These results suggest that they understood the robot's active behavior meant something, but they didn't think it was making a greeting. Discussions 3,4 showed that it was important for users to understand the meaning of the robot's actions exactly, rather than the robot just performing active behavior while subjects don't understand. It was shown that enhancing a robot's intentionality might lead to improvements in overall evaluations on impressions.

5   Conclusion

This study focused on the active behavior of a robot and demonstrated the robot's active behavior design model. We implemented actions that users would expect a robot to make, in order to improve our subject's evaluations of the robot. In the experiment, we implemented greetings as a level 1 active action, and compared evaluations on impressions depending on the presence or absence of those greeting actions. The results revealed that statistically significant differences were observed in the following fields: "activeness", "pleasantness", "affinity", "intentionality" and "continuity".

We should further investigate factors and/or actions that will bring improvements to impressions. In addition, in order to verify the behavioral model that we proposed this time, we would like to implement actions besides greetings to build more general robot behavioral models in terms of human-robot interactions.

Acknowledgement. We would like to thank Tateishi Science Foundation, and MEXT/JSPS KAKENHI Grant 15K00105 for a grant that made it possible to complete this study.

References

1. Nakata, T., Sato, T., Mori, T., Mizoguchi, H.: Generating familiar behavior in a robot. J. Robot. Soc. Jpn. **15**(7), 1068–1074 (1997)
2. Kakio, M., Miyashita, T., Mitsunaga, N., Ishiguro, H., Hagita, N.: How do the balancing motions of a humanoid robot affect a human's motion and impression? J. Robot. Soc. Jpn. **26**(6), 485–492 (2008)
3. Kanda, T., Ishiguro, H., Ishida, T.: Psychological evaluations of interactions between people and robots. J. Robot. Soc. Jpn. **19**(3), 362–371 (2001)
4. RAPIRO official site (2015). http://www.rapiro.com/ja/
5. Honda-Robotics (2015). http://www.honda.co.jp/robotics/
6. Pepper (2015). http://www.softbank.jp/robot/special/pepper/
7. Palrogarden (2015). http://www.palrogarden.net/palro/main/framepage.html
8. Yuriko, N., Okazaki, R., Hachisu, T., Sato, M., Kajimoto, H.: Creating life-like effects in stuffed-toys using micro movements of reflected light in the toy's eyes. In: Interaction, Information Processing Society of Japan (2015)
9. Yano, Y., Ikeda, Y., Okada, A., Nakano, M., Sugaya, M.: Transmitting emotion through movement in a robot's hands. In: Multimedia, Distributed, Cooperative and Mobile DICOMO Symposium 2015, July 2015
10. Kiya, R.: An experiment evaluating robot actions targetting human symbiosis Master's research report (2012)
11. Edward T.: Hall: The Hidden Dimension. Doub – leday (1966) (Translation: Toshitaka Hidaka and Nobuyuki Sato, 1970)
12. Nishida, K.: Construction planning, architecture and practical business based on the distance between people when they communicate, human psychology and ecology (1). Archit. Pract. Bus. **5**, 95–99 (1985)

Machine Agency in Human-Machine Networks; Impacts and Trust Implications

Vegard Engen[✉], J. Brian Pickering, and Paul Walland

IT Innovation Centre, Gamma House, Enterprise Road, Southampton, SO16 7NS, UK
{ve,jbp,pww}@it-innovation.soton.ac.uk

Abstract. We live in an emerging hyper-connected era in which people are in contact and interacting with an increasing number of other people and devices. Increasingly, modern IT systems form networks of humans and machines that interact with one another. As machines take a more active role in such networks, they exert an increasing level of influence on other participants. We review the existing literature on agency and propose a definition of agency that is practical for describing the capabilities and impact human and machine actors may have in a human-machine network. On this basis, we discuss and demonstrate the impact and trust implications for machine actors in human-machine networks for emergency decision support, healthcare and future smart homes. We maintain that machine agency not only facilitates human to machine trust, but also inter-personal trust; and that trust must develop to be able to seize the full potential of future technology.

Keywords: General: HCI methods and theories · Human-machine networks · Agency · Trust

1 Introduction

The term social network is widely understood given the proliferation of communication platforms such as Facebook and LinkedIn. However, non-human component(s) are often neglected. In some cases, this may simply be because they are not obviously visible to end-users. However, increasingly sophisticated ICT systems form networks of both human and machine participants. Machines are not just passive participants in such networks, merely mediating communication between humans; they are increasingly adopting an active role, enabled by technological advances that allow greater autonomy and the performance of increasingly complex tasks.

Here, we refer to a Human-Machine Network (HMN) as a collective structure where humans and machines interact to produce synergistic and often unique effects. Humans and machines are both viewed as actors, given that they interact with at least one other actor in the system. Referring to machines/objects as actors/agents raises issues with agency, which is an ongoing debate in the literature as reviewed in Sect. 2.

While most psychology and sociological models only attribute agency to human actors, more recent models have been proposed that attribute agency also to machines, such as Actor-Network Theory (ANT) [1] and the Double Dance of Agency (DDA)

© Springer International Publishing Switzerland 2016
M. Kurosu (Ed.): HCI 2016, Part III, LNCS 9733, pp. 96–106, 2016.
DOI: 10.1007/978-3-319-39513-5_9

model [2]. Nevertheless, agency definitions still seem insufficient, as Jia et al. [3] argue in the context of the Internet of Things (IoT). Moreover, the scope of research on machine agency is limited. The DDA model was proposed against a background of Information Systems (IS) research and based only on empirical work on Enterprise Resource Planning (ERP) use cases, while Jia et al. [3] focus only on the IoT. Other models, such as captology [4] have a wider scope in terms of empirical applications, but focus solely on human-to-computer interaction.

In this paper, we draw upon the existing literature and propose definitions of human and machine agency (in Sect. 3) for the purpose of understanding and designing HMNs. Further, we discuss the relationship between machine agency and trust. Although traditionally a person-to-person construct, trust in technology has been shown to be accommodating towards technology failings [5, 6]. Further, as a form a social capital, trust may be regarded as an overall organising principle [7]. On this basis, human actors do demonstrate an ability to adapt their concept of trust in response to machine agency [3, 4]. We explore three case studies in Sect. 4 to give a broader view of agency and its impact on the interactions between the different actors.

This work is part of the HUMANE project (https://humane2020.eu/), which is creating a typology and method for the design of HMNs. The aim of this work is to improve public and private services by uncovering and describing how new configurations of HMNs change patterns of interaction, behaviour, trust and sociability. Agency forms part of the HUMANE typology [8], which aims at improving system designers' understanding of the potentially complex interactions that may take place, particularly in terms of emergent phenomena and unexpected behaviour, ultimately leading to HMN designs that contribute innovation and creativity to future network collaborations.

2   Background

In respective sections below, we provide further background on what we mean by an HMN, and review the existing research on agency.

2.1   Human-Machine Networks

We refer to an HMN as a collective structure where humans and machines interact to produce synergistic and often unique effects. Humans and machines are both viewed as actors, given that they interact with at least one other actor in the system. Existing research relevant to HMNs has been conducted in three different areas: Socio-Technical Systems (STS) [9], Actor-Network Theory (ANT) [1] and Social Machines (SM) [10].

As discussed in [11], each of the three areas focus on particular aspects of HMNs: STS on business systems design, providing a body of theory that covers complex interactions between people and technology; ANT on social systems as networks comprising a range of heterogeneous elements, both human and non-human, viewing the actors as networks themselves; SM on online systems mediating social interactions between human users. In this paper, we focus on human-machine interaction, rather than machine mediated human-human interaction.

2.2 Agency

Early cognitive models of human behaviour were based on mechanical and computational processes. These were subsequently modified to include a socio-cultural element [12], whereby contextual interactions could influence responses in the short and long term. This view has evolved into theoretical models seeing human beings as conscious and creative, operating according to belief systems that enable them to set and achieve goals that drive their behaviour and avoid undesirable situations in their lives.

There are different theoretical models and frameworks that address this topic, offering different definitions of agency, which occasionally conflict. For example, in structuration theory (ST), agency is defined as "the capability to make a difference" [13]; in social cognitive theory (SCT) "agency refers to acts done intentionally" [12]. Bandura [12] describes agency according to four attributes: intentionality, forethought, self-reactiveness and self-reflectiveness. Intentionality encompasses the ability to choose to behave in a certain way; in particular with a future course of action in mind. Forethought is related to the temporal characteristic of intentionality, in the sense of setting goals, which affects behaviour in order to achieve desired outcomes and avoid undesired ones. Moreover, it is linked to motivation, which guides the chosen actions and anticipations of future events, which "provides direction, coherence, and meaning to one's life" [12].

We focus on intentionality as it is a key differentiator for definitions of agency. Compared to humans, machines do not have self-generated intention or motivation, do not experience trust or reliance, and do not behave altruistically or irrationally of their own volition; they have no agency in that sense [3, 14, 15]. However, there is a need to refer to machine agency, as machines can participate in HMNs in increasingly significant roles, influencing other actors and the outcomes of the HMN itself [2, 15, 16].

Theoretical positions have been proposed that attribute agency also to machines, such as ANT [1] and the double dance of agency model [2]. As noted above, ANT is a theory that gives equal weight to machine actors compared with human actors [1]. Moreover, Law [1] argue that sociological theories are lacking in fully understanding social effects due to excluding non-human actors, both machines and architectures. Further, ANT only refers to the agency of the network, not of independent actors.

Rose et al. [2, 15, 16] have studied machine agency in the context of Information Systems (IS), finding that neither the definitions in ST or ANT are appropriate for practical application. Rose et al. [16] argue that agency should be acknowledged for both humans and machines, like in ANT. However, unlike ANT, they recognise that their agency is different, due to properties such as self-awareness, social awareness and intentionality, which are considered exclusive to human agency [16].

Rose and Truex [15] propose in their earlier work that machines have perceived agency; neither accepting or denying the notion of machine agency. This relates to the human tendency towards anthropomorphism [17]. Rose et al. [16] also assert agency to machines in terms of the intention of their creators via their endowed potential actions. More research on this aspect forms part of captology, which is the study of persuasive technologies; defined as "interactive technolog[ies] that changes a person's attitudes or behaviours" [4]. Fogg [4] refers to intentionality as a requirement for persuasion, though acknowledging that machines do not have intentions. This semantic predicament is addressed in captology by defining a technology as persuasive when they have been created for the purpose of changing people's attitudes or behaviours [4].

Rose et al. [2] propose a 'Double Dance of Agency' model based on observing the intertwined nature of human and machine agency. That is, there are emergent outcomes stemming from the process of humans and machines interacting and that human agency itself responds to and shapes machine agency [2]. Moreover, Jia et al. [3] argue that both human and machine agency can be balanced and enhanced in order to achieve improvements in interactions and user experience.

In summary, the existing literature on agency has evolved significantly over time. Earlier definitions of agency are bound to the social context in which machine agency does not exist. Later, researchers have argued that machine agency does exist, but that it is different to human agency, and probably the result of human interaction and perception. Building on the existing literature, in the following section we propose an updated definition suitable for the analysis and design of HMNs.

3 Agency in Human-Machine Networks

In the context of designing, evaluating or studying HMNs, we argue the need to consider both human and machine actors in terms of agency. We aim at (a) identifying a shared understanding of both human and machine agency in HMNs, while (b) delineating differences between the two.

Broadly speaking, we understand the agency of an actor, whether human or machine, as the capacity to perform activities in a particular environment in line with a set of goals/objectives that influence and shape the extent and nature of their participation. The environment in this context is bound by the HMN.

SCT distinguishes between three modes of agency [12]. The first, direct personal agency, covers the four characteristics focused on in Sect. 2.2. The second mode, proxy agency, refers to socially mediated agency in which an agent utilises desired resources or expertise in other agents to act on their behalf to achieve goals they cannot achieve on their own. This alone may be the key motivation for human users to participate in a particular HMN, and they may exercise proxy agency via both human and machine agents. Some time after SCT was originally proposed, it was extended to the third mode; collective agency [18]. This mode is based on the premise that many goals are only achievable via socially interdependent effort. Moreover, Bandura [12] notes that group attainments are largely due to interactive, collaborative and synergistic dynamics of the interactions between the people exercising collective agency. We emphasise the importance of synergistic dynamics here as it is integral to the definition and value of an HMN (see Sect. 2.1).

In the context of a HMN, we can refer to actors' having different degrees of agency. For example, the agency of human actors is typically constrained by the respective ICT system of which they form a part and the interfaces they can use for interacting with the system and other actors, e.g., to exercise proxy agency. In practical terms, we can scope agency of both human and machine actors in HMNs according to three key factors: (a) the activities the actor can perform, (b) the nature of the activities, and (c) the ability to interact with other actors.

The activities the actor can perform (a) typically differ between the actors in an HMN; perhaps varied according to roles and responsibilities in the HMN. For example, some may be restricted to viewing content while others may be allowed to generate content, and moderators in online communities typically have higher levels of agency than other community members. In many HMNs, individual machine actors may have low agency as they may be focused on performing a limited number of fixed tasks, e.g., peripheral devices such as sensors.

The nature of the activities (b) concerns actors' ability to behave diversely, unpredictably, freely, and creatively in order to pursue their respective goals/objectives for participating in the HMN. We can distinguish between open or closed activities. A closed activity is one that is restricted or fixed; hence, predictable with an expected pre-defined outcome. An open activity is one in which the actors are able to exercise a degree of freedom, leading to diversity in the HMN. For example, allowing actors to express themselves in free text allows creativity and unpredictability in their activities. Although actors are limited to communicate via 140 characters, Twitter enables individuals and organisations to socialise, perform marketing, customer relationship management, engage in political propaganda, etc. Moreover, machine actors are effectively able to do the same activities as can human actors. While some machine actors are under direct control by human actors to, e.g., schedule tweets to propagate news, other machine actors (bots) act and pose as humans [19, 20] in order to exert influence, e.g., by spreading misinformation and propaganda [19].

The ability to interact with others (c) determines an actor's potential for influencing other actors or the working of HMN itself. The ability to influence others depends on the degree to which the actors are able to communicate with each other and how open the form of communication is. There are examples of HMNs where users may not even be aware that they are in fact a part of a network, such as reCAPTCHA [21]. Nevertheless, they form part of a network of millions of users, mediated via a machine, though they are not visible to one another, and, thus, do not exert influence.

Human agency is important to consider when analysing or designing a HMN as it reflects the ability of the human actors to be creative and use the HMN in unforeseen ways. It also links to the motivations of users. If they are not able to exercise agency in the HMN, in terms of achieving the objectives that underpin their reasons for participating, they may choose not to participate.

While machines cannot exhibit true direct personal agency, due to factors such as intentionality, as discussed above, they can exhibit agency in different ways. For example, it is useful to refer to machine agency in terms of the intentions of their human designers, as interactive technologies may be deployed to change human attitudes or behaviours [4]. For example, in the field of affective computing, emotionally intelligent technologies are developed to respond and adapt to users emotional needs [22].

In practical terms, our definition of machine agency reflects the degree to which machine actors may (a) perform activities of a personal and creative nature (e.g., supporting health care by personalising motivation strategies), (b) influence other actors in the HMN, (c) enable human actors to exercise proxy agency, and (d) the extent to which they are perceived as having agency by human actors. Higher levels of machine agency imply a need to consider the implications of the machine's role in the HMN, which relates to, e.g., the trust relationship between humans and machines. This is discussed further in the following section.

4   Machine Agency and Trust

Any relationship between human and machine agents must be based on trust and reliance in response to trustworthiness factors in machines [23, 24]. Humans may not simply apply social metaphors to machine services [25], although trust transfer, once developed in one area, often occurs across others [7, 26]. Whilst Corritore et al. [27] stress both affective and cognitive dimensions of technology trust, Wiegmann et al. [28] maintain that trust between human agents becomes reliance on machines. Either way, human agents show greater tolerance and adaptation, even in the face of failing or inadequate technology [5, 6, 29]. The interplay between trust and trustworthiness in complex HMNs, especially in light of increasing machine agency and emergent behaviours, therefore merits specific investigation.

4.1   An Evacuation Perspective

Mistrust between operational staff and the public may cause problems [30, 31], whereby operational and emergency services misinterpret crowd behaviours with negative [32], even catastrophic, consequences [33]. The eVACUATE project is going some way to solve this problem (http://www.evacuate.eu). Human actors within the HMN include the members of the public (potential evacuees), operational staff responsible for the general safety of a venue, and, in extreme cases, members of emergency services (fire brigade, ambulance; special forces; etc.). The human and machine actors operate at different levels of autonomy and, therefore, agency; and relations between and within groups may vary contextually from indifference to significant dependence. Therefore, trust becomes an increasingly significant factor. Operational staff and emergency services are reliant on machines such as sensors, smart devices and decision-support engines, while in an emergency, evacuees may vitally depend on them.

The HMN must provide constant data on crowd movement as well as the immediate environment to facilitate not only decision making by those responsible, but the mediation of trust between all actors. For if the original Mayer et al. model is correct [23, 24], then the three main antecedents of trust – ability, integrity, and benevolence – are easily exposed through the interaction between machine and human agents. Sensors, such as CCTV cameras, but also smart objects like floor-level lighting and other signage, can be assumed to provide continuous and objective information back to those responsible (ability). The dynamic and targeted intervention of the latter will be clearly appreciated for what it is: communication based on fact from the sensors (integrity) with the sole purpose of indicating safe and effective evacuation routes (benevolence). Further, if personal devices such as smart phones are recruited as part of the network they can provide alerts and updates which individuals may choose to share with those around them, promoting social cohesion during an emergency, also having the potential to receive additional and more specific contextual information from evacuees about their immediate vicinity. A task-specific exchange is possible allowing the rapid creation of mutually supportive and trust-related connection between evacuees and those tasked with their safety. The HMN in the eVACUATE case therefore has enormous implications for redressing trust issues from previous disasters [34–36] while mediating inter-group communication and cooperation.

4.2 Am I just a Number?

The potential for HMNs to provide mutual support, promoting not only safety and efficiency but also reciprocal trust, are clear not least in enabling communication between actors whilst at the same time providing each with additional information and support. Within healthcare and specifically in machine-mediated patient-doctor communication, the situation is different from the evacuation case. Here, as well as the medical team and patients themselves, an HMN might include monitoring devices such as wearables, mobile applications for self-reporting, a data store, and the related software to interrogate or summarise the data sensibly. The promise is in gathering data reliably and consistently to support specialist nurses and consultants, giving them an overview for their patient during appointments, and freeing them up to focus on the social and personal condition of the patient.

As an IT as a Utility (ITaaU) project, TRIFoRM [37] focused on trust development in technology in the management of chronic conditions such as rheumatoid arthritis. Participants in a small pilot included both patients and a clinician who were asked in semi-structured interviews about their willingness to trust a mobile monitoring application which would automatically log their movements, sending collated information back to the supporting clinical team. Patients acknowledged the benefits of automated tracking: between appointments, they may not always remember exactly how they felt or how things may have changed. Further, if their condition caused specific cognitive impairment, they felt the technology would fill the gaps. Technology is trusted therefore as a reliable mechanism for data collection: its ability to collect and transmit. However, this is not the whole story.

Not least since health data are considered sensitive [38] or special-category [39], surely patients would be concerned at what happens to their data, how it is curated, and who gets to see it? When asked, however, participants showed no such concern: any integrity issues were overwhelmed by an altruistic willingness to share their own data to help others. They trust the technology components in the HMN, but they were concerned that human agents might not continue to provide the interpersonal care they sought. Machine agency within a network should support and enhance trust-related interactions between the human actors.

4.3 How Can You Help Me?

There is much talk about the emergence of smart homes and the potential for home management systems to take over the efficient running of the systems with which our homes are becoming filled. Current home systems are automation systems rather than human machine networks since in essence the machine component is an intermediary, rather than a contributor to the performance of the network. Of interest to us here are future smart home networks in which the machine components exhibit agency, playing an active role in decision making and monitoring, thus, in order to consider a smart home as a true HMN we need to consider the case that devices in the home can learn behaviour, can suggest activity and can operate with some level of autonomy. Such a network would incorporate sensors, controllers and actuators, but also would incorporate "smartness" at the level of interaction with the human occupants and interpretation and management of the output of the various sensors. It is this added component of "smartness" that will distinguish future home networks as HMNs in the sense in which we use it here. Recent reports [40] have highlighted the role of trust and security in home networks, and indeed have suggested that the key driver for uptake of such technology in the near future will be on the basis of security fears, but in order for those fears to be allayed, the owners of smart homes will need to have a high level of trust in the operation of the system and the security of the data which it contains.

In order to consider the key features of an HMN in the home, we need to postulate a format which has not yet arrived, in which the future smart home is one in which the human home dweller communicates directly with the home systems via an intelligent interface, establishing a dialogue with a quasi-intelligent machine agent which forms a proxy for "the home". Thus the home owner would interact with home networks and functions through an interface that operates as an assistant and concierge, tracking movements and collecting behavioural data from the occupants in order to customise its behaviour and responses to changing situations.

Note that, in reality this intelligent interface is a construct representing the home server, data store and connected sensors, actuators and signage. However, the humans in the network relate to the personification of the smart home functions, attributing agency to it. This level of anthropomorphism has been shown to increase levels of both trust and, perhaps surprisingly, tolerance [5, 6, 29].

The family members comprising a household can be regarded as a single human entity, since they are maximally interconnected individuals. They each have personal communication devices for interacting with the world outside, which are also used for communication with the house interface. In turn, this has the effect of putting the house on a similar perceptual level to the humans with which they interact. This contributes to the anthropomorphism by which the human actors are able to apply concepts of trust to the home agent despite its machine nature.

The smart home network of the future can therefore be seen as an example of a human-machine network in which the human actors, the intelligent machine actors and the responsive machine actors occupy different niches, and between which different forms of trust relationship exist. In order for such a network to function effectively we are obliged to postulate a machine agent which can be anthropomorphised and imbued with human characteristics, allowing it to be part of an established trust relationship.

5   Discussion

From health and safety monitoring to the smart gadgets in our homes, the increasing dependence on sophisticated technology implies a fresh look at concepts such as agency. A simple assumption that machines are no more than deterministic automata confined to well-defined tasks is no longer valid. Just as teamwork and crowdsourcing increase human potential [41, 42], the question now becomes how to exploit the power of technology and move toward the creation of synergistic capabilities through human-machine interaction in HMNs.

As a first step, something approaching an equal footing in agency terms between the machine and human actors goes some way to open up the debate. Machine agency is, as we have seen, a much contested idea, and may yet struggle to escape the confines of human perceptions of usefulness and anthropomorphism. Yet, advanced decision-support systems are beginning to demonstrate a level of agency that rapidly becomes a crucial factor in critical situations. Such agency may even lead to a concern that other human actors within a network respond by withdrawing their social concern with other human actors: this may not be machine intentionality, but it certainly demonstrates the possibility for machines to make a difference [13] for human-to-human interactions.

Accepting interactive collaboration as a real possibility, HMNs such as smart homes and advanced socio-technical robotics enable social engagement, encouraging the evolution of mutually supportive networks. For this to become a real and lasting possibility will require the development and maintenance of trust. Only on a trust basis, including a willingness to compromise, to forgive and learn how to overcome shared problems, will the full potential of HMNs become a reality. To become a reality, a revision of the original definition of agency is long overdue, not least to allow the full capabilities of sophisticated technology to combine and develop together in socially motivated HMNs limited only by human imagination.

6   Conclusions and Future Work

We have proposed a definition of agency and discussed its practical application to analysing and designing human-machine networks (HMNs). In support of recent literature, our definitions recognise that machines can both enhance and constrain human agency as well as exhibit agency themselves. Three case studies demonstrated the importance of considering machine agency when analysing or designing HMNs in terms of influencing motivation, participation and trust. As a construct, they suggest not only the traditional view of trust as a prerequisite for technology adoption, but also a mediating role for the machine actors themselves.

Evaluation of the definitions of human and machine agency offered here is already in progress within the HUMANE project. Based on scales used to identify the degree of agency, the challenge is to establish descriptive labels which are both intuitive and useful to system designers. Further, the consistent interpretation of these scales is needed if comparisons are to be made between HMNs with a view to sharing design patterns and experience. However, in considering potential social and behavioural impact as we have done here, it is hoped that some level of prediction about how HMNs will evolve can be attempted.

Acknowledgements. This work has been conducted as part of the HUMANE project, which has received funding from the European Union's Horizon 2020 research and innovation programme under grant agreement No. 645043.

References

1. Law, J.: Notes on the theory of the actor-network: ordering, strategy, and heterogeneity. Syst. Pract. **5**, 379–393 (1992)
2. Rose, J., Jones, M.: The double dance of agency: a socio-theoretic account of how machines and humans interact. Syst. Signs Actions **1**, 19–37 (2005)
3. Jia, H., Wu, M., Jung, E., Shapiro, A., Sundar, S.S.: Balancing human agency and object agency: an end-user interview study of the internet of things. In: Proceedings of 2012 ACM Conference on Ubiquitous Computing, pp. 1185–1188. ACM (2012)
4. Fogg, B.: Persuasive computers: perspectives and research directions. In: The SIGCHI Conference on Human Factors in Computing, pp. 225–232 (1998)
5. Lee, J.D., Moray, N.: Trust, control strategies and allocation of function in human-machine systems. Ergonomics **35**, 1243–1270 (1992)
6. Lee, J.D., See, K.A.: Trust in automation: designing for appropriate reliance. J. Hum. Factors Ergon. Soc. **46**, 50–80 (2004)
7. McEvily, B., Perrone, V., Zaheer, A.: Trust as an organizing principle. Organ. Sci. **14**, 91–103 (2003)
8. Eide, A.W., Pickering, J.B., Yasseri, T., Bravos, G., Følstad, A., Engen, V., Walland, P., Meyer, E.T., Tsvetkova, M.: Human-machine networks: towards a typology and profiling framework. In: HCI International. Springer, Toronto, Canada (2016)
9. Leonardi, P.M.: Materiality, sociomateriality, and socio-technical systems: what do these terms mean? How are they related? Do we need them? In: Leonardi, P.M., Nardi, B.A., Kallinikos, J. (eds.) Materiality and Organizing: Social Interaction in a Technological World, pp. 25–48. Oxford University Press, Oxford (2012)
10. Smart, P.R., Simperl, E., Shadbolt, N.: A taxonomic framework for social machines (2014). http://eprints.soton.ac.uk/362359/1/SOCIAMClassificationv2.pdf
11. Tsvetkova, M., Yasseri, T., Meyer, E.T., Pickering, J.B., Engen, V., Walland, P., Lüders, M., Følstad, A., Bravos, G.: Understanding human-machine networks: a cross-disciplinary survey. arXiv Prepr. (2015)
12. Bandura, A.: Social cognitive theory: an agentic perspective. Annu. Rev. Psychol. **52**, 1–26 (2001)
13. Giddens, A.: The Constitution of Society: Outline of the Theory of Structuration. University of California Press, Berkeley (1984)
14. Friedman, B., Kahn, P.H.: Human agency and responsible computing: implications for computer system design. J. Syst. Softw. **17**, 7–14 (1992)
15. Rose, J., Truex, D.: Machine Agency as perceived autonomy: an action perspective. In: Baskerville, R., Stage, J., DeGross, J.I. (eds.) Organizational and Social Perspectives on Information Technology, pp. 371–388. Springer, New York (2000)
16. Rose, J., Jones, M., Truex, D.: The problem of agency: how humans act, how machines act. In: International Workshop on Action in Language, Organisations and Information Systems (ALOIS-2003) (2003)

17. Nass, C.I., Lombard, M., Henriksen, L., Steuer, J.: Anthropocentrism and computers. Behav. Inf. Technol. **14**, 229–238 (1995)
18. Bandura, A.: Self-Efficacy: The Exercise of Control. Freeman, New York (1997)
19. Boshmaf, Y., Muslukhov, I., Beznosov, K., Ripeanu, M.: The socialbot network: when bots socialize for fame and money. p. 93 (2011)
20. Chu, Z., Gianvecchio, S., Wang, H., Jajodia, S.: Who is tweeting on Twitter: human, bot, or cyborg? In: Proceedings of 26th Annual Computer Security Applications Conference - ACSAC 2010, p. 21 (2010)
21. von Ahn, L., Maurer, B., McMillen, C., Abraham, D., Blum, M.: reCAPTCHA: human-based character recognition via web security measures. Science **321**, 1465–1468 (2008)
22. Picard, R.W.: Affective Computing. MIT Media Laboratory, Cambridge (1995)
23. Mayer, R.C., Davis, J.H., Schoorman, F.D.: An integrative model of organizational trust. Acad. Manag. Rev. **20**, 709–734 (1995)
24. Schoorman, F.D., Mayer, R.C., Davis, J.H.: An integrative model of organizational trust: past, present, and future. Acad. Manag. Rev. **32**, 344–354 (2007)
25. Nass, C., Moon, Y.: Machines and mindlessness: social responses to computers. J. Soc. Issues **56**, 81–103 (2000)
26. King, W.R., He, J.: A meta-analysis of the technology acceptance model. Inf. Manag. **43**, 740–755 (2006)
27. Corritore, C.L., Kracher, B., Wiedenbeck, S.: On-line trust: concepts, evolving themes, a model. Int. J. Hum Comput Stud. **58**, 737–758 (2003)
28. Wiegmann, D.A., Rich, A., Zhang, H.: Automated diagnostic aids: the effects of aid reliability on users' trust and reliance. Theor. Issues Ergon. Sci. **2**, 352–367 (2001)
29. Dutton, W.H., Shepherd, A.: Trust in the internet as an experience technology (2006)
30. Scraton, P.: Policing with contempt: the degrading of truth and denial of justice in the aftermath of the Hillsborough disaster. J. Law Soc. **26**, 273–297 (1999)
31. Taylor, S.P.: The Hillsborough stadium disaster: 15 April 1989: inquiry by the Rt Hon Lord Justice Taylor: final report: present to Parliament by the Secretary of State for the Home Department by Command of Her Majesty January 1990
32. Drury, J., Reicher, S.: Collective action and psychological change: the emergence of new social identities. Br. J. Soc. Psychol. **39**, 579–604 (2000)
33. Nicholson, C.E., Roebuck, B.: The investigation of the Hillsborough disaster by the health and safety executive. Saf. Sci. **18**, 249–259 (1995)
34. Donald, I., Canter, D.: Intentionality and fatality during the King's Cross underground fire. Eur. J. Soc. Psychol. **22**, 203–218 (1992)
35. Canter, D.V.: Fires and Human Behaviour. Wiley, New York (1980)
36. Drury, J., Cocking, C.: The Mass Psychology of Disasters and Emergency Evacuations: A Research Report and Implications for Practice. University of Sussex, Falmer (2007)
37. Pickering, J.B.: TRust in IT: Factors, metRics, Models. http://www.itutility.ac.uk/2014/10/30/trust-in-it-factors-metrics-models/
38. Information Commissioner's Office: Key Definitions of the Data Protection Act (2015)
39. European Commission: Directive 95/46/EC of the European Parliament and of the Council (1995)
40. Sandnell, P.: Dreaming of a connected (and smart) home. http://www.ericsson.com/thinkingahead/the-networked-society-blog/2014/12/22/dreaming-connected-smart-home/
41. Howe, J.: The rise of crowdsourcing. Wired Mag. **14**, 1–4 (2006)
42. Surowiecki, J.: The Wisdom of Crowds. Anchor, New York (2005)

User Perceptions of a Virtual Human Over Mobile Video Chat Interactions

Sin-Hwa Kang[✉], Thai Phan, Mark Bolas, and David M. Krum

Institute for Creative Technologies, University of Southern California,
12015 Waterfront Drive Playa Vista, Los Angeles, CA 90094-2536, USA
{kang,tphan,bolas,krum}@ict.usc.edu

Abstract. We believe that virtual humans, presented over video chat services, such as Skype, and delivered using smartphones, can be an effective way to deliver innovative applications where social interactions are important, such as counseling and coaching. To explore this subject, we have built a hardware and software apparatus that allows virtual humans to initiate, receive, and interact over video calls using Skype or any similar service. With this platform, we conducted two experiments to investigate the applications and characteristics of virtual humans that interact over mobile video. In Experiment 1, we investigated user reactions to the physical realism of the background scene in which a virtual human was displayed. In Experiment 2, we examined how virtual characters can establish and maintain longer term relationships with users, using ideas from Social Exchange Theory to strengthen bonds between interactants. Experiment 2 involved repeated interactions with a virtual human over a period of time. Both studies used counseling-style interactions with users. The results demonstrated that males were more attracted socially to a virtual human that was presented over a realistic background than a featureless background while females were more socially attracted to a virtual human with a less realistic featureless background. The results further revealed that users felt the virtual human was a compassionate partner when they interacted with the virtual human over multiple calls, rather than just a single call.

Keywords: Virtual humans · Smartphones · Video chats · Counseling coaches

1   Introduction

Virtual humans in the digital world are beginning to show promise in applications such as education, training, therapy, and entertainment. In large part, this is due to their ability to evoke social responses in real humans. With the ubiquity of smartphones, the obvious next step for virtual humans is integration into various mobile applications. People create and strengthen their social relationships by communicating each other over video chat services (such as Skype). We believe that virtual humans, presented over video chat services and delivered using mobile phones, can be another effective way to deliver counseling and coaching applications. We suggest that virtual humans who communicate over videoconference services like Skype and Apple's FaceTime have unique advantages over other forms of presentation, including characters in native smartphone

© Springer International Publishing Switzerland 2016
M. Kurosu (Ed.): HCI 2016, Part III, LNCS 9733, pp. 107–118, 2016.
DOI: 10.1007/978-3-319-39513-5_10

apps. The virtual humans may appear to be more realistic since they can communicate using video conferencing, much like real humans, in contrast to the characters running within native smartphone apps.

However, it is well known that users often opt to protect their privacy and are more inclined to share intimate details about themselves when they feel their information will remain confidential. The potential benefit of employing a virtual human in this case is that users experience the nonjudgemental anonymity of a computer not knowing who they are, while still being programmed to behave socially adept enough to maintain an engaging conversation that promotes intimacy [14, 15]. This effect however may be altered when speaking with a counselor who is located far away, as a user might not feel that their conversation is private. Therefore, new research is needed to understand how to effectively present virtual characters on a mobile video platform. We hypothesize that factors such as the context of a smartphone, how the virtual human is presented within a smartphone app, and indeed, the nature of that app, can profoundly affect how a real human perceives the virtual human. Furthermore, video and audio artifacts inherent in Internet based video conferencing may also lower the realism requirements for virtual humans. We have also identified additional design questions involved in developing mobile virtual human experiences. What behaviors, visuals, and utterances might make characters more relatable and increase presence? Can reciprocity and other social behaviors encourage repeated interactions with the virtual character to strengthen social bonds between the character and users?

Our goal is to develop design guidelines for the deployment of virtual humans on smartphones, with a specific focus on mental well-being applications, such as coaching and counseling. To achieve this end, we have developed an apparatus that allows virtual humans to initiate calls and interact over Skype. In this research, we designed two experiments to explore user perceptions of a virtual human interviewer over mobile video chat interactions based on two theories: *Presence* and *Social Exchange Theory*.

1.1 Theoretical Background and Research Questions

Presence. It is desirable to feel presence (being there) with a partner when communicating with him/her via technology such as virtual reality. Previously dominant definitions of this phenomenon of presence with a partner have included the illusion of physically being somewhere together although your partner's physical body is, in fact, not there [5, 18].

Lee [17] later redefines this feeling of "being somewhere" as a mental state in which the users do not notice that their experience is not real. The experience is further described as sensory (or nonsensory) awareness of virtual (para-authentic or artificial) objects as authentic objects. This redefinition is interesting because it separates unsolicited user feelings of presence from the existing definitions of presence [5, 18] in which the term "illusion" may imply a "somewhat undesirable" feeling of presence [17]. Lee suggests three types of presence to represent this concept: physical presence, social presence, and self presence. These three sub-types of presence were coined originally by Biocca [5], but with different definitions from Lee's. Lee contends that Biocca's sub-type definitions were not mutually exclusive and did not explain feelings of presence that could be formulated via low-tech media (e.g. TV). In Lee's definitions, physical presence indicates user feelings of virtual objects as sensory (or nonsensory) awareness of actual physical objects for which user self-transportation is not a requisite. Social presence signifies sensory (or nonsensory) awareness of virtual social entities as actual social actors through both one-way and two-way communication. Self presence includes user feelings of a sensory (or nonsensory) experience of a virtual (para-authentic or artificial) self/selves as one's actual self, for example, perception of an avatar's body as one's own body. In Lee's definitions of presence, both physical and social presence do not require user feelings of being there in virtual reality. Lee argues that his redefinition of presence describes user feelings of presence even when using and communicating over a low-tech medium. We also argue that communicating via smartphone does not require users to feel being transported into another world (i.e. virtual reality), but can demonstrate some forms and levels of presence.

Slater [25] also addresses user feelings of presence in both virtual reality and non-virtual reality situations, such as a desktop. He defines realism and presence using place illusion and plausibility illusion. Place illusion is similar to the prevailing definitions of presence, i.e. the sense of "being there" [5, 18]. Plausibility illusion is defined as the illusion of an event without denying that the event is happening virtually. This relates to consistency and correlations between events in the environment not directly caused by the user, for example, the entities in the environment might move to avoid the user. He states that users could have the plausibility illusion without physical realism, as characters might respond to the user, but might not be realistically modeled. He argues that the measures of presence should be different between systems, such as between a virtual reality setting and a desktop setting (or a setting using a smartphone). This implies that aspects of presence could be applied when there are not user feelings of transportation into another world, which Lee [17] also contended.

We conclude that portions of the existing definitions of presence described above could characterize user feelings of being together with a virtual human displayed on a smartphone. We contend that Lee's concept of social presence applies to sensory (and nonsensory) awareness of a virtual human as a social actor and the smartphone video interaction does not require user feelings of being there through transportation of self into a virtual world (i.e. virtual reality). The notion of social presence has further been explored by other researchers [22] and used interchangeably with "copresence" [2]. Slater also mentions a similar concept and suggests that user feeling of presence may not require physical realism. However, we were interested to examine whether social presence might be influenced and even strengthened by physical realism.

We hypothesized that people might perceive a virtual human to be a responsive animated character and feel some level of presence with the character as it is, but they are more likely to consider the virtual human to be realistic and socially present if they believe the virtual human is in a location that appears to be realistic. Thus, we were specifically interested in Lee's concept of social presence and how strongly people would feel presence with a virtual human based on the type of physical location displayed behind the virtual human. We formulated a question to investigate this subject as follows:

RQ1: How are responses to a virtual human different when individuals interact with a virtual human that is presented with a realistic background, compared to a virtual human with a featureless background?

In addition, gender could be considered as one of the most critical factors for the nature of smartphone use. Geser [8] reports that females use a smartphone more for intimate purposes than males. Females tend to share and express their privacy and emotion with others with long chats and are more likely to articulate their anxieties [23]. Males are more inclined to use a smartphone for functional purposes (e.g. for coordinating meeting times and places) [19]. Exline et al. [7] also suggest that females desire more affection and involvement in their relationships than males. Another finding demonstrates that females are more prone to display affectionate behavior such as immediacy and inclusion through body gesture and orientation as well as gaze in same-sex interactions [11].

These findings imply that female users are inclined to interact with a virtual human displayed on a smartphone more for intimate and anonymous conversations than male users, especially when the female users perceive the virtual human as a counseling interviewer. We formulated an additional research question to investigate this subject as follows:

RQ2: How do responses to a virtual human differ based on gender when individuals interact with a virtual human presented with a realistic background, compared to a virtual human with a featureless background?

Social-Exchange Theory. Social-exchange theory represents human interactions as being driven by a social economics [6]. The theory specifically emphasizes that humans expect to get rewards for what they provide or share with others. The rewards could range from material assets to social currency, such as information, services, etc. Social exchange values social meaning in action rather than material value, which is critical in economic exchange. The reciprocity norm may play a key role in social exchanges between human beings [9] because reciprocity allows people to initiate investment without fear of no rewards [1].

Among many types of reciprocity, self-disclosure reciprocity is known for strengthening social connections [13]. Moon's study [20] showed that reciprocity would encourage communicators to disclose high risk personal information. Moon reported that communicators' self-disclosure reciprocity promoted further self-disclosure and attraction to each other. She defined self-disclosure reciprocity as one of the social rules applied for human interactions. She further described self-disclosure reciprocity that would allow people to interact with computers as if they were humans. It could happen that the exchange may not be even, but it eventually should equalize. That is an essence of the reciprocity norm.

In counseling interactions, it has been reported that patients disclose more intimate information if counselors share their own intimate stories with the patients [14]. Based on the theory, this form of social reciprocity could work successfully. Furthermore, communication researchers [26] suggest that additional interactions could encourage intimate relationships better than just a one-time interaction as social exchanges for relational life occur over time. Bickmore and colleagues developed the *Relational Agent*, a virtual human designed to build long-term, socio-emotional bonds and provide advice on a user's workout behavior [3, 4]. The agent's daily interactions with a user occurred over a long period (e.g. a month). Most of the *Relational Agent* studies explored the use of agents on mobile devices. The results of the studies indicated the *Relational Agent* to be an effective human-agent interface with regard to health education and behavior changes. Bickmore and colleagues also posited that if an app-based mobile agent had the potential to interact with a user for extended periods of time or even constantly, very close relationships with the user become possible [3].

We were particularly interested in the effect of a virtual human on user perceptions of and reactions to the virtual human when s/he has a longer term interaction with the virtual human. Such a study to explore longer term, repeated interactions with a virtual character while also involving smartphone video chats has rarely if ever been performed, due to logistical and technical complexity required. There are two differentiators between our approach and the existing study [3]. One notable difference is that our approach is designed to give users the impression that the virtual human has a presence in the real world like a real human, and has the interest and agency to reach out and contact the user. Another distinction is that Bickmore's virtual human plays the role of a workout coach, while our agent uses a counseling interview style interaction and is meant to ultimately play the role of a coaching counselor working with individuals confronting mental issues.

In our study, a real human user and a virtual human mutually exchanged intimate information, consisting of increasing personal questions. We expected these conversational exchanges could encourage users to engage in self-disclosure reciprocity with their virtual human partner, based on Social Exchange Theory. According to the theory, we would be able to determine whether user preparation for their answers might have enhanced the user's bonds with their partner through the repeated interactions in this study. We further expected that the bonds could affect user feeling of presence with the virtual human. The gifts and rewards were operationally defined as the degree to which each conversant voluntarily disclosed intimate information. We formulated a question to investigate this subject as follows:

RQ3: How are perceptions of a virtual human different when individuals interact with a virtual human more often (multiple calls), compared to interacting with the virtual human less often (a single call)?

1.2 Research Approach and Evaluation

Our approach to mobile counseling is focused on bringing virtual human coaches to smartphones through videoconference services like Skype. This approach could utilize the accessibility of the smartphone and the ability to call users thus allowing exploration of feeling of presence in mediated interactions and longer relationships consisting of repeated interactions and follow-up interventions between users and virtual coaches.

We created an apparatus to conduct Skype calls with users (see Fig. 1).

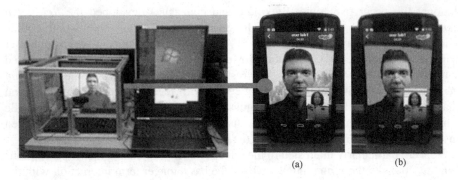

Fig. 1. The apparatus uses a web camera to present imagery of a virtual human in Skype [left]. A male or female version of the virtual human can be presented. The virtual character can initiate a Skype call and communicate to a user over (a) a realistic background or (b) a featureless background on a smartphone [right].

The apparatus allows an experimenter to call a user's Skype ID and transmit video of a virtual human rendered within a Unity game engine application on a desktop computer in our lab. We created both a male and a female virtual human (Caucasians, 35 years of age) to match genders with the human users to control for gender effects. An experimenter remotely controlled a virtual human displayed on the user's smartphone using Wizard of Oz (WOZ) methods. An unseen experimenter would trigger various virtual human verbal behaviors (i.e. questions, intimate back stories, and empathetic feedback) and nonverbal behaviors (i.e. smiles and nods). The virtual human had the ability to display various non-verbal actions, such as small or large nods, and small or large smiles. The virtual human was further able to deliver several variations of verbal empathetic feedback: "OK," "I see," etc. We measured user presence with the virtual human using the *Virtual Rapport* scale (e.g. "I felt I had a connection with my partner."), social attraction toward the virtual human using the *Social Attraction* scale (e.g. "A virtual character would be pleasant to be with."), partner perception using the *Partner Perception* scale (e.g. "compassionate"), and other social perception variables. Participants responded to each question using Likert-type scales. The *Virtual Rapport* scale is constructed from a combination of the *Co-presence* (or Social Presence [16, 22]) scale and the *Rapport* scale [10]. The combined scale has twenty-three items using Likert-type scales with an 8-point metric (1 = Strongly Disagree; 8 = Strongly Agree). The *Social Attraction* scale has six items with 8 point Likert-type scales (1 = Strongly Disagree; 8 = Strongly Agree) [21]. Items include: "I would like to have a friendly chat with a virtual character" and "I think a virtual character could be a friend of mine." The *Partner Perception* scale is a semantic differential with 21 bi-polar pairs of adjectives (e.g. likable-dislikable, threatening-not threatening), each on a 7-point metric [15]. All scales displayed good reliability [14, 15].

2 Experimental Design and Findings

2.1 Experiment 1: Realistic Background VS. Featureless Background

In Experiment 1, we investigated the effects of manipulating the visual backdrop showing the virtual human's location during a Skype call. A detailed and realistic backdrop could allow users to feel an increased sense of presence with a virtual human by perceiving the virtual human to be located in a realistic setting. We also hypothesized that a subjective sense of physical distance could also be a factor that could alter a user's feelings of presence. We examined user perception of a virtual human that was displayed on a realistic background, compared to a virtual human presented on a featureless (less realistic) background during a Skype video call.

We designed two different backgrounds to serve as cues for a virtual human's location in Experiment 1. The experiment is a between-subject design that examined user perception of a virtual human and included two conditions: a realistic animated video background vs. a less realistic featureless gray background (see Fig. 1). The "realistic background" condition used an outdoor scene, videotaped through a window, containing trees that were moving in the wind. The video clip was seamlessly looped during the entirety of the user's interaction with a virtual human. The "featureless background" condition used a plain, grey colored background.

Participants and Procedure. Participants were recruited online, via Craigslist. The qualified participants were over 18 years old and able to communicate comfortably in spoken and written English. We recruited a total of 43 participants (51 % men, 49 % women) whose average age was 35 years (*Mean* = 35, *SD* = 13.13) in the study.

In the experiment, participants were asked to come to our lab and have a conversation with a virtual human coach over Skype. The users were given a Google Nexus smartphone that included a preset Skype ID for the study. An experimenter remotely controlled a virtual human using a WOZ method and presented the character over Skype using the same apparatus as previously described (see Fig. 1). In both of the conditions, users were first asked to fill out a pre-questionnaire to gather demographic information prior to starting an actual interaction session. They were then asked to wait for the incoming call sound from the phone provided by the experimenter. The sound indicated that someone, i.e. the virtual human, was calling. Users were then asked to click the phone call pick-up symbol on the phone. The users were then able to see and converse with the virtual human.

After completing the interaction session described above, user were asked to fill out a post-questionnaire to assess their perception of and responses to interactions with a virtual human. Users were then briefed and compensated $25 for their participation. Participation took about 60 min or so to complete, including filling out a pre- and a post-questionnaires. Questionnaire data was collected through online surveys.

Findings. To detect significant effects within the interaction data, we used 2-way ANOVA analysis using condition and gender as 2 independent variables. We did not find statistically significant differences for user presence with and social attraction toward virtual humans that were displayed with different background types. However, the results showed that there was a statistically significant interaction effect between condition and gender [$F(1, 39) = 7.03, p = .012$] regarding user social attraction toward a virtual human (see Fig. 2). Male users ($M = 5.74, SD = 1.56$) were more socially attracted to a virtual human when they interacted with the virtual human that was displayed with realistic background than female users ($M = 3.80, SD = 1.79$). Meanwhile, female users ($M = 5.60, SD = 1.70$) were more socially attracted to a virtual human when they interacted with the virtual human that was presented with featureless background than male users ($M = 4.77, SD = 1.77$). The results also showed a trend of users tending to feel greater presence with a virtual human that was displayed with realistic background ($M = 5.07, SD = 1.26$), compared to interacting with a virtual human that was presented with featureless background ($M = 4.87, SD = 1.60$) although this trend was not statistically significant.

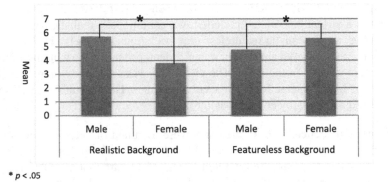

* $p < .05$

Fig. 2. The result of 2-way ANOVA for user social attraction toward a virtual human

2.2 Experiment 2: Single Call VS. Multiple Calls

In Experiment 2, we explored whether virtual humans could establish and maintain long term relationships by leveraging ideas from Social Exchange Theory [6, 26]. The theory postulates that the exchange of gifts and rewards can allow people to strengthen their social relationships.

The experiment used a within-subject design that investigated user reactions to a virtual human displayed on a smartphone over multiple interactions with the virtual human. In the experiment, participants were asked to schedule times to receive 3 calls on their own smartphone from a virtual human coach over the course of 3 consecutive days in any place where the participants could have a private conversation. We expected the interactions could encourage users to feel reciprocity with their virtual human partner, based on Social Exchange Theory. The study would allow us to determine whether user preparation for their answers might have enhanced presence with their virtual partner over the repeated interactions in this study.

Participants and Procedure. Participants were recruited online, via Qualtrics. The qualified participants were over 18 years old, able to communicate comfortably in spoken and written English, and requested access to a smartphone running the Skype app and Wi-Fi or 3G/4G Internet access. We recruited a total of 19 participants (47 % men, 53 % women) whose average age was 32 years ($M = 32$, $SD = 9.88$) in the study.

Potential participants were first asked to fill out a pre-questionnaire to gather demographic information and filter unqualified participants prior to starting an actual interaction. Participation in the study required access to a smartphone running the Skype app and Wi-Fi or 3G/4G Internet access. Qualified participants were asked to schedule their interaction times with a virtual human for 3 sessions over 3 consecutive days. Participants were requested to answer a total of 24 questions over the 3 call sessions in the form of a counseling interview. The virtual human asked 8 questions during each call and shared some personal information before asking each question. The participants were also asked by the virtual human to prepare answers for interview questions given in the next session and promised that the virtual human coach would also prepare answers for the same upcoming questions. The virtual human's verbal questions and responses were pre-scripted using a structure and context adapted from a previous study [15]. During the interaction, users were asked questions of increasing intimacy by the virtual human (e.g. "How old are you?"). The virtual human prefaced questions with its own intimate anecdotes to reciprocate self-disclosure and advance the conversation (e.g. "I am 35 years old.").

The participants were also asked to fill out a post-questionnaire after both the 1st and 3rd call sessions to assess any changes in user responses between the 1st and the 3rd interactions with the virtual human coach. Each session took about 10–15 min to complete, including a post-questionnaire for the first and last sessions. Questionnaire data was collected through online surveys. The participants were given $50.40 compensation when they completed the study.

Findings. To detect significant effects within the interaction data, we used a Paired-samples T-test, an analysis used when the same subjects participated in all conditions (two different occasions) of an experiment.

The results demonstrated that users felt the virtual human was a compassionate partner when they communicated with the virtual human several times [($M = 5.42$, $SD = 1.50$), $t(18) = -2.35$, $p = .031$], rather than just once ($M = 5.05$, $SD = 1.31$) (see

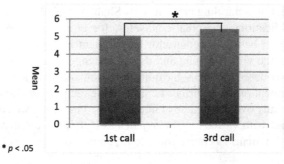

$* p < .05$

Fig. 3. The result of Paired-samples T-test for user partner perception (Compassionate) between the 1st call and the 3rd call

Fig. 3). There were no other significant results for the other variables. In addition, the results showed a trend of users feeling greater presence with the virtual human after experiencing all three calls ($M = 5.80$, $SD = 1.41$), rather than just one call ($M = 5.62$, $SD = 1.24$), although this trend did not reach statistical significance.

3   Conclusions and Implications

In Experiment 1, the results of the experiment demonstrate that overall, the background of a virtual human's location does not significantly affect presence with or social attraction toward the virtual human communicating over a smartphone. However, we discovered that males were more attracted socially to a virtual human that was presented with a realistic background, while females were more socially attracted to a virtual human with a featureless background. Congruent with previous studies, users were not required to transfer themselves to another place (self presence) when using a low fidelity medium such as a smartphone but still felt aspects of presence (i.e. social presence or co-presence). We used the measure of *Virtual Rapport*, which corresponds to social presence (or co-presence), which we argue is an appropriate measurement to assess user presence in this study. According to the results of the experiment, we contend that there would be no difference in perception of a virtual human with regard to their perceived physical location or realism [25]. We further argue that males are more socially attracted to a virtual human presented over a realistic background, because it demonstrates that the virtual human is located somewhere outside the confines of the smartphone. However, females demonstrated greater social attraction toward a virtual human displayed over a less realistic background, which could be expected to decrease feelings of presence in general. Regarding the nature of females' smartphone uses described in Sect. 1.1, we contend that females were drawn to the featureless surroundings, which could be interpreted as more private, less distracting, and more anonymous. Overall, our findings imply that females like to interact with a virtual human who is located in a private setting.

In Experiment 2, the results of the experiment revealed that users felt the virtual human was a compassionate partner when they shared interactions over multiple calls, rather than just a single call. The results further showed a tendency of users to feel greater presence (measured using the *Virtual Rapport* scale) with the virtual human after experiencing all three calls, compared to having just one call. Compassion and rapport are of particular interest in counseling applications. Shallcross [24] noted that compassion is one of the qualifications of a great counselor. Joe et al. [12] also emphasized the importance of rapport between a counselor and a client in psychotherapeutic interactions. In our study, the virtual human and users exchanged their own intimate stories, which could be considered the social meaning in action and a value of social exchange [6, 26]. The experiment protocol further facilitated the reciprocity norm by exchanging intimate stories equally over the course of interactions. Therefore, we contend that users were able to interact with virtual human coaches as if they were real humans [20] and perceive the virtual humans as compassionate partners when the users had more interactions with them.

In conclusion, we argue that there are potential advantages for a virtual human coach to use customized or personalized backgrounds for particular users who receive video calls from the virtual human coach. We also argue that there are potential advantages for the use of a virtual human coach on a smartphone for longer term counseling interactions, specifically when users receive multiple calls initiated by the coach. These conclusions are coupled with other technical advantages of this form of interaction. Since the virtual human can "call" the user, it may grant the virtual human an appearance of greater agency. The common conception of Skype as a communications channel connecting one real world locale to another could also reinforce the belief that the character has a real presence somewhere in the world. We are continuing to explore how to leverage the context of this particular communications channel by running studies that manipulate the context of the communications channel. We plan to begin constructing a theory that captures the significant elements (technical, social, cultural, etc.) that provide context and subtext for real human to virtual human interactions mediated by smartphones.

References

1. Axelrod, R., Hamilton, W.D.: The evolution of cooperation. Science **211**, 1390–1396 (1981)
2. Bailenson, J.N., Yee, N., Merget, D., Schroeder, R.: The effect of behavioral realism and form realism of real-time avatar faces on verbal disclosure, nonverbal disclosure, emotion recognition, and copresence in dyadic interaction. PRESENCE: Teleoperators Virtual Environ. **15**, 359–372 (2006)
3. Bickmore, T., Mauer, D., Brown, T.: Context awareness in a handheld exercise agent. Pervasive and Mob. Comput. Spec. Issue Pervasive Health Wellness **5**, 226–235 (2009)
4. Bickmore, T., Picard, R.: Establishing and maintaining long-term human-computer relationships. ACM Trans. Comput. Hum. Interact. **12**(2), 293–327 (2005)
5. Biocca, F.: The cyborg's dilemma: progressive embodiment in virtual environments. J. Comput.-Mediated Commun. (1997). http://www.ascusc.org/jcmc/vol3/issue2/
6. DeLamater, J.D., Myers, D.J.: Social Psychology. Cengage Learning, Boston (2010)
7. Exline, R., Gray, D., Schuette, D.: Visual behavior in a dyad as affected by interview content and sex of respondent. J. Pers. Soc. Psychol. **1**, 201–209 (1965)
8. Geser, H.: Are girls (even) more addicted? Some gender patterns of cell phone usage. In: Sociology in Switzerland: Sociology of the Mobile Phone (2006). http://socio.ch/mobile/t_geser3.htm
9. Gouldner, A.W.: The norm of reciprocity: a preliminary statement. Am. Sociol. Rev. **25**, 161–178 (1960)
10. Gratch, J., Wang, N., Gerten, J., Fast E., Duffy, R.: Creating rapport with virtual agents. In: Proceedings of Intelligent Virtual Agents (2007)
11. Ickes, W., Barnes, R.D.: The role of sex and self-monitoring in unstructured dyadic interactions. J. Pers. Soc. Psychol. **35**, 315–330 (1977)
12. Joe, G.W., Simpson, D.D., Broome, K.M.: Retention and patient engagement models for different treatment modalities in DATOS. Drug Alcohol Depend. **57**(2), 113–125 (1999). Elsevier
13. Jourard, S.: Self-disclosure: An Experimental Analysis of the Transparent Self. Wiley-Interscience, Hoboken (1971)

14. Kang, S., Gratch, J.: Socially anxious people reveal more personal information with virtual counselors that talk about themselves using intimate human back stories. Ann. Rev. CyberTherapy Telemedicine **181**, 202–207 (2012)
15. Kang, S., Gratch, J.: Exploring users' social responses to computer counseling interviewers' behavior. J. Comput. Hum. Behav. **34C**, 120–130 (2014)
16. Kang, S., Watt, J.H., Ala, S.K.: Social copresence in anonymous social interactions using a mobile video telephone. In: Proceedings of Computer-Human Interaction (2008)
17. Lee, K.: Presence, explicated. Commun. Theory **14**(1), 27–50 (2004). http://onlinelibrary.wiley.com/doi/10.1111/j.1468-2885.2004.tb00302.x/epdf
18. Lombard, M., Reich, R., Grabe, M., Bracken, C., Ditton, T.: Presence and television: the role of screen size. Hum. Commun. Res. **26**, 75–98 (2000)
19. Mante, E.A., Piris, D.: SMS use by young people in The Netherlands. Revista de Astudios de Juventud **57**, 47–58 (2002). http://www.mtas.es/injuve/biblio/revistas/Pdfs/numero57 ingles.pdf
20. Moon, Y.: Intimate exchanges: using computers to elicit self-disclosure from consumers. J. Consum. Res. **26**(4), 323–339 (2000)
21. Nowak, K.L.: The influence of anthropomorphism and agency on social judgment in virtual environments. J. Comput. Mediated Commun. **9**(2) (2004). http://jcmc.indiana.edu/vol9/issue2/nowak.html
22. Nowak, K., Biocca, F.: The effect of the agency and anthropomorphism on users' sense of telepresence, copresence, and social presence in virtual environments. Presence: Teleoperators Virtual Environ. **12**(5), 481–494 (2003)
23. O'Neill, S., Fein, D., Velit, K., Frank, C.: Sex differences in preadolescent self-disclosure. Sex Roles **2**(1), 85–88 (1976)
24. Shallcross, L.: The recipe for truly great counseling. *Counseling Today*. A Publication of the American Counseling Association (2012). http://ct.counseling.org/2012/12/the-recipe-for-truly-great-counseling/
25. Slater, M.: Place illusion and plausibility can lead to realistic behavior in immersive virtual environments. Philos. Trans. Roy. Soc. B (2009). http://rstb.royalsocietypublishing.org/content/royptb/364/1535/3549.full.pdf
26. West, R., Turner, L.H.: Introducing Communication Theory: Analysis and Application. McGraw Hill, New York (2004)

Prototype of Conversation Support System for Activating Group Conversation in the Vehicle

Susumu Kono[✉], Yohei Wakisaka, and Atsushi Ikeno

TOYOTA InfoTechnology Center Co., Ltd.,
6-6-20 Akasaka, Minato-ku, Tokyo 107-0052, Japan
{su-kono,yo-wakisaka,atsu-ikeno}@jp.toyota-itc.com

Abstract. This paper describes the results of our research on a prototype of the conversation support system capable of activating group conversation in a vehicle.

The goal of this system was to enable further activating a group conversation. Based on methodology used in existing technology of utterance analysis, we estimated the intentions and desires of each group member in a vehicle from their conversation, aiming to enhance the overall situation of the group members in the vehicle by providing appropriate reference information corresponding to the situation in a timely manner through a conversational agent system.

Manufacturing a prototype of the system, we verified both its operations involved in the test case and its capability to infer the intentions and desires of each group member and intervene to their conversation in an appropriate timing.

In this research, we have demonstrated that our method used for the prototype was appropriate to a practical use through. In future, we will focus on optimizing the logic and system functions of group situation estimation and the subsequent steps of providing the reference information.

Keywords: Conversation estimation · Group conversation · Utterance feature · Conversational agent · Conversation analysis

1 Introduction

The information retrieval service using speech recognition such as "Siri"[1]and "Google Voice Search"[2] is widely used in a smartphone in our lives, because it enables a user easily to retrieve user's desired information by the user's speaking keywords relevant to the desired information without inputting any characters. However, such existing services require user's button operation with voice commands to initiate information retrieval and information provision.

Considering a user's convenience, it is more desirable to recognize user's intentions spontaneously from utterance contents without user's button operation and commands, and then to intervene to their conversation at appropriate

---

[1] http://www.apple.com/ios/siri/.
[2] http://www.google.com/insidesearch/features/voicesearch.

© Springer International Publishing Switzerland 2016
M. Kurosu (Ed.): HCI 2016, Part III, LNCS 9733, pp. 119–127, 2016.
DOI: 10.1007/978-3-319-39513-5_11

timing. As other existing spontaneous conversation systems and corpus have been examined already in prior research [6–8], here we examined a feasibility of providing services to support a user with a spontaneous conversation.

What particularly motivated us toward this research is to make it feasible by using speech recognition and intention extraction techniques.

Our objective is to clarify the effectiveness of estimating intention of utterances from contents of a group conversation, which is also aimed to lead to an enhancement of group situation with appropriate reference information in a timely manner.

2   Related Work

2.1   Noise Reduction and Voice Separation

Noise reduction function based on a multiple microphone array combined with an adaptive postfiltering scheme has been developed and utilized. The noise reduction function is achieved by utilizing the directivity gain of the array and by reducing the residual noise through postfiltering of the received microphone signals [5,9]. The microphone array system is also helpful for voice separation speaker by speaker in the conversation by plural members.

2.2   Tension Extraction from Utterances

We define *utterance* as the smallest unit of speech of spoken language, that is a continuous piece of speech beginning and ending with a pause, *speech* as the vocal form of human communication, *conversation* as a form of interactive, spontaneous communication between two or more people, typically occurring in spoken communication, and *conversational agent* as a computer system intended to converse with humans.

In existing technology of utterance analysis, the utterance feature values like spectrum of utterance power levels have been used for estimation of member tension in previous research [1]. *Tension* is defined as mental appearances of physiological responses in this paper.

2.3   Intention Extraction from Utterances

We define *intention in spoken dialogue* as a plan or an expectation in a speaker's mind to do something that has been mentioned in their speech, and it can be estimated by comparing the text data between speech recognition results and spontaneous dialogue corpora.

Methods of intention extraction in spoken dialogue utterances have been established by prior research, and the accuracy of intention recognition has recently improved [2–4,10]. The intention of each utterance is extracted from converted text data with speech recognition based on the methods of previous research above, and topics in the conversation and desires of each member is estimated.

3   Methodology

We are studying to enhance the current voice utilizing services as mentioned in Sect. 1, and to develop the support service to the traveling group for the conversation in the vehicle. Then, as a test case, we applied this methodology of conversation support to a group of travelers who needed to make some decisions (e.g., destination, route) while seated in a car. We manufactured a prototype of our system to verify the relevant operations in the test case, and also to estimate the possibility of inferring the intentions and desires of each group member by measuring the utterance characteristics in the group conversations.

We assume to monitor the voice of the conversation by the traveling group in the vehicle continuously, and to estimate topics in the conversation and desires of each member by the extracted intention from converted text data with speech recognition. Thus, we assume to realize that a conversational agent gives a group advice and based on this estimation. The image of the support system and the conversational agent that are applied for conversation in the vehicle is shown in Fig. 1.

Fig. 1. The image of the applied conversation support system in the vehicle.

The methodology we use here, which is based on real-time reactions to spoken speech and its response, is not new, as noted in related work (see Sect. 2). However, our proposed method aims to go beyond previous work and recognize the group status in the conversation; it does not simply provide information to spoken speech.

3.1   Pre-processes of Utterances

We apply the synchronized microphone array system for the noise reduction and the voice separation in our prototype. For the conversation analysis, at the first step, noises such as the sound of the engine or the ventilation of the air-conditioner have to reduce from the input voice signal, and to recognize a voice

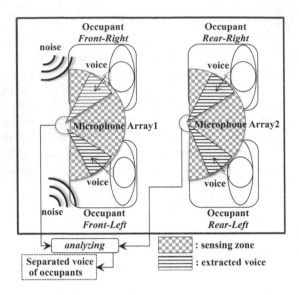

Fig. 2. The image of voice separation process.

speaker by speaker separately by using the microphone array, even in the case of the overlapping of utterances at the same time by plural members. The image of voice separation process is shown in Fig. 2.

3.2   Extraction of Intentions in Utterances

After pre-processes above, utterance sections are detected and each utterance is recognized. Based on the estimated intention by a conversation support system, we assume to choose the information which may be matched with group members from travel information database, and to be informed it to members by a synthetic voice in the vehicle. The flow to the intervention in the conversation is shown in Fig. 3.

After the speech recognition process, "subject (theme)" (e.g., the place to eat lunch, the gift to buy in the shopping mall), "category" (e.g., meal, shopping), "sentence style" (e.g., positive, negative, interrogative), "intention" (e.g., proposal, question, agreement, opposition), and "expected action" (e.g., decision on where to have lunch, searching the shop to buy gifts) are extracted by comparing the text data from the speech recognition results and spontaneous dialogue corpora data. For example, in the case of "Let's talk about where to have lunch," we have the following values: subject; lunch, category; meal, sentence style; positive, intention; proposal, and expected action; decision on where to have lunch.

The politeness level (e.g., polite words used toward elders or superiors in formal speech, or informal terms used toward friends in casual speech) and the existence of childish words (e.g., words often used by children) or instructional words (e.g., words obligatorily used for instruction by someone in a position of

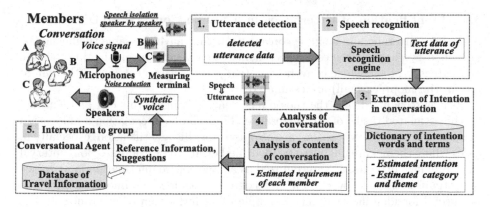

Fig. 3. Flow to intervention in the conversation.

authority) of each utterance are also estimated by comparing them with the dictionary of specific words and terms.

3.3 Extraction of Tensions in Utterances

The tension strength in each utterance is estimated by the utterance feature values (see Sect. 2.2). By combining the extracted intentions of utterances and the indicated tension strength of each utterance, we could identify specific phenomena, such as high tension in negative replies. The proposed method aims to recognize changes in group status through careful monitoring and estimation. The example of member's status extraction from utterance data is shown in Table 1.

Table 1. Example of member's status extraction from utterance data.

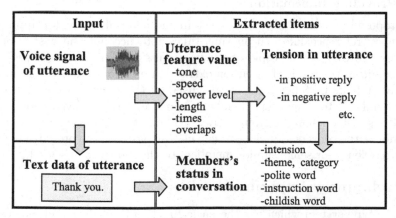

3.4   Identification of Utterances in a Single Conversation

A series of utterances in a single conversation that have the same theme can be identified by checking the estimated theme of each utterance. Then, the theme and category of the whole conversation (e.g., the place to eat lunch, the gift to buy in the shopping mall) are estimated.

If it is recognized that the theme has clearly changed, this can be identified by the estimated theme of each utterance. Time course information and location information (e.g., GPS position) are also used for this identification, especially in cases where themes are unable to be identified clearly. For example, "long interval after previous utterances" is recognized as a time course information, and "place of destination in the conversation" is recognized as a location information. These are useful for identification. The example of identification of utterances in the conversation is shown in Table 2.

Table 2. Example of identification of utterances in conversation.

	Text	Intention	Category	Theme
Utterance-1	A: "Let's talk about place of <u>lunch</u>."	bringing up	meal/lunch	**Conversation-1** - Lunch - meal - Kamakura
Utterance-2	B: "How about the <u>Italian</u> in <u>Kamakura</u>?"	proposal	meal/Italian	
Utterance-3	C: "I prefer the local <u>seafood</u> restaurant rather than <u>Italian</u>."	opposition /proposal	meal/seafood meal/Italian	
Utterance-7	A: "OK, it was <u>decided</u>. We <u>will go</u> to a <u>meal</u> there."	finalization	meal	
Utterance-8	A: "By the way, how is the <u>weather</u> <u>forecast</u> <u>tomorrow</u>?"	question	weather (forecast)	**Conversation-2** - weather - tomorrow

_____ : *"Keyword" for extraction of intentions / categories/ themes*

3.5   Providing Information

Our proposed conversational agent system mechanically provides appropriate and timely reference information that takes into account the wishes of each member according to the topic of group discussion. The members wishes are estimated from the result of intention extraction mentioned above, and location information (e.g., GPS position) are also used for this identification. In this way, the system helps to bring every member's opinion into the conversation, leading to greater satisfaction in the group conversation. In the case of conflict the desires of members, the conversational agent can choose based on the profile of members (e.g., precedence for senior/junior member) or the sequence of seated position.

4   Preliminary Experiment

The prototype system which has the basic function to analyze and intervention to the conversation was developed, and the operation of the prototype system was tested by monitors.

Table 3. Results of the preliminary experiment.

Conversation #	Member	Numbers of utterances	recognized utterances including target words (value, rate)	Extraction of utterances (value, rate)in conversation
1	A-1	4	4/4 100.0%	4/4 100.0%
	A-2	3	3/3 100.0%	3/3 100.0%
2	B-1	4	2/4 50.0%	2/4 50.0%
	B-2	3	2/3 66.7%	2/3 66.7%
3	C-1	4	4/4 100.0%	4/4 100.0%
	C-2	3	3/3 100.0%	3/3 100.0%
4	D-1	4	2/4 50.0%	2/4 50.0%
	D-2	3	2/3 66.7%	2/3 66.7%
Average	–	3.5	78.6%	78.6%

We implemented two kinds of test dialogues (approximately three minutes) with two-member groups (age: 29–51, all males) in November 2015. The theme of the test dialogues were a place of lunch in the downtown of Tokyo as decided beforehand, and conversation was began by expressing preferred food category of each member, and conversational agent intervene to the conversation and inform related restaurant information to each member. In the preliminary experiment, we required to monitors to speak loudly and not speedy, though the function of voice recognition we prepared does not have the availability to deal high speed speech or low voice at the current stage. The results of the preliminary experiment with our prototype system are shown in Table 3 and below;

1. We assume that we will apply the proposed model to group discussion in a car. However, we have not prepared the appropriate noise reduction system for a car driving certain speed as yet. Then, we implemented the test in the stopped car, which is hardly affected by noise at all. In the next step, we will prepare the appropriate noise reduction system, and implement the test in a car driving certain speed.
2. The proportion of speech recognition of words for extraction of intention was 78.6% on average. We assume that this is not a high proportion, but it can be used to extract the intention of almost all conversations.
3. The intention of utterance could be also extracted in 78.6% of all utterances. However, we could identify all utterances in conversation through the extraction of intention and time course information.
4. The extraction of the utterance feature values was quite successful, and we could calculate the strength of the tension using these utterance feature values. We confirmed that the strength of the tension was correctly estimated through human monitoring, excluding any utterances that did not have sufficient length or power to judge the tension.

5. The estimated intention of each utterance could also be used for comparisons with the calculated strength of the tension in conversation, and the strength of the tension could be linked to the intention of each utterance. Thus, we could confirm the possibility of identifying specific phenomena, such as high tension in negative replies.
6. We implement the simple function of informing, which is just picking up the restaurant information related with keywords in the utterance from database and just reading out the corresponded article. At the moment, it took about ten seconds until reading out after speaker uttered the keywords. We plan to further optimize this method by continued testing with many additional kinds of utterance data in future work.
7. The results of our preliminary test show that the basic concept of our proposed method, as outlined above in items 1–6, is generally appropriate.

The proposed system can obtain all utterance feature values and combine them with the extracted intention of each utterance. Thus, we can say that the inferring of the classification and status of groups by measuring the utterance characteristics of their users is possible, as shown by our preliminary experiment.
We also confirmed the possibility of measuring the utterance characteristics of group members as well as a method of providing suitable and appropriate information to group members using our system.

The result of the feasibility test shows basic availability of the noise reduction, voice separation speaker by speaker, speech recognition, extraction of intention and providing the related information timely was confirmed by our prototype system in the specific condition such as the conversation with the voice uttered clearly and loudly.

5   Conclusion

We demonstrated that the conversation support system to infer users' intentions and desires by monitoring utterance data in a group conversation, and to enhance the overall group situation through a conversational agent system by using estimated intentions and desires of each group member. The basic availability of our method to estimate intentions and provide the reference information in the group conversation was confirmed by testing in our prototype system.

In the next step, we will improve noise reduction and speech recognition systems, and perform a test with speedy speech by plural occupants in a car driving certain speed. Even regarding the contents of provided information, we will prepare to extend wider topics for conversation in the car trip, not only about restaurant and food information, but also the related information about historical and sightseeing spots and so on.

Then, we will further verify details of our method and system through continuous field tests, by collecting many additional kinds of utterance test data and further clarifying the appropriate parameters for estimation and information provision using machine learning. In the final step for embodying the method, we will aim to evaluate the effectivity of intervention by conversational agent with comparison of the emotion of occupants before and after the conversation.

References

1. Ariga, M., Yano, Y., Doki, S., Okuma, S.: Mental tension detection in the speech based on physiological monitoring. In: IEEE International Conference on Systems, Man and Cybernetics, ISIC, pp. 2022–2027 (2007). psychology 51(3), 629 (1955)
2. Eckert, W., Levin, E., Pieraccini, R.: Automatic evaluation of spoken dialogue systems. In: TWLT13: Formal semantics and pragmatics of dialogue, pp. 99–110 (1998)
3. Hodjat, B., Amamiya, M.: Applying the adaptive agent oriented software architecture to the parsing of context sensitive grammars. IEICE Trans. Inf. Syst. **83**(5), 1142–1152 (2000)
4. Hodjat, B., Amamiya, M.: Introducing the adaptive agent oriented software architecture and its application in natural language user interfaces. In: Ciancarini, P., Wooldridge, M.J. (eds.) AOSE 2000. LNCS, vol. 1957, pp. 285–306. Springer, Heidelberg (2001)
5. Kaneda, Y., Ohga, J.: Adaptive microphone-array system for noise reduction. IEEE Trans. Acoust. Speech Sig. Process. **34**(6), 1391–1400 (1986)
6. Maekawa, K., Koiso, H., Furui, S., Isahara, H.: Spontaneous speech corpus of Japanese. In: Proceedings of LREC2000 (Second International Conference on Language Resources and Evaluation), vol. 2, pp. 947–952 (2000)
7. Shriberg, E.: Spontaneous speech: how people really talk and why engineers should care. In: INTERSPEECH, pp. 1781–1784 (2005)
8. Stolcke, A., Shriberg, E., Bates, R., Coccaro, N., Jurafsky, D., Martin, R., Van Ess-Dykema, C: Dialog act modeling for conversational speech. In: AAAI Spring Symposium on Applying Machine Learning to Discourse Processing, pp. 98–105 (1998)
9. Zelinski, R.: A microphone array with adaptive post-filtering for noise reduction in reverberant rooms. In: 1988 International Conference on Acoustics, Speech, and Signal Processing, ICASSP-1988, IEEE, pp. 2578–2581 (1988)
10. Zhong, G., Hodjat, B., Helmy, T., Amamiya, M.: Software agent evolution in adaptive agent oriented software architecture. In: IWPSE 1999 Proceedings (1999)

Users' Relational Ascriptions in User-Companion Interaction

Julia Krüger[✉], Mathias Wahl, and Jörg Frommer

Medical Faculty, Department of Psychosomatic Medicine and Psychotherapy,
Otto von Guericke University Magdeburg, Magdeburg, Germany
{julia.krueger,mathias.wahl,joerg.frommer}@med.ovgu.de

Abstract. In a qualitative study in the field of user-companion interaction (UCI), we figured out that users of a system, which was meant to represent a preliminary step towards future Companion-systems, tend to individually ascribe (mostly human-like) characteristics to the system in order to turn it into a potential relational partner. Users' intrinsic motivation to establish and maintain a relationship with these individualized systems was found throughout the analyses and led us to the development of a concept called 'users' relational ascriptions'. In this paper, we present the empirical background of this concept and describe defining characteristics of relational ascriptions, reasons for their formation, factors that influence their content and quality as well as factors, which are influenced by the ascriptions. We sum up with a definition of relational ascriptions and discuss practical implications and future work.

Keywords: Companion-systems · Users' ascriptions · Anthropomorphization · User experience · Mental models · Qualitative research

1 Relational Artifacts and Users' Notions of Them

In recent years, technical systems called 'relational artifacts' [1] gained attention in the field of human-computer interaction. They provide individualized assistive, monitoring or companionship services [2] and are known under terms like, 'artificial companions' [3], 'sociable robots' [4], 'relational agents' [5] or 'Companion-systems' [6]. They share the vision that "the computer is not a tool but a companion" (so-called 'companion metaphor' [1, p. 150]), which aims at supporting the user[1] and maintaining an emotional, long-time social relationship with him [7]. Therefore, on the technical side, implementing features that enable systems to provide the required functionality is inevitable. However, a technical system will only become a 'companion' if the individual user himself *experiences* it as such, including qualities like, e.g., empathy and trustworthiness (e.g., [8]).

Usually, users' notions of technical systems are referred to as 'mental models' [9]. These describe internal system representations focusing on structure and functionality (e.g., [10]). They entail individual notions about the functioning of a system and its

---

[1] In order to simplify readability only male gender will be used.

© Springer International Publishing Switzerland 2016
M. Kurosu (Ed.): HCI 2016, Part III, LNCS 9733, pp. 128–137, 2016.
DOI: 10.1007/978-3-319-39513-5_12

requirements including relevant components of the system, their interrelations and the conditions of their interaction.

Relational aspects aimed at by designers of relational artifacts are not covered in mental models. Thus, a supplementary concept may be beneficial. In [11], the concept of 'anthropomorphization' of technical systems is contrasted to mental models. Literature provides lots of examples for how users think about technical systems as entities with human-like attributes, mental states and behaviors (e.g., [12, 13]). Of course, those ideas may entail information about users' relationship-related notions of a system. This is the case, e.g., when owners of Tamagotchi ascribe to them the human feeling of longing, when they did not spend time with them for a longer period [3]. However, to our best knowledge, a concept that is specially geared to artifacts which are designed to be experienced as 'companions' by their users and hence focuses especially on relational aspects of the interaction is still missing.

In this paper, we propose a concept termed 'users' relational ascriptions' that shall fill this research gap. On the basis of our empirical work presented in [8, 14] we will explain how these ascriptions are formed in the users, we will define them and outline their relevance for user-companion interaction (UCI).

2   Insights from a Qualitative User Study

Besides the theoretical considerations of relational aspects of users' experiences in interactions with relational artifacts, their relevance is supported by empiricism, too.

In a user study we conducted [8, 14], participants underwent a wizard of oz experiment in which they interacted with a speech-based dialogue system. Besides other interaction foci, the system asked for personal information for the purpose of individualization. The system was meant to represent a preliminary step towards future Companionsystems [15]. After the experiment, participants took part in a semi-structured interview focusing on subjective experiences during the interaction.

Our basic assumption in this study was that anthropomorphization of the simulated system is likely to occur in users' reports. This assumption is especially based on the theory of the 'intentional stance' [16]. It describes that users explain and predict the behavior of a technical system by ascribing mental states to it in order to interact effectively with the system, when construction and functioning of the system are far too complex to make explanations and predictions on their basis.

The interview material contained users' ideas about the system as well as users' emotions and reflections upon themselves, which were occurring during the experiment. Its analysis was led by the following two research questions: (1) How do users experience, i.e., what do they ascribe to the simulated Companion-system (system-related experiences)?, and (2) How do users experience themselves in reaction to their individual experiences of, i.e., their ascriptions to it (self-related experiences)?

As described in [14], the analysis of 31 interviews revealed that relational issues are important for users. They tended to think in interpersonal relationship categories and ascribed human like characteristics and behaviors to the system, e.g., support, honest interest in the user or nosiness. Findings regarding the system-related experiences are comprised in Table 1. Therein, categories are listed, which were worked out in the analysis and entail users' ascriptions towards the system.

Table 1. Categories illustrating users' ascriptions in individualization-focused UCI

Category	Range of subcategories
Nature of the system	Between man and machine
Capabilities of the system	Between impressing and frightening
Requirements by the system	Between expectable and strange
Relational offer of the system	Between insensitive and recognizing

We discussed our findings with regard to the system-related as well as the self-related experiences, firstly, concerning users' attempt to regain safety by ascribing familiar human-like mental states to the system and thus, turn it into a predictable counterpart. This is in line with [16] and was explained on the basis of the human inherent need for safety [17]. Secondly, we discussed our findings regarding users' efforts to make the system a potential relational partner they can get into contact with. In literature, this phenomenon is connected to the human inherent need to belong (e.g., [18]). In line with this latter motivation, a lot of private and intimate information was disclosed to the system, even when users' ascriptions to it were negative in quality (e.g., pursuit of own hidden goals, ability to abuse confidence).

3   The Concept of 'Users' Relational Ascriptions' in UCI

Aspects of relationship and attachment are highly relevant for UCI. They are not only aimed at by designers to build up systems as 'relational partners' for potential users, but even arise in users themselves during UCI [14]. Hence, we decided to expand our findings by describing a concept we called 'users' relational ascriptions' for the field of UCI.

In the following, we describe why relational ascriptions are formed in users. Afterwards, we work out the characteristics of relational ascriptions based on our interview data and summarize them in a definition of users' relational ascriptions.

3.1   Formation of Relational Ascriptions in Users

Figure 1 illustrates why relational ascriptions arise in users, from which situation they originated and which goal is aspired by making use of them. The relationships explained here are derived from our user study [14].

The interaction situation is experienced as uncertain regarding both, the system itself representing the interaction counterpart (With whom or what am I interacting here?, What can I expect from it?, What does it want from me?, etc.), and the interaction process (How should I behave in reaction to my counterpart?, How will the interaction proceed?, etc.). In such an uncertain situation, the necessity to adopt relational ascriptions arises in the user and is accompanied by the wish to do so on the basis of the following two needs inherent in humans.

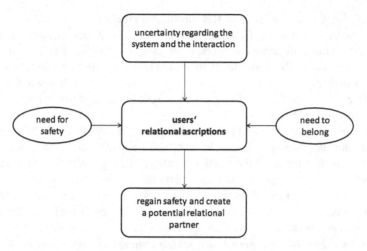

Fig. 1. Formation of users' relational ascriptions

The need for safety marks 'the necessity for relational ascriptions' evolving in the user. Companion-systems are intelligent technical devices providing both, an emotional and a relational dimension of interaction. Thereby, machine-like and human-like aspects can get into conflict and the system may be experienced as an unsettling hybrid [14]. In the sense of the human need for safety [17], the user tries to reduce uncertainty by ascribing human-like characteristics well-known from human-human interaction to the system. Hence, he is able to regain safety by turning the counterpart into something predictable and explainable, including ideas on how to interact effectively and successfully with it.

The need to belong marks 'the wish for relational ascriptions' that is inherent in the user and fundamentally motivates him in addition to the need for safety. It is defined as humans' strong desire to establish and maintain relationships [19]. Based on this need, the user himself is motivated to turn the system into a social, human-like counterpart. On that basis, he is enabled to see a potential relational partner in the system.

3.2 Description of Relational Ascriptions

The interview material gained in our user study revealed a variety of users' ascriptions towards the simulated system [14]. It became apparent that these ascriptions implied users' ideas regarding the relationship between the system and themselves. Hence, we decided to call them 'users' relational ascriptions' to emphasize the importance of the relationship and to contrast these ascriptions to users' internal representation regarding systems' structure and functioning described in mental models. We worked out the characteristics of relational ascriptions, as well as, on the one hand, the factors influencing their content and quality and, on the other hand, the factors which are influenced by their content and quality. All these aspects will be presented subsequently by referencing users' utterances from our interview material.

3.2.1 Defining Characteristics of Relational Ascriptions

It became apparent that even if the ascriptions worked out in the interview material appeared to be similar in groups of users, each user developed individual ones. In our study, e.g., one user ascribes a similarity to human beings to the simulated system *("you do not necessarily expect that it has let's say human-like habits", BH²)*, whereas another user clearly experiences the system as a technical entity *("so it was a computer I was sitting opposite to", FW)*.

For example, [20] report about robots and interface agents that "the perception of a robot/agent and its assigned role can be very different from the perception and role intended by the developer of the artificial entity." [20, p. 20]. Besides differences between developer and user, ascriptions also vary from one user to the other. This implies that there is not 'one bundle of relational ascriptions' every user shares. In fact, each user 'creates' his individual bundle. Thus, relational ascriptions arise from user's subjectivity, rather than representing objective appraisals. Hence, we define relational ascriptions as user's **subjective interpretations, which concern the appearance, the implemented characteristics as well as the resulting behaviors of a Companion-system**.

All these individual interpretations had in common that they are **significant for the relationship between system and user**. This marks the substantial difference between relational ascriptions and mental models, which refer to ideas about function and structure of the system.

According to our empirical analysis [14], the reference to the relationship is entailed in **ascriptions regarding system's nature, its performance, requirements by the system and the relational offer of it**. Whether the system is experienced as a more human- or a more machine-like counterpart ('nature') having more or less advanced capabilities ('performance') influences the user's expectations about the system in the interaction and in the relationship to it *("it mostly understood what I wanted (…) it reasoned (…) I thought (…) cool (…) how advanced this technology is already", CT)*. The way requests by the system are interpreted ('requirements by the system') determines what expectations regarding the user's behavior the user ascribes to the system *("then I thought, oh my god, what does he just want to hear now", UK)*. Finally, the relational offer of the system includes notions about how the system is positioned to the user, how it gets into and stays in contact and which roles the user thinks the system assigns to him *("what is the point of that now (…) I just felt a bit provoked", SP)*.

The content of relational ascriptions was made up mostly by **anthropomorphic characteristics** the user ascribes to the system [14]. For example, one user ascribes interest to the system by saying *"you just felt like someone is really interested in you (…) it was just another kind of experience" (FK)*.

Functional and structural ascriptions are not excluded in UCI contexts, but become secondary. The priority of anthropomorphic ascriptions was explained by referring to two needs inherent in every user: the need to belong and the need for safety (cf. Sect. 3.1). Numerous examples in the literature underline the existence of anthropomorphization by users even when systems provide only small amounts of social cues [18] (e.g., [21]).

---

² User's initials are used in order to ensure anonymity.

Furthermore, relational ascriptions appeared to be often formed on an *implicit level of awareness*. For example, the following utterance allows interpreting the user's implicit ascription of nosiness to the system: *"one feels like being picked ones brains a little bit"(EG)*. This seems to be related with anthropomorphic content of ascriptions. Users tend to adopt an 'as-if-mode' (see also [12]) in reasoning about and interacting with Companion-systems, as if the system would be a human-like counterpart, without really reflecting upon this attitude.

According to [22], subjective denotations regarding systems could occur on a conscious (explicit) level, but also on a preconscious or unconscious (implicit) level. That is, because it has to be differentiated between explicit knowledge about a system and thereby conscious ascriptions on the one hand and the extensive implicitness of ascriptions on the other hand.

Moreover, we observed that relational ascriptions had a *dynamic character* (*"when it asked me I thought (...) that it really cobbles something individual-specific and when I see this in retrospective, I don't know why it needed this", CT*). During an interaction users are able to approve or falsify previous relational ascriptions, but are also able to create new ones. Therefore, the interaction history is the most relevant influential factor: Experiences within the interaction and reflections upon these help to verify, to falsify or to change relational ascriptions made before.

3.2.2   Factors Influencing Content and Quality of Relational Ascriptions

By 'quality' it is meant whether the relational ascription is a positive or negative one. For instance, ascribing to the system to be personally interested in the user and to help him in a certain situation represents a positive ascription. Instead, ascribing nosiness in the sense of following own interests, represents a negative ascription.

Our interview analysis revealed that there are factors influencing the quality of relational ascriptions. For instance, regarding the simulated individualization-focused interaction in our study one user said: *"for example the question for the shoe size and also for the age and one should give the full name (...) I think I didn't answer twice or I said I won't tell that (...) I've been suspicious" (SP)*. This indicates that the user's internal state influences the ascription evolving in the user.

Besides *user's internal state, also the context of an interaction* seems to influence the quality of relational ascriptions. In order to clarify this connection, imagine the following example: a computer crashes during the search for a nearby restaurant. If this happens during the summer holidays while one is relaxing on the veranda of a hotel room, one would probably not be upset or even ascribe malice or intentional provocation to the computer. In contrast, these ascriptions would probably occur while sitting in the office, being stressed because of preparing relevant documents before an important business associate arrives, who could barely fit this appointment into his tight time schedule.

Furthermore, we could recognize that the quality of relational ascriptions is influenced by *user's former experience* regarding human-machine interaction as well as human-human interaction. Previous contacts with humans and machines lead to preconceptions, expectations and assumptions the users adopt when or even before entering the interaction with the Companion-system for the first time (*"it is better than most of the computer voices I heard (...) it filters out more, it knows more, it is more human-like (...) it is not only such a yes-no-principle (...) it rather speaks to you, that was really thrilling", CT).*

Besides experiences with other technical systems (way of use, positive and negative experiences with them etc.), especially interpersonal experiences are supposed to guide the quality of relational ascriptions *("like a child who is taken at the hand without being informed, well, it shall accompany the parents but it isn't told why", SP).* The systems' behavior is interpreted in the sense of what is called "relational schemas" [23] in the user: "cognitive structures representing regularities in patterns of interpersonal related-ness [that consist of] an interpersonal script for the interaction pattern, a self-schema for how self is experienced in that interpersonal situation, and a schema for the other person in the interaction" [23, p. 461]. Because these schemas go back to individual primary interpersonal experiences with significant others, they differ from one person to the other. Based on the "schema for the other person" the resulting relational ascriptions to the system are made up by individual anthropomorphic attributes.

Besides the schema developed for the system, relational schemas also include a self-schema of the interacting person. It seems that the ***user's self-related experiences*** during the interaction are reflected by him on the basis of his self-schema. These reflections reverberate to the quality of relational ascriptions to the system that are created. For example, one female user reported about her feeling during the individualization-focused interaction sequence *"I really felt such a refusal" (SP)*, where a negative ascription arising in her, e.g., a pressure to surrender, may be interpreted.

3.2.3   Factors Being Influenced by Content and Quality of Relational Ascriptions

Users' utterances like *"I tried all the time to speak slow and accented, because I thought it wouldn't recognize my speech otherwise" (SB)* suggest that the quality of relational ascriptions itself influences the **user's behavioral choices during the interaction**.

In [14] it could be shown that regarding an individualization-focused interaction with a Companion-system, the information disclosing behavior of the user is connected to the quality of his ascriptions to it. In this case, the relationship is not always a linear one. Paradox effects were recognized, too, and discussed in the sense of user's need to belong. For example, some of the users disclosed even personal and intimate data although negative ascriptions towards the system appeared. This paradox is illustrated in the following user utterance, where unpleasant persistency is ascribed to the system: *"anyhow it is only a computer and you didn't know what it will do with your information and then you just said anything for making it shut up" (FW).*

Besides influencing the user's behavior, the quality of relational ascriptions seems to influence, if not even makes up the **relationship between user and system**, too *("with the human who speaks, with the voice, you built up a bond really at the beginning when you say 'hello, my name is', FK").* It determines whether or not a relationship is built up, what kind of relationship it is and if is maintained over a longer period of time.

3.3 Summarizing Definition of Relational Ascriptions

In order to sum up our explanation of users' relational ascriptions, a definition of the concept is given subsequently.

Relational ascriptions are

- Mainly unconscious individual user's interpretations with regard to the appearance and the implemented characteristics as well as the resulting behaviors of a Companion-system that are significant for the relationship between system and user.
- They entail interpretations regarding system's nature, its performance, requirements by the system as well as the relational offer of the system.
- They represent mostly notions of anthropomorphic content, which develop in the user before, during and after the interaction with the system.
- They are dynamic; hence, they can be verified, falsified or changed through interactional experiences.

Their quality is influenced by

- The context of the interaction,
- Users' former relational experiences from human-machine and human-human interaction,
- As well as users' self-related experiences during UCI.

The quality of relational ascriptions influences

- Users' behavioral choices during the interaction.
- As well as the question if a relationship between user and system will be established and maintained and how it will look like.

4 Practical Implications and Future Research

Based on empirical investigations, we developed a concept dealing with relational aspects of users' individual notions regarding Companion-systems. For the design and evaluation of relational artifacts, examining users' individual experiences while interacting with them is indispensable. Besides researching individual notions about systems' structure and functioning as represented in mental models, we propose to supplementary consider what we called 'users' relational ascriptions'.

We suggest understanding relational ascriptions as 'interpretation foil' for users' experiences of interactions with Companion-systems. By ascribing to the system the user creates his individual view on it. The ascription-based view on the system is experienced as 'real' and 'objective' by him. This perspective may supplement works on user experience, which focus on investigating relationships between user experience as a summarized overall evaluation and distinct psychological variables [24, 25].

Of course, further investigations are needed to confirm our concept and our findings. In order to examine users' relational ascriptions, we benefitted from using an open, narration-generating user interview as data collection method as well as structuring, interpretation-focused qualitative methods for analyzing the interview material.

Qualitative methods are based on the assumption that spirit and purpose of experiences and actions can only be inferred by subjective meanings the experiencing or acting person ascribes to it [26]. Subjectivity and implicitness of users' relational ascriptions are strong arguments for adopting an idiographic research approach.

Future research is required in many respects. For instance, changes in users' relational ascriptions during long-term interactions with Companion-systems should be investigated. This is highly important when considering the design goal of relational artifacts to provide even long-term companionship to their users.

Moreover, research should face the challenge of making relational ascriptions applicable to the design of Companion-systems. If it is possible to combine these ascriptions with other individual user characteristics, individual user profiles could be build up. Then, it would be imaginable to derive profile-specific dialog strategies that may be implemented in the system. These strategies could be used to foster positive relational ascriptions and reduce negative ones. Thereby, user-companion interactions could be optimized in terms of comfortable long-term interaction patterns suitable for each individual user.

Acknowledgement. The presented study is performed in the framework of the Transregional Collaborative Research Centre SFB/TRR 62 "A Companion-Technology for Cognitive Technical Systems" funded by the German Research Foundation (DFG). The responsibility for the content of this paper lies with the authors.

References

1. Turkle, S.: Sociable technologies: enhancing human performance when the computer is not a tool but a companion. In: Roco, M.C., Bainbridge, W.S. (eds.) Converging Technologies for Improving Human Performance, pp. 150–158. Springer, Dordrecht (2003)
2. Böhle, K., Bopp, K.: What a vision: the artificial companion. A piece of vision assessment including an expert survey. STI Stud. **10**(1), 155–186 (2014)
3. Wilks, Y.: Artificial companions. Interdiscipl. Sci. Rev. **30**(2), 145–152 (2005)
4. Breazeal, C.: Designing Sociable Robots. MIT Press, Cambridge (2003)
5. Bickmore, T.W., Picard, R.W.: Establishing and maintaining long-term human-computer relationships. ACM Trans. Comput.-Hum. Interact. **12**(2), 293–327 (2005)
6. Wendemuth, A., Biundo, S.: A companion technology for cognitive technical systems. In: Esposito, A., Esposito, A.M., Vinciarelli, A., Hoffmann, R., Müller, V.C. (eds.) COST 2102. LNCS, vol. 7403, pp. 89–103. Springer, Heidelberg (2012)
7. Pfadenhauer, M., Dukat, C.: Künstlich begleitet: Der Roboter als neuer bester Freund des Menschen? [Artificially accompanied: the robot as man's new best friend? (in German)]. In: Grenz, T., Möll, G. (eds.) Unter Mediatisierungsdruck: Änderungen und Neuerungen in heterogenen Handlungsfeldern, pp. 189–210. Springer, Wiesbaden (2014)
8. Lange, J., Frommer, J.: Subjektives Erleben und intentionale Einstellung in Interviews zur Nutzer-Companion-Interaktion [Subjective experience and intentional stance in interveiws regarding user-companion interaction (in German)]. In: Heiß, H.-U., Pepper, P., Schlinghoff, H., Schneider, J. (eds.) Informatik 2011. LNI, vol. 192, p. 240. Köllen, Bonn (2011)
9. Norman, D.A.: Some observations on mental models. In: Gentner, D.A., Stevens, A.L. (eds.) Mental Models. Erlbaum, Hillsdale (1983)

10. van der Veer, G.C., Melguizo, M.D.C.P.: Mental models. In: Jacko, J.A., Sears, A. (eds.) The Human-Computer Interaction Handbook. Fundamentals, Evolving Technologies and Emerging Applications, pp. 52–80. Lawrence Erlbaum Associates, Mahwah (2003)

11. Turner, P., Sobolewska, E.: Mental models, magical thinking, and individual differences. Hum. Technol. **5**(1), 90–113 (2009)

12. Turkle, S.: Authenticity in the age of digital companions. Interact. Stud. **8**(3), 501–517 (2007)

13. Weizenbaum, J.: ELIZA – a computer programm for the study of natural language communication between man and machine. Commun. ACM **9**(1), 36–45 (1966)

14. Krüger, J., Wahl, M., Frommer, J.: Making the system a relational partner: users' ascriptions in individualization-focused interactions with companion-systems. In: Berntzen, L., Böhm, S. (eds.) CENTRIC 2015, The Eighth International Conference on Advances in Human-Oriented and Personalized Mechanisms, Technologies, and Services, pp. 48–54. IARIA XPS Press/s.l. (2015)

15. Rösner, D., Frommer, J., Friesen, R., Haase, M., Lange, J., Otto, M.: LAST MINUTE: a multimodal corpus of speech-based user-companion interactions. In: Calzolari, N., Declerck, T., Doğan, M.U., Maegaard, B., Mariani, J., Odijk, J., Piperidis, S. (eds.) LREC 2012, pp. 2559–2566. European Language Resources Association/s.l. (2012)

16. Dennett, D.C.: The Intentional Stance. MIT Press, Cambridge (1987)

17. Maslow, A.: A theory of human motivation. Psychol. Rev. **50**(4), 370–396 (1943)

18. Krämer, N., Eimler, S., von der Pütten, A., Payr, S.: Theory of companions: what can theoretical models contribute to applications and understanding of human-robot interaction? Appl. Artif. Intell. **25**(6), 474–502 (2011)

19. Baumeister, R.F., Leary, M.R.: The need to belong: desire for interpersonal attachments as a fundamental human motivation. Psychol. Bull. **117**(3), 497–529 (1995)

20. Rosenthal-von der Pütten, A.M., Krämer, N.C.: The case of KITT and data - from science fiction to reality? A social psychology perspective on artificial companions. STI Studies **10**(1), 11–29 (2014)

21. Nass, C., Moon, Y.: Machines and mindlessness: social responses to computers. J. Soc. Issues **56**(1), 81–103 (2000)

22. Harper, J.R.: Please do not lean on the computer. It has feelings too: the relationships transferred by humans to technology. Ph.D. thesis, University of Wollongong, Australia (2007)

23. Baldwin, M.W.: Relational schemas and the processing of social information. Psych. Bull. **112**(3), 461–484 (1992)

24. Hassenzahl, M.: User experience (UX): towards an experiential perspective on product quality. In: IHM 2008 Proceedings of the 20th International Conference on l'Interaction Homme-Machine (IHM 2008), pp. 11–15. ACM, New York (2008)

25. Karapanos, E.: Modeling Users' Experiences with Interactive Systems. Springer, Berlin (2013)

26. Frommer, J., Rennie, D.L.: Methodology, method, and quality of qualitative research. Psychother. Psych. Med. **56**(5), 210–217 (2006)

Evolving Framework for Building Companionship Among Human and Assistive Systems

Vikas Luthra[✉], Arvind Sethia, and Sanjay Ghosh

Samsung R&D Institute, Bangalore, India
luthra.vikas07@gmail.com, arvindsethia087@gmail.com,
sanjayghosh@gmail.com

Abstract. The recent progress in artificial intelligence is allowing assistive systems like the voice-based assistant, virtual agents to become more personalized and adaptable. The role of these systems is also shifting from being a mere assistant to a person-al companion. However 'personal companionship' being a subjective term lies open to interpretation, thus posing a challenge for the creators of these assistive systems. This study is an attempt to address this challenge with a user-centric approach. Based on insights gathered from an activity based method called forced photo elicitation techniques with 25 users, we evolved Human Machine Companionship Framework, as a reference tool for designing effective personalized connections between assistive systems and its user. We describe each of the essential behavioural traits that a companion should exhibit and their evolution with time and information gained. Lastly, we establish the use of this companionship framework by discussing its application in case of the social robots.

Keywords: Companionship · Personalization · Elicitation techniques · Assistive systems · Human-Human interaction · Human-Computer interaction

1 Introduction

Be it a personal computer, smartphones, voice-based personal assistants, virtual agents/ companion, robots etc., there is a continuous focus on these systems to be perceived more human-like and natural. These systems have become a part of our daily lives by assisting in numerous activities, making our lives much easier. With recent shifts in the design of such smart technical systems, these are now being looked at, not only from a utilitarian perspective but also in the social and emotional contexts. The attention of Human-Computer Interaction (HCI) community is rapidly growing towards the adaptation of these systems based on the user's needs, habits and mental abilities, and a continuous focus is on ensuring that they are perceived, accepted and utilised by their users as personal and empathetic assistants. Hence, we see an overall shift of technological devices from being considered as mere assistants to behave like the companion systems (CS).

In future, these systems will be our artificial companion [1, 2], behaving more like our personal and empathetic assistants and could be complementing the social roles and

© Springer International Publishing Switzerland 2016
M. Kurosu (Ed.): HCI 2016, Part III, LNCS 9733, pp. 138–147, 2016.
DOI: 10.1007/978-3-319-39513-5_13

needs of our partners, friends, caretakers etc. With recent advances in artificial intelligence (AI) in terms of emotional recognition, natural language and speech processing, it would be possible for these systems to understand our affective states, behaviour, desires, aspirations, personal goals effectively and behave accordingly.

Many studies, especially in the area of Human-Robot Interaction (HRI), have set the development of personal companion as a goal [4–6]. Research has also been conducted to understand the effect of various behavioural traits like empathy [7] social presence [8] in building a human robot companionship. The results of these studies suggest the need for incorporating social sense, emotion and traits of companionship in these cognitive technical systems. Past studies [3, 9] have even shown the relevance of similar emotions in the context of Human-Human Interaction being applied to Human Machine Interaction (HMI) for future companion systems.

Reeves and Nass [10] demonstrated with several experiments that users are naturally biased to ascribe certain personality traits to machines, to PCs, and other types of media. Therefore, it is important to understand how these perceptions of personality influence the interaction and how a coherent personality can be utilised for such technical systems. Further, for a designer and developer of these companion systems, it is important to have directions or framework on how to proceed in designing a personality of these systems.

However, a little effort has been there in understanding the overall process of building a long term companionship among humans and the technical systems. We try to overcome this gap by understanding the meaning of companion and companionship from the human-human interaction point of view, using an activity based exploratory user centred approach called forced photo elicitation technique. Some of the questions we try to address are –

- What are the different expectations or perceptions that people have around the whole notion of companionship?
- What kind of behavioural patterns or traits do people look for in their companions? What is the role of time in terms of building companionship?
- Whom do people consider or relate to as their companions?

In this paper, we have explored the possible answers to these questions by evolving a time and information based Companionship Framework. We describe the Companionship Framework by first discussing the different characteristics of companionship. Then we describe the essential behavioural traits that are required for the building of companionship. Further, we try to explain the expression of each of these traits with time and how each of these develops with an increase in the amount of information and time.

Lastly, inspired by our user-centric understanding of human-human companionship we discuss the application of this Companionship Framework in the context of human-robot companionship.

2   User Study

2.1   Forced Photo Elicitation Technique

The research questions under exploration in this study being abstract in nature and the definition of 'Companionship' itself being very subjective, conventional user-centered design methods were not applicable. We used an activity-based user-centered approach called Forced Photo Elicitation technique [11], which is found suitable for such studies. In this activity, around 120 random samples of photos with abstract content were printed and were displayed to a participant. A total of 25 participants were involved in this study evenly distributed across various age groups and the two genders. Participants were asked to carefully scan through all of those photos, and then were asked the question, 'what is a companion for you?' They were asked to pick minimum five images in prioritized order as their response to the question (Fig. 1). They were then probed to explain their interpretation of each abstract image and how they associated the content of the image with the word 'companion'. Further probing questions were asked during this session to elicit numerous user stories.

Fig. 1. User performing photo elicitation technique

2.2   Research Analysis

All the interactive user sessions were audio recorded and transcribed. The data was then analyzed using grounded theory approach, which included "affinity clusters" of newly generated themes and categories. In the first level analysis of raw user data, numerous behavior *traits* coupled with different *companionship attributes* emerged. These were then regrouped to generate *mega-categories and hierarchy of themes*. Themes were chosen by putting all post-it notes (containing observations and respondents' quotes) together, and then arranging them in piles, in terms of those notes that went together. Each pile or cluster was given a name, according to what best described all the items and contents under it [14].

In order to understand the relationship and connections between the *traits* and *mega-categories* they were analyzed using *Consensus Mapping* technique [12, 13]. In this technique all the identified *mega-categories* were written along with all the associated *traits* for each of the *mega-category* written below them. It was observed that these *mega categories* displayed a hierarchal pattern with incremental progression, i.e. each trait was seen to be supporting the next trait. For instance, *familiarity* as a trait was found to get developed and matured into healthy *curiosity*. At last significant *traits* with greater impact were demarcated leading to the establishment of the hierarchical relationship and the Companionship Framework.

3 Human Companionship Framework

In our research, we considered 'Companionship' to be a connection established be-tween two or more entities that are similar or diverse in nature. Human is always considered to be one among the two entities. Thus, there could be companionship among human-to-human, human-to-another being like the pet or human to an object such as book, music etc. Our study indicated that irrespective of the entities involved, the evolution of companionship may follow a similar high-level progressive path, which became the basic assumption for our proposed Companionship Framework. For the people of HCI community, such framework can be a reference to understand how companionship may develop over time between the involved entities and then create design interventions to support this if one of the entities is an intelligent agent. To cognize the companionship framework it is imperative to know the distinct characteristics of companionship which forms the foundation of such framework, the building blocks and meta-categories involved which bind the numerous behavior traits together and the evolution of these traits based on the amount of information gained and time spent.

3.1 Characteristics of Companionship

In our study, we identified various characteristics of companionship that were re-grouped together to form the four prominent themes: power and control, amplified emotions, sensory immersion and attachment.

There is an equation of power and control seen between the two entities involved in companionship. The equation may be balanced, but there inevitably occurs a tug and pull of power and control between the two entities. Based on the power and control dynamics seen between the two, these two entities were termed as a 'Reacher' and a 'Settler'. Reacher refers to an entity who is reaching for somebody of the higher power, whereas, Settler is the other entity who settles with somebody of lesser power. The equation of Reacher and Settler is very important in building a companionship which would be seen throughout our framework.

Similarly, through our user data, we inferred that whenever a person experiences amplified emotions such as joy, fear, anger, etc., they are inclined to have their companion(s) experience/express emotions alongside them. The expressed emotions would be dependent on the entities existing mental and emotional state, their interpersonal relationships etc.

When companionship matures, there is a certain sensory immersion observed between the entities, where each of them connects by sensorial intimation like touch, smell or visual and become extremely aware of each other presence.

As strong connection begins to develop between the two companions, the attachment becomes stronger. This could lead to the building of trust and a sense of protection between the entities, where the Reacher seeks for protection from the Settler and Settler is the protection provider.

3.2   Companionship Progression and Building Blocks

We identified four major Building Blocks of companionship: 'Compatibility',

'Presence', 'Trust', 'Connect' that binds the numerous behavioral traits. The foundation of companionship starts with establishing compatibility among the companions (Fig. 2). As the entities mature from one trait to another and move in a progressive wavelike pattern, it traverses from compatibility to experiencing a sense of presence to the building of trust and ultimately the formation of strong connects among the companions. This progression is strongly dependent on the level of interaction and time spent together. Drawing an analogy with the human process of ageing, as the entity crosses each stage it retains the compound information gathered in the previous stages and levels. In case a behavior trait is skipped or given insufficient time to develop, the

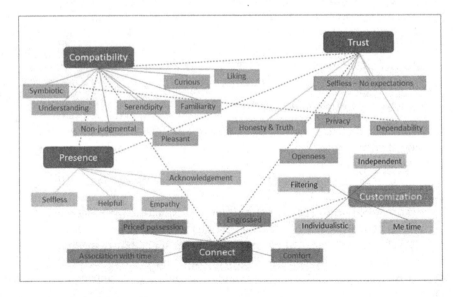

Fig. 2. Consensus mapping for interrelationship among traits

companionship bond may break and a difference of opinion among entities may occur as each level builds on its preceding levels.

3.3 Evolution of Behavioural Traits

The behavioral traits are explained, as factors of the four primary characteristics, i.e. the Reacher-Settler, Amplified emotions, Sensory immersion and Attachment. Figure 3 shows the hierarchical progression of companionship framework. It is a graphical representation of the amount of time the involved entities have spent together to the amount of information gathered about each other.

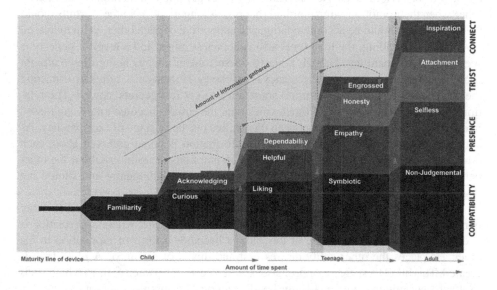

Fig. 3. The hierarchical framework for building companionship

Familiarity in the context of companionship means allowing each other to be their natural self. At this stage of the relationship, both the entities try to find a similar sense of purpose within each other. Similarities could be in terms of interests, likes or dislikes, beliefs, attitude, etc.

In the *curiosity* phase, the entities learn about one another, by noticing or observing actions, language, etc. The learning doesn't mean mimicking, but it's about knowing each other to make the familiarity quotient stronger. Humor is also added to shift the dynamics from formal to casual. Simultaneously, *acknowledgement* makes the presence felt through any noticeable action like gesture, body language, smell, etc. which signifies physical presence. In this phase the casual behavior becomes more pronounced and the companionship becomes stronger owing to each other's' presence. A state of ease is established between companions alongside a degree of acceptance as seen through *fondness* and *liking*. The sensory immersion is also seen, where the Reacher and the Settler recognize each other through their sensory stimuli (like touch, smell, etc.).

Helping or providing assistance to your companion is also an important trait. This help is perceived to be selfless in nature and it is more about increasing the sense of protection. In this case, one entity feels that the other entity is there whenever required, for any support. A sense of *attachment* and *trust* begins to develop at this stage. The Reacher knows the Settler to a certain extent and the Settler starts trusting the Reacher. The Settler becomes dependable on the Reacher for certain tasks and provides a degree of access or autonomy to take certain decisions. The autonomy leads the equation of power and control between the Reacher and the Settler to mature on equal terms. This is the start of the *symbiotic* stage, where the relationship develops in a way that mutual interests grow. The two entities also tend to understand each other much better and empathetic behavior is seen. Here presence is very important. Companions look for each other when their emotions are amplified (happiness, anger, etc.), so the warmth should be felt and they should be accommodating and supportive of each other. With increased level of understanding, the trust level also becomes stronger and a level of honesty is seen among companions. Though honesty doesn't mean always being direct/straight forward and a certain degree of diplomacy is necessary. Honesty also refers to respecting the 'others' privacy and the ability to sometimes forget few secrets as well. The relationship also acquires a sense of timelessness and the entities become totally engrossed in one another. The connection between the entities reaches a stage of transparency. As companionship matures over time, a lot of information is being gathered about each other. This gathered information may lead to assumptions or opinions about the other person's beliefs. However, companions shall remain non-judgmental and should not disrespect other person's belief in any situation.

In final stage power equation between Settler and Reacher is reversed, the Reacher is now the Settler and vice versa. This leads to the *selfless* state, where appreciation is exchanged to increase trust; one of the entities becomes a form of motivation to the other. He places the other entity desires first and thinks of self-next. A blind trust is created. This blind trust creates a strong sense of protection between entities which leads to attachment among them. Finally, the bonding among the companions is at its pinnacle. They become an inspiration to each other and start setting higher goals. This healthy competition keeps them growing and *connected*.

3.4 Social Roles

During our discussions, most of the participants associated companion with various social roles in their lives. We did the frequency mapping of all the social roles and compared it with the categories in our framework. The most prominent roles appeared to be a friend, spouse, siblings, parents, pets, book, music and nature. Spouse as a social role was mostly spoken about.

4 Application of Framework

The proposed Companionship Framework can be applied to various situations that involve companionship relation. In this section, we demonstrate the use of this framework in designing the behavior, interactions and encounters of a social robot with its user. Once the robot is brought and introduced to the family and home scenario, it is programmed to do assistive tasks and behave like an assistant. At this point, in the framework of companionship, it is at the initial stage and on the maturity line of devices, it is at the start, like an infant who is new to the world. Referring to the Settler and Reacher characteristics between companions, it becomes inevitable that the robot is always the Reacher since humans would like to play the role of the controller and the Settler.

In the first stage of the framework, the robot and the user start to establish familiarity between them, by getting to understand each other. Once the familiarity is established, the robot matures to curiosity about various subjects around it. The robot begins to pose subtle questions to the user such as, 'how was your day?' This signifies the start of casual behavior with the user. This casual behavior will also induce a friendly atmosphere around the existence of the robot which could be strengthened through the little use of humor. The acknowledgement develops alongside curiosity, where the robot begins to make its presence felt. As the robot get to know each member of the house, it starts performing simple actions like waking them up every morning, greeting them with a gesture of a smile, etc. These small gestures and questioning mature the companion traits in the robot and a personalized behavior is established with each and every member of the house. When the first three behavior traits are strengthened gradually, a sense of liking is developed towards the robot. The robot is being started to be perceived as a family member, who is able to process certain feelings of the other family members. For example 'I like the dress you are wearing, you look beautiful'. In the previous four stages, the robot is learning and growing up like a child, developing curiosity and a sense of understanding about the environment. With all the information gathered and the time spent to reach the 'liking' stage, a change could be observed in robot's behavior from extremely formal to largely casual and personalized according to the user.

In the next stage, the robot is matured and entered into the teenage stage. It has become helpful, and other than the assistive task it is able to detect problems and provide suggestions to the user, like 'the gas is about to get over, get it refilled'. Here the trust towards the robots has started to develop. This trust is built to such a level, that the robot now has a certain level of autonomy, making way for the dependability stage. In this stage, the robot exercises a degree of freedom to take decisions on the user's behalf. For instance, the robot gets the leaking pipe fixed without asking the user; thereby helping the user in easing the task. This is where both Reacher (robot) and Settler (user) starts to meet on equal terms; the power and control will come to equilibrium, which will be seen in the stage of symbiosis, empathy and honesty. Gradually the robot gets even more autonomous and casual with the user. The robot understands the user's emotional value and becomes more empathetic to situations. It is desired to see the robot mature up to this level. In the stage of non-judgment, self-lessness, attachment and comfort, the table reverses; the Reacher becomes Settler and Settler – the Reacher. It is seen that with more information and time, the robot may have higher control, like a mature adult, understanding the situation and comforting the user.

This storyline is a scenario created to explain the framework, which may differ based on the assumption of the framework. Similarly, this framework can be applied to other applications like conversational agents, voice assistant and mechanical robots as well.

5   Conclusion and Future Work

Our understanding of 'companionship' based on user insights led us to evolve the proposed Hierarchical Companionship Framework. The main applicability of this framework is, as a guideline and a reference for designers and solution developers of intelligent agent systems to systematically define the personality and behavior to transform such systems towards being companion to its end users. We have applied this framework to create several design solutions for a social robot product with an objective of making the product as a user's companion. In further research, we would be evolving the proposed framework to be more concrete reference tool for designing various companionship based products. As part of the next step in our research we have already applied this framework in case of designing a personality for voice based applications.

References

1. Wilks, Y.: Artificial companions as a new kind of interface to the future internet. Chicago (2006)
2. Floridi, L.: Artificial intelligence's new frontier: artificial companions and the fourth revolution. Metaphilosophy **39**(4–5), 651–655 (2008). Chicago
3. Traue, H.C., Ohl, F., Brechmann, A., Schwenker, F., Kessler, H., Limbrecht, K., Walter, S.: A framework for emotions and dispositions in man-companion interaction. In: Coverbal Synchrony in Human-Machine Interaction, pp. 99–140. Science Publishers, New Hampshire, USA (2013)
4. Dautenhahn, K., Woods, S., Kaouri, C., Walters, M.L., Koay, K.L., Werry, I.: What is a robot companion-friend, assistant or butler? In: 2005 IEEE/RSJ International Conference on Intelligent Robots and Systems (IROS 2005), pp. 1192–1197. IEEE (2005)
5. Meerbeek, B., Saerbeck, M., Bartneck, C.: Iterative design process for robots with personality. In: Kerstin Dautenhahn, editeur, AISB2009 Symposium on New Frontiers in Human-Robot Interaction, pp. 94–101 (2009)
6. Ruckert, J.H., Kahn Jr., P.H., Kanda, T., Ishiguro, H., Shen, S., Gary, H.E.: Designing for sociality in HRI by means of multiple personas in robots. In: Proceedings of the 8th ACM/ IEEE International Conference on Human-Robot Interaction, pp. 217–218. IEEE Press (2013)
7. Pereira, A., Leite, I., Mascarenhas, S., Martinho, C., Paiva, A.: Using empathy to improve human-robot relationships. In: Lamers, M.H., Verbeek, F.J. (eds.) Human-Robot Personal Relationships. LNICST, vol. 59, pp. 130–138. Springer, Heidelberg (2011)
8. Tapus, A., Mataric, M.J.: Socially assistive robots: the link between personality, empathy, physiological signals, and task performance. In: AAAI Spring Symposium: Emotion, Personality, and Social Behavior, pp. 133–140 (2008)
9. Walter, S., Wendt, C., Böhnke, J., Crawcour, S., Tan, J.W., Chan, A., Traue, H.C.: Similarities and differences of emotions in human–machine and human–human interactions: what kind of emotions are relevant for future companion systems? Ergonomics **57**(3), 374–386 (2014)

10. Reeves, B., Nass, C.: The media equation: how people treat computers, televisions, and new media like real people and places. Cambridge University Press, New York (1996)
11. Harper, D.: Talking about pictures: a case for photo elicitation. Visual Stud. **17**(1), 13–26 (2002)
12. Zaltman, G., Dotlich, D.L., Cairo, P.C.: How Customers Think. Audio-Tech Business Book Summaries (2003)
13. Hart, S., Boroush, M., Enk, G., Hornick, W.: Managing complexity through consensus mapping: technology for the structuring of group decisions. Acad. Manag. Rev. **10**(3), 587–600 (1985)
14. Ryan, G.W., Bernard, H.R.: Techniques to identify themes. Field Methods **15**(1), 85–109 (2003)

Influence of Personal Characteristics on Nonverbal Information for Estimating Communication Smoothness

Yumi Wakita$^{(\boxtimes)}$, Yuta Yoshida, and Mayu Nakamura

Osaka Institute of Technology, Osaka, Japan
yumi.wakita@oit.ac.com

Abstract. To realize a system that can provide a new topic of discussion for improving lively and smooth human-to-human communication, a method to estimate conversation smoothness is necessary. To develop a process for estimating conversation smoothness, we confirmed the effectiveness of using fundamental frequency (F0). The analytic results of free dyadic conversation using the F0 of laughter utterances in conversation are strongly dependent on personal characteristics. Moreover, F0s without laughter utterances are effective in estimating conversation smoothness.

Both the average value and the standard deviation (SD) value of F0s in smooth conversation tend to be higher than in non-smooth conversation. The differences between the SD of the "smooth" and "non-smooth" segments are shown to be significant when using a t-test, where the confidence level is 95 %.

Keywords: Conversation smoothness · Nonverbal information · Fundamental frequency

1 Introduction

Recently, with more senior citizens living alone and reclusive, many communities, companies, or schools think human-to-human communication is very important. They are interested in a system to aid human-to-human communication. The purpose of this study is to explore a system which provides a topic of discussion for carrying on lively and smooth human-to-human communication.

Several studies have been proposed which use systems to guide smooth communications by introducing some appropriate topics [1, 2]. However the communication atmosphere changes over time. The topic, timing, and method of communicating should be changed when considering the communication atmosphere.

We are developing a system which provides information about suitable timing by considering the communication atmosphere. The system can understand whether or not the human-to-human communication is proceeding smoothly. When sensing there has been little progress during the conversation, the system attempts to provide a topic for leading a smoother discussion. For practical use, it is necessary to find factors which are effective for measuring the communication and developing a process of recognizing the communication atmosphere.

© Springer International Publishing Switzerland 2016
M. Kurosu (Ed.): HCI 2016, Part III, LNCS 9733, pp. 148–157, 2016.
DOI: 10.1007/978-3-319-39513-5_14

2 Conventional Approaches to Estimate the Communication Atmosphere

Several papers illustrated the relationship between communication atmosphere and nonverbal communication [3, 4]. These papers suggest it is possible to estimate communication atmosphere using nonverbal communication. In addition, several methods which can measure the liveliness in human-to-human conversations using nonverbal information have been proposed [5–7]. These papers explain that the system measures liveliness based on whether many people speak at the same time or everyone speaks in turn.

However, more detailed analysis of nonverbal communication is necessary to improve the estimate's accuracy. When thinking deeply or listening attentively, we sometimes keep quiet in free conversation. Even if all member keep quiet, the conversation isn't always deadlocked. Even if only one person continues to speak for a long time, the listeners are not always bored. The conventional methods cannot estimate these communication atmospheres correctly. It is necessary to estimate not only "liveliness," but also "smoothness" to provide a topic of conversation at a suitable time.

On the other hand, in spite of nonverbal communications including several useful factors to understand the communication atmosphere, they have not been used effectively. Several papers suggest that because nonverbal behavior greatly depends on people, it cannot be used. If the system cannot understand whether a nonverbal behavior depends on the person or the communication atmosphere, it would be difficult to estimate the communication smoothness.

We would like to develop a method to estimate conversation smoothness using nonverbal information. To achieve highly accurate estimates, it is necessary to remove personal characteristics from nonverbal information before the estimation begins. For nonverbal information, we selected "fundamental frequency" (F0) and analyzed the relationship between F0 and communication smoothness by considering the factors dependent on personal characteristics.

In this paper, we report the results of our analysis and suggest the most effective factors for estimating conversation smoothness.

3 Ability of Nonverbal Information to Estimate Conversation Smoothness

We made several video recordings of free dyadic conversations and confirmed the probability of the communication smoothness estimate using nonverbal information in the recorded database.

3.1 Conversation Database

We recorded ten sets of three-minute long, free dyadic conversation (between two persons). The conditions are shown in Table 1. All members were not meeting for the first time, but we could make pairs with those who have never spoken before.

Table 1. Conditions of conversation

Number of speakers	7 males, 3 females
Number of conversations	10 (four pairs of males, two pairs of females, four pairs with one female and one male)
Conversation periods	Three minutes
Conversation condition	Free dyadic conversation

We observed video data of two people conversing in two different scenarios. The two scenarios were as follows:

- Smooth conversation (S): the topic had not been decided yet. Speakers searched for a topic which interested both of them.
- Non-smooth conversation (NS): the topic for both of the speakers was already chosen and they spoke smoothly or eagerly.

The results of pairing two people were very similar. The 96 % parts paired both of the speakers in each scenario. Table 2 shows the ratio of "smooth" and "non- smooth" scenarios for all observations.

Table 2. Configuration ratios of each part–"smooth (S)" and "non-smooth (NS)"

Pair	A	B	C	D	E	F	G	H	I	J
S	0.64	0.63	0.82	0.95	0.96	0.96	1.00	1.00	1.00	1.00
NS	0.36	0.37	0.18	0.05	0.04	0.04	0.00	0.00	0.00	0.00

Most "non-smooth" parts were at the beginning part of each conversation. In the case of the pairs A–F, they found a suitable topic in the middle of the conversation, and subsequently, the conversation atmosphere became smoother. In the case of G–J, the speakers explored several topics before initiating their conversations and the conversations were considered "non-smooth" throughout.

We analyzed the A–F conversations by comparing the "smooth" and "non-smooth" scenarios. At first, we noted the "silent interval length (no speech)" and "length of one utterance."

Table 3. Ratio of silent interval length for each scenario

Pair	A	B	C	D	E	F
S	0.14	0.38	0.23	0.13	0.20	0.25
NS	0.20	0.33	0.08	0.33	0.16	0.29

Table 4. Average length of one utterance [Sec.]

Pair	A	B	C	D	E	F
S	2.44	0.89	1.69	2.83	1.72	1.34
NS	1.90	1.04	3.11	1.16	1.63	1.23

In general, it seems that when a conversation progresses smoothly, the silent interval lengths are shorter and utterance lengths are longer. However, the results of Tables 3 and 4 show that both are unrelated to smoothness. The results suggest that other factors should be determined to estimate conversation smoothness.

Examples of silent interval in smoothness are:

- The communication progresses using gestures (hand movements, nodding, etc.)
- Carefully assessing their answers.

Examples of non-smooth conversation intervals are:

- Searching for a conversation topic.
- An ingratiating smile while speaking.

3.2 The Probability of Estimating Conversation Smoothness Using Nonverbal Information

We processed three types of communication data from the original recorded video. The three types of data are as follows:

1. Only images without speech
2. Only speech without images
3. Only nonverbal communication (deleting language information from 2.)

To delete language information, the speech data was processed through low-pass-filter with a cut-off frequency of 300 Hz.

We asked three people to watch or listen to the original video and the three processed conversations, and to select the scenes from each where they could provide a new topic. We also asked that they do not interrupt when they felt the conversation progress was smooth. All the scenes extracted by these three people were included in "non-smooth" parts.

We compared the extracted scenes by using the original video and the processed data. The scenes extracted from the original video were regarded as "correct" and calculated the recall and precision rates of other processed data.

We used only the A–C conversations in Table 2 because the other conversations had very few "non-smooth" segments and we couldn't select the multiple scenes.

The number of correct scenes from the A–C conversations are three from A, four from B, and five from C. We calculated the recall and precision rates for each processed dataset compared to the original data. Each rate is shown in Figs. 1 and 2. The recall and precision rates are the average of three people.

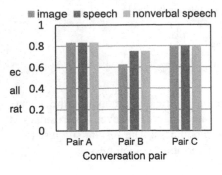

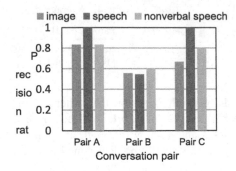

Fig. 1. Recall of each conversation   **Fig. 2.** Precision of each conversation

These figures illustrate the following:

- All of the recall rates are neither perfect nor low. These are all over 60 %.
- The differences of the processes among the pairs are very small.
- The performance of the precision rates depends on the pairs.
- The processed "speech" data has the highest precision rate. However, the differences between using the verbal information and nonverbal information are small for all pairs.
- Comparing nonverbal information, recall and precision rates were higher in "nonverbal speech" than in "image only."

These results indicate the difference between verbal and nonverbal is small. Both recall and precision are high. The nonverbal speech information can be useful for estimating smoothness. However, the estimation accuracy using only one factor of nonverbal information has limitations. Many factors would be necessary to estimate conversation smoothness perfectly.

4   A Study of Estimating Conversation Smoothness Using Fundamental Frequency (F0)

4.1   The Relationship Between the F0 of Each Utterance and Conversation Smoothness

We analyzed the relationship between the F0 and conversation smoothness. We calculated the averages of F0 of each utterance (Ave-F0), and their standard deviations of F0 (SD-F0) for six speakers from the A-C conversations. Figure 3 shows the average of the Ave-F0 and Fig. 4 shows the average of the SD-F0.

These results show that F0 values do not depend on smoothness. The differences between "smooth" and "non-smooth" are small for all six speakers. The standard deviations of F0, which shows the dynamics of F0 for an utterance, tended to illustrate

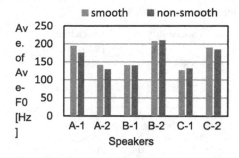

Fig. 3. Average of Ave-F0 for each speaker   **Fig. 4.** Average of SD-F0 for each speaker

that the values of non-smooth are smaller than those for smooth. However, this tendency depends on the speakers. By using a t-test, we can confirm that the differences between smooth and non-smooth are not significant.

4.2 The Influence of F0 on Laughter Utterance for Estimating Smoothness

The conversation data include several utterances of laughter. Figure 5 shows the ratio of laughter utterances in "smooth" or "non-smooth" scenarios to all utterances for each conversation.

The total laughter utterance ratio of both "smooth" and "non-smooth" are about 25 %. The characteristics of laughter utterances should be clear to estimate smoothness correctly.

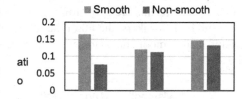

Fig. 5. Ratio of laughter utterances to all utterances

4.2.1 Classification of Laughter in the Data

Nishio and Koyama [8] explained that laughter utterances can be classified in general by "pleasantness" or "sociability." We classified the laughter into two types—basically, "pleasantness" and "sociability." However, several occurrences of laughter include speech. We added two more types, "pleasantness with speech" and "sociability with speech." We asked two people to add a type tag to each utterance of laughter in the data. Before tagging, we explained the meaning of "pleasantness" and "sociability" using Nishio's paper, and confirmed that they understood. The tagging results by both persons are very similar. Table 5 shows the number of laughter utterances for each type. The numbers in Table 5 are only laughter utterances which were regarded as the same type by both taggers.

Table 5. Number of laugh utterances for each class

Total	Pleasantness		Pleasantness with speech		Sociability		Sociability with speech	
Speaker	NS	S	NS	S	NS	S	NS	S
A-1	1	1	1	0	2	7	0	0
A-2	0	0	2	2	0	0	0	3
B-1	6	2	1	2	2	3	0	2
B-2	2	3	0	2	3	1	0	0
C-1	0	5	0	1	5	0	0	0
C-2	0	4	0	0	4	0	0	0

Table 5 shows that "pleasantness" tends to occur in smooth conversation. However "pleasantness" laughs do not always occur in smooth conversation and "sociability" laughs do not always occur in non-smooth conversation. The relationship between the laugh types and smoothness depends on the speakers.

4.2.2   Analysis of Laughter Utterances

The number of laughs for each speaker is not large. But two speakers, 2-A and 2-B, had pleasant laughs in both periods of "smooth" and "non-smooth" conversation. We compared the F0 of the pleasant laughs during "smooth" and "non-smooth" conversation. These results are shown in Figs. 6 and 7.

With both speakers, the F0 of the pleasant laughs in smooth conversation is higher than in a non-smooth one. However the tendency of the standard deviations depends on the speakers.

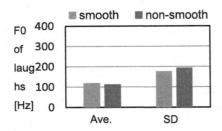

Fig. 6. Comparing the F0 of laughs during "smooth" and "non-smooth" conversation by Speaker B-1

Fig. 7. Comparing the F0 of laughs during "smooth" and "non-smooth" conversation by Speaker B-2

Figure 8 shows the distribution of Ave-F0 and SD-F0 values of two speakers. The results of a t-test show the difference between "smooth" and "non-smooth" is not significant, but the difference between the two speakers is significant when the confidence level is 95 %. These results suggest that the laughter utterances are not useful for estimating smoothness. We should remove these from utterance observations before estimating smoothness.

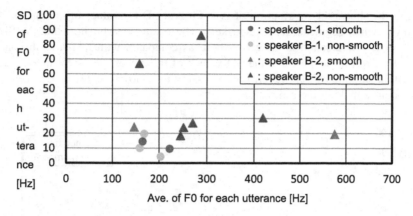

Fig. 8. Distribution of the Ave. and the SD for F0 of pleasant laughs for two speakers

4.3   Relationship Between the F0 of Utterances After Removing Laughter Observations and Conversation Smoothness

As a result of analyzing laughter utterances, we removed the laughter segments from the data and re-analyzed the relationship between the F0 and the conversation smoothness. The results are shown in Figs. 9 and 10.

With all speakers, the average F0s in smooth conversation are higher than in non-smooth conversation. The differences of four speakers are more significant than those of two speakers based on the results of a t-test which has a confidence level of 95 %.

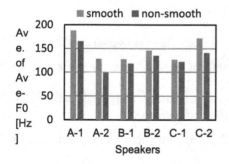

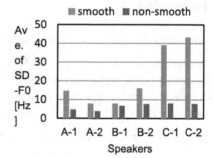

Fig. 9. Average of Ave-F0 for each speaker after removing the laughter segments

Fig. 10. Average of SD-F0 for each speaker after removing the laughter segments

The standard deviations of F0 in smooth conversation tend to be bigger than those of non-smooth conversations. The differences between "smooth" and "non-smooth" are significant as a result of a t-test which has a confidence level of 95 %.

Figure 11 shows the distribution of Ave-F0 and SD-F0 values of utterances after removing laughter segments for six speakers. The results clearly show that the SD of F0 in smooth conversation is increased more as compared with non-smooth conversation. These results suggest that the SD values of utterances are useful in estimating conversation smoothness. However, it is necessary to remove laughter utterances from the data before making the estimate.

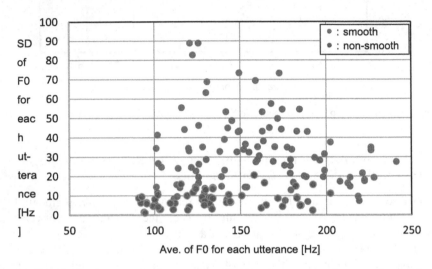

Fig. 11. Distribution between the Ave. and the SD of each utterance after removing laugh parts for six speakers.

5 Discussion

We confirmed the following through analysis of free dyadic conversation data:

- The length of a silent interval and the length of one utterance are not useful for estimating conversation smoothness.
- One may estimate the conversation smoothness using nonverbal information, images of conversation, or nonverbal information with speech removed.

These are our goals for using nonverbal information to estimate conversation smoothness.

Nonverbal information in free conversations includes two kinds of characteristics. One is a factor which depends on the communication atmosphere, and the other depends on personal characteristics. When we use nonverbal information for estimating the communication atmosphere, the personal characteristics should be removed from nonverbal information.

Our analysis results show:

- Laugh utterances depend on speakers more than conversation smoothness
- Standard deviation of the F0 for each utterance is useful for estimating the conversation smoothness.

- It is necessary to remove laughter utterance segments and use only speech utterances for the estimation.

However, there is possibly not enough data to make a clear estimate, especially if we use only two speakers for laugh segment analysis. In the future, the characteristics of laughter observations should be decided more clearly using additional data.

6 Conclusion

We analyzed the relationship between the F0 in free dyadic conversations and conversation smoothness to confirm that the F0 is an effective factor for estimating conversation smoothness. As a result, we confirmed not only that the standard deviation of the F0 for each utterance is useful to estimate conversation smoothness, but that it is also necessary to remove personal, independent utterances such as laughter before making an estimation.

In the future, we will confirm the reliability of our results using a larger quantity of data. In addition, other factors of nonverbal communication such as gestures will be analyzed to obtain a more accurate estimate.

References

1. DiMicco, J.M., Pandolfo, A., Bender, W.: Influencing group participation with a shared display. In: Proceedings of the 2004 ACM Conference on Computer Supported Cooperative Work, CSCW 2004, pp. 614–623. ACM Press, New York, NY, USA (2004)
2. Kim, T., Chang, A., Holland, L., Pentland, A.S.: Meeting mediator: enhancing group collaborationusing sociometric feedback. In: Proceedings of the 2008 ACM Conference on Computer Supported Cooperative Work, pp. 457–466 (2008)
3. Krauss, R.M., Chen, Y., Gottesman, R.F.: Lexical gestures and lexical access: a process model. In: Language and Gesture, pp. 261–283. Cambridge University Press, Cambridge (2000)
4. Wrede, B., Shiriberg, E.: Spotting "hot spots" in meetings: human judgments and prosodic cues. In: Proceeding of INTERSPEECH, pp. 2805–2808 (2003)
5. Gatica-Perez, D., McCowan, I.A., Zhang, D., Bengio, S.: Detecting group interest-level in meetings. IDIAP Research report 04-51, IDIAP, pp. 1–8 (2004)
6. Jayagopi, D.B., Ba, S., Odobez, J.M., Gatica-Perez, D.: Predicting two facets of social verticality in meetings from five-minute time slices and nonverbal cues. In: Proceedings of the 10th International Conference on Multimodal Interfaces, pp. 45–52 (2008)
7. Toyoda, K., Miyakoshi, Y., Yamanishi, R., Kato, S.: Estimation of dialogue moods using the utterance intervals features. In: Watanabe, T., Watada, J., Takahashi, N., Howlett, R.J., Jain, L.C. (eds.) Intelligent Interactive Multimedia: Systems and Services - IIMSS 2012. Smart Innovation Systems and Technologies, vol. 14, pp. 245–254. Springer, Heildberg (2012)
8. Nishio, S., Koyama, K.: A criterion for facial expression of laugh based on temporal difference of eye and mouth movement. IEICE **80**(8), 1316–1318 (1997)

Communication Support via a Collocation Dictionary

Ryota Yaguchi[✉] and Hiroshi Yajima

Tokyo Denki University, Adachi, Japan
15fmi30@ms.dendai.ac.jp

Abstract. In recent years, due to the effects of societal aging, the demand for health-related consultations has been increasing. Recently developments in information technology have made it possible to conduct care consultations by Internet telephony and chat programs. In this study, we propose a remote consultation system that incorporates a collocation dictionary.

Keywords: Collocation dictionary · Remote consultation · Care · Information gap

1 Background

In recent years in Japan, the demand for consultations related to health and nursing care have increased as society has aged. In 2015, Japan's elderly population (those 65 years and older) was 33.84 million people, a record high 26.7 % of the total population [1]. In addition, for the first time, the population of those more than 80 years of age has exceeded 10 million people. Japan has the highest proportion of elderly citizens among developed countries.

In addition to these age-related demands on the care system, the Tohoku region suffered extensive damage during the Great East Japan Earthquake, and this, in concert with other problems, has led to the proposal of a system of regional comprehensive support centers to support elderly residents. The number of health consultations reported for fiscal year 2013 was 17 % higher than that for fiscal year 2011 [2].

In the current system, long-term-care support specialists provide services related to care support, and this is their primary occupation. As part of care, the specialists assist system users, their families, and other professionals, in making appropriate decisions in response to various situations. Recent developments in information technology have resulted in care consultations being conducted via Internet telephony or chat applications, which facilitates remote welfare service. Remote consultations are not used in many fields. For example, remote support for computer users (and particularly for elderly users) is widely available [3]. In addition, research into systems to support remote consultation has been carried out in the financial and medical fields in recent years. In line with this trend, systems for remote provision of financial and legal counseling services have been developed [4].

In the field of health care, the characteristics of remote consultation, in which patients (who are not medical professionals) may live in sparsely populated areas and yet still have problems, have been addressed with the result that several remote providers may

© Springer International Publishing Switzerland 2016
M. Kurosu (Ed.): HCI 2016, Part III, LNCS 9733, pp. 158–165, 2016.
DOI: 10.1007/978-3-319-39513-5_15

collectively provide diagnosis and write a treatment plan [5, 6]. In line with this, the form of care provision has also diversified.

Under these circumstances, the following issues may affect the care manager and the care recipient. (1) The care support specialist cannot successfully talk with the family. (2) Long-term-care support specialists do not know the status of the care recipient. (3) Inexperienced long-term-care support specialist may not be able to recognize or diagnose problems. Additional problems may arise from differences in the abilities of care managers.

Communication with long-term-care support specialists may cause anxiety in some care users and their families. During remote consultation by asynchronous media, such as e-mail, time lags will occur. To overcome this, synchronous communication via telephone, such as the use of a call center system, has been the conventional solution. However, in recent years, various tools to mitigate the problems with asynchronous consultation have emerged, such as electronic bulletin boards. However, during nursing consultations, the levels and areas of knowledge will differ significantly between providers (as experts) and recipients (as lay people). Consequently, large differences in effectiveness are seen between different types of support tools.

Additionally, when care recipients consult with experts, there is often a difference in understanding of the words used according to the environment and because of the difference in position. This may result in consultations that are not smooth, as occurs in communication between different cultures (here, the culture of health experts and that of care recipients). In addition, most people seeking a consultation know little about long-term care. Because of this, they can only listen to the explanation given by specialists and may not feel satisfied with the consultation.

In this study, we propose that communication can be facilitated by bridging the knowledge gap between experts and recipients. For this purpose, we apply a collocation dictionary to remote consultations. In addition to the usual steps for a consultation, reference to the collocation dictionary eases understanding for the person seeking consultation. Additionally, the collocation dictionary can act as a reference during consultation and to improve understanding. By allowing differences in the perception of the keywords to be noticed, it becomes possible to prevent in the consultation.

To generate the collocation dictionary, the sentences of experts are processed by text-mining techniques (see Sect. 5). We propose a method of using the generated dictionary to support communication during remote consultation. The collocation dictionary consists of co-occurrence relations between words, with software presenting these words. In the experiment, we performed pseudo-experiments between an expert consultant and a lay consultee, using the collocation dictionary as a supplement to Internet telephony (Skype). During the consultation, the consultee could reference words from the collocation dictionary in a visual style when desired. As a result, we have identified areas of effectiveness and challenge for use of a collocation dictionary in this way.

2 Previous Research

Iino (of our laboratory) proposed the use of a collocation dictionary to facilitate consultation by deepening mutual understanding [7]. In this study, we experimentally tested the use of a collocation dictionary. However, because of the lower number of trials, and instability in the system and dataset, we were unable to verify the effectiveness of the system.

3 Collocation Dictionary

The collocation dictionary used in this summarizes co-occurrence information for basis text written by experts. Co-occurrence occurs whenever two substrings appear at the same time in any larger string. The collocation dictionary is created by ranking the strength (frequency) of co-occurrences. This makes it possible to generate the distinctive patterns and relations from given sentences. In this study, sentence-level communication is considered, and visual display of the sentences is assumed to improve utility.

4 Conceptual Basis

The basic concept of this study is that, at the time of remote consultation, the effects of knowledge difference between people belonging to different cultures (here, experts and lay people) can be ameliorated by use of a collocation dictionary and that this will facilitate effective communication.

5 Proposed Method

We conducted the same experiment as in previous studies [7], and so it was not possible to quantitatively verify the effectiveness of using the collocation dictionary for remote consultation. Therefore, we performed a qualitative review of the experiment by interview of participants. As a new proposed method, when extracting the collocation information (the KH Coder software package was used for this), irrelevant information is eliminated with the aim of limiting the amount of information used to prepare the collocation dictionary.

6 Experiment

6.1 Preparing the Experiment

In this experiment, we applied the text mining feature of KH Coder to the encyclopedia of care [8] to extract visual collocation information. Then, the produced visual information was extracted by a graphics tool to create the collocation dictionary. This dictionary was used in the experiment (Fig. 1).

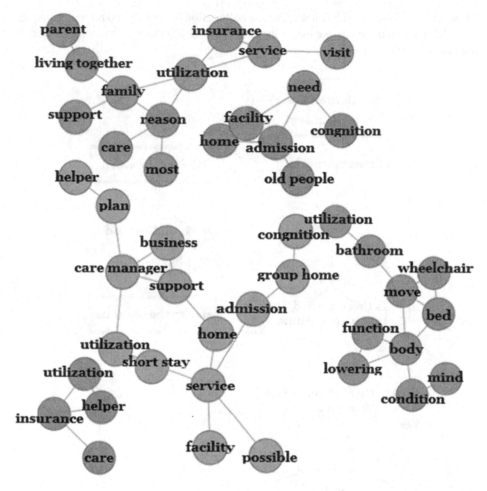

Fig. 1. Example from the collocation dictionary used in the experiment

6.2 Experimental Method

One participant was designated as the expert, and six participants were each designated as a consultee. First, trials were performed without using the collocation dictionary. Then, trials were performed with using the collocation dictionary. The method of the experiment is to distribute the scenario in advance, which allows participants to fully understand their roles. The consultees are told to begin with the position "I have received certification that I need long-term care, but I don't know what to do" in chat (Skype) with the expert and to ask questions for clarification. The expert is to answer that question while introducing the various systems to the consultee. Participants acting as consultees were instructed that when they did not understand the expert's answers, they should ask further questions. When there are no more questions, the interview ends. When using the collocation dictionary, it was displayed in a separate window from the chat screen during the consultation. When not using the collocation dictionary, no references were used. After the experiment, we asked those in the role of consultee to answer a questionnaire (Fig. 2).

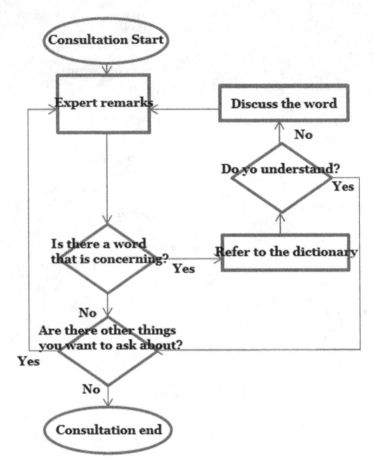

Fig. 2. Flow of consultation

6.3   Experimental Result

After the experiment, we administered a survey questionnaire to participants who had acted as consultees and then interviewed them. The questionnaire items ask for a rating on a 5-point Likert-like scale of the following: depth of consultation, degree of focus, visibility of the collocation dictionary, and effectiveness of the collocation dictionary. In addition, the number of questions and length of consultation was extracted for each consultation from logs, and the averages were calculated (Figs. 3 and 4).

As a result, use of the collocation dictionary seems to improve level of understanding, degree of focus, and reported effectiveness. The average consultation time and the

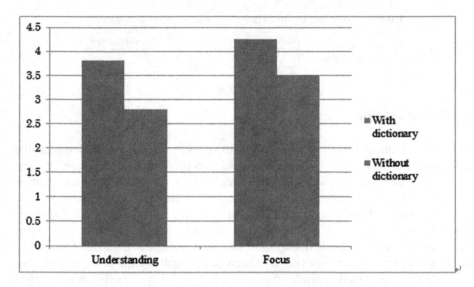

Fig. 3. Understanding and focus (Color figure online)

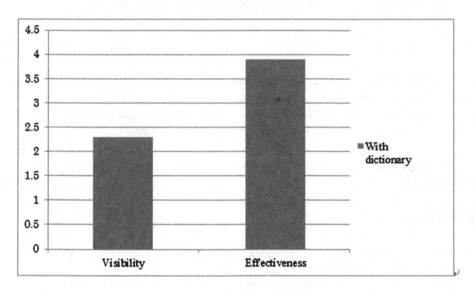

Fig. 4. Reported features of dictionary

average number of questions asked were both increased by using the dictionary. Interviews after the experiment confirmed that using the collocation dictionary improved the degree of focus, resulted in more questions, and achieved better understanding of the consultation. However, the collocation dictionary was seen as difficult use when trying to find words of interest (Table 1).

Table 1. Average number of questions and length of consultation

	With dictionary	Without dictionary
Number of questions	7	4
Consultation time	25 min	21 min

7   Consideration

From the experimental results, it was possible to verify the usefulness of referring to the collocation dictionary. Also, communication was improved in that the number of questions to the expert was increased, which indicates to us that the quality of the consultation was improved. However, feedback on the experiment indicates that the visibility of the system needs to be improved. In particular, we think that it is necessary to improve the procedure used when search for information. Currently, when the words of the expert are unclear, the collocation dictionary must be visually scanned. Because of this, when the amount of information is increased, it becomes difficult to explore the information. To address this, a method to display the information by using a search function should be considered. This would allow instant display of the necessary information, which we think would broaden the potential of the collocation dictionary.

8   Conclusion

Because this study used students as participants, the results do not provide useful data about actual environments. As a next step, we will collect a larger set of data from more participants and consider actual on-site usage. Additionally, we will implement a search function for the collocation dictionary before the next experiments.

Acknowledgement. We thank students at Tokyo Denki University who participated in the experiment.

References

1. Ministry of Internal Affairs and Communications (2015). http://www.stat.go.jp/data/topics/topi900.html. Accessed 20 Oct 2015
2. Kyodo News (2014). http://www.47news.jp/CN/201409/CN2014091001001721.html. Accessed 20 Oct 2015
3. Mori, Y., Fujimaru, N., Egashira, Y.: Online consultation provided by a support software for PC2: a case of elderly users attempt
4. Toshiyuki, I., Yoshihiro, A., Junichi, K., Tsutomu, M.: Remote Consultation and Contract systems using video phone. In: IPSJ 2006, pp. 85–90, 14 Sept 2006
5. Gotoh, T., Takayama, T., Ishiki, M., Ikeda, T.: A support system to consult remote another doctor on assessment and/or medical treatment plan when a doctor has patient not in his/her major. IPSJ **68**, 629–936 (2005)

6. Bratan, T., Clarke, M., Jones, R.W.: Optimum design for teleconsultation systems. In: 27th Annual International Conference of the IEEE Engineering in Medicine and Biology Society EMBS, Shanghai, China from 1-Sep-2005 to 4-Sep-2005, pp. 2178–2182 (2005)
7. Tomotaka, I., Yajima, H.: Communication support system for co-occurrence dictionary. Master's thesis. Tokyo Denki University (2011)
8. Yuichi, S.: Encyclopedia of care. Subarusya (2008)

A Method Using Collective Intelligence for Communication Activation Among Elderly People Living Alone

Hiroshi Yajima[1(✉)], Manabu Kurosawa[1], and Jun Sawamoto[2]

[1] Tokyo Denki University, Tokyo, Japan
{yajima,Kurosawa}@im.dendai.ac.jp
[2] Iwate Prefectural University, Takizawa, Iwate, Japan
sawamoto@iwate-pu.ac.jp

Abstract. Among elderly people who live alone, lack of communication leads to delays in responding to their common medical problems and to the onset or progression of dementia. Here, we propose a communication activation method for elderly people and caregivers. Selection criteria for active communication topics that interest elder people are selected from communication contents, using collective intelligence created by communication among various specialists in elderly care. Results are reported for an evaluation experiment in a Japanese setting.

Keywords: Communication · Elderly people · Living alone · Collective intelligence

1 Introduction

In recent years, the population of Japan has been aging at a rate unprecedented in other countries. The population aged > 65 years now exceeds 30 million people. Roughly one in four Japanese people is elderly. The number of elderly persons is expected to peak in 2042 at 39 million, but the proportion of the population over the age of 75 is expected to continue increasing thereafter [1].

In this context, there is an increased need to care for elderly people living alone. Government policies have also switched from an emphasis on institutional care to home-based care. As a result, there is an increased burden on the people involved with providing care, responding to symptoms of care recipients is difficult. Two elderly people with the same disease can exhibit different symptoms, depending on various factors, such as their environments and medical histories.

For elderly people living alone, lack of communication is a serious issue, because communication is a basic element of daily life. It has been noted that for elderly people living alone, a lack of communication can lead to the onset or progression of dementia or delays in the response when a medical problem occurs. To prevent these situations, elderly people need to have more communication. However, measures for addressing this are limited to volunteers or the relatively few visits by caregivers.

© Springer International Publishing Switzerland 2016
M. Kurosu (Ed.): HCI 2016, Part III, LNCS 9733, pp. 166–175, 2016.
DOI: 10.1007/978-3-319-39513-5_16

Traditionally, institutional care has been the main form of care, meaning that communication with various caregivers and other elderly people was possible. However, for an elderly person living alone, it is difficult to increase communication. For an elderly person who is able to utilize day services and the like, there are opportunities for communication. For an increasing number of elderly people, however, such care services are difficult. Initiatives to increase communication with elderly people have been started in various places, but the current situation is such that these kinds of initiatives are still limited to only a few regions.

Against this background, we developed a means of communication that utilizes ICT without placing a burden on the elderly [2], and the next major challenge is to select topics of conversation for communication with the elderly. Elderly people have a diverse range of characteristics, depending on how they have lived their lives. This means that topics for conversations with elderly people need to be selected with appropriate consideration.

In this study, we propose a method for finding ways to increase communication for elderly people. This study adopts a method of gathering collective intelligence in relation to communication through discussion between diverse caregivers, taking into account the diversity of elderly people. By applying this method, we propose a method for achieving rich communication for elderly people living alone. Finally, we experimentally demonstrate the efficacy of the proposed method for collecting and utilizing collective intelligence through the creation of an appropriate setting.

2   Trends and Issues in Care Observation in the Field

In this study, we consider home-based care, which will increasingly become the focus of care. Home-based care is an arrangement in which the care recipient lives at home and caregivers visit the home to carry out their assigned duties. There are two issues for home-based care, as described in the following subsections.

2.1   Observation Arrangements

Observation is needed in order to track the status of an elderly person and to respond when abnormalities occur. However, the basic approach to this can be broadly classified into the following two types: personal (warm) observation and impersonal (cool) observation.

In personal observation, the elderly person being observed takes the lead in communicating his or her situation. Then, if the information communicated indicates an abnormality, then it is addressed. If the information communicated does not indicate an abnormality, the caregiver is given peace of mind. For this method to work, communication between the elderly person and the observer must be effective, as discussed below. For an elderly person living at home in particular, it is not uncommon for him or her to spend almost all day without talking to anyone, though communication is a fundamental aspect of human life. Having an opportunity for communication is in itself a form of observation, and may also be a way to prevent dementia at the same time.

In contrast, impersonal observation involves tracking the status of an elderly person without regard to the person's volition. In such observation, the elderly person is observed as simply a living creature rather than a human being. In this case, the elderly person is the object of the observation system. There are many cases where the elderly person does not directly understand how he or she is being observed.

In other words, the basic stance of the observer marks the distinction between personal and impersonal observation. With personal observation, the observer treats elderly people as individual human beings. At the same time, this approach also assumes that the observer responds with courtesy and an understanding of the elderly person's psychology. Elderly people, and particularly elderly people living alone, want to be seen as human beings. Elderly people have a desire to be understood through conversation. In other words, elderly people want to have their self-worth as human beings recognized. Personal observation is an approach that meets this desire of elderly people. The central benefit of this approach is a sense of closeness to elderly people. At the same time, this approach is a way of satisfying the various wishes of elderly people. In contrast, impersonal observation universalizes elderly people and observes all elderly people by basically the same method, so that the observations can be done very efficiently. This is because such observation can obtain the same type of information for all elderly people, and with the same timing. This means that the method can be automated. Impersonal observation is extremely convenient for people who develop observation systems and for the bureaucracies that operate observation systems. For bureaucracies, using this system enables the following possibilities: (1) broad trends relating to the elderly can be tracked; (2) bulk management becomes possible; and (3) fixed management becomes possible.

A shortcoming of impersonal observation is that it is difficult to manage abnormal situations that are unlikely to occur. These two types of observations are currently being developed simultaneously and in parallel. However, the key question is not whether only one method or the other is an effective form of observation. Both have advantages and disadvantages. What is important is to strike a balance between the two. How this balance is struck will vary depending on the region and on the community to which the elderly person belongs.

We believe that the fundamentals of observing the elderly consist of the following three points (Fig. 1).

(1) Affirmation
    Elderly people understand and consent to the fact that they are being observed.
(2) Agency of elderly people
    Elderly people explain their own situation themselves, and of their own volition, or indicate that they are unable to explain their own situation.
(3) Activity of elderly people
    Elderly people demonstrate their presence through their own actions, thereby enabling the observation.

To achieve these things, the following three points are likely to be crucial. (1) The observer demonstrates warm-hearted concern, rather than just impersonal monitoring. To do this, the observer must provide messages of concern rather than warning

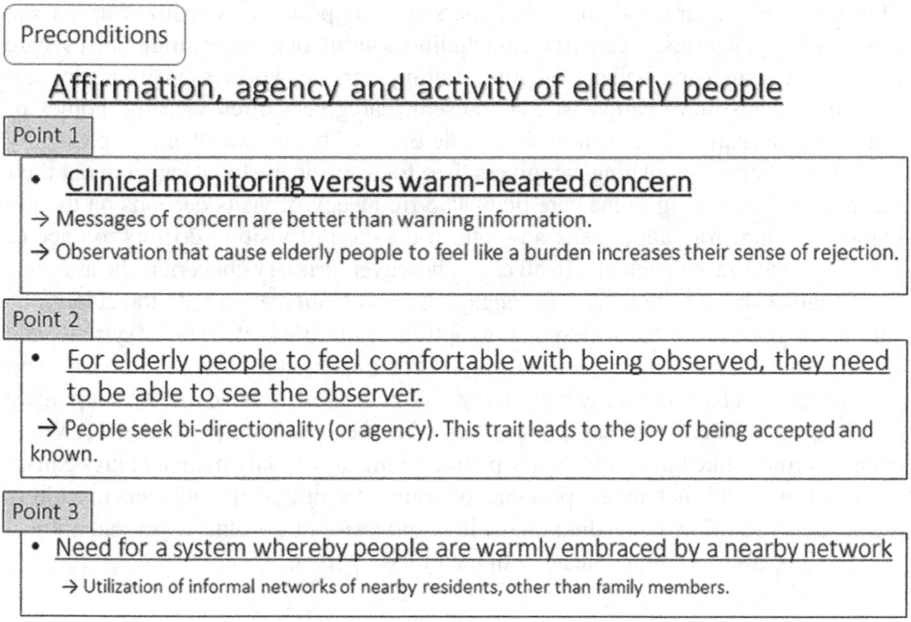

Preconditions

Affirmation, agency and activity of elderly people

Point 1

- **Clinical monitoring versus warm-hearted concern**
  → Messages of concern are better than warning information.
  → Observation that cause elderly people to feel like a burden increases their sense of rejection.

Point 2

- **For elderly people to feel comfortable with being observed, they need to be able to see the observer.**
  → People seek bi-directionality (or agency). This trait leads to the joy of being accepted and known.

Point 3

- **Need for a system whereby people are warmly embraced by a nearby network**
  → Utilization of informal networks of nearby residents, other than family members.

Fig. 1. Key points for observing elderly people living alone

information. Conversely, impersonal monitoring may exacerbate an elderly person's sense of rejection. (2) It is important to establish a sense of being monitored on the part of the elderly person. In general, people tend to desire bi-directionality. Observation based on an understanding of this is required. (3) Observation should be conducted such that the elderly person has a feeling of been enveloped in a nearby warm network. It is important that observation take place through informal close relationships involving people other than family members. From these considerations, the role played by communication in observing the elderly begins to emerge. Broadly speaking, this is significant in two ways.

(1) Dispelling negative emotions in the elderly
    Elderly people tend to harbor various insecurities in relation to finances and other aspects of their lives. Giving elderly people an opportunity to express these kinds of negative emotions as part of warm communication is helpful for dispelling these insecurities. At the same time, this can also provide an opportunity for elderly people to make known detailed physical complaints that they might have.
(2) Enhancing positive emotions in the elderly
    Elderly people often talk about their past experiences. Affirming this gives elderly people a sense of self-worth. At the same time, from these conversations positive feelings about the future can also emerge.

The importance of communication for the elderly has been highlighted in the field of psychology as well. Communication has been identified as an essential factor for improving the quality of life of elderly people.

For home-based care, a single elderly person is supported by experts from a large number of job categories as caregivers, including visiting doctors, visiting nurses, care workers, care managers, helpers, visiting bathing-service workers, visiting physical therapists, and visiting pharmacists. At present, caregivers often visit the homes of people who need care according the schedule determined by the care plan, independently of other caregivers. The visiting caregivers then focus exclusively on carrying out their specific duties, according to the care plan. The frequency of visits depends on the job category, ranging from about once a month in the case of visiting doctors to once or twice a day in the case of helpers. In all cases, however, primary concern is the assigned task. Caregivers have little leeway for engaging in communication with the elderly.

In recent years, with the widespread adoption of the Internet, various systems and communication devices have been developed for impersonal observation. However, elderly people can have difficulty in utilizing ICT because they have trouble keeping up with advances in ICT. At the same, caregivers are often reluctant to utilize ICT. When it comes to communication with elderly people living alone, only human beings can do the job. However, it is not always possible to arrange for sufficient volunteers to address these needs. In addition, depending on the idiosyncrasies of the elderly person, not just anyone will be able to communicate with the elderly person.

3   Proposed Method

In this study, we propose the following: (1) introducing an ICT system for establishing communication without the elderly person having to do anything [1], and (2) then achieving communication to suit the elderly person by appropriately selecting communication topics.

To achieve (1), we have developed a conversation system to facilitate conversations between helpers and the elderly person via a communication television. However, in communication with elderly people, various differences emerge depending on the idiosyncrasies of the elderly person. For this reason, in relation to the communication topics in (2), we propose a method below for using the collective intelligence of caregivers to uncover suitable topics for communication.

3.1   Using Collective Intelligence to Uncover Communication Topics

In this paper, we propose a method for (1) bringing together suitably qualified experts from various fields [3, 4] to have a discussion, and then (2) refining the collective intelligence that emerges from the discussion in relation to the communication topics desired by the care recipients.

The health status of elderly people varies considerably from one person to the next, depending on the experiences they have had over the course of their lives. Often various factors then converge to bring about some health condition. Accordingly, it is extremely difficult for individual doctors or care experts to address these conditions on their own. This is why the expertise and wisdom of multiple medical and care experts is required when establishing communication themes appropriate to each situation. When communicating with elderly people, providing topics of conversation that are close to their hearts is important. To accomplish this, it is necessary to decide topics by viewing the circumstances of the particular elderly person from multiple perspectives. To do this, it is necessary to produce a new collective intelligence, based on the expertise of a diverse range of people involved in medical treatment and care.

During this process, it is important for those involved in medical treatment and care not to shy away from differences of opinion. Each person engages with elderly people from their own standpoint, and so it is common for there to be differences of opinion among experts. When this happens, it is not desirable to give too much regard to authority or position. Collective intelligence may not emerge if people neglect their own unique points of view and agree with the opinions of others too easily. On the contrary, this can lead to a collective folly, which refers to a kind of knowledge where everyone consents to a conclusion at the time but it is clearly incorrect when considered afterward.

Next, we organize some of the terms used in this paper. 'Collective knowledge' often refers to the aggregate of the opinions and knowledge normally held by individuals. However, in this paper we consider a method of wisdom for first producing new ideas ('collective intelligence') by gathering and generalizing collective knowledge. We then propose an environment for promoting active communication by proceeding to the stage of 'collective wisdom', whereby collective intelligence has been consolidated at a higher level. In our considerations below, we define communication topics that are dependent on a particular situation as 'collective knowledge' and topics that do not depend on a particular situation as 'collective wisdom'.

3.2   Conditions for the Emergence of Collective Intelligence

For collective intelligence to emerge, we believe that two conditions are required (Fig. 2), as described below.

An essential element when extracting collective intelligence is the concept of 'setting'. Here we define 'setting' as consisting of (1) the diverse human resources gathered in a place and (2) the atmosphere there, including both the presence of respect for others between these people and an identification of the differences with respect to others. It is important to gather skilled people with differing ideas, while at the same time creating an atmosphere where these people can feel comfortable enough to express their opinions actively. There also needs to be a sense of tension between the people belonging to the setting.

A 'setting' is not a fixed thing. Depending on the type of collective intelligence that emerges in the 'setting', there may be instances where people who can contribute new ideas are sought out and included. It is also necessary to seek and utilize collective intelligence that has emerged in the past.

- Initiate interaction between the setting and collective intelligence

To produce collective intelligence, the first requirement is for each person to clarify, through a process of dialog, the differences between their own ideas (the thesis) and the ideas advocated by others (the antithesis). The next thing is for participants to continue their dialog until they clearly understand the ideas of the others. During this process, the

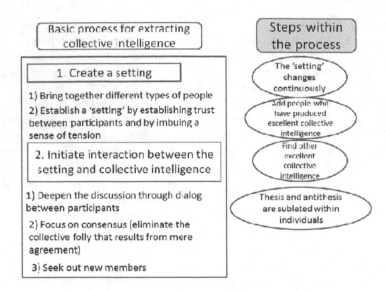

Fig. 2. Conditions for emergence of collective intelligence

facilitator finds areas of overlap between the participants' ideas. The facilitator then strives to arrive at consensus on these overlapping ideas. What is important here is that the result be consensus, not just agreement. As discussed earlier, the sole objective of 'agreement' is to avoid conflict. In contrast, 'consensus' is a realization that emerges through people's internal feelings and the relationships that they share with others. Agreement, in contrast, involves siding with another's position without clarifying one's own ideas. 'Collective folly' can emerge when decision-making is centered on agreement.

The process for forming collective knowledge is shown concretely below (Fig. 3). The facilitator first starts by forming a setting for discussion. In this setting, different types of participants gather. Next, they form the preconditions for the discussion based on each person's individual opinion. Unifying the preconditions makes it possible to prevent the discussion from being disrupted. Next, participants present their own expert opinions, and start discussing these opinions.

In this dialectic process, each individual continuously compares his or her own idea (thesis) to the ideas advocated by others (antithesis). From this process, the work of producing a higher-order synthesis is carried out. The type of collective intelligence that emerges in this 'setting' grows and changes into wisdom through a process of sincere discussion and dialog between participants.

When it comes to the fields of care and medical treatment, the care manager (or someone acting on his or her behalf) is in the best position to play a central role in bringing together the people involved, and encouraging dialog between them. At the same time, the care manager also adds new people to the discussion as needed according to the progress of the discussion. Through this kind of process, communication topics for people who need care are clarified. In the process of discussion, it is essential to share the information held by each individual person involved in providing care.

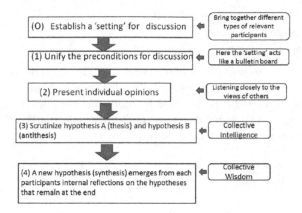

Fig. 3. Process of forming collective intelligence

4 Experiment in Creating Collective Intelligence Relating to Communication Activation for the Elderly

We consider the three measures listed below in relation to collective knowledge. We describe an 'in situ' discussion experiment that took place under these assumptions.

- Discussion is conducted between different types of experts.
- A 'setting' is established where collective intelligence can emerge.
- Through this 'setting', the process is advanced whereby collective intelligence emerges, and collective intelligence is formed from the outcomes of this process.

4.1 Overview of the Experiment

As an example of communication between the elderly and helpers, we created a proto-type communication system using a television [2]. Elderly people converse with helpers, as necessary, through the television that they normally watch. We established a setting for a discussion between different experts on the assumption that this ICT device would be used. We then analyzed and generated conversation topics for communication with elderly people. The specific experimental conditions were as follows.

- Participants: Five individuals—a helper, a geriatric psychologist, a care device researcher, an ICT expert, and a facilitator
- Discussion time: about 2 h 30 min
- A system where the elderly person is not required to do anything but talk to a helper when necessary, and where the helper can unilaterally initiate conversation as appropriate.

4.2 Experimental Results

The results of the discussion were as follows.

- Total number of opinions expressed: 110
- Collective intelligence: 8 items
- Collective wisdom: 2 items

An example of the overall discussion is shown in Fig. 4. Eight items of [[Please confirm this change (it says "Two items of..." in the source)]] collective intelligence emerged from the views and expertise held by individual participants, and these were generalized to generate two items of [[Please confirm the addition]] collective wisdom in relation to communication with the elderly.

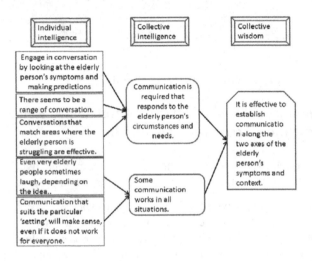

Fig. 4. Example experimental results

5 Discussion

In the process of summarizing the opinions of discussion participants via a questionnaire, we found that it was appropriate to distinguish two types of collective intelligence: collective knowledge and collective wisdom. The possibility of being able to achieve communication that is more versatile based on collective wisdom also became clear.

In this experiment, due to the theme of the discussion and the positions of the participants, the helper took a central role in expressing opinions on the actual situation in the field. The discussion then took the form of the other participants making comments on the expert opinion presented by the helper. The following comment was made by the cognitive psychologist. People's psychological status can be in one of two states. The first is the psychology of ordinary life, whereas the other is the psychology of the extraordinary. The 'psychology of the extraordinary' is the state that emerges, for example, during a festival or when a special visitor comes. It may be necessary to pose communication topics in a way that takes into account these two states.

We also observed that there are two patterns in the situations where collective intelligence emerges. The first pattern is the case where the opinions of multiple participants focus on a particular theme. As a result, this is a case whereby collective knowledge emerges after the details of this theme have been dissected and scrutinized from various angles. The other pattern is the case whereby a new idea emerges suddenly from several conversations between different experts. Both patterns can be regarded as cases where a higher-order idea emerges from an interaction between thesis and antithesis.

6 Conclusion

A lack of communication for elderly people, and those living alone in particular, is becoming more apparent, so here we considered ways to activate communication for elderly people living alone. A distinctive feature of our consideration has been the uncovering of communication themes by obtaining collective intelligence from discussions between multiple experts of different types. We found that this led to the generation of collective intelligence and collective wisdom accepted by the participants. At the same time, we also demonstrated the possibility that a debate within a clearly and realistically defined 'setting' can be effective in generating collective intelligence and collective wisdom.

In the future, we will continue to verify the effectiveness of the protocol by establishing 'settings' for discussion in different regions. At the same time, we will also consider ways of training facilitators for conducting discussions that are even more active. The debate in the experiment reported here took place face-to-face, but it can be difficult to bring various experts together at the same location. Accordingly, we also plan to conduct field work to consider discussions in virtual environments, such as voice chat and video conferencing [[We've used a generic description of Skype]].

References

1. Toward Realization of a Comprehensive Care System for Local Communities (in Japanese). http://www.mhlw.go.jp/stf/seisakunitsuite/bunya/hukushi_kaigo/kaigo_koureisha/chiiki-houkatsu/
2. Suzuki, S., Author, B.B., Author, C.C.: Development of communication tool between elder person and caregiver. National Convention of the Information Processing Society of Japan (2014). (in Japanese)
3. Suzuki, S., Author, B.B., Author, C.C.: Development of a system to support conversations between the elderly and helpers. National Convention of the Information Processing Society of Japan (2015). (in Japanese)
4. Page, S.E.: The Difference. Princeton Press, Princeton (2007)
5. Briskin, A., Author, B.B., Author, C.C.: The Power of Collective Wisdom and the Trap of Collective Folly. Kadokawa (2009). (in Japan)
6. Surowiecki, J.: The Wisdom of Crowds. Kadokawa Shoten, Tokyo (2008). (in Japan)

Narratives and Visualization

MEseum: Personalized Experience with Narrative Visualization for Museum Visitors

Ali Arya[1(✉)], Jesse Gerroir[1], Efetobore Mike-Ifeta[1], Andres Adolfo Navarro-Newball[2], and Edmund Prakash[3]

[1] Carleton University, Ottawa, Canada
arya@carleton.ca, jessegerroir@gmail.com, mikeifeta@gmail.com
[2] Pontificia Universidad Javeriana, Bogotá, Colombia
aannewball@hotmail.com
[3] University of Westminster, London, UK
eprakash@gmail.com

Abstract. The technological enrichment of museums serves as a prime area for research on the changing role of mobile and interactive technologies, and the visualization of personal data. While previous research projects have focused on using mobile technology to act as an electronic guide, or as a means for a user to view additional information about the museum exhibits, in contrast this project takes a different approach. It seeks to develop new methods to create a personalized experience and visualize the data collected from a user's visit as a personal narrative. MEseum, our proposed system, allows the user to plan a visit, follow that plan, and construct a presentation that they can use to reflect, communicate, and share their experiences with others. To this end, a museum guidance system and four visual narrative styles were designed, developed, and successfully tested.

Keywords: Museum · Navigation · Interactive · Personalized · Narrative · Visualization

1 Introduction

The function of the museum in today's society is far removed from what it used to be. The development of museums has been intensely personal and haphazard in plan. The emphasis has been upon collection of the beautiful and the curious [1]. The modern museum now plays a major educational and social role in today's society. This shift in paradigm has seen the visitor's status evolve from mere spectator into an active participant. This has been facilitated in part by the rise and dominance of digital technology. The resultant effect of both evolutions is a dire need to foster a new model of communication, to build a more intimate experience, a new type of relationship between the institution and the individual, between the museum and the visitor.

Advances in interactive technologies are significantly affecting the experience of museum visits; however there is the need for further research to explore how these technologies can be fully optimized to create a better visitor experience. This study looks

© Springer International Publishing Switzerland 2016
M. Kurosu (Ed.): HCI 2016, Part III, LNCS 9733, pp. 179–190, 2016.
DOI: 10.1007/978-3-319-39513-5_17

specifically at the application of interactive digital media in furthering the museum-visitor experience. Efforts made at enriching the modern museum experience have most often than not wound up in the creation or deployment of yet another technological innovation either in the form of interactive installations spread across strategic locations in the museum or virtual simulations expected to increase the level of interaction and engagement between the visitor and a specific artifact. While these advancements have had their places and served their purposes, the issue of enriching the museum visitor experience transcends the context in which such technologies are employed.

The power of narrative is no secret in the museum world where various forms of storytelling have long been employed to engage visitors [2]. However storytelling have been continuously used rather exclusively by the museum in exhibition strategies. A way that may help visitors capture these grand but fleeting experiences and subsequently enrich and extend the museum experience is the construction of personal digital narratives and making explicit the paths of such digital narratives, allowing visitors to later revisit, reflect upon, reorder, and share it. Digital narrative or storytelling refers to a form of digital media production, using a story-like sequence of multimedia content that allows everyday people share aspects of their life's story. Technological advancements can help in the construction of these digital narratives of the museum visit that extends far beyond the single event of arriving at the physical space of the museum. The museum visit encompasses everything; from the intentional or unintentional preparation made before (pre-visit experience) arriving at the physical space, the actual tour of the physical space and its artifacts and everything that occurs after leaving the museum building (post-visit experience). Finally, while indoor mapping and navigation technologies are becoming more available, lack of guidance through complex exhibitions or linear prescribed paths are the two common experiences. Ability to plan a desired visit based on personal interests and reliable suggestions, and then follow that plan, as the base for a personalized narrative, can significantly improve and encourage museum visits.

The problem addressed by this research is the design of an interactive framework that allows the museum visitor plan a personalized visit, effectively record experiences made, and access/share these experiences through visualization of their personal narratives in different styles each suiting a specific purpose.

2   Related Work

Many museums have begun to use technology to make the experience more interactive. Digital touch screens kiosks have become more prevalent along with large screen installations, video walls, smart badge systems, 3D animation, virtual reality, and increasingly sophisticated websites. Such technologies have changed the physical character of the museum [3].

There have been a number of systems developed in order to try and facilitate storytelling in museums. StoryCorps employs a series of fixed and mobile booths where people can record stories, either alone or in the form of interviews, as digital audio [4]. Urban Tapestries [5] allow people to link stories to places using mobile devices. When users create a story, using text, audio and/or still images, it is automatically tied to the place where it was recorded using location-tracking technology. Tate Modern multimedia tours follow the same approach of using location tracking for personalized or contextualized delivery content. Bletchley Park Text [6] goes a step further by allowing museum visitors to construct meta-narratives by combining existing curatorial stories (in the form of interviews with historical figures) [4]. By sending text messages via mobile phone from specific exhibits in the museum, visitors create a personalized web page which links their chosen topics in narrative threads, which could be further explored and rearranged [4].

As novel as these projects are, there is still a lack of provision for actual visitor engagement and co- construction with the museum. What is or has been obtainable is a one way flow of information. In the instances where mobile technology has been employed, models that were essentially built as content delivery systems, providing the audience with contextual information during the course of a tour and sometimes doubling as a GPS device. When storytelling or narratives are mentioned within the museum parlance and in the instances where technology has been employed, we discover that there are no explicit learning goals or incentive to create stories (Story Corps and Urban Tapestry). Presentation of personal narratives of museum visitors in various styles has not been effectively addressed through existing systems.

Marie-Laure Ryan [7] discusses the uniqueness of narrative in digital media and identifies several key elements, including the increased level of interaction and the point of view of the user in regards to the story. Different variations of these two elements can change how the narrative is composed in a drastic fashion [7]. Kosara and Mackinlay [8], provide an example of how narrative visualization requires its own methods in contrast to traditional visualization in the journalistic realm. To this end, new visualization techniques can be found to help convey visual narratives. Hullman and Nick Diakopoulos [9] explore this by examining how visualization can be used to shape meteoric. Edward Segel and Jeffrey Heel [10] also studied different visualizations that the media used to convey stories in print and online, in an attempt to identify and classify broad narrative visualization techniques. They found several different patterns that involved various aspects of presentation such as layout, story structures, and structures used in conveying the story in a visual manner.

3   Research Approach

3.1   Overview

In this paper, we report on the design and evaluation of MEseum (Me-in-the-museum). MEseum has gone through two major phases. In phase 1, the general structure of the system was designed and evaluated. It included general functionality that is required to guide users through a personal experience. While this phase did introduce the notion of timeline as a means of collecting and sharing the narrative information, it included only a simple way of presenting this information. Our phase 2 focused on this presentation and introduced our notion of narrative visualization through various styles. Both phases consists of design, development, and usability studies, as described in the following sections (Figs. 1, 2, 3 and 4).

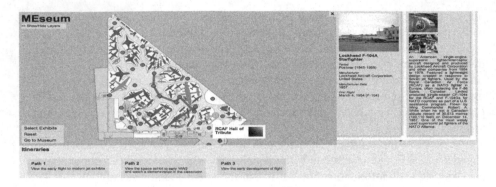

Fig. 1. MEseum Plan

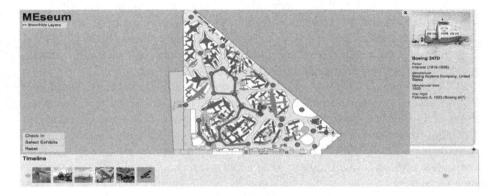

Fig. 2. MEseum Guide

Fig. 3. MEseum Connect

3.2   MEseum System

The research team divided the museum visit into three functionally distinct parts: planning a visit, following the plan, and post-visit access to data. The system and its tools were to correspond to these parts of a visit. MEseum components include:

- MEseum Plan was designed at the tool that provided the visitor with efficient planning information.
- MEseum Guide offered a navigation system that helped the visitor move from one exhibition to the other while digitally creating a narrative trail of things experienced through the help of the check-in and timeline features.
- MEseum Connect becomes the platform where the visitor can access their data and communicate with other visitors and also the museum.

The three components of MEseum are independent but complimentary. The development of a system that is designed to enhance the museum-visiting process will, and by its very nature have a set of tools with functions that overlap. MEseum Plan is the canvass upon which the visitor draws her museum visit based on tailored preferences from information gathered. MEseum Guide in turn implements the visit that has already been constructed by the visitor in MEseum Plan. It does this by using navigational features and other tools that enables the visitor collect digital information and she progresses along her tour. At the end of one's visit, the visitor might decide to share with others, all of the memories that have been made. MEseum Connect provides the platform by which all of the memories made and recorded can be preserved, accessed, edited, and shared.

The key concept in MEseum design is timeline, a collection of personal and museum-provide data that define the user experience. MEseum Guide is the tool that generates timeline content, while MEseum Connect allows it to be packaged and presented effectively.

3.3   Narrative Visualization

Based on seven visualization genres suggested by Segel and Heer [10] and the notions of internal vs. External, and exploratory vs. Ontological presentations [7], we define four visualization styles to be used and evaluated for MEseum. The four narrative visualizations are as follows:

Slideshow: This visualization is a rather simple one. It's meant to mimic the existing method of displaying pictures in a slideshow that is commonly used as a presentation means. It was included to serve as a comparison to the other visualization methods. The pictures are displayed very prominently, and fade into each other as the slide show automatically plays and rotates through them all. There is a small queue underneath the viewing area that displays all the photos along with the comment or title.

Categorical: This visualization is focused around giving a clear sense of the information learned. It presents its information impersonally, like a record of what the user learned and visited. Information is arranged in a scientific way by topic. Where the type and category of information they viewed is all laid out for them and they can gain an understanding of how it is all scientifically related and categorized. Information is presented in a magazine style layout. Information from another source outside the museum is also presented along with a weblink to that source encouraging the user to learn more.

Sequential: This visualization is focused around giving a sense of time and place. Each exhibit is presented like a node on the overall museum floor plan. The user can follow the path they took and view each exhibit they saw and at what time they saw it.

If the user clicks on one of the exhibits a radial menus of nodes is displayed around the central exhibit node. Each child node is a picture of an artefact in the exhibit along with information about that artefact.

Dramatic: This visualization is focused around giving a clear sense of the user's personal experience visiting the museum. There is a sense of linear narrative to it where the user scrolls and is able to see the results of what they saw in the museum in a way that resembles pages of a scrapbook. The background is textured and the font playful. Any pictures the user take are displayed like Polaroid photographs with their comments written on them. Information about the exhibit is kept to a minimum. The system will also comment about what they saw. Such as "Next time try to find the largest meteor on display. It's bigger than you think." If the user missed taking pictures of any prominent exhibits they will be displayed as 'blank' squares next to the Polaroid's. These blank squares are meant give a sense of what the missed.

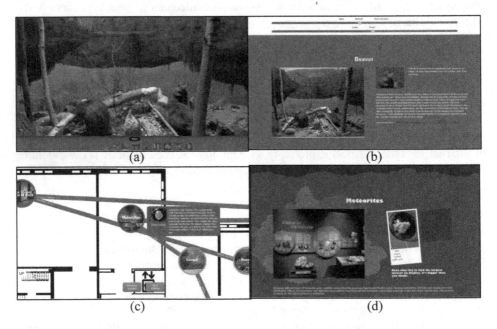

Fig. 4. Narrative visualization styles. (a) Slideshow, (b) Categorical, (c) Sequential, (d) Dramatic

3.4   System Features

MEseum incorporates certain basic features into its design. These features enable MEseum to efficiently perform its primary functions.

3.4.1   Interactive Floor Plan

The floor plan of the Canada Aviation and Space Museum (or any other partner museum) is converted into an SVG map. This allowed for a basic level of interactivity such as 'click and drag' and 'zoom in and out' features using the mouse. The floor plan then became the base layer upon which all other features of MEseum were built upon. The Map contains three layers:

- Content layer, embedded with information (interactive photos, audio, text etc.,) from exhibitions that are currently being displayed on the floor of the museum. The content layer transforms the floor plan into an interactive map where the visitor is able to 'click' or 'tap' on anything that is so desired and retrieve detailed information on that specific object or area.
- Path building / Creation Layer, a procedurally created path connecting points of interest has also been built into the floor plan. This allows the user build paths of interests between two or more tour points, or exhibitions. It becomes essential for building personalized visits based on the visitor's preferences. The user is able to click on various hotspots, get detailed information on these hotspots, which are representative of exhibitions and then build tour paths in whatever order the she desires. These paths can be edited at any time before or during the visit.
- People Layer. This is the third layer that has been built into the interactive floor plan. It ties in neatly with the social media function of MEseum. This layer functions in two ways; Firstly, it shows and allows communication with other museum visitors that might be in the physical space of the museum during a visit and secondly, it acts as a medium through which visitors can engage in continuous interaction at every phase of the museum visit, thus having the potential of fostering a community of like minded individuals.

3.4.2   Check-in

The 'Check in' feature allows visitors who wish to record their arrival at a specific exhibition or particular place in the museum 'click' or 'tap' on a 'check in' menu that automatically updates their timeline. After checking in at an exhibition, the visitor has the option of adding media content (provided by the system or created by the visitor such as photos, notes etc.) to his timeline which in turn starts to progressively build his digital narrative. MEseum provides the visitor with the ability to manually 'check in' so there is no need for expensive infrastructure for location tracking. Various indoor positions systems can potentially be added to automate this process.

3.4.3   Timeline

The Timeline works directly with the 'Check in' feature. It is the container that holds and organizes all the content that is at the disposal of the visitor during her visit. As the visitor navigates her way across the floor of the museum, one exhibition at a time, she is able to build up her timeline with various media contents from different 'Check-in' spots. Once the visitor checks in to an exhibition either automatically or manually, she begins to build up content on her timeline that can later be reviewed, reordered and shared. At the end of a visit or a tour, the visitor has the option of editing and creating a digital story of that particular museum experience and sharing it. The timeline offers multiple formats by which the visitor can output all of the content on the timeline.

4   Experimental Results

4.1   Phase 1

The phase-1 survey participants were invited through posters, mailing lists and word of mouth. Total number of participants was 26. Participation was online and no physical visit to the museum was necessary as the evaluation was focused on the planning and potential uses rather actual real usage in a museum. Participants had almost equal gender distribution (some did not provide the information) and had various occupations from university student to retired. The age range was 23 to 60 with average of 33.

Two URL were shared with the participant. The first URL redirected the participant to the Canada Aviation and Space Museum, our partner museum's Visit Us page. This link was simply used to show the participant what currently exists on the website with regards to tools that support the activity of visiting the CASM. The participant was also provided with a user scenario and a set of user tasks that include locating exhibits, planning paths by using points of interest, checking in (virtually), creating timeline content, and accessing profile features such as sharing and messaging.

Table 1 shows the number of each response options for the significant survey questions. During the pre-survey, 22 participants agreed to some level that having a tool to plan museum visit based on personal interest will enhance their experience (pre-survey question 1). While 23 out of 26 stated that they would consider using a museum visit system, only 17 of them were optimistic about the usefulness of such system. The post-survey responses show that majority of participants found MEseum functional and potentially helpful in achieving its goals. More than 20 participants agreed that MEseum was a successful design for exploring the museum, interaction with content, planning and documenting, and creating a community. On the other hand, only 13 agreed that it was intuitive and easy to use.

Additional comments by participants acknowledged the early state of interface design and mentioned the need for improvements, addition of music and audio, consideration of the Internet connection, supporting video in timeline, and a list of exhibits and features.

Table 1. Distribution of answers to survey questions (Strongly Agree, Agree, Neutral, Disagree, and Strongly Disagree)

	SA	A	N	D	SD
Pre Survey Questions					
Will having the ability to plan your visit based on specific interests/preferences enhance your museum-visitor experience?	12	10	4	0	0
Do you think that having a more customized and personalized approach to planning and experiencing your museum visits will impact the quality of your museum-visitor experience?	10	9	6	1	0
Will a system that offers customizable and personalized tour paths, access to collective museum intelligence (social networking), and the ability to save and share museum memories enhance your museum-visitor experience?	11	6	7	1	0
Do you think that such a system will be of use to you when planning your museum-visit?	10	7	8	1	0
Will you consider using such a system when planning your museum-visits?	9	14	3	0	0
Post Survey Questions					
MEseum was functional in exploring the museum and it's exhibitions.	12	8	4	1	1
Access to the museums exhibitions and layout in this way increased my ability to plan a more efficient museum-visit?	13	6	5	2	0
MEseum provided a more interactive way to engage with the museum and its contents.	10	11	4	1	0
MEseum helped to set expectations for my museum-visit before arriving at the exhibition space.	13	10	2	1	0
MEseum was functional in planning a personalized/customized museum-visit.	9	11	3	2	1
MEseum was functional in documenting and creating a narrative of my museum experience.	9	11	3	2	1
MEseum was functional as an educational tool for the museum and its exhibitions.	10	12	2	2	0
MEseum can help build and foster an online community of aviation enthusiasts.	8	12	5	1	0
MEseum was intuitive and easy to use.	8	5	4	7	2
MEseum makes me feel more of a participant than a mere visitor.	8	9	5	4	0

4.2 Phase 2

The second phase of our study focused on the issue of timeline and narrative visualization. The experiment was broken up into two sub-tests:

- Sub-Test 1, Construction: The first test dealt with a user visiting a virtual (simulated) museum and building a narrative visualization based upon what they experienced. Our hypothesis was that the user would prefer the narrative visualizations to the more traditional methods. Our criteria to verify this hypothesis included effectiveness, operability, satisfaction, and flexibility, all measured through a questionnaire.
- Sub-Test 2, Viewing / Presentation: The second test was based on a user sharing their Visual Narrative with others. In this scenario the user is looking at visualizations of another person's visit to a museum that they have not visited. The two main goals that this user scenario has in mind are *sharing* and *communication*. Our hypothesis was that each visualization would succeed at conveying its themed content in a

satisfactory manner to the user. We used similar evaluation criteria as in sub-test 1, but replaced flexibility (more suitable in case of construction) with sociability (more suitable for this sub-test). We again used survey questions to measure.

20 participants were tested in all. There were 8 females and 12 males and they ranged in age from 20 to 61 with varying degrees of computer literacy that they were asked to rate themselves on (Tables 2 and 3).

Table 2. Sub-Test 1: Construction

Criteria	Result (Combined average rating)	Number of Questions
Effectiveness	5.7 out of 7 with 0.62 std error.	3 seven-point Likert scale
Operability	6.1 out of 7 with 0.2 std error.	3 seven-point Likert scale
Satisfaction	*See Sect. 4.2*	3 Ranking Questions
Flexibility	5.48 out of 7 with 0.29 std error.	3 + (two others detailed below)

Table 3. Sub-Test 2: Viewing / Presentation

Criteria	Result (Combined average)	Number of Questions
Effectiveness	5.65 out of 7 with 0.21 std error.	6 seven-point Likert scale
Operability	45.77 s with 8.09 std error.	Timed Task
Satisfaction	*See Sect. 4.2*	3 Ranking Questions
Sociability	4.6 out of 7 with 0.35 std error.	3 seven-point Likert scale

The ranked satisfaction questions were useful to tell which visualization preformed best in a variety of aspects. Overall the results were a bit inconclusive where for some questions the participants gave all the narrative visualizations clear majorities in terms of rank but for others there would be no clear majority.

Thus three main variables where used to determine the ranking: mode ranking, average ranking, and the various proportions of users who gave it a certain rank versus other ranks. The results, while not wholly conclusive, were analyzed in this regard to determine broad trends which are summarized as follows:

Subtest-1
Reflection: Dramatic, Sequential, Categorical, Slideshow
Uniqueness: Sequential, Dramatic, Categorical, Slideshow
Satisfaction: Dramatic, Categorical, Sequential, Slideshow
Subtest-2
Engagement: Dramatic, Categorical, Sequential, Slideshow, File Browser
Learning: Categorical, Dramatic, Sequential, Slideshow, File Browser
Clarity: Dramatic, Categorical, Sequential, Slideshow, File Browser

5 Conclusion

The research reported in the paper investigated the use of social media and digital technology in enhancing the museum-visitor experience. This has been done through a user study and the design and development of a museum interactive system called MEseum. The system is primarily designed to support the different phases of the museum visit and in the process, give the visitor the capability to build a personal digital narrative that she is able to share with the museum and other visitors.

Overall, the results from the user study conducted show that MEseum can potentially enhance the museum-visitors' experience, with 85 % of participants in favour of such planning and guidance tool. Users were generally able to plan customized visits by defining various paths. Users were also able to document their museum experiences through the creation of digital narratives on their timelines. Features implemented in the system were limited and as such user tasks that involved that part of the system was consequently limited. Based on these initial results as a next step, further research is expected to refine MEseum and also conduct subsequent user studies with real museum visitors in a constructed museum scenario.

- A more streamlined interface where general map, timeline overview, available actions, and information on selected items.
- Check-in process and data collection by visitor can be integrated into one action using object recognition algorithms that can allow the system to know where the visitors are when they take pictures.
- The system should be integrated with existing social networks.

Acknowledgement. This work is funded by Social Sciences and Humanities Research Council of Canada (SSHRC) through IMMERSe Network. The authors would like to thank the Canadian Aviation and Space Museum for the support in phase 1 of the research.

References

1. Alexander, E.P., Alexander, M.: Museums in Motion: An Introduction to the History and Functions of Museums. AltaMira Press, Plymouth (2008)
2. Bedford, L.: Storytelling and the real work of the museums. Curator Mus. J. **44**(1), 27–34 (2001)
3. Griffiths, A.: Media Technology and Museum Display: A Century of Accommodation and Conflict. MIT Communication Forum (2003). Retrieved from web.mit.edu/comm.forum/papers/griffiths.html
4. Walker, K.: Story structures. Building narrative trails in museums. In: Dettori, G., Giannetti, A., Vaz, A. (eds.) Technology-mediated Narrative Environment for Learning, pp. 114–130. Sense Publishers, Rotterdam (2006)
5. Lane, G.: Urban tapestries: wireless networking, public authoring and social knowledge. Pers. Ubiquitous Comput. **7**(3–4), 169–175 (2003)
6. Mulholland, P., Collins, T., Zdrahal, Z.: Bletchley Park Text: Using mobile and semantic web technologies to support the post-visit use of online museum resources. J. Interact. Mediain Educ. (to appear, 2005)

7. Ryan, M.L.: Beyond myth and metaphor - the case of narrative in digital media. Game Stud. Int. J. Comput. Game Res. **1**(1), 1–13 (2001)
8. Kosara, R., MacKinlay, J.: Storytelling: the next step for visualization. IEEE Comput. (Special Issue on Cutting-Edge Research in Visualization) **46**(5), 44–50 (2013)
9. Hullman, J., Diakopoulos, N.: Visualization rhetoric: framing effects in narrative visualization. IEEE Trans. Vis. Comput. Graph. **17**(12), 2231–2240 (2011)
10. Segel, E., Heer, J.: Narrative visualization: telling stories with data. IEEE Trans. Vis. Comput. Graph. **16**(6), 1139–1148 (2010)

Usability Evaluation of the Digital Library DanteSources

Valentina Bartalesi[1(✉)], Carlo Meghini[1], Daniele Metilli[1], and Paola Andriani[2]

[1] CNR-ISTI, via Moruzzi 1, 56124 Pisa, Italy
{valentina.bartalesi,carlo.meghini,daniele.metilli}@isti.cnr.it
[2] Dipartimento di Filologia, Letteratura e Linguistica, Università di Pisa, Piazza Torricelli 2,
56126 Pisa, Italy
paola.andriani@gmail.com

Abstract. In this paper we present DanteSources, a Digital Library of Dante Alighieri's primary sources, i.e. the works of other authors that Dante cites in his texts. Currently, this information is scattered in many books, making it difficult for the scholars to retrieve it and also to produce a systematical overview of the cultural background of Dante. In order to overcome this problem, an ontology expressed in RDF/S was developed to represent this knowledge. Once the ontology had been defined, we populated it with the data included in authoritative commentaries to Dante's works. We stored the resulting RDF graph into a Virtuoso triple store. Finally, on top of this graph, we developed DanteSources, which allows users to extract and display the knowledge stored in the knowledge base in the form of charts and tables. In this paper we present the results of a survey to collect suggestions and comments from end-users on their interactions with DanteSources in order to evaluate its usability.

Keywords: Digital libraries · Digital libraries usability · Semantic web · Human-computer interaction

1 Introduction

In the domain of humanities, scholars analyze old literary works in order to derive several kinds of knowledge. One important kind of such knowledge regards the primary sources, i.e. the works of other authors that an author makes reference to in his texts. Usually, scholars encode this knowledge in natural language, and report it in commentaries, which the readers use to understand several aspects of the literary works. However, encoding knowledge in natural language does not allow using computers to make inferences that could be useful to scholars, for example about the distribution of the primary sources and of the authors cited in a work.

Our study is part of the "Towards a Digital Dante Encyclopedia" project, an Italian National Research project supporting scholars, amongst others, in formally expressing the knowledge about primary sources present in Dante's works and more generally in literary texts. The goal of our work is to represent this kind of knowledge by (i) creating an ontology providing a formal representation of the terms required for expressing knowledge about the primary sources of an author's works, and (ii) developing a

M. Kurosu (Ed.): HCI 2016, Part III, LNCS 9733, pp. 191–203, 2016.
DOI: 10.1007/978-3-319-39513-5_18

semantic digital library based on the ontology that allows scholars to make inferences on the collected data and visualize them in a friendly and easy way.

In the Digital Humanities literature, there are ontologies focusing on different aspects of textual information. Each of these ontologies represents a set of possible interpretations of the source text(s). Up to now, an ontology for representing knowledge about primary sources of literary texts has not been developed. In the previous stages of the project, we developed an ontology [7] using the RDF language [13] to represent Dante's works and the knowledge about their primary sources. Then, we populated the ontology with the knowledge extracted from some authoritative commentaries, obtaining an RDF knowledge base. On top of this knowledge base, we developed DanteSources[1], a focused Digital Library (DL) endowed with web services that allow visualizing information on Dante Alighieri's primary sources in form of charts and tables. In this paper we present the results of a survey, developed using Google Docs, to collect suggestions and comments from end-users on their interactions with DanteSources in order to evaluate its usability.

The paper is structured as follows: Sect. 2 reports a review of related works; in Sect. 3 the functionalities of DanteSources are described. Section 4 presents the results of the evaluation and a discussion of them. Finally, in Sect. 5 we report our conclusive remarks.

2   Related Works

In the last thirty years several major Digital Humanities projects about Dante Alighieri and his works were published online. Most of them focused on offering digital editions of Dante's works with commentaries, textual search, and multimedia.

The Dartmouth Dante Project (DDP)[2] was launched in 1985 with the aim of publishing the full searchable text of the Divine Comedy and several of its commentaries in digital format [10]. On top of the DDP in 2013 the web application Dante Lab[3] was developed. This application allows the concurrent visualization of the original text of the Comedy, some translations i.e. English, French and German, and more than 75 commentaries, each of them fully searchable. The Princeton Dante Project[4] includes the full searchable text of the Divine Comedy, Dante's minor works, several commentaries and multimedia resources [11]. The World of Dante[5] is a multi-media research tool that contains the whole text of the Divine Comedy with a basic semantic annotation that identifies people, places, deities and structures, and connections to digital objects such as images and music. However, the semantic knowledge is not represented through a formal ontology and is not available in a machine-readable format. An interactive timeline of Dante's life and relevant maps are also available [14]. Digital Dante[6] offers the

---

[1]   http://dantesources.org.
[2]   http://dante.dartmouth.edu.
[3]   http://dantelab.dartmouth.edu.
[4]   http://etcweb.princeton.edu/dante/.
[5]   http://www.worldofdante.org.
[6]   http://digitaldante.columbia.edu.

full text of all Dante's works with commentaries, illustrations and recorded readings. It also features a subproject called Intertextual Dante[7], the first digital attempt at connecting passages of Dante's works with the corresponding fragments of cited primary sources. However, the project is limited to the works of the Roman poet Ovid [15]. Dante Online[8] includes the full text of all Dante's works, a biography with an interactive timeline, and a database listing hundreds of manuscripts of the Divine Comedy with bibliographic information. Danteworlds[9] is a multimedia project built around the Divine Comedy, featuring illustrations by historical and contemporary artists, audio lectures and study resources. More recently, two major Italian research projects were published: DanteSearch[10] and Dante Medieval Archive (DaMA)[11]. DanteSearch is a complete lemmatization, grammatical and syntactic annotation of Dante's works allowing users to perform morphological and syntactic queries on the full text of the author's works. On the other hand, DaMA is a digital archive containing the full text of Dante's works, commentaries and several primary sources in XML-TEI format. With the advent of the Semantic Web, several projects were started with a focus on the application of the new semantic technologies (RDF, OWL[12]) to the Humanities. For instance, González-Blanco et al. [9] describe a semantic model to connect repertoires of poetic writings. Vitale [16] presents an ontology for the 3D visualization of cultural heritage; Lana et al. [12] describe an ontology for annotating geographical places in texts. In this context, we developed DanteSources DL, which uses the technologies of the Semantic Web to represent the knowledge included in the works of Dante Alighieri, focusing on primary sources.

3   The Digital Library DanteSources

In the previous stages of the project "Towards a Digital Dante Encyclopaedia", we developed an ontology [7] expressed in RDF language [13] to represent Dante's works and the knowledge about their primary sources. We populated the ontology with the knowledge extracted from the following authoritative commentaries: Vita Nova [3], Vita Nuova [1], De vulgari eloquentia [2], Convivio [5], and Monarchia [6]. The obtained RDF graph was eventually stored in a Virtuoso triple store [8]. The focused DanteSources DL allows extracting and displaying the information stored in the knowledge base to support scholars in discovering and exploring Dante's primary sources. DanteSources is a web application developed in Java using Javascript and Ajax functions. The DL extracts knowledge by running SPARQL queries on the RDF knowledge base. DanteSources shows the knowledge about the primary sources cited by Dante in

---

[7]   http://digitaldante.columbia.edu/digital-projects/intertexual-dante/.
[8]   http://danteonline.it.
[9]   http://danteworlds.laits.utexas.edu.
[10] http://www.perunaenciclopediadantescadigitale.eu:8080/dantesearch/.
[11] http://perunaenciclopediadantescadigitale.eu/istidama/.
[12] https://www.w3.org/TR/owl2-overview/.

the form of tables and column bar charts. In particular, we used the Highcharts[13] Java-Script library to implement these charts. Highcharts allows exporting the charts in various well-known formats: PDF, PNG, JPEG, SVG. Furthermore, we implemented an additional JavaScript function allowing users to automatically export and download all the data in CSV format[14]. This feature is particularly important since it allows scholars to obtain and manage raw data, in order to apply further data analyses in addition to the ones already provided by the DL. Currently, eight different predefined SPARQL queries are available to extract data. They can be distinguished into three different groups. The first group includes three queries. In order to make these queries, a search form allows users to choose either one Dante's work or all his works and, in addition, a specific subpart of the work (e.g. a book). The queries produce column bar charts regarding the distribution of the works, the authors and the thematic areas cited by Dante. For example, Fig. 1 shows the chart of the distribution of some primary sources cited in the first book of Convivio.

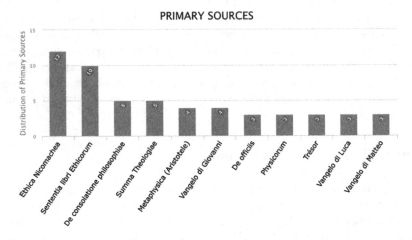

Fig. 1. The chart represents the distribution of some primary sources cited in the first book of Convivio

Additional information about primary sources, authors and thematic areas are available by clicking on their names. In particular, clicking on the title of a primary source, the DL shows a table reporting information about: (i) the book, (ii) the chapter, (ii) the paragraph or poem and (iv) the fragment of the Dante's work in which the primary source is cited, (v) the type of reference, (vii) the reference to a fragment of the primary source cited in the commentary, (viii) the thematic area and (ix) the author of the primary source. An example of this table is reported in Fig. 2.

---

[13] http://www.highcharts.com/.
[14] http://www.w3.org/2013/05/lcsv-charter.html.

Dante's work	Book	Chapter	Paragraph	Fragment of Dante's work	Reference type	Fragment of the primary source	Thematic area of the primary source	Author of the primary source
Convivio	1	8	12	ABBISOGNI	CONCORDANZA STRINGENTE	1155 a 3-6	Aristotelismo	Aristotele
Convivio	1	12	10	COME DICE LO FILOSOFO NEL QUINTO DELL'ETICA	CITAZIONE ESPLICITA	Non disponibile	Aristotelismo	Aristotele
Convivio	1	11	20	CON QUELLA MISURA CHE	CONCORDANZA STRINGENTE	IV 3, 1124 a 20; 1124 b 5-6 e Moore, p. 104	Aristotelismo	Aristotele
Convivio	1	8	11	IN VITA CONTEMPLATIVA O ATTIVA	CONCORDANZA STRINGENTE	I 5, 1095 b 17 sgg.	Aristotelismo	Aristotele
Convivio	1	1	9	LIBERALMENTE	CONCORDANZA STRINGENTE	IV 1, 1119 b 22 sgg.	Aristotelismo	Aristotele

Fig. 2.   Part of the table regarding Ethica Nicomachea cited by Dante in the first book of Convivio

Similarly, when a user clicks on the name of a cited author, the DL shows a table reporting all the works of that author cited in the Dante's text chosen by the user. Furthermore, for each primary source the DL reports the book, the chapter and the paragraph (or poem) of the Dante's text in which the author is cited. Figure 3 shows an example of table related to a cited author.

Dante's work	Book	Chapter	Paragraph	Primary source
Monarchia	1	1	1	Metaphysica
Monarchia	1	1	2	Ethica Nicomachea
Monarchia	1	2	6	Politica
Monarchia	1	2	8	Politica
Monarchia	1	3	2	Ethica Nicomachea
Monarchia	1	3	2	Politica
Monarchia	1	3	3	De caelo

Fig. 3.   Part of the table regarding Aristotle cited in Monarchia

Finally, for what concerns the thematic areas, clicking on one name the user obtains the following information for each thematic area: the primary sources included in that area, their authors and the book, chapter and paragraph (or poem) of the Dante's work where the thematic area is cited.

The three queries of the second group allow visualizing several charts that report the distribution of a particular primary source, a cited author or a thematic area respectively. In order to improve the usability of the DL, we implemented two different search forms for these queries.

(1) An autocomplete menu where the user can type the title of the cited work, the author, or the thematic area;
(2) An alphabetically ordered list in which the user can select the title of the primary source, the author, or the thematic area.

The data regarding the distributions are not only available for an entire Dante's work, like Convivio, but also for its subparts like books, chapters or poems. Indeed, by clicking on one bar in the chart representing the distribution of the information onto a Dante's work, it is possible to visualize information about its subparts. For example, it is possible to visualize the distribution of the selected information on all the books of Convivio and

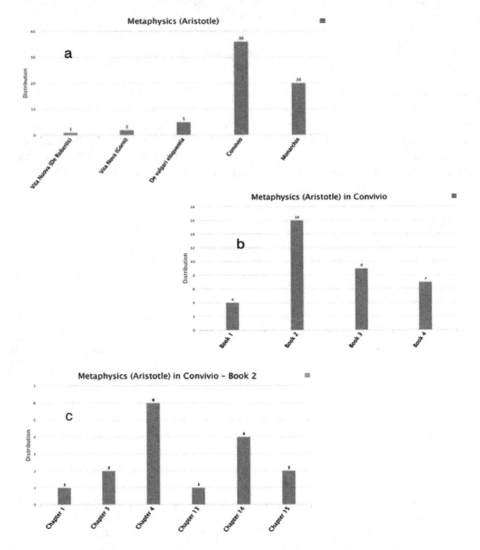

Fig. 4. The distribution of Aristotle's Metaphysics in all Dante's works (a), in the four books of Convivio (b) and in the chapters of the second book of Convivio (c).

also its distribution on each chapter of the second book of Convivio. Figure 4 shows three views of the distribution of a primary source on three different levels: all Dante's works (a), one particular Dante's work (b), a subpart of a Dante's work (c).

The last group includes two queries that allow visualizing the distribution of the three types of reference to primary sources: explicit, strict and generic, focusing either on Dante's works or on a single primary source. Indeed, with the support of Dante's experts we defined three types of reference:

1. *explicit*, if the reference is explicitly made by Dante, e.g. "As the Philosopher says at the beginning of the First Philosophy", where the Philosopher is Aristotle and the First Philosophy is Metaphysics;
2. *strict,* if the reference is indicated by a scholar and refers to a specific work, e.g. "SI MANUCA: it is the bread of the angels, the manna as called in the Old Testament (Ps. 77, 25 Panem angelorum manducavit homo)";
3. *generic*, if the reference is indicated by a scholar, and refers to a concept (e.g. Medieval comments to Aristotle's works).

Figure 5 shows the distribution of the three types of reference in the works of Dante included in our knowledge base.

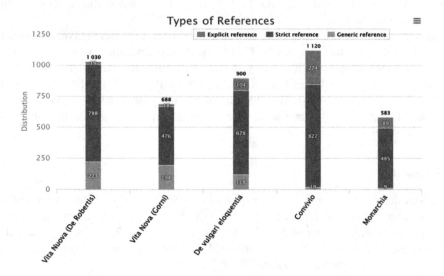

Fig. 5. The distribution of the three types of reference in Dante's works

As for the second group of queries, by clicking on the bars of the chart, the data regarding the distribution of the types of reference are available both for an entire Dante's work and for its subparts, i.e. books and chapters.

4   Evaluation

4.1   The Online Survey

The survey included 28 questions about the main aspects regarding the usability of the DL. After a brief overview to identify the sample, we focused our attention on the features of the DL: the navigation usability, the readability of the charts and tables, the usability of the search functionalities, the satisfaction of the results obtained doing a query. A specific attention was put on the effective responsiveness of the layout and on the use of the DL on different devices, e.g. PCs, smartphones, tablets. Questions were presented through multiple choice and text area. The same questions required a personal judgment on selected features. A Likert 5-scale values from 1 (totally negative) to 5 (totally positive) was used to express the opinion.

4.2   Participants

We collected suggestions and comments from 26 users; some of them did not answer all the questions. Our sample included 18 females and 10 males. 82 % of the participants were in the range of 31–50 years old, 14 % were people between 10 and 30 years old and 3 % were in the range of 51–65 years old.

25 % of the users were students, 20 % were researchers, 12 % were university professors, 4 % were school teachers and the 37 % of the users did not specify their profession. Concerning technological skills, 51 % declared to regularly use smartphones with android system, 18 % an iPhone or iPod touch, 11 % an iPad, 11 % a tablet with Android system, 7 % of the users responded that they never use mobile devices. 100 % of the users said that they use the Internet at least once per day to search information about their interest fields.

4.3   Results

We asked the users to freely use and explore DanteSources. Afterwards, we asked an opinion about the general interaction with the interface: 63 % of the users expressed a totally positive opinion (score 5), 22.2 % assigned score 4, 7.4 % score 3 and the remaining 7.4 % score 2. No one expressed a totally negative opinion (score 1). Figure 6 shows a graphical representation of the results.

1	0	0%
2	2	7.4%
3	2	7.4%
4	6	22.2%
5	17	63%

Fig. 6. Opinions of the users on the interaction with the interface

Regarding the navigation, 55.6 % of the users said that the navigation is simple and clear and the user always knowing where s/he currently and where to go afterwards, 25.9 % assigned score 4, 14.8 % score 3, and only one user score 2. No one expressed a totally negative opinion (score 1). A graphical representation of the results is reported in Fig. 7.

1	0	0%
2	2	7.4%
3	4	14.8%
4	7	25.9%
5	14	51.9%

Fig. 7. Readability of the charts

As far as the readability of the obtained charts is concerned, 51.9 % of the users assigned score 5, 25.9 % score 4, 14.8 % score 3, and the remaining 7,4 % score 2. No one chose score 1. In particular, the users expressed a positive opinion on the possibility to export in CSV format all the data visualized into the charts and on the possibility of visualizing ten results at a time using the scrollbar. On the other hand, some comments reported the continuous use of the scrollbar as a limit, when the results are many.

Then, we asked to evaluate the tables which the user can access from each chart and to leave a textual comment to describe the main observed problems. Regarding the charts about primary sources, several users reported the usefulness and the completeness of the knowledge presented in the tables. Some users highlighted the lack of text visualization for the cited fragment within the text of the primary source. One user said that it is not intuitive that clicking on the title of the primary sources in the chart, it is possible to visualize a table. This possibility is described in natural language below the chart but this user suggested that it could be more useful having it above. As to the tables regarding the cited authors, the majority of the comments reported that the only missing information is the textual fragment of the primary sources.

For what concerns the tables about the thematic areas, many comments reported the lack of a textual explanation on how the thematic areas were defined, as well as the absence of the textual fragment of the primary sources.

For the second group of queries, we asked about the usefulness of the two different search menus, the autocomplete menu and the alphabetically ordered list. 80.8 % expressed a totally positive opinion, assigning score 5, and the remaining 19.2 % assigned score 4. The users reported the usefulness of these search functionalities especially to avoid the failure of the search and the absence of feedback (Fig. 8).

1	0	0%
2	0	0%
3	0	0%
4	5	19.2%
5	21	80.8%

Fig. 8. Usefulness of the two different search menus

Regarding the position of the information on the screen, 25.9 % of the users assigned score 5, 48.1 % score 4, 22.2 % score 3, 3.7 % score 2. No one expressed a totally negative opinion (score 1). The main reported problem regards the presence of too much blank space between the search forms and the results, which forces the users to vertically scroll the page. Furthermore, some comments reported that the explanations about the functionalities of the charts should have a more relevant position on the page.

Only 18.5 % of the users accessed DanteSources from a mobile device. The used mobile devices were: smartphone with Android system, iPhone, iPad. 57.1 % of this 18.5 % declared that interaction on a mobile device was very easy and clear (score 5), the remaining 42.9 % assigned score 4. No problems were reported in the comments.

76.9 % of the users said that the response times of the DL were very fast and they obtained an instantaneous response (value 5). 15.4 % assigned score 4 and the remaining 7.7 % score 3. No one chose the more negative scores 2 and 1 (Fig. 9).

1	0	0%
2	0	0%
3	2	7.7%
4	4	15.4%
5	20	76.9%

Fig. 9. Ease of response of DanteSources

Regarding the data obtained through the search functionalities, 61.5 % of the users said that they obtained all the information they needed, while 34.6 % reported that they obtained a lot of information, although they would like to receive additional data. Only one user said that s/he did not retrieve the information s/he needed. This last user specified that s/he is a linguist and for this reason s/he would need to other types of information, like Named Entities, parsing of the texts and collocations. Unfortunately, our project was focused not on the syntax but on the semantics of the primary sources. Many users expressed the desire to visualize the text of the fragments of the primary sources as well as, on request, the entire text of the primary sources and of the Dante's works. Other comments suggested visualizing the entire text of the commentaries. Unfortunately, they are protected by copyright, so it is not possible to show them.

We asked the user about the major problems encountered using DanteSources. Several users reported that they did not have significant problems, few users suggested making the information more compact on the screen and one user said that the interactive image on the homepage is not intuitive to use.

Finally, the users left suggestions to improve the DL. The three main suggestions regarded (i) the possibility of visualizing the texts of the cited fragments, as well as the entire texts of the primary sources and of the Dante's works; (ii) the introduction of the possibility to directly visualize the information on the primary sources written by a specific cited author; (iii) the enrichment of the knowledge base with other Dante's works, especially with the Divine Comedy.

About the usefulness of DanteSources, 65.5 % of the users declared that the DL is very useful (score 5), 26.9 % assigned score 4, 3.8 % score 3 and the remaining 3.8 % score 2 (Fig. 10).

1	0	0%
2	1	3.8%
3	1	3.8%
4	7	26.9%
5	17	65.4%

Fig. 10. General usefulness of DanteSources

4.4 Discussion

Regarding the answers and the opinions obtained from the users through the survey, we observe that the interaction with the application is generally satisfying. Several users said that the navigation is clear and easy and the results of the queries are complete and well presented. Also the response times of the DL are satisfactory. At the same time, the users made suggestions to improve the interface usability and the user experience. In brief, the suggestions are related to:

a. reducing blank spaces in the layout, especially between the search forms and the results and moving the explanation of additional features of the charts in a more evident position;
b. visualizing the fragments of the primary sources and, upon request, the whole texts of the primary sources and of the Dante's works;
c. visualizing the data shown in the charts also in the form of tables or lists;
d. making available the corresponding works when the users search for a specific author;
e. enriching the knowledge base with other Dante's works.

Regarding the (a) suggestion, we have planned to reduce the blank spaces and modify the position of the explanation of the charts' additional features. About the (b), we have already developed a function that for each Dante's fragment allows visualizing the fragment of the corresponding primary source. Up to now we implemented this function for the primary sources included in DaMA, since this archive contains several primary sources coded in XML-TEI format. Regarding the suggestion to also visualize the entire texts of Dante's works, these are already preset in a dedicated page of the DL as external links to DaMA. However, the users didn't find them easily. For this reason, we have planned to add this links also in the pages of the search results. Concerning the suggestion (c), the users did not consider the possibility to export the data in CSV format in order to have the results in form of simple table. We supposed that the CSV could be a format not very well known and used in the Humanities, so we have thought to replace the current label "Export in CSV" into a more clear label like "Export as a table (in CSV format)". About request (d), when a user searches for a specific cited author, we have decided to add a feature that shows a table of that author's works. Regarding the suggestion (e), at this moment we are working to add Rime [4] in our knowledge base.

5 Conclusions

In this paper we have presented a survey conducted on the interaction with the Dante-Sources Digital Library via PCs and mobile devices to collect suggestions and comments on possible usability issues observed by the users.

We have had a total of 26 users. Positive responses on the general interaction have emerged from the survey: more than 60 % of the users have expressed a distinctly positive response. About 80 % have expressed a satisfactory opinion on the navigation (score 4 and 5) and on the readability of charts and tables (score 4 and 5) as well. 100 % of the users who accessed DanteSources from a mobile device have declared that interaction was easy and clear (score 4 and 5). On the other hand, the users have identified some problems and lacks in the interface, in particular: the presence of too much blank space between the search forms and the results, the hidden position of the explanation of the charts' functionalities, the lack of text visualization for the cited fragments and for the entire texts of the primary sources and Dante's works. Furthermore, the users have suggested adding a functionality that allows visualizing the list of works when the users search for a specific author. The users have also suggested enriching the knowledge base with other Dante's works, especially with Divine Comedy. We have planned to modify and enrich DanteSources taking into account the problems highlighted by the users and the given suggestions.

The Dante's experts who have taken part in our evaluation have said that having the information about primary sources available, for the first time, in digital format, improves and makes more efficient their searches. Indeed, in their commentaries, scholars typically express knowledge on the primary sources in natural language. This limits scholars in their advances insofar as it prevents automatic inferences of new information that may be useful for their studies. For instance, in the case of references to primary sources, the inferences may concern the total amount of references to a certain work or to an author. Eventually, the digitization of the knowledge about primary sources allows experts to have a comprehensive overview of the data, to visualize it as charts and tables, and to export it to make their own analyses. For this reason, DanteSources allows scholars to explore the dynamics of the multi-faceted culture of Dante in relation to the diverse stages of his biography and to study the evolution in time of Dante's cultural background.

References

1. Alighieri, D.: Vita nuova. In: De Robertis, D. (ed.) Milano, Napoli, Ricciardi (1980)
2. Alighieri, D.: De vulgari eloquentia. In: Tavoni, M. (ed.) Opere, vol. I: Rime, Vita Nova, De vulgari eloquentia. Mondadori, Milano (2011)
3. Alighieri, D.: Vita Nova. In: Gorni, G. (ed.) Opere, vol. I: Rime, Vita Nova, De vulgari eloquentia. Mondadori, Milano (2011)
4. Alighieri, D.: Rime. In: Giunta, C. (ed.) Opere, vol. I: Rime, Vita Nova, De vulgari eloquentia. Mondadori, Milano (2011)
5. Alighieri, D.: Convivio. In: Fioravanti, G. (ed.) Opere, vol. II: Convivio, Monarchia, Epistole, Egloghe. Mondadori, Milano (2014)
6. Alighieri, D.: Monarchia. In: Quaglioni, D. (ed.) Opere, vol. II: Convivio, Monarchia, Epistole, Egloghe. Mondadori, Milano (2014)
7. Bartalesi, V., Meghini, C.: Using an ontology for representing the knowledge on literary texts: the Dante Alighieri case study. Seman. Web, 1–10 (2015, Preprint)
8. Erling, O., Mikhailov, I.: RDF support in the Virtuoso DBMS. GI-Edition-Lecture Notes in Informatics (LNI), vol. P-113 (2007). ISSN: 1617-5468
9. González-Blanco, E., Seláf, L., Del Rio Riande, M.G., Martínez Cantón, C.I., Martos Pérez, M.D.: Building a metrical ontology as a model to link digital poetic repertoires (2014)
10. Hollander, R.: The Dartmouth Dante Project. Quad. d'italianistica **10**(1–2), 287–298 (1989)
11. Hollander, R.: The Princeton Dante Project. Humanist Stud. Digital Age **3**(1), 53–59 (2013)
12. Lana, M., Ciotti, F., Magro, D., Peroni, S., Tomasi, F., Vitali, F.: Annotating texts with ontologies, from geography to persons and events (2014)
13. Manola, F., Miller, E., McBride, B.: RDF primer. W3C Recommendation **10**(1–107), 6 (2004)
14. Parker, D.: The world of Dante: a hypermedia archive for the study of the inferno. Literary Linguist. Comput. **16**(3), 287–297 (2001)
15. Van Peteghem, J.: Digital readers of allusive texts: ovidian intertextuality in the 'Commedia' and the digital concordance on 'Intertextual Dante'. Humanist Stud. Digital Age **4**(1), 39–59 (2015)
16. Vitale, V.: An ontology for 3D visualisation of cultural heritage (2014)

Contextual Presentation and Navigation of Historical Artifacts in a Digital Library Design

Joseph R. Galindo and Patricia A. Morreale(⊠)

Department of Computer Science,
Kean University,
Union, NJ 07083, USA
{galinjos,pmorreal}@kean.edu

Abstract. A digital library has been designed to present a historically signifi-cant collection of World War II letters in both temporal and geographical context. Working closely with historical scholars, over 800 WWII historical records have been made publically available for the use of researchers and historians on the web. Digital library design issues encountered as part of this effort dealt with the development of a website from original artifacts and the rendering of this historical content in a visual, geographical, and temporal context, increasing and extending the reach of information previously available only to on-site historical researchers. The current digital library prototype can serve as a model for other developers that are interested in multimodal pre-sentation of varied content.

Keyword: Digital library database user-centered design contextual presentation

1   Introduction

Historical archives are valuable resources for researchers, while also providing support for collective memory, historical context and recall. In order to review and work with such archives, which can include a range of artifacts, researchers must often travel to the location where the artifacts are housed, or settle for a small traveling subset col-lection to work with locally. Both solutions are not ideal, as travel to the site limits access, while a local subset collection limits the range of artifacts which can be con-sulted and examined. In an effort to address both these concerns, a research project was undertaken to overcome the limits of time and space in addressing and identifying correlations in historical collections.

Over 800 letters written by World War II soldiers from the New York and New Jersey region in the northeastern United States have been preserved and successfully incorporated into a digital library, designed to provide contextual information. The soldiers, students at New Jersey State Teacher's College, were contacted by the college librarian during their military service with a request to provide information for an alumni newsletter. The letters received in response to this request for information, serve as the

© Springer International Publishing Switzerland 2016
M. Kurosu (Ed.): HCI 2016, Part III, LNCS 9733, pp. 204–210, 2016.
DOI: 10.1007/978-3-319-39513-5_19

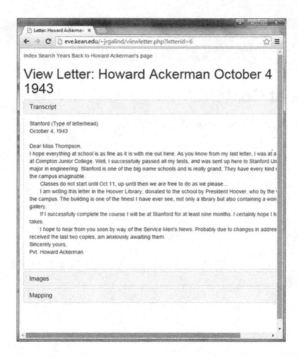

Fig. 1. On retrieval, Transcript (top), Images and Mapping (bottom) links are shown

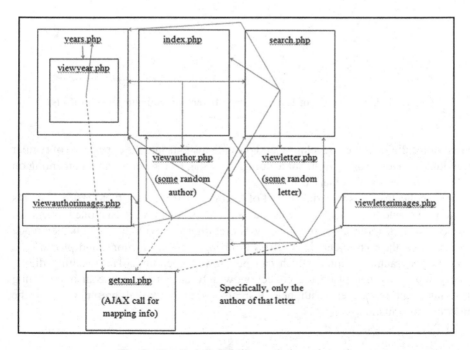

Fig. 2. Detailed digital library design schematic

Fig. 3. A drop-down list of letters, ordered by author, and number of artifacts

basis for the digital library developed, and provide insights into the experience of regular individuals traveling away from home during wartime, facing fears, and commenting on both routine and extraordinary events.

As a collection, this material is a set of historically significant first-person accounts of domestic and international events, as not all soldiers were stationed overseas. Working with historians, this repository was first digitized, with the artifacts then made accessible on the web, ordered for retrieval through search functions, and placed on a map by geographic location, which can be viewed over time. The resulting digital library repository has made the collection widely accessible, while also providing historians and researchers with new insights based on visual presentation of the historical information.

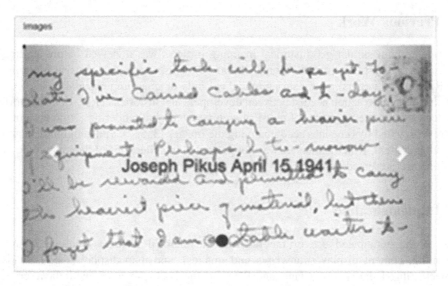

Fig. 4. A letter from Joseph Pikus, April 15, 1941, a scanned artifact, retrieved from the library

Fig. 5. The same letter from Joseph Pikus, in searchable plain text, from the library

2 Previous Work

Literature about similar geo-historical mapping projects was reviewed before starting this project. In particular, an article on the Stanford mapping project (known as Mapping the Republic of Letters) gave a strong model not only of smart implementation choices, but also of the interaction needed between developers and historians [1, 2, 4]. Prior work concentrated on the migration of physical archives to digital renderings, with temporal context provided by timelines accompanying the images [3, 6, 7]. Full geographical and temporal context, with the images, was not presented in collections of the magnitude or significance presented here.

3 Implementation

Due to the anticipated use of the records, the enabled features revolved around searching, content display (transcripts and images), and map display (Fig. 1). This project utilized the scripting language PHP for the back-end work, with JavaScript, HTML, and CSS used to support front-end content. MySQL was used for the database. The resulting design provided the functionality needed (Fig. 2), with the design features supporting search (Fig. 3) and display.

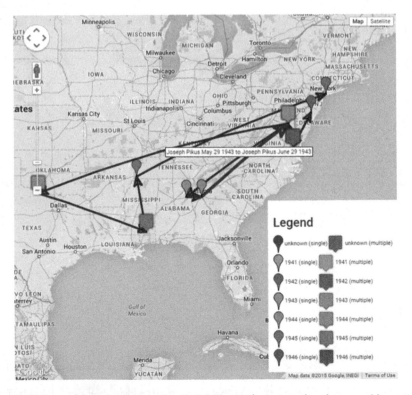

Fig. 6. Letters of Joseph Pikus in the digital library, in temporal and geographic context

In support of the desired user-centered designed, developers worked closely with the anticipated user community to determine how the digital library collection would be used. After detailed discussions with historians, the scanned historical artifacts were placed in a database by author order, for user retrieval and review. The overall design of the digital library was done in multiple iterations, with feedback provided by the historians on how the collection was to be navigated.

4 Features

Once an artifact is selected, users view the actual artifact (Fig. 4), searchable text (Fig. 5), or view the image in a geographical context with added temporal context (Fig. 6) [5, 8]. The use of colored icons (Fig. 6) to denote the progression of years, as well as correlating artifacts in the collection from the same author in the same year is a powerful visual illustration which permits users to understand the chronological development of the materials in the digital library.

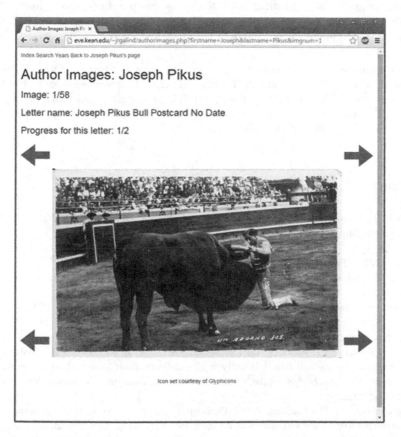

Fig. 7. Postcard from Joseph Pikus in the digital library, with lateral navigation arrows

Users can navigate seamlessly from one view in the digital library to another and from one artifact to another, using lateral display navigation to move through the collection (Fig. 7). The design of the digital library supports identifying correlations or contrasts in the historical record which may not have been identified or clearly understood before.

5   Conclusion

Through close collaboration with historians, this project created a stable digital repository, which can be widely used and remotely accessed in the years to come by both casual users and academic historians. It also provides an active example to other multimedia and digital library developers pursuing similar projects.

Additional materials are being added to the repository and the design will evolve as more information is gathered from user studies, particularly regarding the interactions which historians, researchers, and other members of the public have with the materials. The prototype digital library discussed here demonstrates user-centered information design techniques which illustrate the viability of this proof-of-concept implementation. The historical artifacts in the collection are organized and displayed in an appropriate digital environment designed to support user access and control.

Acknowledgements.   The authors acknowledge the Department of History at Kean University, particularly Dr. Elizabeth Hyde and Dr. Jonathan Mercanti, for providing input crucial to the relevancy of this design to the historical archivist field of research. Kean University, home to the Nancy Thompson World War II collection, provided access and web hosting support for the development of the digital library presented here.

References

1. Brotton, J.: Maps online: digital historical geographies. J. His Geogr. **43**, 169–174 (2014). doi:10.1016/j.jhg.2013.10.003
2. Choi, Y., Syn, S.: An examination of user tags in a digitized humanities online collection (ASIST 2012). Proc. Am. Soc. Inf. Sci Technol. **49**(1), 1–4 (2012)
3. French Revolution Digital Archive. 2012. Stanford University Libraries. Online. http://frda.stanford.edu/
4. Hindley, M.: Mapping the republic of letters. Humanities **34**(20–23), 52–53 (2013)
5. Kumar, S.: Docx to Text convertor, May 15 2014. Accessed 21 October 2014. http://docx2txt.sourceforge.net/
6. Novak, J., Micheel, I, Wieneke, L., During, M., Melenhorst, M., Moron, J.: HistoGraph-a visualization tool for collaborative analysis of networks from historical social multimedia collections. In: Proceedings of the International Conference on Information Visualization, pp. 241–250 (2014)
7. Tomaszewski, B., MacEachren, A.M.: Geovisual analytics to support crisis management: Information foraging for geo-historical context. Inf. Vis. **11**(4), 339–359 (2012)
8. Wisniewski, J.: Improving the search experience with site search. Online **34**(3), 54–56 (2010)

Multi-touch Interaction with Information Visualization Techniques: An Analysis Using Twitter Data

Felipe Eduardo Lammel, Isabel Harb Manssour, and Milene Selbach Silveira[✉]

PUCRS, Faculdade de Informática, Porto Alegre, RS, Brazil
felipelammel@gmail.com,
{isabel.manssour,milene.silveira}@pucrs.br

Abstract. Information Visualization techniques have been aiding in the analysis of large quantities of data that traffics the internet today. Moreover, there is a growing popularization of multi-touch devices that opens up a range of new possibilities of interaction. In this context, and considering the amount of data provided by social networks, the main research question of the work here presented is: Does the multi-touch interaction with information visualization techniques can improve the data analysis? In order to understand this and related questions, a research was conducted in the areas of information visualization and multi-touch technology. User interaction was analyzed with a prototype tool built for this purpose and Twitter was chosen as application domain.

Keywords: Information visualization · Multi-touch · Social networks · Twitter

1 Introduction

With the growing development of the internet and communication and data manipulation technologies, the amount of information that reaches users about these technologies has been increasing greatly. However, not all data that reach them are effectively useful for them, and this excess ends up becoming a problem in understanding the results obtained [18]. In order to facilitate the analysis of these data, Information Visualization techniques are introduced, since a visual representation of the data set makes understanding more simple and intuitive. This reduces the time spent on interpreting the information in addition to reducing the possibility of doing it incorrectly.

For Spence [15], visualization is something that takes place in the mind; in other words, it is a cognitive activity. This author also says that a determined data set can often hide, in a way, relationships that are fundamental for understanding, and a different perspective on this data set can reveal important information. In this case, information visualization is, according to Spence, the process of forming a mental model of a determined data set and through it, one can obtain some knowledge.

A source of data that could be better analyzed by means of visualization techniques is the one obtained through social networks, which accumulate daily a large amount of information. The information contained in these networks has been drawing the attention of common users and businesses, which use them in some way for some personal benefit. Their millions of adepts produce an excessive amount of data, useful or not, and these

© Springer International Publishing Switzerland 2016
M. Kurosu (Ed.): HCI 2016, Part III, LNCS 9733, pp. 211–222, 2016.
DOI: 10.1007/978-3-319-39513-5_20

data are disseminated through the networks. Therefore, depending on the analysis that users need to carry out based on these data, they may need some way to filter the content that is provided to them.

Since information from social networks has been of great value for different areas, various visualization and interaction techniques have been developed and used to present this information using a computational interface. And today, the ubiquity of multi-touch technology [3] opens up a range of new possibilities of interaction.

In this context, the main research question of the work here presented is: Does the multi-touch interaction with information visualization techniques can improve the data analysis? And related to this: How the interaction could improve it? Is this kind of interaction better that the conventional keyboard plus mouse combination?

In order to answer these questions, the main goal of this work is to analyze the use of information visualization techniques allied to the interaction through multi-touch devices. To achieve this goal, we have used the following methodology: first we did a research about information visualization, social networks and multi-touch technology visualization. Then we implemented a prototype and we made a user study to analyze the mentioned interaction issues. Moreover, to implement the prototype, a process was applied to identify the appropriate multi-touch gestures to be implemented.

The next sections describe the research related to that presented in this paper, the process applied to study the gestures and the conception of the prototype developed. After, we analyze user interactions with the implemented prototype and we present some final consideration, concluding this paper.

2   Related Work

Due to the popularity of multi-touch interfaces, some studies have been carried out with the purpose of reconsidering information visualization techniques in order to enable interaction through these new interfaces. According to Isenberg et al. [7], "multi-touch interaction give people additional degrees of freedom to express their intentions and provide more direct access to their objects of interactions".

For example, Kister, Reipschläger and Dachselt [8] discuss multi-touch manipulation using the magic lenses technique. Baur, Lee and Carpendale [1] developed a tool for analyzing stacked graphs that explore multi-touch gestures. Kristensson et al. [9] created a tool for search and photo visualization that uses information visualization techniques such as tag clouds and graphs, and in it, the user has the freedom to use all ten fingers for interaction.

There are also other studies that focus on tasks that are more complicated to carry out through these interfaces, as is the case with the Rizzo tool [17], or even the Touch2Annotate [2]. These studies focus on the weak points of multi-touch interfaces: precision and typing. Precision is also discussed by Thalmann et al. [16].

According to Lee et al. [10], information visualization techniques "do not take full advantage of the possibilities of evolving interaction technologies". Rzeszotarski and

Kittur [13] also explored how interactions different of WIMP "might improve exploratory data visualization through the introduction of physics-based affordances and multi-
touch interaction techniques".

3   Process for Elaborating Gestures

A process based on user opinions [4] was applied to define which gestures to use for
interacting with the information visualization techniques to be implemented. This
process consists of creating a focus group to discuss the data collected by means of a
series of semi-structured individual interviews. Its five stages are described as follows.

3.1   System Definition

In the first stage of the process, the desired system to be used as the basis of study is
chosen. Moreover, a set of initial commands is defined based on the purpose of the
system with which one intends to produce the gesture interactions.

Considering the goal of analyze the use of information visualization techniques allied
to the interaction through multi-touch devices, the main idea was to work with visualization techniques that could both correlate the gathered data and encourage users to
interact with these data to get more information. In this context, the system would present
interactive bubble charts, showing the correlation between distinct data and presenting
more related information by the bubbles resizing.

To present to the users the idea to be developed, the application Ripples[1] was used.
It consists of an information visualization tool in the social network Google +. This tool
allows one to visualize the propagation of a post within this network. The visualization
of post diffusion is composed of various circles and each one represents the profile of
who shared the post. Circles within another circle, connected by arrows, represent the
flow of the shares; i.e., the profiles that shares the post of another profile. As Ripples
was not developed with a focus on multi-touch interfaces, interacting with it was
symbolic, but allowed users to understand the idea to be discussed.

In order to determine user preferences, a set of initial commands was defined to
execute manipulations of simple data. The commands in this process were: selecting
and removing elements that are near to each other; selecting and removing elements that
are far from each other; applying zoom; and translating elements. Moreover, a list of
various illustrated multi-touch gestures [5] was presented to the users and they were
invited to propose specific actions that could be generated based on each gesture.

3.2   Individual Interviews

The next step in the process recommends semi-structured interviews, in a qualitative
approach with a restricted number of users (from five to ten), in order to advance the
discussion.

---

[1] http://www.googleplusdaily.com/2013/02/ripples-explained.html#.VpeXUfkrLGg.

Thus, the interviews were carried out with seven participants[2] from different areas, such as law, economics and computer science. They were between 20 and 33 years of age and all had some type of multi-touch device, with which they interact daily.

Some common gestures were presented to the participants while they were questioned about their experience with the gestures. Users were asked to simulate gestures to interact with Ripples in the multi-touch device. They were also encouraged to use various fingers at the same time, in order to make the most out of this feature. While the participants answered the questions and interacted with the device, video and audio were recorded to register their interactions and expressions. In the second stage of the interview, a new list composed of simple and complex gestures was presented to the participants, in order to ask them about the possible commands that could be created based on these gestures.

3.3   Analysis of Interviews

In the next stage, based on the results of the interviews, an initial set of gestures of interaction should be created. For each command, the proposals can be categorized according to similarity. These categories are then filtered and only one subset of all of the gestures proposed in the interviews will be used in the following stage.

The interviews were extremely useful, since it was possible to bring together various multi-touch gestures based on user opinions. Though they were familiar with these devices, they were instructed to not restrict themselves to the gestures they already knew and were encouraged to be creative in devising new gestures. A set of gestures was created, composed of several different gestures that used different combinations of fingers and movements.

3.4   Focus Group

The next stage is the creation of a focus group to validate, reduce, broaden or improve the set of interaction techniques proposed in the interviews. This focus group was composed of six participants, undergraduate and graduate students from the areas of economics and computer science between 18 and 32 years old.

The moderator showed and simulated the set of gestures proposed in the interviews on a tablet. Therefore, it was possible to discuss each gesture and collect the users' opinions, eliminating gestures that did not meet the requirements of the group.

3.5   Defining the Gestures for Interaction

Concluding this part of the process, we obtained a short list of gestures according to the opinion of the users for later implementation, starting with the interviews and refining it with the focus group. Some of them are:

---

[2] The participants of all stages were recruited through convenience sampling.

- Selection of Elements: To select more than one circle, one of the preferred options was to touch the screen with five fingers to create a circle (or four to create a square) and this defined shape acts as a selection area. Therefore, to select elements, the user can drag them to this shape using one or more fingers simultaneously. The gestures to deselect elements, according to the users, should be the opposite.
- Application of Zoom: To apply the zoom to the elements, the users chose to execute a double touch on the element or to use the traditional zoom.
- Viewing Information: To open information of the profile represented by the circle, users indicated a simple touch with two or three fingers. In this case, a touch with two fingers was used for viewing the text of the tweet and a touch with three fingers was defined for viewing the profiles of those who retweeted

4   Prototype Implementation

As previously mentioned, the main goal of the prototype called TweetStatus, is to allow the analysis of information visualization techniques that use two forms of interaction: multi-touch technology, and keyboard and mouse.

As application area the social networks were elected. The large amount of data created on these networks encourages the use of visualization techniques to their analysis [12]. In this field, the Twitter social network has been widely used due its characteristics of "following" (a friendship link doesn't need to be accepted by both parts) and public data (the data available in this network could be easily gathered).

Because of these, Twitter was chosen as the source of data to be visualized in the prototype. Therefore the prototype is aimed at analyzing tweets, enabling a search for tweets through a keyword to then carry out various analyses on the results found. It is possible to evaluate the feeling expressed in the tweet, the person who created it, how many times it was retweeted, the repercussion and frequency of the topic researched and trends over time.

To use TweetStatus is no need to login, the user just type a keyword of interest, the prototype searches for tweets posted that have this word and then it generates a visualization of the information of these tweets. The user can use two types of information visualization to analyze the search results: a Bubble chart and a Timeline.

4.1   Bubble Chart

Firstly, TweetStatus search the tweets that contain the word typed by the user and, based on the data found, it generates a Bubble chart. In the Bubble chart, each circle represents a tweet and in it, it is possible to see the name of the profile that posted it. Moreover, the size of each circle represents the number of retweets, in other words, the number of shares that the tweet had in the social network. The search can also be done with written tweets in Portuguese and English.

Another feature of TweetStatus is to analyze the feeling expressed in the tweet. Each circle is colored according to the "feeling" contained in the text of the tweet; in other words, green circles represent good tweets or those with a positive message regarding the researched topic. Likewise, yellow represents neutral tweets and red indicates bad tweets or those with negative messages. To implement the characteristic of coloring the tweet according to the feeling expressed, it was necessary to use a lexicon of feelings: the Opinion Lexicon [14]. This lexicon is constituted, basically, of a list of words which were given a determined weight and this expressed the feeling transmitted by them. Each word of the tweet is evaluated according to this lexicon and then the sentimental value of the tweet is calculated by adding or subtracting the corresponding value of each word. For the purpose of evaluating the words, the final value of the feeling is obtained and then a color is attributed to the circle.

In Fig. 1, it is possible to observe the circles representing the tweets and each one has a size and a color according to the information represented by it. Moreover, it is also possible to read the text of some tweet selecting it. Then it is possible to see if it is in accordance with the feeling represented by color.

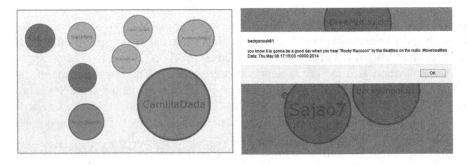

Fig. 1. Bubble chart before (left) and after a tweet selection (right). (Color figure online)

In order for the user to select circles and know how many retweets each one represents or even how many a group of circles represents, it is possible to create a selection circle. Therefore, the circles that represent tweets can be grouped together and an analysis of the total good, bad and neutral retweets can be carried out. The result is presented in a text box above the Bubble chart. Also in the Bubble chart, the user can choose to view the names of those who retweeted the determined tweet, which are also represented by circles, hence the color grey. These two features are demonstrated in Fig. 2.

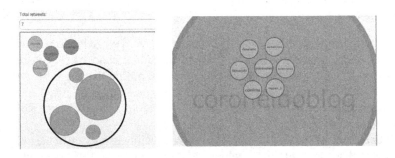

Fig. 2. Circle selection (left) and retweet presentation (right).

4.2   Timeline

With the prototype, the user also has the option of visualizing the tweets on a Timeline, in which they are represented according to the date and time at which they were posted. As in the Bubble chart, the tweets on the Timeline are also colored according to the feeling expressed. In this type of visualization, the user can observe the repercussions of a determined topic over time, such that, for example, the different feelings expressed over the course of a soccer game can be seen.

The Timeline is interactive and the zoom can be applied to find out the exact moment of the post, as well as navigate between the dates. Figure 3 presents an example of Timeline visualization before and after applying the zoom.

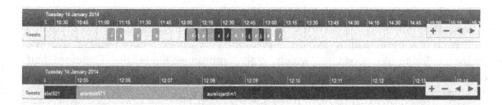

Fig. 3.   Timeline before (top) and after applying zoom (bottom).

5   User Study

In the last phase, in order to discuss the ways of interacting and visualizing that were implemented in TweetStatus, a qualitative analysis was carried out with ten users, based on their use of the developed prototype. The analysis process was structured in four stages, which are detailed below. The interactions in all the stages were filmed and the data recorded in notes.

5.1   User Profiles

Ten users were interviewed, four women and six men with ages ranging from 14 to 54. Of these, two did not complete secondary education, four were undergraduate students, three were graduate students and one was a post-graduate student. Their major expertise areas varied between engineering, computer science, economics, pharmacy and languages. Regarding their skills in using the technology, only one claimed to be a beginner and the rest stated that they were at a level between intermediate and advanced. Questioned about whether they used the social network Twitter, five of them answered affirmatively (four use it daily and one sporadically). Their focus on Twitter is to read news, keep up to date on friends as well as express their opinions and feelings.

5.2 Using the Two Versions of TweetStatus

The participants were invited to use the two versions of the prototype (multi-touch and keyboard plus mouse). To this end, they received a set of tasks, which were posed to them without the intention of receiving "correct" answers as result. The main goal was to stimulate the use of the prototype and not evaluate the accuracy of the data.

The following tasks were carried out: identify the number of good, bad and neutral tweets and retweets; evaluate whether the color of the circle corresponded to the text of the tweets that it represented; evaluate whether the size of the circle corresponded to the number of times that the tweets had been retweeted; evaluate the frequency of the topic researched within the social network; evaluate whether there was, at some moment, a certain "emotional stability", indicated by a sequence of tweets with the same feeling; and, evaluate the repercussion of the topic in general (good, bad or neutral).

Since the users were invited to use two versions of TweetStatus, its use was alternated with each new participant to avoid the possibility of already being familiar with the prototype during the second use, which could compromise the results. Therefore, half of the participants used the conventional interaction and then the multi-touch interaction and the other half did so in the inverse order.

After the tasks execution, a questionnaire was applied intended to collect data about the experience of using the two versions of the prototype: difficulties found, points to improve, user opinions on the use of multi-touch devices with information visualization, in addition to comparative data between the two ways of interaction.

5.3 Data Analysis

After the interviews, an analysis was carried out on the data with the purpose of discovering whether, in this case, using one multi-touch interface was capable of raising the quality of the information visualizations.

According to three users, being able "to touch" the information makes it easier to visualize the information as well as understand it. Some also claimed it was a way of triggering greater interest in visualization and consequently forcing themselves to be more attentive to what they were doing. During the interviews, some comments included *"Touching generates more interest in interacting with the application..."* (Participant 10) as well as *"Normally things that you can interact with, modify, are more interesting than things that are finished products. That is the logic of the touchscreen that is how they win us over."* (Participant 3). Though five of the ten users said that the information perceived in the two interactions was the same, the positive statements suggest that a visualization technique that can be touched adds value to the information or its understanding.

When faced with the statement about the fact that they can drag elements on the screen and if this represented some advantage in information visualization, using the Likert scale, 80 % of users marked "agreed" or marked "totally agreed" with it. Specifically talking about the Bubble charts, all participants agreed that the circle's dragging is an advantage in the visualization manipulation. As Participant 3 said *"It gives an information control feel and encourages interaction"*. However, regarding whether object manipulation was easier through the multi-touch interface, 20 % of users disagreed or totally disagreed with it; one of them reported having problems in manipulating the small objects. This shows that the data resulting from the searches carried out by the participants also influenced the interaction. The information that resulted in small elements on the screen certainly led to a less pleasant interaction for the users.

During the interviews, the users were also asked to give their opinion on the multi-touch version of the prototype being more intuitive than the conventional version and, in this case, there were diverging responses. Some agreed with this statement, though three users disagreed, one of them pointing out that, despite using the keyboard as an aid, with the click of the mouse, the interaction was more intuitive. However, these users also agreed that it was easier to manipulate the elements with the mouse since they were more used to using it. This leads to a reflection on the fact that they are more habituated to using the mouse and, perhaps for this reason, they believed that this version was more intuitive. Analyzing the data on the reported difficulties, five users reported it to be difficult to remember the commands in the traditional version (keyboard plus mouse), and none of them highlighted this in relation to the multi-touch commands.

The users were unanimous in agreeing that the precision of the mouse facilitates the manipulation of small objects. Despite this, alternatives to these techniques can be developed which together with the multi-touch interfaces can provide a positive experience for the user. One example of improving the precision of the multi-touch interaction is Rizzo [17], which simulates the precision of the mouse in multi-touch interfaces.

In using the Timeline, for example, it was claimed that "*it is much easier to move the mouse here*" (Participant 2). We believe that the demand for more precision at the moment of interacting may have caused this feeling, since the space for manipulating the zoom was considerably small. The mouse, despite having only one point of interaction, had a scroll wheel to apply the zoom, making it much more intuitive, since there are many applications that use this same form of interaction.

Concerning to the application domain, the manipulation of tweets and their sentimental analysis through the Bubble charts, the users could easily find information about the amount of tweets and retweets (good, bad and neutrals). They all agreed about the weight fidelity of the circles related to the number of tweets and/or retweets they represent. However, they could perceive that some color was not well employed – they didn't represent the sentiment expressed by the tweet. For example, the tweet selected in Fig. 1 (right) was classified as neutral, but someone could consider it as good. As our main focus in these phases of our research was not in the precision of the sentimental analysis, this fact was saved for future prototype refinements. Considering the Timeline, it allows them to identify the frequency the topic researched appears in the network and also its repercussion. Using the Timeline, 8 of the 10 participants could verify the "stability" of certain sentiment during time ("*some periods with several bad tweets and others neutrals*", as highlighted by Participant 5). Considering this results we observe that these visualizations, combined with the possibilities of multi-touch interaction, could improve the analysis made by users, indicating a research path probably fruitful.

6   Final Considerations

The great increase in the volume of information over the past few years, and the conse-
quent emergence of various information visualization techniques, evidence the importance of this area. The techniques developed for this end are presented in several applications used on a daily basis with the most diverse types of users. However, they are,
for the most part, developed for desktop computers and used through interactions with
the mouse and keyboard. With the popularity of multi-touch devices, due to the massive
use of smartphones and tablets, various elements related to interaction have begun to be
reconsidered and adapted to these types of devices. Among them are information visualization techniques.

Some studies have questioned whether multi-touch devices are capable of improving
the user experience, and thus carried out comparisons with traditional WIMP interfaces
[6, 10, 11]. With respect to the information visualization techniques, their adaptation to
these devices is considered a challenge to be overcome [1]. On the other hand, it is also
considered a more natural way of interaction for data visualization [10, 13].

In this sense, this research aimed to investigate these issues, bringing more data to
the discussion. This technology, as mentioned by some of the participants of the tests
carried out, have the capacity to hold the attention of the users and thus provide better
concentration on their part during the interactions. An information visualization technique on its own is a way of attracting the attention of the users, due to the way the
information is presented. When one interacts with it through a multi-touch interface,
one can say that value has been added, since this interaction helps to maintain the focus
of the user on the visualization. Moreover, when well-executed, these interactions can
make the process for understanding the information more pleasurable for the user. Thus,
we can say that in some way it can improve the data analysis.

In this research we analyzed the multi-touch interaction combined with highly used
visualization techniques, in this case, the Bubble chart and the Timeline. The results
obtained up to this point indicate that multi-touch interactions are capable of making
users more attentive to their activities, thus improving the quality of the information
acquired during these interactions, which is better than using conventional keyboard and
mouse combination. Consequently, one can say that information visualizations have also
benefitted from this improvement and thus its quality has added value as well.

It is interesting that the information visualization techniques undergo a process of
specifying gestures that should be used when they are implemented in multi-touch
interfaces, similar to that applied in this study. This prior specification prevents the
designer from using (and implementing) gestures that may not be well accepted by the
users.

The research also revealed that in tasks that require precision, such as, for example,
selecting and editing long texts, multi-touch should be avoided. On the other hand, since
most tablets and smartphones users do not use mouse and keyboard to interact with these
kinds of devices, a challenge for future research is to find gestures to allow a pleasure
way to do it. Moreover, using multi-touch in devices in which the user is already used
to other types of interactions should not be the only source of interaction; multimodal

interfaces could be an option. And information visualization techniques that are being designed for these devices should be carefully analyzed before being implemented.

With respect to the prototype' domain area, specifically, the participants were unanimous in saying that they would use it to carry out an analysis of the tweets. We can say that it provides better quality in exploring tweets, since some information that could not be seen through the original interface of the social network were contemplated in TweetStatus. Being able to analyze the feeling expressed can make the user focus on the tweets of interest to them, such as, for example, reading only good tweets regarding a product; or reading some bad ones with respect to a store in which one intends to buy some product. A business or public person, such as a politician, for example, can also analyze who was involved and at what time a bad repercussion began about them in the network. This type of information can be very important in a decision-making process.

Since the focus of the research in this paper was not aimed at new information generated by the analysis of the tweets, with future studies, we intend to advance this discussion. We intend to analyze the applicability of the prototype with its use by different kinds of users of Twitter in their daily routine. Users such as businesses and public people, who need to monitor their reputations on social media, can have profiles more interested in analyzing this information than that of users in general, adding value to the results. In this same scope, an improvement to be incorporated in the prototype is the creation of a configurable and personalized lexicon for each user. In this lexicon, each user of the tool could decide which words should be classified as good or bad, attributing their own weights to them.

References

1. Baur, D., Lee, B., Carpendale, S.: TouchWave: kinetic multi-touch manipulation for hierarchical stacked graphs. In: 2012 ACM International Conference on Interactive Tabletops and Surfaces, pp. 255–264. ACM, New York (2012)
2. Chen, Y., Yang, J., Barlowe, S., Jeong. D.H.: Touch2Annotate: generating better annotations with less human effort on multi-touch interfaces. In: CHI 2010 Extended Abstracts on Human Factors in Computing Systems, pp. 3703–3708. ACM, New York (2010)
3. Coram, J.L., Iverson, R., Ackerman, A.: AstroTouch: a multi-touch digital desktop for astrodynamics. In: 2013 ACM International Conference on Interactive Tabletops and Surfaces, pp. 11–14. ACM, New York (2013)
4. Cossio, L.P., Lammel, F.E., Silveira, M.S.: Towards an interactive and iterative process to design natural interaction techniques. In: Stephanidis, C. (ed.) HCI 2014, Part I. CCIS, vol. 434, pp. 19–23. Springer, Heidelberg (2014)
5. Gesture markup language. http://gestureworks.com/icons-fonts
6. Hansen, T.E., Hourcade, J.P.: Comparing multi-touch tabletops and multi-mouse single-display groupware setups. In: 3rd Mexican Workshop on Human Computer Interaction Mexican, pp. 36–43. Universidad Politécnica de San Luis Potosí, San Luis Potosí (2010)
7. Isenberg, P., Isenberg, T., Hesselmann, T., von Zadow, U.: Tang. A.: Data visualization on interactive surfaces: a research agenda. IEEE Comput. Graph. Appl. 33(2), 16–24 (2013)
8. Kister, U., Reipschläger, P., Dahselt, R.: Multi-touch manipulation of magic lenses for information visualization. In: 2014 ACM International Conference on Interactive Tabletops and Surfaces, pp. 431–434. ACM, New York (2014)

9. Kristensson, P.O., Arnell, O., Björk, A., Dahlbäck, N., Pennerup, J., Prytz, E., Wikman, J., Åström, N.: InfoTouch: an explorative multi-touch visualization interface for tagged photo collections. In: 5th Nordic Conference on Human-Computer Interaction: Building Bridges, pp. 491–494. ACM, New York (2008)
10. Lee, B., Isenberg, P., Riche, N.II., Carpendale, S.: Beyond mouse and keyboard: expanding design considerations for information visualization interactions. IEEE Trans. Vis. Comput. Graph. 18(12), 2689–2698 (2012)
11. Leftheriotis, J., Chorianopoulos., K.: User experience quality in multi-touch tasks. In: 3rd ACM SIGCHI Symposium on Engineering Interactive Computing Systems, pp. 277–282. ACM, New York (2011)
12. Rotta, G.C., de Lemos, V.S., da Cunha, A.L.M., Manssour, I.H., Silveira, M.S., Pase, A.F.: Exploring twitter interactions through visualization techniques: users impressions and new possibilities. In: Kotzé, P., Marsden, G., Lindgaard, G., Wesson, J., Winckler, M. (eds.) INTERACT 2013, Part III. LNCS, vol. 8119, pp. 700–707. Springer, Heidelberg (2013)
13. Rzeszotarski, J.M., Kittur, A.: Kinetica: naturalistic multi-touch data visualization. In: SIGCHI Conference on Human Factors in Computing Systems, pp. 897–906. ACM, New York (2014)
14. Souza, M., Vieira, R., Busetti, D., Chishman, R., Alves, I.M.: Construction of a portuguese opinion lexicon from multiple resources. In: 8th Brazilian Symposium in Information and Human Language Technology, pp. 59–66. Brazilian Computer Society, Cuiabá (2011)
15. Spence, R.: Information Visualization. Pearson Education Limited, Essex (2001)
16. Thalmann, F., von Zadow, U., Heckel, M., Dachselt, R.: X-O Arch Menu: combining precise positioning with efficient menu selection on touch devices. In: 2014 ACM International Conference on Interactive Tabletops and Surfaces, pp. 317–322. ACM, New York (2014)
17. Vlaming, L., Collins, C., Hancock, M., Nacenta, M., Isenberg, T., Carpendale, S.: Integrating 2D mouse emulation with 3D manipulation for visualizations on a multi-touch table. In: 2010 ACM International Conference on Interactive Tabletops and Surfaces, pp. 221–230. ACM, New York (2010)
18. Ward, M.O., Grinstein, G., Keim, D.: Interactive data visualization: foundations, techniques, and applications. A.K. Peters/CRC Press, Natick (2010)

History Viewer: Displaying User Interaction History in Visual Analytics Applications

Vinícius C.V.B. Segura[1,2(✉)] and Simone D.J. Barbosa[1]

[1] Departamento de Informática, PUC-Rio, Rio de Janeiro, Brazil
{vsegura,simone}@inf.puc-rio.br
[2] IBM Research, Rio de Janeiro, Brazil
vboas@br.ibm.com

Abstract. Effective and efficient strategies are needed to extract unknown and unexpected information from data of unprecedentedly large size, high dimensionality, and complexity [7]. Only a combination of data analysis and visualization techniques can handle these complex and dynamic data [4]. Visual analytics applications aim to integrate the best of both sides.

After the knowledge discovery process, a major challenge is to filter the essential information that led to a discovery and to communicate the findings to other people. We propose taking advantage of the trace left by the exploratory data analysis, in the form of user interaction history. This paper presents a framework to instrument web visual analytics applications, logging the user interaction during the exploratory data analysis. This paper also presents our solution to display the user interaction history to the user, enabling him to revisit the steps that led to an insight.

Keywords: Visual analytics · User interaction logging · User interaction history · Data visualization · History visualization · Log visualization

1 Introduction

We are now living in a Big Data world. We generate 2.5 quintillion bytes (2.5 10^{18} bytes or 2.5 exabytes) of data every day, meaning that 90 % of the the available data today has been created in the past two years.[1] Research-wise, the bottleneck has shifted from *data acquisition* (when there are poor datasets) to *data analysis* (what to do with the rich datasets recently available) [5].

Human attention is now a limiting resource. Effective and efficient strategies are needed to extract unknown and unexpected information from these data of unprecedentedly large size, high dimensionality, and complexity [7]. Only a combination of data analysis and visualization techniques can handle these complex and dynamic data [4].

---

[1] IBM – What is big data?, available at: http://www-01.ibm.com/software/data/bigdata/what-is-big-data.html.

© Springer International Publishing Switzerland 2016
M. Kurosu (Ed.): HCI 2016, Part III, LNCS 9733, pp. 223–233, 2016.
DOI: 10.1007/978-3-319-39513-5_21

On the one hand, computers can provide intelligent data analysis [6] without cognitive biases [3]. Their enormous processing power [1] and superior working memory [3] guarantee an incomparable mathematical, algebraic, and statistical prowess to handle massive volumes of data. On the other hand, human users can contribute with their analytical capabilities and inherent visual perception [6], which enable them to perform visual information exploration [1].

Visual analytics applications (VAApps) aim to integrate the best of both worlds. They pre-process and analyze data, presenting it to users in a way to take advantage of the user's cognitive capabilities. The final outcome may be an unexpected insight – one only possible by combining computation and cognition.

After the knowledge discovery process, a major challenge is to filter the essential information that led to a discovery and to communicate the findings to other people. We propose taking advantage of the trace left by the exploratory data analysis, in the form of user interaction history. We have devised a framework to instrument web VAApps to log the user interaction during the exploratory data analysis. This user interaction history can be later presented to the user, enabling him to revisit the steps that led to an insight.

In this paper, we start by presenting the framework and its different components (Sect. 2). In the following section (Sect. 3), we discuss the associated log model, which makes the bridge between the VAApp and our history viewer. In Sect. 4 we detail our history visualization idea, elements, and concepts. Next, (Sect. 5) we show how our solution was applied to a weather insights VAApp. Finally, we conclude this paper (Sect. 6) with some final remarks, discussing the current solution limitations and proposing some future work.

2   Framework

Figure 1 summarizes the different components of our framework and the relations between them. We consider that the VAApp architecture is itself comprised of three basic components:

1. A **web UI** – the front-end – responsible for rendering the VAApp in the user's browser. This usually corresponds to the HTML and JavaScript code to be executed in the client's browser.
2. A **data service** – the back-end –, which communicates with the database(s) and sends data back to the web UI according to a given API. The technology used in this component can be various: Node.JS, Java, Python, etc. It is important to notice that this component may not be deployed in the same application as the front-end, or even be developed by the same VAApp team. For example, the VAApp may use a 3rd party API and make transformations to the data only on the client side.
3. Finally, the **data** itself, which is usually stored in some sort of database. Again, there is a multitude of technologies that can be used for this component – from local stored files to cloud-based storage –, which are beyond the scope of this discussion.

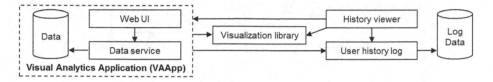

Fig. 1. Framework components diagram.

Our framework considers this basic VAApp architecture, and builds upon it with three components:

1. A **visualization library**, providing reusable basic charts to be used in different VAApps. This component uses d3.js[2] and both the VAApp and the history viewer may use it.
2. An **user history log**, storing the user interaction history. Similar to the VAApp's `data service`, this component handles the queries to the `log data` stored in some sort of database. Section 3 details our current log model.
3. A **history viewer** component, a VAApp itself that presents the user interaction history in a comprehensible way. It corresponds to the VAApp's `web UI`. We will present our visualization in Sect. 4.

3   Log Model

In order to visualize what is being logged by the VAApp, we must define a common log model to be shared between the VAApp and the history viewer. We propose the model illustrated in Fig. 2. It is a hierarchical model, which can be split in two: the definitions and the interactions hierarchy.

On the right-hand side, we can see the **definitions hierarchy**. This hierarchy is established at development time by the VAApp developer. Its root is the **VAApp definition**, which has a collection of `view` and `data service` definitions. A **view definition** represents a view (page) that can be navigated inside the VAApp and contains a collection of `visualization component` definitions. A **visualization component definition** represents a visual element (*e.g.*: a chart, a map, a collection of charts) that appears on the UI. The **data service definition** represents the data service APIs used by the VAApp to gather data for its visualizations.

These definitions consists mostly of a given name, a version, and a URL. The versioning is managed by the VAApp developer. He is therefore responsible for maintaining retro-compatibility (by providing different URL's for different versions, for example). Some definitions (`data service` and `visualization component definitions` – the leaves of the hierarchy) must also provide a class name, so they can be later reused.

---

[2] http://d3js.org/.

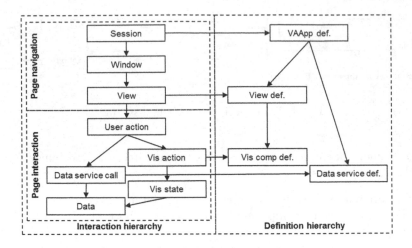

Fig. 2. The log model.

If we take the Gapminder[3] website as an example, the `VAApp definition` would point to the website (http://www.gapminder.org/). For visualization purposes, we could say that there would be only a single `view definition`, pointing to the Gapminder World page (http://www.gapminder.org/world/), ignoring the other pages (video, download, etc.). This page contains a single scatterplot, so it would only have one `visualization component definition`. To keep things simple, we could say that there is only one data service API which returns a time-series data given an indicator. This API would be the only `data service definition` of this example VAApp.

On the left-hand side, we can see the **interactions hierarchy**. It starts with a **session**, when the user logs in to a VAApp. It keeps a reference to the `VAApp definition` and may contain additional information, such as the browser's user agent, for example. During a `session`, the user can open different browser **windows** (or tabs). In each `window`, the user may navigate through many VAApp `views`, each one of which referencing the corresponding `view definition`.

The steps described so far are more related to the page navigation in the browser than an actual user interaction within the page. The first **user action** usually corresponds to the actual page loading and the visualization components' initial state. A user action may trigger a **data service call** to gather new `data` from the `data service` component. Since we focus on changes in the visualization components, a **user action** should always have at least one `visualization action`, indicating what type of change happened to the `visualization component`. Every `visualization action` generates a new **visualization state**, describing the state of the `visualization component` after the action and referencing the `data` currently represented. As the user interacts with the `view`, new `user actions` are recorded every time a `visualization component` is changed.

---

[3] http://www.gapminder.org/.

We believe that the VAApp developer may give some semantics and context to the **user action**, but cannot infer the user's intentions or higher-level goals. We may see this limitation as similar to the affordance levels [9]. At the operational level, we have individual actions (mapped onto **visualization actions**). At the tactical level, we find a sequence of actions that were executed to achieve goals and sub-goals (mapped onto **user actions**). Finally, we cannot log the strategic level, since it relates to the conceptualizations regarding problem formulation and problem solving processes.

The **user actions** therefore can be described by the VAApp developer using terms related to the VAApp instead of more generic ones. For example, in Gapminder, we could describe the change of the y-axis as "Changed y-axis indicator to ACME" instead of generically saying "Changed y to ACME".

We believe that more specific information can make it easier for the user reading the history log to recall the actual actions that took place, since it will be a more contextual description that reflects the actual VAApp UI he first interacted with.

The **visualization actions** are categorized according to a given set of **tasks**, so the VAApp developer does not need to provide any additional information. We are using Brehmer's and Munzner's [2] multi-level typology of abstract visualization tasks, summarized in Fig. 3, to categorize the **visualization actions**. We focused on the "how" part – "families of related visual encoding and interaction techniques" – since the "why" part falls onto the strategical abstraction level previously discussed and is, therefore, outside the scope of this work. The available **visualization actions** are, therefore:

- **Encode**: Codify data in the visual representation.
- **Select**: Demarcate one or more elements in the visualization, differentiating selected from unselected elements (*e.g.*: select, brush, highlight).
- **Navigate**: Alter user's viewpoint (*e.g.*: zooming, panning, rotating).
- **Arrange**: Organize visual elements (*e.g.*: reordering axes, rows/columns).
- **Change**: Alter visual encoding (*e.g.*: size and transparency of points, changing the chart type).
- **Filter**: Adjust the exclusion and inclusion criteria for elements in the visualization.
- **Aggregate**: Change the granularity of visualization elements.
- **Annotate**: Add graphical or textual annotations associated with one or more visualization elements.
- **Import**: Add new elements to the visualization.
- **Derive**: Compute new data elements given existing data elements.
- **Record**: Save or capture visualization elements as persistent artifacts.

By using this typology, we believe it will be possible to compare visualization actions from different interaction paths and even from different VAApps. Moreover, we believe it will also simplify their interpretation, since we limit the number of possible tasks.

Continuing with the Gapminder example, when the user navigates to the Gapminder World page, all the **page navigation** hierarchy is constructed, with

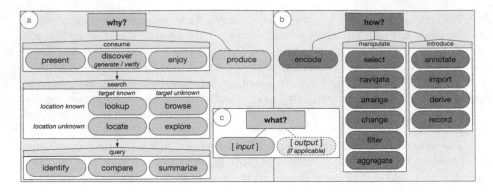

Fig. 3. Brehmer's and Munzner's multi-level typology of abstract visualization tasks.

the `view` referring to the Gapminder World `view definition`. The page loading is mapped to an `user action`, which (considering our simple data API), would trigger three `data service calls` (to gather data for each axis and the circles' sizes using the `data service definition`) and one `visualization action` (the `encoding` of the scatterplot `visualization component`).

If the user hovers the mouse pointer over a data point, a new user action would be created with just a `visualization action` (the `annotation` of the data point), since no new data seems to be gathered. If the user changes an axis indicator, again a new `user action` is created, which would have a single `data service call` (data for only one axis) and a `visualization action` (encoding new data on the scatterplot).

4   History Visualization

After logging the user history, we want to present it back to the user so he can trace back the steps in his interaction. We propose the representation illustrated in Fig. 4. We based our visualization in the GIT commit graph,[4] so users could have some sense of familiarity (at least amongst GIT users). We chose to keep the y-axis as a time axis anchor, so in the "worst-case scenario" the user may just read through the description texts from top to bottom and still relate to the interaction he had with the VAApp.

Each column in the representation groups different `views` if there is no time conflict, *i.e.* the time span of the `view` (time between the first and last `user actions`) does not overlap the time span of another `view`. From the figure, for example, we can notice two parallel `views` (two columns), so we can infer that the user had at least two open `windows`.

`View` navigations are represented as column-wide ellipses breaking the flow. For example, looking at the fourth row, second column, we see that the user navigated from one view to another, given the break represented by the ellipse.

---

[4] http://chimera.labs.oreilly.com/books/1230000000561/ch01.html#fig0101.

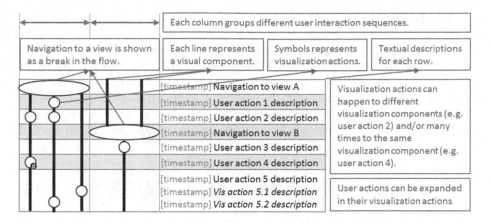

Fig. 4. An annotated history visualization. The elements in blue are not part of the representation, but comments included here to help describe it.

From each `view` representation a different number of lines emerge. Each one represents a `visualization component` of that given `view`. In the first column, therefore, we could say that the `view` has three different `visualization components` and, in the second column, the initial `view` had two `visualization components` and navigated to one with a single `visualization component`.

We chose to represent `views` occupying the whole column to highlight breaks in the flow and changes in the number of `visualization components`. If the second column did not begin with those two lines and simply started with the ellipse on the fourth row instead, we could infer that the user had just opened another `window` at that point in time.

In each `visualization component` line we can have multiple symbols, representing the different tasks associated with the `visualization actions`.

The line in which the symbol appears indicates in which `visualization component` the action took place. The order of the lines, therefore, should be consistent amongst different representations of the same `view`, so the user can create a mental mapping of which line is which `visualization component`.

Finally, each banded row represents a single `user action`. A `user action` may group multiple `visualization actions`. Looking at the figure, for example, we can see that the `user action` 2 comprises of two different `visualization actions` for two different `visualization components` (one symbol in each of the first two lines, on the same row), whilst the fourth `user action` has a number of `visualization actions` for the same `visualization component` (represented by the small '#' badge attached to the circle). If the user wants to look at each individual `visualization action`, he can expand the `user action`, as demonstrated with the `user action` 5 in the figure.

5   Early Implementation

For our first implementation, we chose WISE - Weather InSights Environment [8] as our target VAApp. WISE's main UI (shown in Fig. 5) is composed mainly of three visual components: a map in the background, an event profile at the bottom, and meteograms on the right. We disregarded the top card – a configuration card – since it is only a series of common HTML input elements to choose/display the current parameters (forecast, grid, property, and timestep) and we wanted to focus on the visual analytics aspects.

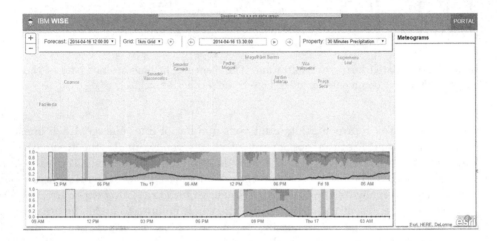

Fig. 5. WISE's main UI.

We started by mapping the available interactivity and visualization changes they generate onto our log model, in order to evaluate how well our approach would fit. The results can be seen in Table 1, with the `visualization action` task inside parentheses.

We proceeded to instrument WISE to generate a log according to our model. We developed helper code to reduce the work needed to be done by the VAApp developer and the impact on the client side. Thus, the instrumentation comprises only four main concerns: (i) keeping the **definition hierarchy** updated; (ii) using the auxiliary **logger class**; (iii) using compatible **visualization components**; (iv) using compatible **data services**.

The `definition hierarchy` is expressed in JSON. We created a simple UI to post this JSON data and get the ids corresponding to the created definitions. These ids should be used at run time to make the `interaction hierarchy` reference the `definition hierarchy`.

The logger class helps to post to the `user history log` component. The developer informs when a `session` starts, the current `view`, and the page interactions. The logger manages saving `session` and `windows` ids, and also doing the actual posting.

Table 1. WISE's user actions and visualization actions study.

User action	Visualization action
Change in the forecast	Redraw map (`Encode`)
Change in the grid	Redraw profiles (`Encode`)
	Redraw meteograms if necessary (`Encode`)
Change in the property	Redraw map (`Encode`)
Change in the timestep	Redraw map (`Encode`)
	Move profiles highlight (`Select`)
	Move meteograms highlight (`Select`)
Panning/zooming map	Update map (`Navigate`)
Mouse over a cell	Show cell tooltip on the map (`Annotate`)
Click on a cell	Highlight cell on the map (`Select`)
	Redraw meteograms (`Encode`)
Mouse over a profile column	Show profile tooltip (`Annotate`)
Mouse over a meteogram	Show property value for the timestep (`Annotate`)

For the `visualization components` and `data services` we established an interface that should be implemented and "abstract" classes that could be used by the concrete implementation. For this implementation, both the `visualization components` and `data services` were developed in the same application as WISE (as opposed to being developed as separate applications). We chose this approach so the development of the VAApp would be clearer to the VAApp development team, with methods adapted to the context instead of a more generic one (for example, the map visualization component has a `selectCell` method instead of a generic `select` one).

All the implementation is done using TypeScript,[5] "a typed superset of JavaScript that compiles to plain JavaScript." This made development easier, with the possibility of defining interfaces to objects and classes, and also enabling the abstract class concept (one not native to JavaScript). Moreover, during development, this approach made debugging easier, with compatibility errors being noticed at compile time instead of run time.

Figure 6 shows a sample interaction log history visualization for the WISE system. We highlight the parameters with monospaced font in the `view navigation` and `user action` descriptions to make it easier for users to distinguish them from regular text. Another change was color-coding the `visualization action` tasks. Together with the "tag-like" appearance (text in a colored background) of the `visualization action` description, we believe this may aid users to establish the mapping with the task (the circle) and with the `visualization component` (the line in which the circle appears), whilst also working as a legend for the graph.

---

[5] http://www.typescriptlang.org/.

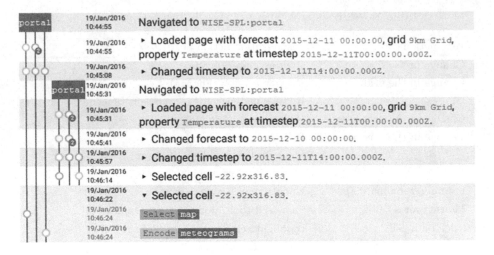

Fig. 6. Sample history view excerpt for WISE interaction.

While developing this early implementation, the history visualization already proved itself useful for the development team, since it enabled visualizing the inner workings of the code. WISE's development team was able to detect some problems with the information flow, such as calls to the `data service` and drawing the `visualization components` in the wrong order or even when not yet necessary.

6   Final Remarks and Future Work

In this paper we provided a complete overview of our solution to record and present user interaction history. We started by introducing how our framework components work, continued to explain the log model that enables the communication between the VAApp and the history viewer, and discussed the main concepts and ideas of our history visualization system. We also presented our early concrete implementation of the solution using WISE as the origin VAApp, the results of such effort, and the unexpected benefit for the VAApp's development team.

The solution is yet in its early stages, needing more use cases and VAApps to strengthen the approach. We also need to evaluate the history visualization with users in order to better assess the visualization's efficacy, efficiency, and understandability.

We currently have plans to enhance the history visualization. We are aware of the scalability issue – when there are many columns, possibly with several VAApps, each with a multitude of view and visualization components. Besides common search, hide, and filter features, we plan to provide a more close-packed representation, for example by collapsing the lines and hiding the nodes, painting the lines themselves. Moreover, we plan to have some sort of mechanism to highlight common `visualization states`, as many different actions can lead to the same state. This could be used to hide sections of user actions (*e.g.*: collapse a sequence of actions that lead to an undo) and also to detect patterns in the user interaction.

Acknowledgement. The authors would like to thank CNPq for the financial support to their work (processes #309828/2015-5 and #453996/2014-0).

References

1. Aigner, W., Miksch, S., Müller, W., Schumann, H., Tominski, C.: Visualizing time-oriented data - a systematic view. Comput. Graph. **31**(3), 401–409 (2007). http://www.sciencedirect.com/science/article/pii/S0097849307000611
2. Brehmer, M., Munzner, T.: A multi-level typology of abstract visualization tasks. IEEE Trans. Vis. Comput. Graph. **19**(12), 2376–2385 (2013)
3. Green, T., Ribarsky, W., Fisher, B.: Visual analytics for complex concepts using a human cognition model. In: IEEE Symposium on Visual Analytics Science and Technology, VAST 2008, pp. 91–98, October 2008
4. Keim, D.A., Mansmann, F., Oelke, D., Ziegler, H.: Visual analytics: combining automated discovery with interactive visualizations. In: Boulicaut, J.-F., Berthold, M.R., Horváth, T. (eds.) DS 2008. LNCS (LNAI), vol. 5255, pp. 2–14. Springer, Heidelberg (2008)
5. Key, A., Howe, B., Perry, D., Aragon, C.: Vizdeck: self-organizing dashboards for visual analytics. In: Proceedings of the 2012 ACM SIGMOD International Conference on Management of Data, SIGMOD 2012, pp. 681–684. ACM, New York (2012)
6. Kohlhammer, J., Keim, D., Pohl, M., Santucci, G., Andrienko, G.: Solving problems with visual analytics. Procedia Comput. Sci. **7**, 117–120 (2011). Proceedings of the 2nd European Future Technologies Conference and Exhibition 2011 (FET11). http://www.sciencedirect.com/science/article/pii/S1877050911007009
7. Mennis, J., Guo, D.: Spatial data mining and geographic knowledge discovery-an introduction. Comput. Environ. Urban Syst. **33**(6), 403–408 (2009). Spatial Data Mining–Methods and Applications. http://www.sciencedirect.com/science/article/pii/S0198971509000817
8. Oliveira, I., Segura, V., Nery, M., Mantripragada, K., Ramirez, J.P., Cerqueira, R.: WISE: A web environment for visualization and insights on weather data. In: WVIS - 5thWorkshop on Visual Analytics, Information Visualization and Scientific Visualization, SIBGRAPI 2014, pp. 4–7 (2014). http://bibliotecadigital.fgv.br/dspace/bitstream/handle/10438/11954/WVIS-SIBGRAPI-2014.pdf?sequence=1
9. Souza, C.S.D., Prates, R.O., Carey, T.: Missing and declining affordances: are these appropriate concepts? J. Braz. Comput. Soc. **7**, 26–34 (2000)

Wayfinding, Mobility, and Transport

The Discussion of Interactive Outdoor Guidance and Appliance on Smart Glasses from the Aspect of Human Computer Interaction: Taking Dihua Street for Example

Hao-Yuan Cheng[1]([✉]) and Chen-Wei Chiang[2]

[1] Department of Information Communication, Yuan Ze University, Taoyuan, Taiwan
s1036402@mail.yzu.edu.tw
[2] Department of Product Innovation and Entrepreneurship,
National Taipei University of Business, Taipei, Taiwan
chenwei@saturn.yzu.edu.tw

Abstract. The research has expanded Augmented Reality (AR) technology by applying the smart glasses "Moverio" with guiding systems, and has use Taipei Dihua Street as an example. After site investigation, interviewing workers, and understanding the historical, environmental and cultural background, the tour routes and associated objects are set. The smart glasses allow its users to see the complete picture of the historical building along with its introduction. This leads them deeper into the historical environment which achieves the goal of outdoor tour guiding. Hopefully, the results can be used in future AR technology researches, or other related interaction designs.

Keywords: HCI · Interaction design · Guide system

1 Introduction

While the ways of tour guiding has increased as technology advances, the purpose remains to draw people's attention, allow them to throw themselves into the atmosphere and then become interested [1]. Thus, the research has place strong emphasis on the "interaction with users" as an important element in designing guiding systems, for an interactive exhibition compared to a traditional one, can appeal to users more.

To achieve this, AR technology is used. It uses photograph calculation and imaginary technique and overlaps the virtual with the real world through the monitor. There are two advantages in using it. Firstly, the user does not need to be fixed in a certain place or equipment which makes the interaction more natural. Secondly, it maintains the original context and spatial perception by adding sensory stimulation into the actual environment which makes it easier for users to adapt and learn.

As for the location, Dihua Street was chosen. It is 800 m long and has being Taipei Tataocheng important trading post for groceries and dry food, tea, Chinese herbs, and cloth since the 19th century. The research combined AR technology with smart glasses to develop a tour guide system that can show users three-dimensional images of the historical buildings, heritages, and information of Dihua Street. For example, it gives

M. Kurosu (Ed.): HCI 2016, Part III, LNCS 9733, pp. 237–247, 2016.
DOI: 10.1007/978-3-319-39513-5_22

introductions, pictures, and voice guidance which can allow the users to become more interested in the history and culture by placing them in the actual historical atmosphere.

Different methods were used in this research. The observation method was one of them. And through interviewing workers and visitors at Dihua Street, needs of both sides were collected and set as the basis of designing the prototype. The textual analysis was also used to integrate domestic and international related cases, and their principles in interaction design.

2 Related Works

2.1 Human-Computer Interaction and User-Centered Design

The human-computer interaction (HCI) is aim to design, evaluate, and operate the system from the users' point of view. Hence, designers should understand the user mental model beforehand, in order for the users to easily interact with the computer system. In other words, to what point users can understand the system. Then, by using the right designing concept, make the system's using experience more fluent, understandable and easy to use. Zhang thinks that human and technology are the core elements of HCI. Therefore, designers should understand the human information processing mode, and cognition, action and limitation theory, as well as related technology development, whereas, the "goal" and "background" are the other elements that gives it its meaning; HCI involves many concept, like the "design", the "usability" and other related issues. However, "interaction" remains its main element [2].

Norman states that a complete human-computer interaction model can be divided into "execution" and "evaluation" which is the well-known execution-evaluation cycle. This means that the users interacts with the system consistently, and by operating and understanding how it works, the system image will become the user's mental model towards the system, and if the conceptual model is closer to the user's mental model, it means it is a more acceptable system for the user [3].

Overall, the research claims that all systems should be equipped with a good human-computer interaction. Achieving it can decrease the problems and obstacles that may occur when users are operating, and satisfy user's needs so that the system can work with high efficiency and function.

User-centered design (UCD) is fundamental to the HCI. It focuses on involving the users within the design and consistently checking whether each part has met the user's user mental model when developing the product. That is to say, UCD stresses the importance of a products usability and learnability [4].

Furthermore, experts view were summarized in the research [5–8], and it has being found that when designing products, it is crucial to find the best mode for the human to interact with the product, and make it a pleasant experience that meets the needs of the consumer. In the same time, the effectiveness and efficacy must be attended to in order to make sure that the product is usable. Thus, by using the usability principle, a user interface that is suitable for the smart glasses to upgrade the experience when using the designed tour guide system has been proposed in the research.

2.2 Related Document Discussion on Tour Guiding

The ways to tour guide has increased, and places other than museums has eventually put more focus on this service. Moreover, the innovation of technology and researches has greatly increased the quality of tour guiding. Thus, the research has looked into different aspect given from scholars.

Tilden states that the goal of tour guiding is to use the original object, firsthand experience and media to highlight the displaying item's meaning and their relevance. It is not only a way to spread facts and information, but also an educational activity. Tilden also thinks that tour guiding must combine the theme and the environment with the tourist personality and experience [9].

Edwards on the other hand states that "tour guiding" is a combination of six services. This includes guiding, educating, providing information, promoting, inspiring, and entertaining. The purpose of it is to lead the spectators to a new field through giving them new knowledge and by obtaining new interest [10].

Therefore, it can be seen from above that a tour guide is the bridge between the product and the viewers. Tour guiding involves more than facts and knowledge, but the understanding of any related medium, environment, equipment, tourist, and resources. The goal is to help users to obtain knowledge and passion.

The research has concluded five elements that are needed in tour guiding which is to lead, to educate, to entertain, to provide information and to raise interest.

- To lead: To lead the viewers through a route that is planned beforehand to decrease their sense of insecurity.
- To educate: Help viewers acquire proper knowledge, and understand the meaning behind the exhibiting object and the relation with its environment.
- To entertain: Allow the viewers to have a pleasant experience, and enhance their ability to enjoy and appreciate.
- To provide information: To give viewers right information regarding to the exhibiting object and it's surrounding.
- To rise interest: Through tour guiding, help viewers obtain knowledge and understanding of the exhibiting object and raise their curiosity.

2.3 AR Technology Development and Its Use on Tour Guiding

AR technology's development started from the year 1960, and till 1990, it stepped into the refined stage of the Virtual Reality (VR) when it was widely used on simulated training, commercial entertainment, and tour guide route planning [11].

Nowadays, there are many cases that can be seen that uses the AR technology in tour guiding. For example, Furmanski et al. have mentioned that the AR technology can use the vision of the spectators and use arrows to help the users to locate their whereabouts, and can even see the internal structure of sealed objects through overlapping images [12]. Figueroa states that experiencing virtual objects through a multi-sensory interface with the sense of vision, auditory and touch can make the displaying objects in museums more attracting then just seeing them through a glass case [13].

Below is a summary of the research and use of AR technology:

- Street Museum App

Street Museum App was released by the London Museum as a tour guiding app. It combines smart phones with GPS positioning and overlaps the historical photos with where the person is at. These intertwining images of the past and present along with words to explain can greatly increase viewer's interest towards the history.

- TimeWarp

TimeWarp is an AR tour guide game. Their aim is to design an adventurous game that fits the local culture by using AR technology. Players must follow directions to move to the corresponding location and interact with the virtual elements. Due to the lack of user's visual experience and to lead them through the routes when playing the game, it also provides sounds to support the players [14].

- Self-Adaptive Animation Based on User Perspective

Papagiannakis and others used the AR technology to create virtual characters, and use them to tour guide. By doing this, they combined the historical environment with virtual images which increased the entertainment level and makes users more involved in it [15].

- ARCHEOGUIDE

Vlahakis et al. have reproduced the ancient Greek palace through the use of AR technology and has upgraded the whole tour guiding experience by increasing its level of entertainment [16].

Overall, this research has summarize the perspective, use and studies of the above professional scholars and combined it with the human-computer interaction theory, "usability" and other related tour guiding elements as the basis of developing the tour guiding system in this research.

3   Methods

Within this research experts of related field are invited to propose and share their point of view of what elements and function the tour guiding should include, as well as how it should be displayed through in-depth interviews. And the outline of the discussion is planned by the results of the literature reviewing.

For the analyzing and integrating of related researches, articles about human-computer interaction, usability, AR technology, and tour guide system designing were used as the reference and basis of designing the system.

Moreover, consulting professionals in the related field, as well as interviewing tour guides who works in historical sites was also conducted by using the semi-structured interviewing method. Before the interview, the questions that will be asked are planned with the respondent's perspective as the main focus. And according to situations, different kinds of open-ended questions are given. This can lead the respondent into a deeper level of discussion.

Then, prototyping was the method chosen to develop the product. Which is to propose a prototype, display it, and after testing it on users, to find out the problems as well as evaluate the actual effectiveness of the product.

The research has followed Laudon four steps of the prototyping [17] and is summarized below:

- Step1: After investigating the human-computer interaction and the tour guide system elements and incorporate it with AR tour guiding literature and cases, propose the concept in designing the system.
- Step2: Develop a smart glasses tour guide system and use literature as reference throughout the process to correct the design.
- Step3: Maintain consistent discussion with users while developing the product to find out problems and correct it.
- Step4: When the prototype is finished, observe the users level of satisfaction, see if there are any feedback, and summarize the final results and start the process of modifying.

To sum up, the research has used smart glasses (Moverio) as a development platform, and AR technology to develop the tour guide system. The interface of AR tour guide is the main focus, and the suitable interface for smart glasses has also been discussed with further hope to be useful for further researches.

4   Design and Implement

As local tourism becomes more and more popular, the use of tour guide, tour guide software and relevant research has started to be focus on. In this research it has being discovered that people may plan their schedule according to the tour guide timetable, and some may even cancel their trip because there are no tour guiding provided at that place.

However, many guiding software can be seen more focus on the navigating then the guiding function. Examples of these apps include the "YuShan National Park", the "Play in PuLi", or the "PingTung Local Cultural Museum" app. Therefore, to develop a system that can guide the users when they reach their destination, and through GPS positioning, 3D display of the AR technique, it can make the users experience a more pleasant trip without the limitation of time that may occur when attending group or person lead tour guiding trips.

4.1   The Components of Forming the Tour Guide System

The smart glasses (Moverio) has been used as a basis in this research to identify the historical sites in Dihua street Taipei through a built in camera within the glasses and achieve the goal of using AR to tour guide. System environment is developed with Unity, and has used Vuforia image recognition technique. In addition, IBeacon was used to estimate the distance that the user had from the object, and through the change of distances, the displayed information and the directions given for the objects location may vary. Nonetheless, IBeacon only supports Bluetooth 4.0, whereas Moverio does not. Due to this reason smart phone was used to receive the Bluetooth signal from IBeacon and transfer the distance data to Moverio through WIFI Fig. 1.

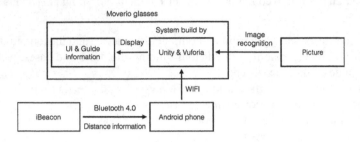

Fig. 1. Framework diagram

4.2   The Contents and Route Designing of the Tour Guiding

The Dihua Street has been Taipei's important trading post for groceries and dry food, tea, Chinese herbs, and cloth since the 19th century. It is Taipei's most preserved traditional street that has nearly all its architectures kept in their original state with four different kinds of style; modernism, western, and Baroque style. The risen of tourism has contribute to the large amount of people visiting Dihua street. This re-search has chosen Dihua Street as the target to tour guide so that its history can be displayed and continued in a good way.

After interviewing three local tour guide workers, the techniques of how to tell the history in an objective way that could allow listeners to understand the history and culture was learned. Furthermore, through analyzing the interviewing script, the actual meaning, procedure, and technique was not only understood, but also from cultural workers point of view the way to display Dihua Streets specialties through the tour routes has been collected and organized in the article below.

To emphasis the connection between Dihua Street and its building, the pieces selected to put into the tour guide all had history, culture, historical important events, and significant historical people to it. The content on the other hand focused on explaining the interrelation or relationship between the historical information given. And to strengthen it with people's knowledge, actual site was connected with virtual image.

The tour guide routes was selected and planned through looking into different aspects. First, actual field investigation was done to understand Dihua Streets local sites and knowledge. Second, experts were consulted to choose the routes and sites. Third, the historical background and local specialties was gathered from experts and put into reference for the tour guiding contents basic material. Thus, the route was planned and numbers were followed to conduct the tour guide as it is shown below (Fig. 2):

1. Lin-Fu-Jhen Trading Company: The earliest merchant that moved to Dihua and ran business was Lan-Tien Lin. However, You-Zao Lin who moved from Bangka due to business failure in the "Dingxiajiao conflict" was the one that established the

blooming economy there. Lin thinks that Dataocheng had the potential to become a commercial port. Hence, three companies Fujhen, Fuyuan, and Fuxing were built there. In the same time, a charity of businessman was formed by Lin to run business with areas in China. For example, Hong Kong, Xia-men, and this contributed to making Dataocheng the most flourished commercial area in Taiwan at that time. Thus, Lin was named as the "Pioneer of Dataocheng".

2. Hanchengtan Pharmacy: The building is in Baroque style which is a representative of Dihua Street, and is constructed with red bricks and granolithic. Tall gable walls, delicate carving of flowers and plants, and glamorous pillars all gives it a wealthy touch.

3. The House of Lan-Tien Lin: In 1985, Lan-Tien Lin moved to Dihua streets from Keelong to escape from the pirates. One of the earliest companies in Taiwanese building style which Lin named Linyishun was built in Dataocheng to trade with China, and at that time Dihua Street was still surrounded by farmland.

4. The Former Home of Wu-Hu Lin: In 1985, the Lin ancestors traveled from Quanzhou, Fujian to Taiwan. The Former Home of Wu-Hu Lin has been classified by the city government as a third graded ancient sites with three halls. The first hall was constructed with no nails in a card tenon structure by using solid wood. This demonstrates the use of traditional craft, and is convenient to take down and put back together for goods to be transferred in.

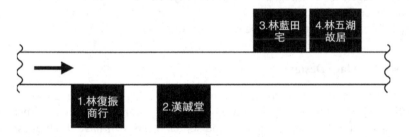

Fig. 2. The route map

4.3   The Designing of the Tour Guide System

It can be seen from literature that device guidance compared to using people to guide is that the latter is often through one to many, and visitors have to move around in groups without the freedom of choosing what they wanted to see. Hence, one of the reasons that the research used IBeacon was to distinguish through the distance in whether the person was interested or not, and then decide to what extent of information should be given. Description is given below: If the distance is 10 m between the person and the object, then only a basic introduction for example the name would be given. If the distance shortens to 5 m, a more detailed introduction with a diorama will be given. Another reason is that image recognition technique has its limitation, for it may be affected by the weather and the lights. Hence, with IBeacon as support, the system can become more stabilized.

Moreover, visual stimulation that the AR provides is not efficient enough [14]. Thus, traditional voice tour guiding function has being kept to increase the usability of the system Fig. 3.

Fig. 3. Testing the system at Dihua Street

The tour guide system instructions:

- Step1. The user wears the smart glasses and walks on the Dihua Street.
- Step2. Users sees or get close to the selected objects by using Moverio.
- Step3. Triggers the event on the tour guiding system and use the interface and voices to introduce the objects.
- Step4. Words and pictures can be read form the screen.

4.4 User Interface Design

The principles that this research has followed in designing the interface was proposed by Tullis [18]. By only putting the necessary details on the upper right corner in the smallest size, with the interface around the screen, users will have the biggest visual range that allows a good tour guide experience. Furthermore, the related interface will be invisible till an event is triggered by the user coming within 10 m close or by the

Fig. 4. Left: The related interface that is shown when there is a successful recognition of the image or if it is within 10 m; **Middle:** Choosing the "more" on the left side will show related pictures and introduction. Through choosing the up and down arrow, other related information can be seen.; **Right:** By using the diorama, structure and space arrangement of the building can be seen.

system recognizing the image. Also, the tour guiding system uses a diorama to let the users see the buildings whole structure and space arrangements Fig. 4.

5   Finding and Informal Evaluation

15 participants with attending tour guide experience were used in this research to anticipate in the user testing of the AR tour guide. The mission was to go through the planned route and a simple route introduction and tour guide system user's instruction was given before setting off. After the test, there were findings and there were adjustments been made.

The general introduction of the voice tour guiding was canceled, and only a short introduction in words would be given at the front. This is because many participants reflected that the sudden voice of the tour guiding was frightening and that from the feedback given, displaying word introduction on the screen is enough for users to make an initial judgment on whether they are interested in the object or not.

The operating and the interface of the device had no significant problems. This may be because that the user interface and the interactive logic is similar to other handhold devices. Thus, the system has matched the learnability principle. However, the participants mostly would stop walking when reading the tour guide information. Meaning that, reading words may be difficult while moving around. Therefore, suggestion was given to cut down the amount of word information given and replaced it with voice introduction. Other than the reason above, other 5 participants said that it can be disturbing when the actual sites and the information can be seen through the glasses in the same time. Moreover, Dihua Street is quite narrow. When people stop to watch the tour guide, they can easily be hit by cars, or bumped by others.

Compliments from 10 of the participants includes that the AR technology tour guide device is better than handhold multimedia tour guide device. For there is no need to hold the machine for a long period of time, and to look down onto the screen constantly to match the displaying image with the actual view. However, the information given is in black and white. Thus, it is not suitable to watch for a long period of time as it can cause user's eyes to fatigue.

Other feedback includes that 7 of the participants out of curiosity would move around to test how big the angle was when seeing the 3 dimensional diorama introduction. But later on they would stop this movement with the feet and only slightly move their eyes. 12 users thought the idea of using 3 dimensional diorama to show the buildings structure and arrangement was interesting, for parts of historical sites was not open to the public, and through 3 dimensional diorama, there can be deeper understanding of the buildings characteristics.

6   Conclusion and Future Work

The use of glasses to display the AR technology tour guide has a better outcome than using a handhold device. It can more easily draw the users into the tour guiding. Nevertheless, problems with users too busy to attend to the real world around them can be seen, and to draw the line in between is the next target of this research. As within the user testing, the original tour guide interface was not visible enough which caused the target object being missed. Hence, improvement of the interface design is another following job to accomplish. Furthermore, users were found to be interested in what the building looked like in the areas that were not opened to the public. Therefore, by combining AR technology with diorama when displaying, has been found as a great advantage in AR tour guiding. As for operating the tour guide system, not much problem was found as the touch screen is design similar to handhold devices. However, the touch screen is installed on a panel not the smart glass this caused some users to feel that the button was difficult to press. To solve this problem, new tangible user interface and models will be developed to upgrade the tour guiding using experience.

References

1. Griggs, S.A.: Evaluating exhibitions. In: Thompson, J.M.A., et al. (eds.) Manual of Curatorship. Butterworth-Heinemann, Oxford (1992)
2. Te'eni, D.: Designs that fit: an overview of fit conceptualization in HCI. In: Zhang, P., Galletta, D. (Eds.) Human-Computer Interaction and Management Information Systems: Foundations. M.E. Sharpe, Armonk (2006)
3. Norman, D.A.: The Psychology of Everyday Things, Basic Books (1988)
4. Xu, Z.M., Li, C.F.: The research of Children's preferences and electronic storybooks
5. Preece, J., Rogers Y., Sharp H.: Interaction Design - Beyond human-computer interaction. Paper presented at the Human-Computer Interaction (2003)
6. Preece, J.: Human-Computer Interaction (1994)
7. Nielsen, J.: Usability Engineering. Morgan Kaufmann, San Francisco (1993)
8. Shneiderman, B., Plaisant, C.: Designing the User Interface – Strategies for Effective Human-Computer Interaction. Addison-Wesley, USA (1998)
9. Tilden, F.: Interpreting Our Heritage. University of North Carolina Press, Chapel Hill (1957)
10. Edwards, A., Civitello, A., Hammond, H.A., Caskey, C.T.: DNA typing and genetic mapping with trimeric and tetrameric tandem repeats. Am. J. Hum. Genet. **49**, 746–756 (1976)
11. van Krevelen, D., Poelman, R.: A survey of augmented reality technologies, applications and limitations. Int. J. Virtual Reality **9**(2), 1–20 (2010)
12. Furmanski, C., Azuma, R., Daily, M.: Augmented-reality visualizations guided by cognition: perceptual heuristics for combining visible and obscured information. In: Mixed and Augmented Reality (2002)
13. Figueroa, P., Coral, M., Boulanger, P., Borda, J., Londoño, E., Vega, F., Prieto, F., Restrepo, D.: Multi-modal exploration of small artifacts: an exhibition at the Gold Museum in Bogota. In: Proceedings of the 16th ACM Symposium on Virtual Reality Software and Technology, pp. 67–74 (2009)
14. Herbst, I., Braun, A., Mccall, R., Broll, W.: Timewarp: interactive time travel with a mobile mixed reality game. In: MobileHCI 2008: Proceedings of the 10th International Conference on Human Computer Interaction with Mobile Devices and Services 2008, pp. 235–244 (2008)
15. Papagiannakis, G., Singh, G., Magnenat-Thalmann, N.: A survey of mobile and wireless technologies for augmented reality systems. Comput. Anim. Virtual Worlds **2008**(19), 3–22 (2008)

16. Vlahakis, V., Ioannidis, N., Karigiannis, J., Tsotros, M., Gounaris, M., Stricker, D., Gleue, T., Daehne, P., Almeida, L.: Archeoguide: an augmented reality guide for archaeological sites. IEEE Comput. Graph. Appl. 2002 **22**(5), 52–60 (2002)
17. Laudon, K.C., Laudon, J.P.: Management information systems: managing the digital firm. Prentice Hall, Upper Saddle River, N.J. (2002)
18. Tullis, T.S.: Screen design. In: Helander, M., Landauer, T., Probhu, P. (eds.) Handbook of Human-Computer Interation, 2nd edn, pp. 503–531. North-Holland, Amsterdam (1997)

Human Factors and Ergonomics Using Anthropometric and sEMG Data in Automotive Gearshift Quality Analysis

Edson Luciano Duque[1,2] and Plinio Thomaz Aquino Jr.[2(✉)]

[1] Global Propulsion Systems – South America, São Caetano do Sul, Brazil
edson.duque@gm.com
[2] Centro Universitário da FEI – Fundação Educacional Inaciana Pe. Sabóia de Medeiros, São Bernardo do Campo, Brazil
plinio.aquino@fei.edu.br

Abstract. Manual transmission shift quality has become extremely demanding due to the higher requirements imposed by drivers in the last years. It is well recognized that manual gearshift operation is a remarkable activity regarding quality perception in passenger vehicles. The available literature presents analytical methods to predict shift quality, but applying only objective variables faced by the driven, and removes the human from the equation. This study introduces the human and ergonomics portion, evaluating the influence of anthropometric variances and muscular activity, though surface electromyography acquisition, on human subjective rating via linear regressions analysis.

Keywords: Electromyography · Manual transmission · Gearshift quality · Human factors · Ergonomics

1 Introduction

Due to the more demanding quality requirements for manual transmissions imposed by the market in the last years, driver sensation during a gearshift has gained a very high importance during the design phase of the shifting systems once it is one of the most remarkable actions in terms of comfort perception in motor vehicles.

Actually, the first article found in the available literature about shifting analysis dates from 1949 and was published by M'Ewen [11] with the very first studies done in this front with the objective to understand the mechanics/behavior of the synchronization system in order to improve and ease the gearshift of war tanks in battle fields. This article is recognized as the first "theory of manual gearshifting". After M'Ewen [11] just one article was found that considers a modeled drive which controls the velocity of the lever during the engagement phase. Kim et al. [2] detailed the dynamics of the synchronizers and gearshift system, applying a proportional, integral and derivative (PID) controller to represent the driver.

Another work performed by Hannemann [5] presented a statistical analysis based on objective results measured from a real situation which aimed to remove the inherent subjective portion of the real driver and his/her respective ergonomics/human factors.

© Springer International Publishing Switzerland 2016
M. Kurosu (Ed.): HCI 2016, Part III, LNCS 9733, pp. 248–258, 2016.
DOI: 10.1007/978-3-319-39513-5_23

The author proposed a non-linear regression to estimate the subjective rating of the drivers for a given vehicle. However, although the author obtained good results, one of the proposed next steps would be to extend this analysis for other countries due to differences among countries around the globe.

Having said that, it is possible to verify in the available literature that no human interaction analysis with the gearshift system considering human factors and ergonomics (HFE) to define its relation to the physical values observed during the process of gearshifting (e.g. efforts, impulses, times, etc.) to support changes in the transmission hardware.

About gearshift quality, one can easily find several definitions, but definitely all lead to a not so clear definition and has been evolving in the last years mainly due to the more demanding market requirements [3, 5, 6].

Moreover, since the pioneer study performed by M'Ewen [11] until the ones presented by Szadkowski [16] and Szadkowski and McNerney [17], the main concern was in the analysis of the influence of the maximum effort demanded to shift gears, and nowadays with the addition of the shift comfort portion [3, 5, 6].

From the studies developed by Duque and Aquino Jr. [3], the model proposed based on HFE aspects plays an important role in the gearshift quality perception and, consequently, the subjective rating given by the driver.

Therefore, the objective of this work is to develop an in-vehicle test protocol, which applies surface electromyography (sEMG) techniques together with anthropometric aspects analysis of the test drivers.

2 Human-System Interface Applied in Manual Gearshifting

According to Czaja and Nair [2], a system can be defined as a set of organized and structured elements, possibly arranged in a hierarchic form, in order to perform tasks and to achieve its objectives. In addition to that, the authors mention that human and machine elements commonly compose a system set to achieve a common aim, with inputs and outputs, and limited by boundaries to define its separation to external and internal elements.

Applying this definition to the vehicle interface, the interaction between driver and vehicle is very wide and cannot be limited in studying only his/her contact with the gearshift lever inside the passenger compartment. However, take into consideration all interactions the drive may suffer while driving would demand a huge amount of time and more detailed and specific studies [6, 18, 19].

Said that, this research deals just with the controls reachability within passenger compartment, being focused on the gearshift lever. Exactly as cited by Robinette [15], reachability analysis is performed through a set of in-vehicle anthropometric studies, and must be the very first activity when designing the interior of a given vehicle [14]. In the available literature [12, 14], all reachability analyses done in a vehicle just guarantee that, statically, a population of drivers is able to reach and operate its controls with comfort and without facing any difficulty. However, these sort of analyses do not consider the loads that, as for example, the gearshift system transfers to driver's hand during a gear change, similar to Parkinson and Reed [12] proposed.

Loads analyses are studied measuring the forces behavior in the lever knob during the entire gearshift, covering both selection and engagement phases [1, 3, 4, 6]. After running these measurements, the gearshift engineer decides if a change is necessary to improve quality, without considering any HFE aspect.

In this work, this analysis is replaced by measuring the muscular activity during the gearshift through sEMG signal acquisition. The details of the protocol applied and the equipment required are further detailed in the next sections.

3   sEMG Methods

According to Konrad [9], kinesiological sEMG can be defined as a discipline that studies the neuromuscular activation during functional movements, work situations and medical treatments. The motor unit is composed by a set of fibers, which are spatially positioned in a random way in different distances from the acquisition sEMG electrode, as shown in Fig. 1.

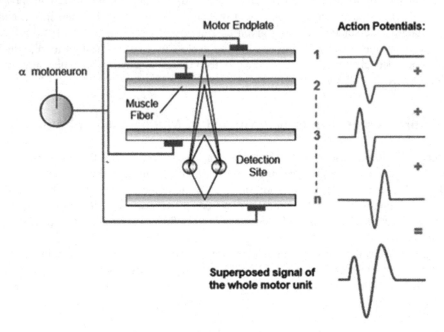

Fig. 1. MUAP representation (Source: Konrad [9], p. 9)

In case of several motor units being activated, the final signal, also known as motor unit action potential (MUAP), will be the sum of all resulting signals from each motor unit [8, 13, 20]. In addition, the MUAP's of all detected motor units are observed as a symmetric distribution with negative and positive amplitudes with zero as average value.

Another point raised by Konrad [9] is that, although the human body is considered as a good electrical conductor, variations on conductivity are observed due to type of tissue, thickness, physiologic changes and temperature, as represented in Fig. 2.

These differences totally forbid the direct comparison among drivers, requiring a normalization of the sEMG signals based on the maximum voluntary contraction (MVC) [8–10].

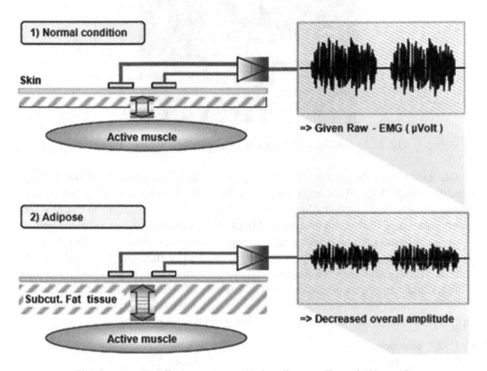

Fig. 2. MUAP differences representation (Source: Konrad [9], p. 12)

The normalization of sEMG signals will be further discussed in Sect. 4 to define the post-processing methods used in this research.

4 Equipments, Test Protocol and sEMG Post-processing

For the sEMG signals acquisition were used the module ML880 PowerLab® 16/30 and the amplifier ML138 Octal Bio Amp®, both manufactured by ADInstruments with the configuration and post-treatment software LabChart® v7.2 (see example in Fig. 3). The equipment was set with a ±5 mV maximum amplitude with an acquisition rate of 1 kHz and filtered within the range of 20 to 500 Hz for the recorded channels.

Fig. 3. In-vehicle sEMG equipment installation (Source: Author)

Cables connect the acquisition module to the surface electrodes of the selected muscular group. With all cabling connections done, the driver sits into the test vehicle, adjusts the seat in a comfortable position, but in a straight posture to avoid any secondary movement during the gearshifts. After these set of adjustments, with the vehicle at rest and engine off, the driver performs some static shifts just for his/her familiarization with the equipment, being used also for the quality check of the sEMG signals. With the sEMG signals behaving accordingly and the adaptation phase concluded, prior to the test trials an acquisition of the MVC for the normalization of the sEMG signals is performed. The MVC acquisition is performed with the vehicle still at rest and the driver applying the maximum effort at the following gearshift lever positions:

- $1^{st}/2^{nd}$ selection;
- $5^{th}/6^{th}$ selection;
- Engagement position of all gears, reverse included;
- Reverse inhibitor activation only.

The time duration of each measurement was about 8 s in order to obtain a stabilized sEMG signal. After the MVC test conclusion, the driver starts the engine and drives the vehicle in a known circuit shifting gears following the vehicle speed profile seen in Table 1.

The sEMG signals are collected and the driver gives his/her subjective evaluation following the ATZ scale presented in Fig. 4, rating the quality perception for each shift.

Due to the availability of the equipment and the drivers, the experiment had to be divided in two data sets, covering different variables. The first one, from now on called test A, was done with 8 drivers (7 female and 1 male) and was performed to evaluate the impacts on human subjective rating due to their differences in terms of anthropometric dimensions.

Regarding test B, just one driver was selected to perform the sEMG signals acquisition to correlate with his subjective rating about quality perception. Only in this

Table 1. Vehicle speed profile per shift.

Shift	Speed
Neutral–1st	0 km/h
1st–2nd	30 km/h
2nd–3rd	40 km/h
3rd–4th	50 km/h
4th–5th	50 km/h
5th–4th	50 km/h
4th–3rd	40 km/h
3rd–2nd	40 km/h
2nd–1st	20 km/h

	not saleable				border line	saleable				
Rating index	1	2	3	4	5	6	7	8	9	10
disturbances	unacceptable			uncomfortable	Improvement required	moderate	slight	very slight	traces	not noticeable
noticeable by...	all customer	average customers			critical customers			experts		none
customer reaction	"walk home" tow away	"walk home" garage	immediate garage	garage as soon as possible	garage at next opportunity	notify during next inspection	none			
customer perception	extremely upset		upset	strongly disstisfied	slightly dissappointed	strongly dissappointed	still satisfied	completely satisfied	positively surprised	enthusiastic

Fig. 4. ATZ rating scale (Source: Hau [6], p. 40)

test, even that no comparison would be made with other drivers, the MVC experiment was performed in order to validate the entire test protocol.

4.1 Anthropometric Measurements

The body dimensions chosen for this research are the height of the driver, and the length from the contact point of the heel with the ground to H-point and from the H-point to the right shoulder (see Fig. 5).

The required measurements are performed prior to the test, just after the briefing done to the driver about the entire experiment.

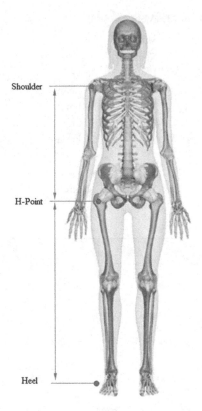

Fig. 5. Body dimensions measured (Source: Author adapted from InnerBody [7])

4.2 Muscles Selection and sEMG Acquisition Preparation

The surface electrodes were positioned in driver's right side Pectoralis Major muscular group, as shown in Fig. 6, following SENIAM recommendations, with the reference electrode being located in the olecranon.

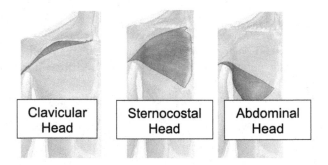

Fig. 6. Pectoralis Major muscular group (Source: Author adapted from InnerBody [7])

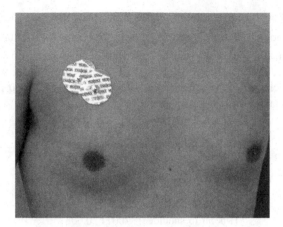

Fig. 7. Surface electrodes (Source: Author adapted from Innerbody)

For the preparation of the interested area, to obtain a good sEMG measurement depends on the condition of driver's skin and electrodes positioning [9].

Regarding skin condition, for evaluations with high dynamic loads it is mandatory to adopt rigid cleanness methods, like the removal of superficial dead cells and use of abrasive cleaning pastes, according to Konrad [9]. Once in this experiment only small/slow movements are performed, a simple alcohol cleaning could be done with hair removal, if needed, to guarantee full electrode adhesion in the area of the target muscle (Fig. 7).

4.3   sEMG Data Post-processing

After the tests, two sets of sEMG data were obtained: one file for the MVC and another file for the regular driving condition. Both files originated by the LabChart® software had to be first converted into two MAT files to be further treated by using scripts created with Matlab® R2013b. As mentioned before, once raw sEMG signal has a mean value around zero, a rectification process had to be applied in all channels. After the rectification, due to the inherent random behavior of the raw sEMG amplitudes, the use of smoothing methods are required in order to obtain the mean trend of the signal. The method chosen was the root mean square (RMS), being recognized as a very good choice for smoothing sEMG signals [8, 9].

This process was performed for all shifts, covering both MVC and regular driving conditions. Moreover, after the RMS calculation for both datasets, it was possible to normalize the signals from regular driving trials.

5   Results

All statistical work in this study was performed using an unidimensional linear regression per selected variable calculated through the statistical tools from Microsoft Excel® 2010.

The way to check the correlation of the selected variable versus the given subjective rating is done by the $\overline{R}^2$ (a.k.a. adjusted R^2), while the checks of the statistical relevance of the linear estimator $\hat{\beta}$ is done by the calculation of p-value considering a 95 % confidence interval. Table 2 shows the statistical results from test A, which is possible to see that the correlation of the linear models based on anthropometric data were very poor, reaching a maximum value of about 3 %.

Table 2. Statistical results from test A

	$\overline{R}^2$	p-value
Height	0.032	0.076
Heel to H-point	0.005	0.244
H-point to shoulder	−0.011	0.608

Additionally to that, the p-values show that the linear estimators for all models do not have statistical relevance, which means that cannot be applied for estimating the subjective rating from bigger populations. About test B, Table 3 summarizes the statistical analysis.

Table 3. Statistical results from test B

	$\overline{R}^2$	p-value
Pectoralis Major sEMG	0.129	0.006

For test B, $\overline{R}^2$ showed a better value, but still too low in terms of pure correlation of the linear model against the explained variable. Meanwhile, the calculated linear estimator showed a very low p-value, meaning that this model has relevance, statistically-wise.

6   Conclusions

Test A results showed that a linear model based only on anthropometric data of the driver does not correlate well to the subjective rating for shift quality perception. Moreover, the model does not present a good statistical behavior failing to generate a linear estimator within the 95 % confidence interval and cannot be used to predict the quality rating to given population.

On the other hand, test B results provided a linear estimator with statistical relevance, and could estimate a bigger population rating. However, the calculated R^2 was very low with just about 13 % of correlation to the real rating.

It means that the model considering the sEMG signal of just Pectoralis Major group could not be used "alone", requiring to be complemented by other variables to explain better the human rating.

Therefore, as a next step of this study, the authors recommend to identify other muscular groups that could be added and propose a multidimensional model instead of the simpler unidimensional approach. Another alternative linked to this one is to follow the non-linear format adopted by Hannemann [4] to define his shift comfort model, leading to a better correlation than the linear approach.

Additionally to that, other HFE-variables, like tactile-sense based, could be further analyzed and added to this new multidimensional model [3]. The results presented are being used in a research project that includes virtual reality interfaces and tele-existence [4] for monitoring data. In this case, the virtual reality resources are also used for simulation test environments.

Acknowledgment. To FAPESP (Fundação de Amparo à Pesquisa do Estado de São Paulo) for financial support.

References

1. Barbosa, G.S.: Análise de sistema manual de controle de caixa de transmissão veicular: uma abordagem ergonômica (in Portuguese), 103 p. Master Thesis – Escola Politécnica, Universidade de São Paulo, São Paulo (2007)
2. Czaja, S.J.; Nair, S.N.: Human factors engineering and systems design. In: Salvendy, G. (ed.). Handbook of Human Factor and Ergonomics, 4 edn., pp. 38–56 (2012). Nova Jersey
3. Duque, E.L., Aquino Jr., P.T.: Human factors analysis of manual gear shifting performance in passenger vehicles. In: 6th International Conference on Applied Human Factors and Ergonomics and the Affiliated Conferences, AHFE 2015 (2015)
4. Goebbels, G., Aquino Jr., P.T., Lalioti, V., Goebel, M.: Supporting team work in collaborative virtual environments. In: Proceedings of ICAT 2000 - The Tenth International Conference on Artificial Reality and Tele-existence (2000)
5. Hannemann, P.: Development of a correlation between subjective and objective shift quality, 147 p. Bachelor Thesis, University of Applied Sciences, Wiesbaden (2012)
6. Hau, C.: Shift Quality simulations, calculations, calibration and evaluation in Matlab/Simulink, 117 p. Bachelor Thesis, University of Applied Sciences, Wiesbaden (2010)
7. Inner Body: Muscles and skeleton images. http://www.innerbody.com
8. Knutson, L.M., Soderberg, G.L., Ballantyne, B.T., Clarke, W.R.: A study of various normalization procedures for within day electromyographic data. J. Electromygr. Kinesiol. **4**(1), 47–49 (1994)
9. Konrad, P.: The ABC of EGM: a practical introduction of kinesiological eletromyography, vol. 1.4. Noraxon USA Inc., Arizona (2006)
10. Mathiassen, S.E., Winkel, J., Hägg, G.M.: Normalization of surface EMG amplitude from upper trapezius muscle in ergonomic studies – a review. J. Electromygr. Kinesiol. **5**(4), 197–226 (1996)
11. M'Ewen, M.: The theory of gear-changing. In: Proceedings of the Institution of Mechanical Engineers: Automobile Division 1949 (1949)
12. Parkinson, M.B.; Reed, M.P.: Optimizing vehicle occupant packaging. In: SAE 2006 World Congress, SAE, 2006, Lyon. França (SAE PAPER 2006-01-0961)

13. Reaz, M.B.I., Hussain, M.S., Mohd-Yasin, F.: Techniques of EMG signal analysis: detection, processing, classification and applications. Biol. Proced. (Online) **8**(1), 11–35 (2006)
14. Reed, M.P.; Parkinson, M.B.; Chaffin, D.B.: A new approach to modeling driver reach. In: SAE 2003 World Congress, SAE, 2003, Lyon. França (SAE PAPER 2003-01-0587)
15. Robinette, K.M.: Anthropometry for product design. In: salvendy, G. (ed.) Handbook of Human Factor and Ergonomics, 4 edn., pp. 330–381 (2012). Nova Jersey
16. Szadkowski, A.: Shiftability and shift quality issues in clutch-transmission systems. In: SAE 1991 World Congress, SAE, 1991, Detroit, Michigan (SAE PAPER 912697)
17. Szadkowski, A., McNerney, G.J.: Engineering method for rating shift quality. In: SAE 1993 World Congress, SAE, 1993, Detroit, Michigan (SAE PAPER 932996)
18. Shinar, D., Meir, M., Ben-Shoham, I.: How automatic is manual gear shifting? Hum. Fact. J. Hum. Fact. Ergon. Soc. **40**(4), 647–654 (1998)
19. Tideman, M., Voort, M.C., Houten, F.J.A.M.: Design and evaluation of a virtual gearshift application 2004. In: IEEE Intelligent Vehicles Symposium. University of Parma (2004)
20. Weiss, J.M., Weiss, L.D., Silver, J.K.: Easy EMG: a guide to performing nerve conduction studies and eletromyography, 2nd edn. Elsevier Inc., Londres (2016)

Service and Usability Engineering Based Approach for Flexible Mobility

Stephan Hörold[1]([⊠]), Robert Kummer[2], Bastian Sander[2],
Cindy Mayas[1], and Heidi Krömker[1]

[1] Technische Universität Ilmenau, Ilmenau, Germany
{stephan.hoerold, cindy.mayas,
heidi.kroemker}@tu-ilmenau.de
[2] Fraunhofer Institute for Factory Operation and Automation IFF,
Magdeburg, Germany
{robert.kummer, bastian.sander}@iff.fraunhofer.de

Abstract. Changing general conditions, e.g. demographic change, rural flight and diminishing funds, and new expectations from mass transit users are compelling transportation companies, especially mass transit authorities, to develop new and flexible mobility services. This paper describes an approach that combines methods of service and usability engineering and also presents the initial results of analyses and specifications. The findings reveal the different views of companies and users and serve to identify the challenges of and opportunities for new flexible and user-centered mobility services.

Keywords: Service engineering · Usability engineering · Mass transit · Public transportation

1 Introduction

Public transportation is tremendously important: People select their places of residence based on the availability of public transportation. Many people's daily routines (e.g. commuters) are significantly dictated by mass transit services. Public transportation also provides socially disadvantaged individuals opportunities to partake in social life. What is more, mass transit presents numerous opportunities over private motorized transportation: Demands for transportation are satisfied cleanly and energy efficiently, traffic is reduced in the public sphere, and customers can use the time in transit to relax or work [1].

German mass transit companies, however, will have to face key challenges in the coming years. Urban flight, continuous decline in the number of school students, and pressure to continually improve profitability are but three examples [2].

While demand for transportation is increasing or will at least remain static in cities, it will continue to decline in rural areas. Public transportation, especially the German mass transit system in its present form with inflexible routes and scheduled timetables, will no longer be financially viable in rural areas in the medium and long term [3]. Moreover, using scheduled means of transportation to meet individual demands for transportation among the populace will be extremely difficult [4]. Disruptive innovations will be

M. Kurosu (Ed.): HCI 2016, Part III, LNCS 9733, pp. 259–268, 2016.
DOI: 10.1007/978-3-319-39513-5_24

essential to the continued provision of high quality transportation services to the rural population [3]. This will require technological innovations such as autonomous driving and especially service innovations.

This paper describes how methods of service engineering [5] and usability engineering [6] can be combined and refined to systematically develop new transportation services for rural areas. The aim is to develop services that satisfy the rural population's transportation needs resource efficiently and provide transportation users easy and flexible access to transportation and information services by designing them user-centered.

The analyses cover the German state of Saxony-Anhalt. This state with only two major cities (Magdeburg and Halle) is particularly being affected by demographic change and migration within Germany. The state lost close to 19 % of its population from 1990 to 2010. Approximately 1.74 million of the state's 2.28 million residents live in rural regions. Its population density of 112 residents per square kilometer, which is comparatively low for Germany, poses major challenges to the German mass transit system [7].

2   Method

2.1   General Approach

The service engineering process model developed by Bullinger und Schreiner [8] has been combined with Mayhew's usability engineering life cycle concept [9] to form an integrated conceptual framework in order to achieve the stated goal of resource efficient, flexible and user-friendly transportation. This entailed cutting the six phases of service engineering (start, analysis, specification, preparation, testing and implementation) put forth by Bullinger and Schreiner down to four phases in order to render the approach highly concurrent. Table 1 presents the approach and the methods used.

The first phase of the integrated conceptual framework covers the development and evaluation of ideas for new transportation services. This entails ascertaining the con-text of use with the specific attributes and demands of transportation users. The second phase is the specification of concrete partial services. Concrete specifications are derived from users' demands and factored into the design of service processes. Parallel to this, mock-ups are created, screen design standards are defined for specific products, and the user interface is developed. The second phase also includes combining the partial services developed in an integrated unified transportation service (system pooling). The third phase covers the testing of the transportation services developed. To this end, the resources required to provide a service (e.g. vehicles, communications infrastructure, control center) are provided, staff is trained appropriately, test users are selected, and the test setting is defined. Then, the test results are analyzed to identify other actions that will improve the service and these are implemented systematically. The fourth and final phase is the implementation and successive improvement of the integrated unified service on the market.

Table 1. Combined methods of service and usability engineering [6, 8–10]

Service Engineering	Set of Methods	Usability Engineering
Start and analysis phase Goal: Create ideas, analyze requirements and assess ideas	Analyze statistics	**Requirements analysis** Goal: Understand and specify the context of use
	Modularize of transportation services	
	Conduct interviews and surveys	
	From focus groups	
	Perform a means-ends analysis	
Design phase Goal: Define detailed and general specifications	Define services and specifications	**Design, testing and Development** Goal: Develop and evaluate design solutions
	Design transportation and information systems	
	Develop user interfaces	
	Develop service systems	
Evaluation phase Goal: Test specifications	Perform tests and evaluations with experts and users	
Implementation phase Goal: Implement solution	Obtain user feedback	**Installation** Goal: Implement solution

2.2 Analysis Phase

This paper concentrates on the first phase of the aforementioned conceptual framework. The goal is to identify starting points for the development and design of new transportation services for rural areas. The methods presented in Table 1 are used.

Secondary Analysis. This analysis is intended to identify typical types of customer structures in the region analyzed. The users are stereotypical in terms of their transportation demands and represent a large number of users in the region analyzed. The analysis of the data sets "Transportation in Germany" [11] and "Transportation in Cities" [12] is used to analyze the population's use of transportation in the region analyzed on the basis of key household and transportation indicators, thus establishing the basis for developing individual and flexible transportation services.

Interviews With Experts. Building upon the quantitative findings on types of customer structures as well as a detailed analysis of literature on the planning and operation of mass transit systems (including [2, 13, 14]), service productivity (including [15–17]), service engineering (including [10, 18–20]) and electric vehicle networks (including [21–23]), interviews with experts are intended to generate qualitative data. The partially standard interviews are conducted with representatives of mass transit companies, mass transit authorities and mass transit networks in order to integrate every relevant stakeholder. The results along with the experts' assessments of the aforementioned topics will also establish the basis for the subsequent online surveys of mass transit companies and customers.

Online Survey of German Mass Transit Companies. The written survey (modeled after [24]) is used to ascertain, among other things, whether companies have already entered collaborative partnerships with other transportation service providers (e.g. car sharing, bike sharing, rideshare agencies), the extent to which electric vehicles are being used, and what forms of flexible services (e.g. dial-a-bus, dial-a-taxi) are al-ready in use now. In addition, the mass transit companies' assessment of their own efficiency and effectiveness is examined. Ultimately, it will be possible to define the current state of responsiveness and the use of innovative transportation services and identify best practices.

Online Survey of Mass Transit Users. The survey of German mass transit system users focuses on the region analyzed and scrutinizes the findings of the secondary analysis from the perspective of transportation users. Among other things, it collects key transportation indicators on different purposes of travel as well as the demands and expectations on current and future transportation concepts. To this end, the respondents are given an opportunity to evaluate existing German mass transit system services on the basis of various criteria such as access and accessibility. The findings enter into the refinement of types of customer structures and the development of service concepts on the level of idea generation of and business model creation.

Focus Groups. Focus groups are intended to help further refine the types of customer structures and facilitate the development of new flexible transportation concepts. In addition, the related factors for the selection of a means of transportation will be identified and weighted for different transportation services. The focus groups repro-duce the types of customer structures relevant to the region analyzed and specify different transportation scenarios and purposes of travel, e.g. tourism, commuter traffic and occasional and daily travel.

3   Results

The overall results of the first phase reveal particularly high potentials for respon-siveness of transportation services in the region analyzed. The secondary analysis revealed the region's failure to exploit its potential for regular German mass transit system customers when compared with the German average. What is more, a large number of routes traveled are shorter than 1 km (0.62 mile). The number of pedestrians and cyclists is significantly elevated. Commuter traffic also harbors potential that transportation service responsiveness can tap.

3.1   Secondary Analysis

The first step of the secondary analysis entailed identifying five types of households in Saxony-Anhalt. They are classified on the basis of the two criteria of car availability and household size (see Table 2). In the second step, these were refined with typical features of transportation, e.g. distance to next mass transit access point or use of transportation services for different routes.

Table 2. Household types in Saxony-Anhalt [11]

		One- person household	Multi-person house-hold without children	Multi-person household with children
	Household size			
Car avability	No car	Retiree over 65, no driver's license		
	One care	Full-time employee, 45-64, driver's license, perhaps a motorcycle	Retired married couple, over 65, both with driver's licenses	
	Two cars		Married couple, part/full time employees, 45-65, both with driver's licenses	Married couple with school age children, part/full time employees, 25-44, both with driver's licenses

The first type of customer structure is a retiree living alone. She has neither a driver's license nor a car and is over sixty-five. She takes trips primarily in the vicinity. Another type of customer structure with the attribute "one-person household" is a working man aged forty-five to sixty-five. A full-time employee, he has a driver's license and a car, and uses them for his daily commute to work.

3.2 Interviews with Experts

Achieving the stated goal of transportation service responsiveness requires factoring in both the customer and the corporate perspective. The significant findings from the two to three-hour interviews conducted with seven experts in the realm of customers on four days are:

- The majority of customers of the companies surveyed are captive users, i.e. customers, primarily older individuals and school students, who have neither a driver's license nor a car and are therefore reliant on mass transit. They primarily use mass transit to travel to school or to medium and large urban areas.
- Typical customer demands include more individualized scheduling, even in off-peak hours, and the reduction of transfers. Universal accessibility of stops, vehicles and information systems are also wishes frequently expressed by customers.
- In particular, the frequency and periods of use, the time spent in transit, the pricing system and perceived inferior flexibility to one's own car were identified as barriers to use.

The following qualitative findings were obtained from the corporate perspective, i.e. the perspective of the mass transit companies, networks and authorities:

- Classic approaches to mass transit responsiveness, e.g. on-demand taxi, dial-a-bus and scheduled taxi, are already in use and will be used more in the future.
- The companies surveyed in the region analyzed do not collaborate with car or bike sharing providers or other alternative transportation providers. Reasons given are the lack of availability of suitable services, the unprofitability of such collaborative partnerships, and fears of cannibalization and crowding out.
- The respondents are fundamentally open-minded about electric vehicles but see numerous obstacles in the requisite charging infrastructure, service garage availability and profitability, which argue the use of electric vehicles in mass transit.
- The respondents have widely varying understandings of efficiency and effective-ness. The target variables hardly have any relevance for daily work. Key indicators that operationalize target variables are either not measured at all or measured on the basis of individual initiatives. The findings are only evaluated and discussed sporadically, if at all.

3.3   Online Survey of German Mass Transit Companies

The findings on mass transit responsiveness, transportation service efficiency and effectiveness and the use of electric vehicles obtained from the survey of experts constitute the foundation for the design of a nationwide survey of mass transit companies. The questionnaire prepared for this contains thirty-two question batteries arranged in six domains:

- Company information, services offered and infrastructure,
- Collaboration with other transportation providers,
- Productivity of the services offered,
- Alternative transportation services, e.g. flexible forms of use and sharing,
- Use of electric vehicles in transportation services, and
- Information on respondents, e.g. position and function in the company.

Since the survey had just started at the time this paper was being written, the response rate is very manageable (N = 20) so far. The portion of the results presented below are therefore preliminary findings intended to illustrate the potential responses when the response rate is commensurate. Table 3 presents select results on the range of services and the vehicles used.

The self-assessment of productivity delivered surprising results. 54 % of the respondents rate the productivity of their own transportation services as low or very low. The respondents are similarly critical of their transportation services' customer orientation. 50 % of the respondents do not concur at all with the statement, "The customer is always able to find information on current departure times, delays and connection (e.g. by smartphone)". Approximately 82 % of the respondents indicated that their companies already employ flexible forms of use. The form of services most frequently used by the respondents is the dial-a-bus in on-demand service [25].

Collaboration with transportation service providers is more advanced than the results of the survey of experts suggested. According to the survey results to date, approximately

Table 3. Select results from the survey of mass transit companies

Subject	Preliminary Results
Permit for regularly scheduled service	• Have a permit for regularly scheduled service: 63 % • Have applied for a permit for regularly scheduled service: 11 %
Types of vehicles used	• Two-axle standard bus: 81 % • Articulated bus: 44 % • Shuttle bus: 31 % • Three-axle standard bus: 19 %
Drive system of the of vehicles used	• Diesel: 63 % • Natural gas: 19 % • Hybrid: 19 % • Electric: 19 %

67 % of the respondents are already collaborating with both car and bike sharing providers. Approximately 87 % of the respondents indicated that they collaborate with taxi companies. 60 % of the respondents collaborate with intercity bus companies. The respondents tend to be restrained in their assessment of the suitability of alternative transportation services to enhance classic mass transit, however. The division of the profits was cited (by approximately 43 %) as the greatest obstacle to collaboration with (other) alternative transportation services. According to the respondents, the greatest potential provided by such collaboration is the related image boost (approximately 33 %).

3.4   Online Survey of Transportation Users and the Focus Groups

The preliminary results from the first focus groups and evaluation of the online survey reveal transportation users' perspective. The typical purposes of travel from the secondary analysis and the expectations already identified by the interviews with experts have been validated.

Moreover, transportation users' expectations of integrated services are growing and easy access and uncomplicated billing and payment as in now common in other sectors, e.g. mail order, is especially important. Concepts with electronic transportation cards that facilitate access to different transportation services are favored. A tendency to view many alternative transportation services as events rather than as transportation options was extracted from the tourism transportation scenario. This aspect could prove to be important for acceptance among transportation users when innovative transportation services are introduced.

4   Discussion

The challenges in the region analyzed and the goal of designing customer-centered flexible transportation services for rural areas necessitate integrating approaches and methods based on service and usability engineering. The development of the conceptual framework in the first phase demonstrated that combining both disciplines is not only theoretically possible but also feasible and practicable. The methods selected represent just a few of the options that will have to be expanded expediently and validated further.

The findings and results obtained by applying the proposed methods already demonstrate, however, that they are essential to the design of new transportation services. The conceptual framework and the methods used additionally make it possible to ascertain the population's demands for responsiveness and interface design thoroughly and to integrate them in development. The approach's sustainable impact will have to be demonstrated in the future by completing every phase and, in particular, by implementing the transportation services. What is more, the approach will have to be discussed further.

5 Conclusion

The integration of different perspectives constitutes a basis for the development of new transportation services. The complex milieu of different stakeholders on the level of transportation service providers and the diversified structure of transportation users will require comprehensive and detailed analysis of demands and basic conditions as well as a detailed analysis from the perspective of service already when development and design commence. The approach presented and the initial results of the phase of demand analysis have revealed the opportunities that arise from combining the approaches.

The next steps will entail further refining the approach and the results in the analysis phase, e.g. by using other methods. What is more, the second phase of the integrated conceptual framework has to be specified in more detail and verified in a real-world case study. Concrete scheduled services will be selected for the region analyzed and new integrated partial services will be developed by applying the methods presented in Table 1. In keeping with the results from the analysis phase, this will both be used to advance the networking of the different transportation providers and to gear user interfaces more toward transportation users' cognitive capabilities and skills and expectations.

Acknowledgements. Part of this work was funded by the German Federal Ministry of Education and Research (BMBF) grant number 01FE14033 and 01FE14034 as part of the project Move@ÖV.

References

1. Bölke, M.: Anspruchsvolle Umweltstandards im ÖPNV fördern: durch Wettbe-werb und eine Reform der Finanzierung. Ein Beitrag auf dem Weg zu einer nach-haltigen Mobilität. In: ifmo, (ed.) Öffentlicher Personennahverkehr. Herausforde-rungen und Chancen, pp. 39–56. Springer, Berlin (2006)

2. Kirchhoff, P., Tsakarestos, A., Hanitzsch, A., Kloth, H.: Methodik für die Planung des ÖPNV im ländlichen Raum, http://www.mobilitaet21.de/wp-content/uploads/m21/OSIRIS_Planung shandbuch.pdf
3. Schnieder, L.: Öffentlicher Personennahverkehr im Jahre 2050 – Was könnte wirklich anders sein? Flexibilisierung des Nahverkehrs. Technikfolgeabschätzung - Theorie und Praxis **23**, 38–45 (2014)
4. Steinbrück, B. Küpper, P.: Mobilität in ländlichen Räumen unter besonderer Berücksichtigung bedarfsgesteuerter Bedienformen des ÖPNV. http://nbn-resolving.de/ urn:nbn:de:gbv:253-201005-dk043302-6
5. Schneider, K., Daun, C., Behrens, H., Wagner, D.: Vorgehensmodelle und Stan-dards zur systematischen Entwicklung von Dienstleistungen. In: Bullinger, H.-J., Scheer, A.-W., Schneider, K. (eds.) Service Engineering. Entwicklung und Ge-staltung innovativer Dienstleistungen, pp. 113–238. Springer, Berlin (2006)
6. DIN Deutsches Institut für Normung e.V.: Ergonomie der Mensch-System-Interaktion – Teil 210: Prozess zur Gestaltung gebrauchstauglicher interaktiver Systeme. Beuth Verlag, Berlin (2010)
7. Statistisches Landesamt Rheinland-Pfalz: Zensus 2011. Bevölkerung nach Ge-schlecht, Alter, Staatsangehörigkeit, Familienstand und Religionszugehörigkeit. Endgültige Ergebnisse, www.statistikportal.de/statistik-portal/Zensus_2011_Bevoelkerung.pdf
8. Bullinger, H.-J., Schreiner, P.: Service Engineering: Ein Rahmenkonzept für die systematische Entwicklung von Dienstleistungen. In: Bullinger, H.-J., Scheer, A.-W., Schneider, K. (eds.) Service Engineering. Entwicklung und Gestaltung inno-vativer Dienstleistungen, pp. 53–84. Springer, Berlin (2006)
9. Mayhew, D.J.: The Usability Engineering Lifecycle. A practitioner's handbook for user interface design. Morgan Kaufmann Publishers, San Francisco (1999)
10. Wolfgang, B.: Markt und unternehmensstrukturen bei technischen Dienstleis-tungen. Wettbewerbs- und Kundenvorteile durch Service Engineering. Springer Gabler, Wiesbaden (2014)
11. Follmer, R., Gruschwitz, D., Jesske, B., Quandt, S., Lenz, B., Nobis, C., Köhler, K. and Mehlin, M.: Mobilität in Deutschland. Struktur – Aufkommen – Emissionen – Trends. Ergebnisbericht (2008). http://www.mobilitaet-in-deutschland.de/pdf/MiD2008_Abschluss bericht_I.pdf
12. Technische Universität Dresden: Mobilität in Städten –SrV (2013). http://tu-dresden.de/die_ tu_dresden/fakultaeten/vkw/ivs/vip/srv
13. Schnieder, L. (ed.): Betriebsplanung im öffentlichen Personennahverkehr. Sprin-ger Berlin Heidelberg, Berlin (2015)
14. Reinhardt, W.: Offentlicher Personennahverkehr Technik - rechtliche und be-triebswirtschaftliche Grundlagen. Vieweg + Teubner, Wiebaden (2012)
15. Grönroos, C., Ojasalo, K.: Service productivity. towards a conceptualization of the transformation of inputs into economic results in services. J. Bus. Res. **57**, 414–423 (2004)
16. Von Garrel, J., Tackenberg, S., Seidel, H., Grandt, C.: Dienstleistungen produktiv erbringen. Eine empirische analyse wissensintensiver Unternehmen in Deutsch-land. Springer, Wiesbaden (2014)
17. Bartsch, S., Demmelmair, M.F., Meyer, A.: Dienstleistungsproduktivität – Stand der Forschung und Zusammenhang zu zentralen vorökonomischen Größen im Dienstleistungsmarketing. In: Bruhn, M., Hadwich, K. (eds.) Dienstleistungspro-duktivität, pp. 35–58. Gabler, Wiesbaden (2011)
18. Bullinger, H.-J., Scheer, A.-W., Schneider, K. (eds.): Service Engineering Ent-wicklung und Gestaltung innovativer Dienstleistungen. Springer, Berlin (2006)

19. Hoffmann, M., Garrel, J.: Service Engineering als strategisches Basisinstrument für Internationalisierungsvorhaben. ZWF Zeitschrift für wirtschaftlichen Fabrik-betrieb **11**, 783–787 (2008)
20. Schenk, M., Garrel, J.: Dienstleistungen kommunizieren. ZWF Zeitschrift für wirtschaftlichen Fabrikbetrieb **6**, 395–399 (2008)
21. Lienkamp, M.: Elektromobilität. Hype oder Revolution?. Springer Vieweg, Berlin (2012)
22. Kasper, R., Leidhold, R., Lindemann, A., Schünemann, M.: Elektrische An-triebsmaschinen. In: Tschöke, H. (ed.) Die Elektrifizierung des Antriebsstrangs, pp. 19–49. Springer Fachmedien Wiesbaden, Wiesbaden (2015)
23. Karle, A.: Elektromobilität Grundlagen und Praxis. Carl Hanser, München (2015)
24. Mayer, H.O.: Interview und schriftliche Befragung Grundlagen und Methoden empirischer Sozialforschung. Oldenbourg, München (2012)
25. Böhler, S., Jansen, U., Koska, T., Schäfer-Sparenberg, A., Christoph, C., Kindl, A., Klinger, D.: Handbuch zur Planung flexibler Bedienungsformen im ÖPNV. Ein Beitrag zur Sicherung der Daseinsvorsorge in nachfrageschwachen Räumen, http://www.bbsr.bund.de/BBSR/DE/Veroeffentlichungen/BMVBS/Sonderveroeffentlichungen/2009/DL_Handbuch PlanungNeu.pdf;jsessionid=8E2C00CAF8EA1CDF4AF9B9E734B3A4F4.live2052?__blob= publicationFile&v=2

A Supporting System for Emergency Vehicles Dispatching Planning Under a Disaster Situation

Yudai Higuchi[1(✉)], Takayoshi Kitamura[2], Tomoko Izumi[2], and Yoshio Nakatani[2]

[1] Graduate School of Science and Engineering, Ritsumeikan University, Kusatsu, Shiga 525-8577, Japan
is0183kf@ed.ritsumei.ac.jp
[2] College of Science and Engineering, Ritsumeikan University, Kusatsu, Shiga 525-8577, Japan
ktmr@fc.ritsumei.ac.jp,
{izumi-t,nakatani}@is.ritsumei.ac.jp

Abstract. Japan is an earthquake-prone country; however, it is also affected by other types of disasters such as typhoons, floods, volcanoes, and landslides. These disasters cause significantly severe damage in affected areas. During large disaster events, the fire departments of affected areas are expected to bring help to these areas. Unfortunately, the number of emergency vehicles and firefighters are limited. Therefore, if emergency calls are handled in a first-in first-out manner, the ability to respond to all calls is compromised. Thus, in order to consider the priority of calls based on the best strategies, call triage is discussed in this study. Call triage requires a thorough investigation of possible situations; however, as a variety of situations exist, investigation on paper is difficult. This study proposes a support system for emergency vehicle dispatch planning using the best call triage. The effectiveness of the system is verified through subject experiment.

Keywords: Call triage · Fire department · Emergency vehicles dispatching · Earthquake

1 Introduction

Japan is an earthquake-prone country, yet it is also affected by other types of disasters, such as typhoons, floods, volcanoes, and landslides. Furthermore, the occurrence of a Nankai Trough Earthquake and a Tokyo metropolitan earthquake are expected by the Japanese government [1]. If such earthquakes were to occur, Western Japan and Tokyo would be significantly affected. Interest in earthquake countermeasures has been increasing in recent years and the government has begun to take various measures.

When a large-scale disaster occurs, firefighting departments must effectively respond to an enormous amount of call-ins from a vast area. However, in reality, firefighters and emergency vehicles are dispatched in the order that the call-ins are received (first-in first-out; FIFO), and seldom is there a strategic approach for emergency vehicle

© Springer International Publishing Switzerland 2016
M. Kurosu (Ed.): HCI 2016, Part III, LNCS 9733, pp. 269–276, 2016.
DOI: 10.1007/978-3-319-39513-5_25

dispatching. However, if firefighters and emergency vehicles are dispatched to each of the call-ins in order, there will be shortage of emergency vehicles and firefighters in that prefecture, making responding to subsequent and more serious cases difficult. To avoid such cases, it is important to get a complete picture of the state of the disaster to dispatch the limited firefighters and vehicles effectively.

A survey conducted on the firefighting head offices in Iwate, Miyagi, and Fukushima prefectures after the Great East Japan Earthquake revealed that more than half of the firefighting head offices did not have an emergency vehicle dispatch plan in order to handle cases where multiple disasters occur simultaneously and there were many call-ins for fire protection and life-saving [2]. The survey also suggested that many of the firefighting head offices recognized the necessity for firefighting strategies and emergency vehicle dispatch plans. One of the most important considerations when designing an effective emergency vehicle dispatch plan is the intensive input of emergency vehicles and firefighters to call-ins of higher priority based on the damage prediction for the area. This type of priority classification of call-ins is called "call triage" or "triage." Triage is defined as a strategy of sorting and allocating aid on the basis of need for or likely benefit from medical treatment [3]. This concept is applied to disaster call-ins by considering the severity and urgency of requests. In the areas affected by the Great East Japan Earthquake, 936 firefighting head offices had triage plans. In sixteen offices, there were cases where triage was required and executed [2]. To ensure that triage is effective, priorities have to be decided among various important factors such as dead or injured persons, firefighting or rescue of buried persons, and firefighting in large dangerous chemical factories or high-density wooden house areas. Since decisions depend on the area, each firefighting head office must decide its own priority strategy considering the characteristics of the area. Although call triage support systems in the medical field have been developed [3], there are few in the field of disaster management.

The decision-making design of a triage strategy and an emergency vehicle dispatch plan require thorough investigation of possible disaster scenarios. A wide variety of possible situations exist, and the evaluation of each triage strategy on paper is difficult. To support firefighting head offices in their design of emergency vehicle dispatch plans, this study proposes a computer simulation based design support system that supports verification of various dispatch strategies by using hazard maps and existing fire department data, in order to solve the problems of lack of available firefighters and emergency vehicles. This system simulates damage in cases of a large-scale disaster based on the earthquakes expected to occur in the area. These assumed damage scenarios are randomly sent out to users as call-ins from citizens, and then the users can consider the dispatch planning of emergency vehicles based on these data and the damage situation and then decide when to dispatch the emergency vehicles and input data to the system. The system simulates the response status in the area damaged by the disaster based on the input data. For example, the system simulates the time required from dispatch of emergency vehicles until patients are transferred to the medical institutions and the time required to put out the blaze. Then, using the simulation results, the system chronologically calculates evaluation data such as the number of sick and injured, time that the fire remained uncontrolled, response rates, number of casualties, and number of injured. In other words, users can not only confirm the damage status of the earthquake and response status visually but also find response rates and the specific number of sick and injured people chronologically on a digital map. Users can assess the response based on the evaluation data calculated. Therefore, users can save the response status of the emergency vehicles to a particular disaster, and compare the data of one strategy with the data of other strategies. Because the proposed system can simulate many strategies and compare various result data, it can help emergency services to create better dispatch strategies if used repeatedly.

In this study, Konan, Shiga prefecture, is considered the target area. We build a prototype system for this area, and then conduct interviews with the firefighting personnel of Konan fire department in Shiga prefecture to evaluate the usability of the proposed system.

2 Related Work

2.1 Development of a Model of the Transportation Time Required to Complete a Transfer to Hospital by the Ambulance System

To calculate a corresponding rate for emergency operations, the emergency lifesaving transportation time is required to be calculated. Kataoka et al. [4] classified this process into five steps from the request for dispatch of emergency services to the arrival at medical institutions in order to grasp the actual situation of emergency lifesaving activities in the present conditions. These steps involve (1) dispatch request, (2) preparation to dispatch, (3) arrival at the site, (4) operation, and (5) transfer to a hospital. They built models to calculate the time required for each step. These models are introduced into this research in order to calculate the time required for each step of operation for selected call-ins.

2.2 Decision Elements of Priority Decision for Dispatch

During the East Japan Great Earthquake, many accidents occurred simultaneously. In deciding the priority of call-ins, the firefighting headquarters chose firefighting teams to be dispatched based on the contents of the received call-ins, taking into consideration the following nine items [2].

(1) Effect on human lives
(2) Degree of urgency of accidents
(3) Scale of accidents
(4) Occurrence point of accidents
(5) Possibility of response by residents
(6) Risk of secondary accidents
(7) Risk of extension of accidents
(8) Severity of injuries to victims
(9) Risk associated with the lapse of time

Our proposed system also considers these items as factors to determine the priority order.

3 System Proposal

Since dynamic disaster situations can change enormously, it is difficult for firefighting planners to form an effective dispatch plan for emergency vehicles and firefighters on paper. There are few systems that support decision-making based on effective priority criteria and planning of effective firefighter dispatch plans in order to respond to the dynamically changing disaster situations. The effectiveness and deficiency of this method are evaluated by simulation of the dispatch of vehicles and firefighters. For the simulation of the dispatch of firefighters, a variety of elements relating to firefighting operations must be modeled, including firefighting facilities, road traffic conditions, collapse situation of buildings, and damage to infrastructure.

First, we clarify the functions required by the system to verify the validity of dispatch planning methods as follows.

(1) The call-ins must be generated rationally and with realism.
(2) The required time from dispatch of ambulances for transporting victims to medical institutions must be calculated rationally.
(3) Progression in the symptoms of victims must be simulated rationally on the basis of transportation time of victims to medical institutions.
(4) The required time from the dispatch of fire engines until their arrival at fire sites must be calculated rationally.
(5) Total operation times must be calculated in order to cope with damage that requires emergency services, such as fires, house collapses, and landslides, on the basis of factors such as the disaster scale and type of house.
(6) Based on (3), (4), and (5), the performance indices such as response rates, waiting time, and death toll must be calculated for each dispatch plan.

The response rate refers to the percentage of dispatched call-ins with respect to total call-ins. The waiting time is the time between the receipt of a call-in and the arrival of an emergency team at the site. A death toll is calculated on the basis of the waiting time of seriously injured persons. When the waiting time of a seriously injured person exceeds sixty minutes, he/she is judged as dead.

This system is a tool for designing a dispatch strategy for emergency vehicles and teams in large-scale disasters by local governments. The system simulates the process of dispatch when the user selects a certain dispatch strategy. Among the six functions to listed in Chapter 3, the functions (1), (2), (3), and (6) are implemented in the prototype system. Figure 1 shows the system configuration.

JavaScript and HTML are used to implement the prototype system on a PC. The Google Maps API is also used to implement the map-based user interface to provide the dispatching process of emergency vehicles and teams.

(1) Event generation unit: All call-ins are generated after the user selects a disaster scenario.
(2) Call-in list unit: When the user presses the "wait button", a generated call-in is selected in the order of occurrence time and is displayed on the computer screen.

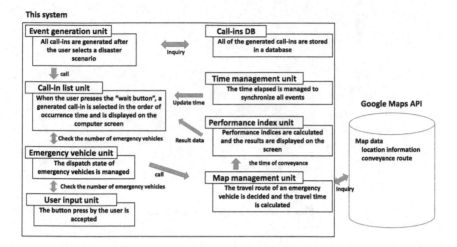

Fig. 1. System configuration diagram

(3) Emergency vehicle unit: The dispatch state of emergency vehicles is managed.
(4) User input unit: The button press by the user is accepted.
(5) Call-ins DB: All of the generated call-ins are stored in a database.
(6) Time management unit: The time elapsed is managed to synchronize all events.
(7) Performance index unit: Performance indices are calculated and the results are displayed on the screen.
(8) Map management unit: The travel route of an emergency vehicle is decided and the travel time is calculated.

At the first step of the simulation, the system generates all call-ins, with the occurrence time and place, according to the scenario selected by the user. Each scenario is formulated on the basis of the damage prediction in the regional disaster prevention plan. When the user presses the "wait button" on the computer screen, a call-in is selected in the order of occurrence time and is displayed on the screen. After the user selects the indicated call-in, an emergency vehicle is selected and dispatched. Then, the time is set forward by the amount of time required for coping with the call calculated by the time management unit. If the user presses the button instead of selecting the indicated call-in, the system selects the next call-in and displays it under the previous call-in on the screen. The user makes this decision (selection of the indicated call-in or press of the button) based on the dispatching strategy. For example, if the user follows the FIFO strategy, the indicated call-in is selected. If the user follows the scenario that gives priority to severe incidents, the user presses the button to confirm if a more severe incident may occur. When the next call-in is listed on the screen, the time is also reset at the time when the call-in occurs. Figure 2 is a screenshot of the system and Fig. 3 shows the flowchart of the event process.

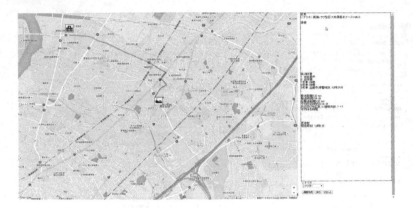

Fig. 2. An example of the screen

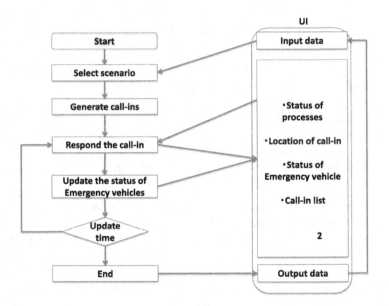

Fig. 3. A flowchart of the event process

4   Evaluation

To validate the efficacy of this system, five specialists in disaster prevention, who are members of Konan Fire Department, Shiga, Japan, performed evaluations. First, the system was explained and demonstrated for thirty minutes. Next, the specialists used the proposed system for five minutes. Following this, the specialists responded to a questionnaire regarding their opinions. The scenario (Table 1) and estimation of earthquake damage (Table 2) that was used for evaluation are given below.

Table 1. Scenario used for validation purposes.

Nankai Trough Earthquake occurred at noon during the summer and its magnitude was 9.0. There are many call-ins from the Konan area.

Table 2. Estimation of earthquake damage used for validation purposes ("—" indicates a number less than 5)

	Kusatsu city	Moriyama city	Ritto city	Yasu city	Total
Maximum seismic intensity	6 lower	6 lower	6 lower	6 lower	
Number of deaths	–	–	–	–	–
Number of injured	35	16	7	27	84

4.1 Specialist Evaluation Results

Five specialists (A–E) validated the efficacy of this system and assessed how realistic the simulation was. The following are the results of the evaluation (Fig. 4) and questionnaires.

(1) Is this system effective for planning the dispatch emergency vehicles during a disaster situation?
(2) Was the simulation close to the real situation?

None of the items received a very positive evaluation.

For "is it close to the actual condition?" we received opinions such as "it would be closer if conditions such as rescue and firefighting activities were added," and "situations in which traffic congestion occurs due to road construction and traffic accidents etc. and hospital acceptance conditions were not taken into account."

For "effectiveness," we received opinions such as "a range of special cases that can occur are required, not just emergency cases," and "if simulations of things that

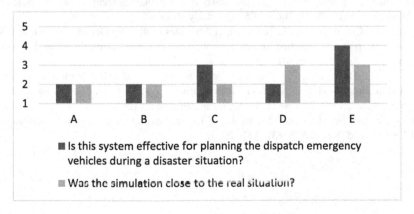

Fig. 4. Results of the evaluation

organizations or young members have not experienced previously are carried out then it is possible to perform activities more effectively." To support examination, disasters that have not yet been experienced and ease of examination need to included.

As all experiment collaborators were experienced persons who have received actual 119 calls, it is concluded that the system is limited from the point of view of sense of reality when compared to real-life situations. As this implementation only considered emergency aid that did not deal with fire and rescue, the difficulty of using the system as an aid in actual disasters, such as the very large landslides that occurred as a result of Typhoon 18 in 2013 was pointed out.

5 Conclusion

The proposed study aims to support planning decisions to carry out effective dispatch of fire brigades by self-governing bodies using triage. This aspect of emergency planning has not been extensively investigated until now. The system allows evaluation through simulation of real situations of disasters and dispatch requests dealt through FIFO or a form of triage. The system was evaluated by fire officials of the Hunan area administration union. The results indicated that, by adding conditions with increased complexity, which have not yet been experienced before by organizations or new members, it was found that activities could be carried out more effectively.

On the other hand, it was identified that further consideration should be given to firefighting or rescue activities, road conditions, and acceptance to hospitals.

Future improvements would include adding conditions that have not yet been experienced by organizations or new members. By adding these conditions, there is not only scope for further investigation but also the possibility of practical usage for training new members.

References

1. Suganuma, K.: Recent trends in earthquake disaster management in Japan. Science & Technology Trends **19**, 91–106 (2006). Quarterly Review
2. Investigation Commission of Effective Initial Activities of the Fire Department in Large-Scale Disasters: Report of Effective Initial Activities of the Fire Department in Large-Scale Disasters, 2012 (in Japanese)
3. Yokose, K., Hamagami, T.: Intelligent call triage system with algorithm combining decision-tree and SVM. In: Rhee, S.-Y., Park, J., Inoue, A. (eds.) Soft Computing in Machine Learning. AISC, vol. 273, pp. 21–31. Springer, Heidelberg (2014)
4. Kataoka, et al.: Development of a model of the transportation time sent to a hospital by ambulance. Prod. Res. **67**(2), 137–142 (2015)

Automotive HUD Interaction Design Based on Lane Changing Scenario

Chen-xi Jin, Fang You[✉], and Jian-min Wang

School of Arts and Media, Tongji University, Shanghai, China
youfang@tongji.edu.cn

Abstract. With the development of society, cars have become indispensable means of our daily transportation. Nowadays,researchers in industrial and academic areas are paying more attention to vehicle safety. This paper focuses on automotive head-up display technology in lane changing scenario. We use research, observation and interviews to analyze the relationship between environment, mentality and behaviors in lane changing scenario. We find that once the unfriendly environment stimulates the drivers, they will make the stress response. If the person does not effectively respond to the environmental stimulation, then he may regard the stimulation as a threat, resulting in anger, fear, anxiety and other emotional responses. These negative emotions will have constraints on people's behavior such as insufficient coping ability. Based on this, we put forward the key points in HUD interaction design. One is the efficient information organization and the other one is good interface design.

Keywords: Head-up display · Interaction design · HMI · Lane changing scenario

1 Introduction

With the continuously development of the society, cars have become indispensable means of our daily transportation. The increasing high rates of traffic accidents have aroused people's concerns. Thus, vehicle safety will be one of the most important directions of future vehicle development. With the wide use of computer and network technology in the field of vehicle transport and the developing car technology, the internal space, HMI (human-machine interaction) design, function operation and interactive process of the vehicle are having revolutionary changes. Nowadays,researchers in industrial and academic areas are paying more attention to artificial intelligence studies about technology improving the interaction between humans and automobiles via smart cars.

The main purpose of vehicle safety and driving-assistance technology is to increase driving safety. This technology uses sensors installed in cars and on roads to collect information about cars, roads, and environmental conditions. Therefore, the system can provide the driver some advice and warning. It can also control the car a little bit better in certain conditions. Now the technology mainly includes: lane departure warning systems, obstacle detection, driver state detection, vehicle control, communication, and so on.

© Springer International Publishing Switzerland 2016
M. Kurosu (Ed.): HCI 2016, Part III, LNCS 9733, pp. 277–284, 2016.
DOI: 10.1007/978-3-319-39513-5_26

This paper will mainly focus on the application of HUD (Heads-Up Display) vehicle safety driving assistance in lane changing scenes. The advantage of HUD is that the driver can read the information he needs without drooping or turning his head. When the driver looks forward through the HUD, he can combine the exterior image with the HUD image easily. This decreases the frequency of head drooping and turning and increases driving safety.

Research shows that vehicle safety and driving-assistance technology can not only reduce the deaths in traffic accidents but also decrease the anthropogenic accidents caused by drivers, which will make the traffic flow more freely. Moreover,this technology can reduce emissions. Thus, vehicle safety and driving-assistance technology will be an important research field of vehicle safety in the future.

2 Background

Head-up display technology can be traced back to the sixties of last century. At that time, it was used on optical aiming and radar aiming. Through development head-up display was widely used in aircraft at the end of the 1960 s. Since 1970 s, it has been used in conveyor, civil aircraft, helicopters and the space shuttle [1] Using this display system, the driver can see the important information on the wind window without bowing, which can help the driver observe emergency situation and take action timely in the status of rising.

Head-up display technology was later ported to vehicles. This technology was firstly used in cars in 1988. GM launched the first head-up display of car, which displays speed and other useful data onto the standard production windshield. Then the Japanese NISSAN and TOYOTA also launched a vehicle head up display system. In 1998, GM launched a night vision system prototype. The head-up display system used in this car can display infrared image on the front windshield view [2]. In 2000, Cadillac had incorporated full-blown thermal imaging into their HUD system. In 2005, GM introduced the world's first four color display system, which is the change of vehicle head up display from monochromatic display to the composite color display. In 2012, Pioneer Corporation introduced a navigation system that projects a HUD in place of the driver's visor that presents animations of conditions ahead, a form of augmented reality (AR). Subsequently, many car manufacturers such as BMW and Volkswagen designed their own head system. BMW has developed vision cameras that can even read temporary or permanent road signs as well as overhead signs. They can project the temporary speed limit or other hazard information onto the HUD.

Internally, the use of HUD system in aerospace has a more in-depth study, but the research for vehicular HUD system has just begun. Dongfeng Nissan Passenger Vehicle Co was the first company to equip the head up display system in China. The head-up display system equipped on Nissan Bluebird was also called the head velocity meter. In 2011, domestic Dongfeng Peugeot 508 brought the head-up display into the ordinary family. It can help the driver to grasp condition and navigation information without the eye away from roads which is more in line with the driver's visual habits and fully improves the driving safety.

3   Research on Lane Changing Scenario

3.1   Preliminary Investigation

According to the literatures, the number of deaths in road traffic accidents is very high each year in China. It ranked seventh after cerebrovascular, respiratory system and other diseases in the total number of deaths. According to the Ministry of Public Security Traffic Management Bureau news, Chinese motor vehicle amounted to 264 million in 2014 and the number of traffic accident death was 58,080. Although the number is decreasing every year, it still cannot be underestimated.

Based on these, we investigated the cause of traffic accidents. According to the annually road traffic accident description which is released by Shanghai Municipal Public Security Bureau Traffic Police Corps, we can see that in a motor vehicle accident, most drivers have 6 to10 years of driving experience, followed by less than 5 years. Besides, motor vehicle drivers' violations in traffic accident mainly dominated by not giving way by rules and the violating traffic signals [3].

Not giving way by rules mainly includes: causing accidents with normal lane vehicle when changing lanes, causing accidents with the opposite lane or normal lane vehicle when overtaking, causing accidents with the traffic going straight when turning a corner through a no-traffic light cross and so on.

In addition, we also had a questionnaire survey and depth interviews for some novice drivers. We found the problems and difficulties encountered in the actual driving are as follows: cannot predict the traffic lights in advance at the traffic light intersection, difficult to change line, motor and non-motor vehicle suddenly appeared, worse sight when meeting haze weather, difficult to reverse.

According to the above analysis, we put forward five key scenes: reversing, changing lane, crossroad, roadside trail and crowded roads. In this paper we focus on HUD design for change lane scenario.

3.2   Study on Environment, Behavior and Psychology

The problem of road traffic safety has always been a focus of concern. Road traffic system consists of the human, vehicle and road. In the past, people focused mainly on the research of vehicle and road characteristics. Until the 1950 s, people began to converse their attention on the characteristics of traffic safety effects. During 1960 s, the United States, Japan and other countries launched the extensive research on various characteristics of the drivers, including their psychological activities while driving [4]. In recent years, with the breakthrough in human physiological and psychological data collection technology, the application of psychology in the field of transportation has been more widely.

In the three elements, driver is the core of the system. In the process of driving, the driver has to complete three driving action, namely, the perception, the judgment and the driving operation. First, drivers will obtain the information through the visual, auditory and tactile perception. Then they will think and judge the traffic situation. Last, they will drive the car by their hands and feet. In this process, the environment contains the vehicle, road and weather conditions, and some other emergencies. The driver's psychology and behavior will be subject to the quality of the environment. Once they have some psychological fluctuations by negative emotions, driving behavior is prone to slow or wrong, which will cause the dangerous consequences. To conclude, the coordination of environment, people and vehicles is the key to achieving safety requirements of road traffic system.

In environmental psychology, environment can affect people's mood and performance, while emotion is a complex concept of psychological changes and subjective experience [5]. Once the unfriendly environment stimulates the drivers, they will make stress response. The so-called stress is the unpleasant action caused by the stress response. The response to stress is the imbalance, that is, the subject copes with the environmental challenges [6]. When the subject is faced with challenges while his coping ability is insufficient, he will make the response to stress. In the beginning of stress moment, due to the survival instinct, the person will mobilize all the physical response to cope with the immediate threat and take the appropriate measures and actions. At this stage, if the person doesn't effectively respond to the environmental stimulation, then the subject may regard the stimulation as a threat, resulting in anger, fear, anxiety and other emotional responses. These negative emotions will have constraints on people's behavior.

For example, in the lane changing scene, due to change the condition of congestion and short distance, if the driver is unable to complete the change, he can easily produce the anxiety emotions. Once the anxiety emotion lasts for a long time, people's feeling and perception ability will drop, muscle strength will decrease, and the control of the car is prone to error. Take another example. When the new drivers change their lanes, big trucks will cause psychological oppression, thus generating the tension. In addition, overload behavior can also cause stimulus constraints. In the road or expressway ramp before changing lanes, the drivers have to observe not only the front and rear of the vehicle but also the signs and instructions and control the speed of the vehicle, so they may cause the slow reaction force. There is one psychological phenomenon named as "psychological confrontation", that is, when some factors interfere with or hinder the people's actions, they will lose their control. Namely, people feel their own action restricted, causing an unpleasant emotion. At this time, people may make the first reaction to re-establish the control of the scene and restore freedom. In the lane changing scene, other vehicle lanes' changing behavior will obstruct the normal driving of drivers of the lane. This interference makes the psychological confrontation to drivers, instinctively do not want to let other vehicles change lanes in, so they may not slow down avoidance behavior, which will cause vehicle collision. The weather may be different in different degrees of stress reaction. The haze rainy weather and low visibility will be easy to make the drivers in the psychological uncomfortable, depressed, depression and other negative emotional reaction of discontent.

Above is about unfriendly environment that will produce psychological impact on people and behavior constraints, but a good environment for safe driving also has hidden dangers. When the traffic environment is very good, there is very little external environmental stimulation. At this time people's physiology and mentality are in flabby condition. Once the stimulation occurs, due to the paralytic psychological for a long time, the low sensory ability and the slow reaction rate may cause accidents.

3.3 Observation

To have a better understanding of drivers' behavior in the process of changing lanes, we took several observations of the drivers and used the v-box to record videos of driving process in different weather and road conditions to do the research.

During driving, the behavior of changing lanes including three process: perceiving information, judging information and performing operation. Perceiving information means drivers use their visual and auditory to get driving information, such as the current car speed, the vehicle distance with a nearby car and the speed of the following car, etc. Judging information is using the current data to make a decision of whether to change a lane. Performing operation is the action of changing lanes. By our observations, we found that new drivers are relatively nervous and not skilled, specially in a changing-lane situation for they are not familiar with the driving speed and the safe vehicle distance between two cars. We also found that experienced drivers conducted more lane change behavior and they may change a lane in some complicated situations. Drivers' perception of car speed on highway is weaker than on the ordinary city road because of the excessive speed on the highway. Moreover, driving blind is another problem worthy to pay attention to during the process of changing lanes. Drivers usually need to turn around to see the blind area, which may cause accidents. According to the observation of driving in different weather condition and brightness, we found that the low visibility at night, in rainy and foggy days increase the difficulty of changing lanes.

4 Automotive HUD Interaction Design

When driving a car, 80 per cent of traffic information is achieved by vision. Usually a driver needs 4 to 7 s to look down to the dash board and then look forward again. During this process, the time the driver spends on dash board is 3 to 5 s. This gap of time can be called blind-vision time which causes driving distraction and is very dangerous. According to statistics, about 30 % per cent of traffic accidents are related with this gap of blind-vision time. If there is a car running on the express way at 100 km/h, it will run 100 m forward during the visual and action distraction time which causes by looking down, reading and looking up. Therefore, Head-up display is very helpful to reduce the visual distraction.

4.1 HUD Information Organization

Information filtration. The information displayed on HUD interface has become richer owning to the technology development. However, overmuch information may aggravate the difficulty of recognition and response which makes the information filtuation more and more important.

Information mainly includes status information and function information [7]. Status information describes the car status and transportation circumstance such as speed, indicator light, temperature, oil consumption, traffic condition, location and so on. Function information is based on the analysis of status information which can instruct drivers to complete the driving mission. The purpose of filtering is to select useful information to the driver.

In lane changing scenario, the purpose of safety and driving-assistance system is to help drivers avoid unsafe factors and complete lane changing safely. According to the previous observation and interview, the distance between cars, the current speed, the target speed, the lane changing path and blind area information are considered important.

Information organization. Information organization is to organize and definite the interface layout, the workflow and the interaction behaviors from interaction framework. It efficiently organizes the information which enables the driver find the needed information quickly and accurately [8]. Only by excellent information organization can the driver keeps the balance between interaction and safety.

In lane changing scenario, information can be divided into several modules and then be displayed on the interface in a tile way. According to the filtered information, we divide them into speed module, danger remaindering module and blind-area module. Besides, we also divide these modules into constant showed module and random showed module. Speed module is constant showed module. Danger remaindering module and blind-area module are only showed when dangers and blind areas appear.

4.2 HUD Interface Design

Overall, HUD interface should observe the general design rules such as clearness, readability, unification, beauty-appreciation and so on. Here we discuss visual symbols, visual color and visual motion in design.

Visual symbols. Visual symbols include character symbols and graphic symbols. Character symbols include numbers and text. Numbers are used to reminder information as speed and distance while text is used to reminder information as destination and street names. Since text needs more time for drivers to read. It is not much recommended in HUD design. The merit of graphic symbols is its readability and strong instruction. For example, in the BMW HUD interface design (as Fig. 1), they use a fork road symbol to convey the dangerous information. Besides, the white arrow shows the direction that the car should keep to the right. In addition, we should also pay attention to the size of the symbols. In the BMW HUD interface design (as Fig. 1), they make "62" much bigger than "km/h" because the "62" is the primary information. Finally, we should keep the visual unity of every symbol like typeface.

In lane changing scenario, we use acceleration as an example. As Fig. 2 showed, we can see four examples. We made a questionnaire to see which one works better. The result showed that arrow symbols are more readable and intelligible than character symbols.

Fig. 1. BMW HUD interface design

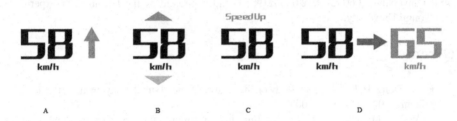

Fig. 2. Acceleration examples

Visual color. According to psychology, color can not only affect physiological reaction but also emotional reaction. In the 1980 s, a scientist proved this opinion. The blindfolded testers were asked to enter three colored rooms. When they came into the red room, their pule pressure got a 12 per cent increase. When they came into the blue room, their pule pressure got a 10 % decrease. When they came into the yellow room, everything keeps regular. Therefore, we should carefully choose the color when we design [9].

In lane changing scenario, we choose red and yellow to remind danger, blue and green to remind speed and instruction. Because in daily transportation, red means stop, yellow means caution and green means go, these colors accord with people's general cognition. As the design in BMW HUD (as Fig. 1), they use red to remind the dangers.

Besides, the saturation of color should be reduced a little in order to merge with the reality. And the color lightness can automatically change with the environment.

Visual Motion. Visual motion in HUD interface design is very important. For example, we can use glint to remind the dangers in lane changing scenario because glint is a more obvious way to catch the driver's attention than color change. However, the frequency of glint can lead to different results. High frequency may make driver nervous which will affect driver's behavior. Therefore, low frequency of glint is better. When we design the visual motion, we should consider the psychology knowledge and make it simple and readable.

5   Conclusion and Future Work

This paper analyzes the relationship between environment, mentality and behaviors in lane changing scenario and finds that unfriendly environment stimulation may lead to drivers' unstable emotion. Then drivers' response time will be increased and driving error rate will be increased too. According to the analysis, we put forward the information organization and design rules in HUD interface design. The important information elements in lane changing scenario is the distance between cars, the current speed, the target speed, the lane changing path and blind area information. The next stage we will do further research on other driving scenarios.

Acknowledgements. This work was supported by the Fundamental Research Funds for the Central Universities (0600219052,0600219053) and supported by the UXlab (user experience lab) of Tongji University.

References

1. Yang, N., Dong, H.T., Yang, S.: Study on installation of head -up display on aircraft. Electron. Opt. Control (04), 117–118 (2007)
2. Xing, W., Qi, Q.: Technologies of head-up display for automobiles. Electron. Opt. Control (01), 55–56 (2014)
3. Shanghai Municipal Public Security Bureau Traffic Police Corps: 2014 Shanghai traffic accidents description. Traffic Transport (03), 75–77 (2015)
4. Tao Pengfei. Modeling of driving behavior based on the psychology field theory, pp. 2–3. Jiling University (2014)
5. Hu, Z.F., Lin, Y.L.: Environment Psychology, pp. 117–119. China Architecture & Building Press, Beijing (2012)
6. Hu, Z.F., Lin, Y.L.: Environment Psychology, pp. 127–129. China Architecture & Building Press, Beijing (2012)
7. Schmidt, A., Spiessl, W., Kern, D.: Driving Automotive User Interface Research. IEEE Pervasive Comput. (1), 85–88 (2010)
8. Zeng, Q.S., Tan, H.: Research on head-up display navigation system. In: Proceedings of the User Friendly 2014 UXPA (2014)
9. Min, A., Yuhong, L., Xiaohong, Q., et al.: The impact of color on human physiology and psychology. China J. Health Psychol., 317–319 (2015)

Development and Evaluation of Mobile Tour Guide Using Wearable and Hand-Held Devices

Doyeon Kim[1,2], Daeil Seo[2(✉)], Byounghyun Yoo[1,2],
and Heedong Ko[1,2]

[1] Department of HCI and Robotics, University of Science and Technology,
Daejeon, South Korea
ehdus0219@imrc.kist.re.kr, yoo@byoo.net, ko@kist.re.kr
[2] Center for Imaging Media Research, Korea Institute of Science
and Technology, Seoul, South Korea
{xdesktop,ko}@kist.re.kr

Abstract. With the popularization of wearable devices, people who are using multiple mobile devices are increasing; a tourist uses a hand-held device, a wearable device, or both to obtain tour information. However, most mobile tour guides provide tour information with little consideration of their hand-held and wearable characteristics. In addition, tour guides that run on multiple mobile devices do not share their touring context. Therefore, tourists have to input their intention separately on each device. To alleviate these problems, we propose a mobile tour guide system that shares the touring context between hand-held and wearable devices, and presents tour information based on the capabilities and usage pattern of the devices. The system guides tourists by compensating the weaknesses of the devices, and also minimizes user interaction between the system and tourists.

Keywords: Point of interest · Touring context · Mobile tour guide · Mobile user interface

1 Introduction

Mobile tour guides help tourists to search and visit their surrounding points of interests (POIs) with their locations and guide information. Recently, mobile tour guides have become popular because the market share for mobile devices, such as wearable glasses and smartphones, has growing rapidly and individual tourists have been steadily increasing. Accordingly, a large amount of mobile tour guides are developed and some of them, such as Google Field Trip [1] and Trip It [2], support both hand-held and wearable devices.

However, these tour guides for multiple devices do not consider the characteristics of the devices, despite it being important to provide information based on the user's device capabilities and usage patterns. The tour guides have similar approaches without utilizing the user interface and interaction for each device. For example, hand-held devices have a large size screen size to provide enough information and a familiar user interface (UI), such as a touch interface and keyboard. However, tourists have

M. Kurosu (Ed.): HCI 2016, Part III, LNCS 9733, pp. 285–296, 2016.
DOI: 10.1007/978-3-319-39513-5_27

difficulties paying attention to their surroundings when they search for or read information on the screen [3]. On the other hand, wearable devices are appropriate for providing information immediately without disturbing their attention because they display information in front of the eye of users (e.g. Google Glass). However, wearable devices have an unfamiliar user interface and wearable tour guides do not provide detailed information due to small screen size on the device [4]. It is also difficult to use both wearable and hand-held devices simultaneously because they do not share their touring context. Tourists have to input their intention separately on each device while entering keywords to search for POIs or pushing buttons to obtain more information. It is supposed that this difficulty is able to be resolved by the sharing tour context between devices.

To alleviate these difficulties, we propose a tour guide system that provides tour information based on the user's device capabilities and shares the touring context between wearable and hand-held devices. The system shares the touring context such as the status of the system, location, orientation, and input of tourists to provide synchronized tour information. Furthermore, we design a screen layout for the devices based on the touring context, and the system provides information according to the characteristics of each device. We also discuss results from a user study to compare them with the proposed approach and others to examine the effectiveness and usefulness of our approach.

2 Related Work

In recent years, many tour guide systems have been researched for mobile device users [5] since Cyberguide [6] was introduced, which designed concept of mobile tour guide. With the prevalence of the smartphone, many studies for mobile tour guides have adopted hand-held devices, which are equipped with built-in sensors for perceiving the location and orientation of users. The previous studies provide tour information with augmented reality (AR) for a first-person view and map for a bird's-eye view. Lee et al. [7] introduced a mobile outdoor AR application to visualize buildings that had disappeared due to the effects of devastating earthquakes. Balduini el al. [8] presented an AR application named BOTTARI for personalized and localized restaurant recommendations. Dünser et al. [9] proved the usefulness of the combination of AR and map interface. Nevertheless, tourists are difficult to obtain surrounding information while they are obtaining tour information from hand-held devices [3]. To avoid the difficulty, we combine multiple mobile devices which are a wearable device for a first-person view and a hand-held device for bird's-eye view.

Wearable tour guides have also researched for a long time. Baldauf et al. [10], Langlotz et al. [11], and Szymczak et al. [12] proposed audio guide systems and they allow tourists to keep their attention on the environment, even when they obtaining information while walking or looking around. Reitmayr and Schmalstieg [13] presented a wearable tour guide with AR technology, and Kerr et al. [14] proposed a wearable navigation system. However, most wearable tour guides do not provide information about remote sites because they only provide visualization with a first person view. In addition, the guides interact with tourists in unfamiliar ways, such as gestural interfaces [14, 15], gaze tracking [10, 16]. These interaction methods help tourists communicate with the tour guides, but tourists do not input their purpose quickly because the interaction is complicated unlike with hand-held devices. To solve this problem, we develop a method for easy and quick interaction with familiar interfaces using the hand-held devices.

Finer *et al.* [17] introduced a touring machine, which is the first mobile outdoor tour guide system. The system was designed as a guide for a university campus with a wearable and a hand-held devices, and they showed the possibilities of combining multiple mobile devices. Vlahakis *et al.* [18] proposed a personalized AR tour guide using multiple mobile devices to virtually reconstruct cultural heritage areas in archeological sites. As mobile technologies have advanced rapidly, a state-of-the-art-approach is needed for combining multiple devices. It is also important to evaluate the usefulness and efficiency of the system.

3 Methodology

In this section, we discuss what kinds of requirements are considered for giving tour information. The section focuses on three topics: type of tour information, characteristics of devices, and conceptual design. The topics will give us insight into what kinds of tour information are needed on tour and how the information should be provided by mobile tour guides.

3.1 Methodology

We divided the status of the tour guide into POI search, navigation, and POI guide as a result of an online survey. The survey was conducted to examine what kind of information is mainly used when they are touring (see Fig. 1 left).

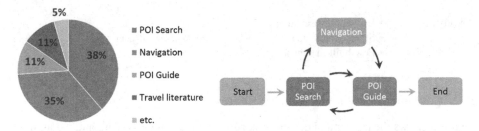

Fig. 1. Online survey result (left) and the status of touring (right)

The participants were composed of 40 people (23 females, 13 males) between 24 and 37 years old (M: 30.58, SD: 3.29). They had experience of searching for tour information with mobile devices through tour guide applications or on the web while traveling. The POI search enables tourists to find POIs such as cultural heritage sites, restaurants, and hotels. The navigation provides route information to go to POIs.

The POI guide helps tourists understand objects or places by providing detailed information of POIs. The status of the touring context is changed as shown in Fig. 1 (right). When a tourist arrives at a travelling area, they search for attractions around them with the POI search and move to the attraction by checking route information. At the attraction, tourists obtain detailed information about the attraction from the POI guide and then search for attractions again with the POI search to decide on their next destination.

3.2   Characteristics of Mobile Devices

The proposed mobile tour guide uses both a wearable device and a hand-held device to compensate for the disadvantages of each device. Table 1 the shows advantages and disadvantages of the devices. A wearable device user immediately receives information because it is displayed in front of the eyes of the user. In addition, wearable devices easily perceive the orientation of the user using their built-in sensors, such as a gyro or compass sensor. However, they do not provide detailed information due to their small screen size. Wearable devices are suitable for providing information in real time without disturbing the touring context. On the other hand, hand-held devices generally have a bigger screen size than wearable devices, which it enables tour guides to provide a lot of information at once. Furthermore, the familiar interfaces of the hand-held devices help tourists quickly search information. With hand-held devices, tourists is able to quickly search for POIs and acquire detailed information without much effort.

Table 1. Characteristics of devices

	Wearable device	Hand-held device
Advantages	• Hands-free • Easily determines what user is seeing	• Familiar user interface • Big enough screen size to show detailed information • Various built-in sensors
Disadvantages	• Unfamiliar user interface • Small screen size • Few built-in sensors	• Hand-held • Blocks view of user

3.3   Conceptual Design and Touring Context

Figure 2 shows the conceptual design of our mobile tour guide system, and we assume that a tourist makes sense of his surroundings with the system. The wearable device gives information using a first-person view aligned with the tourist's sight to provide tour information immediately in front of his eyes. With the wearable tour guide, the tourist is able to easily obtain information on the POIs the tourist is currently seeing. The audio guide for the wearable device provides detailed information such as the name and distance of the POI from the tourist. The hand-held tour guide provides tour information with a map interface that helps tourists obtain tour information by moving and zooming on the map or inputting keywords. The tourist is able to easily interact with the hand-held tour guide to search for and obtain information, and then the system shares touring context between the devices. Touring context is dynamically changed based on the location, orientation of a tourist, state of the system, and interaction with the tourist. By sharing the touring context, the tourist is possible to simultaneously obtain the tour information from multiple devices without inputting their intention separately on each device.

Fig. 2. A tourist obtaining tour information using the proposed mobile tour guide system

4 System Design

4.1 System Architecture

The proposed system consists of four-parts as shown in Fig. 3: a tour contents management system (CMS), a wearable tour guide, a hand-held tour guide, and a route planner server.

The tour CMS stores and manages tour content, and the route planner server helps the tourist to arrive their destination by providing route information. The system interacts with a tourist through the input handler in the hand-held tour guide. The location and the orientation handler perceive the location and orientation from built-in sensors. The tour context analyzer collects data from the handlers, estimates the touring context based on the collected data, and sends the estimated results to the view manager. The view manager displays the tour information using bird's-eye view. The hand-held tour guide communicates with the wearable tour guide through the network module to share the touring context. The wearable device provides tour information using a first person view and audio guide.

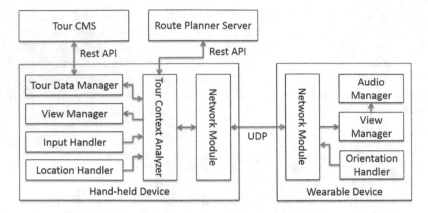

Fig. 3. System architecture

4.2 Prototype Implementation

The mobile tour guide applications are developed with Google Glass and ASUS Nexus7. Figure 4 shows a process overview of the proposed mobile tour guide to explain the usage scenario on tour, and we assume that a tourist is in his traveling area.

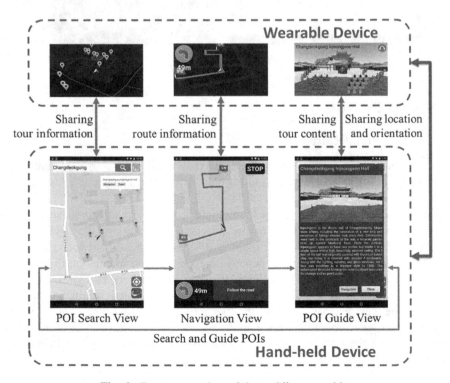

Fig. 4. Process overview of the mobile tour guide

The tourist is able to choose an appropriate view that consists of a first-person view on the wearable tour guide and bird's-eye view on the hand-held tour guide. The tourist identifies his current position and orientation through the arrow icon on the POI search view. The tourist searches for POIs he wants to visit using keyword search and location search, and then the searched tour information is shown as a green POI icon. The navigation view enables tourists to get to the destination POI by providing route information. Route information is composed of route, instructions, and remaining distance. When tourists arrive at the destination POI, the hand-held tour guide provides detailed information with text and related photos, and the hand-held tour guide offers animations and an audio guide. After the tourist has finished sight-seeing, the tourist searches for other POIs by repeating the steps.

5 Evaluation

In this section, we evaluate and discuss the strengths and limitations of the mobile tour guide system. To evaluate the system, we designed a user study to examine its general usability and acceptability while touring.

5.1 Experimental Design

The goal of the user study was to compare usability between the proposed approach and others. The study was composed of three groups that use only a wearable tour guide, a hand-held tour guide, or both, and it was conducted over three days from around lunchtime to approximately 6 pm each day. We selected participants who are used to using mobile devices and have a high interest in them and recruited 15 participants (8 females, 7 males) between 23 and 35 years old (M: 28.86, SD: 3.66) who had little or no knowledge about the test site.

The study was conducted to verify that our approach is possible to quickly provide tour information. To experiment with and observe the usability of our approach, we developed the following null hypotheses.

- POI search: There is no difference for the searching time among a group with a hand-held tour guide, a group with a wearable tour guide, and a group with the proposed tour guide
- Navigation: There is no difference in moving time to their destination among a group with a hand-held tour guide, a group with a wearable tour guide, and a group with the proposed tour guide.
- POI guide: There is no difference in the acquisition time taken to gratify their curiosity among a group with a hand-held tour guide, a group with a wearable tour guide, and a group with the proposed tour guide.

To give the same experience to the participants, we provided ASUS Nexus 7 and Google Glass to the participants for the mobile tour guide and requested they only use these devices when they search for and obtain tour information. Before the study, it was ensured that the participants understood the purpose of the study by giving them an introduction to the study and training for the usage of the tour guide.

The study followed a between-subject design to avoid prior knowledge affecting the study results. During the study, the participants received questions in Table 2 from the manager and then answered the questions using the mobile tour guide. The questions were combined with keywords, locations, and objects related to the types of questions. For the questions, we referred to a study of Kim [19] to compose the questions and modified the tasks which were classified as POI search, navigation, and POI guide. Questions 1 and 8 are classified as POI search because the participants search for the POIs and set as their destination to solve the tasks. While the participants conducted the tasks, the manager measured task completion time. The navigation time was measured while the participants were moving to the next place for another task. To ignore the time taken for the participants to understand the question, the task completion time was measured after the participants understood the question.

Table 2. Questions and combinations for the tasks

Order	Combinations	Question
1	Keyword	How do you get to Injeongjeon?
2	Location	What is the gate in front of you?
3	Location, Keyword	The yard between Jinseonmun and Sukjangmun looks different from the others. What does the yard look like? Who made the gates?
4	Keyword	Passing through Injeongmun, you can see rank stones on each side of the front yard called Pumgyeseok. You are just beginning to wonder why they were divided into two sides
5	Object	While looking around the yard, you find an unknown object. What is the object used for?
6	Object, Location	You find an object on the way to Injeongjeon. While searching for information about the object, it can also be seen on the Daejojeon. How do you get to Daejojeon?
7	Object, Keyword	While seeing the inside of the Injeongjeon, you find a picture behind the throne. What is the name and meaning of the picture?
8	Location	What is the building on the right of Injeongjeon?

After the study, we handed out a post-review questionnaire and the participants wrote down answers to the questions. For a more detailed evaluation, we divided the study results into quantitative and qualitative evaluations to determine how much time was needed to acquire tour information and what user interfaces wered useful. In the quantitative evaluation, participants carried out tasks to obtain information and the manager measured the time taken. For the qualitative evaluation, the manager handed out a post-review questionnaire to check a mainly used device and preferred user interface on each device.

5.2 Evaluation Results

After completing all of the tasks, we asked the participants to answer a number of questions, as shown in Fig. 5. Figure 5(a) is a question for ensuring the relevance of the tasks. The participants recorded the answers on a five-point scale from 1 (completely disagree) to 5 (completely agree) and the results show that all the answers are positive. Figure 5(b) is a question to determine whether participants were influenced by prior knowledge. The participants recorded the answers on a five-point scale from 1 (very much) to 5 (not at all) and the results show that all of the answers are below the average.

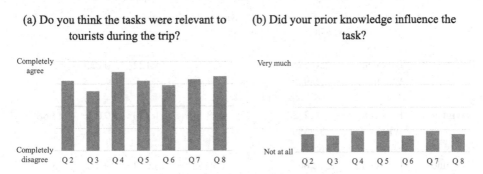

(a) Do you think the tasks were relevant to tourists during the trip?

(b) Did your prior knowledge influence the task?

Fig. 5. Post-study questionnaire results

Figure 6 shows the average task completion time of each task group. The group with a hand-held tour guide took about 391 s (Max: 422, Min: 350, SD: 35) to fulfill all the tasks, and the group with a wearable tour guide took about 448 s (Max: 529, Min: 399, SD: 52). On the other hand, the group with the proposed tour guide took about 329 s (Max: 352, Min: 304, SD: 17), and completed the tasks faster than the other groups; 16 % faster than the group with a hand-held tour guide and 27 % faster than the group with a wearable tour guide.

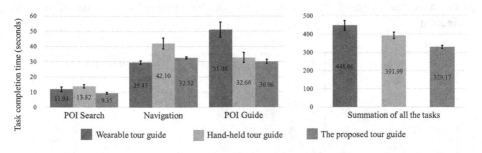

Fig. 6. Tasks completion time

In the case of POI search, the group with the proposed tour guide searched for POIs the fastest. While the participants moved during the tasks, there was a greatly different task completion time between the group with a hand-held tour guide and others. In contrast, the results in the POI guide show a greatly different task completion time between the group with a wearable tour guide and the group with the proposed tour guide.

The task completion time of the participants were analyzed with a one-way Analysis of variance (ANOVA) to determine whether there were any significant differences among the three groups. We set the criterion to 0.05 for the significance level, and the null hypothesis shown in Sect. 5.1 was rejected when the p-level was below 0.05. Table 3 shows the results of the one-way ANOVA.

Table 3. One-way ANOVA results for the task completion time

Task	Source of variation	Sum of squares	DF	Mean square	F-value	P-level	F-critical
POI search	Between	50.323	2	25.162	5.122	0.025	3.885
	Within	58.945	12	4.912	–	–	–
	Total	109.268	14	–	–	–	–
Navigation	Between	436.232	2	218.116	11.250	0.002	3.885
	Within	232.659	12	19.388	–	–	–
	Total	668.892	14	–	–	–	–
POI guide	Between	1312.66	2	656.331	13.217	0.001	3.885
	Within	595.879	12	49.657	–	–	–
	Total	1908.54	14	–	–	–	–
Total	Between	35371.4	2	17685.7	12.339	0.001	3.885
	Within	17200.4	12	1433.37	–	–	–
	Total	52571.8	14	–	–	–	–

Figure 7 shows the questionnaire result for identifying the mainly used devices during the tasks. When the participants searched for their destination POI or obtained detailed information for the tasks, all of the participants mainly used the hand-held device. In contrast, only one person mainly used the hand-held device and the other participants mainly used the wearable device for getting route information for navigation.

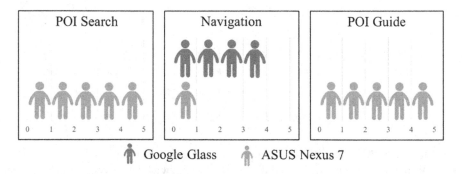

Fig. 7. Questionnaire results for identifying the mainly used devices during the tasks

5.3 Discussion

In the user study, we evaluated mobile tour guides to verify their usability and effectiveness. There were important observations for the behavior patterns of the participants during the study. In this section, we discuss the behavior patterns of the participant group who used the proposed mobile tour guide system.

The participant group recorded the fastest time when they were searching for POIs. In the post-study questionnaire, all of them answered that they mainly used the hand-held tour guide during searching for POIs. They provided reasons such as "The device has a big screen size and convenient user interface" and "It is easy to search for information using the keyboard interface". On the other hand, they searched for POIs with the first-person view by using the wearable tour guide when they did not know the name of the POI but did know the direction, such as in question 8 in Table 2.

In comparison with the POI search, the participants mainly used the wearable tour guide to find the routes to the destinations. They mentioned that "It is useful to get route without disturbing my attention" and "It is easy to find the route because the map rotates to follow the direction of my head". Meanwhile, we observed the group with the hand-held tour guide often stopped at crossroads to obtain their next direction and did not see oncoming people when they looked at the screen of the device.

There is a small difference in the POI guide between the proposed tour guide and the hand-held tour guide. The participants mainly used the hand-held tour guide when they obtained detailed information for the tasks. They also commented that "Listening to the guide is interesting, but it is quite easy to read the guide", "I am used to reading the text for getting information" and "It is faster to read than to listen". The results show that text is more effective than audio when the tour guide offers detailed information.

6 Conclusion and Future Work

Mobile tour guides help tourists quickly obtain tour information. In this paper, we proposed a tour guide system that guides tourists with wearable and hand-held devices by sharing touring context. We also designed a user interface that considered the type of tour information and characteristics of mobile devices. The prototype was implemented and evaluated through a user study. In the user study, we verified the usefulness and effectiveness of the tour guide system.

Even though our approach reduces searching and acquisition time for tour information, some work remain to improve the usability of our mobile tour guide. The user study results show that most people mainly use a mobile device in each task group. In the future, we will conduct a study that automatically selects a mobile device depending on the touring context to provide tour information in a single view. The study may reduce the time spent to select a mobile device to provide tour information.

Acknowledgments. This research was supported in part by the Korea Institute of Science and Technology (KIST) Institutional Program (Project No. 2E26450).

References

1. Google Inc.: Field Trip. http://www.fieldtripper.com (2012). Accessed 16 July 2015
2. Concur Technologies Inc.: Tripit. https://www.tripit.com (2011). Accessed 16 July 16 2015
3. Vadas, K., et al.: Reading on-the-go: a comparison of audio and hand-held displays. In: Conference on Human-Computer Interaction with Mobile Devices and Services, pp. 219–226 (2006)
4. Malu, M., Findlater, L.: "OK Glass?" A preliminary exploration of google glass for persons with upper body motor impairments. In: International ACM SIGACCESS Conference on Computers and Accessibility, pp. 267–268 (2014)
5. Kenteris, M., et al.: Electronic mobile guides: a survey. Pers. Ubiquit. Comput. **15**, 97–111 (2011)
6. Abowd, G.D., et al.: Cyberguide: a mobile context-aware tour guide. Wirel. Netw. **3**, 421–433 (1997)
7. Lee, G.A., et al.: CityViewAR: a mobile outdoor AR application for city visualization. In: 2012 IEEE International Symposium on Mixed and Augmented Reality (ISMAR-AMH), pp. 57–64 (2012)
8. Balduini, M., et al.: BOTTARI: an augmented reality mobile application to deliver personalized and location-based recommendations by continuous analysis of social media streams. Web Semant. Sci. Serv. Agents World Wide Web **16**, 33–41 (2012)
9. Dünser, A., et al.: Exploring the use of handheld AR for outdoor navigation. Comput. Graph. **36**, 1084–1095 (2012)
10. Baldauf, M., et al.: KIBITZER: a wearable system for eye-gaze-based mobile urban exploration. In: Augmented Human International Conference, pp. 1–5 (2010)
11. Langlotz, T., et al.: Audio stickies: visually-guided spatial audio annotations on a mobile augmented reality platform. In: Australian Computer-Human Interaction Conference: Augmentation, Application, Innovation, Collaboration, pp. 545–554 (2013)
12. Szymczak, D., et al.: A real-world study of an audio-tactile tourist guide. In: International Conference on Human-Computer Interaction with Mobile Devices and Services, pp. 335–344 (2012)
13. Reitmayr, G., Schmalstieg, D.: Collaborative augmented reality for outdoor navigation and information browsing. In: Symposium on Location Based Services and TeleCartography (2004)
14. Kerr, S.J., et al.: Wearable mobile augmented reality: evaluating outdoor user experience. In: International Conference on Virtual Reality Continuum and Its Applications in Industry, pp. 209–216 (2011)
15. Caggianese, G., Neroni, P., Gallo, L.: Natural interaction and wearable augmented reality for the enjoyment of the cultural heritage in outdoor conditions. In: De Paolis, L.T., Mongelli, A. (eds.) AVR 2014. LNCS, vol. 8853, pp. 267–282. Springer, Heidelberg (2014)
16. Altwaijry, H., et al.: Recognizing locations with Google glass: a case study. In: 2014 IEEE Winter Conference on Applications of Computer Vision (WACV), pp. 167–174 (2014)
17. Feiner, S., et al.: A touring machine: prototyping 3D mobile augmented reality systems for exploring the urban environment. Pers. Technol. **1**, 208–217 (1997)
18. Vlahakis, V., et al.: Personalized augmented reality touring of archaeological sites with wearable and mobile computers. In: International Symposium on Wearable Computers, pp. 15–22 (2002)
19. Kim, J.: Sharing context between three types of views for effective in-situ exploration. Master thesis. In: Human Computer Interaction and Robitics, pp. 1–58. University of Science and Technology, Daejeon, South Korea (2015)

Releasing a Traffic Light Assistance Application for Public Testing

Michael Krause[1]($\boxtimes$), Walid Fourati[2], and Klaus Bengler[1]

[1] Institute of Ergonomics, Technische Universität München, Garching, Germany
{krause,bengler}@tum.de
[2] TRANSVER GmbH, Munich, Germany
fourati@transver.de

Abstract. The paper's main focus is the requirements and implementations for creating a downloadable traffic light application from a preexisting interaction prototype. The background is the preparation of a public experiment on a test section of a rural road. The paper also contains a proposed taxonomy for classifying Traffic Light Assistants (TLAs). According to this taxonomy, the planned experiment is categorized as a technical feasibility study combined with public participation (field test) in real traffic on a rural road, with a bidirectional internet-connected smartphone application, which implements a full-featured, single-way TLA for one/next traffic light. The signal plans are determined, but should be dynamically switched and optimized depending on traffic. The smartphone-based floating car data doesn't influence the traffic lights, but should improve the speed recommendations for other cars with regard to waiting queues. The TLA is partly context aware (waiting queues, fixed speed limits) and features a speed alert.

Keywords: Traffic lights · Green light · Assistant · Application · App · Field test

1 Introduction

The work presented is part of the European Project (FP7) Local4Global. Local4Global is not limited to traffic lights assistants (TLAs). Section 3 explains how the TLA is embedded into the system-of-systems optimization project.

Many studies examine TLAs. [1], for instance, offers an overview of some of them. Section 2 provides a possible taxonomy for categorizing TLAs. The graphical user interface for the TLA used here was thoroughly assessed during a two-year-long pilot project. Section 4 sheds light on this preparatory work. This paper focuses mainly on the thoughts, requirements, and chosen implementations involved in converting the interaction prototype into a public, downloadable application (Sect. 5).

2 Taxonomy of Traffic Light Assistants

Studies and experiments involving TLAs can be classified according to modes and contents. One category often seen in the field of traffic engineering is *computer*

M. Kurosu (Ed.): HCI 2016, Part III, LNCS 9733, pp. 297–308, 2016.
DOI: 10.1007/978-3-319-39513-5_28

simulations. The researcher makes assumptions about an equipped vehicle's behavior and programs these into a traffic simulation. A parameter often manipulated is the penetration rate. Similar experiments were also part of the Local4Global traffic use case [2]. *Technical feasibility* studies (e.g., proof of concept) constitute another field. Here, different ways can be distinguished for transmitting traffic-light information to the vehicle, *Dedicated Short Range Communications* (DSRC), an *Internet connection* (e.g., to a traffic center), or hybrid solutions. Another aspect is the ecosystem: The TLA could be an original *on-board system* or an *application*, e.g., on an after-market satnav or smartphone. That a hybrid (downloadable application running and visualized in on-board systems) is also possible in the near future is foreseeable.

The traffic lights associated with the TLA can also play a role in categorization. Signal plans can be (simplified) *fixed* or *traffic actuated*. More detailed traffic-engineering classification can become far more complicated (rule based, coordinated, public transport/emergency prioritization, etc.). The information database can be *deterministic* (e.g., assured by the road authority) and/or *probabilistic* (e.g., estimates based on big data). Communication can be *unidirectional* (the vehicle only receives data) or *bidirectional* (vehicles feed floating car data back). Vehicle information fed back can be neglected, used for offline purposes such as quality management, or directly influence traffic lights (*closed loop/fully cooperative*).

TLA visualization is difficult to categorize. Especially basic technical implementations rely on displaying primarily raw numerical values. One approach to categorizing the user interface could be based on available features such as displaying:

- the next traffic light's *current state,*
- the current traffic light's *residual red-light time* (valuable) or residual green time (not recommended), and
- *recommendations for approaching* the traffic light.

Another category is based on whether or not the TLA incorporates current information into calculations for the *next traffic light* or for *multiple* subsequent traffic lights along the route. TLAs can be also divided into those providing *single-way* visualization (e.g., when the route is known from a navigation system or turn indicators) or *multiple-way* visualization (e.g., also showing left- and right-turn lights). The information can be displayed *generally for all drivers* as is the case with dynamic signs on the road side or countdowns, or only for an *individual inside a car*. The TLA can be unaware of context, or partly or fully *context aware* (e.g., awareness of waiting queues, speed limits, heavy rain/snow, construction sites, traffic jam, and so forth).

Incorporating test subjects is essential in the field of human factors engineering. Here, traffic-light experiments can be divided into those involving *driving simulators*, those conducted on *test tracks*, and those taking place in *real traffic*. The TLA's intended place of use (*urban* or *rural*) is also an important categorization criterion.

While DSRC has some limitations such as range, it could represent a viable solution within an urban environment. However, traffic centers having information about dozens or hundreds of traffic lights are often established in cities, which might render Internet connection a better alternative. In urban areas, the distance between traffic lights is typically small, traffic density high during the daytime, and the speed range for adaptations narrow. In addition, there are frequent, vulnerable road users who should receive more attention than the TLA from a driver. This situation could impede a driver's productive *manual* use of the TLA in inner cities; *automated* actions of the car or drive train could be a solution. In urban areas, the driver is also frequently able to observe unaided the behavior of the next one or two traffic lights. Some drivers receive additional clues, such as pedestrian or bicycle lights, or become accustomed to the phase sequences.

The traffic lights on rural roads, which feature large separations, typically lower traffic density, greater speed range, and fewer or no vulnerable road users, would be a suitable use case, but they are usually operated autonomously without communication connections. The organizational and financial effort to reliably get information to or from a rural traffic light is disproportionately high. Many local and regional authorities administer these "outback" lights in Germany. Even when they want to cooperate, the lights are produced by different manufactures and could require (expensive) proprietary upgrades to exchange data.

3   Local4Global (L4G)

The Local4Global European research project is based on the concept of technical systems of systems (TSoS) with machine learning capabilities. A TSoS is composed of specific autonomous constituent systems that work in a local environment, optimizing themselves and mutually improving overall performance at the global level. Constituent systems can be of different natures and aim for different objectives. They enjoy the possibility local decision making to a large extent. Remaining decisions are made after all of the participating systems exchange information to learn from each other and improve overall performance.

A generic, integrated, and fully functional methodology or system with the following attributes is needed to develop and extensively test and evaluate technical systems of systems in real life:

- Full autonomy represented by units that react depending only on their local environment to optimize the TSoS's performance emerging at the global level. This attribute renders unnecessary an elaborate, tedious effort to deploy, redesign, or reconfigure the Local4Global system as well as any need for expensive infrastructure.
- A plug-and-play control mechanism.
- Learning, evolving, and self-organizing capabilities.

Advances will lead to a fully-functional, ready-to-use system (Local4Global final product) delivered in the form of embedded, Web-based, plug-and-play software for a generic TSoS that is mountable locally in each constituent system. This system will be deployed, extensively tested, and evaluated in two real-life TSoS use cases: an efficient-building TSoS use case [3] and a traffic TSoS use case. (cf. the http://local4global-fp7.eu project page)

3.1 Traffic Use Case

In the traffic context, two basic classes of constituent systems are suggested: dynamically signalized traffic junctions and connected vehicles with speed control capabilities. Local traffic-signal control is based on a variant of the max pressure algorithm, while local control of vehicle speed relies on the resulting signaling in-formation. Both controls receive a correction from a global optimizer in a bigger, daily, common control cycle. Figure 1 illustrates the test bed implementation.

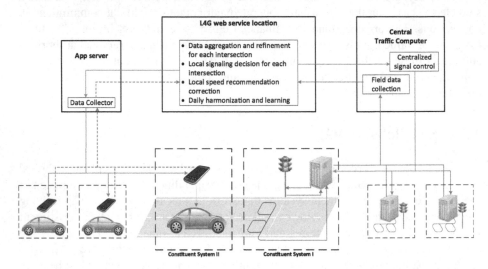

Fig. 1. The real-world implementation's architecture (app server, L4G server, traffic center)

Occupancy and traffic flow data from constituent class I systems (signal control) are gathered and sent to the road authority's central traffic computer. Collected data is subsequently forwarded to the L4G Web service location where data from signal controllers is aggregated and refined. After calculation of new signal plans using a distributed signal-control strategy and optimizer parameters, plans are sent back to the central traffic computer and from there to the signal controllers. The same signal plans are used together with position and speed data collected from mobile telephones to calculate speed recommendations for the constituent class II systems (cooperative vehicles). Data exchange is effected through an application server, where position and speed data are collected together with suggested speed recommendations. To improve the estimation accuracy of speed recommendations, an additional algorithm is integrated for dynamic queue-length estimation.

A microscopic simulation [2] showed that the algorithm effectively adapts automatically to the situation, achieving better performance during evening traffic peak relative to static signaling using an off-peak signaling configuration.

4   Previous Project: KOLIBRI

[4] gives an overview of six human-factors studies and different traffic engineering results from KOLIBRI. The seventh KOLIBRI experiment was reported in [5]. The last stage in KOLIBRI involved an interface that optimized vehicle speed for the next two traffic lights. In L4G, this is simplified to one traffic light; local optimization is also attempted in L4G. The following figures show the display states and visualizations.

The green carpet (Fig. 2a) on the linear speedometer (bottom: 0 km/h, top: 120 km/h; ego car: current speed) shows the range of speeds for getting to the next light while it is green. It is limited to allowed speeds. The display state in Fig. 2b appears if the driver cannot reach the next traffic light while it is green or has to drive too slowly to do so. If the driver drives more than 10 km/h over the limit, the prevailing speed limit appears (Fig. 2c). Figure 2d shows the remaining red-light time (faded out 3 s to 4 s before 0 s) while the driver waits in front of a red traffic light. The sign in the upper right corner shows the traffic light's current state.

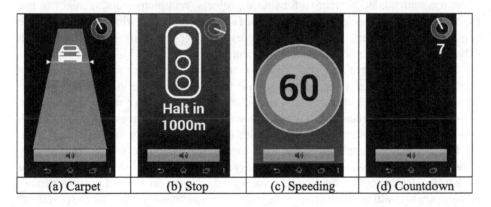

Fig. 2. Display states — human-machine interface

In KOLIBRI, the interface was tested for suitability (driver distraction) with regard to glance durations, mental workload [6], speeding behavior [7], controllability/detection in case of malfunctions [5], and subjective usability ratings ([5] and [8]). The usability ratings and speeding behavior in particular will be used as references for the L4G on-road human-factors evaluation.

In KOLIBRI, the TLA was a prototypical visualization. In L4G, the planned is to make the TLA publically downloadable for testing on this road section. This evolution from a local interface in supervised subject tests (KOLIBRI) to a full downloadable client-server application (L4G) involves remarkable effort. The requirements and implementations are explained in the next section.

5 Application Requirements and Implementation

The requirements imposed on, and the chosen implementation of, the traffic-light-assistant app and server within Local4Global project are explained in the following section.

5.1 General Considerations

The platform/ecosystem was chosen based on the prevalence of Android in Germany. The percentage for Android phones in use was about 70 % at the start of 2015[1]. The market share for sales was typically above 70 % during 2015[2]. The second alternative would have been Apple's iOS with a 15–20 % market share. Some developers nonetheless prefer the Apple ecosystem despite its market share, because Apple's consumers are typically willing to spend more money for applications, which is not an argument for the scientific experiment. Also, the preparatory work in earlier projects was based on Android and even an early prototype with Adobe Integrated Runtime.

A recommendable alternative for future projects (reimplementation) might to use HTML5 sensor and geolocation access. An HTML5 implementation would make the application independent of operating systems (Web application). For this project, a native Android app (Java) has been implemented.

In this project, there was also a discussion about whether or not all calculations should be executed on a central server with the mobile devices displaying only the interface similar to the approach of a thin-client architecture. We retained the system architecture of the former project in which the mobile devices request information such as signal data from a server and execute their calculations locally in the devices. With the thin client architecture, GPS data from the devices would have been continuously transmitted to the server, processed (hopefully) just in time, and the results transmitted back to the device; but on rural roads some signal drops or small dead zones for transmission are not unlikely with a car having no additional antenna. The chosen (fat-client-like) local architecture is more robust against potential transmission/calculation delay and is resilient to some extend if not every request for the slowly changing signal data is successful. The data is transmitted via Internet connection making the system architecture different from other traffic-light assistants, which use Dedicated Short Range Communications (DSRC).

5.2 User Management

Only registered users who accept the terms and conditions will be able to use the app. When first started, the app asks the user about which email address she or he wants to register. A time-limited confirmation link is send to this email address. At each startup, the app checks the authentication with the locally stored email address. The SIM card's

---

[1] http://de.statista.com/statistik/daten/studie/170408/umfrage/marktanteile-der-betriebssysteme-fuer-smartphones-in-deutschland/.

[2] http://de.statista.com/statistik/daten/studie/256790/umfrage/marktanteile-von-android-und-ios-am-smartphone-absatz-in-deutschland/.

serial number is also used during the authentication process in addition to the email address. Manually entering a credential is therefore unnecessary. Due to the fact that the SIM serial number is presented via a software interface from Android and Android is open source, this number cannot be treated as completely trusted data (e.g., when self-compiled Android versions or mods are used). But for normal users, email and the SIM serial number are judged to be enough authentication to exclude potential problematic subjects from this specific experiment. This policy has to be reconsidered for a production system.

The terms of use explain the reason for the project and experiment, informs the user about the tracking, and offer hints for safely mounting the device in the car.

During the experiment, a user database enables problems to be traced back (feedback/incidents/questionnaires), excludes persons, or contacts winners of the feedback tombola. After the experiment, the user table is deleted and the logged data (see Sect. 5.3) is processed anonymized.

5.3 Logging

User data (tracking) is logged on the test section with a radius of 20 m, so detecting the direction from which a vehicle entered or left the experiment would be possible. The GPS data rate on mobile devices is typically one Hz. The logged data also include the calculated recommendation/visualization and an indication of which traffic signal data was used on the phone for the calculation. So every minute, 60 of these data points and one configuration data field are stored. The configuration data holds usage/configuration information such as whether the device is in portrait or landscape mode, the app's sound level, app version, and display size. This congregated data are stored to a file. Before being written, the content is encrypted with a random AES 128 key. The AES key itself is encrypted with a RSA 2048 pubic key and also written to the file. This common splitting (AES/RSA) attempts to achieve a performance benefit by doing the major encryption work using a faster symmetric approach (AES) and exchange the key with slower asymmetric cryptography (RSA). The server has the RSA private key to decrypt the encrypted AES key and afterwards the decrypt message using the decrypted AES key. The local files on the phone are deleted after they are transmitted, but in case of transmission problems they are stored temporarily and synchronized later. This local data is protected by the encryption.

The app server (Fig. 1) consists of two servers. One server (master) runs with an Apache Web server; and both servers operate with a MySQL database in master/slave configuration. The MySQL master/slave configuration should help in backup and analysis situations. For backups, the slave database could be simply stopped and the backup extracted. If scripts need heavy database read access, they can simply use the slave without affecting the running data collection (master).

The lessons below were learned from previous projects.

Saving data on the phone with a local timestamp and using this timestamp on the server side as a primary key in a database might be a mistake. This is due to the fact that the user can easily change the local time on the phone (maybe large changes) or a phone network could change it automatically (typically small changes) possibly rendering the timestamp non-unique or not monotonically increasing. Using automatically increasing data fields as primary keys can mitigate the problem. Own Network Time Protocol (NTP) syncing on the phone also helps. Only (multiple row) database inserts are used for the sake of performance. MySQL's *max_allowed_packet* size had to be adjusted in a prior project with bigger datasets. The database tables were set up with instructions to create multiple-column indexes, to later speed up foreseeable analysis requests. All script inputs are seen by default as untrusted or insecure and handled with SQL sanitization.

All connections from the app to the server, between master/slave and interfaces use Transport Layer Security (TLS). The two servers (master/slave) were tested and hardened to get an A rating (status January 2016) on a common security test site[3]. The public certificate for the master server was hardcoded (certificate pinning) into the smartphone app. Therefore, the app only connects, uploads, and accepts data from the known master server.

5.4   Estimated Server Load/Data Volume

As described in the previous section, a data file transmitted to the servers contains 60 GPS data together with information about what signal information has been used, calculation results and displayed information (altogether about 35 data fields), and one status/configuration message about the app's general use such as sound muted and landscape mode.

The data is coded as comma-separated ASCII values. Unpacked, one data file (one per minute) has about 17–19 kilobytes. Packing (gz) typically reduces this to 6–8 kilobytes. Encryption is subsequently applied.

The script receiving this data on the server is assumed to be the bottle neck. It was observed that 0.1 s to 0.2 s is typically needed to handle (decrypt, unpack, parse, store into database, and conduct some housekeeping) the received data (Fujitsu Primergy RX200S8; Intel Xeon E5-2620v2; 16 GB; SATA RAID1 non SSD). This setup will accommodate about 60 s/0.2 s = 300 simultaneous users assuming no parallelization. Traversing the approximately 15 km test section requires about 15 min. Therefore, 1200 users/h in both directions seems possible. The road administration indicated that the project would be supported during off-peak hours. This is typically fewer than 500 vehicles/h in one direction on this track. The relatively small server therefore seems suitable for this experiment even in the unlikely event of a 100 % penetration rate for the app. With very large numbers of users, recurrent http poll requests for new signal data would also need to be taken into account.

It is likely that the server (6 cores/12 threads) can handle even more load than the rough worst case estimation. With further optimizations such as binary data transmission and removing data fields specific to this experiment, potential later production systems would have room for improvement. The registration and authentication procedure during app startup also enables server load to be managed by refusing some users in case problems arise.

---

[3] https://www.ssllabs.com/ssltest.

5.5   Location-Based Service

For the tests in previous, supervised experiments, it was sufficient for the experimenter to start the app manually while the subject is driving. The version for public download would incorporate an Android service that continuously checks the location, starts the app when the test section is approached, and terminates it sometime after the section is exited.

This is a benefit of the native Android app implementation over a purely Web app (HTML5) approach. For future implementations, a hybrid approach could yield a valuable solution. A native service could check the location and start or terminate the Web application as needed.

The current Android service is only enabled, if the user configures it via checkbox. It starts after the device is booted and checks the location continuously. To save battery power, the check period is adapted based on the distance to the test section. Power-consuming GPS requests are discontinued after several seconds (e.g., indoor), and the coarse phone network location is used instead.

5.6   Time Syncing

The traffic lights use DCF77 for time syncing. In the app, the elapsed real time since the device was booted is used to get a relative time. The app also sends and averages some NTP requests to pin the boot time with an offset to Coordinated Universal Time (UTC). With the current relative time to the boot and the known relation between boot time and UTC, Unix timestamps are calculated app internally.

5.7   Signal Data

The app server constantly polls the L4G server (see Fig. 1) for new data about signal-data programs, queue lengths, and a speed optimization factor from the Local4Global algorithm. The L4G server will not only provide the current signal program for each junction but also the next proposed signal program. To simplify the setup for the test section of (only) seven traffic lights, the app server combines all signal data, queue lengths estimations, and the optimization factor into one (small) single file. A later, large scale production system would probably divide this information based on location. So the app would only requests data that is needed, for example on a specific vehicle's navigation route.

The app constantly polls the app server for new signal data (see Fig. 1). This check is performed via a MD5 hash. If the hash changes, it signals new data is available that are download. The hash is used for an integrity check following download.

If polling fails, for instance due to disconnect or timeout, for some sequential requests, or the last successful transmission is older than a threshold (timestamps), then the app stops showing recommendations and displays an error (fail safe).

5.8   Queue Length/Car Stop

The L4G server runs a queue-length estimator called Transqest, (developed by TRANSVER) to dynamically estimate (scale of signaling cycle time) queue length for each direction at a junction. The estimator inputs the traffic lights' detector to predict queue lengths. The estimations made by Transqest are improved using real positions from participating vehicles communicated through the app server to the L4G server. If a car comes to stop in front of a traffic light, the distance to the stop line is immediately transmitted to the app server. The app server anonymizes this information and forwards an appropriate message to the L4G server. There, the information is used to improve the queue length estimation.

Drivers typically drive near the upper speed recommendation. Therefore, even if no waiting queue is reported or estimated, the green time is nonetheless adjusted locally by several seconds (e.g., about 5 s) on the smartphone. This is done for safety, comfort, and in case (an unpredicted) car is waiting. Otherwise a very confident user could approach the stop line with remarkable speed in some cases exactly when the light (hopefully) switches to green. This evokes stress and could be critical.

These adjustments are only incorporated for the speed-recommendation/calculation (carpet visualization); the graphical visualization of the current traffic lights state is not adjusted.

5.9   Diverse Helpers/Functions

The open source tool LimeSurvey is used for user **feedback questionnaires** and incident reports. The opportunity to win money will be offered to motivate users to participate in recurring surveys.

Different things are checked when the apps starts before it displays recommendations. First, the app requests a minimum required version number from the server and compares it with the app's own version. With this **version number check**, outdated versions can be invalidated and redirected to the app's store for download. Whether locally stored route information such as test section GPS track, stop lines, and speed limits are the same on the app server and locally on the phone is also checked (MD5 hashes). On startup, the app also only proceeds if an **NTP sync** was successful. If something fails on startup, the app makes recurrent trials after some time.

With a hidden feature such as multiple taps on a text field, the app can be temporarily switched to a **debug mode** where app-related debug information is transmitted to and stored on the server. This helped a lot during testing and can be useful later for remote troubleshooting, for instance at a help desk via email or phone.

Server scripts have **plausibility checks/asserts** (e.g., input is well formed and has expected length) that automatically log events and send automated admin emails with script information, which also helped during testing. Another purpose is to detect malicious behavior such as a possible intruder playing around with script inputs.

6   Outlook

At the time of writing, the connections between the systems are set up. The complete system can be tested on the road when the connections are established as well as tested, and the road authority grants permission for the L4G system to send signal recommendations (switch signal plan) to a traffic center. When these tests are successful, the last step will be the public experiment lasting for some weeks or hopefully months.

The usage frequency, drop-out rates, subjective feedback (compared to previous, supervised subject tests), and the speeding behavior (compared to previous, supervised subject tests) are of special interest as human factors. The interface itself was thoroughly checked during a previous project with regard to driver distraction (see Sect. 4). Nor did malfunctions inevitably lead to severe incidents for normal drivers. Unexpected events can nevertheless always happen, especially with new systems. The public tests will be clearly marked and communicated as experiments and participants will be registered. System failures can be viewed like those in satnavs, which are unaware of things like changed road speeds, construction sites, new one-way routing, or a ferry-boat connection that is not in place at night.

The drivers need to be careful and attentive (cf. [9]).

The main aim of transmitting information to cars is to increase comfort (hedonic improvement) in a way similar to that of destination and delay displays at train stations, with more relaxed driving and slightly less speeding [7]. There are also indications that using the system can make the ride on a potentially monotonous rural road a little more interesting (cf. [5]). Pragmatic improvements such as potential fuel savings could represent a minor by-product. Optimization of the traffic lights themselves without TLA communication would provide better leverage for achieving pragmatic goals. Improvements would be available to all road users this way.

References

1. Krause, M., Bengler, K.: KOLIBRI – Ampelassistenz für die Landstraße auf einem Smartphone. Zeitschrift für Verkehrssicherheit 60(3), 135–141 (2014)
2. Aliubavicius, U., Obermaier, J., Fourati, W., Manolis, D., Michailidis, I., Diakaki, C., Kosmatopoulos, E., Krause, M.: Use of system of systems and decentralized optimization concepts for integrated traffic control via dynamic signalization and embedded speed recommendation (submitted). In: Proceedings of 6th Transport Research Arena, 18–21 April 2016, Warsaw, Poland (2016)
3. Sangi, R., Schild, T., Daum, M., Fütterer, J., Streblow, R., Müller, D., Michailidis, I., Kosmatopoulos, E.: Simulation–based implementation and evaluation of a system of systems optimization algorithm in a building control system. In: MED 2016: The 24th Mediterranean Conference on Control and Automation (submitted), Athens, Greece, 21–24 June 2016
4. Dinkel, A., Krause, M., Bengler, K., Ettinger, R., von Dobschütz, A., Bölling, F.: Cooperative optimization of traffic signal control and driver assistance outside urban areas. In: mobil.TUM 2013 (International Scientific Conference on Mobility and Transport), Munich (2013)
5. Krause, M., Weichelt, S., Bengler, K.: Malfunction of a traffic light assistant application on a smartphone. In: Proceedings of the European Conference on Cognitive Ergonomics (ECCE) 2015. ACM Digital Library (2015)

6. Krause, M., Knott, V., Bengler, K.: Implementing the tactile detection task in a real road experiment to assess a traffic light assistant. In: Miller, L., Culén, A.L. (eds.) ACHI 2015, The Eighth International Conference on Advances in Computer-Human Interactions, 22–27 February, Lisbon, pp. 43–38. IARIA XPS Press (2015). ISSN: 2308-4138, ISBN: 978-1-61208-382-7
7. Krause, M., Yilmaz, L., Bengler, K.: Comparison of real and simulated driving for a static driving simulator. Adv. Hum. Aspects Transp.: Part II **8**, 29 (2014)
8. Krause, M., Bengler, K.: Subjective ratings in an ergonomic engineering process using the example of an in-vehicle information system. In: Kurosu, M. (ed.) HCII/HCI 2013, Part II. LNCS, vol. 8005, pp. 596–605. Springer, Heidelberg (2013)
9. Kanz, C., Marth, C., von Coelln, C.: Liability in the case of co-operative traffic and driver assistance systems. Final report (German), Research Project FE 89.0251/2010. BASt-Beiträge (2012/2013)

Ergonomic Systems of Collective Parking in Polish Cities

Robert Masztalski[✉]

Faculty of Architecture, Wroclaw University of Technology, Wroclaw, Poland
robert.masztalski@pwr.edu.pl

Abstract. Individual transportation in Poland is developing very dynamically, effectively blocking the flow of traffic in the centers of large and medium-sized cities. Increasingly, majority of these cities is planning ergonomic parking systems to ensure optimum use of space in downtown. The problem has become so important that a growing number of mayors of medium-sized cities is implementing paid parking zones in city centers as well as thinking about collective parking locations on the outskirts of downtown, including Park @ Ride systems. Many urban agglomerations decide on such a solution and have to designate an area for the strategic parking lots system. Criteria for assessing the quality of the selected location are formulated in general terms and description, and the factors to be assessed are often vague and fuzzy, difficult to delineate, but possible to be reviewed by an expert at a value of linguistic variables.

Keywords: Ergonomic systems of car parks · Collective parking · Large and medium-sized cities in Poland

1 Introduction

Modern cities, due to its extent, are no longer based solely on availability of walking tour. Transport systems which allow to move inhabitants in the city, are mainly based on vehicle and rail transportation. This includes the individual car transportation, public bus transportation and rail transportation (tram, subway, light rail). Cities typically have large developed public transport systems based on vehicle traffic and rail. In medium-sized cities usually dominating transportation is the public transport, based on a network of bus lines serving small part of the displacement of existing residents. Individual transportation in Poland is developing very dynamically, effectively blocking the flow of traffic in the centers of large and medium-sized cities. Increasingly, majority of these cities is planning ergonomic parking systems to ensure optimum use of space in downtown. The problem has become so important that growing number of mayors of medium-sized cities is implementing paid parking zones in city centers as well as thinking about collective parking locations on the outskirts of downtown, including Park & Ride systems.

The plans of urban development of large cities are being developed based on a contemporary trend of limiting vehicular traffic in favor of public transport. For this purpose, the existing urban fabric are determining collective space for the location of parking lots that allow you to leave the car and get to a destination within the city using

© Springer International Publishing Switzerland 2016
M. Kurosu (Ed.): HCI 2016, Part III, LNCS 9733, pp. 309–316, 2016.
DOI: 10.1007/978-3-319-39513-5_29

public transport (i.e. a system of P&R). Many urban agglomerations decide on such a solution and have to designate an area for the strategic parking lots system. Criteria for assessing the quality of the selected location are formulated in general terms or descriptions, and the factors to be assessed are often vague and fuzzy, difficult to delineate, but possible to be reviewed by an expert at a value of linguistic variables. Due to the large number of parameters practice has shown that the selection of the location of these sites in an intuitive way, with no detailed analysis of all conditions, often produces negative results. It happens that the completed buildings are not used as expected.

Considering above issues it should be noted that after the enlargement of the European Union in 2004, including Poland, the issue of implementation of "sustainable transport" in the cities has grown in importance also in our cities. But it is hard for a reliable assessment of the situation, because the system of monitoring transport behavior in Poland is not functioning properly. Model of transport in the city is reflected in many aspects of life for its residents and from the accepted transport solutions it depends largely on what is referred to as "quality of life". No wonder then, that the choice of a particular transport options can result in issues such as noise, the amount of green space, commuting times, pollution, scale accidents etc. It's all to be made up for of what is the nature of the city and the inhabitant's style of life.

Relying polish modern urbanization on conditions of car traffic does not permit the continuation of the traditional model of the city, due to the increasing lack of space. And as rightly observed by Jan Gehl, the quality of urban spaces do not provide the buildings themselves but above all that, life goes on in them and among them. In Europe, shrinking cities are widespread. It is also found in Poland. All this is happening just at a time when Poland has the ability to implement large-scale modern urban development processes. At the same time thanks to the financial support of the European Union, Poland has an unique opportunity to continue the corrective actions of urban technical infrastructure and to support environmental protection.

In this study[1] urban and architectural location of garage objects and parking lot spaces in the Polish cities is diagnosed by very broad group of large and medium-sized cities. The study covered a range of held by the cities transport and parking policies, and also the analysis of the locations and the standards provided in the existing parking facilities.

2 Polish Urban Transformation

Nearest future in Poland will surely be marked with the increased meaning of city structure transformation issues, including revitalization, restoration and sanitation of depreciated downtown building. Nevertheless, the processes of urban sprawl will not be deterred and providing them with opportunities to develop without unnecessary

[1] The research was conducted in the years 2014–2015 by a team from the Department of Urban Planning in the Faculty of Architecture of Wroclaw University of Technology, under the guidance of prof. Robert Masztalski, which comprised from: Dr. Anna Lower, Dr Michal Lower, Dr. Agnieszka Szumilas, Dr. Pawel Pach and Dr. Marcin Michalski.

additional costs appears to be necessary. Unplanned and badly organized building in suburban areas will be an expression of the depreciated urban development phenomenon. Further scattering of urban program in large parts of suburban areas is the most serious threat to the future of spatial structures in polish cities [1].

The above-mentioned phenomena affect directly the way of urban development. Areas of the traditional city centers and downtowns are exposed to gradual extinction and decline of attractiveness. In turn, multifunctional shopping centers are becoming, as indeed the name suggests, the new urban centers, serving not only commercial, but increasingly entertaining and even recreational functions. More and more often we meet other functions growing around shopping centers, which were considered so far by the planners to be closely linked to the city center.

So the problem is current and urgent to solve because of the speed of change in Poland. Democratic procedures are characterized by a certain heaviness resulting from the application of all requirements of the law – they do not let go for shortcuts. Additionally, subjectivity in the process of planning, obtained by Polish citizens in 1989, often manifests itself through a tough opposition to any resolution which can provide order in municipal government actions.

The spatial structure of the city is not fixed and perpetuated in the space once and for all, but it is a subject to constant transformations associated with the vast array of social, economic and environmental conditions [1]. Modern transformations of urban cities in Poland, especially after 1989, after the departure from the centrally planned economy and the introduction of a market economy, are combined with the appearance in this area of hitherto unknown phenomena and spatial conditions. The development of cities and municipalities resulting from changes in civilization and technological progress causes uncontrolled growth of transportation problems in urban areas. Today's pace of development of the automotive industry, and thus resulting increase in the number of vehicles, poses in front of urban planning tasks the primary purpose to reduce conflicts in this area, because in the limited spaces of modern Polish cities there is a huge need for an unconventional solutions in the field of transportation and parking.

The argument confirming the need to address these issues reveals itself in an active and sometimes even enthusiastic participation in our research work of the officials and decision-makers from municipal governments, with whom the research team started to cooperate.

3 Research Objectives

The object of this research was to examine urban planning location of garage and parking objects in Poland and to develop a feasibility study on the location of customizable prefabricated multi-level car park buildings in selected Polish cities.

Area of interest covered by the study is limited to the provinces located in western and central Poland. This includes half of the Polish provinces. Within these provinces is located 58 towns, in which were carried out further detailed analysis (Figs. 1 and 2).

During the work on the research topic a list of cities was set for further analysis of the problem details. The final version of the materials was also established and have

Fig. 1. P&R near the suburban train station in Wroclaw (own)

Fig. 2. P&R near the city stadium in Wroclaw (own)

been devolved to the city decision-makers with a proposal to cooperate in determining the needs and feasibility of multi-level car park buildings, and to base that cooperation on customizable prefabricated multi-level car park buildings system developed during works on a research grant. These materials were intended to encourage the authorities of the designated cities to cooperate and allow them to look more closely into the effects of existing work.

A list of the cities, which could potentially be a subject to further analysis was proposed during the first stage of the research as well as the set of criteria to be used in the next stages to create a catalogue of cities chosen for further examination.

Then, an analysis of existing in polish cities cubic capacity parking facilities, which were not merged with other service functions, was performed. It turned out that there is only 29 such objects. Most of them in Warsaw, slightly less in other provincial cities. A little execution was recorded in medium-sized cities. In this group of cities there were many plans and projects of such implementations, but practically they have no chance of execution. In this study there was no analysis concerning garages or parking lots built in objects of special destination, such as offices and retail services. This is due to the specificity of research on a particular solution, which is customizable prefabricated parking lot building.

Also the literature dealing with multi-level parking garages was reviewed and referrals to domestic and foreign literature were made. Based on this review the most interesting publications and scientific researches were chosen. Also a set of circumstances was established, indicating the need for extension of parking places.

Detailed topics, concerning questions included in the survey forwarded to the municipalities selected by the earlier city analysis, were agreed and developed during discussions in the last part of the study.

Survey issues were built based on the following topics:

1. Questions concerning residential areas
2. Questions concerning large employers
3. Questions concerning business centers
4. Questions concerning shopping centers
5. Questions concerning recreation areas and tourist attractions
6. Questions concerning traffic and parking issues
7. Questions concerning city structure
8. Questions concerning directions of the city development

The survey made it possible to obtain a representative sample range of examined issues and expert opinions used for further simulation studies by using the tools of fuzzy logic.

Analysis of the location possibilities for customized, prefabricated parking facilities has been made primarily on the basis of material obtained in the survey form, as well as on the basis of planning and strategic materials and, in some cases, direct meetings with representatives of the city.

As a result of the survey details from eight Polish cities were obtained: Tomaszow Mazowiecki, Opole, Ostrowiec Swietokrzyski, Kolobrzeg, Jelenia Gora, Bielsko Biala, Bytom and Leszno. Two cities have expressed their desire to participate in the survey and related research, but neither a meeting with representatives of the city nor filling out the survey was organized or completed by those two parties: Walbrzych and Pila. Meetings with city authorities were held in the following cities: Tomaszow Mazowiecki, Opole, Ostrowiec Swietokrzyski, Kolobrzeg and Jelenia Gora. Other cities, i.e. Bielsko Biala, Bytom and Leszno only sent filled in survey materials. In October a further analysis of the cities was performed, using materials obtained through surveys and interviews, as well as own literature and Internet queries research, that is described in the study as well. Simultaneously work on modeling, based on the testing apparatus of fuzzy logic, took place.

One of the most important things was to determine the nature and extent of the needs for parking spaces in selected medium-sized cities in Poland. Based on such data, obtained through cooperation with the city authorities, which helped to determine the real parking needs and by modeling variants of possible solutions using fuzzy logic, the research team was able to develop parking policy scenarios for the selected cities.

Analysis of the current situation and the state of knowledge in Poland within the scope of the project and the needs of the market indicates, that the current market demand for cubic capacity parking facilities is estimated at about 3 million parking spaces [3].

4 Utilization of Fuzzy Logic

Fuzzy logic is based on fuzzy sets [3]. With traditional definition of sets we can encounter some difficulties in determining the membership of some of the items to the set, due to the fact that in the classical definition, we can identify only two states: true or false. An example would be to define a set of women young and old. It is easy to determine the extreme states, i.e. at what age the woman is certainly young (e.g. 20 years), and at what age the woman is certainly old (e.g. 80 years). It is more difficult to determine clearly the border between the two sets. The question is whether a 40-years old woman is young or old? And if the border between the sets runs just on the line of 40 years, why one day later she will be described as old? In such situations, difficult to unambiguously determine, we use theory of fuzzy sets. Fuzzy sets define membership to a set in a fuzzy way. First we need to define some clear states. This is defined based on the knowledge and experience of an expert in his field. For the example above, the expert will determine the age of young women and old, at which he has no doubts (i.e. 20 and 80 years). Then we built up the membership functions, so that we are able to define each intermediate state, as the proportional membership in both sets. E.g. 40-year-old woman is young at 30 % and old at 70 %. The boundary between the collections becomes very fuzzy.

Classic fuzzy inference relies upon the knowledge and experience of the expert. Further application process is described mathematically. When building a model of fuzzy inference it is needed to apply the expert rules. Expert at the beginning of it has to designate a space in which he is sure of the reasoning, and intermediate states between these areas come alone, as a result of further mathematical analysis. Such analyzes are carried by a specialist in the field of fuzzy logic, who is choosing the appropriate functions of fuzzy sets and formulas that will calculate interim results and the final result.

At the current stage the research conducted intention of building a model of the location of parking garages as part of the P&R system in the city. This subject was considered a priority because the majority of the surveyed cities would introduce a system of P&R or see the need to introduce the system, although there are no binding decisions made up yet.

5 Research Effect

All surveyed cities recognized the city traffic problems as one of the key problems for the city, including the problem of parking vehicles in areas of inner-city and strict center areas. In terms of parking policy of the city they presented a variety of approaches for planned solutions.

In the model, the existing urban fabric determines the location of collective parking lots, that would allow to leave the car and get to the desired destination within the city using public transportation (i.e. P&R system) and parking lots located close enough to the destination, so it can be reached on foot (i.e. P&W system).

Many urban agglomerations decide to such solution and must determine the place of the location of car parks system. Criteria for assessing the quality of the selected location are often formulated in general and descriptive way, and the factors to be assessed are often ambiguous and fuzzy, difficult to precisely determine, but possible to assess by the expert at the level of linguistic variables. Due to the large number of parameters, practice has shown that the selection of the location of these sites in an intuitive manner, without detailed analysis of all conditions, often gives negative results. It happens that the completed buildings are not used as expected.

Therefore, in this study it was decided to use fuzzy inference to assess the location of the parking systems based on fuzzy input parameters [5]. The obtained result of the analysis allows to determine the degree of attractiveness of the place on the basis of a broad set of expert's input. The proposed evaluation method has been tested on a few ready-made solutions, for which the effect is already known.

6 Summary

On the basis of the preliminary analysis and as a result of the research presented in the article [3] it can be stated, that fuzzy inference can be widely used in the evaluation of urban indicators, particularly in the assessment of multi-level parking locations. Current assessment of indicators for urban planning was carried out by an expert (human) and based on the parameters difficult to measure, often not supported by precise calculations. Such reasoning was simple for the uncomplicated, clear systems. Mixed structures, which require more complex analysis, were more problematic in making a clear assessment by even an experienced expert. The specificity of fuzzy logic is directed to support exactly such expert actions.

The proposed validation model clearly showed the convergence of the analysis carried out by a large team of experts and user reviews with the methodology based on fuzzy inference model. Such studies were necessary to perform, so that further researches on other cities could be provided with credibility. Cities analyzed in the basic stage of research often have no alternative expert studies and it is planned to use the results of fuzzy inference as the primary localization indicator for multi-level car parks. Even if in some cases such studies are available, they are limited to a few locations. The specifics of the analysis conducted by team of experts is in difficulty of presenting a proposal with a lot of alternatives. Our method [4], because of the calculations and computer analysis, will quickly evaluate alternative locations depending on the potential proposals from the city authorities to determine the input parameters to the model of fuzzy inference allows to evaluate the quality of the selected locations of P&R car parks system. The method is so friendly, that it also enables fast simulation of additional potential situations such as e.g. increasing the running frequency of public transport vehicles.

The results of the research presented in the article [4], shown at an international scientific conference - 17th International Conference on Urban, Regional Planning and Transport, Paris 2015, do confirm the effectiveness of the method. It can be used in spatial planning as a tool to assess the quality of location in a quick and easy way. In the next stage, this method will be extended to investigate potential locations of multi-level car parks in the system of P&W, which is the target parking.

References

1. Ziobrowski, Z. (ed.): Barriers to modernization and development of the city: handbook. Office of Housing and Urban Development, Cracow, Poland (1998)
2. Czapinski, J., Panek, T. (eds.): The social diagnosis 2013. The conditions and quality of life of Poles. The report, Warsaw (2014)
3. Lower, M., Lower, A.: Evaluation of the location of the P&R facilities using fuzzy logic rules. In: Zamojski, W., Mazurkiewicz, J., Sugier, J., Walkowiak, T., Kacprzyk, J. (eds.) Theory and Engineering of Complex Systems and Dependability. AISC, vol. 365, pp. 255–264. Springer, Heidelberg (2015)
4. Lower, M., Lower, A., Masztalski, R., Szumilas, A.: The location of P&R facilities using the fuzzy inference model (2015)
5. Wang, J.Y.T., Yang, H., Lindsey, R.: Locating and pricing park-and-ride facilities in a linear monocentric city with deterministic mode choice. Transp. Res. Part B **38**, 709–731 (2004)

Smart Tourist Guide with Image Understanding Using Visual Instance Search

Minh-Duc Nguyen[1,2]([✉]), Thanh-An Than[1,2], Vinh-Tiep Nguyen[3],
and Minh-Triet Tran[3]

[1] Advance Program in Computer Science, University of Science,
VNU-HCM, Ho Chi Minh City, Vietnam
{nmduc, ttan}@apcs.vn
[2] John von Neumann Institute, VNU-HCM, Ho Chi Minh City, Vietnam
[3] Faculty of Information Technology, University of Science,
VNU-HCM, Ho Chi Minh City, Vietnam
{nvtiep, tmtriet}@fit.hcmus.edu.vn

Abstract. To get useful information on a landmark and to activate appropriate interaction related to that landmark can be a useful utility on mobile devices for travelers, especially in new visiting places. This motivates our proposal to use visual instance search to develop an interactive smart tourist guide system. Our aim is to provide not only a more accurate way to recommend a landmark and its information but also interesting and useful interactions around the landmark in order to seamlessly integrate real life interaction with the retrieved information. First, we develop our visual instance search framework that is optimized for speed and can achieve the accuracy approximating novel methods. Then, we apply our framework to the landmark recognition problem to replace the traditional approach of classification. Lastly, we apply our framework to our smart tourist guide system to identify a landmark, to provide its information as well as related interactions when given a landmark image. By incorporating visual instance search and interactive information, we can provide more accurate and seamlessly natural way of searching and interacting with landmarks for passengers and visitors in tourism.

Keywords: Visual instance search · Smart tourist guide · Landmark recognition

1 Introduction

For travelers, when they arrive at an unknown location, they feel out-of-place because they are not familiar with their surroundings. When they are standing in front of a building, they would want to know basic information about the building, such as opening time, main attractions, registration for upcoming events, or booking for entrance ticket, etc., so that they can participate or plan their sight-seeing trip. When you see images of a beautiful landmark from guide books or the internet, you may want to know the name and location of that landmark, and possible landmarks which look similar to the one you see. You may want instant interaction with that landmark such as making a reservation or asking for services.

© Springer International Publishing Switzerland 2016
M. Kurosu (Ed.): HCI 2016, Part III, LNCS 9733, pp. 317–330, 2016.
DOI: 10.1007/978-3-319-39513-5_30

In reality, there can be many services travelers can use to delight themselves in their journey. Thus, they need a universal guide to provide them with useful up-to-date information so that they can explore their surroundings and take advantage of available services. The guide must also be able to retrieve their location accurately and conveniently so that their travelling experience is not disrupted. Traditionally, they would try to search for their location with either Google or GPS to find out what attractions are nearby. However, these approaches often bring them out-of-date or incorrect results. GPS cannot identify correctly a user's altitude so an indoor environment becomes an obstacle for systems which rely only on localized information. GPS cannot identify what the user is looking at if there are too many landmarks with tagged information in front of the user. Information provided by GPS querying is mostly static and cannot be used as they are not sorted with interactivity in mind. Users cannot interact with the landmark with such information, they can only read and spend their time debating while they could be using that time to explore and enjoy their journey more.

Therefore, we need a smart tourist guide system which can accommodate user's need for accurate and interactive information in real-time. We propose our smart tourist guide application which tackles the stated problems. We propose using visual instance search to accurately recommend the correct information to user when they try to find information about their surroundings when they travel. Using visual instance retrieval serves as another information channel to identify user's landmark of interest. Importantly, we try to optimize our framework to minimize computational cost so that it can run in real-time and in portable device such as mobile, tablet,... with the accuracy as high as that of current state-of-the-art systems. Our proposed framework is based on adjustment of visual instance search with some improvements with novel methods such as natural soft assignment [1], RootSIFT [2], spatial re-ranking [3], query expansion [4], database-side feature augmentation [2]. We also propose the augmentation of interactive information such as: video, image, phone number, reservation booking, and service registration if available at each landmark. This information allows instance interaction with a landmark once the user query the landmark with our system. Our objective with the smart tourist guide is to provide an accurate and interactive way for travelers to explore their surroundings when they are travelling.

In this paper, the main contributions are as follows: We propose the idea and realize successfully a smart tourist guide system which provides users with accurate information corresponding to a landmark image. Furthermore, our system allows users to interact with landmarks in a transparent way. Our visual instance search module is validated with the Oxford 5K dataset [3] and achieves a precision of 0.921 which can approximate the current state-of-the-art of 0.929 [2]. Then we utilize our visual instance search module as the core of our system of smart tourist guide. We create our own dataset of landmarks from Ho Chi Minh City, Montreal, and Toronto and conduct real experiments with volunteers to demonstrate the use of visual instance search in landmark recommendation and interaction.

The remainder of this paper is organized as follows: in Sect. 2 we discuss existing works related to our proposed system. In Sect. 3, we present our proposed system of smart tourist guide by applying visual instance search. In addition, we also discuss our new proposed enhancements for our retrieval system in comparing with previous work of Arandjelović and Zisserman [2]. We analyze and evaluate our proposed system on

3 datasets, including Oxford 5K [3], Zurich building [5], and Caltech building [6] in Sect. 4. Selected real scenarios of usage with volunteers on landmark recognition and interactions in Ho Chi Minh City, Vietnam, and Montreal and Toronto in Canada are also presented in Sect. 4. Finally, we provide our conclusion in Sect. 5.

2 Related Works

GPS location and direction retrieval using compass have been used to recommend information about location by many existing applications in the market such as: Foursquare, and Google. However, the results from using GPS often contain many redundant results which requires user to manually search again to find the correct result. Moreover, GPS and compass information cannot capture the true object which the user is looking at therefore the accuracy of the recommendation may decrease. GPS position's height can be faulty in indoor environment so the landmark which is being focused by the user cannot be accurately identified. The user's orientation is another factor that needs to be considered when recommending a landmark as we should only recommend landmarks that are in front of the user which catch his attention.

We proposed the use of landmark image for accurate landmark recommendation. Using the landmark image, we can identify exactly what is being looked at. In order to achieve our objective of accuracy, we use visual instance search to identify the landmark because of the following reasons. For classification, landmark with the same shape or feature but different in label be hard to classify when in truth we can recommend any label if the provided image contain similar set of feature with the images in the database. Furthermore, classification is not robust to new additional class which is for every additional class we must retrain the classification model. In contrast, visual instance search can overcome classification shortage because it can retrieve images that are similar to the query image. The retrieved image's landmark label can be aggregate to find the correct class of the query image; we can also return multiple classes to the user for variety. When new landmark is added to the system they are simply embedded into the embedding space of the image database without the need to change or retrain any component of the system which make expansion and maintenance less costly compared to the classification approach. In this paper, we have implement a visual instance retrieval system and evaluate it on three dataset Oxford 5K [3], Zurich building [5], and Caltech building [6]. As we plan to adapt our system in real-time usage, we prioritize the ability to scale and the speed of the retrieval operation of the system. We then investigate the best method on how to increase the speed of our system without the sacrifice of accuracy.

Based on the previous tendency, a popular technique to model visual instance search is "bag-of-visual-words" model, which is inspired by text classification problem using bag-of-words. In pre-processing stage, image representation methods widely used are hard-assignment or soft-assignment [3]. However, these methods are not good in case of repeated structure which is usually found in man-made landmark such as building, fences, and attractions... In this work, we use natural soft-assignment which is introduce Akihiko Torii in 2013 to compute visual words and make BOW-vector better for urban landmark recognition [1]. In addition, we also enhance this stage by using burst weighting method to reduce influence of a visual word that frequently occur on image onto computing similarity. In Arandjelović et al.'s framework for landmark retrieval, they introduce and implement the Discriminative Query Expansion (DQE) [2] technique which proves to give better precision than Average Query Expansion [4] at the cost of increasing query time computational complexity. The sacrifice of query computation cost is not acceptable for real-time application because of user experience and server computation cost. Arandjelović et al. also propose the use of database-side feature augmentation [2], which is complementary to query expansion, to enhance database's image representation. Database-side feature augmentation is computed during training so it does not affect the query time complexity.

3   Proposed System of Smart Tourist Guide

3.1   Overview

The smart tourist guide system consists of 3 parts: a mobile application, a server for data communication with the mobile application, and a server for visual instance search.

Our smart tourist guide system receives input from the user's application. When the user's application sends an image of a landmark to our system's server, it retrieves a possible candidate for the landmark. Upon having the landmark identifier, our system searches for interactive and useful information to display to the user. Depending on the landmark, different information and interactions of various kinds can be selected for display. Common information which is available for any landmark includes: phone number, opening hour, address, GPS location, direction guidance, images, and videos. Information that are more specific are ticket information, booking information, and other direct services. In Fig. 1, we demonstrate the work flow of our system and the possible information which can be available with our system.

In Fig. 2, we describe in detail the flow of data in our system. First, a mobile device captures an image from any source. Then, the image is use to retrieve interactive information stored on the server. At the heart of our system is the visual instance search module of the server. We decouple the retrieval server and the content serving server in order to increase the maintainability of our service as the image retrieval module can be duplicated, maintain, and scale for faster and more accurate retrieval.

We implement our user application on Windows Phone 10 platform in order to have a fast development pace as we are experience in the platform. We implemented our content serving server in NodeJS for speed and maintainability. We implemented our visual instance search server in C++ for speed and accuracy. In Sect. 3.2, we present in details our implementation of the visual instance search system. Our visual instance search system is implemented through our study of Philbin et al. [3] and Arandjelovic et al.'s framework [2], we also augmented techniques that are useful in increasing precision while still preserve the time complexity.

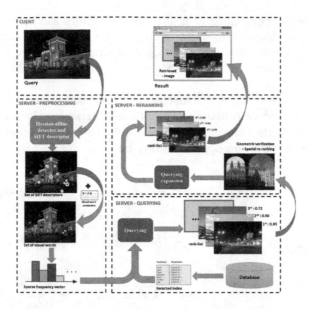

Fig. 1. Query process of the smart tourist guide system

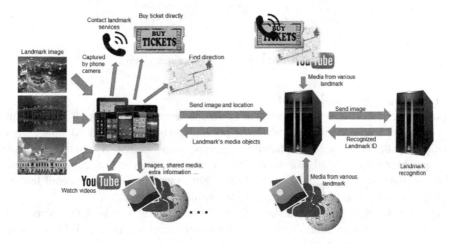

Fig. 2. Interactive landmark information retrieval

3.2 Visual Instance Search System

We build our visual instance search system based on the bag of word model proposed by Sivic and Zisserman [7]. The framework of the bag of word model has three main steps which are feature extraction, codebook training by feature clustering, feature quantization.

In our implementation, we use a modified version of the SIFT feature detector and descriptor proposed by Perdoch et al. [8] as it proves to be effective for feature matching. We use the approximate K-mean proposed by Muja and Lowe [9]. Instead of traditional K-mean algorithm to speed up the K-mean clustering and quantization process. We also use the natural soft assignment strategy proposed by Torii et al. RootSIFT, average query expansion, spatial re-ranking, and database-side feature augmentation techniques.

Figure 3 illustrates the indexing phase of our visual instance search system where each image in the database is assigned a bag of word representation for subsequence retrieval operation. In the indexing phase, we use the inverted document frequency to down weight visual words that appear in many images.

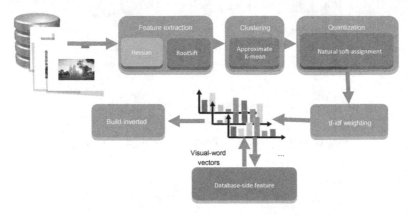

Fig. 3. Build index for image dataset step

3.2.1 Natural Soft Assignment

Repetitive pattern is one of the problem of image representation which is taken into consideration. The bag of word performs poorly when it is applied on images with repetitive patterns because duplicating features over weight a visual word. An over-weighted visual word affects the cosine metric when we calculate difference between image representations. The problem only exacerbates when repeated features are background feature and do not contribute to the object instance.

In order to alleviate the problem of repetitive feature, we need to successfully identify them and treat them differently from other features. Torii et al. [1] proposed using a relational graph between each feature to represent their similarity and treat the graph connected component as similar feature cliques. Let the maximum number of visual word a feature can vote to be n. Depending on the size of the clique, the number of visual word vote per feature is inversely proportional to the size of the clique.

Finally, Torii et al. introduce a new weighting function for each casted visual word vote. Let denote i to be the order proximity between a feature f and a visual word k. The weight for visual word k is w:

$$w = 2^{-(i-1)} \tag{1}$$

Torii et al. also introduce a threshold of 1 over all visual word to further limit the visual word weight to deal with identical features [1].

3.2.2 RootSIFT

RootSIFT [2] is a mapping of SIFT to another space where SIFT descriptor can be measure for difference more robustly. In the original bag of word model, SIFT descriptor is cluster using the K-means algorithm on Euclidean metric though SIFT is originally a histogram. Transforming a SIFT descriptor to RootSIFT is the same as embedding a new metric. The metric which is associate with RootSIFT is the Hellinger distance. Arandjelovic et al. proposed the use of RootSIFT as a replacement for SIFT in every SIFT comparison task and have tested the accuracy of using RootSIFT with SIFT with the feature matching problem. The result shows that more feature were matched correctly.

Let x be the SIFT feature and x' be the RootSIFT feature, the transformation is defined to be:

$$x' = \sqrt{\frac{x}{|x|}} \tag{2}$$

3.2.3 Spatial Re-Ranking

The bag of word model suffer from a basic property of image which is the loss of feature's geometrical information. Geometrical information can describe the shape and size of an object in an image, especially landmark images where building shape plays an important role in identifying the building. Therefore, we use spatial re-ranking [3] to effectively eliminate images that are inconsistent in shape with the query image's landmark. In order to determine the consistency in shape between two buildings, we first perform feature matching by comparing the visual words to which they have been clustered. A match is found when they have at least one common visual word. From the matched key points, we estimate the homography matrix to transform all points from the first image to the second image. Homography matrix is the matrix that transform one point's location to its corresponding matched point's location with possible minor error. The best homography matrix is the matrix that have the most correctly transformed points. After estimating the homography matrix and finding the number of points that the homography matrix can transform correctly, we sort the ranklist by the number of correctly transformed point.

3.2.4 Average Query Expansion

Average query expansion [4] help provide a way to increase recall through the aggregation of the query image and the reliable retrieved images. Chum et al. proposed the family of query expansion techniques and evaluate their effectiveness on the Oxford dataset [4]. Average query expansion achieve the third highest result among 5 methods

Chum et al. proposed. Average query expansion is using the average of the query bag of word vector and the top $m < 50$ bag of word vector to query the dataset.

$$d_{avg} = \frac{1}{m+1} \left(d_0 + \sum_{i=1}^{m} d_i \right) \tag{3}$$

3.2.5 Database-Side Feature Augmentation

While query expansion methods can be viewed as improving the query vector database-side feature augmentation [2] attempt to improve the bag of word vector of all dataset images. We perform a query for each image in the dataset and build a relational graph between each image with each other based on the returned ranklist. The query phase in database-side feature augmentation can contain all previous techniques to enhance the result of the ranklist. The quality of the ranklist directly affect the augmentation as incorrect results may cause the augmentation to be incorrect. Then we augment each image in the dataset with features from adjacent images and build a new bag of word representation for each image with the newly imported features or visual words. The new bag of word vector now contain not only feature from its image but also features from images that is similar to it. The new feature may enhance the main object's visual words so that the weighting of such visual word is increased. Occluded features of the landmark may be augmented for more accurate query result even if the database image suffer from occlusion.

4 Experiments

In Sect. 4, we describe our experiments to validate two goals which are evaluation of the visual instance search system and evaluation of the application of the visual instance search system to landmark recommendation. Through the experiment our system must proves to be accurate for landmark classification and be able to provide interactive information when a user search for a landmark with an image. Evaluation of the visual instance search system provides a baseline for the landmark recommendation as the precision of the visual instance search. In order to evaluate the visual instance search system, we perform instance experiments on standard datasets which are Oxford 5K [3], Zurich building [5], and Caltech building [6]. The detail of the experiment is described in Sect. 4.1. We also conduct experiment on our system as a whole in real-time situation. The experiment is conducted with a predefined scenario which is described in Sect. 4.2.

4.1 Visual Instance Search

In this section, we describe our evaluation of our system with the Oxford 5K dataset. The Oxford 5K dataset contain 5063 images of 11 landmarks building from Oxford. There are 55 query images and a provided ground truth for each query. Each query ground truth have types: Good, Ok, Junk, Absent (Fig. 4).

Fig. 4. Query images from Oxford 5K dataset

For each query image, we calculate the average precision on the returned rank-list. The average precision is the area under the precision-recall curve. We use the mean value of average precisions over all queries to evaluate the efficiency of our system. We run multiple instance of our system in which we progressively integrate more techniques to better illustrate the effectiveness of each technique on the precision of the system. We run our visual instance search system on the Oxford 5K dataset with 4 configuration corresponding to 4 major techniques we implemented which are natural soft assignment, spatial re-ranking, query expansion, and database-side feature augmentation. We use the result from Philbin et al. and Arandjelovic et al. as our baseline for comparison. Minor techniques such as burst weighting, Perdoch et al.'s SIFT are added as a default step in all of our configuration. Our result from these configurations ascertain the effectiveness of the techniques we have studied.

Table 1 illustrate that our system outperforms the base line implementation by Philbin et al. Our best configuration which is comprise natural soft assignment, spatial re-ranking, average query expansion, database-side feature augmentation can approximate the current state-of-the-art method proposed by Arandjelovic et al. The different in mean average precision is the result of using average query expansion in place of discriminative query expansion for time complexity reduction.

After evaluating our visual instance search performance, we evaluate the system's ability to correctly classify a landmark. We use the Zurich building and Caltech

Table 1. Visual instance search result on the Oxford 5K dataset

Methods	Mean average precision
Philbin et al. [3]	0.720
Our bag of word implementation	0.845
Spatial re-ranking	0.846
Average query expansion	0.904
Database-side feature augmentation	0.921
Arandjelovic and Zisserman [2]	0.929

building dataset to evaluate the classification ability of our system. We use the label of the top 1 image in the rank-list to determine the label of the query image. The Zurich image dataset consists of 1005 images of 201 buildings and 115 query images with ground truth label. The Caltech building dataset contains 250 images from 50 building, we use leave one out validation to calculate the accuracy of our system on Caltech building dataset.

Our results on the Zurich and Caltech building dataset proves that our visual instance search system can adapt to the landmark classification problem as the accuracy can approximate current state-of-the-art on the two datasets.

Table 2 shows that the classification accuracy of our method is only second to the state-of-the-art on the Zurich building dataset. As we only take the top 1's label of the ranklist to be the result, the accuracy can be increased if other aggregation on the ranklist is performed.

Table 2. Landmark recognition result on Zurich building dataset

Methods	Accuracy
Our implementation	0.965
Random subwindows [10]	0.960
RGB Histograms [11]	0.940
LAF [12]	1.000

Table 3 shows that our system, which is designed for visual instance search, outperformed classification schemes on the Caltech building dataset. This result proves that visual instance search scheme can be apply to classification problems on landmark. Moreover, visual instance search system can be flexible in its result compared to classification system. The rank-list returned by the visual instance search system can be used to output more than one class of landmark if true landmark resembles other landmarks. We can at the same time do landmark recommendation based on the landmark image that the user query.

Table 3. Landmark recognition result on Caltech building dataset

Methods	Accuracy
Our implementation	0.988
Casanova et al. [13]	0.960
Hedau et al. [14]	0.920

4.2   Smart Tourist Guide

In this section, we describe our experiment of the smart tourist guide system in real situation where a user performs a landmark search with an image. For this experiment, we have built our own dataset of landmarks from Vietnam and Canada. The dataset contains 10 landmarks from Vietnam and Canada.

We conduct experiments based on three main scenarios which was briefly described in Sect. 1. The three main scenarios are: querying image taken from brochure, querying image taken at the landmark, and querying Facebook friend's shared image (Fig. 5).

Fig. 5. Images from Vietnam and Canada landmark dataset

Brochure is popular tool for providing information to traveler. However, brochure has limited information and the cost of creating and updating a brochure is high. Brochure often contains images of a landmark. Therefore, our system can take advantage of brochure to provide information to travelers. Travelers can take an image of the landmark presented in the brochure and our system provides them with interactive information such as direction, videos, image, and booking for the landmark's services. We have experimented with the Royal Ontario museum image and the system correctly return the information of the museum.

Figure 6 shows that phone number, images, direction and the website with latest news about the museum are returned and displayed. The result of the experiment shows

Fig. 6. Royal Ontario museum query and result

that our system can give accurate and interactive information when a landmark image is given for querying. Moreover, our system can perform accurately on a new dataset which proves its flexibility and scalability.

Figure 7 demonstrate our second scenario where we use the Duc Ba cathedral image shared from our friend on Facebook to query information about the cathedral. The smart tourist guide successfully identify the cathedral and returned its information such as: images, videos, and direction. Figure 7(b) shows the information that is returned and its layout on the map for quick navigation.

Fig. 7. Query friend's shared images and result

Figure 8 describes the third scenario where a user capture an image at a landmark. The smart tourist guide immediately recognize the landmark which is the St Joseph observatory in this scenario. Information about location, history, videos, and more are shown to the user. He can browse these information and decide to visit and interact with the landmark.

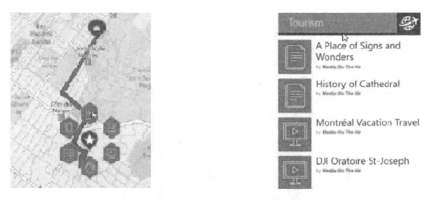

Fig. 8. Query with a captured landmark image

Our experimenting scenarios proves that the smart tourist guide system can successfully provide users with interactive and useful information in different situations. Users do not need to be at the landmark for information they can spontaneously search for information about every landmark they see whether it is on paper or internet. Our experiments demonstrate the immense flexibility of our system in assisting users to discover places and interact with them effectively.

5 Conclusions

In conclusion, we have built an interactive smart tourist guide system using our implementation of a visual instance search system. Our visual instance search system achieve 0.921 in mean average precision which can approximate the current state-of-the-art result of 0.929 on Oxford dataset. When we apply our framework to landmark recognition problem on the Zurich and Caltech dataset, we achieve an accuracy of 0.952 and 0.988 respectively for the 2 datasets which is higher or approximately the best result on these datasets. Our interactive smart tourist guide system successfully provide user with landmark information given a landmark image, the information is useful which allows user to make interaction with the landmark immediately without delay. We demonstrate the use of visual instance search in landmark recommendation can recommend accurately the landmark which is in attention and provide a transparent way to interact with the landmark. We have also build our own dataset of landmark images from Vietnam and Canada. In the future, we plan to integrate more interactive information to allow user to manipulate and receive more information. We want them to share their own experience and make recommendation to other people after they have been to the landmark.

References

1. Torii, A., Sivic, J., Pajdla, T., Okutomi, M.: Visual place recognition with repetitive structures. In: CVPR, Portland, OR (2013)
2. Arandjelovic, R., Zisserman, A.: Three things everyone should know to improve object retrieval. In: CVPR, Providence, RI (2012)
3. Philbin, J., Chum, O., Isard, M., Sivic, J., Zisserman, A.: Object retrieval with large vocabularies and fast spatial matching. In: CVPR, Minneapolis, MN (2007)
4. Chum, O., Philbin, J., Sivic, J., Isard, M., Zisserman, A.: Total recall: automatic query expansion with a generative feature model for object retrieval. In: ICCV, Rio de Janeiro (2007)
5. Shao, H., Svoboda, T., Van Gool, L.: Zubud-zurich buildings database for image based recognition. Technical report 260 (2003)
6. Aly, M., Welinder, P., Munich, M., Perona, P.: Towards automated large scale discovery of image families. In: Second IEEE Workshop on Internet Vision, CVPR, Miami, Florida (2009)
7. Sivic, J., Zisserman, A.: Video Google: a text retrieval approach to object matching in videos. In: Computer Vision, Nice, France (2003)

8. Perd'och, M., Chum, O., Matas, J.: Efficient representation of local geometry for large scale object retrieval. In: CVPR, Miami, FL (2009)

9. Muja, M., Lowe, D.G.: Fast approximate nearest neighbours with automatic algorithm configuration. In: VISAPP (2009)

10. Marée, R., Geurts, P., Piater, J., Wehenkel, L.: Decision trees and random subwindows for object recognition. In: ICML Workshop on Machine Learning Techniques for Processing Multimedia Content (2005)

11. Groeneweg, N.J., de Groot, B., Halma, A.H., Quiroga, B.R., Tromp, M., Groen, F.C.: A fast offline building recognition application. In: Advanced Concepts for Intelligent Vision Systems (2006)

12. Matas, J., Obdrzalek, S.: Object recognition methods based on transformation. In: EUSIPCO (2004)

13. Casanova, C., Franco, A., Lumini, A., Maio, D.: SmartVisionApp: a framework for computer vision applications on mobile devices. In: Expert Systems with Applications, pp. 5884–5894 (2013)

14. Hedau, V., Sinha, S.N., Zitnick, C., Szeliski, R.: A memory efficient discriminative approach for location aided recognition. In: Fusiello, A., Murino, V., Cucchiara, R. (eds.) ECCV 2012 Ws/Demos, Part I. LNCS, vol. 7583, pp. 187–197. Springer, Heidelberg (2012)

Usage Phases in the Development of Product Systems Exemplified by a Route Recommendation Scheme for Cyclists

Sigmund Schimanski[✉]

University of Wuppertal, Wuppertal, Germany
schimanski@uni-wuppertal.de

Abstract. In the course of digitization, users increasingly desire navigation processes with individualized and flexible system solutions or human-machine-systems. This results primarily in early development stages with a vast complexity and growing requirements. For this reason, this paper is based on our self-developed perspective on usage phases in the context of navigation to create sustainable user interfaces with a reduced complexity. The usage phases include the differentiated subject matters of applying technical systems, which need to be considered when designing new system concepts. First of all we agreed on the most important indicators in the usage phases of product and system development in context of mobility, which we then examined in an e-vehicle survey, and modified for the next validation phase. In this phase, we used the example of cyclists to demonstrate the application of usage phases for the derivation of a route recommendation scheme. The results obtained will be presented in this paper.

Keywords: Usage centered design · Human factors engineering · Systems engineering · Product life cycle · Fuzzy front ends

1 Purpose Intention

The observation of the individual usage phases allows a holistic understanding of the application of technical systems in the complete cycle of use. This usage awareness leads developers to comprehensive and constructive approaches regarding requests, ideas and functions etc. for a holistic interaction approach between human and machine as well as a high time efficiency. After respective evaluations, the criteria catalogue is falsified in the usage context, and merged into a universal model. The resulting model is used in the early development stages of other products, systems, services etc. with a key focus on human-computer interaction [5].

2 Design/Methodology

The previously hypothesized usage model is the basis for our analysis. To construct this model, we initially looked at the product life cycle model, which is mainly used in commerce. Typical elements of this cycle are, for example, the extraction of raw

© Springer International Publishing Switzerland 2016
M. Kurosu (Ed.): HCI 2016, Part III, LNCS 9733, pp. 331–342, 2016.
DOI: 10.1007/978-3-319-39513-5_31

materials at the beginning and the disposal at the end. An intermediate element, which is most often included, is the consumption or use. This is (Fig. 1) where our model begins.

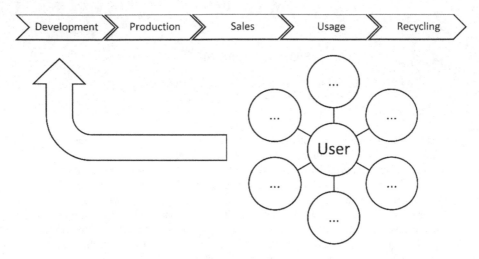

Fig. 1. Usage phase in product life cycle

Our concept, depicted in Fig. 2, is based on the user, who is also part of a system of influence.

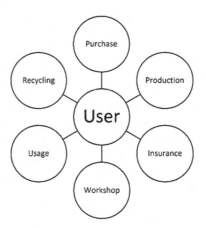

Fig. 2. First elements of the usage model

This system comprises various actors. They consist of different aspects of the product life defined by the interaction with the user. The user represents the consumer, making the user the center of the product system. His wishes, concerns, requirements and behavior are meant to enable the development of new, user-centered services. In this context, the main focus is the identification of beneficial potentials. This allows the creation of innovative solutions in the further process that consequently increase the appeal of interactive products or services.

Crucial for the identification of beneficial potentials, possible innovations and personal ideas was the choice of interview technique.

To be able to implement the requirements of the interview, the only suitable choice was a freeform interview, i.e. a non-standardized or only partially standardized inquiry, which were held in person, orally and took place in a casual environment outside the laboratory. This form of interview technique poses nearly no comprehension problems, and prevent suggestiveness [6, 7].

The conducted interviews started with a neutral introduction of the whole issue of cycling and navigation, and more and more transitioned to a free narrative form, in contrast to standardized question-answer-dialogs between moderator and test person [2, 4]. The moderators explained the topic and the interview process at the beginning, and then gradually withdrew and let the users/experts express themselves freely about the overarching topic of "route optimization for cyclists".

2.1 Model Validation with an E-vehicle Survey

We designed questions for an e-vehicle survey based on e-vehicle owners these actors, aiming to either verify or falsify the assumed factors of influence. Additionally, we wanted to reveal further relevant aspects and the implicit knowledge of the users. For this, we included a variety of rather unspecific questions allowing the users to contribute personally relevant aspects (e.g. asking them about their wishes regarding the interconnection of electric mobility and living).

The final survey about electric mobility consisted of eleven different subject matters: general personal information, general vehicle details, purchase information, act of purchase, use, charging infrastructure, insurance, accidents, maintenance, exploitation and concluding comments. With the exceptions of "general personal information" at the beginning and "concluding comments" at the end, the survey chapters appeared in random order to prevent sequence effects.

The complete survey consisted of 16 open and 69 multiple-choice questions. The great number of open questions is a particular feature of the survey. The open questions give users sufficient space to answer in their own words. As there are no predefined answers, users can freely define length and content of their answer. The purpose of this form of inquiry was to ensure a comprehensive detection of all aspects important to users. The results allow us to extract relevant issues, and examine them closely. Additionally, new subject matters might emerge that other answer formats would not generate. Some questions were only asked if the user had picked a specific answer in the previous question. The intention of these open questions was to allow detailed explanations, and to provide more information about gaps and user wishes.

Some of the multiple-choice questions allowed users to pick more than one answer option. Aiming to provide all participants with a suitable answer, users could often choose the answer option "other", and specify their reply in a blank field. Other multiple-choice questions had rating scales with consistent extremes, if possible. They resembled the school grading system, i.e. "one" representing a positive and "six" a negative answer for electric mobility.

The survey took an average of 30 to 60 min. Although some participants needed much less and others much more time for answering all questions.

We adjusted the user model after the evaluation of the e-vehicle survey. With the replies of the 213 participants, we generated new criteria that considered all relevant factors of influence, especially in the context of mobility. The detailed results will be shown in the chapter "research/practical Effects" (Fig. 3).

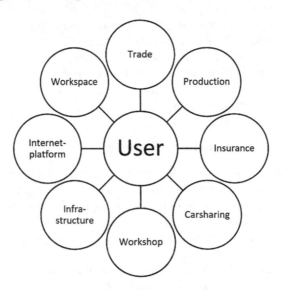

Fig. 3. Custom elements of the usage model

2.2 Usage Model Validation with an E-bike Survey

After the first validation loop, we modified and complemented the usage model and started the second attempt with the focus on a route recommendation scheme for cyclists. In order to identify possible indicators and beneficial potentials for the recommendation algorithm with examples of real use of route preferences in the context of cycling, our next step involved the conduction of expert interviews with daily cyclists, GPS examiners, spokesmen of professional associations, specialists for urban development, mobility and geo applications. In total, we conducted 35 interviews with 16 pedelec users, 7 cyclists, 10 Hardware specialists, 2 electric mobility experts, 2 sport and medicine experts, 2 PR experts, Those interviews only consisted of open questions about requirements, wishes and habits while using e-bikes/pedelecs with regards to usage phases, purchase information, purchase act, use, workplace, rent, charging (infrastructure), insurance, accidents, maintenance, exploitation, information platforms, and concluding comments. With the open, and ocassionally guideded, interview approach, we could especially identify implicit user knowledge, as will be discussed in the next chapter (results). For the evaluation, we detected relations between the statements and grouped them into overarching topics. This resulted in separate using phases within the context of cycling mobility, which were applied to the further system development process. The developed partial concepts were integrated in an innovative route recommendation algorithm, which will be demonstrated briefly in the following (results).

3   Results

3.1   Results of the E-vehicle Survey

Workshops were generally criticized for their minimal offers. An additional request was that special towing services would take care of any completely discharged vehicle, and transport it home. Insurances were generally criticized for not offering sufficient information. Rates should be more transparent and pricier. Also missing is an appropriate way to compare the rates. Some users also wanted a special rate for electric mobiles that considers special attributes, such as batteries and charging technique, as well as a consistent charging rate. Car sharing was considered appropriate, and some users wanted this service to be offered in residential areas. Furthermore, it should be possible to rent private electric cars for days or hours. An enhancement of the subject of car sharing was the request for swarm cars, which can be used by everyone. Especially German manufactures were criticized for the amount and quality of their advertising. An improvement of this situation would be widespread, realistic and honest advertisement in general media. According to user opinion, manufacturers should put more effort in performance and range, and try to offer electric cars at a better price. Time and again the users wanted manufacturers and car dealers to establish central information centers for electric mobility, which should offer all of the important information, and — according to user opinion — counteract a complicated and extensive search for the important facts. But dealers were generally asked to offer diversified information to related topics, such as insurance and charging technology. The dealers should have better knowledge about electric mobility and be motivated to sell them. One user suggested, being the user of an electric vehicle himself, to act as a recruiter and consultant for new customers, i.e. working for the car dealer. An important and often mentioned aspect is the need for test drives. They should be offered proactively, preferably in form of test days or test weeks to convey an everyday concept of electric vehicles. Usual Internet platforms for selling vehicles should have own categories/sections for electric vehicles. This would catch the attention of normal users as well. As the Internet is already one of the most effective sources of information for electric mobility, this function should be enhanced. An especially relevant area is the working place. User asked for charging stations at work or near their working place. The furthermore expressed an interest in having electric company cars or being able to lease such a vehicle from their employer. Electric vehicles should also be used on-site. A major point of criticism was the still insufficient charging infrastructure. The users want more and extensive charging stations that are accessible at all times. Another important aspect is a uniform connector system, and a paying system that works without registration in advance. Everyone should be able to charge at any charging station. Many users mentioned that charging stations were often not working. This shouldn't be the case — but if a malfunction occurs, responsibilities should be clearly specified. A common user wish was an app that would allow direct contact between charging station and vehicle. It could offer route recommendations according to charging points, access the status and other information of the charging station (connector type, payment method and charges, accessibility, current form etc.) Booking the charging station should be possible with the app.

A previously unexpected part of the system in which the user is active is legislation and therefore the government. The gaps and needs discussed here refer to other areas, that's why the government is not included as a separate player but can be regarded as an additional factor in the background. In addition to investing in a meaningful charging infrastructure, users especially wish for statutory regulation. For example, clear towing regulations for the illegal parking of combustion vehicles on charging stations. Accordingly, such parking lots should be indicated more clearly. According to user opinions, new car parks and rental houses should only get building permits if the construction plans include a charging station. The users also want companies from a certain size onward, or in case of an existing demand, to be obligated to offer charging stations. For this, another statutory regulation is needed that permits employers to legally sell electricity to their employers. Private citizens should also be able to sell their electricity to users of electric vehicles. Some users would like the legal opportunity to put up a charging station in a rental house or in a public space. Another request was an inexpensive system for transferable license plates. Some drivers supported benefits and privileges for electric vehicles, e.g. a reduction of vehicle taxation. Desires in the context of road transport were free parking, use of bus lanes and/or other advantages.

3.2   Impacts of the E-vehicle Survey on the Usage Model

First, the survey could confirm and support all previously assumed factors of influence of the usage model.

A complete section consisting of eleven questions concerned the charging **infrastructure**. This section represents the domain of the actual use in the usage model as the use of the vehicle is directly related to the given infrastructure. The frequency of replies as well as the answers themselves justifies the incorporation of the infrastructure into the usage model. For example, 89 % of the participants answered the open questions in the section "Within the context of electric mobility, what are your wishes concerning infrastructure?". The question regarding the necessity of a charging infrastructure yielded a mean value of 1.59 with an available continuum form 1 "very relevant" to 6 "not relevant".

Insurance is already an important aspect of the usage model as insurance is mandatory for vehicle owners. The question about further wishes/desires regarding insurances often generated emotional contributions, which emphasizes the importance of this subject matter to users of electric mobility.

The term **workshop** in the context of maintenance has been mentioned directly in two distinct questions in the survey, and is alluded to in the acquisition of accidents and repairs. 45 % of the users had to have their vehicle repaired; this makes workshops a relevant subject matter. On average the participants answered the question on how satisfied they are with the range of workshops only with 3.27, in a continuum from

1 "very satisfied" to 6 "very dissatisfied". This shows, that this is a crucial topic with obvious gaps, and therefore needs to be integrated into the user model.

Production is not directly brought up in the survey, but the manufacturer is often mentioned by the participants in the disclosed questions "where do you see possibilities of improvements for information capacities?" and "were you satisfied with the information available to you. If so, why?". As users see the manufacturer as their starting point with regards to purchase and further development, it verifies the role of the manufacturer in the user model.

Dealers are twice directly mentioned in the survey. For example, as an answer option for the question "where did you gather information before your purchase?" Almost half of the participants said that they got their information from a car dealer. We also asked for the number of dealer's users visited and got an average result of two – due to the massive Internet use, this can be considered a high value. Moreover, different statements on the topic of car dealers have been made in the context of other open questions. Among them was the question for suggestions to improve the possibilities for gathering information. 39 answers held the car dealers accountable in this field. Good or bad dealers were named 24 times as the reason for the made judgments regarding the received information. Overall, this player is absolutely relevant for our user model.

The section workplace has been addressed with much disclosed questions in the survey (e.g. "which kind of networking do you desire/wish for regarding electro mobility and work?"). This question has been received very well and has been answered by over 78 % of the participants. Overall long and very detailed statements have been made. In the disclosed question "conclusive comments" the workplace has been mentioned as very important multiple times. Users wished a more detailed elaboration for the topic "workplace". This is why the workplace was also incorporated into the user model.

Internet platforms have been mentioned in the survey as an option to the question, "what would be the most likely way on how you would proceed when reselling your electric vehicle?". The option Internet platform has been chosen by 62 % of the participants. Additionally, we asked if users would order a vehicle via Internet, this question was positively answered by more than half of the participants. This shows the relevance of this topic with regards to electric vehicles. Some participants wished for advertisements and presence for sources of information in some of the disclosed questions. Users stated multiple times that the internet – bulletin boards in particular – yielded the most useful bits of information regarding electro mobility. Compliant over 80 % stated to have used the internet as a source of information before the purchase. Also the desire for an App regarding infrastructure has been made and can be seen as an indicator for the relevance of the internet. Therefore, the Internet is incorporated into the user model as a global factor.

Car sharing has not been mentioned directly in the survey. In open questions, such as "what kind of networking do you wish for in the context of electric mobility and living" or "what kind of networking do you wish for in the context of your workplace" however, some users picked car sharing and gave detailed statements. This is why car sharing is incorporated into the user model.

Regarding the recycling of electric vehicles, it can be determined that only 8 participants (3.7 %) have not given an answer to the question on how they plan to resell their electric vehicle. This shows that most users think about recycling their vehicle, which makes it part of the user model. But recycling is not incorporated as an extra player as more than 99 % of the users plan to resell their vehicle over the Internet or via a local dealer, and both are already present in the user model.

Overall, we can derive all sections from the high amount of answers to direct questions or from being frequently mentioned in other open questions. Furthermore, all sections we have detected can also be logically linked to electric vehicles.

While the previously assumed sections in the model have been generally depicted using gerunds, nouns are used in the refitted and optimized model in order to clarify the actors.

In a more detailed elaboration (Fig. 4), the statements, needs and wishes of the participants have been affiliated in the respective sections.

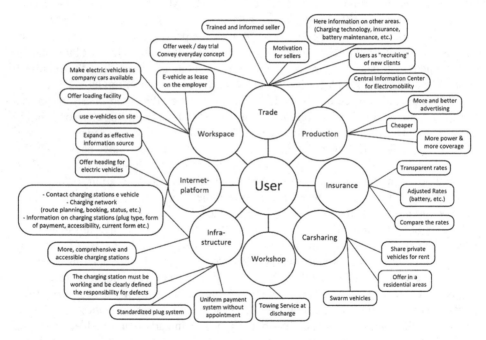

Fig. 4. Replies in corrected usage model

3.3 Results of the Bike Survey

The open interviews with various actors and user groups showed first pattern and content areas, that contribute positively to the further course of the current research project as well as to possible co-operations and follow-up projects with sustainable support of cycling and the "national cycling plan 2020" in the area "Bergisches Land".

The identification of beneficial potentials and current requirements is intended to help all involved actors to better achieve the common goal of a sustainable promotion of climate friendly mobility concepts with the example of e-bikes/pedelecs.

- Importance of cycling and pedelec use in the "Bergisches Land":
  - Cycling has no strong tradition in social life as it has in flat and rural areas
  - Especially in mountainous terrain like Wuppertal, pedelecs are very useful for frequent drivers
  - The mountainous terrain in Wuppertal makes normal cycling unsuitable for many people
  - Pedelecs are superior to conventional bicycles, especially under difficult topography conditions. It also provides a sensible solution for low-income groups by saving money on cars or public transport. But the high purchase price is an obstacle
  - E-bike/pedelec rental systems are only useful if the prices are below those of public transport
  - Potential first car or second car replacement, particularly for inner city driving, everyday work, small purchases and errands
  - Independence, environmental awareness, love for nature
  - Incentive systems and information for employers - inclusion in the operational mobility concept
- Infrastructure – Strengthening existing routes and stirring up regional interest municipally
  - Extension and marketing of existing routes
  - Targeted advertising of gastronomy and POI along bicycle routes
  - Navigation and route planning function for tourists in form of an application
  - Regularly occupied or non-existent public charging stations on well-known routes
  - Accessibility in public transport for cyclists-and pedelec users
  - Better interface to public transport
- Infrastructure – Developing new routes
  - New routes/courses with bike lanes
  - "But I don't like to ride on the main road, I look for secondary roads."
  - Charging stations as well as locking systems, bicycle boxes or storage facilities are necessary along routes
  - "All excursion destinations, such as the zoo, need charging stations."
  - Acquisition of infrastructure in a navigation and route planning function
  - Wuppertal is missing the linkage between University and the "bicycle city Wuppertal"
  - No bike lanes, charging stations and locking system at the University
  - Developing the infrastructure in the altitudes is more purposeful than agglomeration in the valley
- Improving appeal of Wuppertal's mobility concepts
  - Support of e-Bikes/pedelecs with events and theme routes
  - Campaign to improve prominence and acceptance
  - Cycling is a healthy and sporty way of transport and should be supported by the use of e-bikes/pedelecs
  - The use of e-bikes should be encouraged by benefits
  - Not always arrive sweaty and exhausted at the destination
  - Planning routes and tours tree of topography

- "Up the hill - down the hill - up the hill – I was flying! Incredible! Planning our tours used to take so much time and effort."
- Safety and legal basis – Considering risk potentials
  - Car drivers consistently underestimate pedelec cyclists, which recommends the provision of pure or separated bike lanes
  - The 25 km/h limit for e-bike/pedelec users is questionable, alternatively the limitation to 250 W motors has to be reconsidered
  - High risk potential due to operating the control panel while driving. Has to be manageable with both hands on the handlebar
  - In an accident, an emergency program should be activated, which makes the emergency call after a collision if the e-bike user does not respond
  - Incentives for the purchase or for taxation and limitations of CO_2
- Application
  - Application for route recommendation and tourist options
  - Web platform and mobile application for exchange with users, support in case of problems
  - Displaying time, current speed and a battery level indicator
  - Route planning should be based on the battery level

3.4   Impact of the Bicycle Survey on the Route Recommendation Scheme

The following presents already identified topics and content areas of the route recommendation scheme, which we can now gradually investigate further through subsequent agile workshops, interviews and analyses.

By means of the usage phases, we developed a concept, which can calculate routes with a given length. Furthermore, criteria such as duration, rise, traffic volume, traffic interruptions, road situation, road type, road kind and road security and so forth, are weighted depending on their use, and are included in the calculation. In addition, it is possible to automatically incorporate individual or desired points of interests along the planed route.

The practical application of the implemented, use-centered algorithm resulted in a high acceptance rate, which needs to be elaborated in subsequent steps on the part of user guidance and equivalent functions.

To allow a comprehensive design of the algorithms and application, the analysis results are summarized and associated. With the user analysis, we generated requirements for the route recommendation that current applications do not offer. The primary way purposes "work" and "leisure" impose different demands on the navigation in order to meet the "basic needs" of users. The navigation should run on smartphones without Internet connection to allow navigation even with bad or missing reception. This should take as little time as possible to achieve an optimal user experience. In addition to the start and finish of the navigation, the system should be able to calculate courses and routes based on points of interest. Next to the route length, the important factors are, e.g. gradient, position, cultivation of the area and road surface.

4 Conclusion

4.1 Route Recommendation Scheme

Mobility is constantly transforming. With new and more and more performant possibilities of mobility in the shape of pedelecs, electric cars and the combination of multiple means of transportation as well as inter- and multimodal transport with respect to the ever increasing complexity due to user demands, developing an usage-based route recommendation scheme is of great interest and met with immense user approval. Furthermore, the development of such an usage-based recommendation scheme is not only of great value for end users, but also an important communication channel between users on the one hand and economy and communities on the other [1]. According to confirmed statements of experts, this concept significantly supports the maintenance and development of local and regional infrastructure, and also fulfils the requirements in the category of any points of interest.

4.2 Usage Model

In the context of early stages of product system engineering, the developed system proved its reliability.

Based upon mobility-related services, the components of the usage chain have been generalized using field observation, user interviews, etcetera and subsequently methods for pattern recognition. Deriving the usage aspect provides a standardized approach which enables sustainable product and service solutions as well as reliable advances in early development stages in the field of quality assurance. It is therefore possible to

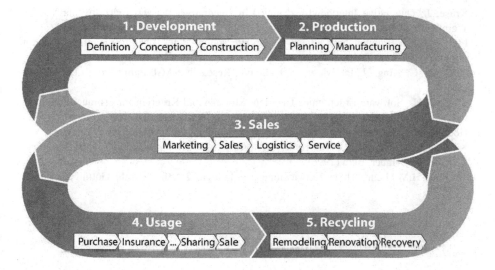

Fig. 5. Usage chain in product life cycle

contrast the derived requirements with the planned functions in order to verify the reliability of the ansatz in the context of human-technology interaction, and to estimate subsequent expenses.

An extensive, individual analysis and the corresponding research requires an increase of time requirements, personal expenses and potential costs within the development phases. But the application of the acquired usage guidelines reduces the required iterations and therefore positively influences the time investment within the development process. The demonstrated application of the usage phases can be embedded in the norm Ergonomics of Human-System-Interaction according to DIN EN ISO 9241-210 [3], and therefore contribute to meeting the usage requirements within the overall solutions (Fig. 5).

Furthermore, the collected methodical results are used as an "extended development approach" for additional product developments which are planned in the fields of "usage centered human-system integration" and/or "usage centered development tools for engineers".

In order to get a more complete picture of the different user-types of the product and therefore get user-groups, the understood (received) development model, the methods or approaches as well as the appropriate communication contents, need to be supplemented and analyzed based upon the environmental differences of the user. A laboratory for innovation-research, in order to investigate the efficiency of development would be an appropriate and expedient tool. Additionally, the transfer of the usage model to a software tool for development processes is planned in further steps.

References

1. Schimanski, S., et al.: Optimization approach and using Bezier-splines in navigation algorithms. In: Automotive, IEEE | ICCE - International Conference on Consumer Electronics, Las Vegas (2016)
2. Kruse, J.: Qualitative Interviewforschung: Ein Integrativer Ansatz. Beltz Juventa Verlag, Weinheim (2014)
3. ISO 9241-210: Ergonomics of human-system interaction - Part 210: human-centred design for interactive systems (2010)
4. Harrocks, C., King, N.: Interviews in Qualitative Research. SAGE Publications Ltd., London (2010)
5. Michael, H.: Software-Ergonomie: Theorien, Modelle und Kriterien für gebrauchstaugliche interaktive Computersysteme, 3 Auflage. Oldenbourg Wissenschaftsverlag (2009)
6. Hoppe-Graff, S.: Tagebücher, Gespräche und Erzählungen: Zugänge zum Verstehen von Kindern und Jugendlichen. In: Keller, H. (Hg.) Lehrbuch Entwicklungspsychologie, pp. S.261–S.294. Huber, Bern (1998)
7. Trautner, H.M.: Lehrbuch der Entwicklungspsychologie, 2 Aufl. Hogrefe, Göttingen (1997)

Evaluation Methods and Results
for Intermodal Mobility Applications
in Public Transport

Ulrike Stopka[✉], Katrin Fischer, and René Pessier

Technische Universität Dresden, Dresden, Germany
ulrike.stopka@tu-dresden.de

Abstract. Against the background of changing social values towards resource efficiency and environmental benefits today's mobility is lived less as an alternative choice between different modes of transport, but rather in their intermodal combination during a trip. The increasing diversity of mobility services is combined by the users under very pragmatic aspects in order to get from A to B as fast, reliable, convenient and cost effective as possible.

Within the scope of the research project "Dynamic Seamless Mobility Information" (DYNAMO) conducted by a consortium of different public transportation, service developing and IT companies as well as scientific institutions such as the Technische Universität Dresden a comprehensive prototype of an intermodal mobility application was developed between 2013 and 2015. The scientific monitoring and evaluation of this process will be presented in the following article.

Keywords: Mobility information · Mobile application · Intermodal services · Public transport · Evaluation methods · User requirements · Operating concepts

1 Project Presentation

The target of the research project DYNAMO was the development and prototypical implementation of dynamic information services to support the travelers before and during their journey. The user is in the focus of the project and provides the basis for the "Design-for-all" concept. The scientific evaluation of the project was divided into three phases, which were conducted at the beginning, during and at the end of the application development (Fig. 1):

Within the scope of the project, the following basic services or core areas had to be designed and integrated into the application:

- dynamic trip guidance (real time information and identification of route deviations)
- indoor positioning (enables navigation in buildings)
- social media (integration of modern interaction channels for networking with passengers)
- routing and navigation (reliable, user-friendly and continuous routing)
- accessibility without barriers (barrier-free routing)

M. Kurosu (Ed.): HCI 2016, Part III, LNCS 9733, pp. 343–354, 2016.
DOI: 10.1007/978-3-319-39513-5_32

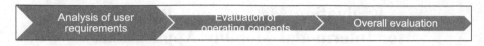

Fig. 1. Scientific evaluation steps in the DYNAMO research project

- intermodal crosslinking (intermodal information including car-/bike sharing, ride sharing and ride selling, taxi)

The development of the intermodal application and the surveys took place in two test regions: in the area of the Rhine-Main Transport Association and the area of the Munich Transport Association.

2 Goals and Methods of the Different Evaluation Phases

2.1 Analysis of User Requirements

The aim of this upstream stage was to elicit requirements for mobility applications with regard to the above mentioned basic services and core topics by using scientific evaluation methods. After an intensive literature review and the development of general requirement catalogs, focus group and individual interviews for the qualitative determination of user requirements for the DYNAMO prototype were conducted. In total 14 guideline-based group or individual interviews with focus on dynamic trip guidance (16 subjects), routing and navigation (13 subjects), intermodal crosslinking (20 subjects) and social media (15 subjects) were performed. The results of the focus group discussions served as a basis for the following standardized online survey. With the help of this survey the insights gained by the qualitative methods (focus group and individual interviews) were supposed to be validated quantitatively.

The questionnaire was distributed electronically via the student and staff mailing center of the Technische Universität Dresden. With 1,985 completed questionnaires an utilizable response rate of 5.3 % was achieved. The features and services found out in the previous interviews were divided and grouped in a reasonable manner and the subjects had to evaluate them by means of a rating scale (5-point scale: very needed … not required). Thereby different scenarios (sections of the travel chain) have been predefined. The sample was made up as follows: 51 % of respondents were male and 49 % female. 73 % of respondents were aged between 16 and 25 years and a quarter between of 26 and 35. 87 % of the subjects stated that they currently pass a training, apprenticeship or study. 6 % were fully employed and 4 % partially employed. The sample cannot be regarded as representative. However, it allows to identify trends in general mobility behavior.

2.2 Operating Concept Evaluation

The aim of the second assessment phase was the evaluation of eight operating concepts with regard to their acceptance by potential users. Operating concepts comprise the operation and interaction features of software users [3]. This second step was very helpful for the iterative approach in the research project, because the results of the survey were sent as feedback to the developers of the application prototype.

1,884 oral interviews in November and December 2014 both at public transport stops and in vehicles of the Rhine-Main Transport Association provided the data base for this evaluation. To participate, the subjects had to use at least one mobility application on their smartphone. The standardized questionnaire was made up of two parts: a first section on mobility behavior, attitudes and personal information and a second section for the actual evaluation of the operating concepts. Following operating concepts had to been evaluated: Menu design, route options overview, route search, route details, social media, modal choice, indoor navigation and map display. The subjects were due to assess their acceptance by evaluating three different screenshots for each operating concept shown on a tablet. The range of the rating scale went from 1 (poor operating features) to 7 (very helpful operating features). Beyond that more in-depth questions were asked especially interesting from a developer's point of view.

2.3   Overall Evaluation

The overall evaluation of the DYNAMO prototype application has the following investigation targets:

1. evaluation of the usability on the functional and application level
2. evaluation of the user acceptance by:
   (a) the intensity of use and their changes
   (b) the willingness to recommend the application
3. elicitation of the potential for improvement of the application
4. assessment of the impacts with regard to mobility behavior by using the application and further mobility service supply options

The usability of an application is a hypothetical feature. After DIN ISO 9241-11 it is defined as "the extent to which a product can be used by specified users to achieve specified goals with effectiveness, efficiency and satisfaction in a specified context of use". For this analysis, the above mentioned three criteria effectiveness, efficiency and satisfaction should be regarded both on the functional and application level. The definitions of these three terms can be found in Table 1.

Table 1. Usability criteria [1]

Criterion	Definition
Effectiveness	Accuracy and completeness with which selected users can achieve defined goals in specific environments
Efficiency	The used resources in relation to the accuracy and completeness of goals achieved
Satisfaction	The comfort and acceptance of the work system to its users and for other people who are affected by the use of it

In order to evaluate software, a variety of methods can be used. Figure 2 provides an overview and also clarifies the trade-off between the greatest possible objectivity and strong user involvement.

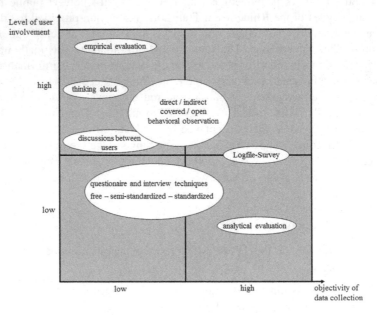

Fig. 2. Evaluation method overview [1]

Table 2. Objectives of the survey and methods used

Objective of the survey/content	Indicator	Used method of collecting data	Used evaluation method
Usability	Effectiveness	• Standardized questionnaire	• Quantitative analysis
	Efficiency		
	Satisfaction	• Semi-standardized (explorative) interview	• Content analysis
Acceptance	Intensity of use	• Logfile-survey • Standardized questionnaire	• Quantitative analysis
	Change of use	• Logfile-survey • Standardized questionnaire	• Quantitative analysis
	Willingness to recommend	• Standardized questionnaire	• Quantitative analysis
Potential for further development and improvement of the application		• Standardized questionnaire • Semi-standardized (explorative) interview	• Quantitative analysis • Content analysis
Impacts with regard to mobility behavior and further service supply options		• Standardized questionnaire	• Quantitative analysis

To minimize this trade-off, a combination of quantitative and qualitative approaches (see Table 2) was used for the present study.

The operationalization of these approaches can be seen in Table 3.

Table 3. Details on surveys in the test region Munich and test region Frankfurt

Type of survey	Details of data collection	Test region Munich transport association	Test region Rhine-Main transport association
Semi-standardized (explorative) interview	Goal questions: • Use problems • Particularly positive/negative implementations • Suggestion for improvement	20 individual interviews, each about 45 min	16 individual interviews, each about 45 min
Standardized questioning (online)	Once, as far as possible identical repetition of the survey for the same sample (panel)	Wave 1: n = 388 (response rate: 40,7 %) wave 2 (+ 3 weeks): n = 148 (response rate: 76,4 %)	Wave 1: n = 207 wave 2 (+ 3 weeks): n = 116

The semi-structured exploratory interviews were characterized by great flexibility in response to statements and behavior of subjects [4]. For the interviews goal questions (see Table 3) were developed as an interview guideline. During the interview the subjects first were confronted with a hypothetical scenario (e.g. trip to work, travel to acquaintances), which corresponded with the information on mobility behavior the subjects had provided before.

The standardized questionnaire (see Table 3) was sent to two times online. Participation criteria for the subjects were the use of a smartphone and an Android operating system so that the prototype could be installed. Furthermore, at least an occasional use of a mobility application was a prerequisite for participation. The questionnaires of the two waves have been very similar. Only questions about travel behavior and personal features have been left in the second survey.

The questionnaire was composed of four parts according to the survey targets. The questions primarily comprised closed response formats:

The question blocks for usability were developed according to the GQM model ("Goal Question Metric") of Hussain and Kutar [2]. This model includes dimensions (usability criteria: effectiveness, efficiency and satisfaction), associated questions and metrics that will finally lead to an overall usability assessment of the tested software. Table 4 summarizes the questions used for the presented study. The response format was a endpoint named 5-point scale with numbered values.

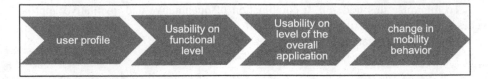

Fig. 3. Questionnaire structure

Table 4. Questions per usability factor of the evaluation questionnaire [2]

	Effectiveness	Efficiency	Satisfaction
Questions	• ease of use • speed of learning • average response time • successful operations from the 1st try • successful solution of the given task from the 1st try • virtual keyboard available	• needed time to solve the task • time until error-free handling the application • suitability of the solutions provided by the app	• sense of security • satisfaction with the user interface • overall satisfaction with the app

3   Results

3.1   Analysis of User Requirements

The following results refer to the quantitative survey described in Sect. 2.1. 60 % of the respondents indicated to use public transport at least once or twice a week for the way to work or training. 53 % of the respondents use public transit regularly (once or twice a week) for leisure trips and 45 % for shopping and other purposes. 70 % of respondents own a smartphone, 60 % use the mobility application once per leisure trip and 33 % once on shopping trips and other routes. After all, nearly one-third shows the same behavior patterns on trips for shopping and other purposes. On trips to job and training the majority (45 %) is using the application only occasionally or rarely.

Within the requirement analysis, the users' needs were investigated with regard to different route sections. Table 5 shows the three most important needs in each section. The most desired user requirements per basic service can be found in Table 8 below.

3.2   Evaluation of Operating Concepts

In this phase of the project should be provided support for the application development by examining eight operating concepts each with the help of three different screenshots shown to the subjects. In the following the results for the operating concept "modal choice" (see Fig. 4) and "maps" (see Fig. 5) belonging to the basic services routing & navigation and intermodal crosslinking are shown.

Table 5. User requirements per route section (priority 1 to 3)

#	Trip preparation	Way to stop/station	Orientation at stop/station	Travel	Transfer	Way to destination
1	Route or stop/station favorites	Alternative route in case of disturbance				Spontaneous change of destination
2	Automatic information in case of delays or disturbances					/
3	Information about special features of the route (replacement services, stations etc. ...)	Spontaneous change of destination	Departure overview	Spontaneous change of destination	Departure overview	/

Fig. 4. Screenshots of the operating concept "Modal Choice"

The left screen shows a tabular list of different means of transport which can be selected by setting or cancelling a check mark. This procedure is taken over in the second (middle) screen by a slider. The right screen use pictograms as a slider for the selection of means of transport (Table 6).

Table 6. Evaluation results of the operating concept "Modal Choice"

	Screen 1 (left)	Screen 2 (middle)	Screen 3 (right)
Mean/standard deviation	5,25/1,65	5,32/1,45	4,99/1,73

The screen in the middle represents the top ranked operating concept. Sliders tend to be assessed with higher values by the subjects than other notations. However, these

Fig. 5. Screenshots of the operating concept "Map"

sliders should have a clear description and should not contain pictograms as in the right screen.

Additionally imposed evaluation criteria include the age of the subjects, the frequency of public transport use and possible disabilities in personal mobility. With regard to these items, it was found that subjects older than 65 years and disabled people rated the left screen as the best to almost 60 %. Also rare public transit users had a clear preference for the left screen.

The screenshots for evaluating the map design show that the left screen has no additional settings by the user, as they can be found in the headline and footer of the middle screen. A deeper detailing and dichotomy of the screen in a graphical representation and a departure monitor can be seen in the right screen.

On average, 475 subjects evaluated the right screen at its highest. Information to be seen on this screen includes stops, departure boards, information about connections from the selected station as well as the possibility to set start and end points. The use of interactive icons on maps is recommended. With regard to the age and the intensity of public transit use was determined that both younger and middle-aged subjects and rare public transit users prefer a map display with larger icons (see left screen). However, elderly subjects and frequent public transport users prefer to split screen composed of a map and the departure monitor (see right screen). That is the same result as the mean rating already showed (see Table 7).

Table 7. Evaluation results of the operating concept "Map"

	Screen 1 (left)	Screen 2 (middle)	Screen 3 (right)
Mean/standard deviation	4,36/1,87	5,04/1,39	5,38/1,58

In the prototype of the intermodal mobility app and its basic services the operating concepts preferred by the majority of the subjects were implemented.

Table 8. Requirements and qualitative evaluation in the test region Frankfurt

Requirements per basic service	Qualitative evaluation by subjects
Intermodal crosslinking:	
Intermodal inclusion of alternative means of transport	• Intermodal combinations perceived partly as interesting • However only reasonable combinations and • Relevant alternatives should be displayed • Clear identification of means of transport with sufficient information about their options are required
Setting options regarding alternative means of transport	• Selection of the relevant means of transport must be very easy to understand and to implement
Routing und navigation:	
Possibility of multimodal comparison	• The decision for transportation does not change due to the presented alternatives (especially in case of individual car traffic alternatives), because with the use of the app the decision for public transport has already been made • If needed, the comparison of different means of transport is well resolved and clear
Specify settings/preferences for route search	• Options should be presented in an easily understandable manner, possibly in the start screen as directly apparent option list • Sidebar as a place for options is very useful • Selection of walking speed is well accepted • Partly great skepticism towards many settings in the options menu (e.g. modal choice, maximum walking distance)
Display all stops/stations nearby	• Very practical for unknown routes • Request for every stop/station to display the serving lines
Detailed information to stops and stations	• No clear opinion because the depth of details on the one hand is perceived as very advantageous and on the other hand as information overload
Indoor-navigation:	
Overview of the whole building	• Up to the moment of writing the paper the available interviews did not focus this aspect
Navigation with the help of pictures and important points in the surroundings	
Barrier-free accessibility	
Barrier-free routing	• Voice response and list display of the route is important for people with disabilities

(Continued)

Table 8. (*Continued*)

Requirements per basic service	Qualitative evaluation by subjects
Social media:	
Combination of calendar and mobility application	• Very useful when the trip can be stored in the calendar
Alarm in case of disturbance on the planned route	• Alarm is an important, useful function
Opportunity to provide feedback about the trip, vehicle, staff, etc. to other users and the transport company	• With the possibility to input the feedback very fast in the application, it is realistic that the feedback function is used intensely • The feedbacks' trustworthiness given by other passengers is rated less than a feedback given by the transport company • The reason of a disturbance is interesting to know in any case, even if it has been given by other passengers and not by the transport company • Subjects requested that customer feedback should be verified in any case by the transport company • It must be clear who is the sender of the feedback
Dynamic trip guidance:	
Real-time information about departure, arrival (push messages)	• Very useful because new departure and arrival times are calculated automatically
Reliable information about the reason and duration of disturbance	• Users need longer time to build confidence and to accept the information as "reliable"
In case of delays automatic display of alternative connections	• Explicit desire of subjects • Only alternatives really relevant for the user should be • Displayed
Storage of routes and corresponding documentations	• The term "travel folder"[a] as a possibility to store route information is difficult to understand • "Favorites" function, however, is far better known and understood, but is confused with the term "travel folder" →Aggregation in a "favorites" function may be reasonable

[a]Virtual folder of planned trips with stored time data; favorites are distinguished from travel folder and store frequent start and destination points.

3.3 Overall Evaluation

At the time of finishing this paper the qualitative and quantitative surveys of the overall evaluation have already taken place in the two testing regions Munich and Frankfurt.

So far, the evaluation results are only partially completed. The following statements therefore comprise only parts of the objectives formulated in the survey.

The qualitative surveys in the Frankfurt region revealed that the multimodal information is very useful in specific situations. The subjects' expectations regarding a public transport application rarely include the offer of alternative modes of transport. The trade-off between the greatest possible depth of information combined with low "overloading" of the application appeared in the interviews repeatedly. Different requirements in different situations require both "slim" solutions as well as highly detailed information. The sender of the information is important for to the subjects. Confidence in reports of other passengers is significantly lower than the confidence in information of transport companies. Moreover, the quality of the data plays an important role. The subjects assess real-time information to be very positive and valuable.

The quantitative results of the overall evaluation show a nearly balanced picture (see Table 9). The effectiveness, that is the accuracy and completeness with which users reached the objectives, is evaluated a little bit higher than the degree of satisfaction and efficiency, but only slightly.

Table 9. Results of usability measurement for the application prototype in total

	Effectiveness	Efficiency	Satisfaction	Usability
Mean of the ratings (Scale: 1 (poor) – 5 (very good), n = 152)	3,78	3,58	3,62	3,66

With regard to the objectives, to gain insights about changes of the mobility behavior due to the use of mobility applications (see Fig. 3), the following statements can be derived from the survey results (n = 154 subjects):

- the likelihood that public transport is used more often with such an application is significantly higher than in the case of other means of transport
- 54 % of the subjects reported that the chance to use public transport more often is at least 80 %, but
- with increasing age and with declining frequency of public transit use this chance is reducing.

4 Conclusions

Within the scope of the DYNAMO research project an intermodal door-to-door application was developed and at the same time this process was accompanied scientifically. The article dealt with the three-stage approach of this scientific evaluation. At the end of the project the great benefit of a broad-based methodology in which all the quantitative and qualitative approaches are combined is visible. In particular, in the development process of a prototype it is very helpful to integrate qualitative user research as often as possible, because it delivers valuable insights for software engineers during the development process. The involvement of the software development teams in these surveys enhances this effect.

All three survey levels showed that during the development of intermodal applications a trade-off between the complex information needs of users and the applications' ease of use always exists. In the future, this trade-off may be handled with the help of specialized applications for individual types of users or groups. Probably, such solutions, however, can be fully implemented on the basis of self-learning systems and artificial intelligence.

References

1. Hegner, M.: Methoden zur Evaluation von Software. IZ-Arbeitsbericht Nr. 29., Informationszentrum Sozialwissenschaften der Arbeitsgemeinschaft sozialwissenschaftlicher Institute e. V., Bonn (2003)
2. Hussain, A., Kutar, M.: Usability metric framework for mobile phone application. In: The 10th Annual PostGraduate Symposium on The Convergence of Telecommunications, Networking and Broadcasting, Liverpool (2009)
3. Rhein-Main-Verkehrsverbund Servicegesellschaft mbH. Projektphasen. http://www.nahtlosmobil.eu/arbeitsplan.html (2016). Accessed 29 Jan 2016
4. Honer, A.: Das explorative Interview: zur Rekonstruktion der Relevanzen von Expertinnen und anderen Leuten. Schweizerische Zeitschrift für Soziologie 20, 3 (1994)

A Simulation System of Experience with a Disaster by Locating Memories on a Virtual Space

Kohki Yoshida[1(✉)], Takayoshi Kitamura[2], Tomoko Izumi[2], and Yoshio Nakatani[2]

[1] Graduated School of Information Science and Engineering,
Ritsumeikan University, Kyoto, Japan
is0147ei@ed.ritsumei.ac.jp
[2] College of Information Science and Engineering, Ritsumeikan University, Kyoto, Japan
{ktmr,izumi-t}@fc.ritsumei.ac.jp,
nakatani@is.ritsumei.ac.jp

Abstract. This study proposes a simulation system to improve awareness of disaster risks for a stranded commuter who is unable to get home from school, work, and the like. It shares the recollections of stranded commuters during a past disaster. The simulation system also presents a scenario for considering potential risks and making appropriate decisions. It takes advantage of the disaster experiences of others and shares them in a virtual space to promote disaster awareness. The system is expected to raise disaster awareness and preparation and allow people to take detailed disaster-avoidance measures.

Keywords: Disaster · Awareness · Stranded commuters · Virtual experience

1 Introduction

Earthquakes, tsunamis, landslides, typhoons, and storms occur every year in Japan. As a result, fire stations, local community bodies, educational institutions, private enterprises, and other groups organize a wide range of drills for disaster preparation for many people in Japan. However, some people remain uninterested in such preparation, as they typically cannot imagine disasters occurring within their own areas of daily life. Even when faced with imminent danger or catastrophe, people usually do not believe what is happening. If people were always sensitive to every event, they would have to be afraid of everything and daily lives would be difficult. Within a certain range, people tend to recognize abnormality as normal. This is the "normalcy bias." People judge a situation as all right, even if danger is approaching. This tendency more strongly exists in daily lives without any symptom of disasters. Therefore, it is necessary to develop a method that encourages people to consider the risks of disaster and become familiarized with them.

To improve people's interest in the disasters that may occur in their area, the most effective method may be getting people to walk around their areas and to meet with others and hear them speak about their experiences of disasters in their own areas. However, such a method requires a great deal of time and effort to match people for learning and teaching.

© Springer International Publishing Switzerland 2016
M. Kurosu (Ed.): HCI 2016, Part III, LNCS 9733, pp. 355–362, 2016.
DOI: 10.1007/978-3-319-39513-5_33

This study proposes a system for simulating people's experiences with a disaster. With this system, learners with no prior experience of a disaster can understand the effects of a disaster occurring in their residential area and destinations to which they commute. Since a user can best understand the effects of a disaster whilst walking around his/her area, the system maps recollections of an actual disaster to a street-view virtual space.

This paper focuses on a system for commuters who become stranded and find it difficult to go home. If a large earthquake directly strikes the Tokyo area, then public transportation will be disrupted all day long and commuters will become stranded. According to the Cabinet Office of the government of Japan [1], a disaster affecting the Tokyo area will cause 6.5 million commuters to be stranded. Figure 1 shows stranded commuters in Tokyo after the Great East Japan earthquake in 2011 [2]. At that time, approximately 5.15 million people were stranded on the road [3]. There is confusion all around the station, bringing a risk of secondary disaster. Tokyo has put in place ordinance for measures concerning stranded persons [1]. The purpose of this law is to prevent people from heading home all at once. However, it is unlikely that this law will contribute to decreasing the number of stranded persons, because most people will want to go home after the disaster occurred, regardless of the laws. Therefore, people should be helped to understand the risks involved in taking immediate action to head home. There are some activities that can improve disaster awareness.

Fig. 1. Stranded people on the Great East Japan earthquake

There are some activities to improve the disaster prevention awareness. A drill is an effective method for people to realize difficulty to cope with the problematic situations in disasters. The Tokyo Metropolitan Government regularly carries out large-scale disaster drills to prevent severe confusion of the commuters (ex., [4]). Neighborhood disaster response group activity and community disaster response study meetings are also recommended [5]. These drills and activities, however, take much cost to carry out and only people who have strong interest in disasters take part in them. It is difficult for the commuters who are busy every day to participate in such drills. Methods of learning what situation may happen just after large-scale disasters and how to cope with such situations more easily are required.

2   Related Works

A few studies have been made on improving awareness of disasters. Yamamoto and Nakatani [6] proposed a disaster education system for the general population to mitigate possible damage by improving awareness of preparation for disasters. As a method to resolve the normalcy bias, their approach is to simulate the kinds of risky situations that may occur in daily life of the user. Although people may know the possible risks as general knowledge, they have difficulty realizing that risky situations may occur to them and that they will face problems. Alternatively, past disaster cases can be used as source of realistic knowledge. The problem here is that some people do not recognize the relationship between past cases and their daily lives. If the system can suggest to the user the possibility of a risky situation at a specific time of day through showing past cases that actually occurred at a similar time of day and in conditions similar to the user's life style, the user can realize that such a situation may occur in their own life.

Figure 2 shows an example of screen image of the system.

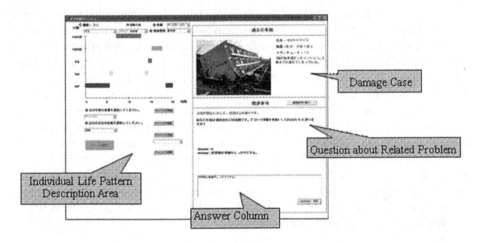

Fig. 2. An example of screen image of the case-based disaster education system

The system provides the timeline of the day at the top-left of the screen, and the user describes his/her life pattern for a typical day as a Gantt chart. The user also describes his/her personal information, such as a residential area, an occupation, a commute method, and so on. Based on these data, in addition to selecting a season and a specific time of day, a potential risky situation is selected. The situation is retrieved from among past disaster cases with most similar conditions to the described life style. Past disaster cases are stored in the case base, indexed by the same information as the life style description.

The effectiveness of this approach was verified by the subject experiment. The result showed the improvement of awareness of preparation for disasters, although the improvement was smaller in people who are optimistic for the disaster.

This research shows the effectiveness of the case-based approach to realize the dangerousness of disasters and necessity of preparation for disaster mitigation from normal times. The system to be proposed in the next chapter also utilizes the past experiences of people who suffered from serious disasters, especially on the streets.

3 Proposal of the System

This paper proposes a photo-based walk-through virtual experience system which supports the user learn how to behave in large-scale disasters, especially when he/she is stranded and tries to return home.

3.1 Overview

The system has two functions as follows.

- Simulated experience of disaster situations
- Vicarious experience of disaster cases of other people

Our focus is on the situation when people might be at a loss about what to do. People are expected to successfully cope with such situations if they know possible problematic situations and consider countermeasures. The system supports the user to know possible problematic situations mainly with the first function, and to consider countermeasures with the second function. Of course the first function is helpful also for considering countermeasures and the second function is helpful for knowing possible situations. Both functions are provided on the photo-based street walk-through interface and the bird's-eye view map-based interface as shown in Fig. 3. The red-circled icon shown in the map-based interface shows the current location of the user. These two types of interface work together, and the location of the user on the map changes as the user walks forward in the walk-through interface, and vice versa. In this screen, the user can refer to past experiences of other people, as balloons on the photo-based street walk-through interface and as icons on the map-based interface, which are located at the places where the corresponding experiences happened.

3.2 Simulated Experience of Disaster Situations

The first function provides the user with a certain evacuation scenario and asks him/her to behave as the scenario. For example, a scenario asks the user to cope with the situation of full suspension of the train service in a big typhoon. The user may drop in at a convenience store. He/she has to decide whether he/she tries to return home on foot, tries to find other transportation, or tries to find a shelter. The user can examine what to do on the area shown on the screen, inspired by photos.

On the streets and buildings shown in the screen, the user can refer to past experiences which were actually had by other people on these sites. These experiences show the user actual situations, which may happen to the user in disasters.

Photos of actual streets and past experiences provide such an environment that shows a wide variety of situations in which difficult decisions are required. The user can realize what kinds of situation may happen and what he/she has to decide.

Fig. 3. An example of the screen image

3.3   Vicarious Experience of Disaster Cases of Other People

The second function supports the user to follow an actual experience of a certain person. The system picks up the past experiences of a certain person and presents them on the walk-through interface and the map-based interface.

The map-based interface supports the user to know the actual route of the person and the environment around him/her. By following the route and viewing the experiences in time series in the walk-through interface, the user can experience for him/her-self what the person has gone through. By viewing the map in the map-based interface, the user can notice alternative countermeasures which could be taken by the person if he/she might knew the environment well.

3.4   System Configuration

Figure 4 shows the system configuration. The system consists of eight units.

(1) Data acquisition device: Ricoh Theta^{TM} is used to capture 360° panorama photos, along with location information.

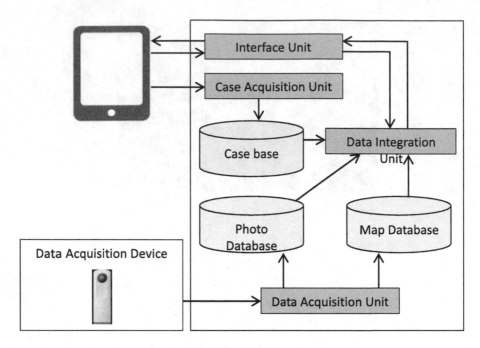

Fig. 4. System configuration

(2) Data acquisition unit: Photo data and location information are stored and in the photo database and are linked with map data stored in the map database.

(3) Case acquisition unit: Experiences of people are acquired along with location data and are sent to the case base.

(4) Photo database: 360° panorama photo data are stored and managed.

(5) Map database: The map data are stored and managed.

(6) Case base: Acquired experiences are stored along with location data.

(7) Data integration unit: The user's location is managed by monitoring the operation on the walk-through interface and the map-based interface, which reflects in the screen, changing a photo in the walk-through interface, changing the location of the user's icon in the map-based interface, changing a displayed area of the map, and changing the balloons and icons from the case base.

(8) Interface unit: The operations of the user are accepted and are sent to the data integration unit. The results of data integration in the data integration unit are sent to the computer screen.

4   Evaluation

4.1   Purpose

As described in Sect. 3, the proposed system presents a scenario of a commuter who finds it difficult to return home. A user should be able to experience a simulated disaster in a virtual space. We must evaluate how well they can relieve the disaster experiences of others.

4.2 Assumption

When large-scale disasters occur in urban areas, there are often problems in public transport, such as when trains are halted for safety checks or to conduct recovery operations. In such instances, people using public transport to commute to school or the workplace must instead walk home, which can be tens of kilometers away. Such people are referred to as stranded commuters. Many commuters can become stranded in city centers, such as in Tokyo during the Great East Japan earthquake, 2011, crowding the roads around the stations. If a large-scale disaster occurs, such an earthquake directly affecting a city, then using public transport like a railway to move many people home, in the absence of other options, will interfere with rescue activities [7]. Therefore, the Tokyo Metropolitan Government developed ordinance to handle stranded commuters in Tokyo; these measures came into force in 2013 [7]. However, in order for people to comply with this ordinance, it is important that they understand the difficulties involved in going home during a disaster and what kinds of issues they may face.

Table 1 shows the experience of an actual stranded commuter during the Great East Japan earthquake.

Table 1. The experiences of stranded commuters in the Great East Japan earthquake

---

- The railroad service was suspended.
- The television broadcast that a tsunami had hit a town and a town caught fire.
- The telephone line was busy and I could not get through.
- Mail was delivered late.
- Hotels had no vacancies.
- The cellular phone shop was full of people wanting to charge their own phones.
- Using the mobile phone did not go as planned because opportunities to charge the phone were rare.
- Long lines formed in front of convenience stores and items of food were sold out.
- Long lines formed in front of the bus station and buses were full.
- Walking was faster than driving the car because of heavy traffic.
- Near the station, I became stuck in crowds.
- As time progressed, I became stressed because things did not go as planned.
- Restroom breaks were always a problem.
- The hotels were full of people wanting to stay.
- Some stores provide places to rest and some drink.
- At night, it was very exhausting because it was cold.

4.3 Method

This study uses records of people's experiences of being stranded commuters in Tokyo, as published on blogs and social networking services on the Internet. The system uses the Google Maps API and web-scripting language released by Google Inc. Furthermore, experiments to evaluate the system will be performed, targeting people who commute in Tokyo yet have never become stranded.

5   Future Activity

Each person must consider the risk of disaster on an individual basis in order to reduce the risk to his/her own life. Therefore, this paper proposed a system for simulating a disaster experience by locating recollections of others within a virtual space. With this system, we expect to improve users' awareness of disasters. We evaluated the system by considering a scenario in which a disaster causes commuters to become stranded in Tokyo, as occurred during the 2011 Great East Japan earthquake.

In the future, we plan to compile recollections of people who have been stranded commuters in the past and to reflect these in the system. Test participants in Tokyo will be recruited and, after a preliminary experiment, an evaluation experiment will be carried out. We also wish to specifically present the experiences of others who in similar situation as that of the user.

References

1. Toriumi, S.: Problem of commuters who have difficulty returning home after a large-scale disaster in the Tokyo metropolitan area, ChuoOnline, The Yomiuri Shinbun (2012). http://www.yomiuri.co.jp/adv/chuo/dy/research/20120315.html. Accessed 26 Feb 2016
2. Dot: Does it become a reality? A New Damage Estimation of Tokyo Metropolitan Earthquake, 3 December 2013 (in Japanese). http://dot.asahi.com/aera/201312260004.html. Accessed 26 Feb 2016
3. Takayanagi, H., et al.: How stranded commuters in Tokyo returned home after the Great East Japan earthquake – analysis of the situation on twitter-. J. JSCE **1**, 470–478 (2013)
4. Tokyo Metropolitan Government: A drill to practice response measures for situations where commuters become stranded, Disaster Prevention Website. http://www.bousai.metro.tokyo.jp/foreign/english/kitaku_portal/2000139.html. Accessed 26 Feb 2016
5. Tokyo Metropolitan Government: Disaster Preparedness Tokyo (2015)
6. Yamamoto, T., Nakatani, Y.: System to improve people's awareness of preparation for disasters considering individual lifestyle. In: Proceedings of the International Disaster Reduction Conference (IDRC Davos 2008), pp. 366–367 (2008)
7. Tokyo Metropolitan Government: Ordinance for Measures Concerning Stranded Persons (Overview). http://www.bousai.metro.tokyo.jp/foreign/_res/projects/gaikokugo/_page_/002/000/188/kitakon_eigo.pdf. Accessed 26 Feb 2016

Media, Entertainment, Games, and Gamification

ImmertableApp: Interactive and Tangible Learning Music Environment

Sandra Baldassarri[1]([✉]), Javier Marco[1], Clara Bonillo[1], Eva Cerezo[1],
and José Ramón Beltrán[2]

[1] GIGA AffectiveLab, Aragon Institute of Engineering Research (I3A),
Universidad de Zaragoza, Zaragoza, Spain
{sandra,javi.marco,clarabf,ecerezo}@unizar.es
[2] Department of Electronic Engineering and Communications,
Aragon Institute of Engineering Research (I3A), Universidad de Zaragoza, Zaragoza, Spain
jrbelbla@unizar.es

Abstract. This paper presents ImmertableApp, an innovative multimodal interface based in tangible interaction in which audio edition is managed through physical controllers. The system is composed by two different main components: a tangible tabletop interface in which the sound parameters can be changed by the manipulation of physical controllers; and a graphic editor interface for setting the configuration of the controllers and their corresponding parameters through a tablet device. In this way ImmertableApp adds to a musical tangible interface the new possibilities of software interfaces: personalization for being adapted to different users, either experts or beginners and, so that it can be used as a didactic tool of different concepts related with sound synthesis. The system has been early assessed with experts in order to obtain feedback about its utility in different fields of music education. The results of the evaluation give the basis for interesting improvements in future versions.

Keywords: Tangible user interface · Music · Audio edition · Education · Object manipulation · Tablet

1 Introduction

Since the development of the MIDI protocol in 1982 there are plenty of sound control and generation hardware and software. The most popular systems to generate real-time interaction are hardware systems that have no problem with real-time interaction but are very constraint in terms of use and interaction due to the specific design of the device: number of potentiometers, buttons, actuators... On the other hand, software-based systems, although very much powerful, are always limited by the traditional interaction with a mouse. This is why, in most cases, musicians, composers and DJs prefer hardware interaction devices to control their music creation applications. Nevertheless, when training novel users the most used applications are controlled by a mouse and a keyboard, or are tactile in the best-case scenario. Due to this virtualization of the sound generation software and devices, users lost the haptic "touch" sensation with the devices, that now

© Springer International Publishing Switzerland 2016
M. Kurosu (Ed.): HCI 2016, Part III, LNCS 9733, pp. 365–376, 2016.
DOI: 10.1007/978-3-319-39513-5_34

are simple represented as images of faders and regulators projected in a screen by the sound software in order to replicate the aspect of their physical equivalents. The relationship between the layout of the different virtual controls and the physical controls of the sound control device, therefore, has been lost. The non-expert user often finds his/herself in front of a window saturated with controls and he/she is not able to comprehend and make use of all the possibilities that are been offered. Moreover, in a graphical interface users usually interact with just one controller, while in physical device it is possible to interact with several controls at the same time.

In order to fill this gap, in this work we propose the use of tangible interaction as a way of recovering the same possibilities that the physical controls offer to the sound edition and generation with the advantages of having also digital information, processing and visualization features. The proposed system is flexible and configurable through a graphical editor, and makes it easy the development of musical educative applications oriented to different kinds of users: children, physical of cognitive disabled people, old people, educators, therapists…

The reminder of the paper is organized as follows. Section 2 presents the state of the art in tangible interaction and music. In Sect. 3, the whole environment is described, giving details about the both main components: the graphical editor and the tangible environment. Following, Sect. 4 presents the results obtained after doing an early evaluation with experts, and finally, the Sect. 5 is focused in the conclusions and the lines of future work that emerged from the assessment.

2   Background and Related Work

In the last years, new interaction techniques have been arisen. These kinds of interaction styles go beyond keyboard, mouse or touch screens, and nowadays are being used in different areas in order to achieve a more natural communication between computer systems and users. Tangible User Interfaces (TUI) are a particular case of natural interaction which joins physical and digital worlds [1] by the manipulation of everyday objects for controlling and representing digital information.

Within TUIs, the tabletops or interactive surfaces digitally augmented [2–4] opened the door to new ways of interaction with computers, more natural and social, since the interactive space of the surfaces is especially suitable for the development of educational and collaborative applications. In fact, most of the works based on physically object manipulation show important benefits in users with difficulties for accessing to conventional technologies, as very young children [5], users with disabilities [6] and elderly persons [7].

In the last years, tabletop solutions have been used in different areas and scopes. Particularly, they offer an interesting tool for the design of musical interfaces, either for execution, composition or control of digital musical instruments [8, 9]. In this area, one of the most well-known tangible interfaces in music creation and execution is Reactable [4, 10]. The instrument is based on tabletop and the manipulation of specific objects over the surface allow performers to combine different elements like synthesizers, effects, sample loops or control elements in order to create a new composition. Although it offers a lot of possibilities, it is developed for being used by DJs or expert musicians, and the control is done with not intuitive controllers. In a similar way, AudioCubes [11] is a tangible user interface that allows to explore and to create dynamically changing sound. Each cube implements a DSP and a sound generator or different musical sound processing techniques. The relative position in space of the different cubes fixes the interaction between the generators or processing cubes. However, the hardware complexity is very high, since each cube has a DSP, an infrared communication module for audio interchange between modules. And the creation process is not intuitively obtained.

Creative musical expression is also the aim of Nielsen et al. [12], who uses modular robotics to create a platform oriented to the music creation process and the control of Ableton Live© software. In this case, the music is prerecorded and depending on the position of the physical building blocks different sounds or styles are played. There is no sound generation process or sound synthesis. A validation of the system has been developed showing that "utilizing music technology in music education and out of school, may give children, or adults, the opportunity to be musically creative and create understanding of musical phenomena and structures".

More recently, Potidis and Spyrou present Spyractable [13], an evolution of Reactable, with a different interface and position and location of the objects but devoted to the sound synthesis process. The objects are "reactable-like" tokens and no didactic or learning approach is presented.

From the analysis of the studied works it can be deduced that, although there are several precedents of the use of musical applications with tangible interaction, in most of the cases the profile of their final users are expert musicians, composers or DJs, and almost all of them used cube objects in order to control the sound. There are also some other tabletop interactive systems for learning or playing with music, especially developed for children and novel users. Most of them are based in cubes or "pucks" [14, 15], objects representing instruments [16], cards [17] or tactile interaction [18]. However, either in the case of applications for experts or for children, none of them considered the usual controllers for music edition for the management of the sound parameters, and none of them allow that the musical environment could be previously configured and personalized. ImmertableApp, instead, propose to include the potential of object manipulation for teaching the didactic aspects of music, adapting it to different user profiles and different levels of knowledge, in an easy and natural way.

3   Description of the Environment

ImmertableApp environment is composed by two main different components (see Fig. 1): a graphic music configuration editor and the tabletop tangible application with physical controllers.

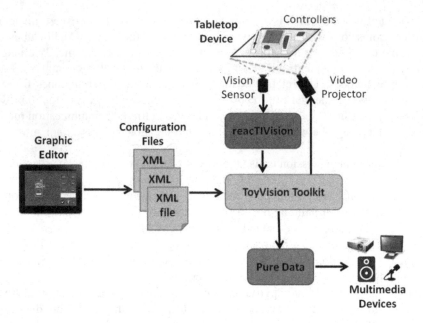

Fig. 1. Description of ImmertableApp's environment

Final users of the tabletop application (usually children and students) can create and modify sounds by manipulating the tangible musical controllers over the interactive surface. Each controller has a fiducial marker that allows that is recognized by the reacTIVision library [19] and processed by the ToyVision framework [20]. In this way, the manipulations produced in the surface of the tabletop generate variations of the synthesis sound parameters, which are processed and can be heard in real time through the sound synthesis generated by an API implemented with the PureData application [21]. The ways in which the controllers will modify the different parameters and sound properties are previously set (usually by teachers) using the graphic editor interface developed for a tablet device.

In the following sub-sections the different components of the system are explained in detail. First, the graphical editor interface is described and later, the tangible interactive environment, detailing the tabletop, the physical controllers and the software developed for managing all.

3.1 The Graphic Editor Interface

The graphic editor interface is an interactive tactile application that runs over a tablet device (Android or iOS). The user, with drag and drop interaction, can configure the interactive environment of the musical application: he/she can define the different control objects involved in the activity and their layout, and also the sound properties he/she wants to associate to each controller for managing the musical creation (see Fig. 2). In this way, the graphical editor allows to personalize and create musical activities in order to generate different modalities of sound generation and edition depending

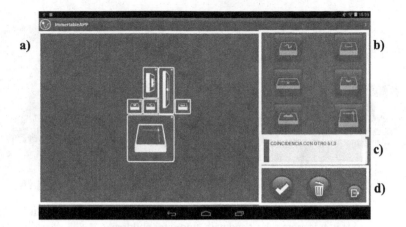

Fig. 2. Graphic editor interface: (a) Work area, that will be visualized later in the tabletop surface, (b) Controllers area, that can be included in the work area dragging and dropping them, (c) Feedback and user information area, and (d) menu area.

on the user knowledges, or with didactic and learning aims, for teaching musical concepts to students of different levels.

Once the configuration of the controllers and properties for a specific activity are defined, the project is saved in two different XML files. These configuration files will be stored, sent to, and later processed by the ToyVision framework [20] for the correct association of the changes in the sound and the visualization of the activity over the tabletop interface.

The editor interface was designed taking into account the recommendations of music teachers and following the style guides for the development of tactile applications. The User Interface was implemented in Adobe Flex, with AdobeAIR technology, in order to be multiplatform and to be executed either in an Android or an iOS device.

3.2   The Tangible Interactive Environment

The tangible interactive surface is based in NIKVision tabletop [5] (see Fig. 3-left) that has been adapted for filling our requirements (see Fig. 3-right).

Technically, the tabletop uses the computer vision framework reacTIVision available for free as open-source software [19] that tracks the objects placed on the surface, provided by a fiducial marker attached to the base of each controller. An infrared light USB camera captures video from underneath the table and streams it to the computer station that executes the visual recognition and the visualization and audio generation software. Active image projection on the table is provided by retro-projection through a mirror inside the table.

For audio generation in the tabletop, ImmertableApp incorporates a system based in PureData [21] and integrated with the ToyVision framework [20] for the management of the audio events and the corresponding visualizations through an Application

Fig. 3. Left: NIKVision tabletop [5]. Right: ImmertableApp tabletop (no monitor, it has a picoprojector inside it, it is more robust and with colors for children).

Programming Interface (API) that allows programmers to easily access to the information coming from the tablet editor and to the tangible controllers.

ToyVision framework reads the XML files previously generated with the graphic editor interface, renders the corresponding visualization over the tabletop surface and change the necessary data into the OSC format in order to be managed by the sound engine. Figure 4 shows the tabletop surface with the visualization of the background layout previously create and with an oscillator physical controller over it. The background color projected into the surface changes according to the fundamental frequency of the sound.

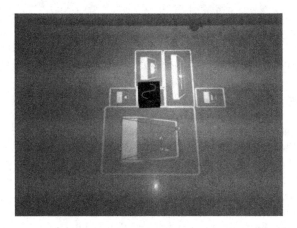

Fig. 4. An activity generated with the graphic editor is rendered in the tabletop surface

As it was explained before, the PureData software was used to develop the sound management. This approximation allows us to implement a sound generator inside the system without the need of another computer or even an external sound module.

For the purpose of sound generation understanding an additive sound synthesis [22] was implemented. Each sound is generated by the weighted sum of a number of harmonics. Then a global envelope with a typical ADSR (attack, decay, sustain and release) pattern is applied to the whole sound. The envelope parameters, the harmonics amplitude, the global volume, the fundamental frequency (pitch) and the duration of the sound are the main characteristics that can be modified by the user by means of the controller objects.

Set of Tangible Controllers. The tangible controllers are conceived as replicas of usual physical controllers used in sound devices and allow to do musical control actions with better response time and feedback that virtual systems based in tactile interaction or image recognition [23].

Within edition and musical composition context there is a well-known set of physical controllers. Therefore, in this work, the design of the interactive objects is based on the physical devices that are usually in synthesis, generation, music and sound composition applications, like faders, potentiometers, buttons, actuators... In this way, we decided to create an intuitive set of controllers, with flexibility and expressivity, for the configuration of the new interactive environment. Each tangible controller set (see Fig. 5) is formed by one or more controllers, which are the physical elements in charge of modifying different sound parameters.

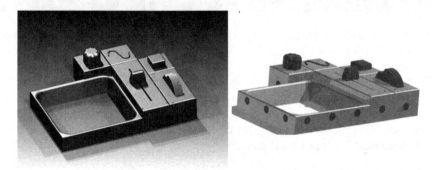

Fig. 5. Tangible controller set

The objects have been prototyped using a 3D printer and, some of them include LEDs illumination and Arduino's sensors and actuators. The different generated objects for sound control are (see Fig. 6):

- Oscillator: It produces a periodic sound signal (wave). There are 4 kinds of waves: sinusoidal, square, triangular and saw-tooth.
- Switch: Button with two states: active/non active.
- Knob: Regulator by 360° turn that allow to increase or decrease a digital variable according to the sense of turning.
- Fader: Vertical or horizontal slider that allow to regulate the value of a digital variable between a minimum and a maximum.
- Regulator: Wheel with an equilibrium position, movable between a minimum and maximum position.

- Touch-pad: Rectangular tactile surface in which the user can regulate a bi-dimensional variable dragging with the finger or with a small piece within the surface. It allows to work with harmonics and envelops.

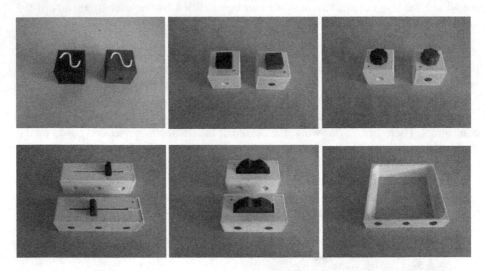

Fig. 6. Different controllers (from left to right and up to down): Oscillator, Switch, Knob, Fader, Regulator and Touch-pad.

The users will make up their different spatial configurations joining several controllers (each one has magnetized laterals) and placing them over the visualization projected in the surface of the tabletop (see Fig. 7). Right now, only one oscillator, that defines the basic sound, is allowed for each set of controllers. All the changes in the sound properties are made over this basic sound.

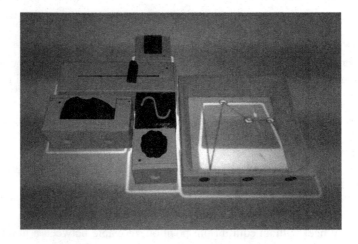

Fig. 7. Set of controllers placed in the tabletop

4   Evaluation and Discussion: First Results

Given the didactic orientation of our system, in this first version we decided to do an informal evaluation of ImmertableApp, only with experts, in order to obtain an early feedback of the utility of the system in different fields of music education. Ten music teachers who work at different level of education (from preschool to university, including special education) attended to a two hours evaluation session in our lab. Four researchers acted as observers in this session, taking notes and recording the comments and discussions between the experts.

The main components of ImmertableApp were tested. The assessment was conducted with several aims in mind. First of all, the value of the tabletop interface as a didactic tool was investigated. Secondly, the usability of the graphic editor was explored. And, finally, the design of the graphic editor and the physical controllers was analyzed.

In the session, first, a presentation of 10 min was given to the music teachers for offering a complete overview of the components. Then, teachers used and played with the tabletop for other 10 min. To assess the didactic possibilities of the tool three activities were carried out: a focus group, a team work and the fulfillment of a questionnaire.

The focus group session lasted 40 min. All the teachers analyzed and discussed the pros and cons of the system, specially focusing in the possibility of using the tabletop device in their classrooms. The teachers most interested in the use of the tabletop were those of special education area, in particular those working with deaf students, autistic children, or very young kids. In particular a teacher of a school for deaf children showed great interest to keep working on this project due to the potentialities that the tabletop offered, since it could allow to "see" the music (for example, by changing the color of the surface depending on the sound that was being reproduced). Most part of her students had partial deafness, and consequently she found really attractive to be able to touch and manipulate the sound parameters by using the controllers.

Following, the experts were divided into two groups of 5 persons each, with the aim of defining, in 40 min, possible didactic activities (for different educational levels) to carry out with the system (editor and tabletop). The results of the two groups were quite different: one rapidly reached a solution that could be easily modulated in complexity in order to be used from primary school to university; the other group, instead, took almost all the time in generating just a proposal since they were continuously engaged into dialogues.

Finally the teachers were given a questionnaire to measure the value of the tabletop interface as a didactic tool. It covered different aspects: functional, pedagogical, esthetic aspects, and accessibility. The results of these enquiries reveal that, regarding functional aspects, the tabletop interface is perceived as easy to use, and that it offers didactic efficacy and flexibility. In the pedagogic aspects the tabletop is considered as a very motivating tool but they also detected potential problems for working in classrooms with more than 10 students. This would be a problem except in special education or very young children classes since they used to work in small groups. In general, as a solution to this problem, they proposed to project the tabletop surface in a whiteboard, or to use it as a collaboration tool only for a small number of students (not more than 5), placing it at tutorial classes, or setting it as rotational activity. Concerning esthetical aspect, almost 60 % of the teachers considered that the tabletop is attractive, but the rest have doubts about its design. Finally, almost all the teachers believe that the tabletop favors accessibility since it takes into account different communication codes.

In order to evaluate the usability of the graphic editor, the teachers had to fill a SUS questionnaire [24] (a popular method to evaluate perceived usability) about their experience while using the editor. The mean of the questionnaires was 76.75 (being 100 the perfect score), assessing a rather high user satisfaction while using the graphic editor. However, there are some aspects that have to be improved. For example, the editor should be more intuitive to use, since almost all the teachers agreed with the fourth question: "*I think that I would need the support of a technical person to be able to use this system*". For a correct verification of the graphic editor usability, a special session with a specific task, like re-creating a classroom activity, must be carried out.

And, finally, about the design of the physical controllers objects teachers said that they were very intuitive and very easy to manipulate although they were a little small for some special cases, like children with motor disabilities. This fact has to be deeper studied in each classroom and group before conducting an evaluation involving children.

5   Conclusions

The system developed in this article is a step in the improvement of teaching and learning music edition without losing the sensations felt using physical controllers through a tangible tabletop interface. The presented system goes further nowadays works allowing the design and personalization of new musical activities by using a tablet to generate them, in and intuitive and simple way. So that, two different components formed this system: a graphical editor and a tabletop interface with physical objects for controlling music edition. Both parts of the system have been early evaluated and the results are very encouraging. The experts highlighted the potential for working with groups with few children, for students with motor or cognitive limitations, and especially for deaf children. However, in this early assessment some aspects result susceptible to be improved, and must be verified with a more rigorous and systematic evaluation. The graphic editor has to be used by teachers for the design of their daily musical activities and later, the activities must be evaluated using the tabletop and the controllers in the classrooms, like in similar works that use tangible interaction with children [25–27]. Moreover, it would be very interesting to use MINUET [9], a framework for musical interface design, in order to position our work in a structured design space, to elaborate ideas and objectives when designing a new musical interface and to guide the evaluation process. This could be a helping tool for analyzing our development.

On the other hand, the physical controllers designed in this work only support passive interaction (they react to users' actions). However, in a near future, they could include active interaction (produced by the system). For this purpose, micro-controllers connected to electronic sensors and actuators and a wireless communication module will be used [28]. In this way, new types of sensors, such as pressure sensors, capacitive sensors and sensors that can vibrate as controllers will be included, making the interaction richer and more motivating.

Acknowledgements. Authors want to thank the ideas given by the ten music teachers that participated in the evaluation session and the support and collaboration of the Education Faculty professors of the University of Zaragoza: Marta Liesa, Sandra Vázquez and Ana Cristina Blasco. This work has been partly financed by the Spanish "Ministerio de Economía y Competitividad" through project No. TIN2015-67149-C3-1R and by the "Diputación General de Aragón" through project: ImmertableApp No. 1004460/2015.

References

1. Ullmer, B., Ishii, H.: Emerging frameworks for tangible user interfaces. IBM Syst. J. **39**(3.4), 915–931 (2000)
2. Smithson Martin. https://smithsonmartin.com/products/emulator-elite/. Accessed 15 Feb 2016
3. Smartable: Gorenje design studio. http://www.smar-table.com/en. Accessed 15 Feb 2016
4. Kaltenbranner, M., Jorda, S., Geiger, G., Alonso, M.: The reactable*: a collaborative musical instrument. In: 15th IEEE International Workshops on Enabling Technologies: Infrastructure for Collaborative Enterprises, WETICE 2006, pp. 406–411 (2006)
5. Marco, J., Cerezo, E., Baldassarri, S., Mazzone, E., Read, J.C.: Bringing tabletop technologies to Kindergarten children. In: Proceedings of the 23rd British HCI Group Annual Conference on People and Computers: Celebrating People and Technology, pp. 103–111. British Computer Society (2009)
6. Li, Y., Fontijn, W., Markopoulos, P.: A tangible tabletop game supporting therapy of children with cerebral palsy. In: Markopoulos, P., de Ruyter, B., IJsselsteijn, W.A., Rowland, D. (eds.) Fun and Games 2008. LNCS, vol. 5294, pp. 182–193. Springer, Heidelberg (2008)
7. Al Mahmud, A., Mubin, O., Shahid, S., Martens, J.B.: Designing and evaluating the tabletop game experience for senior citizens. In: Proceeding of the NordiCHI, 20–22 October 2008
8. Lyons, M.J., Mulder, A., Fels, S.: Introduction to designing and building musical interfaces. In: Proceedings of the Extended Abstracts of the 32nd Annual ACM Conference on Human Factors in Computing Systems. ACM (2014)
9. Morreale, F., De Angeli, A., O'Modhrain, S.: Musical interface design: an experience-oriented framework. In: Proceedings of NIME, vol. 14, pp. 467–472 (2014)
10. Jordà, S., Geiger, G., Alonso, M., Kaltenbrunner, M.: The reactable: exploring the synergy between live music performance and tabletop tangible interfaces. In: Proceedings of the 1st International Conference on Tangible and Embedded Interaction, pp. 139–146. ACM (2007)
11. Schiettecatte, B., Vanderdonckt, J.: AudioCubes: a distributed cube tangible interface based on interaction range for sound design. In: Proceedings of the 2nd International Conference on Tangible and Embedded Interaction, pp. 3–10. ACM (2008)
12. Nielsen, J., Bærendsen, N.K., Jessen, C.: RoboMusicKids. In: IEEE International Workshop on Digital Game and Intelligent Toy Enhanced Learning, DIGITEL 2008, pp. 149–156 (2008). doi:10.1109/DIGITEL.2008.25
13. Potidis, S., Spyrou, T.: Spyractable: a tangible user interface modular synthesizer. In: Kurosu, M. (ed.) HCI 2014, Part II. LNCS, vol. 8511, pp. 600–611. Springer, Heidelberg (2014)
14. Parra-Damborenea, J.: Reactblocks: A 3D tangible interface for music learning. Master thesis, University of Pompeu Fabra (2014)

15. Costanza, E., Shelley, S.B., Robinson, J.: Introducing audio d-touch: a tangible user interface for music composition and performance. In: Proceedings in Human Computer Interaction (HCI). ACM (2003)
16. Bischof, M., Conradi, B., Lachenmaier, P., Linde, K., Meier, M., Pötzl, P., André, E.: Xenakis: combining tangible interaction with probability-based musical composition. In: Proceedings of the 2nd International Conference on Tangible and Embedded Interaction, pp. 121–124. ACM (2008)
17. Francesconi, J.I., Larrea, M., Manresa-Yee, C.: Tangible music composer for children. J. Comput. Sci. Tech. **13**, 84–90 (2013)
18. Patten, J., Recht, B., Ishii, H.: Audiopad: a tag-based interface for musical performance. In: Proceedings of the 2002 Conference on New Interfaces for Musical Expression (2002)
19. Reactivision. http://www.reactivision.com. Accessed 15 Feb 2016
20. Marco, J., Baldassarri, S., Cerezo, E.: ToyVision: a toolkit to support the creation of innovative board-games with tangible interaction. In: Proceedings of the 7th International Conference on Tangible, Embedded and Embodied Interaction, pp. 291–298. ACM (2013)
21. PureData. https://puredata.info/. Accessed 15 Feb 2016
22. Roads, C.: The Computer Music Tutorial. MIT press, Cambridge (1996)
23. Schöning, J., Brandl, P., Daiber, F., Echtler, F., Hilliges, O., Hook, J., von Zadow, U.: Multi-touch surfaces: a technical guide. IEEE Tabletops Interact. Surf. **2**, 11 (2008)
24. Brooke, J.: SUS-A quick and dirty usability scale. Usability Eval. Ind. **189**(194), 4–7 (1996)
25. Villafuerte, L., Markova, M., Jorda, S.: Acquisition of social abilities through musical tangible user interface: children with autism spectrum condition and the reactable. In: CHI 2012 Extended Abstracts on Human Factors in Computing Systems, pp. 745–760. ACM 2012
26. Chen, W.: Multitouch tabletop technology for people with autism spectrum disorder: a review of the literature. Procedia Comput. Sci. **14**(2012), 198–207 (2012)
27. Nikolaidou, G.N.: ComPLuS model: a new insight in pupils' collaborative talk, actions and balance during a computer-mediated music task. Comput. Educ. **58**(2), 740–765 (2012)
28. Marco, J., Cerezo, E., Baldassarri, S.: Lowering the threshold and raising the ceiling of tangible expressiveness in hybrid board-games. Multimedia Tools Appl. **75**(1), 425–463 (2016)

Relationship Between Video Game Events and Player Emotion Based on EEG

Duo Chen[1], Joseph James[2], Forrest Sheng Bao[3], Chen Ling[2(✉)],
and Tianzhe Fan[4]

[1] School of Biological Science and Medical Engineering,
Southeast University, Nanjing, China
230139426@seu.edu.cn
[2] Department of Mechanical Engineering, University of Akron, Akron, OH, USA
jjj27@zips.uakron.edu, cling@uakron.edu
[3] Department of Electrical and Computer Engineering,
University of Akron, Akron, OH, USA
fbao5@uakron.edu
[4] Jackson High School, Massillon, OH, USA
clarkftz@gmail.com

Abstract. Real-time immersive virtual dynamic environments in video game are gaining ground recently. A task is correctly detecting user emotions during video gaming. However, there is a lack of study on emotion changes triggered by events in video games and whether we can predict the potential engagement of players. In this work, we carry out an EEG-based study on the relationship between emotion changes and events in video gaming. Twenty participants played 3 types of video games and their EEG data were used to study two common emotions in game playing: excitement and frustration. Highly linear correlation with statistical significance between game events and emotion changes was found. This relationship may provide game designer valuable reference to improve game designing with better user satisfaction.

Keywords: EEG · Game event · Emotion · Correlation analysis

1   Introduction

Providing gaming experience adaptive to the player's real-time mental states is important to game designing [2]. For example, games can be adapted to match players' emotions in gaming process [6]. Recent study shows that emotion output can be used to give user more immersive experience and more satisfaction in video gaming [9]. However, the relationship between emotion changes and game events remains unclear. In this paper, we hypothesize that emotion changes are consistently triggered by game events. Our goal is to answer how are emotion changes and game events are correlated which can inspire game designers using detectable human emotions to provide better gaming experience.

© Springer International Publishing Switzerland 2016
M. Kurosu (Ed.): HCI 2016, Part III, LNCS 9733, pp. 377–384, 2016.
DOI: 10.1007/978-3-319-39513-5_35

A practical way to quantify human emotion in gaming system is to use electroencephalogram (EEG), which has been tested as part of many gaming systems as a user input or a supplement to traditional inputs [4,6,10]. Existing literature has proven the feasibility to measure "emotions" from EEG [8]. Therefore, in this study, we carried out an experiment of 20 participants with moderate gaming experience and analyzed their emotion changes along with events in the game. Three representative games were used to provide good coverage of this study.

Data analysis focusing on two typical emotions in gaming, namely excitement and frustration, a highly linear correlation ($R^2 = 0.97$ for both emotions) was found between event occurrences and emotion changes in video gaming. On average, a game event is followed by an emotion peak detected in EEG after 35.58 s for excitement, and 24.77 s for frustration.

This research is the first on this topic to the best of the authors knowledge. It proves the strong correlation between emotion changes and triggering gaming events. We hope the conclusion drawn from this study can help game designers altering game characteristics to improve user immersion and satisfaction.

2   Methodology

2.1   Data Acquisition

Emotiv EPOC+ EEG headset was used to record human EEG and to extract the emotions using Emotiv's APIs [9]. Many research studies in the past few years have supported the reliability and accuracy of this head set [1,5] and its capability to detect emotions [3,7]. The sampling rate of 14-channel EEG is 128 Hz. Five emotions can be extracted by Emotiv's APIs: 1. meditation, 2. engagement/boredom, 3. long-term excitement, 4. short-term excitement, and 5. frustration. Emotiv's API measures emotion using *emotion intensity*, a normalized value between 0 and 1.

Twenty participants were recruited for the experiment, consisting of 18 males and 2 female between the ages of 18 and 45, with an average age of 25.5 years. Participants were randomly assigned to one of the 3 games.

Before the test, each participant completed a game experience survey. The summary of their game experience is shown in Table 1.

The participants' average gaming experience was moderately good. Their facial expression and game screen are also recorded for event-emotion correlation analysis.

Our experiment environment was set up to simulate a natural gaming environment like a living room. The gaming device was an XBox One connected to a 32-inch TV. One camera recorded participant's facial expression while the TV screen was also recorded for event annotation afterwards.

2.2   Experimental Design

For each participant, the experiment consists of four states (Fig. 1), beginning with picking one of the 3 games: Battlefield 4 (shooting), Forza 5 (racing), and

Table 1. Game experience survey from 20 subjects

Subject	Game	Gender	Age	Game frequency	Game skill
01	Shooting	Female	2	monthly	Fair
02	Shooting	Male	1	monthly	Fair
03	Racing	Male	1	daily	Fair
04	Shooting	Male	1	yearly	Fair
05	Pool	Male	1	yearly	Bad
06	Racing	Male	2	yearly	Bad
07	Pool	Male	1	daily	Good
08	Pool	Male	3	monthly	Good
09	Shooting	Male	2	daily	Fair
10	Shooting	Male	2	yearly	Fair
11	Racing	Female	2	yearly	Bad
12	Racing	Male	1	monthly	Good
13	Shooting	Male	1	daily	Good
14	Racing	Male	2	yearly	Bad
15	Racing	Male	2	yearly	Bad
16	Pool	Male	2	daily	Good
17	pool	Male	3	daily	Fair
18	Pool	Male	1	monthly	Fair
19	Pool	Male	2	yearly	Fair
20	Racing	Male	1	daily	Good

* Game: Shooting $\sim$ BattleField 4; Racing $\sim$ Forza 5; Pool $\sim$ Pure Pool 8.
* Age: 1 for 18 $\sim$ 25; 2 for 26 $\sim$ 35; 3 for 36 $\sim$ 45.

Pool Game (table). Participants rest for 7 min with eyes closed after every 10 min game playing period.

We also record participants' facial expression and game screen for event-emotion correlation analysis. The simultaneously captured video of participant's facial expression and the game screen are shown in Fig. 2.

2.3   Events & Emotions

Since events and emotion intensity are represented differently–the former is a collection of discrete time points while the latter is a signal of constant sampling rate, some conversion is needed in order to study the correlation between them. Our approach is converting emotion intensity into a time series first.

Event occurrences are annotated on recorded video, e.g., hitting a target in shooting game (Battlefield 4) and relative time points of occurrences are extracted using usability software Morae. We define several events which may cause high

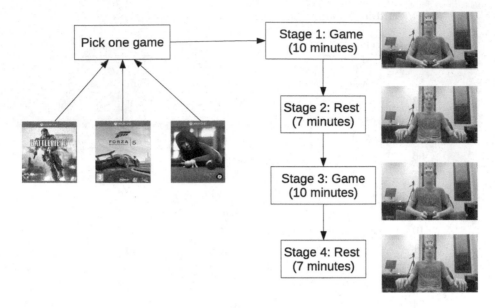

Fig. 1. Experiment flowchart

emotion intensity and extract the events' time from the recorded game. We used three different games in this work, which means the events vary from game to game. In the 5 emotions mentioned above, we choose excitement and frustration in event-emotion correlation analysis. We choose these two emotions because the events they correspond to are easy to be annotated in recorded video. Events associated with short-term excitement and frustration for 3 games are annotated based on video recording of the experiment trials as shown in Table 2.

Table 2. Events used in annotation

	Excitement	Frustration
Battlefield 4	1. hitting target	1. dead
		2. mission failure
Forza 5	1. pass	1. out of lane
	2. good turn	2. getting passed
	3. ranking up	3. collision
Pool	1. goal	1. miss
	2. multiple entries	2. continuous miss

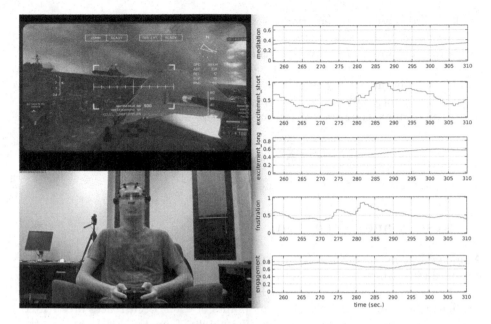

Fig. 2. Game screen (top left), player recording (bottom left) and emotion intensity (right)

2.4   Data Analysis

If game events can regularly stimulate detectable emotion changes, game designers can use emotions as the objective feedback of players to improve game performance. An ideal condition is a single game event can trigger a dependent emotion peak with high likelihood which means the relationship between the time series of event occurrences and emotion peaks should be linear. To test this assumption, linear regression is used for event-emotion correlation analysis.

Events associated with short-term excitement and frustration for 3 games are annotated based on video recording of the experiment trials as shown in Fig. 2. Events vary from game to game. Events associated with short-term excitement and frustration for 3 games are annotated based on video recording of the experiment trials as shown in Table 2. We choose these two emotions since they are easy to be captured and annotated in video recording. Video totally in 6 h 40 mins are annotated manually by two researchers. An event is considered "true event" only if it is marked by both researchers. We use the time points of annotated events to establish a square-wave which is the Y vector of the same length as vector X. Then, we calculate the correlation coefficient between X and Y.

If we denote the event time points as a vector $\mathbf{Y} = [y_1, \ldots, y_N]$ for one type of event in one trial, the emotion intensity for one type of emotion in the same trial is a function I from time points $\{t_1, \ldots, t_M\}$ to intensity values $\{a_1, \ldots, a_M\}$, such that $a_i = I(t_i), \forall i \in [1..M]$.

Then we convert the emotion intensity into a vector of time series $\mathbf{X} = [x_1, \ldots, x_N]$. $\forall y_i \in \mathbf{Y}$, $x_i = \arg\max(a_p, \ldots, a_q)$ such that $y_i \leq t_i \leq y_{i+1}, \forall i \in [p..q]$. In other words, for any event time points y_i, x_i is the time point of the maximum emotion intensity (called *emotion peak*) between an event point y_i and the next event point $y_i + 1$.

With N-point vectors $\mathbf{X}$ representing the emotion peaks and the event vector $\mathbf{Y}$, we can compute the cross-correlation coefficient between event and emotion by

$$r_{xy} = \frac{\sum_{i=1}^{n}(x_i - \bar{x})(y_i - \bar{y})}{\sqrt{\sum_{i=1}^{n}(x_i - \bar{x})^2(y_i - \bar{y})^2}} \tag{1}$$

where $\bar{x}$ and $\bar{y}$ are the means of $\mathbf{X}$ and $\mathbf{Y}$.

3   Results and Discussion

As introduced in Subsect. 2.4, we use time points of annotated events to establish a square-wave which is the Y vector (blue dots in Fig. 3) of the same length as emotion peaks vector X (red dots in Fig. 3). Then, we calculate the correlation coefficient between X and Y. The time points of event occurrences are treated as the independent variable, while the time points of emotion peaks are treated as the dependent variable.

We present results from a typical subject in Fig. 3. Data from other subjects shows similar results. The results reveal a high correlation between events and emotion peaks.

The linear regression between the two vectors reveals a high linear relationship between events and emotion peaks, with an average goodness-of-fit $R^2 = 0.97$ among all subjects for both excitement and frustration (Column R^2 in Table 3). Some subjects do not produce enough emotion data points of excitement or frustration for linear regression (fewer than 5 data points), results of these subjects are denoted as NaN in Table 3.

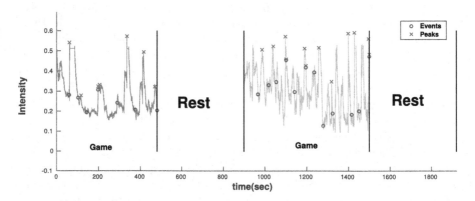

Fig. 3. Emotion intensity of one subject with events and emotion peaks marked. (color figure online)

Table 3. Result of regression analysis (20 subjects)

Subject	Excitement					Frustration				
	Slope	Intercept	STD	R^2	Ratio	Slope	Intercept	STD	R^2	Ratio
01	NaN					1.00	-44.72	93.84	0.97	67.86 %
02	0.96	-20.52	53.01	0.96	55.88 %	NaN				
03	1.02	-39.92	50.54	0.99	56.76 %	1.00	-38.08	41.70	0.94	66.67 %
04	1.06	-105.39	106.42	0.94	54.55 %	NaN				
05	1.05	-99.01	61.69	0.95	81.36 %	0.99	-11.23	20.86	0.99	90.74 %
06	1.06	-117.72	98.92	0.96	62.50 %	0.98	-17.23	28.61	0.99	68.29 %
07	1.00	-12.63	24.38	0.99	89.23 %	1.00	-30.28	64.79	0.98	76.92 %
08	0.98	-24.23	67.23	0.98	63.41 %	1.01	-19.43	44.88	0.91	81.67 %
09	0.99	-22.17	92.33	0.97	63.64 %	NaN				
10	0.99	-17.64	66.31	0.98	80.39 %	0.97	-18.69	75.87	0.97	69.70 %
11	1.01	-43.78	59.16	0.98	66.67 %	0.99	-21.72	0.97	76.09 %	
12	0.99	-10.54	15.46	0.99	79.31 %	NaN				
13	1.01	-27.41	35.53	0.99	64.29 %	NaN				
14	0.96	-30.70	132.35	0.92	43.59 %	1.03	-21.04	43.71	0.99	92.86 %
15	1.00	-26.58	64.35	0.98	75.44 %	1.00	-26.38	42.88	0.99	73.33 %
16	1.00	-12.01	71.96	0.98	88.71 %	0.97	-15.02	53.46	0.97	60.00 %
17	0.99	-19.57	68.35	0.98	66.67 %	1.01	-31.73	29.56	0.99	64.44 %
18	1.03	-31.23	66.90	0.98	72.34 %	0.99	-11.63	15.07	0.99	82.46 %
19	0.95	-3.15	80.45	0.95	58.33 %	0.99	-31.82	79.77	0.96	50.00 %
20	0.98	-11.79	26.53	0.99	77.14 %	0.97	-32.54	51.67	0.99	53.57 %
Average	1.00	-35.58	65.36	0.97	68.43 %	0.99	-24.77	50.86	0.97	71.64 %

A consistent slope of approximately 1 (Column Slope in Table 3) of linear regression results show the time-invariant delay between emotion peaks and events. The delay can be represented by the intercept of linear regression (Column Intercept in Table 3). The average delays across all subjects for excitement and frustration are -35.58 and -24.77 s, respectively, meaning an average delay of less than half minute. The proximity between a blue circle and its following red circle in Fig. 3 illustrates the duration of the delay.

The consistency of delay can be measured by the standard deviation (Column STD in Table 3) of prediction error of the linear regression model on all samples. For most subjects, the standard deviation is under 2 min, meaning the maximum 2 min error between true emotion peak and predicted emotion peak. The maximum standard deviation is 132.35 s for Subject 14 on excitement.

Although the regression result is promising, we need to eliminate the possibility that the high correlation is due to how we constructed the emotion peak vectors (e.g., local maximums between two consecutive events). Hence we calculate the ratio between game event related emotion peaks and all emotion peaks (Column Ratio in Table 3). The average ratio is 68.43 % for excitement and 71.64 % for frustration, indicating that emotion peaks are very likely to be yielded by game events.

4   Conclusion

In this work, we investigated how human emotion respond to game events during video gaming. Two important conclusions drawn from the emotion-event correlation analysis are: first, the human brain is very sensitive to events in video gaming as demonstrated by emotion peaks appearing around half a minute after onset of event; second, the one-to-one correspondence between game events and emotion peaks can be quantitatively and reliably established. The strong correlation between game events and human emotion shows promising evidence that game designers could use event-triggered emotion to design adaptive immersive game for better user experience.

Acknowledgement. We acknowledge Microsoft for its support of this work.

References

1. Badcock, N.A., Mousikou, P., Mahajan, Y., de Lissa, P., Thie, J., McArthur, G.: Validation of the emotiv EPOC (R) EEG gaming systemfor measuring research quality auditory ERPs. PeerJ **3**, e907 (2013)
2. Bernays, R., Mone, J., Yau, P., Murcia, M., Gonzalez-Sanchez, J., Chavez-Echeagaray, M.E., Christopherson, R., Atkinson, R.: Lost in the dark: emotion adaption. In: Adjunct Proceedings of the 25th Annual ACM Symposium on User Interface Software and Technology. ASSOC Computing Machinery (2012)
3. Blaiech, H., Neji, M., Wali, A., Alimi, A.M.: Emotion recognition by analysis of EEG signals. In: 2013 13th International Conference on Hybrid Intelligent Systems (HIS) (2013)
4. Chumerin, N., Manyakov, N., van Vliet, M., Robben, A., Combaz, A., Van Hulle, M.: Steady-state visual evoked potential-based computer gaming on a consumer-grade EEG device. IEEE Trans. Comput. Intell. AI Games **5**, 100 (2013)
5. Ekandem, J.I., Davis, T.A., Alvarez, I., James, M.T., Gilbert, J.E.: Evaluating the ergonomics of BCI devices for research and experimentation. Ergonomics **55**, 592 (2012)
6. Gomez-Gil, J., San-Jose-Gonzalez, I., Fernando Nicolas-Alonso, L., Alonso-Garcia, S.: Steering a tractor by means of an EMG-based human-machine interface. Sensors **11**, 7110 (2011)
7. Khushaba, R.N., Greenacre, L., Kodagoda, S., Louviere, J., Burke, S., Dissanayake, G.: Choice modeling and the brain: a study on the Electroencephalogram (EEG) of preferences. Expert Syst. Appl. **39**, 12378 (2012)
8. Liu, Y., Sourina, O., Nguyen, M.K.: Real-time EEG-based human emotion recognition and visualization. In: 2010 International Conference on Cyberworlds (CW) (2010)
9. Vinhas, V., Oliveira, E., Reis, L.P.: BioStories: dynamic multimedia environments based on real-time audience emotion assessment. In: Filipe, J., Cordeiro, J. (eds.) ICEIS 2010. LNBIP, vol. 73, pp. 512–525. Springer, Heidelberg (2011)
10. Wolpaw, J.R., McFarland, D.J.: Control of a two-dimensional movement signal by a noninvasive brain-computer interface in humans. In: Proceedings of the National Academy of Sciences of the United States of America (2004)

A Practical Evaluation of the Influence of Input Devices on Playability

Lucas Machado[(✉)] and João Luiz Bernardes Jr.

School of Arts, Sciences and Humanities (EACH),
Universidade de São Paulo, São Paulo, Brazil
{lucas2.machado,jlbernardes}@usp.br

Abstract. Innovations being achieved with interactive devices (screens, sensors etc.) allow the development of new forms of interaction for many applications. Videogames played with these devices are completely changing how we use them and taking advantage of intuitive interfaces. Based on that, we ask "What aspects of playability are affected using different input devices for a certain gaming task and how is gaming performance affected?". Our contribution is to present a practical evaluation of four different input devices (Mouse, Gamepad, Kinect and Touchscreen) used to interact with the same game, Fruit Ninja, with our data analysis indicating that changing input device brings significant differences in certain aspects of player experience for this game, such as sensation, challenge and control, while for others there was very little difference since this particular game rarely provides intense experiences for those aspects.

Keywords: Emotions in HCI · Entertainment systems · Evaluation methods and techniques · User experience · Input devices

1 Introduction

Videogames nowadays are relevant both as an economic activity and as a subject of scientific research. Economic relevance is due to, for instance, the large growth of this sector, particularly when compared to the average growth of other areas and of national economies as a whole [1]. Scientific relevance is shown in game research in several areas and applications, such as Human Computer Interaction studies or gamefication techniques being applied in education, among many other examples. Research based on videogames has a ludic nature which keeps user attention for longer periods and provides experiences such as exploration, challenge, competition, and collaboration [2], that are different from the experiences expected from traditional productivity software.

While playability relates to user experience in videogames, there is not a *de facto* definition for it. However, as the traditional usability evaluation heuristics are used with user interfaces in productivity software, several authors have tried to propose frameworks to evaluate Player Experience in videogames, considering the particular properties of this medium [3]. Thus, in the same way that usability

© Springer International Publishing Switzerland 2016
M. Kurosu (Ed.): HCI 2016, Part III, LNCS 9733, pp. 385–395, 2016.
DOI: 10.1007/978-3-319-39513-5_36

in software aims to improve users productivity with a set of heuristics related to ease-of-use and simplification of interfaces and tasks [4], proposals of playability heuristics aim to improve game experience with characteristics like challenge, fantasy, humor, exploration etc. [2].

Human Computer Interaction happens through input and output devices and, as Bonarini et al. [5] notes, the interaction with devices turns out to be more important than perceptual realism of the game in how strong a relationship can be established between the game and the user. Also as Alvarez et al. [6] points out, over the last decades the devices we use to interact with games have evolved considerably, and these changes shaped our usage and, thus, our experience of interaction and play. These studies show opportunities for research on the area of input devices and playability, like the work of Lee and Chung [7], that analyses psychological experiences of gamers, in which the results demonstrated that the controller was significant in the perceived interactivity, spatial involvement, dynamic immersion, and realistic immersion. However, there are still few studies and a gap in literature relating input devices to specific game experiences, especially if compared to usability studies of traditional productivity software, and a question can be elaborated of top of it: "What aspects of playability are affected by using different input devices for a certain gaming task, and how is the gaming performance affected?".

Our objective is to address this question by selecting criteria and metrics of playability evaluation in the literature that relate to interactions and input methods and also to the subjective aspects of player experience, preparing and carrying out observational experiments with a particular videogame, and establishing what are the most appropriate metrics for evaluation of interaction of users with games, under certain devices and tasks, and then conducting an experiment and analyzing the data to investigate whether different devices could produce different game experiences, to establish a framework to facilitate the understanding of the relationship between playability and input devices.

An experiment was then conducted, in which voluntary users were asked to play a game alternating between four different input devices: Mouse, Gamepad, Touchscreen and Microsoft Kinect. After the experiment, the users answered a questionnaire that collected data about their experiences. One limitation is that the chosen game (*Fruit Ninja*) does not have the capacity to strongly generate all the possible experiences (e.g. eroticism or fellowship), and a more extensive experiment is required to analyze them under longer gaming sessions (probably in an immersible Role Playing Game that could emulate all these experiences, or using different games for different experiences). This limitation does, however, provide an opportunity to test the quality of experimental results, since we expect the experiences not evoked by the game to be ranked uniformly low by users and, thus, to show little difference between input devices. We are also purposefully focusing on these experiences separately from questions related to ergonomics or the physical strain of prolonged use, which is why the experiment is composed of only a few short, one-minute play sessions (which is the default duration for one of Fruit Ninja's modes).

As a contribution, our results could help in game development processes, for example by choosing the best interaction devices and techniques based on the desired experiences. The process of evaluation itself can also be reproduced for other games or devices and even during development and can be considered another contribution. Further studies could also help in considering player experiences during controller design.

After a statistical analysis of the data collected on the experiment, differences between user experiences in different devices were found. As expected, several emotions showed very little difference between devices or any intensity at all during this experiment. Sensation, Fantasy, Challenge, Expression and Control, in that order were the aspects which showed the most significant differences between different devices. Kinect was the preferred input device, followed by touch.

2   Related Work

There is not a consensus yet about a most accepted set of heuristics for playability evaluation, but there are some promising studies trying to define it. The set of Heuristic Evaluation for Playability (HEP) by Desurvire et al. [8] is focused on *expert evaluation* during the development phase of a game, as well as on aspects related to gameplay, game story mechanics and usability. Since these heuristics are more direct and objective, and they are not strongly linked to player feelings, it was not adequate to our purposes. The set of heuristics described by Koeel et al. [9] is based on the previous cited HEP and on *expert evaluation* as a test framework and it is also strongly related to game mechanics.

Other research exists relating user experiences and interactions to games and input and output devices. Lee and Chung [7] studied gamer experiences according to display and controller, but focusing more on physical or materially perceived experiences comparing 2D to 3D environments. Bonarini et al. [5] also studies wearability and comfort of devices and their physiological effects on users, and while this could relate to player experience with different devices, it is still distant from players emotions and feelings, that could be mapped do playability heuristics.

Chu et al. [10] proposed a playability matrix based on an analysis of methodologies for evaluating player experience in game play. It was used in this work in conjunction with the previous cited literature research to define our framework of evaluation, based on the playful experiences (PLEX) framework. As described by Lucero et al. [2], the PLEX framework summarized heuristics of playability evaluation of several other theoretical works on pleasurable experiences, game experiences, emotions, elements of play and reasons why people play. Since it deals with experiences as feelings and emotions themselves, it is the best fitted set of heuristics to abstract from the experiences we want to identify on players with different devices.

Thus, since there are no studies specifically treating and comparing the relation of different input devices and user experiences and emotions in games, we try to fill this gap by using PLEX heuristics to evaluate a set of devices under determined tasks.

3   Evaluation of Input Devices

Since different input devices provide different user interactions, different devices could be needed to keep the usability of a system high depending on the user interface and the tasks to be executed. We ask then, for a specific set of tasks and interfaces, how different input devices affect the playability of a game.

Therefore, our objective in the experiment is to propose and establish playability metrics and criteria to evaluate certain input devices (mouse, gamepad, touchscreen and Kinect) for certain tasks in a game.

3.1   Methodology

An experiment was conducted with 13 voluntary users in a controlled environment, in which they were asked to play the game *Fruit Ninja* in arcade mode (for the period of one minute, only once after a training game), alternating between four different input devices: Mouse, Gamepad, Touchscreen and Microsoft Kinect. After the experiment, users anonymously answered a questionnaire ranking their device preference, previous experiences with the devices, and the intensity of their experiences in several aspects with each device. Not all of the emotions and experiences described in PLEX are expected to be present in a game like *Fruit Ninja*, but we chose to use the questionnaire without modification and let the collected data show the truth of this. Therefore, we chose to evaluate experiences of Captivation, Challenge, Competition, Completion, Control, Cruelty, Discovery, Eroticism, Exploration, Expression, Fantasy, Fellowship, Humor, Nurture, Relaxation, Sensation, Simulation, Submission, Subversion, Suffering, Sympathy, and Thrill. The experiment sessions were previously scheduled to prevent conflicts and interruptions and a period of one hour was reserved for each session. Despite the relatively low number of participants, experimental results showed good statistical significance.

Risks. During this experiment, participants were exposed to minor physical discomfort risks, such as aspects of posture, reading distance, illumination and noise, or dirtiness or contamination through devices they touched. Another possible risk is embarrassment by skill confrontation, since the experiment protocol could be interpreted to ask some participants to perform above their skill levels. To mitigate all of these risks, devices were cleaned after each use, adaptations to specific physical conditions of the participants were available, and participants were not encouraged to pay attention to their in-game scores and asked to execute the task in the way they felt most comfortable. They were also told they could ask questions and interrupt or leave the experiment at any time.

Participants. We had thirteen participants recruited in our university. They were mainly students or professors. The average age was 24.5 years (ranging from 17 to 38, with a standard deviation of 6.86), and 7.7 % of them identified themselves as women (92.3 % identified as men).

Table 1. Participants previous experiences on devices

Experience	None	Little	Average	A lot
With Fruit Ninja game	15.4%	23.1%	53.8%	7.7%
With touch screen	7.7%	0%	23.1%	69.2%
With mouse	15.4%	7.7%	15.4%	61.5%
With gamepad	15.4%	23.1%	46.2%	15.4%
With Kinect	38.5%	30.8%	15.4%	15.4%

As we can see in the Table 1, the devices with which participants had more previous experience were touchscreen, mouse, gamepad, and Kinect, in decreasing order. More than half of the participants knew the game well and only 15.4% of them had never played it. Touchscreens were also reported as a more common device than the mouse, perhaps because of their current extensive use in smartphones. Participant experience with gamepad was more varied, probably because videogames have been in the market for decades and, despite not being as ubiquitous as smartphones in Brazil, they are still quite popular. The Kinect device, on the other hand, was unknown or little known for most participants, probably due to the fact that it is a rather new device and available only in a specific platform (the Xbox console).

3.2 Instruments

For each of the forms of input being evaluated and to answer the questionnaire, several devices were used. In the Kinect evaluation, an Xbox 360 console with a Kinect attached to a video projector were used. The setup was that the projected screen size was about 32 in. on its diagonal, and the user was about 4 meters from it. The image was never obstructed by any of the devices. The projector (or a large screen) was necessary because the users have to be at a certain minimum distance from the kinect so it can capture their image, and playing the game in a smaller monitor from this distance would be impractical. For the touch screen evaluation, a third generation iPad was used. In both mouse and gamepad evaluation, a 13-inch MacBook Air running Windows 10 in a virtual machine environment was used, with a common mouse and an Xbox One controller wired via USB. The participants played on the computer screen.

The questionnaire was also answered on the computer. We implemented a simple web service with a wizard interface so the participant could go through the questions and assign a value for the perceived intensity for each of the PLEX categories and for every device. Visual aids and descriptions about the experiences were used to help identifying and understanding them: Captivation (Forgetting one's surroundings), Challenge (Testing abilities in a demanding task), Competition (Contest with oneself or an opponent), Completion (Finishing a major task, closure), Control (Dominating, controlling, regulating), Cruelty (Causing mental or physical pain), Discovery (Finding something new or unknown), Eroticism

(A sexually arousing experience), Exploration (Investigating an object or situation), Expression (Manifesting oneself creatively), Fantasy (An imagined experience), Fellowship (Friendship, communality or intimacy), Humor (Fun, joy, amusement, jokes, gags), Nurture (Taking care of oneself or others), Relaxation (Relief from bodily or mental work), Sensation (Exciting by stimulating senses), Simulation (An imitation of everyday life), Submission (Being part of a larger structure), Subversion (Breaking social rules and norms), Suffering (Experience of loss, frustration, anger), Sympathy (Sharing emotional feelings), and Thrill (Excitement derived from risk, danger). Because all users were native speakers of Brazilian Portuguese, this was the language actually used in the questionnaire.

To adapt gamepad input signals to the game, we used Xpadder software. It maps and simulates controller input as keyboard and mouse. For our tests, we mapped the left analog stick as mouse movement, and the "A" button as a left click. That way, the user should simulate mouse movements by pressing "A" while moving the stick to simulate the cutting blade movement.

For the game installations, we used the official versions of *Fruit Ninja* for iOS and Kinect. For the tests on the computer (with mouse and gamepad), we used an unofficial version that was ported to PC but has the same dynamics and graphics, except for the pomegranate bonus in the end that was missing. Fruit Ninja was chosen because it is possible to run it under different platforms for different input devices and because the game itself is simple to understand and has an arcade game mode that lasts for one minute, standardizing the sessions between players and devices.

3.3   Experimental Procedure

After agreeing to an Informed Consent document, in which participants could also read about aspects of the experiment pertaining to themselves, such as its objectives and risks, they were asked to interact with the game in arcade mode for one minute and only once per device, as the test task. Participants could remove their consent or leave the test at any moment without having to give any explanations. Initially we randomly chose the order of the first three devices between mouse, touchscreen and gamepad. We set Kinect always as the last one since it requires greater physical effort and this could influence the evaluation of other devices.

Before each device evaluation, participants could try the device in a training session in the same game mode (arcade) for one minute. It was an optional choice and they often decided to skip the training if they already had previous experience with the game or with the device.

At the end of the experiment, participants were asked to answer the questionnaire. Participants had to fill in their age, gender identity, and their previous experience with the game and with each of the devices used in the experiment. For these questions, a scale of one to four was used, with one being *no experience* and four *plenty of experience*. This was followed by a series of 22 questions (one for each experience according to the PLEX framework [2] we chose). Participants were asked to evaluate the intensity of their experiences in a scale of zero to ten for each device, for every experience, with zero denoting no intensity and ten full intensity. Finally, participants were asked to sort the devices by how much they enjoyed each to execute the tasks in the game. An optional field allowed participants to write any relevant comments they wanted to express. After each session, devices were cleaned and games were restarted to prepare for a next session.

4 Results

Data collected from the questionnaire answers were extracted and the Analysis of Variance (ANOVA) method was applied to analyze the scores participants provided to the aspects of their experience for each of the devices.

The results show differences between user experiences in different devices. As expected, several emotions (half of the set of experiences) showed very little difference between devices or any intensity at all during this experiment. Sensation, Fantasy, Challenge, Expression, Control, Humor, Thrill, Suffering, Simulation, Captivation and Exploration, in order from most to least difference, were the aspects which showed significant differences between different devices.

Table 2. F-values and P-values of variables with significant difference

	F-value	P-value
Sensation	10.27027027	0.0000245473656
Fantasy	8.528064993	0.0001208619902
Challenge	8.521854305	0.0001215729081
Expression	8.296525097	0.0001505365208
Control	7.230474732	0.0004240317507
Humor	6.399884426	0.0009783774656
Thrill	5.867	0.001696429971
Suffering	5.838978015	0.001746782684
Simulation	4.710676447	0.005819916856
Captivation	3.269876003	0.02907170146
Exploration	3.161100196	0.03292371113

With our data and an alpha of 0.05, an F-critical of 2.798 was calculated in the ANOVA procedure. Figure 1 shows a comparison of the averages of each device for the experiences that had a F-value greater than the F-critical, according to the values of Table 2.

There was also no substantial correlation between preferred devices and previous experience with them. As Fig. 2 shows, Kinect was the preferred input device, followed by touch. Participants disliked using the gamepad a lot, since it was considerably harder to play the game with it, and a few of them reported

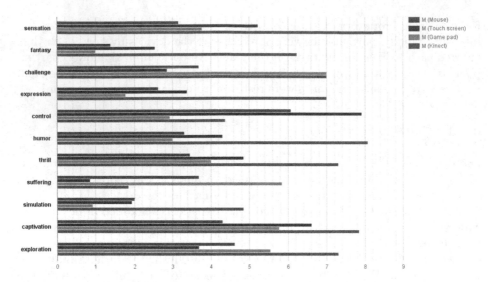

Fig. 1. Comparison of averages between devices for the most significant differences in experiences

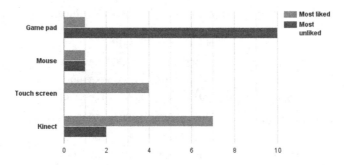

Fig. 2. What devices participants liked and disliked the most

disliking Kinect because they felt it gave them less control over the game due to lack of physical contact with the device.

The raw data obtained in the experiment is available at https://drive.google.com/file/d/0B7274IzRmrS8OS13dVBWbk42NVU.

5   Discussion

We reached our initial objective of evaluating players experiences through different devices. It was clear that almost every experience was more intense when using the Kinect device, except for Control and Suffering. We believe this is related to the use of the whole body (particularly the arms in this case) to control the game, which even allowed the use of both hands, together or separately, in an intuitive way and occasionally led to humorous situations. Other factors may have affected the experience with Kinect. Some of them are common to most videogame experiences with this device, such as necessitating a larger screen and standing some distance from it. Other differences, related to our experimental setup, appear to have had little or no impact. While game versions for Xbox, iPad and PC were different, gameplay, graphics, sound and other features were very similar in all of them except for the method of input. We also investigated whether the lack of experience with this device could be responsible for its high scores, due to some sort of novelty effect, but there was little correlation between these scores and experience with Kinect (and users with average or high experience also scored high on the relevant experience aspects when using it). We believe the aspect of control was low for the Kinect because interactions using it occur without physical contact, so users have no tactile feedback and rely solely on visual and aural cues about how the game reacts to their input. The low intensity of Suffering on Kinect might be caused by the higher intensity of other positive aspects which help prevent emotions of anger and frustration. Touch-screen provided the least Suffering experience, since users were manipulating the game directly and could feel that difficulties they had originated from themselves and not from the device interaction (incidentally, the game was initially developed with this device in mind).

It is also worth noting the high intensity of Challenge and Suffering with the gamepad, since it is a device best suited to directional controls and hard to use in the chosen game. However, The intensity of Captivation and Exploration were also high for this device, suggesting that participants were interested by the difficulties and in learning how to use it for this game.

Touch screen demonstrated the highest intensity of control when comparing to the other studied devices. This is probably because it is a direct manipulation device in which users could directly *feel* their fingertips *cutting* the fruits on the screen. Mouse followed touchscreen closely in Control experience, perhaps because its use is common among all the participants and it feels as natural and easy to control the cursor as with direct manipulation. Despite Kinect also looking realistic and natural with its movements recognition, the game control is indirect since the user has to command a shadow of himself on the screen, therefore not achieving the same level of Control experience. However, Fantasy intensity on Kinect was noticeably high among other devices, being explained by the realism of doing body movements that looked like a ninja (the game's avowed theme).

Overall we can observe that the Kinect device could improve the intensity of player experiences and feelings for games of this type, especially fantasy and humor, but that it reduces the feeling of control (which might be desirable or not depending on the desired game experience). The Gamepad device offers difficulty and challenge since it is not best suited for the chosen game. Mouse tends to follow touchscreen, usually with slightly less intense emotions, and players feel good control on touchscreens since its direct manipulations feels natural.

As this work was conducted with only one game, Fruit Ninja, some experiences such as eroticism and fellowship could not be easily aroused on the participants.

An experiment with a longer gaming session using a game which has the capacity of stimulating all the experiences, such as an immersible and social RPG, or several smaller games, each stimulating different experiences, would be necessary to have a wider understanding of their relations with input devices.

Other input devices were also considered to be for inclusion in this study, but left out due to time and resource limitations. Future work could try to reproduce the experiments with other games and devices such as Leap Motion, Intel RealSense, graphics tablets, game paddles, or even voice control.

Future work in the design of input devices and in game designing could also benefit from our contribution and the contribution of further experimentation along this line in what concerns which specific experiences the designer aims to provide. The better understanding of the relationship between playability and input devices allows the translation of usability concepts to the field of videogame studies and design, but relating to player experiences and feelings and ways to analyze them.

We expect that more studies along these lines will be made since interaction device technology is improving quickly and also becoming more pervasive. In a world of different devices that collect data and commands from users for games, it is valuable to understand how users feel and react to these devices.

References

1. Makuch, E.: Video game industry grows four times faster than US economy, ESA says (2014). http://www.gamespot.com/articles/video-game-industry-grows-four-times-faster-than-u/1100-6423536/
2. Lucero, A., Holopainen, J., Ollila, E., Suomela, R., Karapanos, E.: The playful experiences (plex) framework as a guide for expert evaluation. In: Proceedings of the 6th International Conference on Designing Pleasurable Products and Interfaces, DPPI 2013, p. 221 (2013). doi:10.1145/2513506.2513530, http://dl.acm.org/citation.cfm?d=2513506.2513530
3. Paavilainen, J.: Critical review on video game evaluation heuristics. In: Proceedings of the International Academic Conference on the Future of Game Design and Technology, pp. 56–65 (2010). doi:10.1145/1920778.1920787, http://dl.acm.org/citation.cfm?id=1920787
4. Turner-Bowker, D.M., Saris-Baglama, R.N., Smith, K.J., DeRosa, M.A., Paulsen, C.A., Hogue, S.J.: Heuristic evaluation of user interfaces. Telemed. J. e-Health Official J. Am. Telemed. Assoc. 17, 40–45 (1990). doi:10.1089/tmj.2010.0114. CHI 2009. http://online.liebertpub.com//abs/10.1089/tmj.2010.0114
5. Bonarini, A., Costa, F., Garbarino, M., Matteucci, M., Romero, M., Tognetti, S.: Affective videogames: the problem of wearability and comfort. In: Jacko, J.A. (ed.) Human-Computer Interaction, Part IV, HCII 2011. LNCS, vol. 6764, pp. 649–658. Springer, Heidelberg (2011). doi:10.1007/978-3-642-21619-0-77
6. Alvarez, J., Haudegond, S., Havrez, C., Kolski, C., Lebrun, Y., Lepreux, S., Libessart, A.: From screens to devices and tangible objects: a framework applied to serious games characterization. In: Kurosu, M. (ed.) HCI 2014, Part III. LNCS, vol. 8512, pp. 559–570. Springer, Heidelberg (2014). doi:10.1007/978-3-319-07227-2-53

7. Lee, H., Chung, D.: Influence of gaming display and controller on perceived characteristics, perceived interactivity, presence, and discomfort. In: Kurosu, M. (ed.) HCII/HCI 2013, Part II. LNCS, vol. 8005, pp. 258–265. Springer, Heidelberg (2013). doi:10.1007/978-3-642-39262-7-29
8. Desurvire, H., Caplan, M., Toth, A.F.: Using heuristics to evaluate the playability of games. In: CHI 2004 Extended Abstracts on Human Factors in Computing Systems, pp. 1509–1512 (2004). doi:10.1145/985921.986102, http://portal.acm.org/citation.cfm?d=985921.986102
9. Koeffel, C., Hochleitner, W., Leitner, J., Haller, M., Geven, A., Tscheligi, M.: Using heuristics to evaluate the overall user experience of video games and advanced interaction games. In: Bernhaupt, R. (ed.) Evaluating User Experience in Games: Concepts and Methods, pp. 233–256. Springer, London (2010). doi:10.1007/978-1-84882-963-3. http://link.springer.com/chapter/10.1007/978-1-84882-963-3_13
10. Chu, K., Wong, C.Y., Khong, C.W.: Methodologies for evaluating player experience in game play. In: Stephanidis, C. (ed.) Posters, Part I, HCII 2011. CCIS, vol. 173, pp. 118–122. Springer, Heidelberg (2011). doi:10.1007/978-3-642-22098-2

Haptic Relay - Including Haptic Feedback in Online Video Game Streams

Tony Morelli[✉]

Department of Computer Science, Central Michigan University, Mount Pleasant, USA
tony.morelli@cmich.edu

Abstract. The popularity of streaming video game sessions has been on a constant increase. Players stream their games as well as cameras facing them, while providing a description of the game play to the viewers. Fellow players watch the games to learn tips and tricks, as well as to learn what to expect when playing the game themselves. This is a great learning tool; however, the current rendition of streaming video games is missing a key factor in video game satisfaction - tactile feedback. All mainstream video game consoles contain some sort of haptic feedback in the form of a rumble and provides greater immersion in to the game; however, this modality is missing from the live streams. Haptic information in some games is also essential for game play by people who are visually impaired. This paper presents Haptic Relay, a method of providing real time haptic feedback for online video game broadcasts.

Keywords: Haptic interfaces · Games · Streaming media

1 Introduction

Streaming video games across the internet is becoming more popular; however, the vibration cues contained within all modern day console controllers and phones is not present in the online streams. The research presented here is an approach to broadcast haptic cues to better replicate the gameplay experience and to lower the learning curve of new games experienced by game players who are blind.

In 2010, the United States passed the Communications and Video Accessibility Act. This Act requires advanced communications and video broadcasting to be accessible to people who are deaf, blind and deaf-blind. Although the applicability of this Act to video game streams has not be questioned, video game systems are covered under this Act and in the future video game streams may be considered part of this as well. If that is the case, the ideas presented here may be useful for video streams to be compliant.

This paper is organized as follows. First, background information is given on the use of haptic cues in video games, the rise of internet video game streams, and the use of haptic feedback in video game research. Then an approach is described which could enhance online streams and haptic video game. Finally, future work and a conclusion are described.

© Springer International Publishing Switzerland 2016
M. Kurosu (Ed.): HCI 2016, Part III, LNCS 9733, pp. 396–405, 2016.
DOI: 10.1007/978-3-319-39513-5_37

2   History of Haptics in Games

Although vibration (or rumble as it was first known) is standard in modern day gaming systems, it has not always been present. The first mass release of a vibration unit to be used in video games was the Rumble Pack released for the Nintendo 64 in 1997 [1]. This add-on to the controller allowed developers to vibrate the controller when exciting things happened on the screen such as explosions, or when a car was traveling off the road. This innovation was released with the hopes that players would obtain a more realistic gameplay experience while using the device.

Just a few months after Nintendo released the Rumble Pack, Sony released the Dual Shock controller [2]. The Dual Shock controller was named because it contained a vibration motor located against the palm of each hand when holding the controller. This has become the standard location for vibration motors in current generation gaming systems such as the Xbox One and Dual Shock 4 (standard controller for the Playstation 4) which also contain this same design.

The use of haptic feedback in games has been involved in legal battles that have cost the major players in excess of $100 million in legal penalties [5, 6]. Mainly fighting over patents owned by Immersion Corp [4] and Virtual Technologies [3], Sony and Microsoft have invested a lot of money to ensure haptic capabilities remain standard on their game consoles.

3   Streaming Video Games

Twitch has made streaming video games mainstream and popular. In fact, 1.8 % of internet traffic comes from Twitch live streams [8]. Behind Netflix, Google, and Apple, is Twitch. According to Business Insider [9], Twitch accounts for more than 43 % of all live streaming content on the internet and it is producing enough money that people are making a living live streaming games with some reporting more than $100k in yearly income. Business Insider also reports Twitch has more than 55 million active users and 58 % of them have reported an increase in watching live video streams while decreasing the time spent watching videos from other sources including television, and other non-live streaming sites such as YouTube. Amazon purchased Twitch for just under $1 billion [10].

YouTube's most popular broadcaster is PewDiePie, a person who reviews video games and receives over $4 Million a year in revenue [11]. He has over 42 million subscribers to his channel [12]. Video game streaming is very popular and lucrative; however, the streams contain audio and visuals only, the haptic channel is absent. Any kind of enhancement to the video streams may increase the engagement time of viewers and could result in larger revenues for broadcasters and providers due to the potential of selling more advertising.

4 Haptics in Research

The use of haptic feedback in games has been shown to be important. Players prefer haptic feedback to audio when playing full body 3D interactive games [13]. In general, virtual environments have shown to have a higher level of quality of experience when compared to environments that are only audio and visual based [14]; however, this level of experience has not also increased the performance in games [15].

Haptic cues have also been used when creating games for people with disabilities. These games have been used in rehab [16, 17] where the results of the rehabilitation have been better when haptic feedback is used. Games using haptic cues have also been created for people who are blind [18–20]. It is very important for people who are blind to have this additional method of communication to replace required visual aspects of games that are not represented by sounds.

This paper defines methods of haptic capture and retransmission suitable for online game play session video streams. The following sections describe methods of haptic capture, haptic transmission, and haptic replay demonstrated by a small field test. Standards of encoding text with video are analyzed and modifications are suggested to also carry haptic information and finally limitations of the current prototype and future work are discussed.

5 Haptic Capture

Two methods of haptic capture are described in this section. Direct haptic capture involves embedding methods within the game software in order for the game itself to transmit the haptic information. Indirect haptic capture involves the use of a third party capture device that will be able to capture and transmit haptic information from haptic capable controllers.

Direct Haptic Capture. The direct haptic capture is available to games that have haptic relay capabilities embedded directly within the game's source code. These games are required to have full knowledge of the haptic relay protocol described below, and may often be custom games created to comply with this system. Software developers will have to modify existing game such that any code referencing a change in status of any of the haptic motors will also have to inform the remote server of the change in real time.

Indirect Haptic Capture. This method of haptic capture is used when access to the game's source code is not available. A hardware modification to the controller is performed such that the intensity of the vibration motors is recorded and transmitted to the helper service for web disbursement.

A prototype of this method was created using an Xbox 360 wired controller attached to a PC running Windows 8. The Xbox 360 controller contains two different vibration motors located near the bottom of each side of the controller (Fig. 2). The intensity of these motors can be individually controlled through software and is electronically controlled by varying the voltage presented to each of the motors. The higher the voltage, the higher the intensity of the rumble, or the faster the counter weight spins. In order to capture this intensity value, the variable voltage can be measured and used to identify the current state of each of the vibration motors.

In this case, a jumper wire was attached to the positive terminal of each motor and extended through the controller case. During installation of the jumper wires it was noted that the vibration motor on the right of the controller spins counterclockwise, and as a result the ± terminals were swapped in the factory controller. To obtain the positive voltage values, the jumper wire was attached to the negative terminal.

An interface board is required to translate the varying voltage values into something that can be processed by a computer for transmission to a remote device. In this case, an Arduino Duemilanove board was used (Fig. 1). This board contains 6 analog inputs and an USB interface to communicate data to a computer. This provides a standard interface and more than enough analog inputs to handle the 2 values needed to represent the state of the vibration motors contained within the Xbox 360 controller. This board has enough inputs available to capture haptic data from three Xbox 360 controllers. Although this paper presents results using an Xbox 360 controller, the standard Xbox One, Playstation 3 and Playstation 4 controllers also contain 2 vibration motors and a similar modification can presumably be performed to capture data from those controllers as well.

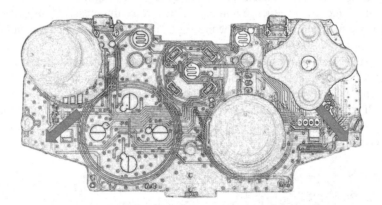

Fig. 1. Indirect haptic capture - read haptic data from XBox 360 controller. Arrows indicate solder points to retrieve left and right haptic values.

The arduino board contains custom firmware which is responsible for reading the values of the analog inputs and pass those values on to the host computer via USB for further processing. The firmware is a simple small infinite loop that reads the analog inputs every 10 ms, formats them in a comma separated string, and then writes them out the USB port. Through basic testing, it was discovered that each of the vibration pins sending voltage to the motors behaved in a similar way when the motor was vibrating vs idle. The arduino board contains a 10 bit analog to digital converter. When the vibration motor was idle, the analog pin on the arduino board reported back a value of 1024. When the motor was at its fastest, the analog pin contained a value of 10. This was the same for both motors within the Xbox 360 controller. Thus a simple formula was created to take those values and normalize them to the range of 0 (no activity) and 1 (full speed).

This was done to eliminate any variation of non-standard values that different interface boards may report back to the host.

6 Haptic Helper Service

The Haptic Helper Service (HHS) is responsible for taking the data from either the direct or indirect haptic capture methods and transmitting them to a remote server such that remote devices can receive this information and replicate the haptic state of the device. Messages passed to the HHS describe the behavior of the haptic motors. The message includes an index of the controller, an index of the haptic motor, and a value of the intensity. This message is passed to the HHS on an as needed basis. Whenever the haptic value changes for a particular haptic motor, a message is passed to the HHS.

In order to prevent a run away haptic situation, the game program is required to ping the HHS every 1000 ms in order for the HHS to acknowledge that any lapse in communication from the game is intended.

All messages include a sequence number, which the game program is responsible for incrementing. The HHS will acknowledge every message by sending back an ACK or a NACK, along with the sequence number. If the game program receives an ACK or NACK with an incorrect sequence number, it must retry the message until an ACK is received. Once the HHS has ACK'd the message, the game program no longer needs to keep this message in its buffer.

The capture methods present data in the format of a comma separated string representing up to six different haptic motors. This allows up to three controllers worth of data in the format Controller1Left, Controller1Right, Controller2Left, Controller2Right, Controller3Left, Controller3Right. The values of each of these are floats within the range of 0.0 (not active) to 1.0 (fully active). The HHS is configured with the URL of the remote HTTP server and when started, it has the option to create a new session ID or use an

Fig. 2. Complete haptic capture controller modification with arduino board

existing session ID. The session ID allows for multiple haptic streams occurring simultaneously as the client must identify the session ID to obtain data from the desired game play session.

7 Methods

Client Real Time Streams. The transmission of the data in the functioning prototype is through a simple protocol using HTTP posts passing each variable as a separate parameter to the post. The variables include the session ID, controller ID, and the six motor state variables. When a client receives the response from the HTTP post, it must assume that the values returned are the real time values of the haptic motors. As a result, the client must poll often to retrieve updates in real time. When using haptic relay locally, the client expects to receive the data in real time such that the delay between when the player feels the vibration and when the spectator feels the vibration is minimal. As a result, the message to the local controllers is sent at the same time as the message sent to the HTTP remote host, which makes those write at roughly the same speed. Any delay would come from the polling cycle of the client, which was set to fire off along with video frame updates at the rate of 30 times per second.

Using a hardware capture method introduces more delay as the intensity of the motors is also periodically polled at 100 times a second. Depending on network conditions, this could result in 10 ms delay on the capture, and a 34 ms delay on the client, with any additional delay occurring due to network traffic. Although there is some delay that may surpass 100 ms, it is negligible when paired with an online streaming session over a streaming network such as Twitch.tv. Twitch is typically delayed by 30 s. Even if there are lengthy delays on the haptic capture server, it is expected that any of these delays will be several orders of magnitude lower than the video delay presented.

In order to properly match up the haptic stream with the video, the client replay service has an option to delay the presentation of the vibration cues to the player, allowing for proper synchronization. In the prototype this is a manual process. The client viewer must adjust the slider from 0 to 120 s until he finds the value that is correct. No matter what the delay is, the client is always polling the server to receive the real time updates and queues them up until the presentation time has arrived.

The hammering of the server by the clients is not scalable. When not using a haptic capture device, it is possible to limit the amount of traffic. In this case, if the client software knows how long the vibration cue will be presented to the player, it can deploy a message to the server indicating the entire duration. For example, the game may know it will present a 5 s 100 % intensity cue on vibration motor 1. When the client reads this message, it knows that there is no need to keep polling for the next five seconds and will hold off repeatedly requesting information. This becomes much harder in the case of a hardware capture because the future of the haptic stream is not known and a polled method must be used.

The current prototype relies on streaming the haptic information through different servers than the originating video. Even after going through a manual sync process, the two streams can become out of sync. In order to avoid this issue, protocol modifications are suggested to follow similar streaming techniques for closed captioning. Two standards for synchronizing text to video are described below and then an addition to these is proposed to utilize haptic information streams in a similar fashion.

WebVTT: The Web Video Text Tracks Format [22] was last updated at the end of October, 2014 and describes captions or subtitles for video and audio content distributed across the internet through HTML. The text tracks can be passed alongside a video by using the <TRACK> tag. WebVTT streams are in the following format:

00:11.000 –>00:13.000
<v Roger Bingham> We are in New York City

This entry in the stream indicates that from seconds 11 until seconds 13, the string shown in the second line should be displayed. Haptic information can be encoded in this exact same format. Using the same time encoding, the second line can contain information about the state of the motors during that time. A proposed addition to this specification would allow the definition of haptic states. The following encoding would indicate that the haptic motor on controller 0 with identifier 0 should vibrate at half of its capacity between seconds 11 and 13:

00:11.000 –>00:13.0000,0,0.5

This could be extended to identify a sequence of haptic signals that could be performed over the time defined. For example, the following json encoding would indicate that vibration motors 0 and 1 should pulse at full intensity for 1 s, followed by a half a second of silence for the time period of 11 s through 21 s:

00:11.000 –>00:21.000 "pulses": ["duration": 1, "pulse": ["id": 0, "value": 1, "id": 1, "value": 1], "duration": 0.5, "pulse": ["id": 0, "value": 0, "id": 1, "value": 0]]

These types of enhancements to WebVTT will work best when the gameplay session is archived as all instructions will include a start time and end time. This type of encoding could potentially be used in the scenario where the client is streaming these commands in real time (as shown in the prototype) and the actual video delay is larger than the longest pulse. For example, if the video delay was 30 s, and the haptic stream was occurring in real time and depended on the client to buffer and present the vibrations to the player in synchronization with the video broadcast, as long as any piece of data did not take place longer than 30 s, the full haptic capabilities would be relayed to the player without any perceivable difference.

There are times when this might not be sufficient and directly embedding the haptic data into the video stream may be preferred. Text can be directly embedded into MPEG 4 video streams using the definitions shown in Part 17 and Part 30 of the standard. Part 30 defines the embedding of text as WebVTT into MPEG4 video streams. Enhancing Part 30 to include definitions for haptic streams will provide a convenient mechanism for packaging video and haptic together, however it still may suffer from some of the issues that come with requiring to know the start time and end time of a piece of haptic information. Part 17 defines the use of encoded text as 3GPP Timed Text [23]. This text standard embeds the text into the video stream at the appropriate times. This can be enhanced to embed haptic status whenever the status changes. It will create a low overhead as nothing will be polled, and the stream will not be filled with repetitive information. It will allow the live broadcasting to continue without the need to synchronize time with the live stream and the haptic stream as they both will be carried in the same structure.

8 Limitations

Client Haptic Reproduction.   There may be hardware and software limitations when the client attempts to reproduce a haptic stream. If the broadcaster and the receiver are using the same hardware, then the stream should be replicated in very near real time. An issue with replicating the stream becomes important when the client is either using a different hardware controller than the broadcaster, or the client is using a different hardware controller than the original software was designed for.

Different types of controllers have various types and number of motors. The Xbox 360, Xbox One, Dual Shock 3 and Dual Shock 4 are all similar in that they each have two vibration motors in each controller. That should make haptic broadcasts designed for these controllers and replayed by these controllers interchangeable for the most part. They do use different types of motors so a player broadcasting a haptic capture of an Xbox 360 controller may feel slightly different to a player who is receiving the stream with a Dual Shock 4 controller. Hardware limitations may be present when the hardware capabilities of the controllers differ significantly. For example, if a hardware capture of an XBox 360 controller is being replayed by a player who is holding a Wii Remote, the client side may lose some of the detail that the player is feeling. The Wii Remote only contains one vibration motor and it may not be able to replicate the same feeling as two vibration motors. The same issue goes for someone who is using a cell phone as the client. Phones typically also only have one vibration motor and may not be able to replicate the stream accurately.

There are also software issues when attempting to replicate a haptic stream. Certain devices may be locked out of certain haptic features. The most common feature that clients may lack is in the replication of the intensity of the vibration. iPhones and Wii Remotes generally only allow either an ON or OFF setting with no varying intensity being available to developers. This differs greatly from the Xbox and Playstation controllers as they can vary the intensity and duration as needed. The current iPhone SDK even limits the duration of the pulse of available to developers to 1 s. Techniques such as starting and stopping the motors prior to them getting to their full speed may produce a feeling of different intensities; however, these techniques are unavailable in the default SDKs.

Capture Device Limitations.   The current hardware prototype for capturing haptic signals from controllers has a limitation. The prototype shares a common ground between the controller and the arduino board. This allows for a simple and quick circuit to be developed that involves only the positive terminal of the vibration motor being connected to the analog inputs on the ardiuno board. If the controller and the capture device were connected to different ground sources, the circuit may have to be slightly more complex. For example, if the shown circuit was used to capture the haptic signals from an Xbox One controller powered by batteries, the circuit would have to be modified. All tests performed with the haptic capture board for the purposes of this paper were performed with the arduino board and the controller both powered by the same USB source.

9   Future Work and Conclusion

The work presented here demonstrates the need and feasibility of transporting haptic information along with video streams of games. Future work will involve implementing the suggested haptic channel encodings into video transmission standards and to evaluate their performance. Performing a round trip test using a standard video streaming site, such as Twitch.tv, may require assistance from Twitch as they may re-encode videos on their end to maintain end user expectations, and during this re-encoding process the new haptic information may be lost.

In addition to games, this haptic encoding may be able to take movie viewing to the next level. Smart phones with haptic capabilities are common place, and it may be useful to consider using that personal technology while watching a movie. For example, if movie viewers were able to log into a haptic stream for whatever movie they were watching, and when an explosion on the screen occurs, a phone in the user's own pocket would vibrate giving the viewer a directed cue about onscreen activities. This paper presents a prototype and suggested enhancements to video transmission standards such that haptic information is also included in video streams. It can be used for enhancements for online video game streams.

References

1. Johnston, C.: Rumble Pak Titles On the Rise, GameSpot.com 23 May 1997. http://www.gamespot.com/articles/rumble-pak-titles-on-the-rise/1100-2466717/. Accessed 10 Jan 2015
2. maru-chang, SCPH, maru-chang.com 8 February 2004. http://maru-chang.com/hard/scph/index.php/english. Accessed 10 Jan 2015
3. Tremblay, M.R., Yim, M.H.: Tactile feedback man-machine interface device US Patent US6088017 A. Filed 24 April 1998, 11 July 2000
4. Tremblay, M.R., Yim, M.H.: Tactile feedback man-machine interface device US Patent US6424333 B1. Filed 18 April 2001, 23 July 2002
5. Jenkins, D.: Immersion Wins Sony DualShock Patent Infringement Suit. GmaSutra.com, 22 September 2004. http://www.gamasutra.com/view/news/95287/ImmersionWinsSonyDualShockPatentInfringementSuit.php. Accessed 15 Jan 2015
6. Riddell Williams: Microsoft Corp. Vs Immersion Corp., 18 June 2007. http://blog.seattlepi.com/microsoft/files/library/immersionmicrosoft.pdf. Accessed 9 Jan 2015
7. Skillman, A.: Immersion Issues Patent Licenses for Tactile Feedback Video Game Console Peripherals, 11 July 2007. http://ir.immersion.com/releasedetail.cfm?ReleaseID=253387. Accessed 12 Jan 2015

8. Fitzgerald, D., Wakabayashi, D.: Apple quietly builds new networks. Wall Street J. (2014)
9. Eadicicco, L.: 10 Facts About Twitch, The Company That Amazon Is Buying, That Will Blow Your Mind. Business Insider, 25 August 2014. http://www.businessinsider.com/statistics-about-twitch-2014-8. Accessed 12 Jan 2015
10. Amazon.com. Amazon.com to Acquire Twitch. Amazon.com Press Release, 25 August 2014
11. Grundberg, S., Hansegard, J.: YouTube's biggest draw plays games, earns $4 million a year. Wall Street J. (2014)
12. PewDiePie, PewDiePie - Youtube. https://www.youtube.com/user/PewDiePie. Accessed 20 Jan 2015
13. Charbonneau, E., Hughes, C.E., LaViola Jr., J.J.: Vibraudio pose: an investigation of non-visual feedback roles for body controlled video games. In: Sandbox 2010, Los Angeles, California, 28–29 July 2010
14. Hamam, A., El Saddik, A., Alja'am, J.: A quality of experience model for haptic virtual environments. J. ACM Trans. Multimedia Comput. Commun. Appl. (TOMM) **10**(3), Article No. 28 (2014)
15. Nesbitt, K.V.: Multi-sensory game interface improves player satisfaction but not performance. In: AUIC 2008 Proceedings of the Ninth Conference on Australasian User Interface, vol. 76, pp. 13–18 (2008)
16. Alahakone, A.U., Senanayake, S.M.N.A: Vibrotactile feedback systems for rehabilitation, sports and information display: a review. In: International Conference on Advanced Intelligent Mechatronics, AIM 2009, pp. 1148–1153 (2009)
17. Xu, Z., Yu, H., Yan, S.: Motor rehabilitation training after stroke using haptic handwriting and games. In: iCREATe 2010, Proceedings of the 4th International Convention on Rehabilitation Engineering Assistive Technology, Article No. 31 (2010)
18. Morelli, T., Foley, J., Column, L., Lieberman, L., Folmer, E.: VI-Tennis: a vibrotactile/audio exergame for players who are visually impaired. In: FDG 2010, Proceedings of the Fifth International Conference on the Foundations of Digital Games, pp. 147–154 (2010)
19. Morelli, T., Foley, J., Folmer, E.: Vi-bowling: a tactile spatial exergame for individuals with visual impairments. In: ASSETS 2010, Proceedings of the 12th International ACM SIGACCESS Conference on Computers and Accessibility, pp. 179–186 (2010)
20. Morelli, T., Foley, J., Lieberman, L., Folmer, E.: Pet-N-Punch: upper body tactile/audio exergame to engage children with visual impairments into physical activity. In: GI 2011, Proceedings of Graphics Interface 2011, pp. 223–230 (2011)
21. Kendzierski, D., DeCarlo, K.: Physical activity enjoyment scale: two validation studies. J. Sport Exerc. Psychol. **13**, 50–64 (1991)
22. WebVTT, WebVTT: The Web Video Text Tracks Format. WebMedia Text Tracks Community Group, 30 October 2014. http://dev.w3.org/html5/webvtt. Accessed 12 Dec 2014
23. 3GPP, 3GPPSpecification detail. Spec26.245. http://www.3gpp.org/DynaReport/26245.htm. Accessed 20 Jan 2015

Approaches of Participatory Design in the Design Process of a Serious Game to Assist in the Learning of Hospitalized Children

Eunice P.S. Nunes[1(✉)], Alessandro R. Luz[1], Eduardo M. Lemos[1], and Clodoaldo Nunes[2]

[1] Laboratório de Ambientes Virtuais Interativos (LAVI) – Instituto de Computação, Universidade Federal de Mato Grosso (UFMT), Cuiabá, MT, Brazil
eunice.ufmt@gmail.com, alsrluz@gmail.com, emartinslemos@gmail.com
[2] Departamento da Área de Informática (DAI) – Instituto Federal de Educação, Ciência e Tecnologia de Mato Grosso (IFMT), Cuiabá, MT, Brazil
clodoaldo.nunes@cba.ifmt.edu.br

Abstract. Although the literature shows initiatives of conception of serious game for the support learning of hospitalized children, generally, the design process stays on the draftsman responsibility, exclusively, being based on the initial requirements set-up. In this scenario, this article presents the design process of Three-Dimensional Virtual Environments (3D VEs), based on games, here considered as serious game, to assist in the learning of hospitalized children. The serious game is grounded in the Reference Model for conception of 3D Virtual Learning Environments (3D VLE) to assist hospitalized children [4] and counted on Participatory Design (PD) approaches. From the approaches of Contextual Inquiry (PD technique) with health professional, including the hospital class teacher, it was possible to identify the main needs and expectations related to the conception of a pedagogic, interactive and ludic tool that supports learning on children who stay long periods hospitalized. However, the serious game proposal can be extended to all the childish public interested in learning by means of serious games. In the next stage of PD process, we will apply the Mockups technique with the patient (children) using the prototype developed.

Keywords: Serious games · Participatory Design · Three-dimensional · Learning virtual environment · Hospitalized children

1 Introduction

Serious games are a category of interactive games, which allied to Virtual Reality (VR) and Human-Computer Interaction (HCI) have as purpose going beyond entertainment, because they offer a wide possibility of simulations of daily situations, for example, simulating critical situations that involve some kind of risks, as well as being

© Springer International Publishing Switzerland 2016
M. Kurosu (Ed.): HCI 2016, Part III, LNCS 9733, pp. 406–416, 2016.
DOI: 10.1007/978-3-319-39513-5_38

applied in human awareness about social problems. Serious games can be applied in many knowledge areas, as business, governmental, politics, engineering, health, among others [8].

However, one of the areas that had most benefit within the usage of serious games, mainly combining training and virtual education, is the health area [5, 6]. Several surgery procedure simulators based on games are being used by medicine students for virtual training, in order to reduce physical laboratory costs and accelerate the learning of students. In the context of hospitalized children, are found initiatives of Three-Dimensional Virtual Environments (3D VEs) conception, based on games, with educational purpose [1–3], once the long periods of internment interrupts the process of school learning and the social interaction between the children and their teachers and classmates.

Although the literature shows initiatives of conception of 3D VEs, based on games, for the support learning of hospitalized children, generally, the design process stays on the draftsman responsibility, exclusively, being based on the initial requirements set-up. In this scenario, this article presents the design process of a three-dimensional serious game to assist in the learning of hospitalized children. The 3D VE based on games, here considered as a serious game, due to its pedagogic proposal, is grounded in the Reference Model for conception of 3D Virtual Learning Environments (3D VLE) to assist hospitalized children [4] and counted on Participatory Design (PD) approaches.

Participatory Design (PD) offers techniques that favor the dialogue between designers and users, in order to build technology collaboratively [7]. PD is a method in which participants are invited to cooperate and interact with designers, researchers and developers during the design process. According to [12] "…they can participate during several stages of the creative process, e.g. they participate during the initial exploration, problem definition, and requirements elicitation, in order to help to define the problem and to focus ideas to get valid solutions. They also can contribute during development, aiding at the evaluation of proposed solutions".

In hospital context, the PD aids the designer to investigate and understanding the relation of the hospitalized children with the technology being proposed, starting with the collaboration of the own child and the health professional that live with the hospitalized children.

Following this introduction, the paper is structured in four sections, as follows. Section 2 presents the materials and methods used in the research; in Sect. 3 we show the interface design of serious game proposed and, finally, Sect. 4 focuses on the conclusions of this study.

2 Materials and Methods

Initially, we conducted a Systematic Review (SR) in the specialized literature, in order to answer the following research question:

- Which the main methodologies/techniques of Participatory Design are being applied in the process of 3D VE design with educational focus to the childish public?

The SR included three stages: planning, conduction and results extraction. In each stage the steps were aligned with the PRISMA [10] methodology. In the planning phase, the SR protocol was established, which includes the SR objectives, the research proposition, the keywords, the search strings combination employed on the research, the main database indication, the inclusion and exclusion of articles criteria and the procedures to be applied on the stages of preliminary selection and final selection.

To answer the research question, it was used combination of search strings, applying in the IEEE and ACM databases. Out of 220 works found during the SR conduction stage, 31 works were selected on the preliminary selection stage and 12 works were included on the final selection stage, the ones who seek to answer the referred research question. Figure 1 shows a distribution of the works included and excluded from Systematic Review.

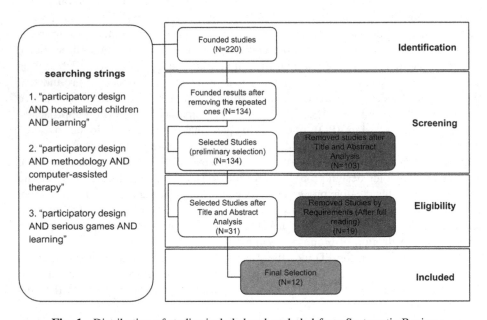

Fig. 1. Distribution of studies included and excluded from Systematic Review

From the results obtained with the SR, we could identify the main techniques that have been applied to conceive design project centered on the user, including the know-how of the interested parts and their needs. Table 1 presents the identified Participatory Design techniques and their main characteristics.

Considering the Participatory Design approaches presented in the Table 1, we select the Contextual Inquiry and Mockups techniques because they were the only techniques found in the SR that are applied in the beginning of the interface project development. The approach of successive meetings of Participatory Design follows the same principles of Contextual Inquiry technique. In sequence, the Sects. 2.1 and 2.2 present a brief description of the selected techniques.

Table 1. Classification of Participatory Design Techniques

Technique	Approach	Expected Results
Contextual Inquiry [7, 14, 15]	The interviewer observes and questions the user in his natural context of work (brainstorm reunions and interviews)	• Detailed understanding about the work process, contextualized in the users natural environment; • Needs assessments; • Suggestions from potential users
Mockups [7]	The interviewer observes what the users have to say through prototypes development in different levels of detail and fidelity.	• Production of prototypes in paper with the possible alternatives that meet the client requirements.
Cooperative Cognitive Course [7]	The interviewer applies a formulary with questions to be answered about the Cognitive Course of a determined activity that is implemented on the already prototyped interfaces.	• It is obtained an evaluation about the interfaces related to the learning facility and verifies possible design fails related to the requirements originally specified.
Creative Participatory Design [11]	The interviewer presents the prototype under testing and align with the ideation/brainstorming.	• Prototype' Refinement.
Successive meetings of participatory design [13]	Discussion, negotiation and exchange among stakeholders and real users.	• Creation of several products (documents, diagrams, prototypes, notes, etc.).
Creative Participatory Design [11]	Storyboarding, low-fidelity prototyping technique	• Users develop design concepts and ideas which are translated into design directions for the development of the game.

2.1 Contextual Inquiry

Contextual Inquiry technique consists on field interviews conducted with the final users in their real work context. In this study, the final users are health professionals and hospitalized children. The application of Contextual Inquiry involves the whole development team with the stakeholders through brainstorms reunions and interviews. The technique also foresees quiz applications with the users, in order to collect the maximum amount of possible data to be analyzed in the future. The Contextual Inquiry technique is based in four main principles[1]:

- Focus – inquiry planning phase, grounded on a clear comprehension of your intention;
- Context – observer the customer do their job inside his own workplace;

---

[1] http://www.usabilitybok.org/contextual-inquiry.

- Partnership – dialogue to customers about their job and try to make they talk about any failures in the process;
- Interpretation – try to share with the customer an understanding about the aspects in the job that actually matter.

This way, applying the Contextual Inquiry technique includes a high reliability in the obtained information, considering that it focuses in the interfaces development totally geared to the needs and diversities of the final users.

2.2 Mockups

Mockup is a final prototype of the object to be developed, with the goal of testing, studying or sampling of its artifices. Usually, it presents all the components that will be part of the product final version in development by clear and objective ways, avoiding dual interpretation.

This technique counts on information collected by the developing team with stakeholders, seeking conception concepts, layout and/or content. Mockups are usually resulting processes of the Contextual Inquiry technique application, starting from the premise that the final product should to suit the users' needs, besides of foreseeing the users diversity and different everyday situations.

2.3   Application of Design Participatory in the Serious Game Proposed

From approaches of Participatory Design selected, the design process was divided in two steps:

- first step – we applied the **Contextual Inquiry** technique [9] that counted on brainstorm reunions and interviews with the project multidisciplinary team, involving computing and health areas professionals. The stakeholders contributed collaboratively with the game design process (defined topic, main characters and interaction strategies), considering the emotional/social state of hospitalized children and serious games native aspects. During this step, we identified the main characters role in the process of interaction with the child, seeking to improve their emotional/social state, beyond investigating how characters could motivate learning, even the children being in a situation of pain and fear.
- Second step – this step still will be applied to include the design practice centered on the child participation. The hospital team will select children that are hospitalized longer time (7 to 10 years), in order to have access to the serious game initial prototype. The register of interactions in the game will be realized through video recording, for posterior data analysis. In this step the game design process will count on another PD technique, **Mockups** [7], which notices what users have to say through prototyping in different detail and simulation levels. Participate on this technique the users of technology; in this case, we consider as users children/teacher. The interviewer (designer) observes the users during exploration on 3D VE. In sequence, the multidisciplinary team stimulate the children to express

their ideas and wishes drawing (paper prototyping) what they would want to change in the game, which scenarios they would like to discover in the next stages and which characters they would like to be part of the context.

3   Interface Design of Serious Game Proposed

Serious game proposed interfaces were designed considering the data collected on the Contextual Inquiry sections (first step). During the brainstorm reunions and interviews, we identified the necessity to develop a 3D VE to assist in the learning of hospitalized children who are kept away from the school routine for medical treatments.

Highlight the 3D VE here proposed, is grounded in the Reference Model 3E Virtual Learning Environments conception to assist hospitalized children [4], which predict the application requirements, the interaction strategies that can be applied in the VE and the human factors involved in the process.

We present below the main characteristics of the prototyped interfaces for the proposed serious game, which were designed with the participation of the health area team from the partner institution of this project (Hospital Universitário Julio Muller in Brazil). Therefore, the game is being developed only in Portuguese:

- in search of a 3D VE that combines learning, entertainment and socialization, it was proposed a 3D VE based on the following strategies of interaction: learning based on games and avatar;
- the serious game scenario starts in a hospital room, as observed in Fig. 2, which was modeled from interviews realized with the health professionals. Additionally, the development team personally met a room from the pediatric wing;

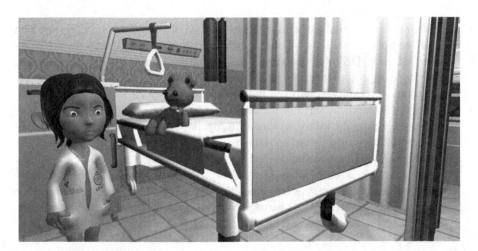

Fig. 2. Initial interface of the serious game (context hospital room)

- the child begins the navigation in the game selecting his/her own avatar to represent himself/herself in the VE. Through the avatar, the child explores the environment and interacts with virtual objects. Highlighting that by selecting the avatar, this one shows up dressed with a white coat, usually, used by health professional, in order to familiarize the children with the hospital team;
- given the diversity of users (children) that will play the serious game, the health team asked to be modeled avatars from different ethnicities (white, black and indigenous). This way, the game counts with six avatars, being a boy and a girl for each ethnicity (Fig. 3);

Fig. 3. Avatars for selection

- considering that hospitalization is not a trivial task for children, for carrying with themselves not only their sick body, but their costumes, routine and main characteristic: "playing" [16], the scenario for the curricular learning process happens in a square to bring joy, so named "Joy Square" (Fig. 4). The transition between the initial scenario (hospital room) and the square, occurs by an interface transition;
- in the first development stage of the serious game, the hospital class teacher suggested us to explore the following theme "Recycling and Environment", for treating an interdisciplinary subject, cover Mathematics and Science contents, propitiate the environmental awareness and include risky situations to alert the children about the presence "dangerous trash". The Math discipline was included in the interdisciplinarity because to progress in the game, the child needs, for example, in one of the game situations, to verify if the garbage bin still have space to throw the trash in. Each garbage bin has capacity for 10 units of trash and each kind of trash has its own units (Fig. 5).
- On request of the hospital class teacher, we had insert a non-playable character in the serious game (Lady Rose), who has the responsibility to collect the trash

Fig. 4. Interface "Joy Square" (learning based on games)

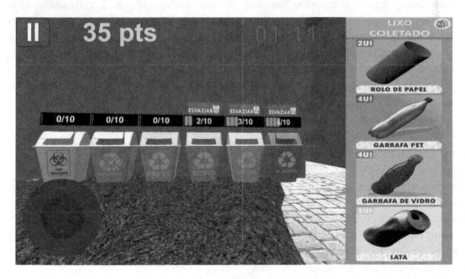

Fig. 5. Interface with the garbage bin of the "Joy Square" to selective collect

considered dangerous for the child. Lady Rose executes the task to collect and put in the right garbage can named "dangerous trash", if she is called by the player (child). The player asks for the intervention of Lady Rose every time he/she encounters a dangerous trash and the alert siren is triggered in the VE. To ask Lady Rose's help, the player only needs to click on the character that is walking on the square (Figs. 6 and 7).

Fig. 6. Lady Rose (non-playable character)   **Fig. 7.** Lady Rose collecting "dangerous trash" (syringes, medicine, others)

- Other requirements were collected to the interface project during the PD technique application – Contextual Inquiry, such as the score system definition, type of environment sounding, format of the dialogues between player and non-playable characters, scenario composition and avatars appearance and caricatures that accompany the dialogues. The health professionals suggested for the dialogues to have an easy vocabulary for the expected age group, so it influences not only the reading but text interpretation as well, but also the understanding of the concepts related to the serious game "Recycling and Environment". Other two phases of the game, also related to the theme, were defined with the multidisciplinary team support.

4   Conclusions

From the approaches of Participatory Design with health professional, including the hospital class teacher, it was possible to identify the main needs and expectations related to the conception of a pedagogic, interactive and ludic tool that supports learning on children who stay long periods hospitalized. Therefore, techniques of PD enabled to develop a game designed closer to the hospitalized children reality and health professionals' needs.

However, the serious game proposal can be extended to all the childish public interested in learning by means of a 3D VE based on games.

The initial prototype was validated by the health professionals involved in the interfaces project. In the next stage of Participatory Design process (Mockups), we will include the patient participation (children) in prototype tests, as presented in Sect. 2.3, in order to seek the improvement of the serious game interfaces and its functionalities.

Considering the final users are children who are part of a generation that uses mobile and electronic devices since their early years, their participation during the serious game development is effective to produce consistent interfaces with the target audience interests, even before providing the game widely to the society.

We intend to apply the game in real situations of learning with hospitalized children, seeking to investigate the knowledge acquisition level acquired through the game, in order to validate the tool as a pedagogical instrument.

Finally, this study represents a relevant social contribution to the Health and Educational areas that use the 3D VE for different matters. For the Computer area, this study represents a reflection about the best practices of interfaces project of 3D VEs, as well as it identified the need of methodologies proposition grounded on PD approaches for the conception and evaluation of 3D VEs, specially, based on games.

Acknowledgments. This research was supported by the Institutional Program of Scholarships for Scientific Initiation of Federal University of Mato Grosso (UFMT-Brazil) and by the State of Mato Grosso Research Foundation (FAPEMAT-Brazil).

References

1. Di Fiore, F., Jorissen, P., Vansichem, G., Van Reeth, Frank: A 3D virtual learning environment to foster communication for long term Ill children. In: Hui, K.-C., Pan, Z., Chung, R.C.-K., Wang, C.C.L., Jin, X., Göbel, S., Li, E.C.-L. (eds.) Edutainment 2007. LNCS, vol. 4469, pp. 92–103. Springer, Heidelberg (2007)
2. Jorissen, P., et al.: A virtual interactive community platform supporting education for long-term sick children. Cooperative Design, Visualization, and Engineering. vol. 4674, PP. 58–69. Springer, Heidelberg (2007)
3. González-González, C., et al.: Design and analysis of collaborative interactions in social educational videogames. Comput. Human Behav. **31**, 602–611 (2014)
4. Kawakami, R., Nunes, E.P.S., Maciel, C.: Ambientes Virtuais Tridimensionais que Apoiam o Aprendizado de Crianças Hospitalizadas. In: XVII Symposium on Virtual and Augmented Reality, São Paulo, Brazil (2015)
5. Machado, L.S., Moraes, R.M., Fátima, L.S.N.: Serious games para saúde e treinamento imersivo. Abordagens Práticas de Realidade Virtual e Aumentada, 31–60 (2009)
6. Machado, L.S., et al.: Serious games based on virtual reality in medical education. Rev. Bras. Educação Méd. **35**(2), 254–262 (2011)
7. Melo, A.M., Baranauskas, M.C.C., Soares, S.C.M.: Design com Crianças: da Prática a um Modelo de Processo. Rev. Bras. Educação Méd. **16**(1) 43–55 (2008)
8. Rankin, J.R., Sampayo S.V.: A review of Serious Games and other game categories for Education (2008). Unpublished manuscript
9. Holtzblatt, K., Jones, S.: Contextual inquiry: a participatory technique for system design. In: Participatory Design: Principles and Practices, Hillsdale, pp. 177–210 (1993). apud Muller et al. (2007)
10. Moher, D., et al.: Preferred reporting items for systematic reviews and meta-analyses: the PRISMA statement. Ann. Intern. Med. **151**(4) 264–269 (2009)
11. Tan, J.L., et al.: Child-centered interaction in the design of a game for social skills intervention. Comput. Entertainment (CIE) **9**(1), 2 (2011)
12. Silva, C.C., et al.: Developing 3D human-computer interfaces and serious games for health education in the Brazilian countryside using participatory design and popular education. In: 2014 IEEE International Conference on Systems, Man and Cybernetics (SMC), pp. 2971–2976. IEEE (2014)

13. Kechaï, H.E., Pierrot, L.: Participatory design in EU-TOPIA: a serious game for intercultural competences during work mobility. In: 2015 IEEE 15th International Conference on Advanced Learning Technologies (ICALT), pp. 127–131 (2015)
14. Druin, A.: Cooperative inquiry: developing new technologies for children with children. In: SIGCHI Conference on Human Factors in Computing Systems, pp. 592–599. ACM (1999)
15. Tellioglu, H.: Coordination design. In: 20th International Conference on Advanced Information Networking and Applications (AINA) (2006)
16. Silva, S.H., et al.: Humanização em pediatria: o brinquedo como recurso na assistência de enfermagem à criança hospitalizada. Pediatr. mod [Internet] 46.3, 101–104 (2010)

A Field Study: Evaluating Gamification Approaches for Promoting Physical Activity with Motivational Models of Behavior Changes

Xin Tong[✉], Diane Gromala, Chris D. Shaw, and Amber Choo

Simon Fraser University, Surrey, Canada
{tongxint,gromala,shaw,achoo}@sfu.ca

Abstract. Wearable trackers and mobile applications can facilitate self-reflection of doing physical activity. The gamification process incorporates game design elements with persuasive systems in order to encourage more physical activity. However, few gamification strategies have been rigorously evaluated; these investigations showed that using the same gamification mechanism to promote physical activity could have contradictory effects. Therefore, I developed FitPet, a virtual pet-keeping mobile game for encouraging activity. I evaluated its effectiveness, and compared it with the goal-setting and social community strategies in a six-week field study. The findings revealed social interaction were the most effective intervention. Contrary to prior research, goal-setting was not perceived as an effective way to provide motivation compared to social interaction overall. Although FitPet was not able to promote significantly higher activity, participants showed great interests in this approach and provided design insights for future research: implementing social components and more challenging gameplay.

Keywords: Gamification · Motivation · Physical activity · Serious game · Social interaction

1 Introduction

Tools such as mobile devices and wearable technologies have been shown to help people manage their health and wellness. Of particular interest are technologies that are designed for activity tracking and promoting behaviour changes in everyday life. These technologies hold the potential to assist with counteracting the lack of regular physical activity by motivating people to develop and maintain a more active and healthier lifestyle.

Numerous persuasive systems aimed at promoting physical activity have been developed and researched in recent years. These systems capture and measure activity-related parameters and present the measured data to the user in various ways. In particular, mobile and wearable technologies can offer a host of sensing technology and data visualization tools, which allow for captured and quantified data to be stored, analyzed and communicated. Furthermore, researchers and commercial companies alike have been developing various systems designed to promote physical activity.

© Springer International Publishing Switzerland 2016
M. Kurosu (Ed.): HCI 2016, Part III, LNCS 9733, pp. 417–424, 2016.
DOI: 10.1007/978-3-319-39513-5_39

Individual behaviour change, including physical activity, has become a subject of active investigation in the areas of cognitive science and clinical psychology. One of the most accepted theoretical models from psychology community of how changes happen is the Transtheoretical Model (TTM) introduced by James Prochaska [1]. TTM argues that individuals change their behaviour gradually, by advancing along a series of steps. These steps vary from pre-contemplation in which individuals have not realized the need for change, to termination in which the new behaviour has become so habitual that there is no longer any danger of relapse.

In the light of the criticism toward gamification and a relative lack of rigorous studies evaluating its effectiveness, in this paper, we set out to evaluate people's acceptance of gamified strategies, motivation models and behavior changes. Through the six-week field study, we tested three gamification approaches and evaluated participants' motivation changes.

2   Related Work

Digital technology is increasingly being adopted to promote physical activity and reduce sedentary behaviour in the general population. It offers a practical way to motivate self-managed physical activity. However, for any behaviour change technology to be effective, the strategies that promote change need to be examined along with reasons that undermine to behaviour changes.

In the past decade, a number of innovative health-related programs designed to promote an increase in physical activity introduced novel technologies to reduce the cost of continuous involvement of clinical personnel required to promote and maintain healthy behaviours in patients. Many of these include techniques that transform physical exercise into engaging the individual or social games that often mix real and virtual environments [2]. In an alternative approach, pedometers – small electronic devices that monitor individual step counts, have been used as a ubiquitous and unobtrusive motivational technique available anytime and anywhere [3–5].

Some of these "quantified systems" provide numerical numbers for self-knowledge and self-reflection, which has been termed as "personal informatics". Such quantified systems can facilitate the collection and storage of personal information. It is believed that self-reflection leads individual to reconsider and possibly change their attitudes towards lifestyle changes. However, there are other systems that present physical activity data using game-based mechanics, defined as gamification. This approach has been assumed to be more fun and enjoyable, thus motivating users or players to become more physically active.

Gamification has the potential to engage people at an emotional level, which is considered to be far more powerful than typical transactional engagement strategies [6]. The gamification techniques – points, virtual rewards, levelling up, badges, peer obligation, social currency, missions and challenges – are part of the new area of gamification, with early signs of great potential for lifestyle improvements [7]. Concluded from the definition and applications of gamification, gamification is not about applying technology to old engagement models. Rather, gamification is thought to create entirely new engagement models, targeting new communities of people and motivating them to achieve goals they may not even know they have.

Gamification approaches have become popular in recent years [6] and are utilized as a design trend in applications for promoting healthy behavior changes. Nevertheless, many researchers have also criticized gamification mechanics. Furthermore, current research has not covered or evaluated most gamification techniques yet. Therefore, it remains unclear whether certain gamification approaches are effective in the context of physical activity.

Therefore, the major research question of this research is: will certain gamification approaches, including goal setting, social interaction, and a game-based virtual pet-keeping mobile application, be effective for promoting more physical activity? If there is an effective gamification method, how can that strategy provide motivation and why? Besides, I also wanted to figure out the design challenges and opportunities for developing such research prototype and persuasive technologies for encouraging motivation for lifestyle behavioral changes.

3   FitPet Game Design and Gamification Approaches Overview

3.1   FitBit Website Community and Mobile Challenge

Social Interaction Type One: Online Website Community: Fig. 2 (the second image) introduces the layout of Website Community. At the top of this image is a leaderboard which visualizes all group members' step data into bar charts and ranks each member from the most to the least with the member's name and the step number. Members may post their questions in the Discussion area and add friends with others.

Social Interaction Type Two: Challenges on Mobile Phones: Fig. 2 (the third image) demonstrates what the Mobile Challenges look like in a mobile App and how the communication and interactions among members can be. Four types of Mobile Challenges are included. *Daily Showdown* is a one-day competition, and *Weekend Warrior* takes effect only during the weekend, whereas *Workweek Hustle* is effective for competition during the five weekdays. *Goal Day* is about how many participants can reach their daily steps goal. For all challenges, the one who has the most steps will win the competition. After a Mobile Challenge starts, participants can chat with each other, cheer-up or nudge each other. The system will send notifications to the main screen once there are major changes happening, such as "Tom just surpassed you!", "You just have 1000 steps more than Jerry!", or "You rank first currently."

3.2   FitPet Mobile Game

Therefore, in *FitPet*, goal-setting is the key to designing and playing this virtual pet-keeping game. The relationship between goal-setting and virtual creature's wellness and evolvement is the core mechanics that incorporate the users' daily physical activity goal into the wellbeing of their virtual pet. The tight connection is designed for player engagement so that during the 'user-pet interaction', users will grow emotional attachment to their virtual pet. *FitPet* also asks its users to break larger goals (like a long-term fitness or activity goal) into smaller practical challenges – a daily steps goal. This is to encourage players to stay motivated through the growth progress of their virtual pet and engages them *emotionally* to achieve their best to attend to the virtual pet.

In order to motivate users to engage with the pet more frequently, and grow an emotional attachment to the pet, individual's daily progress towards their goals was mapped to the development of the virtual pet in two ways. Firstly, the daily step count

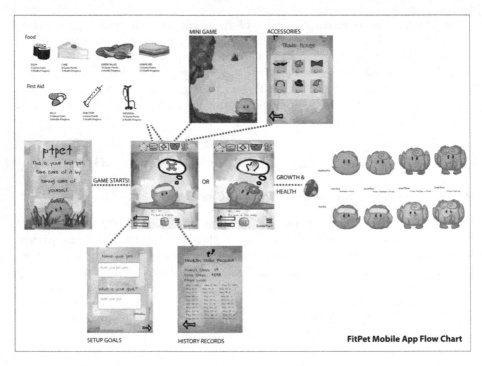

Fig. 1. Flow chart of FitPet mobile game

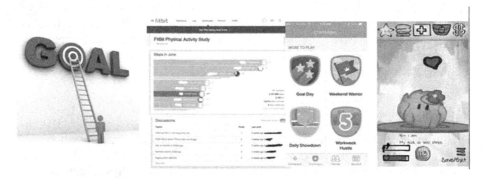

Fig. 2. The three gamification approaches for each study group: control group (left, goal-setting task), social group (middle, goal-setting task and Website Community as well as Mobile Challenges), and FitPet group (right, goal-setting and the mobile game)

can be converted to game coins, and then the users can use their coins to play with their pets, feed their pets, and provide medical help when the pet is sick. Secondly, the growth level of this virtual pet is related to the accumulated total steps and the users' daily step goal. The general idea of this mobile application is to take care of the pets by taking care of the player himself. Figure 1 shows the flow chart of *FitPet* mobile App.

4   Research Method

A six-week long between-subject field study was conducted with 23 participants (8 females and 15 males). The six-week period was divided equally into the study's three phases: pre-test observation, intervention, and post-test observation. During the intervention phase, the participants used the system and reported their experiences. This mixed-design study consisted of four quantitative questionnaires and three semi-structured interviews. Three conditions were designed to assess the engagement and effectiveness of separate gamified solutions: (1) goal-setting with *FitBit*, (2) social Website Community and Mobile Challenge condition with *FitBit* applications and (3) the *FitPet*.

Pre-test Observation (2 weeks): Before the pre-intervention stage, participants were asked to fill in a questionnaire about their daily lifestyle, physical activity level and routines, and familiarity with technologies and games. During the pre-intervention phase, the participants were given a *FitBit* wearable device worn on the wrist. The participants were asked to wear the *FitBit* as much as possible. The participants were also encouraged to maintain their regular lifestyles.

Intervention (2 weeks): During the experimental phase, the participants were randomly assigned to one of the three conditions. The control group has the FitBit data self-monitoring features and the goal-setting task. The first experimental group was also given the goal-setting task with FitBit data self-monitoring features, as well as social features (activity groups and Mobile Challenges). While the second experimental group could still wear FitBit (for capturing data), they were instructed to focus on the mobile app FitPet and not pay attention to FitBit anymore.

Post-test Observation (2 weeks): At the end of week 4 in the study, the goal-setting, social Website Community and mobile game interventions ended for the experimental groups. But the participants were asked to adopt the most helpful methods to keep themselves motivated and stay physically active.

The steps data were measured during all three phases by the *FitBit* devices and FitPet mobile App. After each session, the participants were interviewed for 20 min regarding their experience of using *FitBit* and how the intervention might impact their physical activity.

5   Results, Analysis and Evaluations

The study used a between-subjects design; a participant either belonged to the control group, the social group, or the *FitPet* group. Time was a within-subjects factor, as every participant's step was measured after each study phase. Therefore, in order to evaluate the effectiveness of the three gamified conditions, a Two-way Mixed-ANOVA test was conducted to compare before-intervention and after-intervention step changes. Independent variables were intervention conditions (goal-setting, social Website Community and *FitPet*) and time phases (pre-intervention and post-intervention). The dependent variable was the step count data collected throughout the six-week user study. To compare the effectiveness of three interventions, only steps data from before-intervention and post-intervention phases were included and analyzed.

A significant main effect of time was found, $F(2, 22) = 4.17$, $p = .02 < .05$, $r = .53$. Then to figure out where the significant differences existed, a Tuckey HSD test was run. It showed that the social group had significantly more steps than the *FitPet* group $p = .03 < .05$, and between the social group and the control group, $p = .03 < .05$. However, there was no significant difference between the *FitPet* group and the control group. Figure 3 shows steps increased during post-intervention phases compared with pre-intervention phases among three study groups.

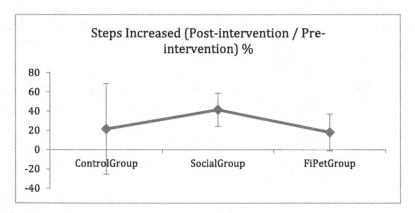

Fig. 3. Steps increased: percentages of three conditions after intervention compared to pre-intervention phase

The main effect of condition was non-significant, $F(2, 22) = 2.23$, $p = .12 > .05$, $r = .20$. This indicated that when the time at which step count was measured is ignored, the initial step level of participants in each group was not significantly different.

There was a significant Time * Group interaction effect, $F(2, 22) = 5.31$, $p = .02 < .05$, $r = .33$, indicating that the changes of step count in the groups were significantly different from each other. Specifically, there was a significant increase of steps in the social group. In the social group, the post-test step count was significantly higher than pre-test step data, $p = .03 < .05$. Also, in the post-test analysis, significant differences were found between *FitPet* group and social group. The social group had a significant increase of steps over *FitPet* group, p = .04 < .05. No other differences were revealed by the tests. These findings indicate that the social group was significantly more effective than the goal-setting control group and the *FitPet* experimental group.

6 Discussion and Conclusion

From the interview results, we found that the effectiveness of goal-setting strategy relied highly on individual's personality. Social interaction and communication gamification strategy were the most effective one in terms of promoting more steps. Although the FitPet game-based approach was not successful at encouraging significantly more steps compared to the control group, participants accepted and enjoyed the generally game design idea. However, more game mechanics should be implemented in order to keep players within the flow channel of engaging with the game. The findings of the study revealed how people liked various gamification design strategies and what should be taken into specific consideration when designing for motivation and behavior change. Hopefully, these design challenges and opportunities may shed light on gamification design and provide other designers and researchers with enlightening insights.

The lessons learned from this research could inform the design of applications for promoting physical activity or behavior changes. From the analysis, we found that emotional engagement played a significant role in motivating individuals as well as to keep them checked in and to stay motivated during the study. The social aspects are evaluated as an effective strategy if used properly and under certain circumstances. For example, some social aspects can involve participants in an active and engaging way, such as socializing and having fun with each other. Conversely, the passive communication afforded in the Website Community has not proven very effective in promoting physical activity. Moreover, besides social competition, opportunities for positive collaborations should be considered as an important type of social interaction when designing for gamification. Specifically, social components should be implemented into a FitPet-like game approach, and its effectiveness should be investigated and evaluated. Furthermore, since FitPet-ish games hold the potential to engage people and we see people's enthusiasms about making achievement in a larger context than their personal-goals. More mechanics and dynamics are needed in order to enhance the level of players' awareness and engagement.

Attending to these issues will help in the ways in which ubiquitous and persuasive technologies can be used to encourage physical activity and promote healthy behavior changes. The reflections of this research and critiques of others in the same fields helped us understand: in order to be effective and efficient, the context where gamified approaches are used matters. The contexts and prerequisites of what gamification strategy should be deployed, how to use it, and when, are critical to the success of designing gamification strategies for behavior changes.

References

1. Prochaska, J.O., Velicer, W.F.: The transtheoretical model of health behavior change. Am. J. Health Promot. **12**(1), 38–48 (1997)
2. Björk, S., Holopainen, J., Ljungstrand, P., Akesson, K.-P.: Designing ubiquitous computing games – a report from a workshop exploring ubiquitous computing entertainment. Pers. Ubiquitous Comput. **6**(5–6), 443–458 (2002)
3. Tudor-Locke, C.E., Myers, A.M., Bell, R.C., Harris, S.B., Wilson Rodger, N.: Preliminary outcome evaluation of the first step program: a daily physical activity intervention for individuals with type 2 diabetes. Patient Educ. Couns. **47**(1), 23–28 (2002)
4. Chan, C.B., Ryan, D.A.J., Tudor-Locke, C.: Health benefits of a pedometer-based physical activity intervention in sedentary workers. Prev. Med. **39**(6), 1215–1222 (2004)
5. Consolvo, S., Everitt, K., dSmith, I., Landay, J.A.: Design requirements for technologies that encourage physical activity. In: Proceedings of the SIGCHI Conference on Human Factors in Computing Systems, New York, NY, USA, pp. 457–466 (2006)
6. Burke, B.: Gamify: how gamification motivates people to do extraordinary things. Bibliomotion (2014)
7. McCallum, S.: Gamification and serious games for personalized health. Stud. Health Technol. Inform. **177**, 85–96 (2012)

Personalized Annotation for Photos with Visual Instance Search

Bao Truong[⊠], Thuyen V. Phan, Vinh-Tiep Nguyen, and Minh-Triet Tran

Faculty of Information Technology, University of Science,
VNU - HCM, Ho Chi Minh City, Vietnam
{tmbao,pvthuyen}@apcs.vn, {nvtiep,tmtriet}@fit.hcmus.edu.vn

Abstract. Emotional and memorable moments are usually kept and shared on different online services such as Facebook, Flickr, Instagram, and Google Photos. As a result, one of users' practical needs is to have their photos annotated automatically, especially with personalized tags. This motivates the authors to propose a system that can suggest personalized annotations for a photo uploaded to online services. Our system provides 2 major features. First, the system automatically recommends personalized annotations for newly uploaded photos based on visually similar photos uploaded in the past. Second, our system propagates manual annotations of users to other similar photos existed in their albums. To evaluate the performance of our system, we use the Oxford 5K Building Dataset and our own dataset consisting of personal photos collected from Facebook. Our systems achieves the mean Average Precision of 0.844 and 0.749 respectively on these two datasets. This demonstrates that our proposed solution can be potentially integrated as a useful utility or extension for online photo sharing services.

1 Introduction

In our lives, there are many emotional and memorable moments that worth keeping and sharing with others. Therefore, services allowing users to upload and share their personal photos are always ones of many notable products of different companies such as Facebook, Flickr, Instagram, and Google Photos. This shows that sharing photos is one of greatest demands of users on the Internet.

Online photo services usually allow users to attach some memos to their photos as well as to search their photos more easily using text queries. Currently, the most common way for users to do so is to tag their photos manually which consumes a lot of time and effort. There are also some proposed methods [3,5] and smart systems which are able to automatically identify noticeable landmarks or locations related to the photos such as Google Photos and Flickr. However, these automated annotation systems suggest tags that are identical for all users and thus do not reflect one's own memories, feelings, or characteristics. For example, these systems would recommend phrases like "Eiffel Tower", "a dog", or "a cat" rather than "where I first met my lover" or the name of your pet.

© Springer International Publishing Switzerland 2016
M. Kurosu (Ed.): HCI 2016, Part III, LNCS 9733, pp. 425–435, 2016.
DOI: 10.1007/978-3-319-39513-5_40

Therefore, it is necessary to automatically tag users' photos with personalized captions corresponding to their memory and personal characteristics.

In this paper, we propose a system that can suggest appropriate annotations for each photo uploaded by users using Visual Instance Search. In our system, users can assign their personalized annotations for some photos as initial examples, then, the system automatically propagates these annotations to other existed photos in their collection based on visual similarities among the photos. For each uploaded photo, the system bases on visual similarities between that photo and already-annotated photos of the corresponding user to propose a list of suitable annotations for the new uploaded photo in descending order of similarity. Then, the user can choose to approve reasonable annotation for the uploaded photo. In addition, if a user uploads more than one photo and change the annotations, the system has more samples for reference and thus, it tends to better adapt to user's interests. As a result, our system is not only able to recommend proper annotations which are unique for each user but also to interactively and incrementally learn and adapt as users change annotations.

Since the problem of retrieving similar images in a collection corresponding to a single image has been developed for years, there are many different approaches to the problem. One of them is template matching method, i.e. a technique for finding small parts of an image which match a template image [2,4,16]. Another popular technique is to evaluate the similarity of two images by comparing some regions which appear to be critical parts of the images, namely features matching [1,17,23]. In this paper, the authors develop our own Visual Instance Search framework using Bag-of-Words (BoW) model. In Bag-of-Words model, each image is represented as a histogram of pre-trained visual words (codebook). Since Bag-of-Words allows parts of a query image to appear in a flexible way in the result images, it is a potential approach that is widely used in many Visual Search systems.

Together with the exponential increasing of the number of uploaded images, the system faces lots of difficulty adapting those new images. Since re-training the codebook requires changing Bag-of-Words vectors of users' existing images and is also computationally expensive, the authors propose to use a fixed codebook trained with different types of features (e.g. vehicles, animals, buildings...) and use it universally. Because of the varieties of those different features, it is appropriate to compute and represent any new images' Bag-of-Words vectors without changing the codebook. Therefore, we train our codebook on Oxford Building Dataset and use this codebook for our system.

Our main contributions in this paper are as follows:

- We propose the idea and realize the system that can recommend annotation for photos with visual instance search.
- Our system allows recommended annotation to be personalized and to vary from user to user.
- Our system is interactively user adaptive, i.e. the more a user annotates his/her photos via our system, the more accurate the recommended annotations are.

The rest of this paper is organized as follows. In Sect. 2, we review the background and related works in image retrieval and image classification. Detailed steps of the automatic annotation system and how we use the BoW model is described in Sect. 3. Section 4 contains our experiment result. Conclusion is presented in Sect. 5.

2   Background and Related Works

There are many approaches to build an Image Information Retrieval System. Some methods aim at high precision, i.e. to achieve high quality of top retrieved results, while others focus on high recall, i.e. to retrieve all positive results. Among them, the first effective and scalable method is Bag-of-Words, proposed by Sivic and Zisserman [20], which is inspired by the correspondence algorithm using in text retrieval. Before going into details of BoW model in Subsect. 2.2, we first introduce some different methods for image retrieval problem in Subsect. 2.1.

2.1   Different Approaches for Image Retrieval Problem

One of many popular methods is histogram comparison which compares 2 different images based on their color histograms. Some early works of this approach using a cross-bin matching cost for histogram comparison can be found in [12,19,24]. In [12], Peleg et al. represent images as sets of pebbles after normalization. The similarity score is then computed as the matching cost of two sets of pebbles based on their distances.

Another well-known technique is template matching, i.e. seeking a given pattern in an image by comparing to the pattern with candidate regions of the same size in the target image. By considering both the pattern and candidate regions as a length-N vector, we can compare these two vectors using different kinds of distance metrics, and one such metric is the Minkowski distance [10]. The major disadvantage of 2 listed methods is that they require the query and target images to share a similar stationary interrelation, which means that components of the given image are not allowed to change freely in a certain extent. Bag-of-Words, the method that is discussed in this paper, is another approach that can tolerate the flexibility in structures of the object and thus, has a wider variation of applications in many problems.

2.2   Bag-of-Words

Since Bag-of-Words is originally a text retrieval algorithm, we first introduce some backgrounds about BoW in text retrieval problem in Subsect. 2.2 before discussing using BoW in image retrieval in Subsect. 2.2.

Bag-of-Words in Text Retrieval. In text retrieval, a text is represented as a histogram of words, also known as BoW [6]. This scheme is called term frequency weighting as the value of each histogram bin is equal to the number of times the word appears in the document. Moreover, some words are less informative than others since those words appear in almost every document. Therefore, we need a weighting scheme that address this problem. Such weighting scheme is called inverse document frequency (idf) and is formulated as $log(N_D/N_i)$, where N_D is the number of documents in the collection and N_i is the number of documents which contains word i. The overall BoW representation is thus weighted by multiplying the term frequency (tf) with the inverse document frequency (idf) giving rise to the tf-idf weighting [6]. In addtion, extremely frequent words, "stop words", can be removed entirely in order to reduce storage requirements and query time.

Bag-of-Words in Image Retrieval. When applying BoW to image retrieval, a major obstacle is the fact that text documents are naturally broken into words by spaces, dots, hyphens, or commas. In contrast, there is no such separator in images. Therefore, the concept of "visual word" is introduced where each visual word is represented as a cluster obtained using k-means on the local descriptor vectors [20].

The bigger the vocabulary size is, the more different the visual words are. Hence, the vocabulary helps us distinguish images more effectively. Nonetheless, with bigger vocabulary size, slightly different descriptors can be assigned to different visual words thus not contributing to the similarity of the respective images and causing a drop in performance examined in [9,15,18]. Philbin et al. [15] suggests "soft assign" method where each descriptor is assigned to multiple nearest visual words instead of using "hard assignment", i.e. only assign a local descriptor to only one nearest visual word. Despite its effectiveness, this method also significantly costs more storage and time.

3   Proposed System

In this section, we present how our system can learn to annotate different photos and briefly describe main steps in our BoW model.

3.1   Learn from Manual Annotations and Automatic Annotation for New Photos

Figure 1 illustrates the overview of our proposed system to automatically recommend personalized annotations for newly uploaded photos. First, a user simply uses his or her smartphones camera to capture scenes or objects in real life such as books, dogs, or buildings. A photo is then sent to the annotation server for processing and the server returns the list of visual similar photos. Additionally, each photo attaches a list of annotations and these possible personalized annotations are re-ranked and sent to the user. The user can review and approve these personalized annotations before sharing the photo to social networks such as Facebook, Flickr, or Google Plus along with the approved personalized tags.

Figure 2 shows how our system learns to annotate a photo from samples provided by a user in the past. First, a user manually chooses suitable tags for some photos and these photos along with the tags are then sent to the server. Subsequently, our server process identifies and recommends the user to also apply these changes to visually similar photos in his or her albums. The user can approve before these changes take effect in the database. From this point of time, our system automatically annotates new photos for that user based on these new configurations.

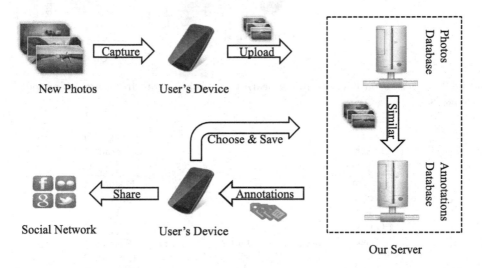

Fig. 1. Overview of our proposed system to automatically recommend personalized tags.

3.2 Visual Instance Search Method

Feature Extraction. To detect and extract features from images, there are many methods that have been proposed (Harris-Affine, Hessian-Affine detectors [8], Maximally stable extremal region (MSER) detector [7], Edge-based region detector [21], Intensity extrema-based region detector [22] ...). The authors choose to use Hessian-Affine detector, for detecting and extracting features from images. In our version of BoW model, we use Perd'och's implementation of SIFT detector, which is shown to perform best on Oxford Building Dataset [13] (Figs. 3 and 4).

Dictionary Building. Treating each descriptor as an individual visual words in the dictionary results in a worthless waste of resources and time. In order to overcome this obstacle, the authors therefore build the dictionary by considering some similar descriptors as one. In other words, all descriptor vectors are

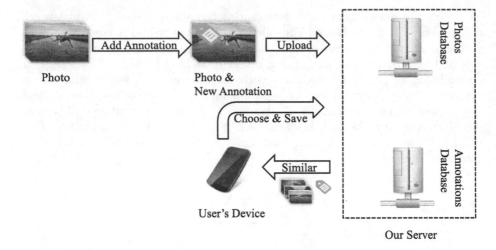

Fig. 2. Overview on how our system learn to annotate photo from samples provided by users.

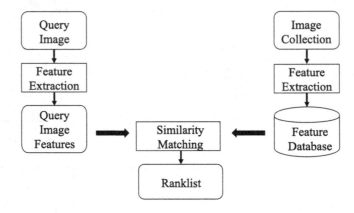

Fig. 3. How an Image Retrieval System works

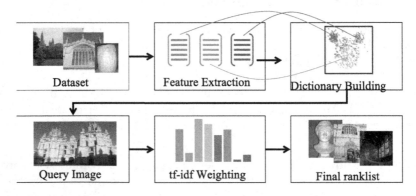

Fig. 4. Proposed framework

divided into k clusters, each representing a visual word. There are many algorithms that are proposed to solve this kind of problem. However, the authors use the approximate k-means (AKM). AKM is proposed by Philbin et al. [14]. Comparing to the original k-means, AKM can reduce the majority amount of time taken by exact nearest neighbors computation but only gives slightly different result. Also, in [14], Philbin et al. shows that using 1M dictionary size would have the best performance on the Oxford Building 5K Dataset [11].

Quantization. Subsequently, each 128-dimension SIFT descriptor needs to be mapped into the dictionary. Commonly, each descriptor is assigned into the nearest word in the dictionary. Thus, when two descriptors are assigned to different words, they are considered as totally different. In practice, this hard assignment leads to errors due to variability in descriptor (e.g. image noise, varying scene illumination, instability in the feature detection process ...) [15]. In order to handling this problem, the authors use soft assignment instead of hard assignment. In particular, each 128-dimension SIFT descriptor is reduced to a k-dimension vector of their k nearest visual words in the dictionary. Each of these k nearest cluster is assigned with weights calculated from the formula proposed by Sivic et al. [15], $weight = \exp(-\frac{d^2}{2\delta^2})$, where d is the distance from the cluster center to descriptor point. Then, by adding all these weights to their corresponding bins, we have the BoW representation of an image.

In this work, k and δ^2 are chosen to be 3 and 6250, respectively.

tf-idf Weighting Scheme. As mentioned in Sect. 2, tf-idf is a popular weighting scheme that is used by almost any BoW model. In this section, the authors show how this scheme is applied to our system.

For a term t_i in a particular document d_j, its term frequency $tf_{i,j}$ is defined as follow:

$$tf_{i,j} = \frac{n_{i,j}}{\sum_k n_{k,j}} \tag{1}$$

where $n_{i,j}$ is the number of occurrences of the considered term t_i in the document d_j. The denominator is the sum of the number of occurrences of all the terms in document d_j.

The inverse document frequency idf_i of a term t_i is computed by the following formula:

$$idf_i = \log \frac{|D|}{|\{j : t_i \in d_j\}|} \tag{2}$$

where, $|D|$ is the total number of documents in the corpus, $|\{j : t_i \in d_j\}|$ is the number of documents where the term t_i appears, i.e. $n_{i,j} \neq 0$

The tf-idf weight of a term t_i in a document d_j is then calculated as the product of tf and idf:

$$tfidf_{i,j} = tfi, j \times idf_i \tag{3}$$

The tf-idf weight is then used to compute the similarity score between an image d_i and a query q:

$$s_{d_i,q} = \boldsymbol{tfidf}_i \cdot \boldsymbol{tfidf}_q = \sum_{j=1}^{|T|} tfidf_{i,j} \times tfidf_{q,j} \tag{4}$$

Finally, by sorting the list of images corresponding to their similarity score with a query, we achieve the raw ranked list of this query which is then used for the Spatial Rerank step.

4   Experiment and Result

In this section, first, we present our experiment result on Oxford 5K Building Dataset to prove that our BoW implementation can achieve good enough performance on standard benchmark. The experiment shows that our version of BoW achieves the mean average precision of 0.844 on Oxford 5K Building Dataset with nearly one second average time for each query. This dataset was constructed by Philbin et al. in 2007 [14]. It consists of 5,062 images of resolution 1024 × 768 belongs to 11 different Oxford buildings. Images for each building are collected from Flickr by searching using text queries. Along with the dataset, there are also 55 queries along with their ground-truth, 5 for each landmark. The ground truth of 55 queries are manually constructed. For each query, images are classified into 4 groups: (1) *Good*: the building appears apparently, (2) *OK*: more than 25 % of the building is present, (3) *Bad*: the building is not shown up, and (4) *Junk*: less than 25 % of the building is captured. The reason why the authors use this dataset is because of its popularity, it is used by many previous works in this field. Thus, we can easily compare our systems with those previous works.

Secondly, we also present and illustrate several typical scenarios of our automatic annotation system with the dataset consisting of our personal photos taken from Facebook. This dataset includes 5 different classes corresponding with 5 social events that are personally annotated. There are 2 classes that share a common annotation. Photos in each class share some particular attributes such as background, mascots, logos. As a result, whenever users create or edit the annotation of these common objects, other photos in the same class can also be tagged similarly thanks to theses mutual attributes. The details of these 5 classes in the dataset are described below:

1. #APCS_Party: Photos taken at a party of our university. Photos in this class contain nearly the same group of people and have similar background and decoration on the stage.
2. #First_time_in_Singapore: These photos are taken at the Merlion in Singapore. They all contain the merlion statue.
3. #Hoi_An_with_family: Consisting of photos taken at Hoi An town in Vietnam with one of the authors' family. The people appearing in them and the background are their common attributes.

#APCS_Party

#First_time_in_Singapore

#Hoi_An_with_family

#My_favorite_competition

#My_first_Regional

(a)   (b)   (c)

Fig. 5. Our personal dataset. Column (a) shows 5 queries of 5 classes in the dataset. Column (b) and (c) are some examples in the returned result of the queries.

4. #My_favorite_competition: These are taken at multiple times I have taken part in the ACM-ICPC, a really famous collegiate programming competition. The mutual characteristic of these photos is the logo of the competition.
5. #My_first_regional: Photos taken at my ICPC regional contest in Phuket, Thailand. The photos all accommodate the mascot of the competition.

We then performed experiment on 5 different queries corresponding to 5 different classes. These queries and some sample result are given in Fig. 5. In the experiment, each query also takes our system nearly one second on average and the mean average precision over 5 queries is 0.749. The detail result is shown in Table 1.

Table 1. Experiment on personal dataset

APCS query	Singapore query	Thailand query	ACMlogo query	HoiAn query	**mAP**
0.690	0.775	0.798	0.754	0.728	**0.749**

5 Conclusion

In this paper, we have proposed our idea to use Visual Instance Search to create a system that can help user in 2 different tasks: automatically suggested personalized annotations for uploaded photos and propagate users' annotations for their photos to similar images. To realize this, we build our system based on Bag-of-Words model. To evaluate the performance of the system, we have used Oxford 5K Building Dataset, a really popular benchmark for Visual Instance Search task. In addition, we have also experimented and illustrated our systems with some scenarios taken from personal photos along with their tags on Facebook. Our system has achieves the mAP of 0.844 and 0.749 respectively on these 2 datasets with the processing time less than 1 second for each query. In the future, the authors believe that the system can further be developed to become a valuable extension for online photo sharing services.

References

1. Belongie, S., Carson, C., Greenspan, H., Malik, J.: Color- and texture-based image segmentation using EM and its application to content-based image retrieval. In: 1998 Sixth International Conference on Computer Vision, pp. 675–682, January 1998
2. Brunelli, R.: Template Matching Techniques in Computer Vision: Theory and Practice. Wiley, New York (2009)
3. Chen, M., Zheng, A., Weinberger, K.Q.: Fast image tagging. In: Dasgupta, S., Mcallester, D. (eds.) Proceedings of the 30th International Conference on Machine Learning (ICML 2013), vol. 28, pp. 1274–1282. JMLR Workshop and Conference Proceedings, May 2013. http://jmlr.org/proceedings/papers/v28/chen13e.pdf
4. Gharavi-Alkhansari, M.: A fast globally optimal algorithm for template matching using low-resolution pruning. IEEE Trans. Image Process. **10**(4), 526–533 (2001)

5. Lan, T., Mori, G.: A max-margin riffled independence model for image tag ranking. In: IEEE Conference on Computer Vision and Pattern Recognition (CVPR), June 2013

6. Manning, C.D., Raghavan, P., Schtze, H.: Introduction to Information Retrieval. Cambridge University Press, Cambridge (2008)

7. Matas, J., Chum, O., Urban, M., Pajdla, T.: Robust wide baseline stereo from maximally stable extremal regions. In: Rosin, P.L., Marshall, A.D. (eds.) BMVC. British Machine Vision Association (2002)

8. Mikolajczyk, K., Schmid, C.: Scale & affine invariant interest point detectors. Int. J. Comput. Vis. **60**(1), 63–86 (2004)

9. Nister, D., Stewenius, H.: Scalable recognition with a vocabulary tree. In: Proceedings of CVPR (2006)

10. Ouyang, W., Tombari, F., Mattoccia, S., Di Stefano, L., Cham, W.K.: Performance evaluation of full search equivalent pattern matching algorithms. IEEE Trans. Pattern Anal. Mach. Intell. **34**(1), 127–143 (2012)

11. http://www.robots.ox.ac.uk/~vgg/data/oxbuildings/

12. Peleg, S., Werman, M., Rom, H.: A unified approach to the change of resolution: space and gray-level. IEEE Trans. Pattern Anal. Mach. Intell. **11**(7), 739–742 (1989)

13. Perd'och, M., Chum, O., Matas, J.: Efficient representation of local geometry for large scale object retrieval. In: 2009 IEEE Conference on Computer Vision and Pattern Recognition, CVPR 2009, pp. 9–16, June 2009

14. Philbin, J., Chum, O., Isard, M., Sivic, J., Zisserman, A.: Object retrieval with large vocabularies and fast spatial matching. In: Proceedings of CVPR (2007)

15. Philbin, J., Isard, M., Sivic, J., Zisserman, A.: Lost in quantization: improving particular object retrieval in large scale image databases. In: Proceedings of CVPR (2008)

16. Rosenfeld, A., Vanderburg, G.J.: Coarse-fine template matching. IEEE Trans. Syst. Man Cybern. **7**(2), 104–107 (1977)

17. Rubner, Y., Tomasi, C., Guibas, L.: The earth mover's distance as a metric for image retrieval. Int. J. Comput. Vis. **40**(2), 99–121 (2000)

18. Schindler, G., Brown, M., Szeliski, R.: City-scale location recognition. In: Proceedings of CVPR (2007)

19. Shen, H.C., Wong, A.K.: Generalized texture representation and metric. Comput. Vis. Graph. Image Process. **23**(2), 187–206 (1983). http://www.sciencedirect.com/science/article/pii/0734189X83901123

20. Sivic, J., Zisserman, A.: Video google: a text retrieval approach to object matching in videos. In: Proceedings of ICCV (2003)

21. Tuytelaars, T., Gool, L.V.: Content-based image retrieval based on local affinely invariant regions. In: International Conference on Visual Information Systems, pp. 493–500 (1999)

22. Tuytelaars, T., Gool, L.V.: Wide baseline stereo matching based on local, affinely invariant regions. In: Proceedings of BMVC, pp. 412–425 (2000)

23. Viola, P., Jones, M.: Rapid object detection using a boosted cascade of simple features. In: 2001 Proceedings of the 2001 IEEE Computer Society Conference on Computer Vision and Pattern Recognition, CVPR 2001, vol. 1, pp. I-511-I-518 (2001)

24. Werman, M., Peleg, S., Rosenfeld, A.: A distance metric for multidimensional histograms. Comput. Visi. Graph. Image Process. **32**(3), 328–336 (1985). http://www.sciencedirect.com/science/article/pii/0734189X85900556

Videogame Technology in Architecture Education

Francesc Valls[1], Ernest Redondo[1], David Fonseca[2(✉)], Pilar Garcia-Almirall[1], and Jordi Subirós[1]

[1] Barcelona School of Architecture, UPC - BarcelonaTech, Barcelona, Spain
{francesc.valls,ernesto.redondo,pilar.garcia-almirall}@upc.edu,
jordi.subiros@estudiant.upc.edu
[2] Architecture School, La Salle Universitat Ramon Llull, Barcelona, Spain
fonsi@salle.url.edu

Abstract. Videogame technology is quickly maturing and approaching levels of realism once reserved to 3D rendering applications used in architecture, in real-time and with the capacity to react in real-time to user input. This paper describes an educational experience using videogame technology in architecture education, exploring its applicability in the field in architecture compared to more traditional media. A prototype application modeling a proposed urban space was developed using Unreal Engine and a group of architecture students were asked to use the software to navigate the virtual environment. The development process of the applications is discussed as well as the design of the survey to assess the participants' experience in four key areas (a) player profile, (b) experience using the beta version, (c) use of videogame technology as an educational tool, and (d) applicability of game engines in Architecture.

Keywords: Gamification · Education · E-learning · Architecture · Videogame engine · Visual representation · Interactivity · Immersion · Urban space

1 Introduction

Videogames are increasingly part of our life; while in the past playing videogames was considered an activity restricted to the young male demographic segment, the average age of a "gamer" (a person who plays videogames) is currently 35 years old and the gender distribution is remarkably balanced [1]. Moreover, the use of smartphones for leisure activities have widened the game-playing population spectrum while introducing new genres labeled as "social gaming" (games with emphasis on social interactions, usually with friends) and "casual gaming" (games designed to be played without needing special skills or strong player commitment, in contrast to "hardcore games").

The progressive importance of videogames in our lives is influencing our cultural expression; for example, Machinima Theater [2] uses videogames in performing arts, enacting classic plays using videogames, while indie (as in "independent") games [3] often use videogames to explore complex issues in their narrative [4], and can be a vehicle for expressing extremely deep emotions such as witnessing the suffering of a child with a medical condition [5].

© Springer International Publishing Switzerland 2016
M. Kurosu (Ed.): HCI 2016, Part III, LNCS 9733, pp. 436–447, 2016.
DOI: 10.1007/978-3-319-39513-5_41

Videogames have also been used in sports training, where a virtual partner increases the motivation of the subject while doing exercise in a virtual environment [6], and is beginning to find its place in the educational programs of Universities [7]. At the same time, the way games themselves are played is also evolving; the rise of livestreaming is influencing how games are designed and played [8], and game-playing is becoming a spectator sport [9].

1.1 Videogames in Educational Contexts

Gamification is the use of game mechanics in non-game situations [10], using the elements that make game-playing engaging (e.g. competition, reward system, immersion) to improve learner motivation. On the other hand, serious games [11] simulate situations to practice specific skills, usually in training where practicing in a real setting is difficult, expensive or dangerous. Some educational experiences incorporate both gamification and serious games elements in different degrees.

The constructivist paradigm [12], where learners internalize new knowledge into their internal framework through accommodation (reframing existing knowledge to fit new one) and/or assimilation (incorporating new knowledge without altering existing one) has been applied in a gamified environment [13], where students produce in-game artifacts in a self-directed hands-on approach. Along these lines, the videogame Minecraft [14], and specifically its variant Minecraft Education [15], has been used as an educational tool [16], and the character from the TV series Doctor Who has been used in an online game to teach computer programming [17] to schoolchildren.

Other educational experiments confirm that using videogames in education can be a vehicle to promote reasoning in sciences [18], especially when using simulations [19, 20], and can be a valuable asset when used in e-learning [21], although some effort is necessary in its implementation to achieve the desired motivation [22]. Beyond school education, gamification has also been used in higher education [23] and workplace training [24], and videogames have even been used in machine learning to teach computers how to play a game [25], with a teacher agent instructing a student agent.

1.2 Videogame Technology in Architecture Education

Today, photorealistic synthetic imagery in architecture is almost undistinguishable from reality [26], but achieving comparable results in real-time is still challenging. The experience described in this paper describes a prototype exercise to test the applicability of teaching Architecture students using videogame technology.

The use of architecture-related content in videogames is not uncommon; beyond using the built environment as a background for the action taking place in a game, both at urban and architectural scales, we can find examples where elements of the architectural practice are central to the game mechanics, such as city-building games [27] which, beginning at the end of the 1980 decade with the SimCity [28] series to the more recent Cities Skylines [29], place the simulation of the life in a city as the core gameplay element. Beyond pure entertainment, the simulated environment of this game genre, although heavily simplified and mainly focused on mobility and infrastructure development [30], can help urban planners grasp basic concepts of their practice.

Regarding urban planning education, the Artificial Intelligence (AI) that power the agent-based models in the simulations of these games can be valuable in urban planning education [31], helping students assess the outcomes of their proposed policies in a "what-if" scenario, in a constructivist educational approach. In addition, three-dimensional geospatially referenced virtual environments [32] have also been proposed as an experimental approach to geographic analysis. These advances are made possible by advancements in 3D visualization [33] in Geographic information Systems (GIS), which in turn can benefit from the vast amount of urban data currently available [34].

Other experiences focus on the visual representation instead of the functional aspects of the simulation, and the realistic environments modern videogame engines are capable of producing have been used to explore the decision-making processes in landscape planning [35] and to support collaborative landscape planning [36].

Multiple teaching strategies can be used to deal with the complexity of education in the field of architecture, and the advantages of using 3D representations using Virtual Reality (VR) in contrast to the more traditional 2D plans in built environment education [37] can be beneficial, as well as using Augmented Reality (AR) to improve student engagement while promoting public participation [38].

2 Objectives

Architectural design has benefited from innovations in representation technologies, from the invention of conical perspective in the Renaissance to more recent introduction of Computer Aided Design (CAD) and, at the same time, these innovations have influenced directly or indirectly both the design workflow of the architectural practice and the formal language of the buildings.

This experience developed previous work by the authors [39], which proposed using videogames as an educational tool with two distinct strategies: (a) as a gamification experiment, through the incorporation of challenging and/or competitive elements to improve motivation, and (b) as a tool to promote critical thinking in architecture students placing them in simulated environments, to stimulate reflection on multiple aspects that are often overlooked in the design of public spaces, taking advantage of the Proteus effect [40] where self-representation in virtual worlds can affect the behavior of the participants.

The educational objective of the experience described in this paper was to test the applicability of using videogame engines in architecture education, specifically to research the students' perception on using this technology, and specifically to study if it could improve their motivation.

The application was an early beta prototype, following the software design philosophy of "release early, release often" [41] to enable a tighter feedback loop between the students and the instructors, which should be beneficial to both, producing better results that fulfill the requirements of the users while at the same time avoiding developing unneeded content.

In this version, the students' opinion was gathered through an online anonymous survey; in future iterations, they will be asked for permission to have their behavior logged in-game (using game analytics tools), and some elements of the survey will be incorporated into the executable.

As a secondary objective, the application laid the groundwork of a data-gathering tool to track the users' behavior in virtual space, to (a) find out if their behavior diverges from the behavior observed in a real (non-simulated) environments, and (b) to be used as a tool to perform controlled experiments, manipulating the simulated environment (i.e. lighting intensity, simulating disabilities, placing the user in crowded situations using AI-controlled avatars) and observing the changes in the behavior of the test subjects.

3 Prototype Development

3.1 Case of Study

The simulated environment was in a lot next to the building of the Barcelona School of Architecture of the Technical University of Catalonia (BarcelonaTech). This lot is currently the roof of an underground facility connected to the Engineering School of the same campus. The working premise was that this roof would be transformed into a public space, which would give access to the two towers of the Engineering School, that would be repurposed as multiple-use buildings with student dormitories and related facilities for the hosted students as well as other students in the campus (laundry, meeting rooms, convenience stores, etc.).

The site location was chosen because it was easy to visit by the architecture students, and allowed the comparison between the simulated proposed environment and the real built environment easily. In addition, it was expected that the familiarity with the site would make possible to identify contextual elements (visual or audio cues) that should aid in the sensation of being in a specific place.

3.2 Choice of Game Development Platform

A review of the leading game engines available, considering three main factors (ease of development, feature set and licensing requirements) resulted in two main choices: Unity 5 [42] and Unreal Engine 4 [43]. The platform of choice was Unreal Engine 4.10 (UE) over Unity because it seemed more adequate for the purposes of the application to be developed. The main reasons of this choice were:

- While the new Unity version 5 supported Physically-Based Rendering (PBR), UE allowed programming complex shaders in a visual node-based editor like other 3D modeling and rendering packages commonly used in Architecture
- Most of the functionality needed for the application was built-in in UE (navigation, behavior trees, node-based scripting) and therefore more tightly integrated than Unity, which relied on third-party solutions

- Both platforms had a marketplace with downloadable free and paid content, and while Unity had more content at the time of writing, the UE marketplace content was sufficient
- UE was free [44] for Architecture Visualization (ArchViz)
- The development language in UE was either Blueprint (node base scripting) or C++, instead of C# and UnityScript, which arguably allowed non-programmers access to advanced scripting
- Both platforms had a strong user community, and good documentation and training materials, and therefore this factor was not factored in the decision

Overall, it seemed that UE was more artist-friendly and less a developer tool, and could eventually be taught to Architecture students. However, the tool could actually have been developed in Unity as well, and newer versions of the application might use this platform instead.

3.3   Rebuilding 3D Assets

Based on a SketchUp Model developed by the students on another course, the 3D assets had to be re-modeled in a 3D package, because the SketchUp model was not ready to be used in the game engine: (a) the geometry was not optimized (it contained too many triangles), (b) many of the elements (i.e. windows, pillars) were repetitive and therefore there was a lot of potential for asset reusability, (c) the objects were not UV unwrapped, and (d) materials were not assigned to faces.

The modeling phase involved breaking the geometry into simple objects that could be reused: the objects were remodeled with their geometry optimized, using multiple Levels of Detail (LOD) when necessary and given sensible pivot points (local transform), unnecessary non-visible faces were removed (since UE works with single-sided faces), normal maps were baked onto simplified geometry to simulate detail without increasing triangle count, materials were assigned to faces, objects were unwrapped using two UV channels (one for textures, and a second non-overlapping UV for lightmaps), hard and soft edges were defined, custom colliders were created when necessary, and finally the objects were exported to FBX files (the 3D asset file interchange format used by UE).

This way the geometry could be reduced from one 800 MB FBX file to 55 FBX files with a combined size of less than 1 MB. These 3D assets were the building blocks of the simulated environment.

3.4   Environment Setup

The environment design consisted in the following phases: (a) inserting the 3D objects into the scene, (b) defining the materials, (c) lighting setup, (d) reflection environment setup, and (e) visual effects.

The 3D objects were inserted into the scene using the UE editor. For repetitive assets, a custom construction script procedurally created a 3D array of instances of the meshes with definable number of copies and separation intervals for the X, Y and Z axes.

In addition, a class system was defined to help creating variants of compound objects (modules made of multiple 3D assets) to take advantage of inheritance from a parent class, adding or removing components when necessary.

The material setup consisted in assigning materials to the corresponding parts of the objects and defining the shaders and the texture assets each material should use. Instanced materials were defined to reuse the same material definition while allowing to change the scale of the object UV mapping to account for the different mesh dimensions.

Lighting was setup as two light sources, one directional light to account of sunlight and another skylight to account for the diffuse lighting from the sky. The lighting information (direct and indirect lighting, as well as shadows) was baked (pre-calculated) into lightmaps for all static (non-movable) objects in the environment.

Finally, some effects were added to improve immersion: eye adaptation (taking advantage of the High Dynamic Range (HDR) rendering of UE), bloom effects to compensate for the limited dynamic range of computer monitors when viewing very bright objects, flare effects to simulate the view from a physical camera, dynamic moving clouds in the sky dome, and reflections from the environment on materials such as glass (using spherical reflection probes).

3.5   Avatar Control Definition

The user avatar (pawn) inherited from the built-in character class in UE, adding a camera component at eye level, emulating a first-person perspective. Therefore, the pawn inherited the rigid body physics simulation functionality from the parent class and had the ability to collide with objects in the environment (using the capsule collider inherited from the character class) and climb stairs and ramps.

Since the movement functionality was inherited form the character parent class, the pawn had walk functionality and only the controls had to be defined. The controls replicated the standard First Person Shooter (FPS) functionality using the mouse and WASD keys:

- Moving forward/backwards: mapped to W and UP arrow (positive) and S and DOWN arrow (negative)
- Moving sideways: mapped to D and RIGHT arrow (positive) and D and LEFT arrow (negative)
- Turning the camera left/right: Mapped to horizontal movement of the mouse (X), controlling yaw (rotation around the vertical local axis of the avatar)
- Looking up/down: Mapped to vertical movement of the mouse (Y), controlling pitch (rotation around the left-right local axis of the avatar)

4   Results

The standard point of view when designing an architectural space is either a top-down perspective when working in 3D (either modeling on a computer or building a physical model) or a plan view when working in 2D (either in a CAD program or sketching freehand). Perspective representations are generated in a computer using a 3D rendering package or hand-drawn, but the results are either static images or non-interactive videos.

To find out the benefits that the use of game engines in architecture can provide to architectural visualization, focusing on (a) the use of a first-person perspective, and (b) the real-time interactivity, the resulting application was compiled into an executable and deployed to the students through the university Moodle-based intranet, where a Dropbox link was posted due to the maximum file size limitation of the platform. The students were asked to execute the application on their own computers and fill a survey after the experience.

On application launch, the avatar spawned facing the (virtual) building of the Barcelona School of Architecture to provide a familiar landmark to give the participants a contextual cue on the simulated environment. Therefore, the first-person camera was initially placed looking in the opposite direction of the place the students were expected to explore, to encourage them to walk around to get their bearings.

Placing the camera at the same eye-level as in the real world, added to the possibility of looking around emulating the head movement, was expected to mimic the sense of being in an architectural space more successfully than the traditional top-down view with orbit control commonly used in architecture, while providing a better sense of human scale (Fig. 1).

Fig. 1. In-game screenshots of the application visiting the virtual space

The participants were able to walk around the space, and had to navigate the environment avoiding obstacles (trees, pillars, buildings) and cross bridges over pools filled with water to reach some sections of the scene. The lighting when visiting the spaces underneath the buildings was dimmer and had to wait for their eyes to adapt to the relative darkness (Fig. 2).

Fig. 2. In-game screenshots of the application featuring eye adaptation to dark environments

5   Survey Design

To gather data about their experience, the students were asked to fill a survey, using Google Forms. They were asked about four key aspects, using questions ranked in a 5-point Likert scale where applicable:

- Player profile
- Experience using the beta version
- Use of videogame technology as an educational tool
- Applicability of game engines in Architecture

The questions about the player profile tried to identify the motivation [45] of the participants and categorize them into six main profiles following a previous example of game motivation survey [46–48]: action, strategy, achievement, social, fantasy and creativity. The participants were also asked the average hours played daily in different platforms (computers, consoles and mobile devices) and their year of birth and gender.

The questions about the experience in the beta application asked about its usability (controls, speed and immersion), its graphics (materials, illumination, shadows, models, reflections and color) and the improvements that users would value in the next version of the software (more interaction, better visuals, sound cues, better sense of urban context, simulation of seasons or day/night cycles).

As and educational tool, the students were asked if the simulation promoted thinking differently about some aspects of the space, such as its size, proportions, materials or functionality.

Finally, the participants were asked about the applicability of game engines in architecture in different contexts (design, urban planning, visual representation, heritage) and to compare game engines to other technologies used by architects (rendering, Computer

Aided Design, physical models, 3D printing, hand-drawn sketches, photomontages, videos).

The analysis of the responses of the survey should give the authors insight on the participants' experience, which should improve the quality and usability of the next version of the program.

6   Conclusions and Future Work

The initial results show that students valued the experience of using videogame engines in architecture education, and the authors speculate that this acceptance will increase as engines improve and become easier to use. I this sense, in the 2015–16 academic year of the Architecture degree of the Barcelona School of Architecture, the students will be introduced in how to use UE in the context of the Multimedia course.

The next version of the application is expected to target HTML5 and run on modern browsers, to allow user participation over the Internet and increase the pool of participants while simplifying the distribution of the executable. This experience should be carefully designed taking advantage of gamification elements to increase involvement, to avoid participants dropping out of the experiment early, as some research suggests [49].

Actively manipulating the environment instead of just passively wandering in it should increase the engagement of the students because the resulting object will be built by themselves [50]. In the next iteration of the experience, it is planned to allow the participants not only to visit the virtual environment, but also interact with some elements, adding modular building blocks to create objects in-game which will allow the students to produce artifacts.

Finally, in future iterations of the experience, the changes in the perception of the space using realistic rendering compared to stylized (non-realistic) rendering [51, 52] will be assessed.

6.1   Gathering Experimental Data in a Virtual Environment

Tracking individual persons in public spaces is challenging; although it is possible to accurately track their movement using RFID or other technologies [53], it is technically difficult, and it raises privacy concerns when gathering data in public spaces. In areas such as economics, synthetic experiments are performed to model real situations, even though in some cases participants do not understand the rules fully [54].

The next phase of the development will include the capacity of tracking (with their consent) the users' behavior in virtual space (position and gaze along time), which will allow the application to be used as a research tool [55] to conduct controlled experiments. This experiments will focus on estimating movement parameters in pedestrian models [56], exploring wayfinding and search behavior [57], the mental representation of urban spaces [58, 59], as well as gaze behavior [60].

Acknowledgments. This research was supported by the Non-Oriented Fundamental Research Project EDU2012-37247/EDUC of the VI National Plan for Scientific Research, Development and Technological Innovation 2008-2011, Government of Spain, titled "E-learning 3.0 in the teaching of architecture. Case studies of educational research for the foreseeable future".

References

1. Entertainment Software Association: 2015 Essential Facts About the Computer and Video Game Industry. Entertainment Software Association (2015)
2. EK Theater: Retelling Classical Stories through Video Games. http://www.ektheater.com/
3. Pajot, L., Swirsky, J.: Indie Game: The Movie (2012)
4. Pope, L.: Papers, Please. 3909 LLC (2013)
5. Osit, D., Zouhali-Worrall, M.: Thank You for Playing (2015)
6. Irwin, B.C., Scorniaenchi, J., Kerr, N.L., Eisenmann, J.C., Feltz, D.L.: Aerobic exercise is promoted when individual performance affects the group: a test of the kohler motivation gain effect. Ann. Behav. Med. **44**, 151–159 (2012)
7. Conditt, J.: "Citizen Kane" to "Call of Duty": The rise of video games in universities. http://www.engadget.com/2015/10/01/video-games-film-history-education-ashley-pinnick/
8. Orland, K.: Twitch plays everything: How livestreaming is changing game design. http://arstechnica.com/gaming/2015/10/twitch-plays-everything-how-livestreaming-is-changing-game-design/
9. Free to Play (2014)
10. Deterding, S., Dixon, D., Khaled, R., Nacke, L.: From game design elements to gamefulness: defining "gamification." In: Proceedings of the 15th International Academic MindTrek Conference: Envisioning Future Media Environments, pp. 9–15. ACM, New York (2011)
11. Davidson, D. (ed.): Beyond Fun: Serious Games and Media. lulu.com, Pittsburgh (2010)
12. Papert, S.: Mindstorms: Children, Computers, and Powerful Ideas. Basic Books Inc, New York (1980)
13. Weintrop, D., Holbert, N., Horn, M.S., Wilensky, U.: Computational thinking in constructionist video games. Int. J. Game-Based Learn. **6**, 1–17 (2016)
14. Persson, M.: Minecraft. Mojang (2011)
15. Microsoft: Minecraft Education. Microsoft (2016)
16. Stuart, K.: Minecraft Education Edition: why it's important for every fan of the game. http://www.theguardian.com/technology/2016/jan/22/minecraft-education-edition-why-its-important-for-every-fan-of-the-game (2016)
17. BBC Learning: The Doctor and the Dalek. www.bbc.co.uk/cbbc/games/doctor-who-game
18. Holbert, N.R., Wilensky, U.: Constructible authentic representations: designing video games that enable players to utilize knowledge developed in-game to reason about science. Tech. Know. Learn. **19**, 53–79 (2014)
19. Honey, M., Hilton, M.L. (eds.): Learning Science Through Computer Games and Simulations. National Academies Press, Washington, D.C. (2011)
20. Aldrich, C.: Simulations and the Future of Learning: An Innovative (and Perhaps Revolutionary) Approach to e-Learning. Pfeiffer, San Francisco (2003)
21. Domínguez, A., Saenz-de-Navarrete, J., de-Marcos, L., Fernández-Sanz, L., Pagés, C., Martínez-Herráiz, J.-J.: Gamifying learning experiences: Practical implications and outcomes. Comput. Educ. **63**, 380–392 (2013)

22. Villagrasa, S., Fonseca, D., Romo, M., Redondo, E.: GLABS: Gamification for learning management systems. In: 2014 9th Iberian Conference on Information Systems and Technologies (CISTI), pp. 1–7 (2014)
23. Iosup, A., Epema, D.: An experience report on using gamification in technical higher education. In: Proceedings of the 45th ACM Technical Symposium on Computer Science Education, pp. 27–32. ACM, New York (2014)
24. Garcia-Panella, O., Badia-Corrons, A., Labrador-Ruiz, E., Fonseca-Escudero, D.: Pleasant learning experiences: augmenting knowledge through games and interaction. In: Jia, J. (ed.) Educational Stages and Interactive Learning: From Kindergarten to Workplace Training, pp. 369–386. IGI Global, Hershey (2012)
25. Taylor, M.E., Carboni, N., Fachantidis, A., Vlahavas, I., Torrey, L.: Reinforcement learning agents providing advice in complex video games. Connect. Sci. **26**, 45–63 (2014)
26. Parkin, K.: Building 3D with Ikea. http://www.cgsociety.org/index.php/CGSFeatures/CGSFeatureSpecial/building_3d_with_ikea
27. Moss, R.: From SimCity to, well, SimCity: The history of city-building games. http://arstechnica.com/gaming/2015/10/from-simcity-to-well-simcity-the-history-of-city-building-games/
28. Wright, W.: SimCity. Maxis (1989)
29. Korppoo, K.: Cities: Skylines. Colossal Order (2015)
30. Goodwin, D.: 10 Things The "Cities: Skylines" Video Game Taught Us About Modern Urbanism. http://www.archdaily.com/619567/rebuilding-simcity-10-things-cities-skylines-says-about-modern-urbanism/
31. Hjorth, A., Wilensky, U.: Redesigning your city – a constructionist environment for urban planning education. Inform. Educ. **13**, 197–208 (2014)
32. Lin, H., Batty, M., Jørgensen, S.E., Fu, B., Konecny, M., Voinov, A., Torrens, P., Lu, G., Zhu, A.-X., Wilson, J.P., Gong, J., Kolditz, O., Bandrova, T., Chen, M.: Virtual environments begin to embrace process-based geographic analysis. Trans. GIS **19**, 493–498 (2015)
33. Yin, L.: Integrating 3D visualization and GIS in planning education. J. Geogr. Higher Educ. **34**, 419–438 (2010)
34. Valls Dalmau, F., Garcia-Almirall, P., Redondo Domínguez, E., Fonseca Escudero, D.: From raw data to meaningful information: a representational approach to cadastral databases in relation to urban planning. Future Internet **6**, 612–639 (2014)
35. Bishop, I.D.: Landscape planning is not a game: Should it be? Landsc. Urban Plann. **100**, 390–392 (2011)
36. Herwig, A., Paar, P.: Game engines: tools for landscape visualization and planning? In: Buhmann, E., Nothhelfer, U.G., Pietsch, M. (eds.) Trends in GIS and Virtualization in Environmental Planning and Design, Proceedings at Anhalt University of Applied Sciences 2002. Wichmann Verlag, Heidelberg (2002)
37. Horne, M., Thompson, E.M.: The role of virtual reality in built environment education. J. Educ. Built Environ. **3**, 5–24 (2008)
38. Fonseca, D., Valls, F., Redondo, E., Villagrasa, S.: Informal interactions in 3D education: Citizenship participation and assessment of virtual urban proposals. Comput. Hum. Behav. **55**(Part A), 504–518 (2016)
39. Valls, F., Redondo, E., Fonseca, D.: E-learning and serious games. In: Zaphiris, P., Ioannou, A. (eds.) LCT 2015. LNCS, vol. 9192, pp. 632–643. Springer, Heidelberg (2015)
40. Yee, N., Bailenson, J.: The proteus effect: the effect of transformed self-representation on behavior. Hum. Commun. Res. **33**, 271–290 (2007)
41. Raymond, E.S.: The Cathedral & the Bazaar: Musings on Linux and Open Source by an Accidental Revolutionary. O'Reilly Media, Sebastopol (1999)

42. Unity Technologies: Unity 5. Unity Technologies (2015)
43. Epic Games: Unreal Engine 4. Epic Games (2012)
44. Epic Games, Inc.: Unreal Engine End User License Agreement. https://www.unrealengine.com/eula
45. Yee, N., Ducheneaut, N., Nelson, L.: Online gaming motivations scale: development and validation. In: Proceedings of the SIGCHI Conference on Human Factors in Computing Systems, pp. 2803–2806. ACM, New York (2012)
46. Yee, N.: How We Created the Gamer Motivation Profile (2015). http://quanticfoundry.com/2015/06/18/how-we-created-the-gamer-motivation-profile/
47. Yee, N.: How We Developed The Gamer Motivation Profile v2 (2015). http://quantic foundry.com/2015/07/20/how-we-developed-the-gamer-motivation-profile-v2/
48. Yee, N.: Most popular games by gaming motivations (2015). http://quanticfoundry.com/2015/08/11/most-popular-games-by-gaming-motivations/
49. Sauermann, H., Franzoni, C.: Crowd science user contribution patterns and their implications. In: PNAS 201408907 (2015)
50. Norton, M.I., Mochon, D., Ariely, D.: The IKEA effect: When labor leads to love. J. Consum. Psychol. **22**, 453–460 (2012)
51. Sloan, P.-P.J., Martin, W., Gooch, A., Gooch, B.: The lit sphere: a model for capturing NPR shading from art. In: Proceedings of Graphics Interface 2001, pp. 143–150. Canadian Information Processing Society, Toronto (2001)
52. Grabli, S., Durand, F., Sillion, F.X.: Density measure for line-drawing simplification. In: 12th Pacific Conference on Computer Graphics and Applications, 2004, PG 2004, Proceedings, pp. 309–318 (2004)
53. Kravets, D.: How the NFL—not the NSA—is impacting data gathering well beyond the gridiron. http://arstechnica.com/tech-policy/2015/09/the-nfl-is-reshaping-the-surveillance-society-xbox-one-experience-and-gambling/
54. Burton-Chellew, M.N., Mouden, C.E., West, S.A.: Conditional cooperation and confusion in public-goods experiments. PNAS **113**, 1291–1296 (2016)
55. Kuliga, S.F., Thrash, T., Dalton, R.C., Hölscher, C.: Virtual reality as an empirical research tool — Exploring user experience in a real building and a corresponding virtual model. Comput. Environ. Urban Syst. **54**, 363–375 (2015)
56. Vafayi, K., Muntean, A., Corbetta, A.: Parameter estimation of social forces in pedestrian dynamics models via a probabilistic method. Math. Biosci. Eng. **12**, 337–356 (2014)
57. Pingel, T.J., Schinazi, V.R.: The relationship between scale and strategy in search-based wayfinding. Cartograph. Perspect. **77**, 33–45 (2014)
58. Hölscher, C., Tenbrink, T., Wiener, J.M.: Would you follow your own route description? Cognitive strategies in urban route planning. Cognition **121**, 228–247 (2011)
59. Schinazi, V.R., Epstein, R.A.: Neural correlates of real-world route learning. NeuroImage **53**, 725–735 (2010)
60. Wiener, J.M., Hölscher, C., Büchner, S., Konieczny, L.: Gaze behaviour during space perception and spatial decision making. Psychol. Res. **76**, 713–729 (2012)

Spatio-Temporal Wardrobe Generation of Actors' Clothing in Video Content

Florian Vandecasteele[1], Jeroen Vervaeke[1], Baptist Vandersmissen[1],
Michel De Wachter[2], and Steven Verstockt[1(✉)]

[1] ELIS Department - Data Science Lab, Ghent University IMinds,
Sint-Pietersnieuwstraat, 41, 9000 Ghent, Belgium
{florian.vandecasteele,steven.verstockt}@ugent.be
[2] Appinness, Hertshage 10, 9300 Aalst, Belgium

Abstract. In this paper, we propose a methodology for spatio-temporal wardrobe generation for video content. The main goal is to suggest relevant matches between clothes worn by actors and images originating from a set of e-commerce clothing sites. The semi-automatic generation of fine-grained spatial metadata for each video sequence is based on shot detection, keyframe detection, feature matching and clothing type classification based filtering. The result of this annotation process is a spatio-temporal database consisting of videos and the corresponding actor clothing. This database can be queried in various ways depending on the intended target application.

Keywords: Video summarization · Shot detection · Clothing annotation · Metadata enrichment · Deep learning

1 Introduction

The clothing industry amounts for one of the most important selling segments in e-commerce worldwide[1]. Furthermore, the majority of online shopping happens spontaneously, often based on popular trends displayed on television (TV) [1], i.e., consumers actively search based on what their role models wear on TV. Currently, no automatic tool exists that is able to link the digital wardrobe of an actor to the same clothes visually displayed on a TV screen. The consumer's search for similar clothing is mostly based on the actors branding and a rough textual description of the type and color. Such strategy does not enable people to efficiently find similar clothes. In this paper, we propose a solution for spatio-temporal recognition and annotation of clothing in video content. Our system significantly reduces the required efforts for consumers to find interesting items. The main focus of this paper is on the spatio-temporal recognition of clothes in video shots. In addition, we also introduce a novel keyframe selection mechanism, effectively reducing the set of relevant frames. By limiting the amount of

---

[1] http://bit.ly/1F2zC9M.

© Springer International Publishing Switzerland 2016
M. Kurosu (Ed.): HCI 2016, Part III, LNCS 9733, pp. 448–459, 2016.
DOI: 10.1007/978-3-319-39513-5_42

keyframes, while still maintaining all relevant information present in the video, significant time, needed to label and predict clothing matches for a video shot, can be gained.

The remainder of this paper is organized as follows. Section 2 gives an overview of the proposed framework. Subsequently, Sect. 3 proposes the workflow of the video summarization algorithm. Furthermore, Sect. 4 focuses on the clothing annotation and recognition. In Sect. 5, we present the tool for manual verification of the clothing tagging and we demonstrate our approach on an exemplary TV application. Finally, Sect. 6 lists the conclusions.

2 Framework

The proposed architecture, shown in Fig. 1, consists of 3 main building blocks: (a) a low-complexity video summarization algorithm; (b) a region-of interest (ROI) selection based on face detection; and (c) feature-based clothing object annotation. The generated results are stored in an XML or JSON file depicting the different clothing matches, the video timestamp (frame number) and the spatial location in the keyframe.

The video summarization, i.e., the first building block, is subdivided into three steps, namely: a keyframe selection mechanism (Sect. 3.1), followed by a quality analysis in order to find the best representative frame of a shot (Sect. 3.2), and finally a keyframe similarity mechanism (Sect. 3.3) to reduce the amount of similar keyframes. The final set of distinct keyframes is used as input for the second part of our architecture, i.e., the face detection module (Sect. 4.1), and clothes region selector (Sect. 4.2). The predicted ROI (depicting the region of clothes) and the information concerning the coordinates of the face are used as inputs for the final step of our system, namely the clothing matching based on a coarse to fine strategy (Sect. 4.4).

3 Video Summarization

The automatic understanding and summarization of video content is a challenging problem. The main goal is to reduce the amount of data (frames) by filtering out redundant and unnecessary frames, while preserving only those frames, distinctive and essential to capture the entire video content. A lot of research has been done in the area of video summarization. Ajmal et al. [2], for example, give an overview of the different techniques and classification methods that are commonly used in literature, e.g., feature classification [3], clustering [4], shot selection [5] and trajectory analysis [6]. The focus of this paper will be on shot selection and detection [7–9]. The main research challenge is to properly cope with camera movements within a shot. In order to tackle this issue, we present a grid-based histogram shot detection method. In combination with an additional quality analysis step, this technique gives us the best frame for each shot, i.e., the frame with the most optimal lightning and contrast. Finally, we generate a list of keyframes, where each frame represents a new viewpoint of a scene. A camera

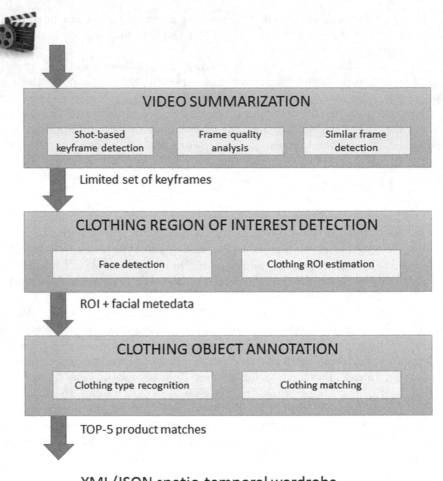

Fig. 1. Modular architecture for spatio-temporal wardrobe generation of video content

shift between one actor to an other, for example, results in two shots. The proposed mechanism is suitable for non-fixed camera movements and works without significant content knowledge. Compared to Baraldi et al. [10], which recently proposed a novel hierarchical clustering based video summarization algorithm, we focus on finding the best representative keyframe within each shot, while they focus on segmenting broadcast videos into coherent shots/scenes.

3.1   Keyframe Selection

The proposed approach for keyframe selection is based on local histogram analysis on a 5-by-5 grid. Compared to state-of-the-art temporal shot selection algorithms [7–9] it is able to cope with fast camera movements, zoom gestures, gradual shot transitions, and similar scene discrimination. An evaluation on a dataset of 400 scenes from different kinds of commercial video content (cooking programs, TV series, clothing styling programs, film trailers) results in a recall of 96 % and a precision of 90 %. The proposed algorithm performs especially well on detecting hard and gradual shots, making it suitable to process multiple types of video content. The main limitation of the histogram grid based shot detection is that it fails to cope with similar scenes. However, this problem is tackled in Sect. 3.3. Furthermore, in order to cope with gradual shots, such as blends and fades, the amount of frames after the last detected transition is counted. By comparing this amount to an experimentally defined threshold, we decide whether to consider it as a new or the same transition. In this way, we successfully manage to detect both gradual and abrupt scene transitions.

3.2 Keyframe Quality Analysis

The clothing recognition algorithm only uses the most representative keyframe per shot as input, i.e., the frame predicted to have the highest quality within each shot. Therefore, a weighted combination of three no-reference quality metrics (blur, contrast and brightness) is computed and used as a real-time image quality measure. Currently, multiple image quality metrics are available [11]. However, most of the existing metrics require a reference image or are not suitable for real-time quality measurement. The proposed no-reference blur, contrast and brightness metrics are evaluated on a variety of television programs. The blur-metric is based on an edge strength analysis. The sharpness of an image is computed by summing the partial differentiate in vertical and horizontal direction. Finally, the shift and spread of the histogram are analyzed to evaluate the brightness and contrast of the image. The combination of those metrics achieves performances that match the human perception for best frame selection, which is proven by a subjective evaluation on our dataset of TV shots.

3.3 Similar Frame Detection

To ensure a robust, reliable, and scalable setup, and in order to avoid recurrence of similar queries, i.e., processing overhead, the detected keyframes are filtered on similarity. We note that in this context similar or near duplicate frames are defined as frames originating from the same scene but showing a different viewpoint or change in illumination.

Numerous approaches detecting near-duplicate images or frames have been published in literature. Chum et al. [12], for example, propose a color histogram local sensitivity hashing (CH-LSH) as the best method for near duplicate image search. They assume that the Euclidean distance between two images (described by their color feature vectors) is a meaningful measure of image similarity. However, the Euclidean distance is found not to be robust and local occlusions can cause a significant change in an image's color histogram. Tasdemir et al. [13] describe a motion vector based approach for copy detection in video content. Experimental results, however, do not seem promising in our context. Sarkar et al. [14] compare

YCbCr histograms, Compact Fourier-Mellin Transform (CFMT) and Scale Invariant Feature Transform (SIFT) for video fingerprinting and large scale similar video retrieval. Their results show that CFMT features perform best for providing quick, accurate retrieval of duplicate videos. Our proposed near duplicate recognition system follows a similar strategy and is built upon LIRE, a light weight open-source library for content based image retrieval (CBIR) [15].

The best results for similar keyframe comparison are achieved with a combination of color and edge directivity descriptor (CEDD) [16] and the fuzzy color and texture histogram feature (FCTH) [17]. The combined compact descriptors mentioned by Kumar et al. [18] show that the fusion of several smaller local descriptors improves the overall results for image indexing and retrieval. Our combination of CEDD and FCTH features for duplicate detection is evaluated on several video sequences, starting from the generated keyframes as described in Sect. 3.1. Finally, we end up with an automatically selected representative set of keyframes. This set could be visualized in an application, effectively summarizing any video. Those keyframes are then used as input for the clothing recognition mechanism, which is proposed in Sect. 4.

4   Clothing Recognition and Annotation

In recent years, the research community has actively been focusing on the automatic classification and detection of clothes in digital content [19–21]. Unfortunately, due to the large visual differences between images on e-commerce websites (photographed on a clean, white background with clear lighting conditions) and those retrieved from in-the-wild videos, this problem is still largely unsolved. In this paper, we propose a novel algorithm to find the best match between clothes in a keyframe and related images found on e-commerce websites. The proposed methodology uses a coarse to fine strategy, which is inspired by the current search mechanisms of popular e-commerce sites. By adding metadata elements like gender, color, texture, and clothing type we filter clothing indexes and predict the most likely matches.

4.1   Face Detection

On each keyframe, returned by the video summarization tool, a face detection algorithm is executed. Face detection and face metadata generation is still an active research domain. However, nowadays multiple commercial solutions are available (e.g. Betaface [22] and openbiometrics [23]). Since improving face detection algorithms is out of scope for this paper, we make use of the commercial Face++ algorithm [24]. An evaluation is done by first comparing the output of several commercial detectors, and additionally evaluating the estimated face coordinates. Furthermore, Face++ outperforms the other approaches on age and gender classification. Both features are used as filters on our indexed clothing datasets to guide and improve the clothing search process. Important to mention is that further improvements on face descriptors would be beneficial to optimize our global architecture.

4.2   Clothing Object Segmentation

Due to different body poses, clothing colors and textures, clothing object segmentation is still an active research problem. Simo-Serra et al. [25], for example, propose a promising CRF model to parse clothes in an image. However, similar to the majority of state-of-the-art approaches, this method fails when the frame only contains upper body parts. For this reason, we propose an alternative approach which is able to cope with this issue.

Based on the position of the detected face we construct a region-of-interest (ROI) that can be used for the proper selection of a clothing patch. The automatic ROI selection takes into account the Face++ results for position, orientation and dimension of the face to proportionally estimate the most probable clothing location in the image. The coordinates of the ROI are based on the position of the lowest neck pixels. By computing a histogram of the face, we obtain a descriptor of skin like pixel colors. These values can be compared to those of the neck pixels, resulting in an estimation for accurate clothing boundaries.

Given a ROI depicting the clothing object(s), our architecture contains three different methods to perform clothing patch generation. Our first method makes use of a superpixel segmentation of the ROI. These superpixels are groups of perceptually meaningful pixel regions which reduce the image complexity into homogeneous regions that align well with object boundaries. Based on a thorough evaluation of different superpixel strategies, simple linear iterative clustering (SLIC) [26] is currently found to perform best. Finally, we merge the superpixels into our clothing query object using a graph based approach [27], focusing on texture, Lab color and location similarities. The main problem with this automatic approach, however, is its inability to cope with differing colors and textures withing a same clothing piece. The merging of superpixels can potentially result in a patch without any meaningful part of the clothing. To avoid this problem, a second approach is developed based on taking a proportional crop of the given ROI. The third and final approach relies on manual input selection by a domain expert. Future work will focus on further optimizing/automizing the clothing segmentation.

4.3   Clothing Type Recognition

Even though color and texture information derived from a clothing patch are essential pieces of information to detect the exact clothing wear, determining the type of clothing can also greatly aid to reduce the target search space. In this subsection we will briefly describe our approach towards automatic clothing type recognition. Important to mention is that we use one of the pretrained Visual Geometry Group (VGG) networks of Simonyan et al. [28], that has proven to be suitable for general image understanding and different classification tasks. The VGG network is a successor of Alexnet, significantly increasing the depth of the convolutional network (up to 19 layers). While Alexnet achieved a top-5 accuracy of 80 % on the ImageNet test set, VGG improved this to 89 % by using a deeper network with very small filters (3x3).

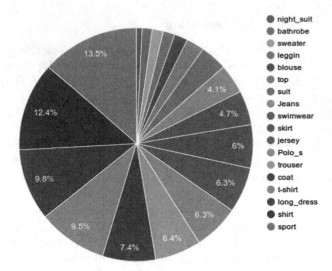

night_suit
bathrobe
sweater
leggin
blouse
top
suit
Jeans
swimwear
skirt
jersey
Polo_s
trouser
coat
t-shirt
long_dress
shirt
sport

Fig. 2. Class distribution of collected clothing dataset

The dataset was collected from Zalando, containing 7210 samples, distributed over 18 different classes. Figure 2 shows the class distribution. We replace the 1000-dimensional softmax layer of the 16-layer pretrained VGG network with an 18-dimensional softmax layer to adapt the network to our needs. First, 10 % of the dataset is randomly left out and used as a validation set, while the other 90 % represent the training set. Images are preprocessed by subtracting the mean image values and generating randomly cropped, mirrored and shifted images to augment the dataset. Minibatch gradient descent in combination with momentum and a degrading learning rate is used to fine tune the network. This network was tested on keyframes originating from different television shows. The clothing type classification using an entire image as input achieves a top-1 accuracy of 35 % and a top-3 accuracy of 47 %. Results on the region of interest based classification task results in a top-1 accuracy of 15 % and a top-3 accuracy of 49 %. The accuracy of the clothing type classification task is relatively low, but similar results are obtained in state-of-the-art approaches [19, 20]. This accuracy shows the necessity for manual verification of the classification results. This will be further explained in Sect. 5. In future work, we will fine-tune our network for the classification of the clothing type by incorporating the manual verification data in a feedback loop.

4.4   Clothing Matching

Finally, the algorithms described in Sects. 4.1 to 4.3 result in several input parameters for the coarse to fine clothing matching. First of all, we incorporate the Face++ metadata as an index filter, i.e., we use the returned attributes to filter the clothing indexes on gender and age. By incorporating this information, we

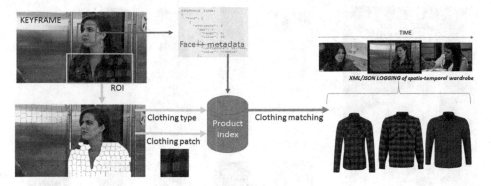

Fig. 3. Overview of the proposed clothing matching strategy - experimental results based on "Keeping Up with the Kardashians".

can already significantly improve the results. Furthermore, we also generated LIRE based clothing indexes for each predefined clothing type (similar to those of the classification task). Based on the recognized clothing type, we use global image features of the clothing patch to find the best visual match within the particular index. Finally, by reranking the CEDD [16], FCTH [17] and PHOG [29] features, we are able to generate decent results, i.e., the majority of top-3 matches in our test cases are subjectively marked as relevant by our lead users. Figure 3 gives a general overview of all different steps involved in finding a clothing match.

5   Demonstrator

In order to facilitate manual verification of the clothing type and the proposed clothing patch, we have built a validation tool (shown in Fig. 4). First, gender and clothing type is predicted based on an input frame. Wrong predictions can

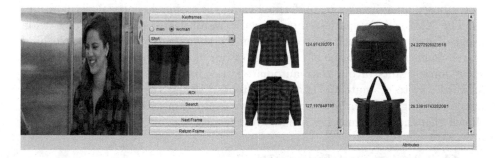

Fig. 4. Tool for manual verification and correction of the clothing match showing the keyframe (left), the best clothing matches based on the adaptable gender and clothing type estimation (middle), and a proposal of similar fashion accessories (right).

Fig. 5. Corresponding keyframes (left) and top-5 matches (right) for actors wardrobe based on the Zalando dataset.

easily be corrected by the evaluator. Second, a clothing patch is suggested. If the proposed patch is incorrect, a new region of interest can be drawn manually. Third, the search query shows the best matches with their corresponding matching rate. The lower the rate, the higher the visual features correspond. Furthermore, some fashion accessories are proposed that are similar to the color and texture of the best clothing match. This will facilitate the e-commerce shopping by enabling shopping for a complete look. Finally, The matches from our clothing tagging are stored in XML/JSON format and they are labeled with the corresponding video timestamp, location, matching accuracy, and the actors id. Actor-based querying can be performed using the trainable Face++ recognition.

The XML/JSON spatio-temporal actor wardrobes can be used in a wide range of applications, such as second screen TV shopping apps and video clothing search engines. To show the effectiveness of our clothing tagging framework, we show some results of our semi-automated tool in Fig. 5. There is no straight forward way to evaluate the clothing matches because there is no exact match in the clothing dataset. However, subjective evaluation with our lead users have shown that the given matches are highly relevant.

6   Conclusion and Future Work

In this paper we proposed a novel methodology for linking clothing of actors to their corresponding keyframe. The proposed spatio-temporal actor wardrobes help improving the viewing experience and facilitate e-commerce shopping by making the TV content interactive and allowing you to shop what you see.

Currently, it is not possible to fully automate the clothing recognition pipeline. However, based on the proposed methodology a large reduction of the manual tagging effort is already achieved. Future work will optimize the clothing type classification and the overall scene understanding. Furthermore, a larger evaluation of the proposed shot detection and keyframe generator will be performed. Finally, it is important to stress that the continuous evolution in fine grained image understanding and classification is expected to further improve the proposed methodology in the upcoming years.

Acknowledgments. SpotShop   (http://www.iminds.be/nl/projecten/2015/10/01/spotshop) is a research project facilitated by iMinds and funded by the Institute for the Promotion of Innovation by Science and Technology in Flanders (IWT).

References

1. Liaukonyte, J., Teixeira, T., Wilbur, K.C.: Television advertising and online shopping. Mark. Sci. **34**(3), 311–330 (2015)
2. Ajmal, M., Ashraf, M.H., Shakir, M., Abbas, Y., Shah, F.A.: Video summarization: techniques and classification. In: Bolc, L., Tadeusiewicz, R., Chmielewski, L.J., Wojciechowski, K. (eds.) ICCVG 2012. LNCS, vol. 7594, pp. 1–13. Springer, Heidelberg (2012)
3. Wang, F., Ngo, C.-W.: Summarizing rushes videos by motion, object, and event understanding. IEEE Trans. Multimedia **14**(1), 76–87 (2012)
4. dos Santos Belo, L., Caetano, C.A., do Patrocínio, Z.K.G., Guimarães, S.J.F.: Summarizing video sequence using a graph-based hierarchical approach. Neurocomputing **173**, 1001–1016 (2016)
5. Uchihachi, S., Foote, J.T., Wilcox, L.: Automatic video summarization using a measure of shot importance and a frame-packing method. US Patent 6,535,639 (2003)
6. Qiu, X., Jiang, S., Liu, H., Huang, Q., Cao, L.: Spatial-temporal attention analysis for home video. In: IEEE International Conference on Multimedia and Expo, pp. 1517–1520. IEEE (2008)
7. Chalamala, S.R., Kakkirala, K., Dhillon, J.: A robust video synchronization method based on hierarchical shot detection. In: International Conference on Audio, Language and Image Processing (ICALIP), pp. 206–210. IEEE (2014)
8. Liu, T.-R., Chan, S.-C.: Automatic shot boundary detection algorithm using structure-aware histogram metric. In: 19th International Conference on Digital Signal Processing (DSP), pp. 541–546. IEEE (2014)
9. Thomas, S.S., Gupta, S., Venkatesh, K.S.: An energy minimization approach for automatic video shot and scene boundary detection. In: Tenth International Conference on Intelligent Information Hiding and Multimedia Signal Processing (IIHMSP), pp. 297–300. IEEE (2014)
10. Baraldi, L., Grana, C., Cucchiara, R.: Shot and scene detection via hierarchical clustering for re-using broadcast video. In: Azzopardi, G., Petkov, N., Yamagiwa, S. (eds.) CAIP 2015. LNCS, vol. 9256, pp. 801–811. Springer, Heidelberg (2015). doi:10.1007/978-3-319-23192-1_67

11. Joy, K.R., Sarma, E.G.: Recent developments in image quality assessment algorithms: a review. J. Theoret. Appl. Inf. Technol. **65**(1) (2014)
12. Chum, O., Philbin, J., Isard, M., Zisserman, A.: Scalable near identical image and shot detection. In: Proceedings of the 6th ACM International Conference on Image and Video Retrieval, pp. 549–556. ACM (2007)
13. Taşdemir, K., Cetin, A.E.: Content-based video copy detection based on motion vectors estimated using a lower frame rate. Signal, Image Video Process. **8**(6), 1049–1057 (2014)
14. Sarkar, A., Ghosh, P., Moxley, E., Manjunath, B.S.: Video fingerprinting: features for duplicate and similar videodetection and query-based video retrieval. In: Electronic Imaging 2008, pp. 68200E–68200E. InternationalSociety for Optics and Photonics (2008)
15. Lux, M.: Lire: open source image retrieval in java. In Proceedings of the 21st ACM International Conference on Multimedia, pp. 843–846. ACM (2013)
16. Chatzichristofis, S.A., Boutalis, Y.S.: CEDD: color and edge directivity descriptor: a compact descriptor for image indexing and retrieval. In: Gasteratos, A., Vincze, M., Tsotsos, J.K. (eds.) ICVS 2008. LNCS, vol. 5008, pp. 312–322. Springer, Heidelberg (2008)
17. Chatzichristofis, S., Boutalis, Y.S., et al.: Fcth: fuzzy color and texture histogram-a low level feature foraccurate image retrieval. In: Ninth International Workshop on Image Analysis for MultimediaInteractive Services, WIAMIS, pp. 191–196. IEEE (2008)
18. Praveen Kumar, P., Aparna, D., Venkata Rao, K.: Compact descriptors for accurate image indexing and retrieval: fcthand cedd. In: International Journal of Engineering Research and Technology (2012)
19. Wang, H., Zhou, Z., Xiao, C., Zhang, L.: Content based image search for clothing recommendations in e-commerce. In: Baughman, A.K., Gao, J., Pan, J.-Y., Petrushin, V.A. (eds.) Multimedia Data Mining and Analytics, pp. 253–267. Springer, Heidelberg (2015)
20. Kiapour, M.H., Han, X., Lazebnik, S., Berg, A.C., LBerg, T.: Where to buy it: matching street clothing photos in online shops. In: Proceedings of the IEEE International Conference on ComputerVision, pp. 3343–3351. IEEE (2015)
21. Nogueira, K., Veloso, A.A., dosSantos, J.A.: Pointwise and pairwise clothing annotation: combining features fromsocial media. Multimedia Tools Appl. **75**, 4083–4113 (2015)
22. Šaloun, P., Stonawski, J., Zelinka, I.: Automated face comparison with facebook friend's faces and flickr photos. In: Zelinka, I., Duy, V.H., Cha, J. (eds.) AETA 2013. LNEE, vol. 282, pp. 349–362. Springer, Heidelberg (2014)
23. Klontz, J.C., Klare, B.F., Klum, S., Jain, A.K., Burge, M.J.: Open source biometric recognition. In: IEEE Sixth International Conference on Biometrics: Theory, Applications and Systems (BTAS), pp. 1–8. IEEE (2013)
24. Fan, H., Yang, M., Cao, Z., Jiang, Y., Yin, Q.: Learning compact face representation: packing a face into an int32. In: Proceedings of the ACM International Conference onMultimedia, pp. 933–936. ACM (2014)
25. Simo-Serra, E., Fidler, S., Moreno-Noguer, F., Urtasun, R.: A high performance CRF model for clothes parsing. In: Cremers, D., Reid, I., Saito, H., Yang, M.-H. (eds.) ACCV 2014. LNCS, vol. 9005, pp. 64–81. Springer, Heidelberg (2015)
26. Achanta, R., Shaji, A., Smith, K., Lucchi, A., Fua, P., Susstrunk, S.: Slic superpixels compared to state-of-the-art superpixel methods. IEEE Trans. Pattern Anal. Mach. Intell. **34**, 2274–2282 (2012)

27. Yang, J., Gan, Z., Li, K., Hou, C.: Graph-based segmentation for rgb-d data using 3-d geometry enhanced superpixels. IEEE Trans. Cybern., 927–940 (2015)
28. Simonyan, K., Zisserman, A.: Very deep convolutional networks for large-scale image recognition (2014). arXiv:1409.1556
29. Bosch, A., Zisserman, A., Munoz, X.: Representing shape with a spatial pyramid kernel. In: Proceedings of the 6th ACM International Conference on Image and Video Retrieval, pp. 401–408. ACM (2007)

Does Online Game Community Matter?

Fan Zhao[(⊠)] and Hang Shi

Florida Gulf Coast University, GP Technologies, Fort Myers, USA
fzhao@fgcu.edu, Usa@imagicsmart.com

Abstract. With the rapid growth of online games, online game communities has been used to explain game players' loyalty to the game. The purpose of this paper is to review the current literatures and summarize the constructs to explain game players' behaviors in online game communities. In this paper, we propose a research model to predict online games continuance play. We believe this framework will help both researchers and practitioners in game research, design and development.

Keywords: Online game · Loyalty · Game community

1 Introduction

Computer games and video games turn to one of the key entertainment media our life. With the development of network, online games now become the leader in the market. According to the new Online Game Market Forecasts report by Statista Incorporation (2012), online game market will reach $41.4 billion at the end of 2015. In another report by Holodny (2014), online gaming in the US is expected to be a 5.2 billion business by 2020. Along with the blooming age of online games, there are some concerns raise by different parties. Game developers concern about how they can make a certain game life longer. Players concern about how to find a better game to play. Game stores or retail stores concern how to sell more games and subscribing licenses to the consumers. For all three parties, the key connect them is customers' loyalty to the game, so that game developers are happy with the current game, retailer will have enough customers to buy, and players will keep playing a game they like.

A number of studies have been conducted in this area. Researchers believe that high quality of the online games, including a good game story, high quality of geographic design, proper length of the game, ease of use, and a good online service, social norms, enjoyment feeling, etc. Will increase players' loyalty to the game (Holsapple and Wu 2008; Sweetser and Wyeth 2005; Wu et al. 2008; Zeschuk and Muzyka 2004). However, only a few studies have focused on social media impact to the game loyalty. The goal of this research was to examine the function of social media played in the loyalty context in online game playing.

2 Literature Review

There are two categories of social media channels in the online game playing. The first one is all the channels in the game named synchronous communication mediator. When

© Springer International Publishing Switzerland 2016
M. Kurosu (Ed.): HCI 2016, Part III, LNCS 9733, pp. 460–466, 2016.
DOI: 10.1007/978-3-319-39513-5_43

players are playing the game, they can adopt different channels to communicate with other players instantly, such as online chatting or texting function provided by the game or chatting/texting with cell phones or other devices if the players know each other in person. These channels are efficient especially when players need corporations in the game. Besides the channels provided by the game, players most likely communicate to each other based on self-organized communications. For example, players enrolled to a same game guild will have a special guild channel to communicate while anyone else outside the guild will not be able to see or hear the communications. The second method is named asynchronous communication mediator. Players often share playing experiences, communicate, develop social network, and search additional useful information of the game playing at a special virtual place named virtual community. These virtual communities usually are built by the game developers. They use a number of artifacts and tools, such as online forums, discussion boards, chat rooms, video channels, and so on. These tools can help game players to gain more information about the game and share their game knowledge.

An online community is defined as social groups of people who communicate with each other via network technology, such as Internet. Typically, each online community has a community theme, such as purposes or reasons why people are here, to attract more members. The theme of online game community is focus on the game to share information about game news, game experiences for different tasks and different types of actors, stories related to the certain game, social network communications, and so on. Through the online game community, players share their game information, seek helps from the community for game activities, and even build their social network beyond the game. The better quality of online game community motivates more players to gather and share information in the community, and in return stimulates even higher quality of the community. Players will feel comfortable and enjoyable if they have a social network in the game, which they build through the online game community. This community network also encourages their intentions to play the game and eventually increase their loyalty to the game (Hsu and Lu 2004).

Current studies focus on players' behaviors in the community. Some researcher adopted social capital theory believing that some aspects of a social structure can create valuable consequences for an individual and facilitate the players' actions within the social system (Coleman 1998). Hsiao and Chiou (2012a) merged social capital into social exchange theory and develop a social capital framework (Fig. 1) to support that social trust and confidence come from game players' strong embeddedness with an online game community. They point out that through normative, relational and utilitarian processes, players' social capital in online game communities affect their loyalty to the game.

On the other side, other than a virtual information sharing community, an online game community could also be recognized as a self-organized guild in the game. From this point of view, Ho and Huang (2009) identify different position in the guild may affect game playing satisfaction differently. They state that relationship between the guild leader and members is significantly associated with member satisfaction with the game. Additionally, the level of game involvement of the leader positively impacts members' attitude toward the guild. Furthermore, Hsiao and Chiou (2012b) argue that

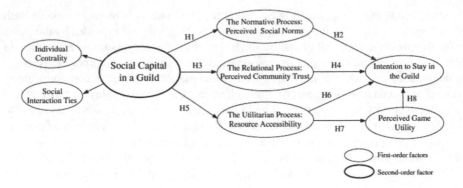

Fig. 1. Social Capital research model from (Hsiao and Chiou 2012a)

a player's position in the guild could impact his or her continuance intention toward an online game playing. Based on social capital theory, they develop a research model (see Fig. 2) to demonstrate relationships among the community position, trust, social value and the continuance intention. The findings are very supportive that community position significantly affects community trust and social value and indirectly positively impacts online game continuance intention.

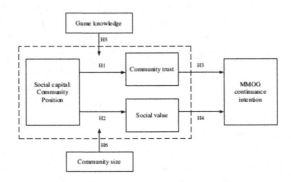

Fig. 2. Community position model by Hsiao and Chiou (2012b)

To confirm that online games are socially driven, Badrinarayanan et al. (2015) conduct a survey study from 970 online game players. The results confirm the influence from game environment characteristics and players' characteristics to players' identification and game community will be influenced by both players' characteristics and identification. Knowledge sharing is another key characteristics in online game community, especially the external user community provided by the game developer. To study players' knowledge sharing behaviors, Hau and Kim (2011) develop a modified model based on the theory of planned behavior. After analyzing 1244 players' information, they suggest that intrinsic motivation, shard goals, and social trust are critical factors encouraging players to share their experiences and game knowledge in the community, whereas extrinsic motivation and social tie have the opposite effect toward knowledge sharing.

In this study, we focus on external game community which helps game players gain game information, share experiences, store game knowledge, and provide discussion forums.

3   Theoretical Background and Proposed Framework

Many previous research adopted Technology Acceptance Model (TAM), Theory of Reasoned Action (TRA), or Social Capital theory to exam the link among beliefs, intentions, and behaviors in IT adoption. Obviously, these theories help understand consumers' acceptance behaviors and reveal key factors and issues at different circumstances. However, these theory are less applicable in explaining the continuance outcome after the intension of adoption. Therefore, we are trying to adopt a theory that can assist us both understand the behaviors of customers and show the predicted outcomes from these behaviors. Melville' belief-action-outcome (BAO) framework links human behavior, social structure, and environmental context together to explain the relationships among both macro and micro variables in the social system (Melville 2010).

The BOA describes the impact of macro-level constructs (environmental/social variables) on micro-level constructs (individual beliefs), and lead to actions (intention to adopt/consumption), and eventually reveal outcomes. We believe this theory framework is suitable for our study to relate game players' beliefs, actions, and behavior outcomes.

Based on the BOA framework and previous online game studies, we propose a conceptual online game continuance model as depicted in Fig. 3. This model integrates the motivational perspective into the original BOA framework. We proposed that micro (game indicators including game quality, game reputation, and critical mass of the game) and macro (usefulness of the community, extrinsic benefits players gain, and intrinsic

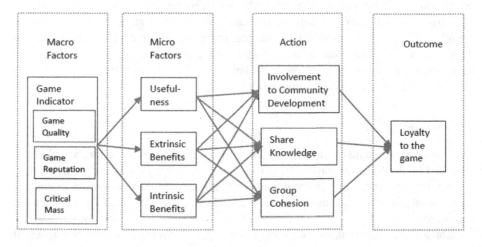

Fig. 3. Propose research model

benefits players gain) influence online game community acceptance and usage, including involvement of community development, share knowledge, and group cohesion, which can increase players' loyalty to the game. Discussions of this model are presented in the following sections.

3.1 Macro Factors

Product quality is one of the crucial factors influencing customers' consumption (2000). For online products, since most purchasing and service activities are completed over the Internet, both product quality and service quality are important determinants of customers' behavioral intentions (2006). As online products, online games' quality is important. It includes but not limited to game story, game graphics, game length, and game operations.

3.2 Micro Factors

Usefulness is one critical factor adopted in TAM models. When game players recognize the usefulness of the online game community when they are looking for certain game knowledge, such as how to defeat a monster, or game solutions, such as how to get out from a maze in the game, they gradually believe the usefulness of the community to help them in game playing.

Extrinsic benefits refer to a game player's desired outcome resulting from doing an activity (Porter et al. 2003). Access to in the game community allow game players to gain more knowledge of the game, review other players' experiences, stories and shared knowledge. Therefore, the game players can adopt all the information to the game and enhance their game playing, eventually obtain the enjoyment they are looking for. Besides, they will expand their social network and interact with more players who is playing the same game and build more relationships among the players. This social benefit offers more mental enjoyment to the players. Therefore, we believe that extrinsic benefits are the beliefs from the players who access to the online game community.

Intrinsic benefits include satisfaction and pride when a game player achieve or complete a certain task/activity. For example, the game player stuck at certain point in the game for a long time, and suddenly found out a solution from the game community, besides the usefulness of the community, he/she will satisfy with the community and also enjoy the feelings of completing a tough task.

3.3 Action

The main purpose of involvement in online game community is for leisure and pleasure (Hsu and Lu 2004). Once game players believes the benefits from the community, they will try to participate more in the community and develop the community to make it more useful. Therefore, the more they involved, the more beliefs they will gain from the community.

Knowledge sharing is the behavior when a player disseminates his/her acquired knowledge or experiences to other players in the community. After game players enjoy the knowledge from community provided by other community members, they will most likely begin to provide their knowledge and experiences to share within the community. Therefore, the more knowledge shared among game players, the higher value the community will be recognized, and the higher binding between the game and the players who shared their knowledge and experiences.

Group cohesion refers to a sense of game players' attraction to the group (Hogg 1992). When people in a community perceive that some common desired goal or objectives can be achieved through some group activities, the cohesion in the group increases. In the online community, under a certain group, players have many common goals, such as defeat a certain monster, find out the best solution for a maze, or discuss the same event or issue in the game. By doing this, once the degree of their interaction reach to a certain level, cohesion will increase and show a better interaction environment to the players. Therefore, group cohesion, in many cases, has been linked to a number of positive outcomes, such as high commitment to the group activities (Klein and Mulvey 1995).

3.4   Game Loyalty

As suggested by Semeijin et al. (2005), maintaining customer loyalty not only lowers the cost of acquiring new customer, but also brings in substantial revenues. A typical revenue model of an online game is to charge subscribing fee every month. However, to attract more players, who are not willing to pay fees, most of the current online game developers start to offer the online games for free to the consumers. In the free games, their revenue model changed from collecting subscribing fee to allure customers buying virtual goods in the games. Therefore, the longer time players play the online games, the more money they possibly will spend on the game, and this will bring more revenue to the game vendors or developers.

4   Conclusions

The purpose of this study is to develop a theoretical research model regarding the key factors affecting customers' online game continuance usage based on a literature review. There are studies developed IS continuance research model and models for applications in mobile technology usage, social network adoption, and e-learning technology. However, there is no study focusing on the online game continuance playing area. This paper summarizes the previous IS continuance studies and proposes a complete research model to explain our research question: why there are online games that last over than 10 years while most of the online games only had short life less than 2 years.

References

Boyer, K., Hult, G · Customer behavioral intentions for online purchases: an examination of fulfillment method and customer experience level. J. Oper. Manage. **24**, 124–147 (2006)

Chinen, K., Jun, M., Hampton, G.: Product quality, market presence, and buying behavior: aggregate images of foreign products in the U.S. Multinational Bus. Rev. **8**(1), 29–38 (2000)

Coleman, J.: Social capital in the creation of human capital. Am. J. Sociol. **94**, 95–120 (1998)

Hogg, M.: The Social Psychology of Group Cohesiveness: from Attraction to Social Identity. New York University Press, New York (1992)

HOLODNY, E.: Online Gaming in The US Could Be A \$5.2 Billion Business By 2020 (2014). http://www.businessinsider.com/morgan-stanleys-online-gaming-market-forecast-2014-9

Holsapple, C., Wu, J.: Building effective online game websites with knowledge-based trust. Inf. Syst. Front **10**, 47–60 (2008)

Hsiao, C., Chiou, J.: The effect of social capital on community loyalty in a virtual community: test of a tripartite-process model. Decis. Support Syst. **54**, 750–757 (2012a)

Hsiao, C., Chiou, J.: The impact of online community position on online game continuance intention: do game knowledge and community size matter? Inf. Manage. **49**, 292–300 (2012b)

Hsu, C., Lu, H.: Consumer behavior in online game communities: A motivational factor perspective. Comput. Hum. Behav. **23**, 1642–1659 (2004)

Klein, H., Mulvey, P.: Two investigations of the relationships among group goals, goal commitment, cohesion, and performance. Organ. Behav. Hum. Decis. Process. **61**(1), 44–53 (1995)

Melville, N.: Information systems innovation for environmental sustainability. MIS Q. **34**(1), 1–21 (2010)

Porter, L., Bigley, G., Steers, R.: Motivation and Work Behavior, 7th edn. McGraw-Hill, New York (2003)

Semeijn, J., Riel, A., Birgelen, M., Steukens, S.: E-services and offline fulfillment: how e-loyalty is crated. Managing Serv. Qual. **15**(2), 182–194 (2005)

Statista Inc.: Market volume of online gaming worldwide (2012). http://www.statista.com/statistics/270728/market-volume-of-online-gaming-worldwide/

Sweetser, P., Wyeth, P.: GameFlow: a model for evaluating player enjoyment in games. ACM Comput. Entertainment **3**(3), 3–24 (2005)

Wu, J., Li, P., Rao, S.: Why they enjoy virtual game words? an empirical investigation. J. Electron. Commer. Res. **9**(3), 219–230 (2008)

Zeschuk, G., Muzyka, R.: Why don't people finish games? (2004). http://www.gamestar.com/12_04/features/fea_finish_jadeempire.shtml. Accessed October 2008

Exploring the Motivational Affordances of Danmaku Video Sharing Websites: Evidence from Gamification Design

Yuxiang Zhao[1]([⊠]) and Jian Tang[2]

[1] School of Economics and Management,
Nanjing University of Science & Technology, Nanjing, China
yxzhao@vip.163.com
[2] School of Information, Central University of Finance and Economics,
Beijing, China
jiantangruc@gmail.com

Abstract. Danmaku video sharing website is a kind of popular social media used by digital natives in China. Very few existing studies or research models explain the psychological and behavioral aspects of user behavior in danmaku websites. The paper aims to explore the motivational affordances of Chinese danmaku websites from the gamification design perspective. Using the qualitative Delphi method and follow-up interviews, we leveraged the knowledge and experience of 18 panel members who were labelled as "UP主" in the ACG communities. Some key research findings have been drawn from the analysis.

Keywords: Danmaku · Motivational affordance · Game elements · Gamification · Delphi analysis

1 Introduction

Social media have promoted the emergence and development of diverse subcultures among the younger generation who are labeled as digital natives (Prensky 2001). ACG (Animation, Comic, and Game) is such an adolescent subculture that is fascinating to a group of digital natives, named Otaku. This subculture was first found in Japan. Through various media it spread to other Asian countries (e.g., China) and even to the United States. Danmaku video sharing website is a kind of important social media for those fans of Otaku to communicate and collaborate in virtual community. Compared with regular user-generated content websites such as Youtube, users can synchronously post comments when watching ACG video on danmaku websites, and these comments will immediately slide over videos in the form of commentary subtitle (Shen et al. 2014). So far, danmaku websites receive great attention and interest from digital natives and rapidly accumulate a large number of users in a short time period.

Danmaku websites allow users to communicate and collaborate with each other while watching videos. This shared watching experience may lead to a strong perceived social presence and sense of virtual community. Danmaku websites, as an emerging UGC style, have been welcomed by mass digital natives, especially those who have a

© Springer International Publishing Switzerland 2016
M. Kurosu (Ed.): HCI 2016, Part III, LNCS 9733, pp. 467–479, 2016.
DOI: 10.1007/978-3-319-39513-5_44

hallmark of ACG subculture. From human-computer interaction perspective, the elements of user-centered design and (sub) culture-centered design are well represented in the design process of danmaku websites. Zhang (2008) proposes the motivational affordance theory to elaborate on the positive design principle for ICT adoption and use. Hamari et al. (2014) indicate that gamification is a desired way to support user engagement and enhance positive patterns in service use. Deterding et al. (2011) highlight that the affordances implemented in gamification will lead to some positive outcomes of product/service use. We argue game elements embedded in the human-focused design process enable the motivational affordances of an IT artifact. To our best knowledge, few studies or research models explain the psychological and behavioral aspects of user behavior in danmaku websites (Shen et al. 2014). Our study is the first attempt to investigate the motivational affordances of Chinese danmaku websites. Therefore, we would like to explore what motivates digital natives to use danmaku websites, especially the driving factors for their contributing behavior. In this paper, we posit to adopt gamification design as a theoretical lens and view the game elements in danmaku websites as a reflection of related motivational affordances. We conducted an exploratory investigation on four Chinese Danmaku video sharing websites, i.e., AcFun, Bilibili, Tudou, and Kankan, to answer the following research question:

What is the current status for the gamification design in Chinese danmaku websites and how it relates to the underlying motivational affordances?

2   Motivational Affordances via Gamification Design

2.1   Motivational Affordance

From the design science research paradigm, Zhang (2008) adapts the concept of affordance and proposes the concept of motivational affordance to examine the positive design of ICT, arguing that people tend to use and continue to use ICT to fulfill various psychological, cognitive, social, and emotional needs. Therefore, features or functions of an IT artifact that support these internal motivational needs can influence whether, how, and how much this artifact will be used (Zhang 2008). The design principles of motivational affordances are proposed for ICT design in general to fulfill the five different motivational sources, including psychological (autonomy and self), cognitive (competence and achievement), social & psychological (relatedness), leadership and followership, and emotional (emotion and affect). We consent that the motivational affordance framework and design principles can and should be selectively applied to enhance the motivation of ICT users. In this study, danmaku video sharing website is one kind of social information systems, which targets at a unique user group and reflects an obvious hedonic characteristic of usage. Thus, the design and support of the motivational affordances is an important determinant of the successful adoption and continual use of danmaku websites.

2.2   Reviewing Motivational Affordance in Gamification Design Process

In recent years, gamification has drawn the attention of academics and practitioners in various domains, such as business, education, information systems, health informatics, and human-computer interaction, etc. (Seaborn and Fels 2015). Deterding et al. (2011) define the gamification as "the use of game design elements in non-game contexts", and suggest that gamification aims to apply elements of "gamefulness, gameful interaction, and gameful design" with a specific intention in mind (p. 9, p. 10). Huotari and Hamari (2012, p.19) define gamification as "a process of enhancing a service with affordances for gameful experiences in order to support user's overall value creation". Seaborn and Fels (2015, p.17) survey the gamification studies and define gamification as "the intentional use of game elements for a gameful experience of non-game tasks and contexts", and game elements are conceptualized as patterns, objects, principles, models, and methods directly inspired by games.

Blohm and Leimeister (2013) proposed a framework to elucidate how gamification design can elaborate on the incentive of intrinsic and extrinsic motives to result in behavioral change. This research endeavor established the connection between game elements (both the mechanics and dynamics) and human motivations (e.g., curiosity, achievement, social recognition, and social exchange, etc. Aparicio et al. (2012) developed a gamification framework based on self-determination theory (Ryan and Deci 2000), and game elements are categorized into three dimensions, namely autonomy, competence, and relation. Other researchers, for example, Nicholson (2012) and Sakamoto et al. (2012), also focused on the intrinsic or internal motivation when designing their gamification framework. Some previous studies have identified the key relevant game elements, such as points, badges, leaderboards, levels, rewards, progress, status, feedback, challenge, and roles, etc. (Seaborn and Fels 2015).

The implementation of game elements can enhance the motivational affordances and lead to better user experiences and performances. Gamification indicates sequential steps comprised of implemented motivational affordances, resulted psychological outcomes, and further behavioral outcomes. Hamari et al. (2014) created a framework for examining the effects of gamification, and found that gamification really works. From our standpoint, we argue that the gamification design is a cirtical way to enhance motivational affordances.

Table 1. Motivational affordances via gamification design (Adapted from Chou (2015)

Motivational Affordances Source	Description	Game Elements	Theoretical Evidence
Epic Meaning & Calling	Meaning is the core drive where a user believes that she/he is doing something greater or she/he was chosen to do something.	Story/theme/narrative (Halan et al. (2010); Smith and Baker (2011))	Situational Relevance; Self-determination theory; Beginners luck

(Continued)

Table 1. (*Continued*)

Motivational Affordances Source	Description	Game Elements	Theoretical Evidence
Development & Accomplishment	An internal drive of making progress, developing skills, and eventually overcoming challenges.	Points (Cheong et al. (2013); Hamari and Koivisto (2013)); Badges (Anderson et al. (2013); Denny (2013); Domínguez et al. (2013)); Leaderboards (Thom et al. (2012)); Progress bar (Farzan and Brusilovsky (2011))	Flow theory; Goal theory; Self-efficacy theory
Empowerment & Feedback	This is when users are engaged a creative process where they have to repeatedly figure things out and try different combinations, including self-expression and timely feedback.	Feedback (Dong et al. (2012)); Milestone unlock; Boosters; Blank fills; Real-time control	Self-determination theory; Organismic integration theory
Ownership & Possession	This is the drive where users are motivated because they feel like they own something.	Virtual goods (Smith and Baker (2011)); Avatar; Earned Lunch	Social capital theory
Social Influence & Relatedness	This drive incorporates all the social elements that motivate people, including: mentorship, acceptance, social responses, companionship, as well as	Friending; Group quest; Mentorship; Social Prod; Social treasure; Touting	Social interaction theory; Social identity theory; Social proof theory

(*Continued*)

Table 1. (*Continued*)

Motivational Affordances Source	Description	Game Elements	Theoretical Evidence
	competition and envy.		
Scarcity	This is the drive of wanting something because you can't have it. The more scarcity the users feel, the more patience and desire they will hold for that product.	Appointment; Fixed intervals; Dangling; Count down; Moats	Resource-based view; Relative deprivation theory
Unpredictablity & Curiosity	This is a the drive of wanting to find out what will happen next. If you don't know what's going to happen, your brain is engaged and you think about it often.	Glowing choice; Easter eggs; Random rewards; Sudden rewards; Obvious wonder	Flow theory; Cognitive absorption theory
Loss & Avoidance	This core drive is based upon the avoidance of something negative happening. In addition, opportunities that are fading away have a strong utilization of this Core Drive.	Visual grave; Scarlet letter; Status quo Sloth; Progress loss; Weep tune	Fear of missing out; Stimulus-Organism-Response (SOR)

In this study, we will use Octalysis, a gamification framework proposed by Chou (2015), to guide our data analysis. Chou (2015) defined the gamification as the craft of deriving all the fun and engaging elements in games and emphasized the important role played by the human motivation in the process. The framework consists of eight core drives that form an octagon shape. Table 1 shows how the Octalysis framework aligns with specific theoretical foundations and how specific game design elements facilitate the eight motivational affordances.

3   Research Design

In this study, we employed the Delphi method to investigate the status quo of gami-fication design in four popular Chinese danmaku websites, AcFun, Bilibili, Tudou, and Kankan. We attempted to identify how game elements can support or enhance various motivational affordances. The Delphi method aims to achieve consensus from a group of experts using repeated responses of questionnaires and controlled feedback. Some researchers in the IS field have demonstrated that the Delphi method can be used to forecast and identify critical issues as well as to develop concepts/frameworks (Okoli and Pawlowski 2004).

The process used in our study involved a panel of versatile content contributors in danmaku websites, and their followers call them "UP主" in the ACG sub-culture. Most of the participants in danmaku video sharing websites are young people with the characteristics of the digital natives. They are fascinated about the new technologies and are easily adapted to the digital environment. Some researchers indicated that those digital natives have a better multi-tasking capability compared with their older generations (Zhao et al. 2014). For instance, in our case, the participants who are watching the danmaku videos can simultaneously post their comments and interact with other peers for various reasons. Regarding the "UP主"selected in our Delphi study, they are technology savvy and have strong digital competence and social media literacy. In particular, they should be good at video processing and editing, and sometimes they need to adapt the original videos in an innovative way to arouse interest and attention from other audience. Therefore, those "UP主" should be acquainted with the creation and communication of danmaku resources, and are familiar with the functions and features of those danmaku websites. During their past interaction with the danmaku websites, they have accumulated some usage experience and are more likely to identify the game elements explicitly or implicitly designed or embedded in those platforms. Participants in this study were carefully selected from the ACG communities in China. In selecting them, our criterion was to find "UP主" involved with some successful danmaku video producing and sharing activities, and having authority and a large number of fans in the ACG communities. At completion of the selection process, the panel of participants comprised 18 veteran "UP主" with age from 19 to 28. Most participants are college students and are well-educated. Each panelist was contacted by email and instant messenger in order to invite him or her to participate in the research explain the scope and objective of the study.

Following the traditional Delphi procedures, this study was carried out in two parts: (1) a focus group phase to generate a list of game elements, and (2) a rating phase to identify the specific motivational affordances of the four Chinese danmaku websites by marking a score for each of the eight dimensions and listing the most impressive game elements accordingly. After completion of the study, in-depth interviews were conducted with panel members to gain some further understanding towards the interaction with the danmaku websites from the gamification design perspective.

During the focus group stage, six participants were selected to discuss their usage experience of danmaku websites. Firstly, we gave a detailed introduction about the gamification design, and listed some well-known game elements. Then, the participants were asked to recall what are the most impressive game elements, features, and functions when they use the danmaku websites. Each of the focus group members had the task of identifying a minimum of six game elements that are pertinent to danmaku websites. The participants were also asked to give a short description of each of the elements they proposed. We then designed the questionnaire based on the framework proposed by Chou (2015) in Table 1, and also consolidated all of the game elements identified by the focus group members into a single list on which a definition of each element was also provided. We highlighted that those game elements listed in the questionnaire are only for reference when they are rating the danmaku websites rather than an exhaustive taxonomy. Finally, the 18 participants were asked to use the Octalysis tool proposed by Chou (2015), to rate the extent of each motivational affordances by a ten-point scale for the four Chinese danmaku websites, as well as justified their answers by providing the specific game elements for each of the motivational affordances dimensions.

As the goal of a Delphi study is to achieve consensus among its panel members, Kendall's W was used to measure agreement in the rating stage (Schmidt et al. 1997). As a general guideline, the interpretation of Kendall's W are as follows: scores closer to 1 represent a very strong consensus; $0.7 < W < 0.9$ for strong agreement; $0.5 < W < 0.7$ for moderate agreement; $0.3 < W < 0.5$ for weak agreement (Schmidt et al. 1997). In this study, after the first round, the W indicated weak consensus. Panel members were therefore asked to modify their rating carefully on the basis of the group's average score provided for scrutinizing. After the second round, consensus have improved (W = 0.63; $p < 0.001$) and detailed explanations were provided when individual ratings differed substantially from the group's average. We finished our Delphi study in the third round with a strong consensus (W = 0.78; $p < 0.001$) among the 18 panel members. It is important to note that, since the ten-point scale is adopted by the Octalysis tool (all of the ratings are in integer form), we computed the mode of ratings instead of the mean in the final round.

4 Findings from the Delphi Study

The data analysis results show that Bilibili receives the highest rating scores in terms of eight core drives, followed by AcFun, Tudou, and Kankan. All four websites have relatively low scores of epic meaning and calling, indicating those websites don't attach great meaning to the website development. Compared to Tudou and Kankan, AcFun and Bilibili applied more game elements, such as various virtual properties, to trigger the drive of accomplishment and achievement. AcFun, Bilibili, and Tudou allows users to upload self-developed contents, yet Kankan only provides purchased contents from other sources. All four sites have reward systems to record users' participation and contribution. Specific measurements include points, badges, member levels, and leaderboards, etc. AcFun and Bilibili have well-constructed membership systems. For instance, users of these two sites have to pass some entry tests to fully enjoy the rights for members. At the same time, AcFun and Bilibili established clear standards for penalty. Users will have to behave themselves and follow the rules to avoid any loss of rights to view, post, and comment. Yet on the other two websites, Tudou and Kankan, loss of rights is not set up to be a serious concern for users. Figure 1 shows the detailed ratings for each of the danmaku websites.

According to the Octalysis graph, AcFun have a good balance in promoting the eight core drives of gamification. AcFun aims to promote the ACG subculture and build a space for peers who share common interest in subculture. It implements a point system that measures users' accomplishment with multiple indicators, such as number of clicks, bookmarks, followers, amount of virtual properties (e.g., bananas). To show the privilege of full membership, AcFun also requires an entry test for new registered users and only provides some advanced function to those high-level members, such as colorful danmaku. Users who upload or view videos continuously receive feedback or danmaku comments from other users, reflecting a lasting process of user-generated contents. The synchronized danmaku helps to establish connections among users, which in turn leads to a close social circle, as they can instantly notice users who share similar opinions and interests. Users of AcFun continuously go back to check content updates to ensure they follow the trend and never miss any amusing posts. Figure 2 presents the specific game elements for each of the motivational affordances cores from the Delphi study.

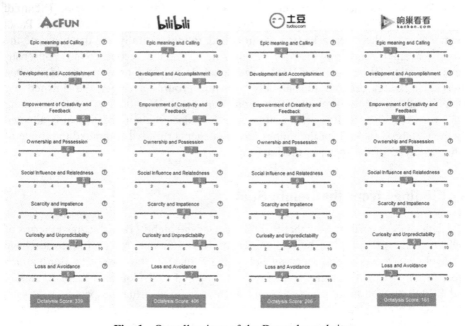

Fig. 1. Overall ratings of the Danmaku websites

The Octalysis graph of Bilibili have a balanced shape to showcase eight core drives, with a bolder shape. Bilibili goes beyond a video sharing websites, as it aims to promote subculture and support crowdfunding to award users who contribute to video contents. It implements a similar point system as AcFun to measure users' accomplishment. What's more, Billibili allows owners of videos to redeem their "shell" (a kind of virtual

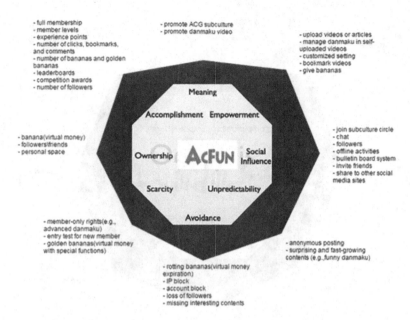

Fig. 2. Motivational affordances of AcFun based on gamification design

properties) for monetary rewards. Similarly, Bilibili also requires an entry test for new registered users and only provides some advanced function to high-level members. The danmaku elements allow users to instantly communicate with other users who are watching the same content, and they can also share their words through connection icons with other social media sites. Figure 3 provides the details.

The Octalysis graph of Tudou has a smaller size, compared to AcFun and Bilibili, indicating Tudou receives relatively low rating scores in all aspects of eight core drives. Tudou makes every user aware the idea of self-development and respect, and it also supports crowdfunding for owners of videos. Tudou also applies game elements, such as badges, to symbolize members' levels in the system, and award users for completing certain tasks. Yet, users also need to follow rules and avoid being blocked. In addition, Tudou helps users to expand their social influences through social media. Figure 4 shows the motivational affordances of Tudou based on gamification design.

The Octalysis graph of Kankan has the smallest size among the four websites, indicating Kankan has the lowest scores of core drives. Kankan only provides purchased contents from other sources, so users are not motivated to upload self-development contents. Other than that, Kankan has a similar point system to award users with virtual properties, such as film voucher. Users can also follow each other and share their thoughts through social media connections. Figure 5 specifies the motivational affordances based on the eight core drives.

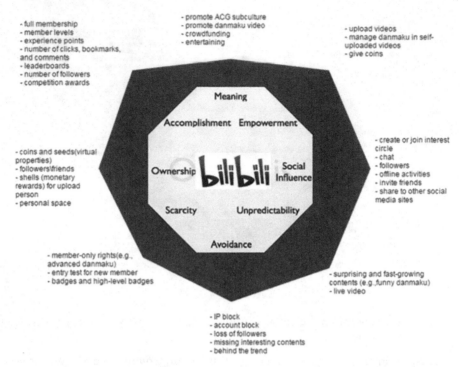

Fig. 3. Motivational affordances of Bilibili based on gamification design

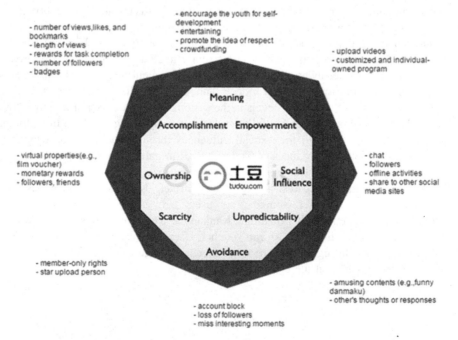

Fig. 4. Motivational affordances of Tudou based on gamification design

Fig. 5. Motivational affordances of Kankan based on gamification design

5 Discussion and Conclusion

Our goal was to investigate the motivational affordances of Chinese danmaku websites from the gamification design perspective. Using the qualitative Delphi method and follow-up interviews, we leveraged the knowledge and experience of 18 panel members who were labelled as "UP主" in the ACG communities. Some key research findings have been drawn from the analysis.

First, the extent of gamification design in the four Chinese danmaku websites varied according to the eight core drives on motivational affordances. As shown in Fig. 1, Bilibili and AcFun stay ahead of the other two danmaku websites in almost every aspects of the motivational affordances. Second, some core drives of motivational affordances have been well facilitated by the gamification design and fully incorporated with the game elements, such as the accomplishment, social influence and relatedness, and unpredictability. In other words, the traditional game elements, i.e., points, rewarding systems, leaderboards, and fans groups etc., have been well designed in the danmaku websites. However, some other dimensions, such as avoidance, meaning, and scarcity, did not attract enough attention. For example, some panel members said that the punishment system is important for the governance and maintenance of the danmaku websites; Otherwise, those who obey the rules and regulations of the ACG community will lose passion and motive to contribute the qualified resources. Third, it is interesting to note that, the gamification design should be viewed as a journey rather than an event, which is consistent with Chou's finding (Chou 2015). Since users may get boring after a period time of usage, the gamification design should constantly launch some new attempts and keep up with the trend and fashion of ACG subculture. In other words, some classical incentives may lose their effects and change to the hygiene factors, and there is no way to accomplish the whole design task at one stroke.

Our study was not without limitations. The theoretical mapping between motivational affordances and game elements needs further literature supports and arguments. Furthermore, some critical questions regarding how ACG subculture may influence the gamification design and its underlying motivational affordances were not addressed. The contribution of our work is in identifying and investigating the motivational affordances of Chinese danmaku websites from the gamification design perspective. In future work, we will conduct some quantitative studies to extend and validate our findings.

Acknowledgement. The authors acknowledge the research funding received by National Science Foundation in China (No. 71403119 and 71390521), and the Ministry of Education, Humanities, and Social Sciences Council in China (No. 13YJC870033).

References

Anderson, A., Huttenlocher, D., Kleinberg, J., Leskovec, J.: Steering user behavior with badges. In: Proceedings of the 22nd International Conference on World Wide Web, pp. 95–106. International World Wide Web Conferences Steering Committee (2013)

Aparicio, A.F., Vela, F.L.G., Sánchez, J.L.G., Montes, J.L.I.: Analysis and application of gamification. In: International Conference on Interacción Persona-ordenador, vol. 44, pp. 101–102 (2012)

Blohm, I., Dr, P., Leimeister, J.M.: Design of it-based enhancing services for motivational support and behavioral change. Bus. Inf. Syst. Eng. 5(4), 275–278 (2013)

Cheong, C., Cheong, F., Filippou, J.: Quick quiz: a gamified approach for enhancing learning. In: Pacific Asia Conference on Information Systems, 18– 22 June 2013, Jeju Island, Korea, pp. 1–14 (2013)

Chou, Y.: Actionable Gamification: Beyond Points, Badges, and Leaderboards. Octalysis Media (2015)

Denny, P.: The effect of virtual achievements on student engagement. In: Proceedings of the SIGCHI Conference on Human Factors in Computing Systems, pp. 763–772. ACM (2013)

Deterding, S., Dixon, D., Khaled, R., Nacke, L.: From game design elements to gamefulness: defining gamification. In: International Academic Mindtrek Conference: Envisioning Future Media Environments, pp. 9–15. ACM (2011)

Domínguez, A., Saenz-De-Navarrete, J., De-Marcos, L., Fernández-Sanz, L., Pagés, C., Martínez-Herráiz, J.J.: Gamifying learning experiences: practical implications and outcomes. Comput. Educ. 63(1), 380–392 (2013)

Dong, T., Dontcheva, M., Joseph, D., Karahalios, K., Newman, M., Ackerman, M.: Discovery-based games for learning software. In: Sigchi Conference on Human Factors in Computing Systems, May 5–10, 2012, Austin, Texas, USA, pp. 2083–2086. ACM (2012)

Farzan, R., Brusilovsky, P.: Encouraging user participation in a course recommender system: an impact on user behavior. Comput. Hum. Behav. 27(1), 276–284 (2011)

Halan, S., Rossen, B., Cendan, J., Lok, B.: High Score! - motivation strategies for user participation in virtual human development. In: Safonova, A. (ed.) IVA 2010. LNCS, vol. 6356, pp. 482–488. Springer, Heidelberg (2010)

Hamari, J., Koivisto, J.: Social motivations to use gamification: an empirical study of gamifying exercise. In: Proceedings of the European Conference on Information Systems, June 5–8, 2013, Utrecht, The Netherlands (2013)

Hamari, J., Koivisto, J., Sarsa, H.: Does gamification work? – a literature review of empirical studies on gamification. In: The 47th Hawaii International Conference on System Sciences (HICSS), 2014, pp. 3025–3034. IEEE (2014)

Nicholson, S.: A user-centered theoretical framework for meaningful gamification. In: Proceedings of Games + Learning + Society 8.0. Madison, WI (2012)

Okoli, C., Pawlowski, S.D.: The delphi method as a research tool: an example, design considerations and applications. Inf. Manag. **42**(1), 15–29 (2004)

Prensky, M.: Digital natives, digital immigrants part 1. On the Horiz. **9**(5), 1–6 (2001)

Ryan, R.M., Deci, E.L.: Self-determination theory and the facilitation of intrinsic motivation, social development, and well-being. Am. Psychol. **55**(1), 68–78 (2000)

Sakamoto, M., Nakajima, T., Alexandrova, T.: Value-based design for gamifying daily activities. In: Herrlich, M., Malaka, R., Masuch, M. (eds.) ICEC 2012. LNCS, vol. 7522, pp. 421–424. Springer, Heidelberg (2012)

Schmidt, Roy C.: Managing delphi surveys using nonparametric statistical techniques. Decis. Sci. **28**(3), 763–774 (1997)

Seaborn, K., Fels, D.I.: Gamification in theory and action: a survey. Int. J. Hum Comput Stud. **74**, 14–31 (2015)

Shen, Y., Chan, C.H., Hung, I.W.: Let the comments fly: the effects of the flying commentary presentation on consumer judgment. In: Proceedings of the Thirty Fifth International Conferences on Information Systems, Auckland (2014)

Smith, A.-L., Baker, L.: Getting a clue: creating student detectives and dragon slayers in your library. Ref. Serv. Rev. **39**(4), 628–642 (2011)

Thom, J., Millen, D., Dimicco, J.: Removing gamification from an enterprise SNS. In: Proceedings of the ACM 2012 conference on Computer Supported Cooperative Work, February 11–15, 2012, Seattle, Washington, USA, pp. 1067–1070. ACM (2012)

Zhang, P.: Motivational affordances: fundamental reasons for ICT design and use. Commun. ACM **51**(11), 145–147 (2008)

Zhao, Y., Xu, X., Sun, X., Zhu, Q.: An integrated framework of online generative capability: interview from digital immigrants. Aslib J. Inf. Manag. **66**(2), 219–239 (2014)

User Studies

Study of Middle-Aged and Youth Users' Preference for Smart Homes

Jianxin Cheng, Yixiang Wu[✉], He Huang, and Xinhui Kang

School of Art, Design and Media, East China University of Science and
Technology, NO. 130, Meilong Road, Xuhui District, Shanghai 200237, China
cjx.master@gmail.com,
{wuyixiang_15,nbukxh}@163.com

Abstract. Nowadays Smart home will optimize traditional life style and life
habit, it brings brand new experience and feeling, and it will become future's main
life style and life habit. But now smart home products are still at start-up period of
product's development life cycle. What functions can attract consumption and are
necessary? What functions are necessary but have no attraction? These function
demands of users are not understood thoroughly. So far, there is no much study to
differentiate varieties of function demands of smart home. In addition, their
preference for requirements of smart home is different as different groups are
different in consumption psychology and consumption behavior. For example, the
consumption behavior of middle-aged group is rather conservative and youth
group is active in thinking and likes to buy some new products and try new life.
Therefore how to position the development of relative smart home products
according to different target groups is an important subject needed to think.

This study tries to employ positive and negative questionnaire survey form to
survey on users' requirement satisfaction degree to obtain key properties of
attracting two consumption groups based on Kano Model theoretical basis and
the study objects are middle-aged and youth consumers. Traditional Kano model
overlooks users' uncertain thinking, and for a question having uncertain choices,
questionnaire design must be conducted combining with fuzzy theory. Besides,
as the range of smart home industry is too wide, in this study the author takes
smart home air healthy products as an example, conducts user interview about
home air purifier, collects expert and experienced product designer's suggestions, screens out 10 secondary indexes to build key properties of home air
purifiers and judges the property and category of 10 functions by Kano model to
infer middle-aged and youth consumers' demand preference difference for home
air purifier thus finally providing references for future's smart home products
according to analysis results.

Keywords: Smart homes · Fuzzy-Kano model · Air purifier · Target group

1 Background and Motives

With the fast growth of sensor chip, big data, cloud computing, internet of things and
mobile internet, people's daily life combines with smart life technology closely. In
recent years, China released a series of policies, listed smart home in 9 major fields of

© Springer International Publishing Switzerland 2016
M. Kurosu (Ed.): HCI 2016, Part III, LNCS 9733, pp. 483–493, 2016.
DOI: 10.1007/978-3-319-39513-5_45

demonstration projects clearly to establish emerging industries aiming to improve people's life quality by the promotion of intelligent life technology. And related software and hardware innovative application and products are developed. Range of intelligent home products includes intelligent light system, health care, security guarding, monitoring system and internet home appliance system and other new fields.

With the development of sensing and interaction technology, intelligent products are embedded in all kinds of home devices, and these hardware products constitutes a multi—functional hardware system. Software system and hardware system are integrated to build a smart management system with strong multi-functions. Comfort, safety, happiness and other elements are added into home life application to design vision, smelling, hearing, touch and heart moving smart home life products to make home living environment more safe, comfortable, healthy, energy-saving, happy, warm and sweet by control, scene, linkage, study, adaptation, analysis, strategy and other functions and it can even improve life quality and art yearning.

Smart home will optimize traditional life style and life habit, it brings brand new experience and feeling, and it will become future's main life style and life habit. Smart home has characteristics of safety, automation, health and entertainment. By far, there is no much study to differentiate what can attract consumption and is necessary and what is necessary but has no attraction among multi-functions of smart home. In 1984, Noriaki Kano, a professor of Tokyo University of Science, proposes the concept of Kano model. In this study, the author figures out the demands of users based on Fuzzy-Kano Model and survey questionnaire data to obtain key elements of attracting consumers. Fuzzy-Kano Model combines Kano model and fuzzy theory. Compared with traditional Kano model, fuzzy theory must be used to count fuzzy weight for uncertain question evaluation. In this study, air healthy products of smart home are taken as an example, survey on home air purifier is conducted, expert and experienced product designers' suggestions are collected, and present 10 functions are selected to explore key elements of home air purifiers. In this study, Kano model is tried using to account for the properties of these 10 functions to provide references for future users and system providers. In addition, as different consumption groups are different in consumption psychology and behaviors, they have different preferences for functions of smart home. For example, middle-aged group is conservative in consumption behavior; while youth group is active in thinking and likes to buy some new products and try new life. Therefore, how to position development of smart home considering different target groups is an important project needed to think.

2   Demand Category Based on Fuzzy Kano Model

2.1   Fuzzy Kano Model

In 1984, Noriaki Kano, a Japanese famous quality management expert, Tokyo University of Science professor, is inspired by Herzberg's two-factor theory and proposes the concept of Kano model. Professor Noriaki Kano believes that two-dimensional model is needed to be adopted for quality cognition: objective representation characterized by satisfaction in character and subjective feeling characterized by customer satisfaction, thus obtaining non-linear relationship between user satisfaction and product/service performance.

Figure 1 is Kano analysis model. Horizontal ordinate represents realization rate of user demand and vertical coordinate represents satisfaction degree of users.

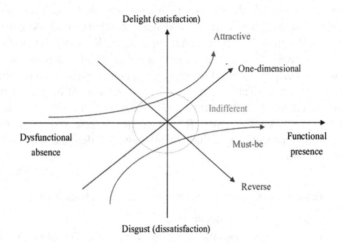

Fig. 1. An illustration of the Kano model

Users'one-dimensional requirements: such quality elements generally change in linear relationship. If products and services provided by enterprises have more characteristics and functions, then users will be more satisfied. When products and services provided by enterprises don't include such characteristics and functions, users will not be satisfied. The products and services with this kind of quality elements are rather excellent, but they are not necessary quality element, it is more possible that users'requirements on some quality elements are fuzzy but they hope to get them.

Attractive requirements curve in the figure is product and service property which is quite unexpected. Users will not clearly express the desire for this kind of quality elements, at the same time they will not expect excessively. But this kind of quality element is uncommitted benefit provided by enterprises for users. If products or services provided by enterprises include this kind of quality element, user will be satisfied, thus improving users' loyalty index.

Must-be requirements curve means users will have dissatisfaction emotion when the products and services provided by enterprise don't include this kind of quality element; on the contrary, when such quality elements like products and services provided by enterprises represent fully, products and services are qualified, users will not have dissatisfaction emotion. At the same time, even the presentation of this kind of quality elements surpass the users' demand, it will not cause the improvement of users' satisfaction degree, because in users' eyes these quality elements are most fundamental elements that products and services should have.

Indifferent requirements: this kind of quality elements are those elements users don't care. Whether the products and services satisfy the elements will not cause users' satisfaction or disaffection.

Fuzzy Kano model demand category method mainly targets at the character that customers' satisfaction degree for demand is fuzzy. Certain fuzzy satisfaction degree value in the range from zero to one represents customers' satisfaction degree for products' survey items, which makes customers' demand category survey more accurate. In order to differentiate customers' demand category better, Matzler etc. made revised Kano model demand category evaluation table. Kano model designs 2 questions which are positive and negative for product property. Customers' demand category for product property is obtained by analyzing Kano's questionnaire table filled by customers. It is seen from Table 1 that "M" represents must-be requirements, "O" represents one-dimensional requirements, "A" represents attractive requirements, "I" represents insignificant requirements, "R" represents reverse requirements and "Q" represents question requirements. Values of all items of demand satisfaction degree range from zero to one.

Table 1. Kano model requirement category evaluation table

Positive questions	Negative questions				
	Like	Go without saying	Don't care	Tolerable	Dislike
Like	Q	A	A	A	O
Go without saying	R	I	I	I	M
Don't care	R	I	I	I	M
Tolerable	R	I	I	I	M
Dislike	R	R	R	R	Q

2.2   Fuzzy Kano Model for Customers' Demand Category Method

Among traditional Kano model survey, testers give a single answer to a positive or negative question, which overlooks testers' uncertainty of thinking. When customers give uncertain answer for product property, survey data on this part of customers by traditional Kano model is not correct. Considering uncertainty of customer satisfaction degree, fuzzy Kano model demand category method is proposed.

Fuzzy Kano model and traditional Kano model are used to survey on customer satisfaction degree by employing positive and negative questionnaire table and the biggest difference lies in the design of survey questionnaire. One most satisfied answer is permitted to chose for positive and negative questions in traditional Kano questionnaire, and fuzzy Kano questionnaire permits customers to have fuzzy satisfaction degree value for dozens of survey items(percentage form is employed, and the value is between zero and one, and the sum of the line elements is one). Traditional Kano model and fuzzy Kano model questionnaire survey table are seen in Tables 2 and 3.

Table 2. Traditional Kano questionnaire survey table

XX Function of products	Like	Go without saying	Don't care	Tolerable	Dislike
Realizable	$\checkmark$				
Unrealizable					$\checkmark$

Table 3. Fuzzy Kano questionnaire table

XX Function of products	Like	Go without saying	Don't care	Tolerable	Dislike
Realizable		0.7	0.1	0.2	
Unrealizable			0.8	0.1	0.1

For traditional Kano model (Table 2), customers tick in certain item to represent that they agree to this item, and other blank places are expressed by zero. Realized function matrix is supposed to be X = [1 0 0 0 0], unrealized function matrix is Y = [0 0 0 0 1] and interaction matrix S is generated. Matrix S is compared with Kano model category evaluation table, "one" in matrix S corresponds to "O" in Kano model category evaluation table. Therefore, the demand category for this property of the product is one-dimensional requirement. Fuzzy Kano model is similar to traditional Kano model method in data process, and the basic steps are as follow:

Certain tester's fuzzy Kano questionnaire table (Table 3) is taken as an example, realized function matrix is supposed to be X = [0 0.7 0.1 0.2 0], unrealized function matrix is Y = [0 0 0.8 0.1 0.1] and generated fuzzy interaction matrix is.

Above fuzzy interaction matrix X^TY is one-to-one correspondent to Table 1, and subordinated vector $t_a = 0$, $t_m = 0.1$, $t_o = 0$, $t_i = 0.9$ of A, M, O and I are known.

$$
X^TY = \begin{bmatrix}
0 & 0 & 0 & 0 & 0 \\
0 & 0 & 0.5600 & 0.0700 & 0.0700 \\
0 & 0 & 0.0800 & 0.0100 & 0.0100 \\
0 & 0 & 0.1600 & 0.0200 & 0.0200 \\
0 & 0 & 0 & 0 & 0
\end{bmatrix}
$$

As the same factor attributes to varieties of Kano property category at the same time generally. In order to obtain more accurate data and more reliable data, threshold value α is introduced to screen out data in subordinated vector T of demand category obtained from fuzzy Kano questionnaire. For the valuing of α, most scholars employ comparison method, Meng Qing Liang etc. (2013) found that $\alpha = 0.4$ is the most ideal valuing by setting a different value for α, thus guaranteeing the undistortion of information and less intersection of information. In this paper, according to opinions of Meng Qing Liang etc., threshold value $\alpha = 0.4$ is set. According to threshold $\alpha = 0.4$, data in subordinated vector T of fuzzy Kano demand category is screened out; and when subordinated vector T value of Kano property category is bigger than α, property vector of this property category is set to represent by "1", otherwise represent by "0".

Count each tester's demand preference category for products by repeating above steps and the highest preference frequency for products is demand category corresponding to this product character. If two kinds of categories are same in frequency, demand categories are must-be requirements, one-dimensional requirements, attractive requirements and indifferent requirement according to priority order from high to low.

3 Kano Model Is Used to Build User Home Air Purifier Requirements

Home living is an important place in people's mind. People require home air to be clean and healthy and require a fresh and comfortable environment. Home air purifier not only exists because of its function of purifying air, and with the development over time, some new requirements occur and the design of air purifier evolves and changes. Besides the most basic air purifying function, nowadays air purifier has added some other functions, and the addition of each new function requirement aims to provide a healthy and comfortable indoor environment better for people. In another hand, air purifiers with different functions need to be chosen for different indoor air pollution situations and different people groups have different focuses on air purifier and different use methods. In order to study the requirement differences on home air purifiers of different people groups, an air purifier requirement Kano model is built to help finish the design in this paper.

Home air purifier function requirement table is designed starting from behavior and psychology feeling of youth and middle-aged people. Card category method, focus group method, questionnaire survey method and user interview method are adopted to obtain users' requirement list. Finally 10 function requirements are screened out to explore key factors of a home air purifier referring to the suggestions of experts and experienced product designers. User requirement table is seen in the following table (Table 4).

Table 4. Function list of an air purifier

Grade1 index	Grade2 index	Description of index
Intelligent interaction	Remotely control air purifier by APP of a mobile phone.	A remote control can be replaced by a mobile phone with App installed to reach the function of operating air purifier by using Wifi, infrared ray or Bluetooth method
	Voice identification operation	Human can communicate with device smoothly. Voice identification operation can be converted to order of operating air purifier
	Operate with touch-sensitive panel	According to users' operation thinking habit, actions of a user are anticipated and converted into the pictures of operating air purifier interface, which makes users experience products by intuition, experiences and easy operation

(Continued)

Table 4. (*Continued*)

Grade1 index	Grade2 index	Description of index
Healthy	Intelligent air purifying	Remove methane/PH2.5/peculiar smell/lampblack/secondhand smoke, plasmacluster and degerming
	Greenery energy saving	Greenery energy saving
	Real time detect air quality	It is connected with a mobile phone. Real-time indoor air quality is fed back to a user and "starting on" or "starting off" can be set according to air quality. Air quality is reported by voice and graphic change
Mobile and convenience	Mobile mode design	Mobile mode: how to innovate design methods like roller/hand-held
Modularized design	Modularized design: water changing device and filter net change etc.	Modularized design: how to modularize water changing device and filter net change etc.
Comfortable and affinity feeling	Mute/light mode/starting on method and vision presentation method etc.	Continual innovation in comfortableness, anti-interference and easy sleeping
Multi-function	Function expansion of air purifier	Multi-function such as: disguising as a flower pot, playing like a stereo and integrating humidification function.

The following Table 5 is the function requirement evaluation questionnaire table designed based on fuzzy requirement table. In the table, two-way questions about the attitude of having that function and the attitude without having that function are designed to obtain users' attitude at each requirement from different angles.

Table 5. Two-way question evaluation questionnaire table based on fuzzy Kano model

	1. Like	2. Go without saying	3. Don't care	4. Tolerable	5. Dislike
If modularized design is provided, what will you feel?	0.6	0.3	0.4		
If modularized design is canceled, what will you feel?			0.2	0.2	0.6

Face to face interview for answering the above questions is conducted. First explain function and specification, and then let testers choose the keys to the positive and negative questions about each function requirement. Conduct careful survey interactively during answering questionnaire questions to obtain real preference of users for home air purifier requirements. Finally carry on the statistics for requirement information collected from users' requirement survey tables, make data table and obtain demand property of testers for home air purifier and classify it. Results of attractive requirements, one-dimensional requirements, must-be requirements and indifferent requirement are seen in Table 6.

Table 6. Youth home air purifier requirement property category result

Factor	M	A	I	O	R	Q	Category
Remotely control by App of mobile phone	1	9		8			A
Voice identification operation		7	10	1			I
Operate using touch sensitive panel	6	4	9	6			I
Purify air intelligently	4	5	3	10			O
Greenery energy saving	3	1	5	7			O
Real-time monitor air situation	1	3	6	11			O
Mobile and convenient	3	4	12	2	1		I
Modularized	2	4	5	8			O
Comfort and affinity feeling	2	4	4	7			O
Function expansion		7	17				I

Table 7. Middle-aged people's home air purifier requirement property classification result

Factor	M	A	I	O	R	Q	Category
Remotely control by App of mobile phone	1	6	9	1			I
Voice identification operation	1	6	9	1			I
Operate using touch sensitive panel	3	4	8	3			I
Purify air intelligently	1	6	4	7			O
Greenery energy saving	9	4	3	5			M
Real-time monitor air situation	5	4	5	3			MI
Mobile and convenient	3	2	10	2	1		I
Modularize	3	2	8	5			I
Comfort and affinity feeling		8	3	7			A
Function expansion	1	4	12	1	2		I

Kano model classification method. For youth group, by statistics, it is known that attractive requirements are remote controlling by App of a mobile phone; one-dimensional requirements include 5 items, which are purifying air intelligently, greenery energy saving, real-time monitoring air quality, modularizing design and providing affinity feeling; indifferent requirements include 4 items, which are voice identification operation, operating by using touch sensitive panel, mobile convenience and function expansion. For middle-aged group, attractive requirements are comfort and affinity feeling; one-dimensional requirements are purifying air intelligently; there are 6 items of indifferent requirements: remotely controlling by App in a mobile phone, voice identification operation, operating by using touch sensitive panel, mobile convenience, modularization and function expansion; and must-be requirements are greenery energy saving and real-time monitoring air situation. For the item of real-time monitoring air situation, must-be requirements and indifferent requirements have same statistic result; if frequencies of two categories are same, the priority of requirement categories are must-be requirement, one-dimensional requirement, attractive requirement and insignificant requirement in order from high to low. Therefore, real-time monitoring air situation is judged to be must-be requirement (Table 7).

4 Discussion and Analysis on Results

Each question item is classified and its property is judged according to If Noriaki Kano professor thinks that life cycle of quality element is indifferent quality stage, attractive quality stage, one- dimensional quality stage and must-be quality stage. When products have certain new quality element, consumers are not familiar with it at the beginning; even this quality element exists, consumers can not aware it and feel there is no difference, then this time is indifference stage. After educating consumers over time, consumers feel satisfied for quality elements gradually, and this time is attractive quality stage. As Kano model needs property judgment, when frequencies of two categories are close, some information will lose if screening, thus the attitude of certain number of consumer groups will be overlooked; after all, for the same concept, different people have different cognition and acceptation degree. If transitivity description is used, the concepts with similar frequency type are more reasonable. Therefore using preferred transitivity description is more reasonable because the propaganda of this concept has no overwhelming advantages among users.

This study shows that products in the fields related to smart home are at introduction stage of product's life cycle. The products have not been accepted by market still; and consumers do not accept products still, waiting for system providers to educate consumers how to use in order to make consumers feel satisfied for products gradually. Undifferentiated qualities with same results among youth group and middle-aged group include 4 items: voice identification operation, using touch sensitive panel to operate, mobile convenience and function expansion. Deep problems involved in voice are large transformation of human-machine interaction. And users of function expansion can not produce good association, function expansion is not found to be valued so it needs to be publicized to make consumers understand it more. Touch sensitiveness and mobile convenience are insignificant for them, perhaps customers do not care them really because touch sensitiveness and mobile convenience appear in all kinds of products widely, users understand these two concepts and have operating experience but users attribute them in indifference property and it only shows that users have no interest in them really. Strengthening of touch sensitive design has no enough attraction for users but design of touch sensitiveness interface is close to life and makes products convenient to use. We should reduce cognition burden of users and design interfaces catering for users and we should not make users adjust their own habits to adapt your products.

For youth group, attractive quality elements are remotely controlling air purifier by App in a mobile phone. There is some controversy in this aspect, and counting result shows that the results of A and O are similar, so it is known that remotely controlling air purifier by App in a mobile phone is understood and known by users after long time propaganda. At present, remotely controlling air purifier by App in a mobile phone is at a stage transiting from attractive stage to one-dimensional stage, therefore attraction of remotely controlling air purifier by App among smart home products decreases. While middle-aged group is different, statistic result shows that comfort and anti-interference and affinity are attractive for middle-aged group. Air purifier can adjust automatically according to air quality and users' sleep status. As middle-aged group likes quietness, their anti-interference ability from outside environment in physics is worse, and they are not so good at operating smart mobile phones, they have no strong desire for remotely controlling home appliances by a mobile phone. Therefore this item is attributed to indifference property.

The item real-time monitoring air situation is attributed to must-be requirements among middle-aged group. The author understands from interview that middle-aged group believes that air purifier is a product used to purify air and it must have the function of monitoring air quality. But another part of middle-aged group has the attitude of indifference, it shows that quite a part of middle-aged group has not so high purchase passion for air purifier as youth group, their demand for air purifier is not very strong, their consumption idea is rather conservative, and their consumption impulse for unnecessary daily goods is not large, even some middle-aged group think that they do not need air purifier products, because they hold the opinion that nowadays air is polluted but it is not necessary to purify air indoor, they think natural air is good and purified air is not sure to be good and air pollution problem should be solved by government's strict control from root, and only improving indoor air has no much effects. Obviously there is misunderstanding and blind rejection psychology existing in their opinion on air purifiers. At present the function characteristics of an air purifier has not been accepted wholly by middle-aged group. It is needed to greatly publicize function characteristics of an air purifier and promote more middle-aged people to experience them by manufactures. The category of greenery energy saving is different among two groups. Energy saving consciousness is approved and popular among middle-aged people, and even it transits to must-be property.

For results of purifying air intelligently, the two groups both attribute it into one-dimensional requirement. Middle-aged people have different understanding degree for air purifying products, a part of people think it is attractive but insignificant when this character is not adequate; but users who have higher education background, higher income and like to contact new things are familiar with air purifier, therefore there is big difference among middle-aged group, statistic results show that frequencies of attractive requirements and one-dimensional requirements are similar, but one-dimensional requirements frequency of youth group is very prominent, which shows that although both two groups have desire for intelligently purifying air but their progress at the same stage is different.

Modularized design such as water changing device and filter net changing is desired very much for youth group. Taking Shanghai as an example, a filter net needs to be changed frequently, if not, it is better not to use air purifier because normal service cycle of a filter net is three months to six months therefore purchasing an air purifier is equal to purchasing purifying ability and purchasing a filter net, and a filter net needs to be changed regularly. The net change is a complicated thing; and our filter net with modularized design is easy to change. Middle-aged group is not very clear about modularized design compared with youth group and they have no big interest in it.

References

1. Kano, N., et al.: Attractive quality and must-be quality. J. Jpn. Soc. Qual. Control **14**(2), 39–48 (1984)
2. Liang, M.Q., Lin, H.: Quality property category method and application based on fuzzy Kano model. Ind. Eng. **16**(3), 121–125 (2013)
3. Jun, W.: An Essential Guide of Smart 3.0 Smart Home. Chinese International Book Publisher (2015)
4. Yang, X.Y.: Study on Customers' Satisfaction Degree of Mobile Phone Purchasers Based on fuzzy Kano Model. Academic Dissertation of Donghua University (2015). 61
5. Berger, C.: Kano's methods for understanding customer defined quality. Center Quality Manage. J. **2**(4), 3–36 (1993)
6. Tao, B., Zhongkai, L.: The important degree calculation method of customer demand based on Kano model. China Mech. Eng. **8**(4), 975–980 (2012)

Analysis of Different Types of Navigational Structures for Machine Tool Controlling

Julia N. Czerniak[✉], Tobias Hellig, Alexander Kiehn,
Christopher Brandl, Alexander Mertens, and Christopher M. Schlick

Institute of Industrial Engineering and Ergonomics,
RWTH Aachen University, Aachen, Germany
{j.czerniak, t.hellig, a.kiehn, c.brandl, a.mertens,
c.schlick}@iaw.rwth-aachen.de

Abstract. The rapid technological developments in the manufacturing industry and an increasing demand for more and more complex and individual products has led to the development of modern machine tools from simple tools to highly automated technical products. The trend towards cyber physical production systems will intensify this development in the machine tool sector in context with the so-called fourth industrial revolution. In particular, the increasing quantity of mechatronic components in machine tools has led to a high amount of different functions that need to be controlled by the user. Empirical research has shown that user oriented Human-Machine-Interface-design (HMI-design) reduces error rates and cognitive load for the machine operator and can lead to an increase in effectiveness and efficiency with regard to the interaction. In this paper we introduce a study which points out the impact of user centered design by analyzing the differences of workflow-oriented and function-oriented HMIs. The results of the study show that work task performance can be enhanced by workflow-oriented HMI by improving the time needed and diminishing the number of clicks and errors for specific work tasks.

Keywords: Human-machine-interaction · Function-oriented navigation structure · Graphical user interface · Machine tool controlling · Workflow-oriented navigation structure

1 Introduction

Over the last few years, machine tools have developed into exceedingly complex high-tech systems in order to fulfill the increasing demands that have risen up lately from the manufacturing industry. This trend is set to continue, as machine tools will ascend in their complexity and quantity since cyber physical production systems yield a real-time optimization of value-added chains as a result of intelligent monitoring and decision making processes.

The number of physical input elements on numerically controlled machine tools has approximately tripled since their market launch in the early 1960 s, due to a rising amount of functions the machine needs to fulfill [1]. More specifically, the ever-increasing number of mechatronic parts in machine tools has led to a high amount of

© Springer International Publishing Switzerland 2016
M. Kurosu (Ed.): HCI 2016, Part III, LNCS 9733, pp. 494–504, 2016.
DOI: 10.1007/978-3-319-39513-5_46

different functions that need to be operated by the user [2]. However, the corresponding controlling concepts have only been slightly revised, resulting in significant cognitive demand on the user which is attributable to a lack of intuitiveness [3].

Empirical investigations have revealed that, in comparison to a function-oriented design, a workflow-oriented design of a human-machine-interface notably reduces the error rates and cognitive load for the machine operator [1]. Additionally, this design usually has a lower software complexity, reducing the initial training and execution time. Furthermore, regarding the HMI, it can also create a boost in effectiveness and efficiency [4]. In order to properly design an interface, human needs and capabilities already ought to be properly deliberated during the development process. If this recommendation is followed, contemporary workflow-oriented HMI concepts have the ability to improve usability by simultaneously offering a more intuitive handling of the machine and lowering the cognitive load in everyday controlling operations.

A possible approach to designing a workflow-oriented HMI is derived from the information and telecommunications sector. Widely spread on smartphones, application programs (Apps) could be incorporated into interfaces on machine tools. Unfortunately, apps are traditionally characterized by a minimalist structure with only one function. While this makes apps intuitive and easy to use, with reference to the complexity of a machine tool, this concept is limited. However, it is possible to combine several elemental apps to so-called "container apps" so that the reduced app concept can be displayed on a multifaceted HMI. Therefore, this study analyzed the usability for machine tool controlling based on general ergonomic implications for designing Human Machine Systems given in standard series DIN EN ISO 9241.

Taking this concept a step further, there may be cases in which different types of workflows are optimal for different age groups. It is conceivable that the younger generation that was born and grew up during the information era has a better grasp of modern HMI concepts than the elderly and thus has a different understanding according to workflow structures [5]. This phenomenon is dubbed the technology generation effect and could be utilized to construct an individualized adaptive HMI in terms of expected conformity to age-related mental models.

1.1 User-Oriented Human-Machine-Interface-Design

According to DIN EN ISO 9241-12, a graphical user interface (GUI) needs to meet the following seven design aspects in order to be guarantee an efficient and effective usage. Firstly, it needs to display the visual information in a clear and concrete way to enable a simple information intake by the user. Secondly, differentiability of the information is of importance. Also, the information needs to be presented in a compact form, i.e. only relevant information is shown. Additionally, consistency is the key success factor in order to avoid confusion. Furthermore, the attention of the operator needs to be drawn to the relevant information. Lastly, the information presented obviously needs to be easily legible and comprehensible. [6].

Often, a multitude of visual information that needs to be processed is presented to the user. In order to simplify the task of information intake, information can be clustered on the GUI according to the gestalt laws of grouping. These principles, as summarized by Wagemans et al. (2012), were first proposed by gestalt psychologists in the 1920 s and assist in emphasizing the relevant information and distinguishing between the different information clusters. The first principle, the law of proximity, states that objects that are seen as close together are perceived to form a group. The law of similarity asserts that similar objects are grouped together. Similarity can be based on color, shape, shade or various other attributes. Lastly, the law of closure maintains that people see objects (i.e. letters, shapes) as a whole even when they are incomplete. Using these principles, information can easily be grouped on a GUI, helping to direct the attention of the user to the information relevant in the specific context. [7].

Moreover the user can be supported by context sensitive help systems, that are dependent on the current processing status [8], for example greyed buttons, that are not necessarily needed for the actual task.

Furthermore, a GUI should be designed according to the user's attention. To this end, information should be presented in an area of the interface where it is most expected, for example, by placing a close button in the top right corner [6].

1.2 Function-Oriented and Workflow-Oriented Human-Machine-Interface

The complexity of machine tools increases with every passing year as they are required to perform more complex tasks with function-oriented HMIs. However, empirical studies have shown that human mental models are based on actions and not on functions or data types [9]. The traditional function-oriented approach to design a machine tool HMI does not appropriately assist the operator, who is left with a high level of cognitive load. Hence, initial training times need to be prolonged and daily tasks are more inefficient [1]. These problems can be alleviated with a contemporary workflow-oriented approach that assists the user by reducing transfer capacity to his mental model. Thus operating times should decrease in total for workflow-oriented HMI concepts by reducing execution times, the amount of clicks to fulfill the work task, as well as the number of mistakes made during performing the work task.

The field of telecommunication has given rise to a new possibility for designing machine tool HMIs: the app concept. Typical smartphone apps are characterized by their minimalist structure, where every app has a certain purpose and therefore limited functionality. This means an app is easy to operate as the manageable size makes it easy to find functions. However, at the uppermost operating level (i.e. the desktop) the complexity is increased dramatically due to the accumulation of apps. Furthermore, no operating steps are presented to the user, which is critical for a machine tool HMI. Thus, the typical smartphone app concept needs to be adapted in order to be a useful fundament for a user-oriented machine tool HMI. At the most elementary level, where tasks cannot be divided in subtasks any further, the apps concept can be directly adopted. Then, in order to describe more complex tasks, several elementary apps are combined in a container app to create a sequential workflow that can be carried out without much cognitive effort. [1].

Since the user does not need to remember the order of tasks or their position in the whole process and continuously look for them, this app design saves time as well.

If necessary, container apps can then also be combined. This combination of apps ultimately results in the reduction of complexity on the uppermost levels of the HMI even when there are a large number of possible functions while retaining the simplicity of apps in the lower ones. Further, these apps can also be adapted to suit each individual user, for example displaying the most used functions more prominently [10].

2 Method

In order to develop a laboratory study to analyze the impact of different HMI designs on the working performance and the worker's load, a video of a common machine tool workflow of "setting machine coordinate origin" was recorded for a Hermle machine tool with SINUMERIK controlling. The workflow was analyzed based on the Hierarchical Task Analysis (HTA) [11] and was then abstracted to a simplified workflow that can also be handled by novices (Fig. 1). Two different HMIs were implemented, a function-oriented HMI reflecting the current HMI design of the machine tool and a workflow-oriented HMI according to the principals of optimized graphical user interfaces and navigation structures (see Sect. 1.1). The main objective of the study was to test the workflow-oriented HMI compared to the function-oriented HMI design for machine tools. Therefore we used clickable computer-based mockups for both HMI versions. As independent variables we assessed the function-oriented approach in condition 1 and the workflow-oriented approach in condition 2 of the study. The depending variable of the study is *user performance* (distinguished in *execution time*, *number of clicks* to perform the work task and *number of errors*).

2.1   Participants

For the study 19 participants (aged between 20 and 34 years) with an average age of 27 years were tested. Ten of the tested participants were male, whereas 9 participants were female. All participants reported being experienced with mobile devices. About half of all participants reported to be unexperienced in using milling machines, while six participants worked at a milling machine at least once. Table 1 shows the demographic information of the participant group, including self-reported knowledge with milling machines and smart devices.

2.2   Procedure and Task

The study was conducted in a laboratory of the Institute of Industrial Engineering and Ergonomics at RWTH Aachen University. All people participated in both conditions and completed the same task with both mockup versions. The participants were introduced to the task by a verbal description and pictures of the scenario. The participants were given a text-based step-by-step instruction of the workflow to be performed, and sufficient time to become familiar with the workflow. After the participants read the instruction, they started performing the task "Set machine coordinate origin" with the first HMI design. The starting task was permuted between condition 1 and 2

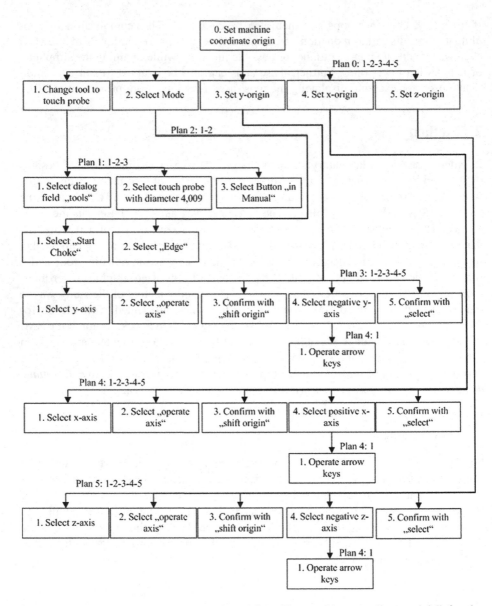

Fig. 1. Selected simplified machine tool workflow "Set machine coordinate origin" for the laboratory study.

for each participant. After performing the workflow on both HMI designs, an additional questionnaire was handed out to collect subjective impressions of each participant with respect to the different HMI designs, supplementing the objective data collected during the task performance.

Table 1. Characteristics of Participants, Mean (and Number)

Age	Gender		Knowledge Milling Machine					Knowledge Smart Device	
27	F	M	1	2	3	4	5	1–4	5
(Mean)	(9)	(10)	(5)	(3)	(4)	(7)	(0)	(0)	(19)

Note. M = male; F = female; Knowledge Milling machine and Knowledge Smart Device were counted from 1 = "I have never seen a milling machine/mobile device in my life" to 5 = "I regularly use milling machines/mobile devices".

For condition 1 a function-oriented HMI of a milling machine controlling was rebuilt by a computer-based mockup version. For condition 2 a workflow-oriented HMI was designed as a mockup considering gestalt laws of grouping [6, 7], as well as contextsensitive menustructuring [8]. Furthermore, the visual design of the workflow-oriented mockup is based on mobile devices in order to adapt their advantage of intuitivity [12].

Figure 2 shows screenshots of the function-oriented mockup version for condition 1. The buttons to operate the mockup of the function-oriented HMI were arranged in a row at the bottom and in a column at the right edge of the interface according to the interface

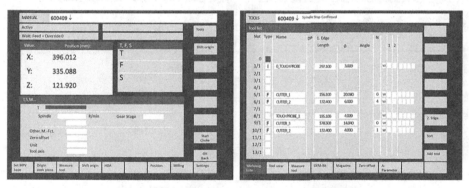

(1) Start Screen	(2) Tool Selection

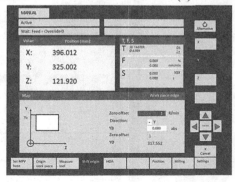

(3) Set axis direction

Fig. 2. Screenshots of the rebuilt function-oriented SINUMERIK-Mockup (condition 1)

layout of the real machine tool (e.g. see screenshot (1) in Fig. 2). In the "tool selection" menu the tools were arranged by their slot in the tool changer (screenshot (2)). Additional elements needed to operate the mockup were implemented by hard buttons on the HMI, e.g. the directional pad, depicted in screenshot (3).

Figure 3 shows the workflow-oriented mockup version realized for condition 2. The start screen in this condition shows several container apps (screenshot (1)) including different apps with elementary functions with the same context (screenshot (2)). In this version we also implemented a control area for all tasks, where all buttons are placed, at the bottom of the interface (see screenshots (3) and (4)). To compare both conditions we maintained the look-alike of the display and all control elements as buttons or the control cross in conformity with condition 1. Buttons belonging to the same context were arranged in proximity to each other according to gestalt principles [6, 7]. The buttons to control the actual workflow part, as well as corresponding operations, were arranged in the top row of the key pad. Selection buttons were placed in the middle row and the bottom row contains functions that do not affect the actual workflow. The menu buttons were greyed out according to context sensitivity [8]. Unlike the interface in condition 1, tools were sorted by type on the first level and by

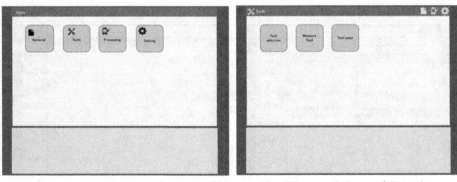

(1) Start Screen (Container Apps)   (2) Elemental Apps of Container
                                                    App "Tools"

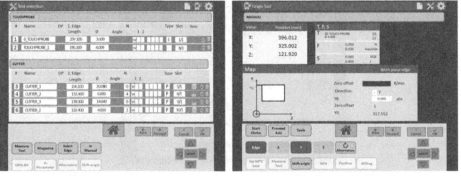

(4) Tool Selection   (3) Set axis direction

Fig. 3. Screenshots of the workflow-oriented mockup (condition 2)

name on the second level in the tool selection menu instead of slot numbers (3). Buttons that refer to specific tools, e.g. "delete tool" or "tool wear", were replaced by descriptive icons, which were placed at the end of each tool row.

2.3 Statistical Analysis

Descriptive results were further analyzed with inference statistical methods, to check, if statistically significant differences for the tested HMI types in performing indicators could be proven. A one-way repeated measures ANOVA with a Greenhouse-Geisser correction was conducted to compare the effect of the independent variable function-oriented versus workflow-oriented HMI structure on the dependent variables execution time, clicks and errors at a level of significance of 0.05.

3 Results

For each participant, the execution times in each condition, the number of clicks needed to perform the entire workflow and the number of errors made were collected as dependent variables. Table 2 shows the descriptive results of the 19 participants. Then we calculated the minimum, maximum, mean and standard deviation for each dependent variable (see Table 2 and Fig. 4). Results show that the minimum of the execution time, clicks and errors is lower in condition 1 compared to condition 2. The maximum of the execution time, clicks and errors is higher in condition 1 than in condition 2. For condition 2, the mean and standard deviation is lower for each dependent variable.

Table 2. Descriptive Statistics for Condition 1 and 2 of the *Execution times*, *Clicks*, and *Errors*

	N	Min	Max	Mean	Std. Error	Std. Deviation
Execution time Condition 2 [sec]	19	84.00	556.06	202.21	27.59	120.25
Execution time Condition 2 [sec]	19	43.28	329.13	156.13	15.82	68.97
Clicks Cond.1	18	21	96	32.33	4.45	18.89
Clicks Cond.2	18	4	53	27.61	2.57	10.91
Errors Cond.1	18	2	77	14.94	4.54	19.28
Errors Cond.2	18	0	33	9.22	2.18	9.23
Valid N (listwise)	18					

Regarding the execution time, the participants needed 202 s in average with a standard deviation of 120.248 to perform the working task with the function-oriented HMI, while the workflow-oriented HMI led to an average execution time of 156 s with a standard deviation of 68.97. The better performance of the workflow-oriented HMI is confirmed by the mean values of the clicks and errors. Concerning the clicks, participants needed 27.61 clicks on average (SD = 10.907) to perform the given task with

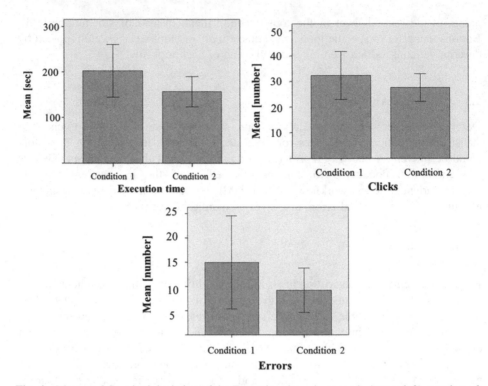

Fig. 4. Mean and Standard deviation of the Execution times in seconds (upper left), number of clicks (upper right) and number of errors (bottom center) in Condition 1 and 2

the workflow-oriented HMI and 32.33 clicks on average (SD = 18.89) to perform the same task with the function-oriented HMI. The mean value for errors made by all participants during the working task was 14.94 in condition 1 (SD = 19.28) and 9.22 in condition 2 (SD = 9.23). The evaluation of the subjective questionnaire approves these findings. 73.68 % of the participants answered, that the workflow-oriented condition (2) was more intuitive and clearly arranged than the function-oriented condition (1).

However, the ANOVA determined that neither the mean length of execution time did differ statistically significantly ($p = 0.189$) between time points ($F(1.000, 18.000) = 1.861$, $p > 0.05$). Nor the mean number of clicks differ statistically significant ($p = 0.378$) between time points ($F(1.000, 17) = 0.819$, $p > 0.05$), nor the mean number of errors differ statistically significant ($p = 0.288$) between time points ($F(1.000, 17) = 0.288$, $p > 0.05$).

4 Discussion

As it becomes obvious, the mean execution time is 46 s lower in condition 2 (workflow-oriented) than in condition 1 (function-oriented). These descriptive results point out that the workflow-oriented HMI leads to an average time saving of about 20 %

in comparison with the function-oriented design. Also, the standard deviation of execution time in condition 2 is considerably lower, which allows a more efficient time planning in production planning and scheduling by using workflow-oriented HMIs. The mean of clicks and errors can also obtain as an initial estimate for the improvements of workflow-oriented HMI approaches. Both means (as well as standard deviations) were lower in condition 2 than in condition 1 (4.72 on average for clicks and 5.72 on average for errors). Most of the clicks and errors were made in the workflow step "set axis direction" for all axes with the arrow keys of the directional pad, which nevertheless was adopted from the function-oriented approach and could be replaced by a more intuitive control element, for example a touch button, which allows a direct input of the axis value. To eliminate additional errors, for example made when selecting one of the axes, an enhanced visualization of the current workflow, i.e. depiction of the next task to perform, will improve the user orientation and will result in lower error rates. None of the dependent variables was statistically significant, which can be explained by characteristics of the test design of this preliminary study. Our study only comprised a single and brief work task with low complexity that was intended to be solved by the participants without any previous knowledge by just executing the written step-by-step instruction. Furthermore the average task execution time only lasted 179 s. According to the descriptive findings a subsequent study will be conducted, in which disturbance variables are going to be eliminated. Beyond that the rework of the workflow-oriented HMI, based on the results of the preliminary study and especially on the analysis of the subjective questionnaires, should lead to meaningful and significant results.

5   Conclusion

Prior research has documented the advantaged of workflow-oriented HMI design to support the user by carrying out human thinking structures [1]. However, these works did not study the actual effects caused by redesigning HMIs using an app concept empirically. This study can be seen as an explorative preliminary study to gain first important findings of the impact of workflow-oriented HMI design. In this study we tested effects among a group of novices for the work task "Set machine coordinate origin". The descriptive analyzes revealed that the workflow-oriented HMI resulted in a decrease of all dependent variables (execution time, clicks, errors). These findings extend those of Herfs et al. (2013), confirming that the work task becomes easier to solve for the participant with a workflow-oriented HMI. In addition, the improvements noted in our study were unrelated to gender. This study therefore leads to the conclusion that the benefits from workflow-oriented HMIs will be valid across a wide range of the HMI's users. However, some limitations are worth noting. Although our study has descriptively shown an improvement of performance, results only show a tendency, but no significance. To emphasize inference statistically effects, future work should therefore consider conducting an extended, optimized study with a longer procedure time as well as more short term task and an optimized HMI design. Moreover, further work should incorporate age-differentiated studies to analyze a possible Generation effect.

Acknowledgements. The Research is funded by the German Federal Ministry of Education and Research (BMBF), Project: MaxiMMI, according to Grant No. 16SV6237, supervised by the VDI/VDE Innovation + Technik GmbH. The authors would like to express their gratitude for the support given.

References

1. Chittaro, L.: Visualizing information on mobile devices. Computer **39**(3), 40–45 (2006)
2. DIN EN ISO 9241–12: Ergonomic requirements for Office Work with Visual Display Terminals Part 12: Presentation of Information, zuletzt geprüft am 2/20/2016 (2011)
3. Herfs, W., Kolster, D., Lohse, W.: Handlungsorientiertes Werkzeugmaschinen-HMI. atp edition **55**(11), 32–41 (2013)
4. Kolster, D.: Handlungsorientierte, multimodale Werkzeugmaschinen Benutzerschnittstellen. 1. Aufl. Aachen: Apprimus-Verl. (Edition Wissenschaft, Bd. 2014, 23) (2014)
5. Kuzgunkaya, O., ElMaraghy, H.A.: Assessing the structural complexity of manufacturing systems configurations. Int. J. Flex. Manuf. Syst. **18**(2), 145–171 (2007)
6. Lee, J., Bagheri, B., Kao, H.A.: A cyber-physical systems architecture for industry 4.0-based manufacturing systems. Manuf. Lett. **3**, 18–23 (2015)
7. Lim, C.S.C.: Designing inclusive ICT products for older users: taking into account the technology generation effect. J. of Eng. Design **21**(2), 189–206 (2010)
8. Mayhew, D.J.: Principles and Guidelines in Software User Interface Design. Prentice Hall, Englewood Cliffs, N.J. (1992)
9. Riediger, D., Hinrichsen; S., Schlee, A.: Ergonomic design of graphical control elements on production machines. In: 5th International Conference on Production Engineering and Management. Trieste (2015)
10. Schlick, C.M., Bruder, R., Luczak, H.: Arbeitswissenschaft. Springer, Berlin Heidelberg, Berlin, Heidelberg (2010)
11. Stanton, N.A.: Hierarchical task analysis: developments, applications, and extensions. Appl. Ergonomics **37**(1), 55–79 (2006)
12. Wagemans, J., Elder, J.H., Kubovy, M., Palmer, S.E., Peterson, M.A., Singh, M., von der Heydt, R.: A century of gestalt psychology in visual perception. I. perceptual grouping and figure–ground organization. Psychol. Bull. **138**(6), 1172–1217 (2012)

Designing Effective Teaching Interventions with Semantic Annotation

Zainb Dawod[(⊠)] and David Bell

College of Engineering Design and Physical Sciences,
Department of Computer Science, Brunel University, Uxbridge UB8 3PH, UK
{zainb.dawod,David.Bell}@brunel.ac.uk

Abstract. Semantic web technology promises a number of benefits for a future in many different fields and especially within education. There is, however, a considerable gap in Semantic Web research between the contributions in the educational field and the research carried out in the special educational needs area. Semantic web techniques have been applied in education to retrieve the relevant material, and add semantic annotation to documents. However, special needs schools still rely heavily on manual methods. This paper presents a design of SEN teaching platform based on a semantic web annotation tool (Amaya) coordinated with a web application. This design evaluated by conducting pilot study in schools caring for special needs students SEN.

Building on a pilot study at two schools and interviewing nine participants (Teachers, Teaching Assistant) in UK, the findings indicate that Semantic Web technology can benefit the education of special needs by utilizing semantic web annotation tools.

Keywords: Semantic web · Semantic web annotation (Amaya) · Special educational needs (SEN) · Design educational platform · Effective teaching

1 Introduction

Rapid evolution of the World Wide Web has attempted to support a variety of users in different fields and contexts with different requirements and experiences such as, e-learning, distance learning, digital libraries and medical field. The Semantic Web initiative could have an impact on educational research with a number of promising characteristics such as allowing data to be shared and reuse by the teaching staff and students. There is, however, a considerable gap in Semantic Web research between the contributions in the educational field and the research carried out in the special educational needs field. The teaching methods available in a special needs school typically utilise manual methods. This paper examines the impact of Semantic Web Annotation tool (Amaya) on enhancing their educational performance. Consequently, the motivations for promoting semantic web annotation tools in the education of special needs motivated the design of a new system which could support varied special needs students. The new system - SEN Teaching Platform (STP) - synthesises the core Web language for creating applications (HTML) and semantic Web Annotation Tool (Amaya). Concerning the STP design, a set of criteria are based on the previous

© Springer International Publishing Switzerland 2016
M. Kurosu (Ed.): HCI 2016, Part III, LNCS 9733, pp. 505–518, 2016.
DOI: 10.1007/978-3-319-39513-5_47

research in paper [4]. This earlier experiment tested different annotation tools and selected Amaya as a most suitable tool to conduct further work in schools. A major concern from this earlier study was to allow the STP model to consider the important factors and barriers that might influence semantic web annotation adoption.

The identified criteria for a proposed STP focused on designing a teaching platform that is easy to use; support/replace the current manual teaching methods, coordinate with different abilities and requirements and available as required. The experimental content used in this study and implemented in the STP is poetry. Poetry is used in the design because it has certain qualities that make it an excellent vehicle through which to teach SEN students. Poems that rhyme offer an excellent opportunity to listen for and find rhyming words [5]. Consequently, it is one of the more difficult areas to understand for special needs students especially students with ASD [11]. Poetry has a sizable vocabulary with underlying meanings that are especially difficult for autistic students [6].

Twenty five schools were contacted to volunteer for this research. The target age group in this research is two and a half to sixteen years old. Two schools offered to participate in this study (Nursery, Special needs High School). Building on a comprehensive pilot study at two schools accommodating special needs students in the UK, nine interviews were conducted with teaching staff (teachers and teaching assistant) to experience and understand their personal point of view. All of the data gathered from the two schools was thematically analysed resulting in a design brief that has a number of required elements. Firstly, communications including engaging students, increasing the concentration and reducing behavior problems. Secondly, understanding certain words, especially for autistic students, and accommodate different abilities in class using visual resources are important for greater understanding. Finally, class management, resources availability as required and staff training are important to prepare each lesson for special needs. The pilot study examines all these categories with their themes using the SEN Teaching Platform (STP). STP proved to be a useful tool in enhancing SEN teaching.

The study follows a design science research approach composed of three phases. The first phase "Identify and build the STP", is accomplished in three steps. The first step started by identifying the problem area from literature and the previous research [3]. Secondly, a vision was formulated and feasibility study undertaken that includes identifying the participant (Teaching staff) requirements and understanding the special needs student requirements. Thirdly, preparing and scoping stage to design the STP. Designing STP include design an educational poetry website imported into Amaya. In the second phase, Semantic annotation was applied to poetry from the first step. This process includes annotating all the poems with different types of annotations. The annotations included are the symbol systems currently used for special needs (Makaton, Widget and Picture Exchange Communication System PECS), images, sound and information [4, 10]. The second step involved conducting data collection and filtering. This process itself includes managing the required information which includes all the data gathered from the participant's interview, class observations and field's notes. All the data gathered is then thematically analysed. The last phase is evaluating the STP performance to see if it achieved the design targets/criteria.

The findings indicate that Semantic Web technology can benefit the education of special needs by utilizing semantic web annotation tools. The semantic web annotation tool (Amaya) has a considerable impact on enhancing their educational performance and reducing the effort required from the teaching staff to design and prepare for each lesson. All participants chose to use STP and recognised the benefit of STP. However, some recommendations suggested improvement that could be made.

2 Research Design and Platform Process

The study follows a design research approach through which learning of the problem space is accomplished through artefact evolvement and evaluation. Hevner [7] described the process as an effective solution to a problem. Effective solutions may not match with the optimum result. The effectiveness of the solution must be provable through an iterative evaluation of the design artifact(s). The artefact resulting from the Design Science Research (DSR) in this work was to induce the characterisation of the new STP model from observation of practice. The process which derives the discovery of semantic web annotation technique to design SEN Teaching Platform (STP) is refining and extending the structure of the website produced in [4]. The input for the first step is the poetry website and the output will be the refined poetry website which will be the input for the second step. In second step manual annotation using Amaya will be conducted which produced poetry annotated website. This website will be the input for the participant's requirement in order to modify according to the teachers lesson requirements. This annotated website with the consideration of the participant's requirement will be input for the final step to produce the STP as described in Table 1.

Table 1. Iteration steps- input output model

Steps	Method	Input artefacts	Output
1. Refine and extend the structure of the website	Build, amend and extend HTML Website	Poetry Website, Anotea/Amaya, Mozilla browser, images, SEN symbols	Improved HTML Poetry website (Model) & (Method) (Instantiation)
2. Identify the text required for annotation/type of annotation	Manual annotation	Improved HTML Poetry website (Model) & (Method) (Instantiation)	Annotated text (Method)
3. Identify the teaching staff requirements to teach poems	Interview (Semi structured interview questions)	Annotated text (Method)	The teaching staff requirements for teaching poems (STP Model)
4. Develop and extend the STP model by incorporating the current symbol systems used to support SEN students and variety of SEN needs	Build Amaya Application	Web service artefact/STP Model	Prototype application (Instantiation) New STP

3 Artefact Building and Development (Pilot Study)

The STP Design proposed is based on the findings from the previous work of [4] study. The study was based on literature review and the experiment conducted on two tools and results in choosing Amaya for this study. Hence, a set of evaluation criteria listed for the proposed STP in this study.

1. The platform model should be simple to use to make the platform model usable by staff with different IT skills and to avoid any technical problems.
2. The platform model should **support the staff with the class management skills**, including the ability to reduce behaviour problems and increase student's engagement level in class.
3. The STP model should be able to support/replace the manual methods as a huge effort required to prepare lessons.
4. The STP should include the symbol systems currently used for helping SEN in schools to assist with symbol systems training.
5. The platform model should **support/replace the symbol cards** existent.
6. The platform model should coordinate with different abilities and needs.
7. The platform model should improve the **understanding the poems**, since poetry is one of the difficult topics to explain for SEN students.
8. The platform model should have **flexibility** to benefit in different subjects.
9. The platform model should **increase the student's motivation and engagement** in class.
10. The platform model should be **easy to use, edit and maintain.**
11. The platform model should **offer different types of annotations** (image, information, bigger text, sound and symbols).
12. The platform saved on the local server at this stage because some schools have no internet in class.

3.1 Data Collection

This section covers all activities to produce the platform assessment. The primary goal of data collection is to prepare data for assessing the STP model. The data used in this study was collected from February 2012 to October 2012. The particular technique used to collect the data was through a series of semi-structured interviews. The interviews provide the opportunity to explore that cannot be directly observed from the participants' or the researcher point of view [8, 12]. In this study, data collection activities described as follows:

Participants Recruitments. Pilot study interviews were carried out in two schools, a nursery for children ages 3–5 years and a secondary school for children ages 11–16 years. The interviews conducted with nine participants. They sampled according to two categories, two Teachers and seven Teaching assistants Table 2. Illustrates the composition of the interviewee sample across the two schools.

Table 2. Participants overall description in the Pilot Study

Description	Total
Sample Size	9
Gender Female	9
Age Range SEN Children	(2.5–4), (11–16)
Preschool (2.5-4)	5
Manager/Staff Teacher	1
Teaching Staff	4
Secondary School (11-16)	4
SEN Teacher	1
Teaching Assistant	3

4   Extended Amaya and STP Implementation

This section presents a demonstration of the practical application of STP with the use of the semantic annotation (Amaya). First, the class teacher chooses the poem and the type of annotation rewquired for the class demonstration. The platform prepared accordingly with the kind of annotation required. The annotation offered will be in a wide range depending on the SEN age and needs. In this study "The Zoo" selected for the Nursery school without any changes suggested. "Bed Time" poem was chosen by the secondary class teacher with symbol annotation requirement for the class and image annotation for one-to-one support. Figure 1 presents the first user interface of STP. Figure 2 presents the poem page with different styles of poems depending on the age and style. Figure 3 presents the children poems page with various types of poems that can be changed according to the class requirements.

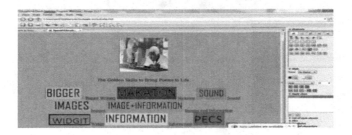

Fig. 1. STP user Interface

Fig. 2. Different styles of poems

Fig. 3. The children poem home page

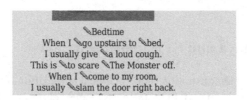

Fig. 4. The screenshot of Amaya annotation penci

When the teacher clicks on the pen mark as illustrated in Fig. 4. "The Zoo" is the poem tested in the pre-school caring for special educational needs as illustrated in Fig. 5.

Fig. 5. The result of clicking the word 'Polar bear'

5   Analysis, Results and Discussion

In this study, the data collected was thematically analysed. The results grouped into common themes in the following sections to facilitate comparison between the categories.

5.1   Adopting Thematic Analysis as a Research Approach

The practical purpose of this analysis is to confirm and evaluate the STP design with Amaya annotation tool technology. Step one in developing the analysis plan for this research is to be familiarised with the data. Data familiarization through the transcription process, by listening to the interviews and reading through the data, while thinking about possible themes [1]. Thereafter, first codes generated from the transcript information [2]. Qualitative data analysis software NVivo10, used to facilitate the thematic analysis in the pilot study. All the data exported to NVivo10, which coded the interesting features of the entire dataset. Additionally, identify themes and review them. Each theme captures something important about the data in relation to research questions. All the data relevant to each theme is extracted to ensure all the relevant data are connected first with individual codes and then with the theme. This process will build a framework of themes to show the connections and relationships between themes and subthemes [1]. Table 3 outlines the eight codes, themes and sub-Themes along with the number of times each theme and sub-theme was mentioned by the participants.

During the interviews, participants identified various ways of teaching poems which is either using the computer or the manual way. The theme for current teaching method among these categories is labelled Current Teaching Methods. The observation shows that using images is the method that all participants use in their teaching. Moreover, from reviewing the participant's interviews it shows that current teaching methods requires time, preparation, and it should be visual. The participants signposted the current teaching requirements during the interviews by expressing their current concerns, current issues and the main issues in teaching SEN. The theme for the requirements is labelled understanding current teaching requirement.

A key issue observed from participants was that behavior problems, time, preparation and the underline meaning, in addition to other concerns such as staffing and understanding. Concurrently, the need for different ways of learning to increase understanding and to improve SEN mood was expressed by most of the participants. Finally, most of the participants pinpointed ASD as a major issues required effort to manage in SEN class.

Table 3. Open-coding concepts categorisation

CODES	Themes	SUB-THEMES	DEFINITION
Current teaching methods	-Manual Methods (93), computer programs/Internet (9), Time Consuming (5), Preparation Demands (4), Visual (5), Required Individual Support Required more staff (1)	- Computer programs (4), internet (4), Visual using Images (18), Symbol Systems (6), Designed Booklet (5) and document created (1)	What is the scope of study? Explore the current teaching methods used in schools for SEN

(Continued)

Table 3. (*Continued*)

CODES	Themes	SUB-THEMES	DEFINITION
Understanding current teaching requirement	-Support Teaching Staff, Understanding (5), Resources (42), Time (9), Support (2), Visual, Class Management, Staffing (2), Communication And Language (2), Personal Social And Emotional (2), ASD, Learning Progress (2)	-Understand Underline Meaning (9), SEN Understanding Poems (5), Behavioural Problems (9), Time Demand (9), Preparation (6), Accommodate Different Abilities (2), Reading (4), Numeracy (1), Writing (1), Communication (3), Engaging (2), Lack Of Staff (5), Training (6), Organization (4), SEN Mood (4)	Understand the current teaching needs and what they require Managing and interpreting the SEN and teaching staff requirements
		-English As A Second Language (1), Support ASD (2), Concentration (1)	
Important teaching factors for SEN in school	-Resources, Class Management, Understanding, Group Size (One To One Or Small Group), Communication(2), Personal Social And Emotional	-Concentration (1), Understand Underline Meaning (1), Differentiation (1), Routine(1)	Categorise the demands based on requirements Managing and interpreting the SEN students requirements
		-Visual (5), Time Management (1), Prepared (1), Engaging (2), Demonstration Layout (5), Working In Small Groups Or One To One (5), Resource Layout (2), Mood (4), Poems (7), Language (3), Simple and short poems (2)	

(*Continued*)

Table 3. (*Continued*)

CODES	Themes	SUB-THEMES	DEFINITION
Poems	-Importance, Support, Difficult	-Essential For Pre-School (1)	Categorise the demands
		-Support SEN Students In Teaching And Learning (2), Supports With Talk (1), Can Teach All Subject In Pre-School (2), Difficult To Explain The Underline Meaning (2)	
ASD	-Resources, Class Management	-Concentration (1), Understand Underline Meaning (1), Routine, Visual, Prepared, Demonstration Layout	Categorise the demands Managing and interpreting the ASD requirements
The use of semantic web annotation tool (SEN teaching prototype)	-Aid All Types Of Sen (9), Preparation (3), Class Management (16), Resources, Setting (Sen Mood), Teaching, ASD(4), Concentration (2), Learning Process (150), Availability (1), Support (6)	-Understanding (6), Support With Preparation (5), Reduce Pressure On Teaching Staff (10), Support Teaching Staff (5), Save Preparation Time (7), Help With Staffing Problems (Lack Of Staff) (4), Support For Autistic (ASD) Children (5), Accommodate Different Abilities (16)	Undertake pilot research and Evaluating SEN prototype in schools
		- Support/Replace Re-sources (11), can replace cards (1), Support Manual Methods (6), Reduce Behavioural Problems (7),	

(*Continued*)

Table 3. (*Continued*)

CODES	Themes	SUB-THEMES	DEFINITION
		Better Mood, Support With Reading, Differentiate Numeracy, Can Be Used For Different Subject (25), Can Support ASD (12), Better Concentration (2), Effective Learning (216), Useful In Teaching Poems (7), Motivation (11), Writing (2), Engaging(1), Better teaching results (4)	
Evaluation	-Layout (8), Content (9), Participants Suggestions For Future Work	-Bright Colours (4), Suitable Font and colour (4), Short Rhymes (2), Images (1), Bigger Images (4), Adapted To Younger age (11), Adapted To Be Used By SEN Independently (2), Special Version For Teachers (1), Can Be Used For Different Subjects Such As Maths (1), Popular Characters Within The Prototype (1), Use real pictures (1), Small Text (2), To Have A Choice Of Annotate Words Or Lines (7_), Use different languages for annotation (1), Choose to use it in future (9)	Evaluate SEN prototype if it support the teaching staff and enhance the teaching and learning of poems in class

It was observed through the interviews that the participants felt that Autistic is one of the main factors require attention in SEN schools. Another observation was the change faced by the teaching staff with an autistic child who has a short concentration time, difficult to understand underline meaning and can work in small groups.

The interviews reflect on the suitability of using STP in teaching poems to SEN students. The observation made from group demonstration and one-to-one support during assessments with worksheets.

Several principal themes developed during coding through the links among categories. Moreover, the interview observation of the main points that participants focused on which have more impact on SEN teaching and learning. The results from the coding outlines the scope of the research that was pinpointed main themes required to achieve for the new STP design. Table 4 presents nine themes assigned to three categories of dimension 2: SEN students and teaching staff interaction.

Table 4. Categories and themes relating to SEN and teaching staff interaction

Category	Theme
5.5.2 Communication	1. Engaging
	2. Concentration
	3. behaviour problems
5.5.3 Understanding	1. understand underline words
	2. Accommodate different abilities
	3. visual resources
5.5.4 Preparation	1. management
	2. resource availability
	3. staff training

Communication.   The themes in Communication category was 'Engaging', 'Concentration' and 'Behavior problems'. These themes secured agreement from all the participants. The teaching assistant from the special school express the significance of engaging, concentration in the progress of learning for the whole class.

> TA1: "obviously behavioral of certain students because if one student not doing what he supposed doing, it has effect on the rest of the class, but once you actually get to know that child".

Understanding.   Theme one gained shared agreement from the participants on understands underline words especially with poems. The teacher from the special school expressed the difficulty of Autistic students to understand the underline words as follows;

> "They understand it face value as it is literal not the underlining meaning of what the authors trying to get out, that is quiet difficult for them to understand" "To understand the underline meaning in the poem, so with some of our ASD pupil they would understand what they read as literal".

Theme two shows the significance of accommodating different abilities in class. The general opinion was that the teaching resources should benefit all types of abilities as clarified in the interview feedback below:

"To support with behavior...yhaa... Umm and understanding for the ones that have low understanding or communication problems".

Theme three, expressed strong opinion of all the participants that SEN students can understanding required visual resources as labelled by the teacher from the special secondary

"Which of the above you consider more important for this type of support? "Visuals..images.. visuals..visual images".

Preparation.   Theme one in preparation category was management which is raised as main issue by all the participants. The teachers expressed their needs for staffing, time and resources to manage the load of preparation required before each lesson as expressed by the teaching assistant.

TA3: *"pause.., no there aren't enough hours in the day so, times, because there is always lots of preparation to do and lot of things to get ready and resources, they will never be enough resources no matter how much you got, you will always".*

Resource availability is the second theme raised by the teaching assistant which said:

TA1: *"well in my class in particular, we have a lot of ASD students, so it's making sure that we have all of the work set beforehand, so if we have to do a class lesson with the whole group has to listen? We just have to make sure that we have everything ready, first thing for the ASD students, and prepare them what have to be next because you want to include everybody into the lesson if we can, so just preparation"*

Research participants pointed to the staff training as an important issue to teach SEN students as said below:

TA3: *"yes, definitely because (student) does Makaton, I picked up a bit of it but I never done it, I wish I had".*

5.2   Evaluation of STP

The new STP designed is evaluated according to the criteria and the results from the thematic analysis. The STP can accomplish all the criteria as illustrated in Table 5:

Although all the participants found the STP to be a useful resource for enhancing SEN education. There are some recommendations mentioned by the participants to improve the design of the STP such as bright colours, bigger font, short poems, more images.

Table 5. STP evaluation findings

Criteria	STP
1. Simple to use	✓
2. Support the staff with the class management skills	✓
3. Support/replace the manual methods	✓
4. Saving preparation time	✓
5. Support/replace the symbol cards	✓
6. Support different types of SEN students' needs and abilities	✓
7. Understanding	✓
8. Utilised for other class subjects (flexible)	✓
9. Increase the motivation and engagement	✓
10. Easy to use, edit and maintain	✓
11. Offer different types of annotations (image, information, bigger text, sound and symbols)	✓
12. Saved on local server	✓

6 Conclusion and Future Works

There is a considerable gap in Semantic Web research between the contributions in the educational field and the research carried out in the special educational needs field. The teaching methods available in a special needs school are typically based on manual methods. This paper examines the impact of Semantic Web Annotation tool (Amaya) on enhancing their educational performance – designing educational content. Consequently, the motivations for promoting semantic web annotation tools in the education of special needs motivated a design of a new system which could support special needs education. The new system - SEN Teaching Platform (STP) – synthesises of the core Web language for creating applications (HTML) and semantic Web Annotation Tool (Amaya).

The study follows a design science research approach composed of three phases. The first phase "Identify and build the STP", is accomplished in three steps. The first step started by identifying the problem area from literature and the previous research [3]. Secondly, a vision was formulated and feasibility study undertaken that includes identifying the participant (Teaching staff) requirements and understanding the special needs student requirements. Thirdly, preparing and scoping stage to design the STP. Designing STP include design an educational poetry website imported into Amaya. In the second phase, Semantic annotation was applied to poetry from the first step. This process includes annotating all the poems with different types of annotations. The annotations included are the symbol systems currently used for special needs (Makaton, Widget and PECS), images, sound and information. The second step involved conducting data collection and filtering. This process includes managing the required information which includes all the data gathered from the participant's interview, class observations and field's notes. All the data gathered will be thematically analysed. The last phase is evaluating the STP performance to see if it achieved the design targets/criteria.

References

1. Braun, V., Clarke, V.: Using thematic analysis in psychology. Qual. Res. Psychol. **3**(2), 77–101 (2006). ISSN 1478-0887
2. Braun, V., Clarke, V.: Teaching Thematic Analysis, look at overcoming challenges and developing strategies for effective learning. Psychologist **26**(2), 120–124 (2013)
3. Communication Matters: Using Symbols and Communication. ISAAC (UK) (2012)
4. Dawod, Z., Bell, D.: Adaptive Special educational needs (SEN) education on the Semantic Web. In: Proceedings of the U.K. Academy for Information Systems, 16th Annual Conference (2011)
5. Dillon, W.: Using Poetry in Teaching Reading to Special Education Students. Yale-New Haven Teachers Institute (2016). Accessed 8 Feb 2016
6. Gill, P., Stewart, K., Treasure, E., Chadwick, B.: Methods of data collection in qualitative research: interviews and focus groups. Br. Dent. J. **204**, 291–295 (2008)
7. Hevner, A., March, S., Park, J., Ram, S.: Design science in information systems research. MIS Q. **28**(1), 75–105 (2004)
8. Maxwell, J.A.: Designing a Qualitative Study, Chap. 7, pp. 214–253 (2008). http://www.sagepub.com/upm-data/23772_Ch7.pdf
9. Osteen, M.: Autism and Representation. Tailor & Francis Group, Routledge (2008)
10. Published online: 22 March 2008. doi:10.1038/bdj.2008.192. http://www.nature.com/bdj/journal/v204/n6/full/bdj.2008.192.html
11. Punch, K.F.: Introduction to Social Research: Quantitative and Qualitative Approaches. Sage, Thousand Oaks (1998)
12. Khandkar, S.H.: Open Coding, pp. 1–9 (2014). http://pages.cpsc.ucalgary.ca/ ~ saul/wiki/uploads/CPSC681/open-coding.pdf. Accessed 26 Oct 2014
13. Slimani, T.: Semantic Annotation: The Mainstay of Semantic Web (2013)
14. Randi, J., Newman, T., Grigorenko, L.E.: Teaching children with autism to read for meaning: challenges and possibilities. J. Autism. Dev. Disord. **40**(7), 890–902 (2010)

Effect of Visual Emphasis on Important Parts of Texts

Yuta Fukui[1(✉)], Toru Nakata[2], and Toshikazu Kato[3]

[1] Industrial and Systems Engineering, Graduate School of Science
and Engineering, Chuo University, Hachioji, Japan
all.tjek@g.chuo-u.ac.jp
[2] National Institute of Advanced Industrial Science
and Technology (AIST), Tsukuba, Japan
toru-nakata@aist.go.jp
[3] Chuo University, Hachioji, Japan
kato@indsys.chuo-u.ac.jp

Abstract. This paper investigates the effect of visual emphasis on important parts of texts to support readers' comprehension. Our experiment showed that changing color and enlarging font size of important parts shorten reading time and improve accuracy of comprehension. We, however, also found a negative effect of visual emphasis that the readers less understand contents of not-emphasized area. This paper reports influences of those cognitive effects quantitatively.

Keywords: Reading comprehension · Visual emphasis of texts

1 Introduction: Does Emphasizing of Important Text Parts Help Understanding?

In recent years, we have become forced to read many documents in our workplace and daily life. However, we cannot read all documents carefully because of time limitation. Some recent researches, therefore, has investigated methods that can automatically summarize documents to aid the comprehension of long documents [1, 2].

A problem takes place after the extraction of important parts: we have to consider about how to display of the texts.

In some cases, less important parts are simply hided, while important parts are left. Even though some parts are evaluated as unimportant by the system, they still have certain information that might be crucial. So we should avoid hiding them.

Another way is visual emphasis that highlights important parts of texts without hiding unimportant parts.

Today we can extract important parts from texts by using some automatic software. Also we do not feel difficulty to emphasize important parts by applying conventional typographical techniques. The problem is that we are not sure about cognitive effects of emphasis of important parts: are they really helpful for comprehension or not?

© Springer International Publishing Switzerland 2016
M. Kurosu (Ed.): HCI 2016, Part III, LNCS 9733, pp. 519–526, 2016.
DOI: 10.1007/978-3-319-39513-5_48

The purpose of this paper is to confirm our expectations that the visual emphasis increases the degree of comprehension and shortens the reading time. We also examine side-effects of visual emphasis.

2   Preparation: Extraction and Emphasis of Important Parts

2.1   Automatic Methods to Detect Important Parts of Texts

For the experiment, we can consider the following three methods to automatically evaluate and extract important texts.

- Method A: Extracting sentences containing terms that appear most frequently in the document.
- Method B: TF-IDF method, which extracting sentences with a high Term Frequency Inverse Document Frequency (TF-IDF) sum.
- Method C: Improved TF-IDF method [3]. Extracting sentences containing not only many instances of frequent terms, but terms that tend to appear together with the frequent terms, and terms evaluated by the TF-IDF measure.

We used Total Environment for Text Data Mining (TETDM) [4] to implement Method C.

In the experiment, we set 30 % as the ratio of compression of the text length, so that 70 % of original sentences will be evaluated unimportant.

Our research interest does not aim at the discovery of an excellent method to automatically evaluate and extract important texts. We use these three methods to confirm that the visual emphasis increases the degree of comprehension and shortens the reading time even if the extracting methods are any methods.

2.2   Ways of Visual Emphasis on Important Parts

We apply following three types of visual emphasis simultaneously on the parts evaluated as important (Fig. 1).

1. Important sentences are displayed with red letters.
2. The important sentences are enlarged from 11pt font-size to 13pt.
3. The most frequent terms used in the important sentences are typed in blue.

The purpose of this paper is to confirm that the visual emphasis increases the degree of comprehension and shortens the reading time. Therefore, we do not care about the difference of ways of visual emphasis on important parts (Fig. 2).

本文

　思えば子どものころから意気地もなければ根気もない。通信簿に担任の先生が書く所感の欄があるけれど、そこにはよく「あきらめずに最後までやりとげましょう」なんて書かれていた。学校の先生というのはえらいもので、ちゃんと見ているものだ。いや、まったくその通り。我ながら今までの人生、中途半端ばかりだった。

　中学のとき剣道部に入ったけど、半年でやめちゃったし、高校のときは一時の気の迷いで演劇部に入り、一、二回、端役で舞台に立ったけれど、その後、なんとなくやめちゃった。もし、あのとき人前で演じることの醍醐味みたいなものを味わっていたら、また違っていたかもしれないけれど、そういうこともなかった。

　大学時代はなんとなく過ごし、叔父さんのツテで入った小さな会社でしばらく営業をやらされていたが、成績はあんまりパッとせず、部長から、お前はやる気に欠けているって、いつも言われていた。結局、2年ほどで首にされちゃった。

　それからいくつもの職場を転々としたけれど、やっぱり長続きしなくて。

　だけどそんな俺にもじつは夢がある。人に聞かれたら笑われそうだけど、自分にとっては、けっこう本気でね。それはフルマラソンで完走すること。

　走るのはもともと嫌いじゃなかった。中学時代、陸上部じゃなかったけれど、学校対抗の駅伝大会の選手に駆り出されて上位に入賞したこともある。だからといって、このトシにとって、いきなりフルマラソンで完走できるとは思ってないけれど、自分では挑戦するに値する目標だと思っている。

　この夢を思いついたのが、2度目のリストラに遭った半年前のこと。それから毎朝トレーニングを始めて、最初は3キロ走るのがやっとだったけれど、少しづつ距離をのばして、いまやっと20キロ完走できるところまできた。まだ夢は半分だけど、ダブついていたお腹はへっこんだし、脚もしまってだいぶ筋力がついてきた。当面の目標は来年の市民マラソンに出場して完走すること。それがだめでも、へこたれない。夢を果たすまで挑戦を続けるつもり。

　もし 42,195 キロを走り抜くことができたら、人生をリセットできるような気がするから。中途半端な生き方と、おさらばできるような気がするから。

(a)

本文

　思えば子どものころから意気地もなければ根気もない。通信簿に担任の先生が書く所感の欄があるけれど、そこにはよく「あきらめずに最後までやりとげましょう」なんて書かれていた。学校の先生というのはえらいもので、ちゃんと見ているものだ。いや、まったくその通り。我ながら今までの人生、中途半端ばかりだった。

　中学のとき剣道部に入ったけど、半年でやめちゃったし、高校のときは一時の気の迷いで演劇部に入り、一、二回、端役で舞台に立ったけれど、その後、なんとなくやめちゃった。もし、あのとき人前で演じることの醍醐味みたいなものを味わっていたら、また違っていたかもしれないけれど、そういうこともなかった。

　大学時代はなんとなく過ごし、叔父さんのツテで入った小さな会社でしばらく営業をやらされていたが、成績はあんまりパッとせず、部長から、お前はやる気に欠けているって、いつも言われていた。結局、2年ほどで首にされちゃった。

　それからいくつもの職場を転々としたけれど、やっぱり長続きしなくて。

　だけどそんな俺にもじつは夢がある。人に聞かれたら笑われそうだけど、自分にとっては、けっこう本気でね。それはフルマラソンで完走すること。

　走るのはもともと嫌いじゃなかった。中学時代、陸上部じゃなかったけれど、学校対抗の駅伝大会の選手に駆り出されて上位に入賞したこともある。だからといって、このトシにとって、いきなりフルマラソンで完走できるとは思ってないけれど、自分では挑戦するに値する目標だと思っている。

　この夢を思いついたのが、2度目のリストラに遭った半年前のこと。それから毎朝トレーニングを始めて、最初は3キロ走るのがやっとだったけれど、少しづつ距離をのばして、いまやっと20キロ完走できるところまできた。まだ夢は半分だけど、ダブついていたお腹はへっこんだし、脚もしまってだいぶ筋力がついてきた。当面の目標は来年の市民マラソンに出場して完走すること。それがだめでも、へこたれない。夢を果たすまで挑戦を続けるつもり。

　もし 42,195 キロを走り抜くことができたら、人生をリセットできるような気がするから。中途半端な生き方と、おさらばできるような気がするから。

(b)

Fig. 1. (a) Text with visual emphasis and (b) plain text

Choose the correct answer

Agree : This sentence agrees with the original text.

Disagree : This sentence disagrees with the original text.

No Relation : This sentence has no relationship with the original text.

1. The author can escape from the disappointing life by attaining his dream.
   ☐ Agree ☐ Disagree   ☐ No Relation
2. If the author can not run the whole race, he will give up his dream.
   ☐ Agree ☐ Disagree   ☐ No Relation
3. If the author can run the whole race, he does not glow up mentally.
   ☐ Agree ☐ Disagree   ☐ No Relation
4. We can not attain the each dream easily because we have weak wills.
   ☐ Agree ☐ Disagree   ☐ No Relation

Fig. 2. The example of the admission tests

3 Experiment: Visual Emphasis and Degree of Understanding

3.1 Source Texts and Applied Visual Emphasis

We select eight documents for this experiment. Those documents are used for admission tests on comprehension ability in Japanese (ISBN 978-4-86248-938-8) (Table 1).

Table 1. Text extraction method for each document

Document Number	Method to Extract Important Sentences
1	A
2	A
3	A
4	B
5	B
6	C
7	C
8	C

For each document, we prepare two versions of appearance: texts with visual emphasis and plain texts without emphasis (Fig. 1).

3.2   Subjects and Order of Sessions

Twelve university students participate in our experiment. We assign the two document groups to two corresponding groups of subjects (Fig. 3). The order in which the subjects read the texts is changed randomly for each subject to eliminate the order effect.

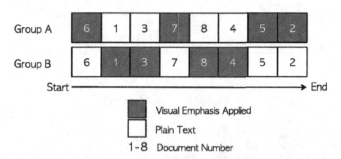

Fig. 3. Example of a random document order presented to a subject

First, each subject seat 45 cm away from a screen and is instructed to read the document on the screen quickly. After reading it, the document disappears from the screen. The subject answers four questions to check the degree of understanding of the contents.

3.3   Results and Discussion

Comprehension Performance. Table 2 shows the result of the rate of correct answers. When the questions relate contents written in the emphasized area, the subjects answered more correctly. The attentions of the subjects were strengthened toward the emphasized area. This tendency was verified as significant with t-test ($p < 0.05$).

This suggests the proposed method can support reading comprehension for this problem type (Fig. 4).

Table 2, however, also shows the result of the rate of correct answers. When the questions relate contents of not-emphasized area, the subjects answered less correctly. The attentions of the subjects were strengthened toward the emphasized area, so they may not pay attention toward the not-emphasized area carefully. Though this difference is not proven as significant by using the t-test, we value this tendency as a negative effect (Table 3).

Reading Time. The reading times of three documents with visual emphasis were slightly shorter than those of plain text (Fig. 5), but this difference is not proven as significant by using the t-test.

Summarizing all of the experimental result, we find that the proposed method cannot shorten reading time greatly, but we can use our method to support reading

Table 2. Correct answers rate

Mean Rate of Correct Answers (%) (± S. D.)	Types of Problems	
	Related to Contents in Visually Emphasized Areas	Independent to Contents in Visually Emphasized Areas
Visual Emphasis Applied	74 (± 10)	53 (± 19)
Plain Text	61 (± 16)	66 (± 20)

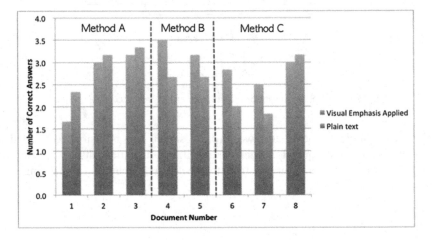

Fig. 4. Means of correct answers out of the four questions

Table 3. Means and standard deviations of number of correct answers

Document Number	Method to Extract Important Sentences	Mean # of Correct Answers (± S. D.)	
		Visual Emphasis Applied	Plain Text
1	A	1.7 (±0.9)	2.3 (±0.7)
2	A	3.0 (±0.8)	3.2 (±1.2)
3	A	3.2 (±0.7)	3.3 (±0.5)
4	B	3.5 (±0.5)	2.7 (±0.7)
5	B	3.2 (±0.4)	2.7 (±0.9)
6	C	2.8 (±0.9)	2.0 (±0.8)
7	C	2.5 (±1.3)	1.8 (±1.1)
8	C	3.0 (±1.2)	3.2 (±0.4)

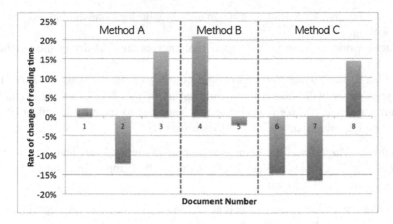

Fig. 5. Rate of change of reading time for each document

Table 4. Reading time and reading speed, normalized by the number of document characters

Document Number	Method to Extract Important Sentences	Text Length	Mean of Reading time (s) (± S. D.)			Reading Speed (character/s)	
			Visual Emphasis Applied	Plain Text	Diff	Visual Emphasis Applied	Plain Text
1	A	1032	100 (± 28.5)	98 (± 28.5)	2	10	11
2	A	990	96 (± 28.7)	109 (± 25.8)	-13	10	9
3	A	697	61 (± 11.6)	52 (± 15.7)	9	11	13
4	B	714	70 (± 17.8)	58 (± 16.8)	12	10	12
5	B	740	60 (± 15.3)	61 (± 15.1)	-1	12	12
6	C	775	60 (± 16.8)	70 (± 19.9)	-10	13	11
7	C	901	68 (± 22.1)	82 (± 19.6)	-14	13	11
8	C	1261	94 (± 14.1)	82 (± 16.8)	12	13	15

comprehension for visually emphasized areas. That means proper selection of emphasis area is crucial to proper comprehension of readers (Table 4).

4   Conclusion and Future Work

These results of this experiment suggest that the proposed method could support reading comprehension in visually emphasized areas.

We, however, also found a negative effect of visual emphasis that the readers less understand contents of not-emphasized area.

These two results suggest that we should increase the emphasized area on important parts of texts to support readers' comprehension.

We, however, know that too many emphasized areas disturb reader's comprehension.

In future work, we plan to investigate that appropriate quantity of the emphasized area of each user.

We plan to investigate that appropriate quantity of the emphasized area of each user. Therefore we will attempt the quantification of an effect of visual emphasis on important parts of texts. We plan to use two variables to quantify an effect of visual emphasis on important parts of texts of each user.

- Variable 1: The ratio of the emphasized areas to the total text length.
- Variable 2: The grammatical classification of the emphasized area, e.g. word, phrase, sentence and paragraph.

In future work, we plan to investigate that whether these variables are appropriate. Also we plan to look for the other variables.

Acknowledgement. This work was partially supported by JSPS KAKENHI grants (No. 25240043) and TISE Research Grant of Chuo University.

References

1. Erkan, G., Radev, D.R.: LexRank: graph-based lexical centrality as salience in text summarization. J. Artif. Intell. Res. **22**, 457–479 (2004)
2. Kitajima, Risa, Kobayashi, Ichiro: Graph based multi-document summarization with latent topics. J. Jpn. Soc. Fuzzy Theory Intell. Inf. **25**(6), 914–923 (2013)
3. Sunayama, W., Yachida, M.: A panoramic view system for extracting key sentences discovering keywords that express the features of a document. Syst. Comput. Jpn. **34**(11), 81–90 (2003)
4. Sunayama, Wataru, et al.: Development of total environment for text data mining. Trans. Jpn. Soc. Artif. Intell. **28**(1), 1–12 (2013)

Accessing Effects of Various Depth-Cue Combinations on Hand Control Movement in a Virtual Environment

Ray F. Lin[(⊠)] and Huei-Yun Cheng

Department of Industrial Engineering and Management, Yuan Ze University,
135 Yuan-Tung Road, Chungli, Taoyuan 32003, Taiwan
juifeng@saturn.yzu.edu.tw

Abstract. To assess the effect of depth cues on hand-control movements in a virtual environment, Fitts' law has been commonly used. However, Fitts' law has the limitation of effectively discriminating how the depth cue independently affects performance of speed and accuracy. Hence, this study aimed at testing the ballistic movement method for assessing the effects of depth cues. Six participants performed ballistic movements in six scene settings manipulated with three depth cues, comprising background gradient, shadows, and drop line. These ballistic movements were performed with six distances and in six movement directions. The results showed that scene had no significant effect on ballistic movement properties, comprising movement time, constant errors, and variable errors. The ballistic movement method was helpful for assessing the effects of movement directions. Future research should measure the time before executing ballistic movements to verify if different scenes have effects on the corrective reaction time.

Keywords: Ballistic movement method · Virtual reality · Depth cues · Input device · Aiming movement

1 Introduction

Since the early of 1990s, virtual reality technologies have been gradually developed and widely applied. These technologies utilize computer graphics to create a realistic-looking world in which users interact the virtual world via various tools and get real-time feedback. The advantage of rapid prototyping of high-cost or imaginary environments makes these technologies widely and successfully applied to the areas of medicine, education, game, rehabilitation, commercial, etc.

Although the techniques of virtual reality seem matured and beneficial, perception of depth has been a critical issue while interacting with a virtual environment. Studies show that the poor perception of depth would degrade hand control movement performance in a virtual environment. To generate depth information, several depth cues, such as texture gradient, shadows, and drop line, were developed and used.

To evaluate these depth cues, although Fitts' law is a widely accepted method, the application of Fitts' law has a limitation that only allows practitioners obtain the performance information confounded with the two movement properties: speed and

© Springer International Publishing Switzerland 2016
M. Kurosu (Ed.): HCI 2016, Part III, LNCS 9733, pp. 527–537, 2016.
DOI: 10.1007/978-3-319-39513-5_49

accuracy. To overcome the limitation, Lin and his colleagues [1, 2] proposed the ballistic movement method. Hence, this study aimed at testing the application of the ballistic movement method for assessing the effects of depth cues on hand-control movement in a virtual environment.

1.1   Applications of Various Depth Cues in Virtual Environments

In the real world, people use a variety of information, such as the changes of luminance, contrast, and size, to determine the distance from an object. Hence, it is critical to generate same or similar depth information via two dimensional devices. Helpful aids commonly used include background grid, object shadow, drop line, size change and inter-reflections.

By using the method of distance estimation, several studies investigated depth cues. Hu, Gooch, Creem-Regehr and Thompson [3] showed that shadows and inter-reflections could improve depth perception. Waller [4] found that the application of background grid greatly help the performance. Bülthoff and Mallot [5] compared the integration of the depth cues of stereo and shading. Kenyon, Sandin, Smith, Pawlicki and Defanti [6] showed that the size change is a helpful depth cue. Witmer and Kline [7] reported that floor pattern and object size were helpful for distance estimation.

To directly assess the effects of these cues on hand-control movement in virtual environments, Fitts' law has been the most common method applied. Teather and Stuerzlinger [8] applied pointing tasks to show that texturing and support cylinders did not significantly influence performance. Liao and Johnson [9] found that droplines helped participants navigate straighter paths and benefited range dimension acquisition.

1.2   Fitts' Law and Its Limitation

As shown in Eqs. 1 and 2, Fitts' law [10] predicts that the movement time (*MT*) required to execute a Fitts-type aiming movement is linearly related to the index of difficulty (*ID*) of that movement, defined as the dyadic logarithm of the quotient of amplitude of the movement and target width (Eq. 2).

$$MT = a + b \times ID \tag{1}$$

$$ID = log_2 \frac{2A}{W} \tag{2}$$

where *A* is movement amplitude, *W* is target width, *a* and *b* are experimentally determined constants. Because Fitts-type aiming movements are easily tested and the measured data can be well predicted by Fitts' law, Fitts' law thus become one of the most popular evaluation methods in the domains of Human Factors and Human Computer Interaction.

Although Fitts' law is easy to apply, as mentioned by Lin and colleagues [1, 2], Fitts' law has the limitation. The application of Fitts' law only allows practitioners obtain the performance information that is confounded with the two motor properties:

speed and accuracy. A Fitts-type aiming movement that takes a longer movement time could result from lower motor speed, lower motor accuracy, or a combination of both. However, Fitts' law has difficulty discriminating the extent to which the two motor properties contribute to the overall movement time.

1.3   Ballistic Movement Method

In recent year, the general model proposed by Lin and colleagues [2, 11, 12] indicates that a Fitts-type aiming movement is composed of ballistic movements, which are basic movement unit. The movement time and the endpoint variability of a ballistic movement are two essential factors that directly affect the speed and accuracy of a Fitts-type aiming movement. Lin and Drury [13] tested two ballistic movement models for describing how these two properties are associated to ballistic movement distance.

Ballistic movement time represents the required time for performing a ballistic movement. In an experiment in which participants performed hand control movements on a drawing tablet, Lin and Drury [13] verified that Eq. 3 (the ballistic movement time model), proposed by Gan and Hoffmann [14], can effectively describe and predict the relationship between ballistic movement time ($t_{ballistic}$) and the squared root of ballistic movement distance ($\sqrt{d_u}$).

$$t_{ballistic} = i + j \times \sqrt{d_u} \tag{3}$$

where i and j are experimentally constants.

Ballistic movement variability describes the endpoint variability of a ballistic movement. No matter endpoint errors are measured in the movement direction or perpendicular to the movement direction, Lin and Drury [13] found that the probability of endpoint location formed a normal distribution around the aimed point. In order to predict two directions of endpoint variability, Lin and Drury [13] verified the application of Eq. 4 (the ballistic movement variability model).

$$\sigma = e + f \times d_{ballistic} \tag{4}$$

where e and f are experimentally constants. As shown in the equation, the endpoint variability is linearly related to the square of movement distance ($d_{ballistic}$).

The two ballistic movement models (i.e., Eqs. 3 and 4) have been tested in several conditions by Lin and his colleagues [2, 13]. Lin and Drury [13] originally verified the two models by asking participations to perform ballistic movements using a drawing tablet. Further, the models were tested by Lin and Tsai [2] to show that the two models could be used as an additional method to assess performance of computer mice.

According to Lin and Tsai [2], a self-paced aiming movement is composed of one or more than one ballistic movement. By measuring ballistic movements, practitioners not only can predict the performance of self-paced aiming movements, more importantly, practitioners can obtain separated performance of motor speed and motor accuracy.

1.4 Research Objectives

This study aims at accessing the effects of depth-cue combination on hand-control movement. More specifically, the ballistic movement method was used to obtain independent measurements of ballistic movement time, constant errors, and variable errors so that the effects of depth-cue combination could be independently accessed.

2 Method

2.1 Participants and Equipment

Three female and three male graduate students, aged from 19 to 20 years, participated in this study. They were all right-handed with normal or corrected-to-normal vision.

Experimental apparatus included a personal computer (PC), a 54.6" LED (Light-Emitting Diode) television (TV), a motion capture system (Flex 3, Opti-Track^{TM}), and a self-developed program. The PC ran Unity3D and the motion capture system using the self-developed program that both displayed the experimental tasks on the TV and measured task performance.

2.2 Experimental Procedures

After informed consent procedures, as shown in Fig. 1, the six participants used a stylus to perform ballistic movements in conditions with different depth-cue combination. To reduce training effect, the participants had sufficient time to practice all the experimental combinations. To reduce the fatigue effect, the participants finished only a measurement (totally 4 measurements) in a half-day. A measurement took approximately 30–40 min.

To perform ballistic movements, as shown in Fig. 2, the participants quickly moved from a starting point to the center of the green cross target with a certain distance. The movements were performed at manipulated distances, but with the same midpoint set approximately 20 cm in front of body at elbow high. The tasks started by moving the stylus tip, attached with a 6.4 mm reflection marker, to control the cursor within the starting point. Once the cursor was at the starting point, the program generated a signal sound and showed the green cross target. The participants then moved the cursor toward the center of the target as quickly as possible. Once the cursor was moved away from the starting point, the cursor and the cross target disappeared and the movement time started to record. When the movement stopped, the cross target and the endpoint of that movement were immediately displayed on the screen. The experimenter clicked the space key to continue on the next trial.

2.3 Experimental Variables

The independent variables were scene (Scene), movement direction (Direction), movement distance (Distance). As shown in Table 1, three depth cues, comprising

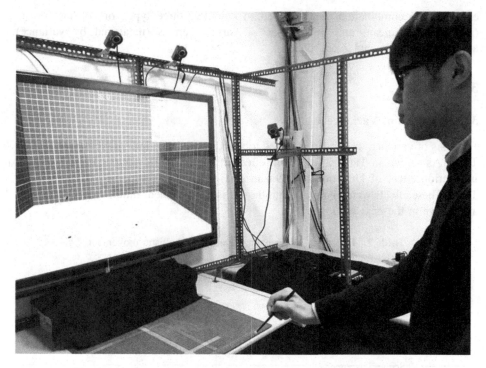

Fig. 1. The execution of ballistic movement in a virtual environment

background gradient, shadows, and drop line, were used to generate six scenes with different combinations. Movements were performed in six directions, comprising anterior, posterior, right, left, superior, and inferior. For each direction, six movement distances, comprising 50, 100, 150, 200, 250, and 300 mm, were tested. Each experimental combination was replicated eight times, resulting in a total of 1,728 trials.

Table 1. Six virtual reality scenes with six combinations of depth cues

Scene	Depth cue		
	Gradient	Shadows	Drop line
1	▦	▦	▦
2	▦	▦	
3	▦		▦
4		▦	▦
5			▦
6		▦	

The dependent variables were movement time (Time) and the endpoint errors measured at X (left-right), Y (up-down), and Z (back-front) coordinates. The errors consisted of constant error and variable error. To analyze whether the independent variables had significant effects on these two types of errors, eight replications of each experimental combination were utilized to calculate three types of constant errors (measured by mean) and three types of variable errors (measured by variance) according to X, Y, and Z coordinates.

3 Results

3.1 Analysis of Variance

Analysis of variance was first performed to test the effects of independent variables on Time. As shown in Table 2, the main effect of Distance ($F_{5,\ 25}$, $p < 0.001$) and the interaction effect of Direction and Distance ($F_{25,\ 125}$, $p < 0.05$) were significant on Time. These effects were analyzed with the ballistic movement time model (Eq. 3) and are shown in the next section.

Table 2. Effects of independent variables on ballistic movement

	Time	Constant error			Variable error		
		X	Y	Z	X	Y	Z
Scene							
Direction		***	***	***	***	***	***
Distance	***	*			***	***	***
Scene*Direction			**				
Scene*Distance							
Direction*Distance	*	***	***	***	***	***	***
Scene*Direction*Distance							

Note: *($p < 0.05$); **($p < 0.01$); ***($p < 0.001$)

Analysis of variance was then performed to test the effects of independent variables on six types of endpoint errors, comprising Constant-X error, Constant-Y error, Constant-Z error, Variable-X error, Variable-Y error, and Variable-Z error. Regarding constant errors, as shown in Table 2, the main effect of Direction ($F_{5,\ 25}$, $p < 0.001$) and the interaction effect of Direction and Distance ($F_{25,\ 125}$, $p < 0.001$) were significant on three types of constant errors. As shown in Fig. 2, three types of constant errors differed among six movement directions. These errors were greater when movements were performed in anterior, left, and right directions. There was a trend that constant errors increased with increased movement distance, especially for Constant-X error. This explains the significant main effect of Distance on Constant-X error ($F_{5,\ 25}$, $p < 0.05$). However, the rate of increase of constant errors differed among different movement directions. Furthermore, there was an interaction effect of Scene and Direction ($F25, 125$, $p < 0.05$) on Constant-Y error. As shown in Fig. 3, Constant-Y error varied according to different movement direction and these rates of difference were different in different scenes with depth-cue combinations. Regarding variable errors, the main effects of Direction ($F_{5,\ 25}$, $p < 0.001$) and Distance ($F_{5,\ 25}$, $p < 0.001$) and the interaction effect of Direction and Distance ($F_{25,\ 125}$, $p < 0.001$) were significant on three types of variable errors. These effects were analyzed with the ballistic movement variability model (Eq. 4) and are shown in the next section.

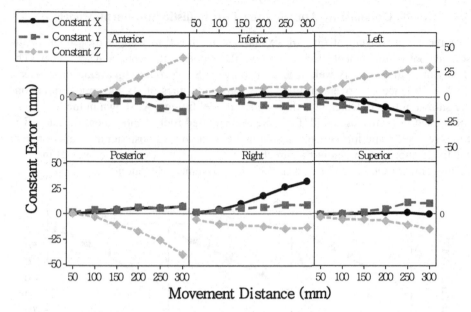

Fig. 2. Relationships between three types of constant errors and ballistic movement distance for six movement directions

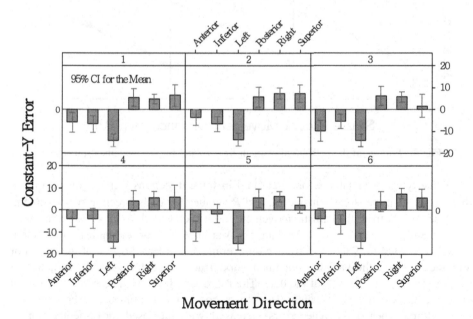

Fig. 3. The interaction effect of movement direction and scene on Constant-Y error

Since there were the main effect of Distance and certain related interaction effects of Distance on Time and three types of variable errors, in the next section, the two ballistic movement models were applied to show these effects.

3.2   Results Obtained by Applying the Two Ballistic Movement Models

The means of movement time of six movement direction were regressed on to the square root of movement distance to give the slopes, intercepts, and R^2 values. The model fitted the data very well. It accounted for 97.8 % variance on average and at least 97.2 % variance of movement time. The regression lines of six movement directions are shown in Fig. 4, which also shows good model fittings. As shown in the figure, the movement time increased with the increased squared root of movement distance. The times required to perform the movement in the directions of posterior and superior were relatively shorter than that in the direction of the left. However, these rates of increase of movement time were different in different movement directions.

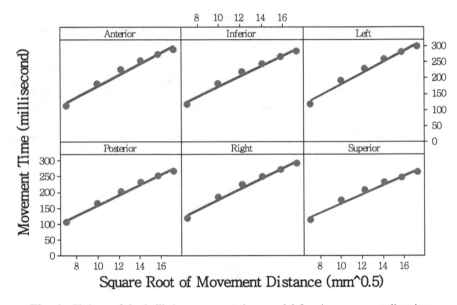

Fig. 4. Fittings of the ballistic movement time model for six movement directions

Three types of variable errors measured in three directions were regressed on the distance to give the slopes, intercepts, and R^2 values for each direction of movement. For Variance-X error, the ballistic movement model accounted for 98.17 % variance on average and at least 94.5 % of the data. For Variance-Y error, the ballistic movement model accounted for 98.27 % variance on average and at least 96.7 % of the data. For Variance-Z error, the ballistic movement model accounted for 99.17 % variance on average and at least 97.7 % of the data. The regression lines of three types of variable error are shown in Fig. 5, which also shows good model fittings. As shown in the figure, three types of variable errors increased with increased movement distance. However, these rates of increase of variable errors were different in different movement directions. The ranking of three types of variable errors differed among movement directions. However, Variable-X error was relatively less than Variable-Y and Variable Z errors. Furthermore, variable errors were relatively less when movements performed in left-right directions.

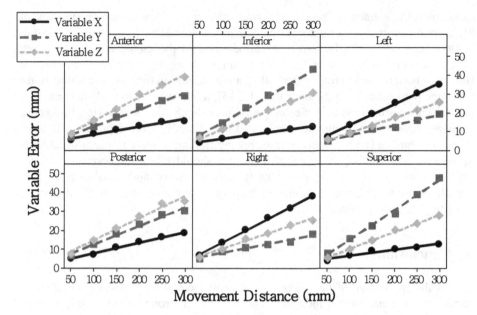

Fig. 5. Fittings of the ballistic movement variability model of three types of endpoint variability for six movement directions

4 Discussion

This study attempted to use the ballistic movement method to assess combinations of depth cues on hand-control movements in a virtual environment. Surprisingly, there was no significant effect of six depth-cue combinations on ballistic movement properties, comprising movement time, constant errors, and variable errors (Table 2). It is expected that depth cues should affect hand-control movements. Hence, we hypothesize that the effect of depth cues might be on the corrective reaction time [15]. The corrective reaction time represents the time required to process visual information for executing a sub-movement to modify an ongoing hand control movement. An evidence was found by Mather and Smith [16] who found that the effect of depth cues was on reaction time.

This study showed that the ballistic movement method is helpful for assessing the effect of movement directions. By applying the ballistic movement method that proposed by Lin and Tsai [2], we were be able to assess how movement direction affect motor properties of ballistic movement time, movement endpoint constant errors and variable errors. The ballistic movement time model and the ballistic movement variability model predicted well the data (Figs. 4 and 5), which allow practitioners to measure and apply the human capabilities and limitations while executing hand control movements in a virtual environment.

This pilot study showed some interesting findings, but with certain limitations, suggesting modifications of experimental designs for future research. First, the ballistic movement method has potentials for assessing the effects of movement direction on hand-control movements. To provide sound references of the human capabilities and limitations, to increase the number of participants is necessary. Moreover, in this study, constant errors and variable errors were measured in the global coordinate system, which allows us to study how these errors differ among the six movement direction. However, because these errors differ if they are measured in the movement direction or measured perpendicular to the movement [2, 13], it is necessary to analyze these errors in the local coordinate system. Second, only three depth cues, comprising background gradient, shadows, and drop line, were tested in this study. More depth cues should be tested in future research. Finally, one surprising finding arises a research question for future research. That is, the effect of depth cue should be on the corrective reaction time, but not on ballistic movement time, constant errors, and variable errors. This hypothesis needs further investigation with appropriate measurement of the time before executing ballistic movements.

5   Conclusions

To test the application of the ballistic movement method for assessing the effects of depth cues on hand-control movements in a virtual environment, this study recruited six participants to perform ballistic movements in six scene settings manipulated with six depth-cue combinations of background gradient, shadows, and drop line. Surprisingly, there was no significant effect of six combinations of depth cues on ballistic movement properties, comprising movement time, constant errors, and variable errors. However, the results showed that the ballistic movement method is helpful for assessing the effect of movement directions. We suggested that the effects of depth cues should be on the corrective reaction time, but may not on ballistic movement time and ballistic movement endpoint variability. This hypothesis needs further investigation by measuring the time before executing ballistic movements.

Acknowledgments. We would like to acknowledge the grant support from Taiwan Ministry of Science and Technology (MOST103-2221-E-155-053-MY3) for funding the paper submission and presentation.

References

1. Lin, J.-F., Drury, C.G.: Verification of two models of ballistic movements. In: Jacko, J.A. (ed.) Human-Computer Interaction, Part II, HCII 2011. LNCS, vol. 6762, pp. 275–284. Springer, Heidelberg (2011)
2. Lin, R.F., Tsai, Y.-C.: The use of ballistic movement as an additional method to assess performance of computer mice. Int. J. Ind. Ergon. **45**, 71–81 (2015)
3. Hu, H.H., Gooch, A.A., Creem-Regehr, S.H., Thompson, W.B.: Visual cues for perceiving distances from objects to surfaces. Presence Teleoperators Virtual Environ. **11**(6), 652–664 (2002)
4. Waller, D.: Factors affecting the perception of interobject distances in virtual environments. Presence Teleoperators Virtual Environ. **8**(6), 657–670 (1999)

5. Bülthoff, H.H., Mallot, H.A.: Integration of depth modules: stereo and shading. J. Opt. Soc. Am. **5**(10), 1749–1758 (1988)
6. Kenyon, R.V., Sandin, D., Smith, R.C., Pawlicki, R., Defanti, T.: Size-constancy in the CAVE. Presence Teleoperators Virtual Environ. **16**(2), 172–187 (2007)
7. Witmer, B.G., Kline, P.B.: Judging perceived and traversed distance in virtual environments. Presence **7**(2), 144–167 (1998)
8. Teather, R.J., Stuerzlinger, W.: Visual aids in 3D point selection experiments. In: Proceedings of the 2nd ACM Symposium on Spatial User Interaction (2014)
9. Liao, M.-J., Johnson, W.W.: Characterizing the effects of droplines on target acquisition performance on a 3-D perspective display. Hum. Factors **46**(3), 476–496 (2004)
10. Fitts, P.M.: The information capacity of the human motor system in controlling the amplitude of movement. J. Exp. Psychol. **47**, 381–391 (1954)
11. Lin, J.-F., Drury, C.G., Karwan, M., Paquet, V.: A general model that accounts for Fitts' law and Drury's model. In: Proceedings of the 17th Congress of the International Ergonomics Association, August 9–14, Beijing, China (2009)
12. Lin, J.-F., Drury, C.G.: Modeling Fitts' law. In: Proceedings of the 9th Pan-Pacific Conference on Ergonomics, November 7–10. The Ambassador Hotel, Kaohsiung (2010)
13. Lin, R.F., Drury, C.G.: Verification of models for ballistic movement time and end-point variability. Ergonomics **56**(4), 623–636 (2013)
14. Gan, K.-C., Hoffmann, E.R.: Geometrical conditions for ballistic and visually controlled movements. Ergonomics **31**, 829–839 (1988)
15. Lin, R.F., Hsu, C.-H.: Measuring individual corrective reaction time using the intermittent illumination model. Ergonomics **57**(9), 1337–1352 (2014)
16. Mather, G., Smith, D.R.R.: Combining depth cues: effects upon accuracy and speed of performance in a depth-ordering task. Vision. Res. **44**(6), 557–562 (2004)

Investigating Communal Interactive Video Viewing Experiences Online

Lili Liu[✉], Ayoung Suh, and Christian Wagner

School of Creative Media, City University of Hong Kong,
Hong Kong SAR, China
{llili2, ahysuh, c.wagner}@cityu.edu.hk

Abstract. A new generation of online video systems increasingly integrates online video content with social media communication interfaces, creating a communal (or quasi-communal) interactive viewing experience. This study seeks to enrich our understanding of why and how the communication features work to attract users to this new experience. Drawing on the affective response model, this study identifies antecedents of users' affective and cognitive states and examines how these factors influence user satisfaction and intention to continue the experience. The model was tested using data collected from 212 users who had such communal interactive viewing experiences online. The results show that extraversion, display augmentability, and comment relevance are positively associated with playfulness, but negatively associated with cognition load. The results also reveal that playfulness positively influences satisfaction, whereas cognition load negatively influences satisfaction, which in turn positively influences intention to continue. Potential theoretical and practical implications of our findings are discussed.

Keywords: Communal interactive video viewing · Affective response model · Extraversion · Display augmentability · Comment relevance · Playfulness · Cognition load · Satisfaction · Intention to continue

1 Introduction

Online video systems have been recently augmented to provide a more socialized online viewing experience [11], which combines the individual and passive act of viewing with the social, active aspect of commenting, thus creating a discourse around the video content. YouTube, for instance, exemplifies a moderately social environment where viewers can share opinions about videos through commenting and rating features. Other online video sites such as ClipSync and Bilibili extend this logic, by adding text chat features to the videos, which supports active viewing, and encourages viewer participation as well as social engagement. Such sites are pioneers in the integration of communication features with online video content, creating the experience of a communal process of viewing videos together [25], even if in reality the social interaction online is not same-time and same-location, but serial and highly fragmented. In addition, the interactive experience allows users to enjoy videos in greater depth and interpret them along more diverse perspectives, since viewers are

© Springer International Publishing Switzerland 2016
M. Kurosu (Ed.): HCI 2016, Part III, LNCS 9733, pp. 538–548, 2016.
DOI: 10.1007/978-3-319-39513-5_50

privy to other users' impressions, interpretations, and feelings about the video content [12]. This new viewing experience appears to be desirable to users, according to market share information for corresponding video sites. Bilibili, for instance, is listed among the Top 10 most popular video sites in China [5], despite a late launch (2009), notwithstanding minimal advertising, and a highly competitive environment.

Despite growing scholarly and industry attention towards communal interactive video viewing online, little is known about the reasons for its attractiveness, and specifically why and how the associated communication features achieve to attract users. Although viewing video content and user comments simultaneously (a hallmark of these sites) might be thought to cause cognition overload and destroy video aesthetics, many users are enthusiastic about using these communication features. Users explain that viewing videos whose content is enriched by augmented displays of user comments elicits specific affective experiences, such as playfulness [12]. Furthermore, although research suggests that people often exhibit greater similarity in affective reactions toward technological features than in cognitive assessments, the literature in the information system (IS) literature frequently overlooks non-cognitive factors such as affect [21]. As such, a significant research gap still exists in understanding communal interactive viewing experiences online (CIVEO), especially the affective and cognitive experiences of video sites that provide communication features. This study thus raises the important questions of (1) what the antecedents of users' affective and cognitive states in CIVEO are; and (2) how affective and cognitive states influence user satisfaction and intention to continue using sites offering CIVEO.

Drawing on the affective response model (ARM) [31], this research identifies the antecedents of a user's affective state (i.e., playfulness) and cognitive state (i.e., cognition load). More specifically, we posit that extraversion, display augmentability, and comment relevance influence users' perceptions of playfulness and cognition load. We also posit that playfulness and cognition load influence satisfaction, which in turn influences users' intention to continue. User satisfaction has been widely considered as a critical factor that determines a user's intention to continue using an IS [3], and continuance intention has been regarded as a promising concept for explaining continued IS use across various types of IS [30]. Thus, understanding the factors that contribute to video sites user satisfaction and continuance intention has both theoretical and practical implications. We expect that the findings of our study can be referenced by video website managers to improve their service quality and to enhance their competitive advantage.

The remainder of this paper is organized as follows. First, we briefly review the theoretical background. Second, we present our research model and then develop our hypotheses. Thereafter, we describe the research design, present the results of the analyses, and finally conclude the article with implications and limitations.

2 Theoretical Background and Hypothesis Development

2.1 Affective Response Model

ARM is a theoretically bound conceptual framework, which provides a systematic and holistic map for studies that consider affect [31]. It focuses primarily on the affective aspect rather than on cognitive and behavioral aspects. The ARM indicates how affect is manifested and eventually turned into affective evaluations. In the ARM, the antecedents of a user's affective state are grouped into two categories: human factor and technology stimulus. The human factors refer to the characteristics reside within a person, which is not dedicated to any specific stimulus. The technology stimuli refer to the objective attributes or properties of technological features of an IS. The ARM suggests that human factors and technology stimuli trigger specific affective states. Subsequently, induced affective states may contribute to the formation of affective evaluations. Affective evaluation is a general term that represents user attitudes toward objects and behaviors. As defined in previous studies [29, 31], affective evaluations consist of user attitude toward objects and attitude toward behaviors. Accordingly, in this study, we investigate user satisfaction and intention to continue using online video sites in order to capture affective evaluations.

Researchers have employed the ARM as a robust and parsimonious framework for predicting user attitudes in various contexts (e.g., web interfaces) [9]. However, the ARM only focuses on affective factors and ignores cognitive factors, thus potentially limiting a comprehensive understanding of user attitudes toward technological features. In this study, we extend the ARM by adding a cognitive factor (cognition load) and investigate how the involvement of a non-affective factor influences users' affective evaluations. To this end, the study attempts to provide insights into design strategies for a video site seeking to facilitate desirable affective and cognitive states.

3   Research Model and Hypotheses

By applying the ARM to CIVEO, we identify a personal trait, extraversion, as a human factor; display augmentability and comment relevance as technology stimuli. We also identify playfulness and cognition load as induced affective and cognitive states. Furthermore, user satisfaction and intention to continue are examined as affective evaluations. The research model is depicted in Fig. 1. The extended ARM model contributes to (1) the provision of a parsimonious and theoretical justification for investigating extraversion, display augmentability, and comment relevance as antecedents and (2) the examination of the role of playfulness and cognition load in predicting users' satisfaction and intention to continue using online video sites.

Antecedents of Induced Affective/Cognitive States. Extraversion refers to the personality of an individual who is outgoing and personable [26]. In general, extraverts are usually less timid and hesitant in communication with others and they tend to initiate more conversations and talk more than others. Extraverts enjoy interacting with others in a group or a collective of people. In this study, playfulness refers to the perceived hedonic value of an online video site, as amplified by associated fun, excitement, creativity and pleasure [4]. Cognition load is defined as the load imposed on memory by information being presented [24]. Cognitive overload can occur when the degree of mental effort exceeds processing capabilities. However, since extraverts actively pursue social connections with others, they are capable of interacting with others, despite having to process a lot of information during their communication. Thus, we propose the following hypotheses:

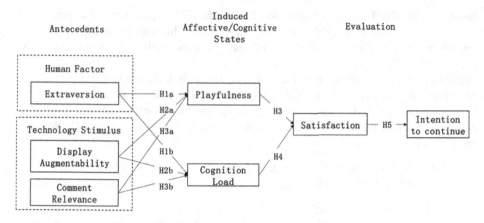

Fig. 1. Research model

H1a. Extraversion positively affects users' playfulness when using online video sites.
H1b. Extraversion negatively affects users' cognition load when using online video sites.

Display augmentability is defined as the extent to which the communication features of a video website support the augmented display of video, audio, and text. Online video sites with high display augmentability allow users to communicate with multiple people, which is desirable for higher playfulness [32]. Previous studies claim that if too many individuals attempt to communicate simultaneously, they are more likely to be distracted and less attentive to the focal communication partners [15]. Besides, greater effort is needed to conduct simultaneous interactions. Thus, we propose the following:

H2a. Display augmentability positively affects users' playfulness when using online video sites.
H2b. Display augmentability positively affects users' cognition load when using online video sites.

Comment relevance is defined as the extent to which the communication features of a video site support the adjustment of comments on videos, thereby making them relevant to the video content. When the comments on videos are relevant, useful, important, meaningful, or helpful to audiences, reading comments will result in enhanced pleasure [33]. Since users have limited ability to process novel information, reading comments that seem to have no relevance to the videos requires extra mental effort [19]. In contrast, the better the fit between comments and videos, the less effort is needed to process the information, thus mitigating the required mental effort. Therefore, we hypothesize the following:

H3a. Comment relevance positively affects users' playfulness when using online video sites.
H3b. Comment relevance negatively affects users' cognition load when using online video sites.

Induced Affective/Cognitive States and Evaluation. Playfulness is considered as the intrinsic motivation associated with using any IS [28]. Individuals in a state of playfulness are involved in an activity for intrinsic benefits, such as pleasure and enjoyment, rather than extrinsic rewards [27]. Such experience may result in better evaluation of the technology use. For example, research demonstrated that playfulness or enjoyment was positively related to user satisfaction in the post-adoption of social network services [15, 17]. In contrast, the literature also indicated that the greater the cognitive burden, the lower the users' satisfaction with the learning [24]. We thus propose the following:

H4. Playfulness positively affects users' satisfaction with online video sites.
H5. Cognition load negatively affects users' satisfaction with online video sites.

Satisfaction is defined as an individual's evaluation and affective response to his or her overall experience with a service or product [20, p. 29]. In decades, user satisfaction has been demonstrated as one of the vital constructs predicting behavioral intentions [3, 19]. For example, many studies have provided evidence that user satisfaction with ISs, such as web-based learning systems [8] and online brokerage services [2], is associated with continuance intention. Thus, propose the following:

H6. Users' satisfaction positively affects their intention to continue using online video sites.

4   Method

CIVEO is spreading rapidly among Chinese video sites. In particular, the introduction of Danmaku technology to video sites has provided new opportunities for richer communal viewing experiences [16]. Danmaku technology—a communication feature that overlays user comments directly on the video screen and augmentedly displays comments alongside videos [12]—enables users to simultaneously view and add comments to videos. The technology synchronizes the comments to the video playback time and displays them to the current and future viewers as a stream of moving subtitles overlaid on the video screen [5]. By viewing time-synchronous comments (semantic information) together with videos, users feel as if they experience the video as part of an interactive community of (anonymous) viewers, across differences in time and space [25]. Figure 2 presents a screenshot of a video with Danmaku comments enabled on Bilibili.com.

Data was collected through an online survey from users of Chinese video sites that had implemented a Danmaku system (including IQIYI, LETV, Tudou, Bilibili, Acfun, Souhu, and Tecent Video). Users who had experience of activating the Danmaku system on their video site were considered for the survey. To ensure the validity of the instruments, we adapted all items from previous research. Extraversion measurement items were adapted from Balaji and Chakrabarti [1]. Measurements for display augmentability drew on Tang et al. [26]. Additionally, measurements for comment relevance were initiated by Zimmer et al. [33]. Items of playfulness were adapted from Celik [4], while items of cognition load were derived from Hart and Staveland [14]. Furthermore, measurements of satisfaction and intention to continue were drawn from Bhattacherjeee [3].

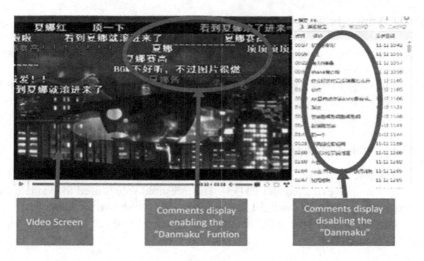

Fig. 2. A screenshot of a video on Bilibili.com (source: http://www.bilibili.com/video/av715040/)

All items were measured using seven-point Likert scales ranging from strongly disagree (1) to strongly agree (7). A web-based survey solution provider (http://www.sojump.com/) was used to distribute the questionnaire. 284 users with experience of online communal viewing with the Danmaku function enabled were identified and selected as subjects to complete the questionnaire. The respondents consisted of a range of users, some of whom liked the Danmaku function and other who disliked the function. A total of 212 valid responses were received, representing a response rate of 74.6 %. The demographics of the research sample are displayed in Table 1.

Table 1. Subject demographics

Item	Category	Frequency	Percentage
Gender	Male	94	44.34
	Female	118	55.66
Age	15–20	5	2.36
	21–25	51	24.06
	26–30	82	38.68
	31–40	73	34.43
	>40	1	0.47
Education	College or below	12	5.66
	Bachelor	174	82.08
	Master	25	39.90
	Ph.D and above	1	0.47
Internet Experience	<2 years	1	0.47
	3–5 years	38	17.93
	5–10 years	108	50.94
	>10 years	65	30.66

5 Data Analysis and Results

The data analysis was conducted in two stages. In stage one, the appropriateness of measurement model, including reliability, validity, and common method bias, was examined. In stage two, the structural model and hypotheses were assessed and tested respectively [7]. Data was analyzed using SmartPLS 2.0 [23].

5.1 Measurement Model

Reliability was assessed by examining Cronbach's alpha, composite reliability (CR), and average variance extracted (AVE) [13]. The threshold values used to evaluate these three indices were .70, .70, and .50, respectively [6]. As shown in Table 2, all item loadings were significant (p < .001) and ranged from 0.64 to 0.93, indicating adequate convergent validity [10].

Table 2. Item means and loadings

Construct	Item	Mean	Loadings	T-value	Cronbach's Alpha	Composite Reliability
Extraversion	EXT1	5.34	0.90	56.00	0.89	0.92
	EXT2	5.27	0.93	91.71		
	EXT3	5.75	0.80	26.34		
	EXT4	4.15	0.74	15.90		
	EXT5	5.00	0.81	22.26		
Display Augmentability	DA1	6.27	0.83	30.27	0.81	0.89
	DA2	6.06	0.88	53.12		
	DA3	6.08	0.85	36.58		
Comment Relevance	CR1	5.56	0.77	18.03	0.89	0.92
	CR2	5.60	0.87	62.52		
	CR3	5.34	0.87	54.57		
	CR4	5.50	0.84	41.41		
	CR5	5.63	0.82	32.90		
Playfulness	PLAY1	5.27	0.64	7.84	0.75	0.84
	PLAY2	5.67	0.81	23.07		
	PLAY3	5.50	0.78	22.11		
	PLAY4	5.90	0.80	32.64		
Cognition Load	CL1	2.33	0.84	25.47	0.94	0.95
	CL2	2.17	0.91	53.94		
	CL3	2.03	0.93	75.63		
	CL4	2.05	0.89	43.33		
	CL5	2.09	0.92	60.37		
Satisfaction	SAT1	5.85	0.84	31.05	0.79	0.88
	SAT2	5.83	0.86	46.17		
	SAT3	5.83	0.82	14.69		
Intention to Continue	CONT1	6.24	0.83	28.69	0.82	0.88
	CONT2	5.58	0.64	10.75		
	CONT3	6.27	0.87	39.98		
	CONT4	6.15	0.87	22.63		

Discriminant validity of the constructs can be verified by confirming the square root of the AVE to be higher than the inter-construct correlations [10]. The result in Table 3 shows that the square roots of the AVE of all the constructs were higher than all the correlations, suggesting good discriminant validity. Subsequently, following Podsakoff and Organ [22], we tested common method bias (CMB) to prevent artifactual covariance between variables. The results reveal that no single factor emerged from the Harman's one-factor analysis and there was no one single factor that accounts for the majority of the covariance in the independent and criterion variables, revealing that CMB did not pose a major threat to this study [18].

Table 3. Discriminant validity

Construct	AVE	EXT	DA	CR	PLAY	CL	SAT	CONT
Extraversion	0.84	0.84						
Display Augmentability	0.85	0.26	0.85					
Comment	0.84	0.51	0.44	0.84				
Playfulness	0.76	0.50	0.49	0.62	0.76			
Cognition Load	0.90	-0.36	-0.47	-0.43	-0.36	0.90		
Satisfaction	0.84	0.47	0.53	0.70	0.67	-0.56	0.84	
Intention to Continue	0.81	0.43	0.61	0.64	0.56	-0.59	0.64	0.81

Note: The square root of average variance extracted (AVE) is shown on the diagonal of the correlation matrix.

5.2   Structural Model

The results of the structural model test are summarized in Fig. 3. As hypothesized, extraversion, display augmentability and comment relevance were positively associated with playfulness. Moreover, extraversion, display augmentability, and comment relevance were negatively associated with cognition load.

The proportions of variances explained were 48.1 % for playfulness, and 30.6 % for cognition load. H1a, H1b, H1c, H2a, and H2c were supported at significance levels of $p < 0.05$ or better. In addition, playfulness had a positive effect on satisfaction, while cognition load negatively influence satisfaction. Playfulness and cognition load jointly explained 56.5 % of the variance in satisfaction. H3 and H4 were supported at $p < 0.001$. Finally, satisfaction was positively associated with intention to continue, accounting for 54.1 % of the variance in intention to continue. H5 was supported at $p < 0.001$.

6   Discussion

The purpose of this study was to examine the antecedents of users' affective/cognitive states, and the impacts of these states on user satisfaction and intention to continue, in video websites which have provided communication features during video watching. The results showed that that extraversion, display augmentability and comment relevance enhanced playfulness, indicating that the communication features, which allow

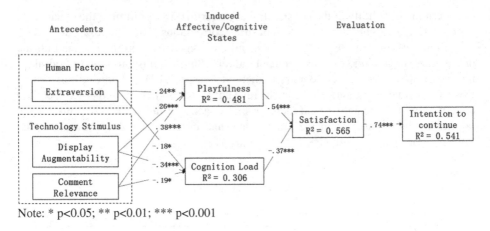

Note: * p<0.05; ** p<0.01; *** p<0.001

Fig. 3. Structural model

users to interact with others, provide an enjoyable experience. This study also revealed that extraversion and comment relevance, helped to reduce users' cognition load. Surprisingly, the results implied that display augmentability negatively influenced cognition load. This is a novel finding, which implies that when highly relevant additional information is provided in a way users prefer, they are able to process more information at the same time, without feeling interrupted or mentally overwhelmed. The results also indicated that playfulness had positive impacts on user satisfaction, while cognition load had a negative influence on user satisfaction. Furthermore, satisfaction was positively associated with intention to continue, which determined the success and sustainability of video websites [32].

Drawing on ARM, this paper was intended to take a first step in empirically investigating CRIVEO. The main contributions of our paper are summarized as follows. First, it contributes to the ARM by incorporating a cognitive factor (cognition load) and empirically examining the parallel role of cognition load with playfulness in determining user satisfaction in the context of video sites. Second, it provides empirical evidence of the role of a human factor (extraversion) and technology stimuli (display augmentability, comment relevance) in predicting affective and cognitive states. Third, it contributes to extending the research on the sustainability of video sites by examining the antecedents and consequences of users' affective and cognitive states.

A robust understanding of affect and cognition has practical implications for the design, acceptance, use, and management of communication features in online video sites. The work indicates that in order to develop innovative communication features and to improve video site performance, practitioners should focus on improving display augmentability and regulating additional information to make it more relevant to video content.

Our research has several limitations, which suggest opportunities for future studies. First, the results might be limited by the sampling, as the data was collected only from Chinese Danmaku video websites. Although Danmaku technology is popular in East Asia, it does not seem to have been adopted by video sites serving other cultures.

Second, antecedents other than extraversion, display augmentability and comment relevance may contribute to playfulness and cognition load. Third, our results might also have suffered from inadequate consideration of third-variable effects. Although the survey respondents were users who had different experience of using Danmaku video sites and were thus appropriate for the present study, the results would be more generalizable by incorporating some control variables, especially personal characteristics of the subjects. We expect to overcome above shortcomings in a future study.

Acknowledgement. This paper was partly supported by the National Research Foundation of Korea Grant funded by the Korean Government (NRF-2013S1A3A2054667) awarded to the second author.

References

1. Balaji, M., Chakrabarti, D.: Student interactions in online discussion forum: Empirical research from 'media richness theory'perspective. J. Interact. Online Learn. **9**, 1–22 (2010)
2. Bhattacherjee, A.: An empirical analysis of the antecedents of electronic commerce service continuance. Decis. Support Syst. **32**, 201–214 (2001)
3. Bhattacherjee, A.: Understanding information systems continuance: an expectation-confirmation model. MIS Q. **25**, 351–370 (2001)
4. Celik, H.: What determines Turkish customers' acceptance of internet banking? Int. J. Bank Mark. **26**, 353–370 (2008)
5. Chen, Y., Gao, Q., Rau, P.-L.P.: Understanding gratifications of watching danmaku videos – videos with overlaid comments. In: Rau, P.-L.P. (ed.) CCD 2015. LNCS, vol. 9180, pp. 153–163. Springer, Heidelberg (2015)
6. Chin, W.W.: The partial least squares approach to structural equation modeling. Modern Methods. Bus. Res. **295**, 295–336 (1998)
7. Chin, W.W., Marcolin, B.L., Newsted, P.R.: A partial least squares latent variable modeling approach for measuring interaction effects: Results from a Monte Carlo simulation study and an electronic-mail emotion/adoption study. Inf. Syst. Res. **14**, 189–217 (2003)
8. Chiu, C.M., Chiu, C.S., Chang, H.C.: Examining the integrated influence of fairness and quality on learners' satisfaction and Web-based learning continuance intention. Inf. Syst. J. **17**, 271–287 (2007)
9. Deng, L., Poole, M.S.: Affect in web interfaces: a study of the impacts of web page visual complexity and order. MIS Q. **34**, 711–730 (2010)
10. Fornell, C., Larcker, D.F.: Structural equation models with unobservable variables and measurement error: Algebra and statistics. J. Mark. Res. **18**, 382–388 (1981)
11. Geerts, D., et al.: Are we in sync?: synchronization requirements for watching online video together. In: Proceedings of the SIGCHI Conference on Human Factors in Computing Systems. ACM (2011)
12. Goto, M.: Music listening in the future: augmented music-understanding interfaces and crowd music listening. In: Audio Engineering Society Conference: 42nd International Conference: Semantic Audio. Audio Engineering Society (2011)
13. Hair, J.F., et al.: Multivariate Data Analysis, vol. 6. Pearson Prentice Hall, Upper Saddle River (2006)
14. Hart, S.G., Staveland, L.E.: Development of NASA-TLX (Task Load Index): Results of empirical and theoretical research. Adv. Psychol. **52**, 139–183 (1988)

15. Homburg, C., Koschate, N., Hoyer, W.D.: The role of cognition and affect in the formation of customer satisfaction: a dynamic perspective. J. Mark. **70**, 21–31 (2006)
16. Johnson, D.: polyphonic/pseudo-synchronic: animated writing in the comment feed of nicovideo. Jpn. Stud. **33**, 297–313 (2013)
17. Kang, Y.S., Lee, H.: understanding the role of an IT artifact in online service continuance: an extended perspective of user satisfaction. Comput. Hum. Behav. **26**, 353–364 (2010)
18. Liang, H., et al.: Assimilation of enterprise systems: the effect of institutional pressures and the mediating role of top management. MIS Q. **31**, 59–87 (2007)
19. Oliver, R.L.: A cognitive model of the antecedents and consequences of satisfaction decisions. J. Mark. Res. **17**, 460–469 (1980)
20. Oliver, R.L.: Measurement and evaluation of satisfaction processes in retail settings. J. Retail. **57**, 25–48 (1981)
21. Pham, M.T., et al.: Affect monitoring and the primacy of feelings in judgment. J. Consum. Res. **28**, 167–188 (2001)
22. Podsakoff, P.M., Organ, D.W.: Self-reports in organizational research: Problems and prospects. J. Manage. **12**, 531–544 (1986)
23. Ringle, C.M., Wende, S., Will, A.: SmartPLS 2.0 (beta). Hamburg (2005)
24. Segall, N., Doolen, T.L., Porter, J.D.: A usability comparison of PDA-based quizzes and paper-and-pencil quizzes. Comput. Educ. **45**, 417–432 (2005)
25. Shen, Y., Chan, H., Hung, I.: Let the Comments Fly: The Effects of Flying Commentary Presentation on Consumer Judgment (2014)
26. Tang, F., Wang, X., Norman, C.S.: An investigation of the impact of media capabilities and extraversion on social presence and user satisfaction. Behav. Inf. Technol. **32**, 1060–1073 (2013)
27. Van der Heijden, H.: User acceptance of hedonic information systems. MIS Q. **28**, 695–704 (2004)
28. Venkatesh, V., Bala, H.: Technology acceptance model 3 and a research agenda on interventions. Dec. Sci. **39**, 273–315 (2008)
29. Wixom, B.H., Todd, P.A.: A theoretical integration of user satisfaction and technology acceptance. Inf. Syst. Res. **16**, 85–102 (2005)
30. Zhang, K.Z., et al.: Understanding the role of gender in bloggers' switching behavior. Decis. Support Syst. **47**, 540–546 (2009)
31. Zhang, P.: The affective response model: a theoretical framework of affective concepts and their relationships in the ICT context. MIS Q. **37**, 247–274 (2013)
32. Zhao, L., Lu, Y.: Enhancing perceived interactivity through network externalities: An empirical study on micro-blogging service satisfaction and continuance intention. Decis. Support Syst. **53**, 825–834 (2012)
33. Zimmer, J.C., et al.: Investigating online information disclosure: Effects of information relevance, trust and risk. Inf. Manage. **47**, 115–123 (2010)

Establishing Determinants of Electronic Books Utilisation: An Integration of Two Human Computer Interaction Adoption Frameworks

Boniswa Mafunda[1(✉)], Aaron Bere[2], and James Swart[1]

[1] Faculty of Engineering and Information Communication Technology, Central University of Technology, Bloemfontein, Free State, South Africa
{bmafunda,aswart}@cut.ac.za
[2] Melbourne Institute of Technology, Melbourne, Australia
aaronbere@gmail.com

Abstract. Rapid technological developments led to the development of eBooks. The high propagation of pervasive technologies creates opportunities for eBook utilisation over traditional textbooks, thus providing students with learning resources everywhere and anywhere at a cheaper price. This study developed a model for assessing determinants for eBook adoption based on the Task-technology-Fit theory and the Technology Acceptance Model. The developed model is validated using factor analysis and path analysis statistical methods. Findings of the study suggest that usability of eBooks is influenced by learning task characteristics, technology characteristics and individual student characteristics. Furthermore, the study provides insights into the effects that eBooks adoption exerts on student academic performance.

Keywords: Task technology fit · Technology acceptance model · eBooks adoption

1 Introduction

The hasty expansion and popularity of wireless Internet and mobile telecommunication technology has significantly contributed to the growth of electronic learning. The advent of digital content has altered many readers' attention and perception towards the use of electronic books (eBooks).

Despite the availability of eBooks, most African countries are lagging behind on the adoption and use of eBooks for academic purposes. Allen and Kaddu [1] proclaim that, in spite of Africa's remarkable growing interest and use of ubiquitous technologies, social media and blogs, it is surprising that eBooks are somewhat in their nascent phase. Therefore, it is necessary to establish factors that foster eBooks adoption and utilisation in Africa. This study aims to establish some of these factors that may influence eBook adoption and use among South African university students.

The field of technology adoption has largely been researched. Several Human Computer Interaction (HCI) researches have investigated determinants for technology use and acceptance [2–4]. The most common research frameworks that have been used

© Springer International Publishing Switzerland 2016
M. Kurosu (Ed.): HCI 2016, Part III, LNCS 9733, pp. 549–562, 2016.
DOI: 10.1007/978-3-319-39513-5_51

for technology use and acceptance are the Technology Acceptance Model (TAM), the Unified Theory of Acceptance and Use of Technology (UTAUT) model and the Task Technology Fit (TTF) theory. A limited number of studies have focused on eBooks adoption and use in Africa. Two HCI frameworks for technology acceptance and use, TAM (limited to user perceptions) and TTF (its scope does not include user perceptions) were amalgamated in this study in order to develop an appropriate integrated framework model (IFM) that may be used for eBook usability adoption.

The paper is structured as follows: Appropriate literature is discussed in line with eBooks, followed by a discussion of the key frameworks underpinning this study. Based on the literature, a conceptual framework will be developed leading to the research model of the study. The study then reports on the data collection instrument and the procedure used for collecting data. A correlational study procedure follows to present the study results. The study sums up with a discussion of the results and a conclusion is included.

2 Literature Review

The literature for the study is on eBooks adoption, TAM and TTF theory.

2.1 Technology Adoption Contextualized

Technology adoption is defined in terms of how well a given type of technology has been accepted by users (Davis et al., 1989). Venkatesh et al. [5] proclaim that adoption can be a resultant from a user's perception of the technology after having used it. According to Goswami and Chandra [6], adoption refers to the acceptance and one's willingness to use a given type of technology. De Silva et al. [7] denotes adoption as explaining decisions of persons by applying perceptive and social models of decision making. Shroff et al. [8] argue that adoption is a person's conduct concerning using an information technology (IT). In this study, adoption refers to acceptance and use of eBooks for academic purposes.

According to Sarker and Valacich [9], the complexity of a technology may have serious implications for technology adoption. Chong et al. [10] proclaim that irrespective of higher institutions' demands to implement eBooks in their academic libraries, literature has demonstrated the toil in perusing and reading an eBook using unfriendly user interfaces. According to Foasberg [11], an eBook is "a digital object with textual and/or other content which arises as a result of integrating the familiar concept of a book with features that can be provided in an electronic environment". Kahn and Peter [12] identified features of eBooks as inclusive of the following: hypertext links, bookmarks, multimedia objects, interactive tools, annotations, highlights, and search and cross reference functions. Preliminary investigation indicates that students prefer to use eBooks due to their portability, financially affordability and easy of navigation on different electronic devices. Following this background, usability is defined in this study as the degree to which eBooks, learning and individual characteristics provides a fit suitable for promoting eBooks adoption.

2.2   Technology Acceptance Model

The TAM is the most prominent extensions of Azjen and Fishbein's Theory of Reasoned Action (TRA) which was developed by Fred Davis in 1986. Davis et al. [13] TAM has been widely applied using its two major constructs; perceived usefulness (PU) and perceived ease of use (PEOU). The model suggests that when users are presented with a new technology, a number of user perception factors influence their decision about how and when they will use it [13]. The TAM is depicted in Fig. 1.

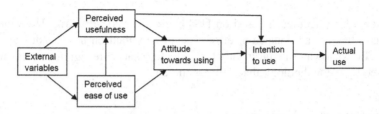

Fig. 1. Technology acceptance model (source: [2])

Previous studies indicate that TAM is the most influential model in technology usability and adoption [14–16]. Since this study aims to investigate eBook usability, it is appropriate to consider TAM constructs. Furthermore current studies have applied TAM in investigating eBook adoption [5]. According to Poon [17] the triumph of eBook adoption is dependent upon the application of a scholastic model that addresses scholar needs, relevant content and enhances student performance. Poon [17] utilised the TAM in investigating the intention of college students to use eBooks and the findings provided improved understanding on student conduct intention to adopt eBooks.

2.3   Task Technology Fit

Goodhue and Thompson [18] established this theory to examine the link concerning IT and individual performance. They anticipated confirming the supposition that usage and task-technology fit composed can better clarify the effect of IT with regards to performance than usage. According to Goodhue and Thompson [18], TTF ascertains that for a technology to have an encouraging influence on performance, it is necessary for the technology to be used and there should be a 'good fit' with the tasks it supports.

The constructs of TTF are, task characteristics, technology characteristics, TTF, performance impact and utilization. The TTF model is depicted in Fig. 2.

In a study of mobile learning of information systems, Gebauer et al. [3] reported that the findings established that the TTF and usage together well clarified the influence of an IT on individual performance. Gebauer et al. [3] proclaimed that there was user-perceived accomplishment of individual tasks than usage alone. Lee et al. [19] proclaims that TTF is among the most widely used models for measuring performance enhancement using technology. This study seeks to establish the effect of eBooks usability on students' performance, application of TTF seems to be appropriate for

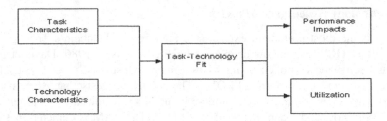

Fig. 2. Task technology fit model (source: [18])

investigating this phenomena based on [19] claims mentioned above. D'Ambra et al. [15] suggest that the acceptance of eBooks shall be reliant on how academics remark the fit of eBooks toward the tasks they take on and what more significant functionality is provided by the technology that delivers the content.

2.4 The Conceptual Framework

Wentzel et al. [20] argue that TAM is limited in scope. Rogers (1995) and Wentzel et al. [20] warn researchers of the bias associated with studies that apply TAM since they concentrate solely on user perceptions as an independent factor necessary for technology adoption. Similarly, D'Ambra et al. [15] criticized TAM for its lack of task focus. The TTF has been criticized for lack of focus on individual perceptions affecting a user's choices about technology [5].

An integration of TAM and TTF theory may result in a model strong enough to eliminate the weakness of both TAM and TTF and hence capitalizing on their strengths. The study's contribution to the HCI body of knowledge involves the development of an integrated model for technology adoption. The study's practical contribution may involve an improved eBooks adoption by the South African University students. Figure 3 represents the integrated IFM which incorporates the TAM and the TTF constructs.

The hypothesis for this study is listed below. The hypothesis indicates how the constructs in the IFM influence one another.

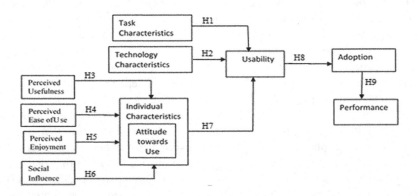

Fig. 3. Integrated framework model

Task characteristics. Goodhue and Thompson [18] define tasks as actions performed by a user in transforming inputs into outputs. Tasks can vary in a number of dimensions: task no routineness, task interdependence, and time criticality [15]. The attributes of these tasks form task characteristics. Task characteristics that may influence a student's decision to depend more on eBooks and its associated technologies are of interest in this study [15]. The following hypothesis was therefore developed.

H1: Task characteristics have a positive influence on usability.

Technology characteristics. Technology refers to tools in the form of hardware and software that can be used in performing a learning task [15, 18]. The attributes of these technologies can affect usage and users' perception of the technology [15]. In this study technology involves eBooks and the eBooks readers used by the participants. We therefore develop the following hypothesis.

H2: Technology characteristics have a positive influence on usability.

Individual characteristics. Individual characteristics encompass a user's perceptions based on their attitude towards eBooks usage in learning. The individual characteristics are categorised into four dependent variables (PU, PEOU, Perceived enjoyment (PE), and Social influence (SI)) on an (independent variable) individual's attitude towards use.

Perceived usefulness. PU refers to the potential user's subjective probability that applying a given type of technology will improve his or her task performance [13]. In this context PU refers to students' subjective probability that using eBooks for academic purposes will enhance their learning performance. Therefore, the following hypothesis was formulated.

H3: PU has a positive influence on individual characteristics.

Perceived ease of use. PEOU is defined as the degree to which the potential user expects the target system to be free of effort [13]. In this study PEOU refers to the extent to which university students expect the eBook system to be free of effort on its usage. We therefore formulated the following hypothesis.

H4: PEOU has a positive influence on individual characteristics.

Perceived enjoyment. PE is defined as the degree to which using a computer system is perceived to be personally enjoyable in its own right, aside from the instrumental value of the technology [21]. In this study, PE refers to the extent to which the activity of using eBooks is perceived to be personally enjoyable on its own right aside from the instrumental value of education. Therefore the following hypothesis was developed.

H5: PE has a positive influence on individual characteristics.

Social influence. SI is defined as the degree to which an individual perceives that important others believe he or she should use the new system [22]. In this context, SI refers to the extent to which a university student perceives that important others, like peers, family and lecturers believe he or she should use eBooks for learning purposes. Therefore the following hypothesis was developed.

H6: SI has a positive influence on individual characteristics.

Attitude towards use.   Attitude refers to a subjective or mental state of preparation for action. In this study, attitude towards use refers to a students' mental state of preparation for using eBooks. Therefore following hypothesis was formulated.

H7: Attitude towards use of eBooks has a positive influence on usability.

Usability.   Usability refers to the degree that a particular type of technology assists the users in accomplishing particular objectives with efficiency and fulfilment [19]. In this study, usability refers to a perfect coordination among the learning task characteristics, eBooks characteristics and individual characteristics for the purposes of enhancing learning objectives. Therefore following hypothesis was formulated.

H8: Usability has a positive influence on adoption.

Adoption.   Adoption is an act that enables hesitant users to successfully accept and use technology [13]. In this study, adoption refers to the student's decision to accept and use eBooks for learning purposes. Therefore following hypothesis was formulated.

H9: Adoption has a positive influence on performance enhancement.

Performance enhancement.   Performance refers to the accomplishment of a portfolio of tasks by an individual. Performance enhancement implies some mix of improved efficiency, improved effectiveness, and/or higher quality [18]. In this study performance enhancement refers to an improvement in effectively completing learning tasks using eBooks as a learning resource.

3   Methodology

3.1   Study Procedure

The participants for this study were IT Bachelor of Technology (B.Tech) students registered at a University of Technology in South Africa. This group of students was chosen because they all possess at least a laptop. The participants in this study used their eBook readers (e.g. laptops, Tablets, IPads and smartphones) for downloading and accessing the eBooks. A participant was allowed to use more than one gadget. The project targeted computer security subject (B.Tech subject). This subject was chosen because it has the highest number of students compared to other B.Tech subjects in the IT department. The study was conducted for a period of twelve weeks which constitute a full semester. It was conducted on the first semester in 2015. The university provided eBook licenses for computer security prescribed textbooks. Furthermore, the university provided software for downloading and accessing eBooks.

Participation was voluntary and participants were allowed to withdraw from the study at any stage. Students who chose to use traditional textbooks had an option of borrowing the textbook from the library or buy their personal copies. At the end of the semester data was collected from participants.

3.2 Participants

The study was conducted amid the time, in which the institution providing the context of the study weighed the possibilities of migrating from utilising traditional textbooks to eBooks. All the students registered in the targeted subject chose to participate in the study. Their ages ranges from 20–34. Among other things, the university provides Wi-Fi around campus to facilitate ubiquitous access of eBooks by students and staff. A total of 144 students participated in the study. The male participants were more than females. The most dominating race was Black African followed by mixed race commonly known as coloured in South African context. The detailed demographics of the participants are shown in Table 1.

Table 1. Demographics

Participants Groups	Frequency	Percentage	Cumulative percentage
Number of participants	144	100	100
Gender			
Male	102	72.3	72.3
Female	39	27.7	100
Race			
Black African	131	92.9	92.9
Coloured	5	3.5	99.5
White	4	2.8	99.3
Other	1	.7	100
Age Distribution			
20-24	122	86.5	86.5
25-29	18	12.8	99.3
30-34	1	.7	100
Device Used			
Desktop computer	51	36.2	36.2
IPad	5	3.5	56
Smart Phone	35	24.8	91
Tablet	21	14.9	112
Laptop	96	68.1	208

3.3 Instrument Development

The questionnaire instrument was grounded on the TTF and TAM constructs endorsed in [13, 15, 18]. A complete 42 questions survey questionnaire was constructed. The questionnaire utilised a 7 Likert scale ranging from "strongly agree" to "Strongly Disagree". The variables measured include PU, PEOU, PE, SI, attitude toward use, task characteristics, technology characteristics, usability, adoption and performance.

3.4 Data Analysis

The statistical method used for this study was the structural equation model (SEM). The SEM is a general statistical modelling technique which is used in the studies of behavioural sciences, social science, studies of education and in other fields [23]. It is a combination of the factor analysis and the path analysis. SEM is used to determine whether a certain model is valid and analyses relationships among variables, hence used in this study to look at the research model and hypotheses. The SEM analysis is provided by linear structural relations (LISREL) and AMOS. Both LISREL and AMOS are software analysis tools for analysis covariance.

The LISREL is used in SEM for manifest and latent variables [24]. The LISREL is mainly syntax-based, although recent versions have featured a graphical user interface (GUI).

The AMOS enables one to specify, estimate, assess and present models to show hypothesised relationships among variables. The software lets one build models more accurately than with standard multivariate statistical techniques. It also allows one to build attitudinal and behavioural models that reflect complex relationships. The component analysing software, partial least squares (PLS) PLS-Graph and SmartPLS also provide SEM analysis. The PLS is a variable based technique. Hair, Sarstedt, Ringle and Mena [25] proclaim that PLS maximizes the explained variance of the endogenous latent variables by estimating partial model relationships in an iterative sequence of ordinal least regressions. A significant aspect of PLS is that it estimates latent variable scores as precise linear amalgamations of their related apparent variables and handles them as impeccable substitutes for apparent variables [25, 26]. The PLS has two sets of equations, the measurement model and the structural model.

4 Results

4.1 Measurement Model Analysis

The measurement model is comprised of equations representing the relationships between indicators and the variable measure [27]. It is used for examining all the measured variables. It also includes estimating the internal consistency for each block of indicators and evaluating construct validity. Internal consistency is evaluated using composite reliability (CR) and average variance extracted (AVE). The questionnaire instrument is validated in terms of reliability and construct validity.

Straub and Carlson [28] argues that construct validity examines whether the measures chosen are true constructs describing the event or merely artifacts of the methodology itself. If the constructs are valid in this sense, one can expect relatively high correlation between measures of constructs that are expected to differ [28]. According to Clark and Watson [29] reliability is an evaluation of measurement accuracy which is the extent to which the respondent can answer the same or approximately the same questions the same way each time. The questionnaire instrument included 40 items of which 3 were deleted. They were deleted they did not satisfy a loading item of at least 0.70 as specified in literature [27, 30, 31]. The remaining items that were examined represent the fundamental construct demonstrating to the content validity of the questionnaire instrument. Table 2 represents the results of the items loading, weights, composite reliability (CR) and average variance extracted (AVE).

Table 2. Individuals loadings, weights, CR and AVE

Construct	Items	Item loadings	Construct CR	Construct AVE
Task	TsC1	0.8210		0.634
Characteristics (TsC)	TsC2	0.7903	0.836	
	TsC3	0.7817		
	TsC4	0.5807		
Technology	TecC1	0.8380		0.563
Characteristics (TecC)	TecC2	0.8866	0.869	
	TecC3	0.7743		
	TecC4	0.8348		
Perceived	PU1	0.8091		0.763
Usefulness (PU)	PU2	0.8736	0.957	
	PU3	0.7956		
	PU4	0.7687		
Perceived Ease	PEoU1	0.7925		0.665
of Use (PEoU)	PEoU2	0.6210	0.821	
	PEoU3	0.8168		
	PEoU4	0.8133		
Perceived	PE1	0.9215		0.774
Enjoyment (PE)	PE2	0.8331	0.943	
	PE3	0.8827		
	PE4	0.5209		
Social	SI1	0.7306		0.584
Influence (SI)	SI2	0.7727	0.811	
	SI3	0.7947		
	SI3	0.7226		
Attitude Towards	ATU1	0.8248		0.656
Use (ATU)	ATU2	0.7429	0.7985	
	ATU3	0.7772		
	ATU4	0.7111		
Usability (U)	U1	0.8296		0.647
	U2	0.9123	0.892	
	U3	0.7948		
	U4	0.7535		
Adoption (A)	A1	0.8281		0.689
	A2	0.8600	0.835	
	A3	0.9125		
	A4	0.7601		
Performance (P)	P1	0.7236		0.734
	P2	0.7602	0.861	
	P3	0.7157		
	P4	0.8711		

Baum et al. (2001) proclaims that the foremost indicators for measuring convergent validity are CR and AVE. The results indicate a satisfactory CR for every latent variable since they are all over 0.70 [32]. The higher the CR, the higher the internal consistency of a latent variable. The AVE is greater than 0.5 which also adheres to the suggestions made by [32]. The higher the AVE, the higher is the convergent reliability. Table 2 depicts the individual loadings, weights, CR and AVE.

Chin [23] argues that, if the diagonal components demonstrating the square root of the AVE are suggestively greater than the off-diagonal values in the corresponding rows and columns, discriminate validity is confirmed. Following Chin [23] sentiments, our study confirms discriminate validity. The results for this study (see Table 3) depict good consistency because for each latent variable AVE values range between 0.7 and 0.9. This reveals that the latent variables in the study indicate a good convergent reliability. The bold diagonal numbers represent the square root of the AVE of each of the latent variables. Table 3 depicts the AVE for the study model constructs.

Table 3. The average variance extracted (AVE) for the study model constructs

	TsC	TecC	PU	PEoU	PE	SI	ATU	U	A	P
TsC	*0.792*									
TecC	0.542	*0.823*								
PU	0.663	0.652	*0.776*							
PEoU	0.557	0.596	0.452	*0.753*						
PE	0.554	0.665	0.511	0.462	*0.789*					
SI	0.578	0.452	0.512	0.624	0.536	*0.763*				
ATU	0.654	0.615	0.596	0.562	0.542	0.558	*0.729*			
U	0.785	0.693	0.523	0.504	0.458	0.567	0.662	*0.894*		
A	0.594	0.452	0.632	0.426	0.624	0.598	0.623	0.661	*0.759*	
P	0.556	0.521	0.547	0.511	0.488	0.577	0.598	0.520	0.531	*0.743*

The study reveals satisfactory reliability and validity hence it is suitable to perform the hypotheses test concerning the correlations on the latent variables and predictability of the model's explanatory power [14].

4.2   Structural Model Analysis

Structural model analysis is primarily performed for examining path coefficient and R2 within latent variables of the research model [33]. Zimmerman [33] proclaims that path coefficients measure the comparative forte and sign of casual relationship within latent variables. The R2 represents the total variance explained of independent variables on dependent variables. Predictability of the research model is also represented by R2. The R2 values are depicted on top of each variable. The R2 values of 42.30, 64.10, 58.30 and 74.20 have been recorded for attitude towards use, usability, adoption and performance enhancement respectively. The research model explained over 50 % of the total variance in usability and performance enhancement which supports the opinion that the research model holds a good predictability and explanatory power for the task-technology fit for the eBooks utilisation (Fig. 4).

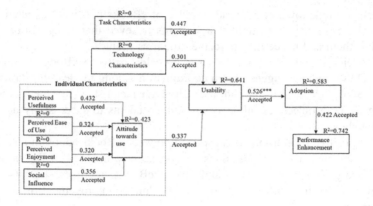

Fig. 4. Structural model

The path coefficients of each research model path per given hypotheses have been indicated. The study presented a total of 9 hypotheses. The results of the study indicate that all the 9 hypotheses were significant. The path coefficients for the 9 hypotheses were 42.20, 52.60, 44.70, 30.10, 33.70, 35.60, 32.00, 32.40 and 43.20.

5 Discussion

The results show that task characteristics and technology characteristics positively affected usability. These findings are consistent with [15, 18]. These findings suggest that students believe that learning characteristics such as self-study and sharing of learning resources influence usability of eBooks in higher education. Findings about technology characteristics suggest that features such as portability of eBooks, hyperlinks, and low costs contribute to eBooks usability. Task characteristics had stronger effects to usability than technology characteristics, suggesting that task characteristics are considered more important in the eBooks usability.

Considering the individual characteristics domain, findings of the study confirmed TAM related hypotheses. PU and PEOU positively affected students' attitude to use eBooks. These finding supports previous studies' reports [13, 14]. However, PU had a stronger effect on students' attitude towards use compared to PEOU. This suggests that, the students' mental state of preparation for learning using eBooks is strongly influenced by the extent they perceive that eBooks will improve their learning performance. Yet the degree to which the students expect the eBooks technology to be free of effort also contributes to students' subjective preparation of learning using these technologies.

The study results further reveals that PE and SI positively affect students' attitude towards eBooks usage. These findings imply that, apart from academic benefits students enjoy using eBooks. To them reading eBooks is just a fun activity. A strong relationship was revealed between SI and students' attitude towards the use of eBooks. This relationship signifies that peers and lecturers played a significant role in preparing students' mental states for learning using eBooks.

Students' attitude towards the academic use of eBooks positively affected eBooks usability. These findings shed light that students believed that using eBooks can be beneficial to them and hence they perceived them as usable.

The model's strongest relationship was revealed between eBooks usability and adoption. These findings suggest that a coordination among the learning task characteristics, eBooks characteristics and individual characteristics for the purposes of enhancing learning objectives influences hesitant students to successfully accept and use technology.

Another positive relationship was revealed between eBooks adoption and students performance enhancement, these findings are consistent with [15, 18]. The significance of these findings is that acceptance and use of eBooks improves students learning performance. These insights are vital for the continuous improvement of the instructional systems.

6   Conclusion

The correlational study reported in this paper sought to provide answers concerning suitable determinants for eBooks adoption. In providing these answers, the following contributions were made:

- The study contributed to the human computer interaction (HCI) body of knowledge specifically in the eBooks adoption context by developing a model suitable for evaluating determinants for eBooks adoption.
- The development and validation of an eBooks technology adoption based on the integration of the TTF theory and the Technology acceptance model.
- The findings provided insights that eBooks acceptance and use may significantly contribute to students' enhanced academic performance.

References

1. Allen, M., Kaddu, S.: A Report on the Survey of the eBooks and eLending in African Countries (2014)
2. Davis, F.: Perceived usefulness, perceived ease of use, and user acceptance of information technology. MIS Q. **13**(3), 319–340 (1989)
3. Gebauer, J., Gribbins, L., Shaw, J.: Task − Technology Fit for mobile information systems (2006)
4. Vankatesh, V., Morris, G.: Why don't men ever stop to ask for directions? Gender, social influence, and their role in technology acceptance and usage behaviour. MIS Q. **24**(1), 115–139 (2000)
5. Venkatesh, V., Thong, J., Chan, F., Hu, P., Brown, S.: Extending the two-stage information systems continuance model: incorporating UTAUT predictors and the role of context. Inf. Syst. J. **21**, 527–555 (2011)
6. Goswami, S., Chandra, B.: Convergence Dynamics of Consumer Innovativeness Vis-à-Vis Technology Acceptance Propensity: An Empirical Study on Adoption of Mobile Devices (2013)

7. De Silva, H., Ratnadiwakara, D., Zainudeen, A.: Social influence in mobile phone adoption: evidence from the bottom of the pyramid in emerging Asia. Inf. Technol. Int. Dev. **7**(3), 1–18 (2011)
8. Shroff, H., Deneen, C., Ng, E.: Analyzing of the Technology Acceptance Model in examining students' behavioural intention to use an e-portforlio system. Australas. J. Educ. Technol. **27**(4), 60–618 (2011)
9. Sarker, S., Valacich, S.: An alternative to methodological individualism: A non-reductionist approach to studying technology adoption by groups1. MIS Q. **34**(4), 779–808 (2010)
10. Chong, P., Lim, P., Ling, S.: On the design preferences for Ebooks. IETE Tech. Rev. **26**(3), 213–222 (2009)
11. Foasberg, M.: Adoption of e-book readers among college students: A survey. Inf. Technol. Libr. **30**(3), 108–128 (2011)
12. Kahn, M., Peter, G.: Issues related to the adoption of e-books in academic libraries: a literature review. SA J. Libr. Inform. Sci. **79**(2), 10–17 (2013)
13. Davis, F., Bagozzi, R., Warshaw, P.: User acceptance of computer technology: A comparison of two theoretical models. Manage. Sci. **35**(8), 982–1003 (1989)
14. Chang, C., Yan, C., Tseng, J.: Perceived convenience in an extended technology acceptance model: Mobile technology and English learning for college students. Australas. J. Educ. Technol. Soc. **28**(5), 809–826 (2012)
15. D'Ambra, J., Wilson, S., Akter, S.: Application of the task-technology fit model to structure and evaluate the adoption of e-books by academics (2013)
16. Gómez, A., Ros, S., Hernández, R., Tobarra, L., Caminero, C., Agudo, J.: User acceptance of a proposed self-evaluation and continuous assessment system. Educ. Technol. Soc. **18**(2), 97–109 (2015)
17. Poon, J.: Empirical analysis of factors affecting the e-book adoption—research agenda. Open J. Soc. Sci. **2**, 51–55 (2014)
18. Goodhue, D., Thompson, R.: Task-technology fit and individual performance. MIS Q. **12**(2), 213–236 (1995)
19. Lee, Y., Hsieh, Y., Chen, Y.: An investigation of employees' use of e-learning systems: applying the technology acceptance model. Behav. Inf. Technol. **32**(2), 173–189 (2013)
20. Wentzel, J., Diatha, K., Yadavalli, V.: An application of the extended Technology Acceptance Model in understanding technology-enabled financial service adoption in South Africa. Dev. South. Afr. **30**(4–5), 659–673 (2013)
21. Kim, T., Suh, Y., Lee, G., Choi, B.: Modelling roles of Task-technology Fit and Self-efficacy in hotel employees usage behaviours of hotel information systems. Int. J. Tourism Res. **12**, 709–725 (2010)
22. Venkatesh, V., Zhang, X.: Unified theory of acceptance and technology: U.S. vs. China. J. Glob. Inf. Technol. Manage. **13**(1), 5–27 (2010)
23. Chin, W.: The partial least squares approach for structual equation modelling. Modern Methods for Business Research, p. 448 (1998)
24. Williams, R.: Brief overview of LISREL & related programs & techniques (optional), Brief Overview of LISREL (2015)
25. Hair, F., Sarstedt, M., Ringle, M., Mena, J.: An assessment of the use of partial least squares structural equation modeling in marketing research. J. Acadademic Mark. Sci. (2010)
26. Henseler, J., Ringle, M., Sinkovics, R.: The use ofpartial least squares path modeling in international marketing. Adv. Int. Mark. **20**, 277–319 (2009)
27. Gayar, O., Moran, M., Hawkes, M.: Students' acceptance of tablet pcs and implications for educational institutions. Educ. Technol. Soc. **14**(12), 58–70 (2011)
28. Straub, D., Carlson, L.: Validating instruments in MIS research. MIS Q. **13**(2), 147 (1989)

29. Clark, L., Watson, D.: Constructing validity: Basic issues in objective scale development. Psychol. Assess. **7**(3), 309–319 (1995)
30. Clarke, C.: Paths between positivism and interpretivism: an appraisal of Hay's via media. Politics **29**(1), 28–36 (2009)
31. Murtagh, F.: Multivariate data analysis (2012)
32. Fornell, C., Larcker, D.: Evaluating structural equation models with unobserved variables and measurement errors. J. Mark. Res. **18**(1), 39–50 (1981)
33. Zimmerman, M.: Toward a theory of learned hopefulness: A structural model analysis of participation and empowerment'. J. Res. Pers. **24**, 71–86 (1990)

Taking the Advantage of Smartphone Apps for Understanding Information Needs of Emergency Response Teams' for Situational Awareness: Evidence from an Indoor Fire Game

Vimala Nunavath[✉] and Andreas Prinz

Department of ICT, University of Agder (UiA), Grimstad, Norway
{vimala.nunavath, andreas.prinz}@uia.no

Abstract. In search and rescue (SAR) operation, a lot of information is being shared among different emergency response groups. However, one of the key challenges experienced by these rescue groups during SAR operation is obtaining the complete awareness of the situation from the shared information. Moreover, one of the key actions of rescue leaders is to get the needed information in order to coordinate effectively with other teams and perform well. So, in this study we conduct an indoor fire drill with the help of Smartphone application with two settings (without SmartRescue smartphone application and with SmartRescue smartphone application) to find out what type of information is mostly communicated in both scenarios and needed by response teams. The presented results combine observations, qualitative and quantitative data analysis on videotaped data after the game. The results indicate that information categories which are formulated more recurrent in second scenario than first scenario. This might be explained as technology is more effective for sharing the information which is available on the smartphone application for obtaining situational awareness and for coordination.

Keywords: Information sharing · Mobile HCI · Emergency management tools · Situational awareness · Indoor fire game · Smartphone applications · Information needs · Information categories

1 Introduction

During any kind of disaster response, information sharing plays a vital role in spreading the information. But the volume and velocity of information shared during crises today tend to be extremely high, making it hard for emergency response teams to process the information in a timely manner. Furthermore, shared information tends to vary highly in terms of subjects and usefulness i.e., from information that could be entirely about critical information that augments situational awareness or information that contain rescuers safety or about resource information. Finding precise information from the shared information could accelerate the emergency response activities and alleviate both property and human losses.

© Springer International Publishing Switzerland 2016
M. Kurosu (Ed.): HCI 2016, Part III, LNCS 9733, pp. 563–571, 2016.
DOI: 10.1007/978-3-319-39513-5_52

Besides, in Search and Rescue (SAR) operations, first responders are often fragmented into different teams to carry out the different tasks (such as fire-fighting, saving victim, evacuation, getting the overview of the situation and so on) at different geo-locations. Due to geographical dispersion, these divided teams must share information within or among (intra-inter) teams to obtain or help to get the overview of the situational as well as to cooperate effectively [1]. However, to obtain the situational awareness is a challenging task as it requires first response teams to have access to the emergency related information. Without having enough and the right type of information, it is difficult to gain situational awareness (SA) [2–4]. Particularly, in dynamic and time critical situations, it becomes difficult for the first response teams to adequately decide which information might be relevant for other teams to support overall coordination. Hence, Information sharing and Task Assignment errors may occur and hence give poor awareness of the situation [5].

Furthermore, in order to support the accurate formation of SA, critical information needs should be identified [6]. In addition, when making decisions in emergencies, good information flow is required. The information which is being shared must be acquired from different sources to create a correct mental picture of what is going on. Moreover, decisions based on low-grade information can lead to poor emergency response [7, 8].

Seppänen et al. [6] have collated the major factors that hampered the Search and Rescue (SAR) organization in achieving adequate SA. These influential factors were information gaps, the lack of fluent communication, and the fact that there was no common operational picture in use. They also found out that the factors affecting information gaps were agencies focusing only on their own tasks, unclear information delivery processes, shortages of incident information, agencies passivity, and a lack of up-to date information.

Therefore the goal of this paper is to find out what type of information emergency rescue teams often needed and communicated during SAR operations in order to get the overview of the situation, to support coordination and to manage their emergency response successfully.

To understand and identify the information needs, a reality indoor fire game was conducted with voluntary participants with the help of smartphone applications. However, augmented reality games are excellent instruments particularly for emergencies to help the researchers and practitioners to better understand the communicated content and information flow patterns emerging within and across emergency response teams [9].

The rest of the paper is organized as follows: first we begin with the description of the developed game with two emergency scenarios which was used to collect the data and then the paper explains the research method that we used for analyzing the collected videotaped data. The results part shows the extracted information categories and the frequency in both scenarios. Finally, the conclusion part summarizes the lessons learned from this research and discusses directions for future research.

2 Game Design and Scenario Development

The developed scenario was about search and rescue operation in an indoor fire setting. This game was played with 23 voluntary participants to identify the information needs of different emergency leaders and their corresponding teams from the communicated content during emergency response. The duration of the game was 30 min and played inside the university building. In this game execution, 11 observers (i.e., 4 fire-fighters and the rest university staff) were present.

For this game, the research team divided these 23 voluntary participants into three teams, one as crew manager (CM), and one as medical care unit (MCU). In these divided three teams, each team consists of three members: one as smoke diver leader (SDL) and other two as smoke diver members (SDs) and the rest 12 as victims. The participants were briefed about their goals and tasks before the game start. The design of the game and division of the teams were done according to the obtained knowledge from the interviews with the real firefighters and also from the provided documents [10, 11].

In this game, two scenarios were designed. In the first scenario, only first responders and MCU got the smartphones with installed Zello application [13] and that was used as information sharing tool. Moreover, first responders further supplemented with a map of the floor layout in the building where the incident occurred to get an idea of the view of the floor. While in the second scenario both the players and victims got smartphones with installed SmartRescue application [14], but not MCU. However, walkie-talkies (WT) were given to only first response players and it was used as information sharing tool. However, the detailed description of the tools and the first responder groups division for both scenarios can be seen in the previous research [5].

However, in fact the game was designed to test a developed smartphone application called SmartRescue. This app is an Android based application which allows both first responders as well as victims to send and receive emergency-related data such as the location of the fire and the victims with the help of embedded sensors of the smartphone such as accelerometer, gyroscope, GPS, humidity, thermometer, and so on.

In the game development process, three main requirements are taken into account: complexity (the scenario must be complicated enough to involve multiple teams); concreteness (the scenario must include sufficient details to allow the participants to identify the relevant actors); and realism (the scenario must be realistic) [12].

The developed scenario was as follows: fire accident happened inside the third floor of A' block of the university building. The building consisted of many students (who might be normal, disabled, and sick), library, laboratories and storage rooms. Most of the students noticed smoke, flames, and screams inside the building. Some of the victims also report fire intensification. Due to the fire, the emergency site became rampageous and many students inside the building were wounded and traumatized. The number of people inside the building was unknown. But, the people who were running out of the building were giving information about the seen victims [9].

3 Research Methodology

3.1 Emergency Responders' Roles

From the interviews and provided documents, the research team got to know that only SDs enter inside the burning building in pairs to start search and rescue process to evacuate the victims from the affected area. However, SDLs does not enter into the affected building. They stay at the near to the building entrance to obtain the overview of the situation. Furthermore, SDLs are responsible for guiding his team members (SDs) by providing the needed information. SDL reports to the CM and receives orders and information from CM. If any of the SDs is injured, SDL inform to the CM and replaces his role with SD role. While, CM in charge of all crew members' safety. He orders and shares/provides the needed information with SDLs. However, Medical Care Unit is responsible for noting down the brought victims (either injured or found or dead or conscious or unconscious) and informing to the CM.

3.2 Video-Taped Data Collection

During the game, the research team utilized four video recording cameras to record the entire game sessions for both scenarios. In both scenarios, these four cameras were placed in all corners of the building where the indoor fire game was conducted. In addition, the research team gave smart glasses and GoPros to the participants who imitated first responders' roles to record the entire SAR operation. The reason for using video recorders, smart glasses and GoPros for data collection was that the entire game session of both scenarios can be retrieved from the recorded tapes. These tapes can provide the researchers a unique opportunity to revise them again and again. Yet, videos can be played, replayed, speedup, allowed or paused, discussed, analyzed and re-analyzed. Thus, provides the insights of the shared information with the actions [16]. Furthermore, after the game, the research team had a chance to discuss the key points with the players and with the observers. And then the players were given the opportunity to make any further comments on their experience and difficulties during game experiment if they felt to discuss. The discussion lasted approximately 30 min for both scenarios.

3.3 Video-Taped Data Analysis

The verbal content of the exchanged emergency information was analyzed through the thematic analysis which is a basic method for qualitative analysis method. Thematic analysis is a method for identifying, analyzing and reporting patterns (themes or categories) of the data [17]. The analysis was inductive with themes driven from the data collected. So, after the game, we retrieved all data from video cameras which were used to capture both scenarios. To analyze the video data, first all the data from video cameras were carefully retrieved, stored and later examined to ensure that all the communication done during the game is captured and later uploaded to our personal computer to analyze them. After uploading, we have played the videos, again and again, to extract and transcribe the shared information in the excel sheets for both scenarios.

After transcribing the shared information, the research team has done coding in NVivo 10.0 (QSR International) [15]. Here, coding is one of the several methods of working with and building knowledge from the abundant data. In coding, first node and sub-nodes are made. Each line of the transcripts gets coded into these nodes and sub-nodes. However, code is an abstract representation of an object or phenomenon or a way of identifying themes in the transcribed text. Coding the text for qualitative analysis is a way of tagging or indexing the text to facilitate later retrieval and allows re-contextualizing the data [18]. Before coding, transcripts were first read, and the content familiarized. Coded sections of the transcripts were then organized into preliminary categories.

As we code, Nvivo tool indexes (adding or tagging flags to) the text or videos by storing the references to the document at the node. In this tagging process, Nvivo is not making a copy of the text at the node, but connecting the concepts or categories with the data. The data that have been coded will be accessible from the nodes. In coding process, transcripts were re-read and double-coded and · discussed with other researchers to maximize the reliability.

4   Results

In this section the results of information needs of emergency responders in both scenarios are presented with the help of qualitative and quantitative analysis.

4.1   Information Categories

The information sharing in scenario 1 was done 75 times and in second scenario the information sharing was done 68 times. The extracted shared information was separated into 3 columns in excel sheet. The data which was listed in column 1 of the excel sheet was about the information categories that were triggered. Second column was about the frequency of communicated information categories of first scenario and 3rd column was about the frequency of communicated information categories of second scenario. The data which was exchanged during the game divided into 6 categories to simplify the exchanged data, which is documented in Table 1.

In both scenarios, information categories which are listed in Table 1 were exchanged mostly. Whenever rescue teams find a victim, they exchange information about the victim status and location of the victim to their leader to make him obtain the situational awareness. Furthermore, when the rescue teams need 'Resources' during SAR operation, they exchange information about the needed resources from bottom to top (group members to leader) and available information from top to bottom (Leader to group members). Moreover, when the fire location is spotted, it is reported to the leader or inform to the other rescue members by giving the direction of the floor in the building. During SAR operation, rescuers have to check their own safety to achieve all the coordination activities.

Table 1. Extracted Information categories from both scenarios

Information category	Description
Victim status	Information about victim whether he is ok or injured or dead
Victim location	Information about the location of the victim
Resources	Information about needed resources and available during SAR operation
Building floor directions	Information about directions of the building floor (i.e., south, north, west, east) used to either to search for the victim
Fire location	Information about location of the fire development
Rescuers safety	Information about Rescuers status and location

4.2   Frequency of Information Categories for Both Scenarios

In the first scenario, the most exchanged information categories by emergency response teams were victims' status and fire location. Whereas, in the second scenario, victims location and fire location information categories were mostly exchanged between rescue groups to obtain the situational awareness. This is because, in second scenario, the rescuers were given with smartphones with SmartRescue application. In this SmartRescue app, rescuers can see on the given mobile screen, where the victim is, fire development and status of the victims.

From the Table 2 it is visible that, *Victim Status* frequency is higher in the second scenario than in the first scenario i.e., from 30.66 % to 39.70 %. It is because rescue teams could find the victims with the help of SmartRescue application and pass the information to their related leaders. Moreover, MCU can also inform or confirm the victim status with the CM.

Considering *Victims' Location* information category frequency, it is higher in second scenario than first scenario i.e., from 20 % to 65.33 %. The reason is from the given SmartRescue application, the rescue teams could see the location of the victim including the room number and name. When emergency rescue teams spot the victims on the SmartRescue application screen, these teams share that information with their corresponding leader. Furthermore, the leaders might have given the orders to the emergency team members by giving victims' location information to save the victims.

When it comes to *Resources* information category, in scenario 2, emergency response teams exchanged information about this information category is 4 %. But, in first scenario, less than 2 % information about resources was exchanged. The reason might be that emergency teams were busy searching for the victims in first scenario than in second scenario.

As explained in the earlier paragraph, with the help of SmartRescue application, emergency rescue teams could spot the victim location. Due to the access to the victims' location, emergency rescue teams could exchange the information about the building directions to describe the location of the victims. Therefore, from the exchanged information, *Building Directions* information category is acquired. So, from the Table 2, it is clearly evident that the frequency of this category is higher in second scenario i.e., 24 % than in the first scenario i.e., 16 %.

Table 2. Frequency of Information categories from both scenarios

Category	Scenario 1	Scenario 2	Total	Frequency of S1	Frequency of S2
Victim status	23	27	50	30.66	39.70
Victim location	15	49	64	20	65.33
Resources	1	3	4	1.33	4
Building directions	12	18	30	16	24
Fire location	*17*	28	45	22.66	37.33
Rescuers safety	*3*	16	19	4	21.33
Total	**75**	**68**	**143**		

While *Fire location* information category in the obtained results, it is clearly visible that the frequency is 22 % in first scenario and 38 % in second scenario. So, this information category is higher in second scenario than scenario 1 as most of the information in scenario 2 is visible on the smartphone's screen, whereas in scenario 1, rescue teams have to search themselves for the location of the fire.

But when it comes to *Rescuers Safety* information category, in second scenario this information category was mostly communicated i.e., 21.33 %, but only 4 % in first scenario. The reason is teams were working together in first scenario, whereas the frequency results got impacted with the distribution of SmartRescue application in the second scenario.

5 Discussion and Conclusion

In this paper, we have investigated and analyzed the data that was collected during an indoor fire game. The game was designed to test a developed Smartphone application called SmartRescue. From this study, the research team wanted to identify the information categories from the exchanged information. However, this study was done with voluntary students, and therefore some extra guidance and training of SmartRescue application were given before the game start.

The obtained results are based on from both qualitative and quantitative analysis. The acquired results provide knowledge about the critical information categories in receiving and sharing the information to obtain and maintain the situational awareness. However, the results show that emergency rescue teams and their related leaders had easy interaction with the smartphone application called SmartRescue and it helped them to obtain the SA. Therefore, the frequency is high in second scenario than in first scenario (without SmartRescue application).

Based on the results of our study, it is anticipated that emergency responders get an impression of what is being communicated during search and rescue operation. By knowing this, emergency responders can learn and understand what information was difficult to obtain and what not. Moreover, this learning can help emergency responders in real emergencies.

Our further research will be to play the same game with real fire-fighters and examine their information needs to enable a better understanding during search and rescue operations in situational awareness formation. And then compare the obtained results with the present study results for developing ICT systems.

Acknowledgments. This study is carried out in collaboration with the SmartRescue project led by Prof. Ole-Christoffer Granmo and co-funded by Aust-Agder utviklings-og-kompetansefond (AAUKF, projectnr. 2011-06). We would like to owe our gratitude to the Grimstad fire station personnel who supported us during the development of different stages of the experiment, to the students that took part in the game, and to Mehdi Lazreg Ben, Jaziar Radianti and Tina Comes for their constant support in the data analysis process. Finally, we thank the observers who provided their valuable suggestions after the game.

References

1. Netten, N., et al.: Task-adaptive information distribution for dynamic collaborative emergency response. Int. J. Intell. Control Syst. **11**(4), 238–247 (2006)
2. Endsley, M.: Theoretical underpinnings of situation awareness: a critical review. In: Endsley, M., Garland, D.J. (eds.) Situation Awareness Analysis and Measurement. Laurence Erlbaum Associates, New Jersey (2000)
3. Kuusisto, R.: From Common Operational Picture to Precision Management. In: Managemental Information Flows in Crisis Management Network. Publications of the Ministry of Transport and Communications 81/2005, Helsinki (2005)
4. Toner, S.: Creating situational awareness: a systems approach. In: Altevogt, B.M., Stroud, C., Nadig, L. (eds.) Medical Surge Capacity: Workshop Summary. National Academies Press, Washington (2009)
5. Nunavath, V., Radianti, J., Comes, T., Prinz, A.: The impacts of ICT support on information distribution, task assignment for gaining teams' situational awareness in search and rescue operations. In: Thampi, S.M., Bandyopadhyay, S., Krishnan, S., Li, K.-C., Mosin, S., Ma, M. (eds.) Advances in Signal Processing and Intelligent Recognition Systems. AISC, vol. 425, pp. 443–456. Springer, Heidelberg (2016)
6. Seppänen, H., Mäkelä, J., Luokkala, P., Virrantaus, K.: Developing shared situational awareness for emergency management. Saf. Sci. **55**, 1–9 (2013). doi:10.1016/j.ssci.2012.12.009
7. Busby, S., Witucki-Brown, J.: Theory development for situational awareness in multi-casualty incidents. J. Emerg. Nurs. **37**, 444–452 (2011)
8. Endsley, M.R., Jones, W.M.: A model of inter- and intrateam situation awareness: Implications for design, training and measurement. In: McNeese, M., Salas, E., Endsley, M. (eds.) New Trends in Cooperative Activities: Understanding System Dynamics in Complex Environments. Human Factors and Ergonomics Society, Santa Monica (2001)
9. Nunavath, V., et al.: Visualization of information flows and exchanged information: evidence from an indoor fire game. In: The Proceedings of 12th International Conference on Information Systems for Crisis Management and Response (ISCRAM) (2015)
10. Beredskap, D. f. s. o.Veiledning til forskrift om organisering og dimensjonering av brannvesen (2003)
11. Beredskap., D. f. s.Veiledning om røyk og kjemikaliedykking (2003)
12. Eide, A.W., Haugstveit, I. M., Halvorsrud, R., Borén, M.: Inter-organizational collaboration structures during emergency response: a case study. In: Paper presented at the Proceedings of the 10th International ISCRAM Conference. Baden-Baden, Germany (2013)
13. Zellowalkie-talkieapp. Zello walkie-talkie software application. http://zello.com/app

14. SmartRescueProject. SmartRescue project, Center for Integrated Emergency Management (CIEM). http://ciem.uia.no/project/smartrescue
15. Nvivo tool, software application. http://www.qsrinternational.com/product
16. Morse, J.M., Pooler, C.: Analysis of videotaped data: Methodological considerations. Int. J. Qual. Methods **1**, 62–67 (2008)
17. Braun, V., Clarke, V.: Using thematic analysis in psychology. Qual. Res. Psychol. **3**, 77–101 (2006)
18. Bazeley, P., Jackson, K.: Qualitative Data Analysis with Nvivo, pp. 1–305 (2013)

Field Immersion on Fitness Activities
in Urban India

Sarita Seshagiri, Aditya Ponnada, Minal Jain[✉], and Simran Chopra

Samsung R&D Institute India, Bangalore, India
{Sarita.s,minal.jain,simran.c}@samsung.com,
aditya1990.p@gmail.com

Abstract. In this paper, we present our initial findings from a dipstick carried out in urban India with 24 users to understand their fitness related needs and activities. We highlight some key findings in terms of motivation, social influences and problems that evolve with this user segment while they carry out their fitness activities. Moreover, we have put forth four key personas that encompass a major portion of user profiles relevant to personal fitness and health in India. Through this dipstick study, we intend to lay the foundation for other researchers and designers interested in exploring fitness technology for Indian users.

Keywords: Fitness · Health · Wellness · Motivation · Personas

1 Introduction and Background

Health care related human computer interaction studies in India have primarily focused on diagnosis technologies [1], maternal care systems [2, 3], personal health record [4] and so on. Design interventions too have focused on assistive health care services [5]. However, there is a dearth of research and literature on personal fitness, which is critical for a healthy lifestyle and health indices of a country. Besides, rapid increase in lifestyle diseases such as obesity, depression and diabetes to name a few [6, 7] has caused more and more people to develop a positive attitude towards fitness activities and engage in healthy habits. Personal fitness hence is seen as an additional responsibility that every individual should undertake to lead a fulfilling life.

We took the opportunity to identify design avenues for personal fitness in urban India. In order to build better fitness technologies, it is essential to understand needs and challenges of users, while they undertake their fitness activities. However, there is a paucity of such research on urban Indian users that highlights their fitness needs. In this paper, we present a dipstick study carried out on fitness enthusiasts in urban Bengaluru (India). We identified several challenges and corresponding workarounds undertaken by users. Through this study, we highlight key design and research opportunities for further research in the domain. We have identified certain user personas to showcase fundamental and evolving fitness needs and challenges that designers and researchers in the field of fitness technology, products, services and applications should consider in order to increase stickiness of their offerings.

© Springer International Publishing Switzerland 2016
M. Kurosu (Ed.): HCI 2016, Part III, LNCS 9733, pp. 572–579, 2016.
DOI: 10.1007/978-3-319-39513-5_53

We undertook an exploratory study [8] with the following general objectives. Firstly, to understand how people undertake fitness activities in urban India. Secondly, to identify challenges they face in undertaking their fitness activities and reaching fitness goals (including tracking/logging fitness activities). Finally, to learn how users cope with these challenges. The overall aim of our study was to explore design opportunities that can enhance overall experience of undertaking fitness activities among users in emerging markets.

Data was gathered in three ways – open discussions, guided user interviews and situational observations (inside gyms, post workout sessions, organized events such as marathons and exclusive sports retail outlets). One-on-one guided interviews with participants were undertaken to gain clarity on observations made during situational immersions. Data was analysed through cluster or affinity analysis. In parallel, the ecosystem of fitness for various personas was detailed out, to identify opportunity areas.

Urban Bengaluru was chosen for the study given its recent population boom, increased employment opportunities, changing lifestyles and the inevitable advent of lifestyle diseases [9]. It is worthwhile to note that urban Bangaloreans are gradually taking fitness seriously, despite the threat of modern lifestyle diseases [10].

24 participants were chosen for the study. All participants followed fitness work-outs with varying rigour, regularity and regimen including diet control, exercising, jogging, cycling, swimming, yoga and even sport activities. Such a mix of users was critical for exploring fitness requirements and challenges across user profiles and thereby identifying opportunity spaces. 12 participants actively undertook daily fitness activities, while the rest did not, or had just resumed their workouts after a long hiatus. Respondents were between the age groups of 20 to 50 years. Of these, 13 were male and 11 were female respondents.

2 Findings

2.1 Managing Time for Regimen

Users undertook fitness activities in little time windows away from work. It was either for a few hours on the weekend or in a few cases during weekdays. However, users who were innately motivated to undertake fitness activities on a regular basis would manage it at specific times of the day despite their work and study schedules.

2.2 Group Fitness Activities

Users undertook fitness activities often as a group. One of the advantages of group fitness regimen was the feeling of camaraderie, along with competitiveness and appreciation. Apart from this, members of a fitness group would even exchange fitness-related information with each other (diet-related tips, regimen-related information, health advice, etc.).

While this was true for most users, there were some who preferred to undertake fitness activities alone. Many participants mentioned that it was a personal activity and they preferred to do in solitude. In fact, the presence of another person was considered distracting. This was even quoted as one of the reasons why people did not prefer going to a gym.

2.3 Sharing and Seeking Information

Apart from group fitness activities, users also mentioned sharing of fitness related information. However, we learnt that people preferred to share their fitness achievements, rather than otherwise unless users were seasoned fitness participants, in which case their performance would already be above a certain level.

Serious fitness enthusiasts with high fitness performance were motivated to obtain better fitness information and hence preferred to receive tips and suggestions from not just close friends or family, but even from proven fitness experts. There was not much concern for privacy, since it was understood that everyone in the group was motivated by the same goal of fitness. Moreover, sharing not just health/fitness tips, but even fitness performance was seen as the means of gaining competitive edge.

2.4 Challenges and Pain-Points

One of the primary pain-points with undertaking fitness activities was the lack of motivation towards undertaking fitness activities regularly. Motivation was a critical challenge especially when users had to begin a regimen after a long break, which is when fundamental motivational shifts were required. But, motivation was also a problem when a fitness regimen was too rigorous.

Undertaking fitness activities in a group was also considered a problem by many users, since it often meant that people would have to slow down or increase their pace in undertaking a workout session to suit other group members. It also meant people changed their routine to suit that of their fitness partner/s.

Monitoring one's performance either through devices or manually was yet another problem area for our respondents. It was challenging to weave monitoring into the exercise/fitness regimen. Often, it was not possible to monitor one's performance or routine while still undertaking it (sweaty hands/body, non-conducive posture of the body and so on). Even the time-lag in monitoring (since users would often check their performance or monitor their regimen) would lead to inaccurate results. Probably diet monitoring was the most challenging, since it had to be manually entered. Besides, Western food and beverages were more likely to have calorie and diet information, as compared to Indian food items. Diet was monitored mostly through user's own alternate manual or physical means.

Yet another problem with monitoring was that most devices were designed for specific workout and monitoring of specific parameters in those exercises. This meant that measuring of certain parameters which were relevant to a specific workout, would be irrelevant for another. This resulted in people using minimum wearables or undertaking regimens through exercises that could be easily monitored by the same device. People often lost out on monitoring important aspects of their parameters while thus working out.

2.5 Workarounds Devised by Users

Device shortcoming was a significant challenge, because it means that the device was unable to accurately measure certain parameters during a regimen. It would over-project a specific performance or parameter. To overcome this problem, users would often set high goals for a particular workout and thereby balance the device's tendency to overestimate. Similarly, the lack of an accurate digital dietary planner would make users draw out manual or mental food plan. They would compensate a supposedly high carbohydrate meal of the afternoon with a fibre rich dinner, or even skip a meal.

At other times, respondents faced the problem of being unable to meet the set goals of a workout session. When they realized this, they would increase intensity or effort at that workout midway or towards the end of the session.

There were also problems like not being able to regularly undertake fitness activities, due to lack of time or lack of access to fitness resources. At such times, users would find alternate ways to engage in fitness activities. These would include ways like climbing up and down the stairs everyday at work, instead of using the elevators, or sprinting everyday to the bus-stop.

Often users would play sports every weekend, or joined an adventure/trekking/biking club so that they would continue to be in touch with fitness activities, despite not being able to do workout sessions regularly.

3 Key Personas

From the needs and coping strategies that users had developed for themselves, it is obvious that they had certain expectations built around fitness technologies. They wanted a fitness device that was personal equipment – either a handheld device or a wearable. But most importantly it had to be personalized to a user's physical parameters and thereby give information related to the user's physical attributes, rather than generalized and aggregated inputs. It also had to be dynamic, i.e. take into immediate context and situation surrounding a user. Users also wanted their fitness apps to take into account their previous engagement with fitness activities or health-related regimen. In this way, fitness recommendations could even be smartly predictive. It is worth considering the right time window to provide recommendations to users i.e. whether it should be between workouts, or at the end of a week's session of workouts. Finally, users wanted inputs from even non-exercising activities to be considered, for e.g. running up and down the stairs, or running to the bus stop or behind a bus (to catch the bus) to name a few. It was felt that a true and complete picture of people's physical activities in a day can be captured by considering these activities, rather than dedicated fitness activities alone. As far as diet related fitness applications are concerned, the expectation is that it should be culturally relevant for Indian food databases. Most diet apps are cognizant of American and European food data bases, which make it difficult for Indian users, who have to manually enter Indian food preferences and items.

Competitive Beginner

- 20-30 years
- Seeking competition
- Active on social media, social support important
- Difficult to start fitness regimen

Passive Practitioner

- 35-45 years
- Wish to weave fitness in day-to-day activities due to time constraints.
- Require passive logging and tracking of fitness data.

Active Reviver

- 30-35 years
- Resuming fitness after a long break.
- Seek social support.
- Require fitness apps to consider their prior experience in fitness.

Challenge Seeker

- 30-40 years
- Into fitness activities since a long time.
- Seek new avenues in fitness and new information from fitness devices.

Fig. 1. Schematic diagram of key personas

Based on such needs and expectations of users that are built around their everyday lives, we arrived at a set of personas. These personas encompass a range of users by virtue of their diverse lifestyle as well as fitness goals. Considering such personas will help build solutions that are not only in accordance with user expectations, but also closely tied to user contexts.

3.1 Competitive Beginner

Competitive beginners were people, who typically belonged to the age range of 20–30 years. They would spend a major chunk of their time on social media including Facebook, Quora etc. They seek competitive environments and are keen on beginning some fitness activity in the near future. Work or academic engagements had stalled their engagement in physical activities till now but concern for physical appearance and the desire to gain social approval drives them to engage in some now. Diet was not an important consideration for them and they indulged in junk food sometimes. Users belonging to this persona often found it difficult to voluntarily engage in fitness activities. Consequently, they relied heavily on their social circles to motivate and drive them towards fitness. They found it convenient to mentally track their fitness activities and did not set any concrete targets for themselves. Instead, they just contemplated on taking action in the near future.

3.2 Passive Practitioner

This persona comprised of people who wished to weave fitness into their day-to-day activities. Belonging to higher age groups (35–45 years) and married, along with domestic responsibilities and day jobs they could not devote specific time slots for fitness activities. Being past their youth, they started experiencing minor health problems that drove them to exercise on weekends and monitor their dietary intake. During their daily chores and job, such users tried to make minor attempts at fitness (climbing up the stairs rather than taking the elevator, avoiding mid-day snacks, maintaining a balanced diet and so on). They also engaged in discussions related to health and fitness in their limited time windows with friends and colleagues. Logging and tracking fitness activities was an extra effort for them given their hectic time schedules. Such a persona was most likely to appreciate a technology that can passively understand minor fitness attempts users make and can offer a comprehensive summary after a period of time.

3.3 Challenge Seeker

Challenge seekers were fitness enthusiasts who had been into fitness activities for a long time and had grown beyond novice level in their regimen. Typically in the age range of 30–40 years, they would have been following a fitness regime for over a year and would have sought advice from experts in their peer group. They would have begun fitness activities with a particular goal in mind (for e.g. losing weight). However, after having reached that goal, these users wished to explore new avenues of fitness. They are most likely to find their regular regimen monotonous and want to explore new regimen or modify their current one in different ways. Over time with familiarity with their regimen, the use of fitness devices would have decreased for these users. They would probably find information provided by such devices and apps as being redundant and mundane. They now seek new and more relevant information from their fitness devices, which can also reduce overall monotony of their fitness activities.

3.4 Active Reviver

These were users who wished to resume their fitness after a long break. Usually belonging to the age range of 30–35 years, people belonging to this persona had a hiatus in their regimen due to pregnancy, physical injuries (wear and tear of bones/muscles) or even a long sabbatical. Having completed their break, these users now had a strong desire to resume their fitness activities that had been compromised for long and wanted to get back in shape. Family and friends for this group of users acted as prime motivators to help them get back on the fitness track. Having engaged in fitness activities earlier, a lot of basic information offered or tracked by fitness apps were considered redundant by these 'Active Revivers'. Instead, they wanted feedback from apps and devices to consider their prior experience with fitness activities. In addition to reviving their fitness level, these users also hold a strong desire to revive their social circle so as to include fitness enthusiasts.

Figure 1 represents a brief schematic diagram of different personas emerging from this study.

4 Conclusions

In this case study, we have presented our findings and potential personas related to fitness eco-system in urban India. Findings of the study reveal that user needs with respect to fitness technologies may not be limited to health related information needs. It also involves social factors such as motivation and group presence. This highlights the potential of emerging user engagement tools such gamification and social media to build successful fitness technologies.

There is a definite need for a pervasive personal trainer or coach who could also suggest regimen based on user's past activities. It should provide personalized recommendations on power workouts to fit the user's present lifestyle and time crunch (as in case of passive practitioners). Since needs of all four personas are significantly different, personalisation of training and instruction becomes vital.

A user's goals could also be broken down into shorter incremental goals for personalised progress tracking in terms of time and effort required. For some personas (e.g. active reviver), having a mode wherein a user could compete with their earlier or future version of themselves for setting their target goals could be beneficial. It could also be encouraging for some personas (competitive beginner, challenge seeker) to know the present performance of others in the user's social circle with a similar body type and regimen.

For many users, vicarious learning through the activities performed in their social network acts as a motivator. Sociality during exercise regimen like collectively performing activities and sharing work-out information within certain closed groups can go a long way in motivating users. To minimize monotony, workout results can be presented at irregular times to create a "surprise element". Also, in the middle of a regimen, alternate relevant activities could be suggested which require similar effort to break the monotony (crucial in case of challenge seekers). Entry of dietary intake should be made more efficient and user-friendly while also allowing log in of outliers' data.

Ultimately, the evolving personas discussed in this study lay the foundation for a more in-depth study for this user segment. We hope to recruit our in-house respondents to approximately fit these personas. Such an exercise of persona creation from field studies will be particularly useful in user trials and interviews within the corporate set up. It will also help facilitate informed brainstorming sessions for use cases and scenarios without losing track of learning from the field.

We believe this method of defining potential personas can be useful, where the domain and its user segments are ambiguous and motivation levels varied. Motivation levels for both competitive beginners and Active Revivers is low, while it is high for Challenge Seekers. However, it is ambivalent for Passive Practitioners. Ideally, fitness technology solutions should address these varying levels of motivation among people and thereby ensure sustained usage.

References

1. Bhasker, R., Kapoor, A., Vo, A.: Pioneering the health-care quality in India using six-sigma: A case study on Northern India Hospital. J. Cases Inf. Technol. **14**(4), 41–55 (2012)
2. Ramachandran, D., Goswami, V., Canny, J.: Research an reality: using mobile messages to promote maternal health in rural India. In: Proceedings of ICTD 2010. ACM Press (2010)
3. Maitra, A., Kuntagod, N.: A novel mobile application to assist maternal health care worker in rural India. In: Proceedings of SEHC 2013, pp. 75–78. ACM Press (2013)
4. Palasamudram, D., Avinash, S.: ICT Solution for managing electronic health record in India. In: Proceedings of ICSEM 2012, pp. 65–74. ACM Press (2012)
5. Ramachandran, D., Canny, J., Das, P.D., Cutrell, E.: Mobileizing health workers in rural India. In: Proceedings of CHI 2010, pp. 1889–1898. ACM Press (2010)
6. Bharadwaj, S., Misra, A., Khurana, L., Gulati, S., Shah, P., Vikram, N.K.: Childhood obesity in Asian Indians: a burgeoning case of insulin resistance, diabetes and sub-clinical inflammation. Asia Pac. J. Clin. Nutr. **17**(S1), 172–175 (2008)
7. Sharma, M., Majumdar, P.K.: Occupational Lifestyle diseases: An emerging issue. Indian J. Occup. Environ. Med. **13**(3), 109–112 (2009)
8. Glaser, B.G., Strauss, A.L.: The Discovery of Grounded Theory: Strategies for Qualitative Research. Aldine Transaction (1999)
9. 4 out of 10 Bangaloreans are obese. http://timesofindia.indiatimes.com/city/bangalore/4-out-of-10-Bangaloreans-are-obese/articleshow/17221891.cms. Accessed on April 2014)
10. Fitness centers are mushrooming, but do they give you results? http://bangalore.citizenmatters.in/articles/1645-fitness-centres-mushrooming. Accessed on April 2014

Supportive Technology for Managing Relevant Information in the Medical and Nursing Care Field

Yuya Totsuka$^{(\boxtimes)}$, Hayato Oiwa, and Hiroshi Yajima

Tokyo Denki University, Tokyo, Japan
12fI101@ms.dendai.ac.jp

Abstract. In Japan, the aging of society has become a serious problem that has increased the importance of being able to flexibly share information between medical and nursing care workers. In this study, we examine the real needs of workers in this field and devise and construct a support system that can assist in collecting and acquiring information of interest at work sites. We additionally consider how to apply psychology to improve information sharing. Our aim is to create an environment that facilitates smoothly sharing information, and we propose a comprehensive system of information sharing toward that aim.

Keywords: Aging society · Care · Team care · Information sharing · Conditions of interest · Filtering

1 Introduction

The number of people in Japan who are 65 years or older recently reached 32.77 million people, a rate of about one in four people. The aging of society is progressing at a much faster speed in Japan than in other countries. In the future, it is expected that and increasingly large portion of the population will be over 75 years of age [1]. The aging of society has rapidly increased the needs of the home care and nursing care field. The Ministry of Health, Labour and Welfare of Japan has been promoting the construction of a comprehensive support system at the local level, a so-called regional comprehensive care system, to be complete around 2025. It is important that medical and nursing care workers can share information between them to better serve the elderly. The regional comprehensive care system is aimed at those who need long-term care and support in order to continue living life in their preferred way [1].

The goal of the study described in this paper is to facilitate sharing, via groupware, of information about elderly care recipients. This sharing is among teams of different medical and nursing care professionals and is intended to allow providing better service in the medical and nursing care field.

2 How to Realize a Comprehensive Community Care System

To realize a local comprehensive care system, it is important that health, medical, and welfare teams cooperate closely. The degree of information sharing that is achieved in the Japanese system by using the conventional contact notes is insufficient. It is

© Springer International Publishing Switzerland 2016
M. Kurosu (Ed.): HCI 2016, Part III, LNCS 9733, pp. 580–589, 2016.
DOI: 10.1007/978-3-319-39513-5_54

necessary for those in health and welfare support to coordinate with the medical facilities where medical care is rendered [2]. Although the goal of providing medical care is being addressed, improving the quality of life (QoL) of care recipients is now seen as increasingly important. Doing so is essential in order to realize a regional comprehensive care system.

3 Information Sharing in the Home Care and Nursing Care Field

3.1 Questionnaire Survey

To clarify problems with information sharing in the home care and nursing care field, we surveyed health care and long-term care workers (62 people) by questionnaire. The questions and the results are listed here.

Question 1. When you share information to health care and long-term care workers, what method do you use routinely and during emergencies? (Multiple answers allowed)

Question 2. Are you satisfied with your means of information sharing?

Table 1. Means of sharing information ordinarily

Dialogue	Phone	FAX	E-mail	Web-system	Other
26	32	19	4	1	9

Table 2. Means of information sharing during emergencies

Dialogue	Phone	FAX	E-mail	Web-system	Other
17	42	7	1	0	1

3.2 Interviews

We interviewed medical and nursing care workers (visiting doctors, visiting nurses, social workers, and care managers). During interviews, we asked about what problems they are facing with the current system to information sharing. The following problems were identified by informants.

- Inability to obtain necessary information at the time it is needed
- Lack of simple method to share information
- Insufficient support for acquiring and storing information
- Importance of information is difficult to assess

4 Problems

In this study, using the questionnaire survey and interviews as a base, we focused the research on the following two problems.

4.1   Information Sharing

At present, the primary medium of sharing information is paper (e.g., contact notes, documents sent by fax). However, this paper-centric system means that information sharing is not simple, and it is particularly difficult to share information in real-time between those in different roles.

4.2   Information Overload

Medical and nursing care workers are busy and require large amounts of information. Because of this, information is often not available when needed. In addition, it is hard to find the important information within a set of information.

5   Proposed Method

In this study, we propose the following system. Medical and nursing care workers designate the conditions of interest [3] (hereinafter, COI) for potentially interesting information. Using this method, information that is relevant to the COI can be rapidly disseminated to those medical and nursing care workers who have expressed interest.

Using the above-mentioned problems as a starting point, we re-surveyed workers about what information they need. We set the COI on the basis of survey results.

5.1   Information Sharing Using Groupware

Conventionally, information sharing in the medical and nursing care field uses analog media, such as telephone and fax. In this study, sharing of information occurred via a free groupware application, Cybozu Live. Cybozu Live allows creating and managing a group space suitable for use by small teams. One reason for using Cybozu Live in the medical and nursing care field is that it can be used free of charge. We decided to adopt Cybozu Live as the groupware application because of its combination of performance and function.

5.2   Setting of COI

Using questionnaire surveys and interviews, we determined the relative priorities of information for each role in medical and nursing care and assigned these priorities as the COI. The priority of each type of information for each role is shown in Table 3.

5.3   Support for Receiving Information of Interest

Cybozu Live has a function that notifies members of new information by e-mail. However, all members are notified of all information, even information that is not of interest. This means that workers who should be receiving the information may miss it among other information, and workers who do not need the information are notified of it anyway. In this study, we combined information-sharing using Cybozu Live with filtering in Gmail to support receiving information of interest only.

First, medical and nursing care workers create a Cybozu Live account, using a Gmail address that has been created in advance. Notices of information newly entered into Cybozu Live is are sent to the Gmail addresses associated with the occupational roles by Cybozu Live. Then, a COI filter (i.e., a filter that is based on the COI of each worker's point of view) is applied to each address associated with an occupational role, and the messages identified by the COI filter are given specific labels. Figure 1 shows the setting screen for the COI filter in Gmail. Figure 2 shows the conceptual flow of the COI filters.

Table 3. Priority of information types, by occupational role

Role	High ⬅———————	Priority———————➤		Low
Home doctor	Status of a patient	ADL*	Follow-up of prescription	Care situation of family
Home nurse	Status of a patient	Situation of medication	Future directions	ADL*
Care manager	Status of a patient	Wishes of the patient and family	ADL*	Drug side effect
Care helper	ADL*	Drug side effect	Status of a patient	Wishes of the patient and family
Physiotherapist	Status of a patient	ADL*	Care situation of family	Follow-up on rehabilitation
Pharmacist	Status of a patient	Follow-up on prescription	Situation of medication	—

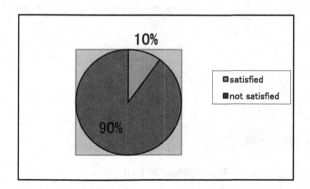

Fig. 1. Answers to Question 2: Are you satisfied with your means of information sharing?

Settings

| General | Labels | Inbox | Accounts and Import | **Filters and Blocked Addresses** |

The following filters are applied to all incoming mail:

☐ Matches: **from:(no-reply@cybozulive.com** 緊急
   Do this: Skip Inbox, Apply label "【実験】○○△△○○", Mark it as important

☐ Matches: **from:(no-reply@cybozulive.com** 状態
   Do this: Skip Inbox, Apply label "【実験】○○△△○○", Mark it as important

☐ Matches: **from:(no-reply@cybozulive.com** 服薬
   Do this: Skip Inbox, Apply label "【実験】○○△△○○", Mark it as important

☐ Matches: **from:(no-reply@cybozulive.com** 処方
   Do this: Skip Inbox, Apply label "【実験】○○△△○○", Mark it as important

☐ Matches: **from:(no-reply@cybozulive.com** 今後
   Do this: Skip Inbox, Apply label "【実験】○○△△○○", Mark it as important

Fig. 2. Setting screen for COI filters in Gmail

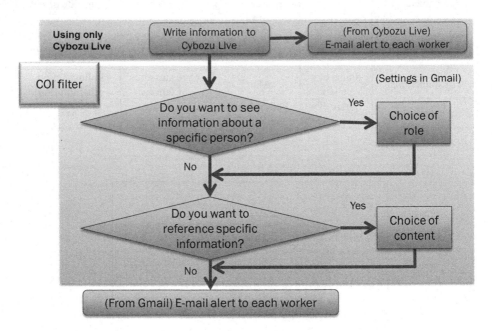

Fig. 3. Flow of COI filters

6 Information Sharing by Team

As described above, it is important for the realization of the regional comprehensive care system that information can be closely shared within the teams involved in home care and nursing care. However, our interviews show that there are obstacles to workers sharing information in the fields of home care and nursing care. This includes obstacles such as each occupational role using different systems and the specific information required for each occupation being different.

This study aims to eliminate barriers as much as possible when sharing information and to apply psychological insights about teamwork to the information system so as to be able to share information smoothly. An overview of the groupware information-sharing system is shown in Fig. 4.

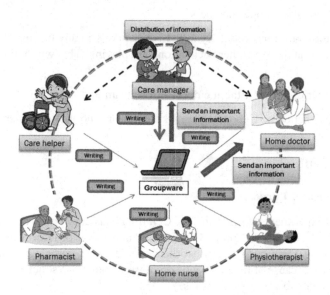

Fig. 4. Flow of sharing information in teams

6.1 Psychology of Teamwork

For teamwork, it is important to consider the elements to be provided as part of team formation. This study targeted adapting to these elements to create teams. The following elements are necessary for team formation.

1. The presence of clear objectives to be jointly achieved
2. Cooperation and interdependence between members
3. Allocation of roles among members
4. Clear boundaries between the members of the team and other people

6.2   Application of Psychology to Teamwork

In this study, we apply the psychology of teamwork to the information systems. Specifically, we considered whether the specific functions of the groupware (Cybozu Live) suitably address the psychology of teamwork, as described below.

1. The presence of clear objectives to be jointly achieved

The objects are to building a comprehensive community care system and to provide better services to the elderly.

2. Cooperation and interdependence between members

Workers will keep in touch via the chat function of Cybozu Live, which will help them tackle the challenges.

3. Allocation of roles among members

By using the to-do function of Cybozu Live, workers in any occupational role can confirm the role that those in other occupations are playing. This will build recognition of role allocation.

4. Clear boundaries between the members of the team and other people

The group function of Cybozu Live makes it clear who the team members are.

7   Experiment

7.1   Experimental Purposes

We performed experiments to verify that the COI filter had been applied correctly and that acquisition of information was properly supported at the time of information sharing.

Ideally, medical and nursing care workers would act as participants in the experiment. However, because of time demands on these workers, we solicited Tokyo Denki University students to act as participants.

7.2   Participants

Six students of Tokyo Denki University participated in the experiment. Six positions were represented, with one student assigned to each: home-care doctor, home-care nurse, care manager, care helper, physiotherapist, and pharmacist.

7.3   Procedure

Using tablet terminals, each participant transmits information to other participants in Cybozu Live according to a scenario of previously prepared information. Then, the other participants confirm whether they have been notified as specified by the COI filter, which is set in advance.

The duration of the experiment was one week.

7.4   Experimental Results

Twenty-three entries were submitted to Cybozu Live, and it was confirmed that each generated e-mail had been given the correct label in Gmail.

7.5   Evaluation

After the experiment, we asked participants to evaluate the effectiveness. The evaluation can be separated into benefits and drawbacks, as follows.
   Feedback about benefits:

- It makes the information that we want easy to see.
- Because receiving a lot of e-mail often causes important information to be buried, the system is convenient.
- I prefer to collect information freely by changing the filter.
- If we filter using COI for each type of content, I feel that work becomes smooth.
- It is convenient to save time looking for information that I want.
- Feedback about drawbacks:
- Synonyms are not applied to the filter.

Five of the six participants expressed a desire to use the system. The other participant reported a favorable impression of the system.

8   Considerations

8.1   Consideration of the Entire System

In this study, we devised a prototype of an information-sharing system that combines existing groupware (Cybozu Live) with an e-mail system (Gmail).
   However, both are existing systems, and they are not specialized to medical and nursing care. Therefore, from the results of interviews and questionnaires, we consider it important to develop a system from an occupational point of view for future use in the medical and nursing care fields.

8.2   Discussion of Problems

The following is a discussion of the two issues that were considered in this study.

– Information sharing

   Information-sharing in the fields of home care and medical care is primarily done via analog media. A method that uses groupware could address the need for information-sharing in real time.
   However, at present, nursing care staff collectively exhibit low information literacy. Therefore, it will be necessary to develop simpler information systems.

– Information overload

The COI-filter method used in this study enables medical and nursing care workers to acquire only relevant information, and more generally allows busy workers in any occupation to preferentially obtain only important information.

However, the scope of this study means it is possible that information that was not caught in the COI filter has been overlooked. It remains to apply the method to medical and nursing care at work sites.

8.3   Psychology of Teamwork

This experiment employed the psychology of teamwork in applying the functions of the groupware. However, a future system could be developed with explicit consideration of the psychology of teamwork. Specifically, there is a need to design the interface of the information system to emphasize team aspects.

8.4   Experiment

The experiment in this study used students of Tokyo Denki University as participants. This should be extended to medical and nursing care workers in the future. The teams of medical and nursing care workers involved elder care contain many people, and so it will be necessary to seek cooperation from various medical care workers and perform demonstration experiments.

The present experiment did not compare between cases in which we adapted the COI and cases in which we did not. It will be necessary to consider both cases when performing the experiments at work sites.

In addition, participants entered information prepared in advance on the basis of the information-sharing scenario into the groupware in this experiment. Therefore, there is a possibility that information will not be appropriately filtered by the COI filter when workers use the system at work sites. This was pointed out by participants as a drawback of this system. A possible solution is to increase the accuracy of filter by testing the system at work sites and performing demonstration experiments until the system is practical for us in the medical and nursing care fields.

8.5   Setting the Conditions of Interest

In this study, we set the COI, but we think that a universal COI will not be suitable for all people. To address this, it is necessary to create a standard model of interest conditions by collecting more data on the COI. Further, there is a possibility that the COI will need continual change. This is difficult to carry out via changing settings each time in Gmail.

For a future system, it is desirable to have a mechanism to simply set the COI to control information sharing.

9 Conclusion

We conducted a study of a system to support acquiring information, for use in sharing information among medical and nursing care workers. However, parts of the system are likely to be unsuitable for medical and nursing care workers at this time. Information sharing that uses COI filtering may be desirable to realize and develop in order to provide the best system in the future.

Acknowledgements. We thank Mr. Nishimura of Ltd. MELPHIS, Mr. Sasaki of Medical Corporation Yushou-kai, and all of the medical and nursing care workers who cooperated in this study.

References

1. Ministry of Health, Labour and Welfare
2. http://www.mhlw.go.jp/stf/seisakunitsuite/bunya/hukushi_kaigo/kaigo_koureisha/chiiki-hou katsu/. Accessed 15 Dec 2015
3. Japan Health Enterprise Foundation, http://ikss.net/enterprise/images/194.pdf. Accessed 10 Dec 2015
4. F Hayes-Roth, "VALUED INFORMATION AT THE RIGHT TIME (VIRT): WHY LESS VOLUME IS MORE VALUE IN HASTILY FORMED NETWORKS," (2006). http://www.nps.edu/cebrowski/docs/virtforhfns.pdf. Accessed 9 Oct 2015
5. Yamaguchi, H.: Ti-muwa-ku no Shinrigaku Yoriyoi shuudan dukuri wo mezasite [Psychology of teamwork Towards a better population planning]. Saiensu-sha Co., Ltd., Publishers, Tokyo (2008)

Proposal for a System of Mutual Support Among Passengers Trapped Inside a Train

Ryohei Yagi[(⊠)], Takayoshi Kitamura, Tomoko Izumi,
and Yoshio Nakatani

Graduate School of Science and Engineering,
Ritsumeikan University, Kusatsu, Shiga 525-8577, Japan
is0192vh@ed.ritsumei.ac.jp,
{ktmr,izumi-t,nakatani}@is.ritsumei.ac.jp
http://www.sc.ics.ritsumei.ac.jp/

Abstract. The Japanese railway system has the greatest accuracy and safety in the world, with a low frequency of delays and a small number of accidents. However, even in such a railway system, a train must sometimes make an urgent stop in emergencies, as a result of an earthquake or other accidents. Most railroad companies have a safety measure in which a train must make an urgent stop in order to confirm safety during emergencies. In the worst cases, passengers have been trapped in a train for a period greater than 24 h. In such a situation, some passengers, such as the elderly or pregnant women, may suddenly become ill, as a result of chronic illnesses, poor conditions, or stress due to the tense situation. In case of emergencies, the limited number of crewmembers on a train are not able to deal with passengers efficiently. Therefore, we suggest an extempore community formation system for passengers who are trapped inside a train in order to promote mutual support during an emergency. Results of an evaluation experiment reveal the usability of the proposed system.

Keywords: Support system · Community formation · Mutual support · Trapped passengers · Train

1 Introduction

Japan has a highly advanced railway system, which services both urban and rural areas. Hence, many people use trains for their commute and the Japanese railway system is deemed as one of the most important modes of transportation. However, Japan is also a nation prone to earthquakes or suicide, a train is required to make an emergency stop. Consequently, passengers may become trapped inside a train during emergencies. Japan is a nation prone to earthquakes and experiences more earthquakes compared to other countries. When an earthquake occurs, a railroad company must urgently stop a train to ensure safety. Meanwhile, approximately 600 accidents are recorded annually, with at least one suicide attempt on the railroad occurring per day. During such situations, affected trains are urgently stopped. The effect of this urgent stop spreads to other trains, and passengers in these trains may be trapped inside and have to wait until the situation is resolved. The length of time they may be trapped depends on the cause

© Springer International Publishing Switzerland 2016
M. Kurosu (Ed.): HCI 2016, Part III, LNCS 9733, pp. 590–598, 2016.
DOI: 10.1007/978-3-319-39513-5_55

of the emergency situation of the train. If a train stops at a place in between stations, the passengers may be trapped inside for a long period of time.

In such a trapped scenario, there is a likelihood that problems may arise in passengers, owing to an increase in stress, worsening of a chronic disease, or emergence of poor health. Generally, in such situations, the crew in the train deal with emergencies. However, in a trapped situation, it is possible that more than one emergency will occur at a time. Typically, the crew consists of only one or two people, and this limited number may not be able to attend to all the emergencies that may occur. Therefore, a mutual support system among passengers is important to aid in the response to emergencies.

This research formed a community plan to perform mutual support among passengers in the case of an emergency stop. In using this system, when a user is trapped with person they do not know, anxiety and impatience can be softened by sharing information. In addition, It's possible that the users go to passengers location that is problem occurred in case of emergency. Furthermore, this system is improved and the problem is simulated via an evaluation experiment.

2 Related Works

2.1 A Disaster Management Platform Based on a Social Network System Oriented to the Self-Relief of Communities

Dominguez-Rios et al. conducted a study on a disaster management platform based on a social network system (SNS) to promote mutual support in communities [1]. This system performed multilingualization using a universal design approach. Moreover, the system was devised such that the interface was user-friendly. The system classified users into the following four groups in order to enable smooth mutual support:

1. Medical Group: These are users with medical skills that may be useful to perform a task and assist other users in need.
2. Search and Rescue Group: These are users who officially belong to a search and rescue agency. If the helper is near the location of the person needing help, these individuals can assist others directly and inform others about rescue efforts in a specific area.
3. Communication Group: These are users who are witnesses to an event and can communicate about the event with other users in the system. These users should have important skills such as knowing a foreign language or skills with appropriate media in order to access important information that may be useful.
4. Evacuation Group: Agencies such as fire departments, public health agencies, and public utilities impart preventive efforts. Using the reports generated by this system with the aid of feedback from the community, public agencies can perform their tasks.

This research reveals the usefulness of the formation of a community based on an SNS. The use of SNSs has increased over recent years. It is very effective in the formation of a community, as the attributes of a user and their social aspects are included. This research confirms the importance of mutual support by a community. However, there is currently a lack of research into community formation in limited space.

2.2   The Necessity of Mutual Support During an Emergency

Mutual support is cooperation between members of a family, company, or local community [2]. The necessity of mutual support during an emergency has been made evident in previous studies [3]. For example, an individual will have to share information and perform self-help and mutual support when a large earthquake occurs, as administrative relief and rescue efforts may be late in arriving. In such a scenario, the only way to protect oneself is to cooperate with people nearby. During the 1995 Hanshin Awaji earthquake disaster, approximately 80 % of survivors in need of rescue were assisted by their families and/or neighbors [4].

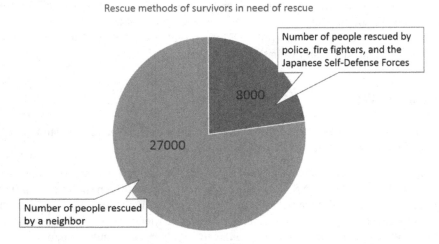

Fig. 1. Number of people rescued in the 1995 Hanshin Awaji earthquake according to the type of savior.

Figure 1 shows the importance of mutual support in emergency situations. Furthermore, self-help is a basis of protection against disasters and is a very important factor during an emergency. Community is not only people's lives more prosperous. It is vital that people cooperate when faced with an emergency. Daily activities performed by a community revitalize that community. Daily activities by a community will form a basis to protect the lives of the people during a disaster.

3   System Proposal

3.1   System Summary

In this research, we propose a system that provides mutual support through the formation of an instant community via vehicles. No such system has been previously proposed. Therefore, it is necessary to consider a system that everyone can use effectively when passengers are trapped inside a train (which is a scenario that can occur any time). Therefore, the following three criteria should be satisfied by this system:

1. It should be possible to form a community immediately during an emergency situation;
2. The position of a train with trapped passengers in trouble can be specified; and
3. The system is easy to use even during an emergency situation.

The solutions for these three criteria are described below:

1. It is necessary to form an original community. The Twitter [5] and Facebook [6] SNSs exist, but it is difficult to use these to detect a problem on a specific vehicle. Therefore, this system forms a community by accessing a designated URL on the train that experiences trouble. Consequently, passengers are able to access this system and connect mutually.
2. In this system, there are a number of images representing individual vehicles. When a patient experiences an emergency, the image changes to an image that indicates an emergency. In addition, even if the passengers in the emergency situation cannot use the system themselves, it is possible that a nearby user can report the situation.
3. This problem is resolved by using pictograms in the system. It is believed that a system with a simple design is easier for users. Even if a single user is in an urgent situation, he or she can transmit information by tapping his or her smartphone several times.

This research does not focus on specifying the position of a user in a train and the communication environment. Because this research is inspection of system's effectiveness. Thus, the system uses an external system for these functions.

3.2   Development Environment

This system is a web application that is built using HTML, PHP, and JavaScript. Data acquisition from a database and input of data to a database are implemented using a PHP script.

It is assumed that most passengers have access to a smartphone. Hence, this system makes a community that shares information via smartphones. In order to use the system and respond to an emergency situation, it is assumed that a user knows the system URL.

3.3   System Operation

This system allows a rescue to be performed even if the user is on a vehicle of anywhere. The system is arranged as follows:

- Main Screen:
  The initial screen is the main screen of the system, and all procedures are mainly conducted from this screen. The system has a simple design and therefore can be used during an emergency situation. A user can grasp the situation of the train through the change of the vehicle image (see Fig. 2).

- Rescue Request Button:
  This button is to be used when the degree of urgency is high (*i.e.*, an emergency situation). This action then changes the vehicle image into an image that informs of an emergency.
- Bulletin Board:
  Users can access this bulletin board from a vehicle image when an emergency occurs. The user may contribute detailed date and ID information, severity of an illness, and vehicle location (Fig. 3).

Fig. 2. Image change

```
id:130 投稿時間2016-01-16 16:17:51
車両位置:真ん中 病気の程度:軽度
コメント:
おなかの調子がすぐれず、トイレも空いていません！薬など持っている方は助けてください！

id:129 投稿時間2016-01-16 16:16:40
車両位置:前 病気の程度:軽度
コメント:
電車が止まった際に転んで擦り傷ができてしまいました。近くにいる方で絆創膏をもっているかたがいればいただきたいです。

id:128 投稿時間2016-01-16 16:15:31
車両位置:後ろ 病気の程度:中度
コメント:
妊婦です。少し体調がすぐれません。

id:127 投稿時間2016-01-16 16:14:32
車両位置:真ん中 病気の程度:軽度
コメント:
どなたか水を少しいただけませんか

id:126 投稿時間2016-01-16 16:11:56
車両位置: 病気の程度:
```

Fig. 3. Bulletin board

3.4 System Flow

This section describes the system flow (Fig. 4), as follows:

1. The user starts the application.
2. When a problem occurs, the user taps the HELP button on the main screen. The vehicle image in the system then changes to another vehicle image that informs of the occurrence of a problem. This system assigned value to vehicle image. This is retained by the system as a value representing the vehicle image. This value is stored in an "image" table in the database.
3. When users contribute to a bulletin board, information on the vehicle location, severity of the illness, and other relevant data are used as inputs. This data is then stored in a "member" table in the database.

4. The contribution to the bulletin board is stored in a "posts" table in the database.
5. At the same time, the contribution time and ID are assigned and inserted in the "posts" table.

An example of the system flow is shown in Fig. 5.

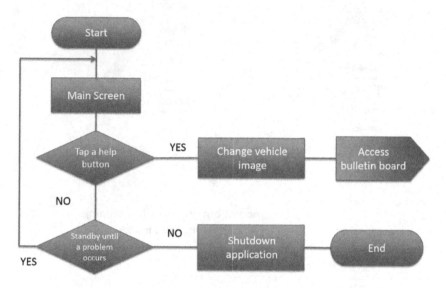

Fig. 4. System flowchart

4 System Evaluation

4.1 Experiment Flow

The experimental procedure is as follows:

1. The URL of the system is conveyed and a role is assigned in advance.
2. The subjects board an appointed vehicle, after which the experiment commences.
3. Subjects in the role of dealing with the medical crisis use the system and are informed of the problem.
4. The other users go to the rescue using the system.
5. The experiment concludes upon the arrival of a user at the scenario of the medical crisis.

4.2 Attributes of the Subject

A role (two emergency patients, two passengers, one doctor, one nurse) and a vehicle were assigned by an experimenter to each subject at random, after which the experiment commenced. The subjects were named A–F and the results are summarized in Table 1.

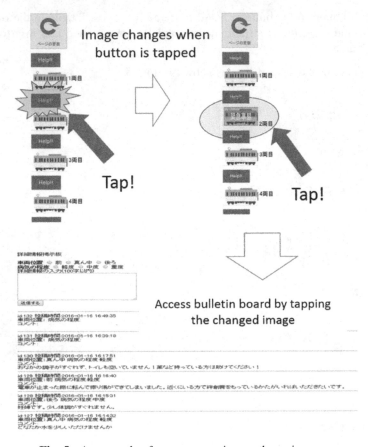

Fig. 5. An example of system operation on the main screen

Table 1. The attributes of the experimental participant and the roles

Subject ID	Age	Gender	Role (going)	Role (returning)
A	21	Man	Passenger	An urgent case (A fit)
B	22	Man	Passenger	Doctor
C	22	Man	Nurse	An urgent case (Giddiness and nausea)
D	21	Woman	Doctor	Passenger
E	21	Woman	An urgent case (Giddiness and nausea)	Nurse
F	22	Woman	An urgent case (A fit)	Passenger

4.3 Experimental Results

To confirm the usefulness and specification of the system and the validity, I conducted questionnaire.

The questionnaire and its results are presented in Table 2.

Table 2. The results of the experimental questionnaire.

Question	A	B	C	D	E	F
① How many times do you take a train every month?	Almost every day	2 or 3 times a week	Do not take it so much	1 or 2 times a week	1 or 2 times a week	1 or 2 times a week
② Have you experienced being "trapped inside a train" for more than 1 h?	No	No	No	No	No	No
③ Did you think this system is simple?	3	3	3	3	3	3
④ Were you able to easily operate this system?	1	2	4	4	4	4
⑤ Can you quickly specified a vehicle as occurring a problem?	2	2	3	3	3	3
⑥ We assume that you are a medical practitioner. Can you hurry in a vehicle to the place of the medical crisis using this system?	2	3	2	2	3	3
⑦ Can you perform mutual support by using this system?	3	3	3	4	4	4

4: Strongly agree 3: Agree 2: Disagree 1: Strongly disagree

As there were only a few test subjects, there was no one who had experienced the situation of being trapped inside a train. Therefore, it appears that they have no techniques for dealing with this problem. Furthermore, all the subjects stated that suggestions can be viewed easily in the main screen. As a result, a user was able to quickly distinguish the location of a person who had experienced a problem (4/6 persons). However, two people stated that the system was difficult to operate. I think, it is the rescue request button was located near to the vehicle image, and incorrect operations resulted. Other opinions in conjunction with the user interface were provided. These provided a good evaluation of the usefulness of mutual support using this system. Hence, the results of the questionnaire indicated the effectiveness of this research.

5 Conclusion

This paper proposed a system for the formation of a mutual support community for passengers in the event of passengers being trapped inside a train. The problem was formulated under the assumption that a limited number of crewmembers cannot deal with many passengers efficiently. The importance of mutual aid between passengers was confirmed from a mutual assistance point of view. It is believed that this study is necessary for the future of the Japanese society, which can be referred to as a railroad society.

In the future, meetings will be held with railroad companies and evaluation experiments will be performed with individuals who have experienced the situation of being trapped inside a train. Furthermore, the user interface of the system will be improved.

References

1. Dominguez-rios, L.E., Izumi, T., Nakatani, Y.: A disaster management platform based on social network system oriented to the communities self-relie. IAENG Int. J. Comput. Sci. **42**(1), 1–16 (2015)
2. Cabinet Office disaster prevention charge. http://www.moshimo-bosai.com/info/help
3. City of Kobe, Comprehensive Strategy for Recovery from the Great Hanshin-Awaji Earthquake (2010)
4. White Paper on Disaster Management
5. Twitter. https://twitter.com/
6. Facebook. https://www.facebook.com/

Author Index

Printed in the United States
By Bookmasters